Jean-Claude **Corbeil**
Ariane **Archambault**

THE FIREFLY
VISUAL
DICTIONARY

FIREFLY BOOKS

A FIREFLY BOOK

Published by Firefly Books Ltd., 2002

Copyright © 2002 QA International

First Printing

National Library of Canada Cataloguing in Publication Data

Corbeil, Jean-Claude, 1932–

   The Firefly visual dictionary / Jean-Claude Corbeil, Ariane Archambault.

Includes index.
ISBN 1-55297-585-1

   1. Picture dictionaries, English. 2. English language—Dictionaries.
I. Archambault, Ariane, 1936– II. Title.

PE1629.C62 2002   423'.1   C2002-901160-4

Publisher Cataloging-in-Publication Data (U.S.)

The Firefly visual dictionary / Jean-Claude Corbeil, and Ariane Archambault. —1st ed.
[960] p. : col. ill. ; cm.
Includes index.
Summary: A comprehensive general reference dictionary including sections on astronomy, geography, the animal and vegetable kingdoms, human biology, food and kitchen, art and architecture, clothing and accessories, communication, energy, science, sports, society, transportation and handling.

ISBN 1-55297-585-1

1. Picture dictionaries, English. I. Corbeil, Jean-Claude. II. Archambault, Ariane. III..Title.
423 /.1 21   CIP   AG250.F57 2002

Published in Canada in 2002 by
Firefly Books Ltd.
3680 Victoria Park Avenue
Toronto, Ontario M2H 3K1

Published in the United States in 2002 by
Firefly Books (U.S.) Inc.
P.O. Box 1338, Ellicott Station
Buffalo, New York 14205

Printed and bound in Slovakia

ACKNOWLEDGMENTS

Our deepest gratitude to the individuals, institutions, companies and businesses that have provided us with the latest technical documentation for use in preparing The Firefly Visual Dictionary.

Arcand, Denis (réalisateur); Association Internationale de Signalisation Maritime; Association canadienne des paiements (Charlie Clarke); Association des banquiers canadiens (Lise Provost); Automobiles Citroën; Automobiles Peugeot; Banque du Canada (Lyse Brousseau); Banque Royale du Canada (Raymond Chouinard, Francine Morel, Carole Trottier); Barrett Xplore inc.; Bazarin, Christine;Bibliothèque du Parlement canadien (Service de renseignements); Bibliothèque nationale du Québec (Jean-François Palomino); Bluechip Kennels (Olga Gagne); Bombardier Aéronautique; Bridgestone-Firestone; Brother (Canada); Canadien National; Casavant Frères ltée; C.O.J.O. ATHENES 2004 (Bureau des Médias Internationaux); Centre Eaton de Montréal; Centre national du Costume (Recherche et de Diffusion); Cetacean Society International (William R. Rossiter); Chagnon, Daniel (architecte D.E.S. – M.E.Q.); Cohen et Rubin Architectes (Maggy Cohen); Commission Scolaire de Montréal (École St-Henri); Compagnie de la Baie d'Hudson (Nunzia Iavarone, Ron Oyama); Corporation d'hébergement du Québec (Céline Drolet); École nationale de théâtre du Canada (Bibliothèque); Élevage Le Grand Saphir (Stéphane Ayotte); Énergie atomique du Canada ltée; Eurocopter; Famous Players; Fédération bancaire française (Védi Hékiman); Fontaine, PierreHenry (biologiste); Future Shop; Garaga; Groupe Jean Coutu; Hôpital du Sacré-Cœur de Montréal; Hôtel Inter-Continental; Hydro-Québec; I.P.I.Q. (Serge Bouchard); IGA Barcelo; International Entomological Society (Dr. Michael Geisthardt); Irisbus; Jérôme, Danielle (O.D.); La Poste (Colette Gouts); Le Groupe Canam Manac inc.; Lévesque, Georges (urgentologue); Lévesque, Robert (chef machiniste); Manutan; Marriot Spring Hill suites; MATRA S.A.; Métro inc.; ministère canadien de la Défense nationale (Affaires publiques); ministère de la Défense, République Française; ministère de la Justice du Québec (Service de la gestion immobilière – Carol Sirois); ministère de l'Éducation du Québec (Direction de l'équipement scolaire- Daniel Chagnon); Muse Productions (Annick Barbery); National Aeronautics and Space Administration; National Oceanic and Atmospheric Administration; Nikon Canada inc.; Normand, Denis (consultant en télécommunications); Office de la langue française du Québec (Chantal Robinson); Paul Demers & Fils inc.; Phillips (France); Pratt & Whitney Canada inc.; Prévost Car inc.; Radio Shack Canada ltée; Réno-Dépôt inc.; Robitaille, Jean-François (Département de biologie, Université Laurentienne); Rocking T Ranch and Poultry Farm (Pete and Justine Theer); RONA inc.; Sears Canada inc.; Secrétariat d'État du Canada : Bureau de la traduction ; Service correctionnel du Canada; Société d'Entomologie Africaine (Alain Drumont); Société des musées québécois (Michel Perron); Société Radio-Canada; Sony du Canada ltée; Sûreté du Québec; Théâtre du Nouveau Monde; Transports Canada (Julie Poirier); Urgences-Santé (Éric Berry); Ville de Longueuil (Direction de la Police); Ville de Montréal (Service de la prévention des incendies); Vimont Lexus Toyota; Volvo Bus Corporation; Yamaha Motor Canada Ltd.

QA International wishes to extend a special thank you to the following people for their contribution to The Firefly Visual Dictionary:

Jean-Louis Martin, Marc Lalumière, Jacques Perrault, Stéphane Roy, Alice Comtois, Michel Blais, Christiane Beauregard, Mamadou Togola, Annie Maurice, Charles Campeau, Mivil Deschênes, Jonathan Jacques, Martin Lortie, Raymond Martin, Frédérick Simard, Yan Tremblay, Mathieu Blouin, Sébastien Dallaire, Hoang Khanh Le, Martin Desrosiers, Nicolas Oroc, François Escalmel, Danièle Lemay, Pierre Savoie, Benoît Bourdeau, Marie-Andrée Lemieux, Caroline Soucy, Yves Chabot, Anne-Marie Ouellette, Anne-Marie Villeneuve, Anne-Marie Brault, Nancy Lepage, Daniel Provost, François Vézina, Brad Wilson, Michael Worek, Lionel Koffler, Maraya Raduha, Dave Harvey, Mike Parkes, George Walker and Anna Simmons.

The Firefly Visual Dictionary was created and produced by
QA International, a division of
Les Éditions Québec Amérique inc.
329, rue de la Commune Ouest, 3e étage
Montréal (Québec) H2Y 2E1 Canada
T 514.499.3000 F 514.499.3010

EDITORIAL STAFF

Publisher: Jacques Fortin

Authors: Jean-Claude Corbeil and Ariane Archambault

Editorial Director: François Fortin

Editor-in-Chief: Serge D'Amico

Graphic Design: Anne Tremblay

PRODUCTION

Mac Thien Nguyen Hoang

Guylaine Houle

TERMINOLOGICAL RESEARCH

Jean Beaumont

Catherine Briand

Nathalie Guillo

ILLUSTRATIONS

Art Direction: Jocelyn Gardner

Jean-Yves Ahern

Rielle Lévesque

Alain Lemire

Mélanie Boivin

Yan Bohler

Claude Thivierge

Pascal Bilodeau

Michel Rouleau

Anouk Noël

Carl Pelletier

LAYOUT

Pascal Goyette

Janou-Ève LeGuerrier

Véronique Boisvert

Josée Gagnon

Karine Raymond

Geneviève Théroux Béliveau

DOCUMENTATION

Gilles Vézina

Kathleen Wynd

Stéphane Batigne

Sylvain Robichaud

Jessie Daigle

DATA MANAGEMENT

Programmer: Daniel Beaulieu

Nathalie Fréchette

REVISION

Marie-Nicole Cimon

PREPRESS

Sophie Pellerin

Tony O'Riley

Jean-Claude Corbeil is an expert in linguistic planning, with a world-wide reputation in the fields of comparative terminology and socio-linguistics. He serves as a consultant to various international organizations and governments.

Ariane Archambault, a specialist in applied linguistics, has taught foreign languages and is now a terminologist and editor of dictionaries and reference books.

The Firefly Visual Dictionary

A DICTIONARY FOR ONE AND ALL

The Firefly Visual Dictionary closely links pictures and words.

The pictures describe and analyze today's world: the objects of our everyday life, our physical environment, the animal and vegetable life that surrounds us, the communication and work technologies that are changing our lifestyles, the means of transportation that are transcending geographical barriers, the sources of energy on which we depend to name a few.

Illustrations play a critical role in our dictionary: they serve to define words, enabling dictionary users to "see" immediately the meaning of each term. Users can thus recognize the objects they are looking for and, at a single glance, find the corresponding term.

The Firefly Visual Dictionary provides you with the terms or vocabulary you need to accurately name the objects that make up the world around you.

AN EASY-TO-CONSULT DICTIONARY

You can use *The Firefly Visual Dictionary* in several ways:

By going from an idea to a word. If you are familiar with an object and can clearly visualize it but do not know the name for it you have two choices. If you want to find out what the squiggles on a weather map are actually called, you can consult "international weather symbols" in the table of contents or the opening page of the Earth chapter. *The Firefly Visual Dictionary* is the only dictionary that allows users to find a word from its meaning.

By going from a word to an idea. If you want to check the meaning of a term, refer to the index where you will be directed to the appropriate illustration. For example, by looking up "mesothorax" in the index, you will find the page reference for the illustration of a chrysalis where you can find the word.

For sheer pleasure. You can flip from one illustration to another, or from one word to another, for the sole purpose of enjoying the illustrations and enriching your knowledge of the world around us.

STRUCTURE OF THE FIREFLY VISUAL DICTIONARY

The contents of *The Firefly Visual Dictionary* is divided into 17 CHAPTERS, outlining subjects from astronomy to sports. More complex subjects are divided into THEMES, 94 in all. For example, the Animal Kingdom chapter is divided into 17 themes including insects and arachnids, mollusks, and crustaceans.

The TITLE (658 in all) has a variety of functions: to name the illustration of a unique object, of which the principal parts are identified (for example, honeybee); to bring together under one designation illustrations that belong to the same conceptual universe, but that represent a variety of elements, each with its own designations and terminology (e.g. the morphology of a honeybee).

At times, the chief members of a class of objects are brought together under the same SUBTITLE, each with its own name but without a detailed terminological analysis (e.g. castes in honeybees).

The ILLUSTRATION shows realistically and precisely an object, a process or a phenomenon, and the most significant details from which they are constructed. It serves as a visual definition for each of the terms presented.

TERMINOLOGY

Each word in *The Firefly Visual Dictionary* has been carefully verified at the required level of specialization. Sometimes different words are used to name the same object and in these cases the word used in the most highly regarded sources was chosen.

ILLUSTRATIONS

The highly realistic illustrations in *The Firefly Visual Dictionary* were created by artists using computers. Instead of being limited by the constraints of photographs, the illustrations allow us to highlight essential features of each object and correspond more closely to the vocabulary. The graphic precision of *The Firefly Visual Dictionary* makes it an excellent encyclopedia and lexographical reference tool.

COLOR REFERENCE
Each chapter is color-coded for easy reference.

TITLE
If the title appears on subsequent pages it is shown in gray.

THEME
Most chapters are divided into themes.

ILLUSTRATION

honeybee

morphology of a honeybee: worker

wing
thorax
abdomen
compound eye
pollen basket
mouthparts
sting
antenna
hind leg
middle leg
foreleg

hind leg (inner surface)

pecten
pollen packer
auricle
pollen brush

foreleg (outer surface)

coxa
femur
trochanter
tibia
velum
metatarsus
antennae cleaner

middle leg (outer surface)

spur
pollen brush
claw
tarsus

honeybee

anatomy of a honeybee

heart
dorsal aorta
Malpighian tubule
nerve cord
rectum
brain
pharynx
salivary duct
venom sac
ventriculus
esophagus
salivary gland
honey stomach

head

simple eye
compound eye
antenna
labrum
mandible
maxilla
labial palp
glossae

castes

queen
worker
drone

ANIMAL KINGDOM

CHAPTER

TERM
Each term is indexed.

Contents

Contents

List of chapters

ASTRONOMY

solar system

ASTRONOMY

outer planets

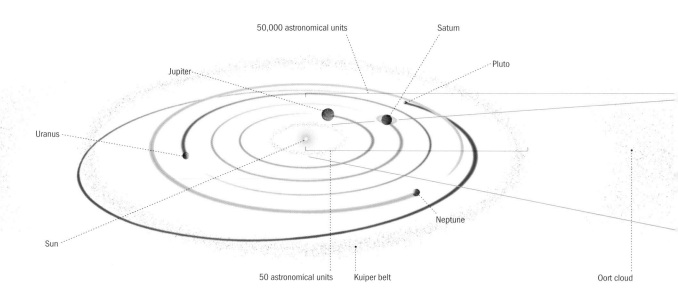

50,000 astronomical units

Saturn

Jupiter

Pluto

Uranus

Sun

Neptune

50 astronomical units · Kuiper belt

Oort cloud

planets and moons

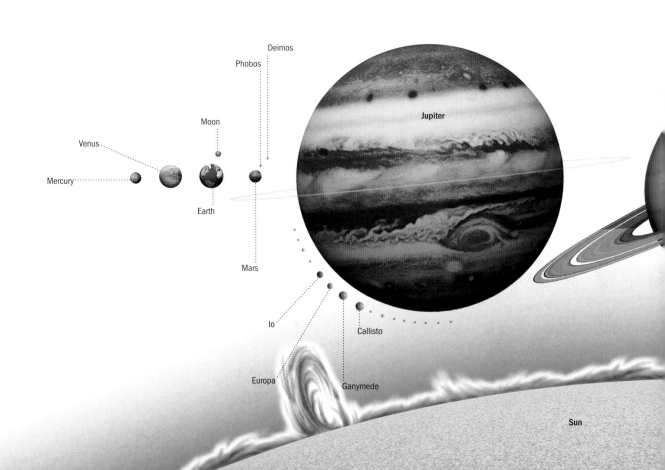

Deimos

Phobos

Moon

Venus

Mercury

Earth

Mars

Jupiter

Io

Callisto

Europa

Ganymede

Sun

inner planets

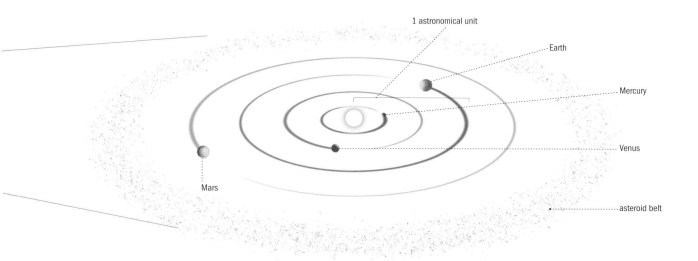

1 astronomical unit

Earth

Mercury

Venus

Mars

asteroid belt

planets and moons

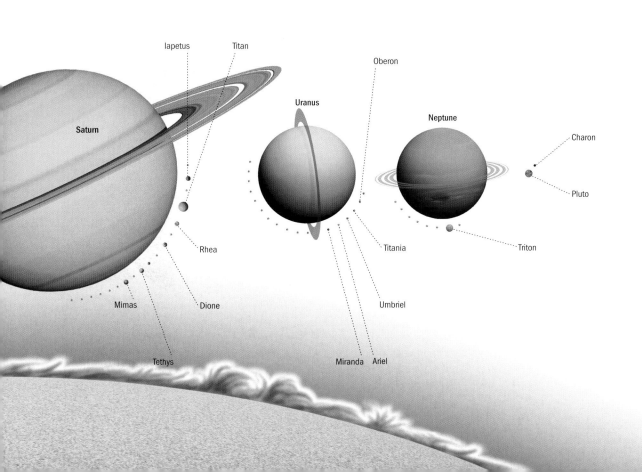

Iapetus

Titan

Oberon

Uranus

Neptune

Charon

Saturn

Pluto

Rhea

Titania

Triton

Mimas

Dione

Umbriel

Tethys

Miranda   Ariel

Sun

structure of the Sun

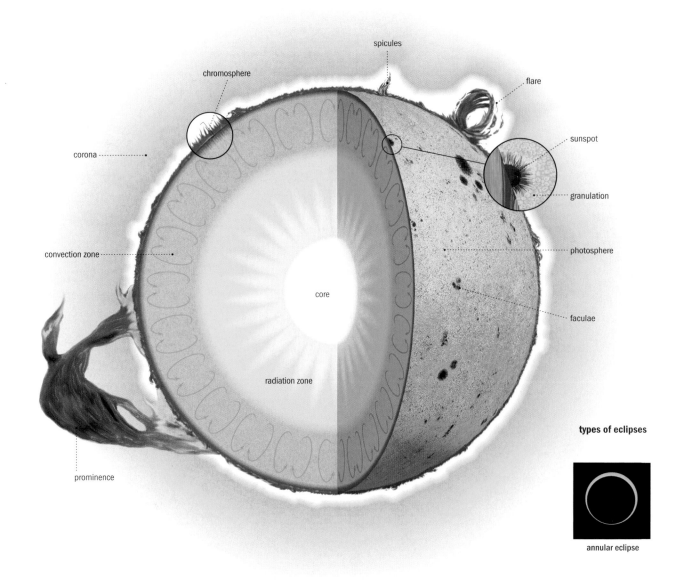

spicules

chromosphere

flare

corona

sunspot

granulation

convection zone

photosphere

core

faculae

radiation zone

prominence

types of eclipses

annular eclipse

solar eclipse

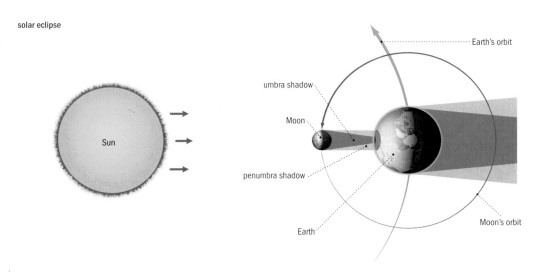

Sun

Earth's orbit

umbra shadow

Moon

penumbra shadow

Earth

Moon's orbit

partial eclipse

total eclipse

Moon

types of eclipses

lunar features

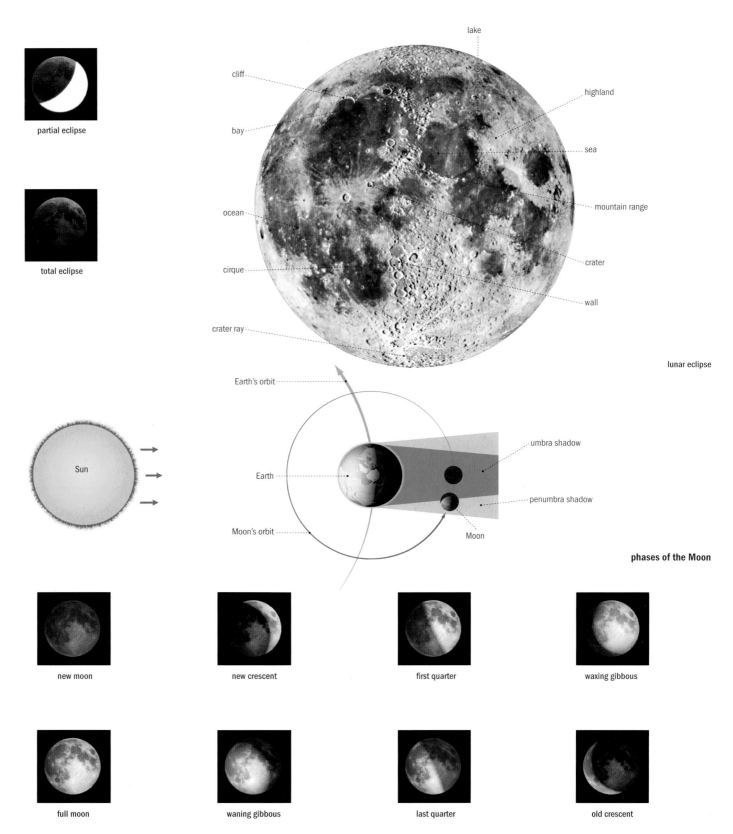

partial eclipse

total eclipse

lake

cliff

highland

bay

sea

ocean

mountain range

cirque

crater

wall

crater ray

lunar eclipse

Earth's orbit

Sun

umbra shadow

Earth

penumbra shadow

Moon's orbit

Moon

phases of the Moon

new moon

new crescent

first quarter

waxing gibbous

full moon

waning gibbous

last quarter

old crescent

meteorite

iron meteorite

stony-iron meteorite

stony meteorites

chondrite

achondrite

comet

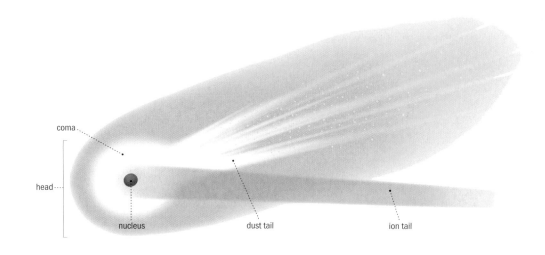

coma

head

nucleus

dust tail

ion tail

star

▨ **low-mass stars**

■ **massive stars**

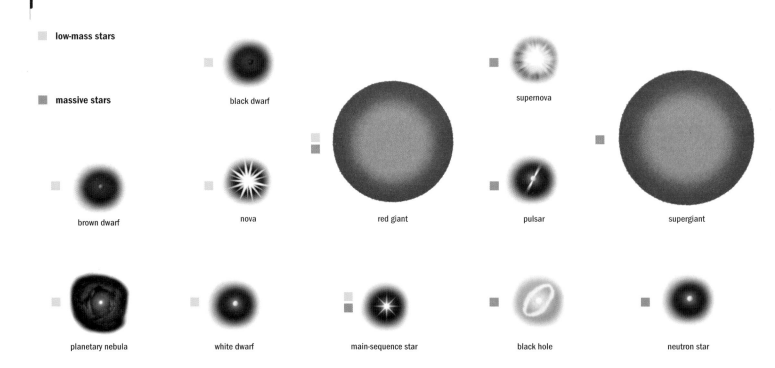

black dwarf

supernova

brown dwarf

nova

red giant

pulsar

supergiant

planetary nebula

white dwarf

main-sequence star

black hole

neutron star

Hubble's classification

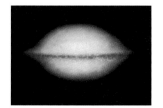

elliptical galaxy

lenticular galaxy

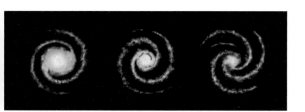

normal spiral galaxy

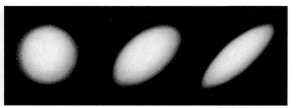

barred spiral galaxy

type I irregular galaxy

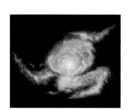

type II irregular galaxy

Milky Way (seen from above)

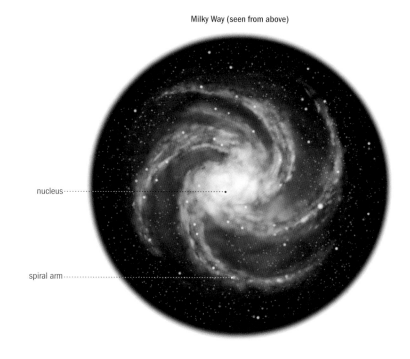

nucleus

spiral arm

Milky Way (side view)

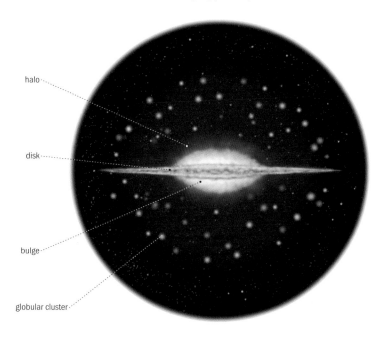

halo

disk

bulge

globular cluster

ASTRONOMY

planetarium

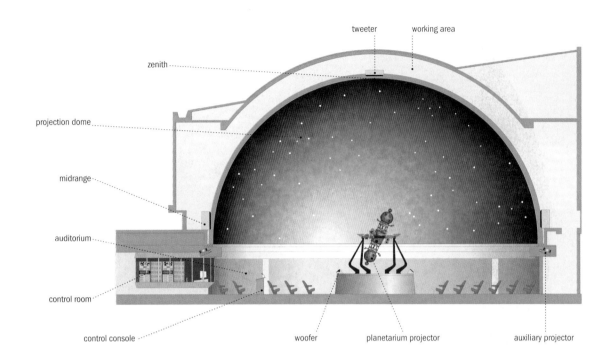

tweeter   working area

zenith

projection dome

midrange

auditorium

control room

control console   woofer   planetarium projector   auxiliary projector

constellations of the southern hemisphere

1 Whale Cetus	**8** Sculptor's Tools Sculptor	**15** Indian Indus	**22** Altar Ara
2 Water Bearer Aquarius	**9** River Eridanus	**16** Telescope Telescopium	**23** Southern Triangle Triangulum
3 Eagle Aquila	**10** Furnace Fornax	**17** Southern Crown Corona Australis	**24** Bird of Paradise Apus
4 Sea Goat Capricornus	**11** Clock Horologium	**18** Archer Sagittarius	**25** Octant Octans
5 Microscope Microscopium	**12** Phoenix Phoenix	**19** Shield Scutum	**26** Sea Serpent Hydrus
6 Southern Fish Piscis Austrinus	**13** Toucan Tucana	**20** Scorpion Scorpius	**27** Table Mountain Mensa
7 Crane Grus	**14** Peacock Pavo	**21** Carpenter's Square Norma	**28** Net Reticulum

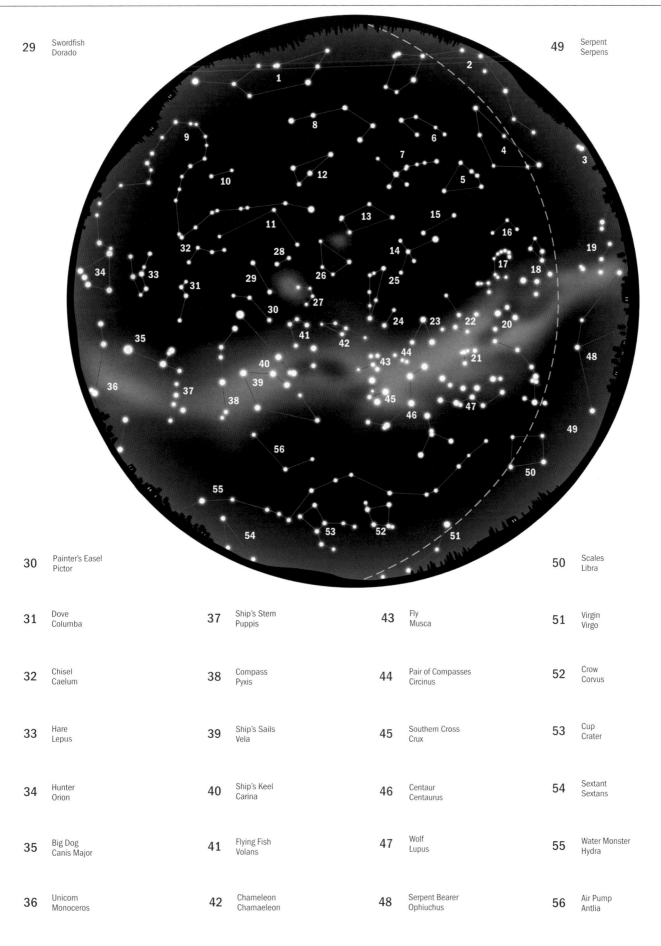

29	Swordfish Dorado					49	Serpent Serpens

30 Painter's Easel
Pictor

50 Scales
Libra

31	Dove Columba	37	Ship's Stern Puppis	43	Fly Musca	51	Virgin Virgo
32	Chisel Caelum	38	Compass Pyxis	44	Pair of Compasses Circinus	52	Crow Corvus
33	Hare Lepus	39	Ship's Sails Vela	45	Southern Cross Crux	53	Cup Crater
34	Hunter Orion	40	Ship's Keel Carina	46	Centaur Centaurus	54	Sextant Sextans
35	Big Dog Canis Major	41	Flying Fish Volans	47	Wolf Lupus	55	Water Monster Hydra
36	Unicorn Monoceros	42	Chameleon Chamaeleon	48	Serpent Bearer Ophiuchus	56	Air Pump Antlia

constellations of the northern hemisphere

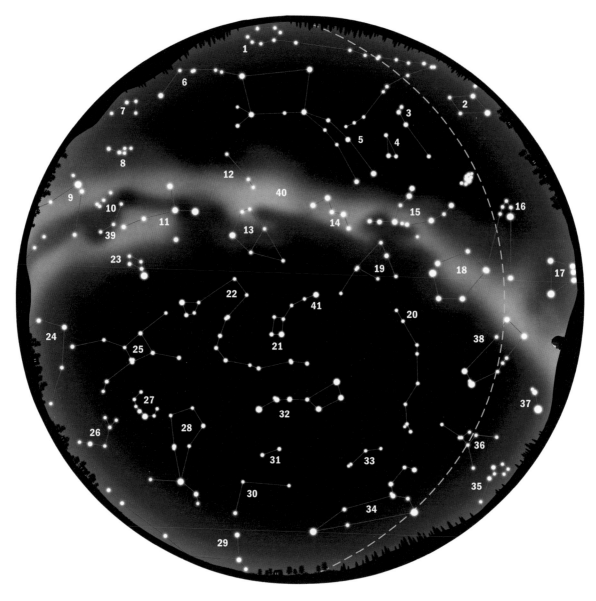

1	Fishes Pisces						

2	Whale Cetus	**7**	Little Horse Equuleus	**12**	Lizard Lacerta	**17**	Hunter Orion
3	Ram Aries	**8**	Dolphin Delphinus	**13**	King Cepheus	**18**	Charioteer Auriga
4	Triangle Triangulum	**9**	Eagle Aquila	**14**	Queen Cassiopeia	**19**	Giraffe Camelopardalis
5	Princess Andromeda	**10**	Arrow Sagitta	**15**	Hero Perseus	**20**	Lynx Lynx
6	Flying Horse Pegasus	**11**	Swan Cygnus	**16**	Bull Taurus	**21**	Little Bear Ursa Minor

constellations of the northern hemisphere

22	Dragon Draco	27	Northern Crown Corona Borealis	32	Great Bear Ursa Major	37	Little Dog Canis Minor
23	Lyre Lyra	28	Herdsman Boötes	33	Little Lion Leo Minor	38	Twins Gemini
24	Serpent Bearer Ophiuchus	29	Virgin Virgo	34	Lion Leo	39	Fox Vulpecula
25	Strong Man Hercules	30	Berenice's Hair Coma Berenices	35	Water Monster Hydra	40	Milky Way
26	Serpent Serpens	31	Hunting Dogs Canes Venatici	36	Crab Cancer	41	North Star Polaris

celestial coordinate system

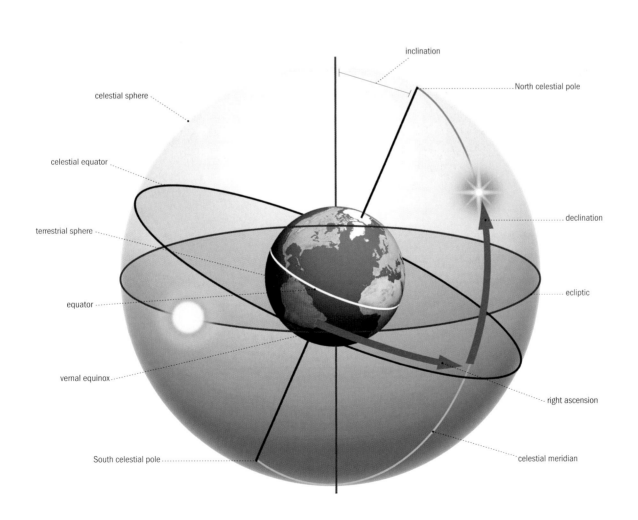

refracting telescope

finderscope

cradle

main tube

dew shield

eyepiece

eyepiece holder

star diagonal

declination setting scale

azimuth clamp

focusing knob

altitude clamp

azimuth fine adjustment

right ascension setting scale

altitude fine adjustment

counterweight

fork

tripod accessories shelf

tripod

cross section of a refracting telescope

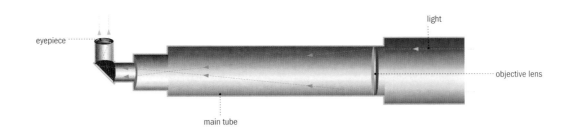

eyepiece

light

objective lens

main tube

reflecting telescope

finderscope

eyepiece

cradle

support

main tube

focusing knob

declination setting scale

right ascension setting scale

azimuth fine adjustment

azimuth clamp

altitude fine adjustment

altitude clamp

cross section of a reflecting telescope

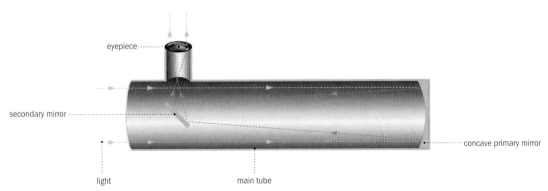

eyepiece

secondary mirror

concave primary mirror

light

main tube

radio telescope

steerable parabolic reflector

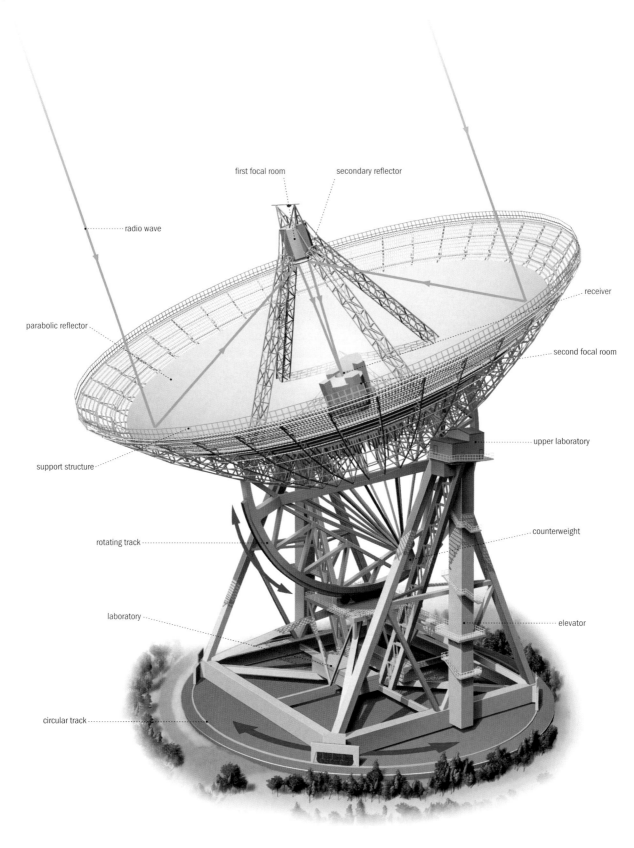

first focal room

secondary reflector

radio wave

receiver

parabolic reflector

second focal room

upper laboratory

support structure

rotating track

counterweight

laboratory

elevator

circular track

Hubble space telescope

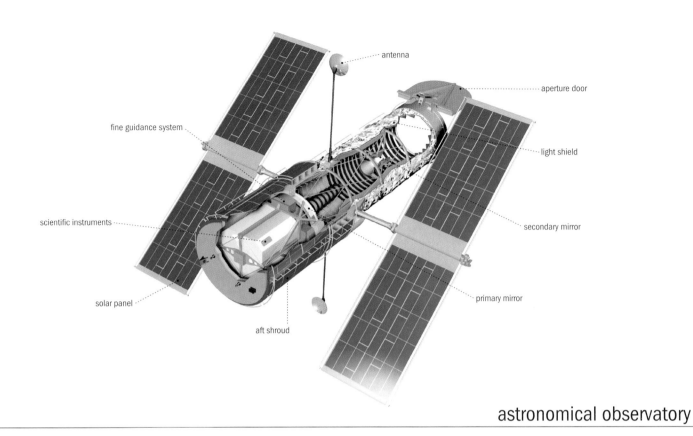

antenna

aperture door

fine guidance system

light shield

scientific instruments

secondary mirror

primary mirror

solar panel

aft shroud

astronomical observatory

cross section of an astronomical observatory

observatory

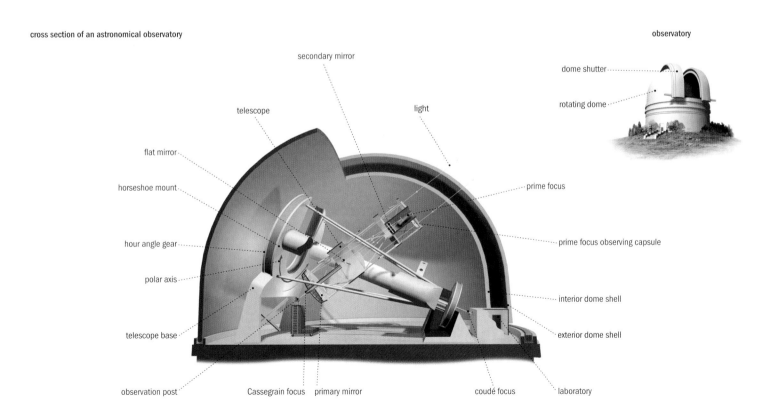

secondary mirror

light

dome shutter

rotating dome

telescope

flat mirror

horseshoe mount

prime focus

hour angle gear

prime focus observing capsule

polar axis

interior dome shell

exterior dome shell

telescope base

observation post

Cassegrain focus

primary mirror

coudé focus

laboratory

space probe

orbiter (Viking)

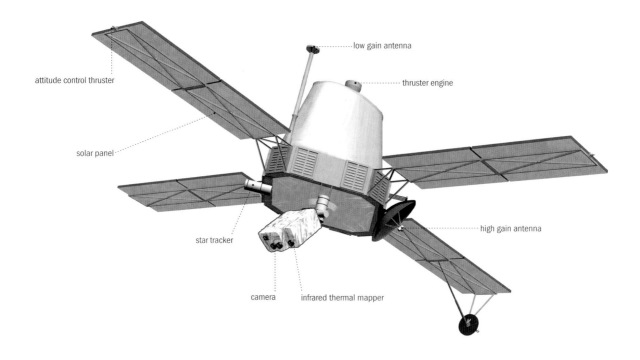

low gain antenna

attitude control thruster

thruster engine

solar panel

star tracker

high gain antenna

camera

infrared thermal mapper

lander (Viking)

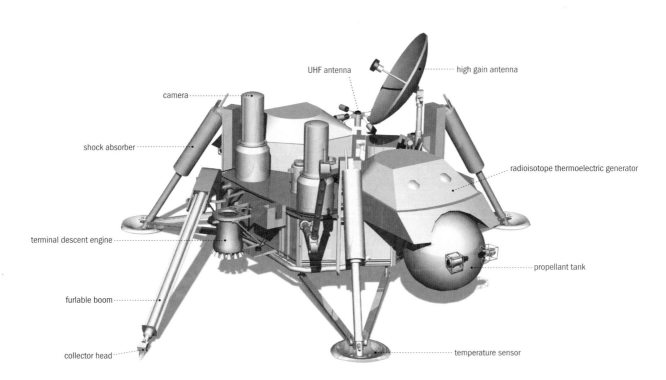

UHF antenna

high gain antenna

camera

shock absorber

radioisotope thermoelectric generator

terminal descent engine

propellant tank

furlable boom

collector head

temperature sensor

examples of space probes

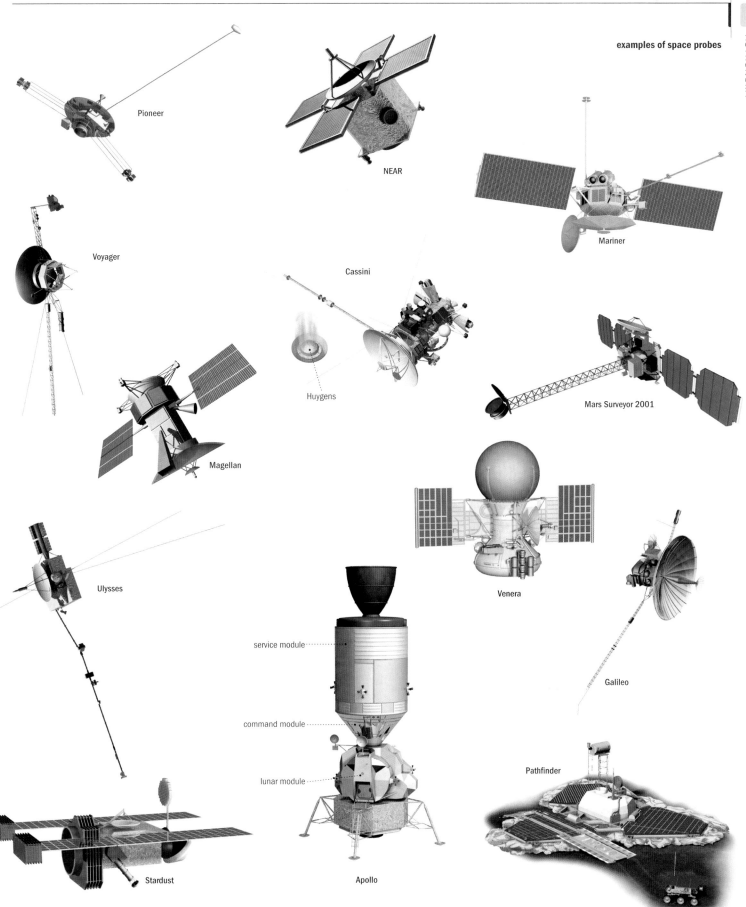

Pioneer

NEAR

Mariner

Voyager

Cassini

Huygens

Mars Surveyor 2001

Magellan

Ulysses

Venera

Galileo

service module

command module

lunar module

Pathfinder

Stardust

Apollo

spacesuit

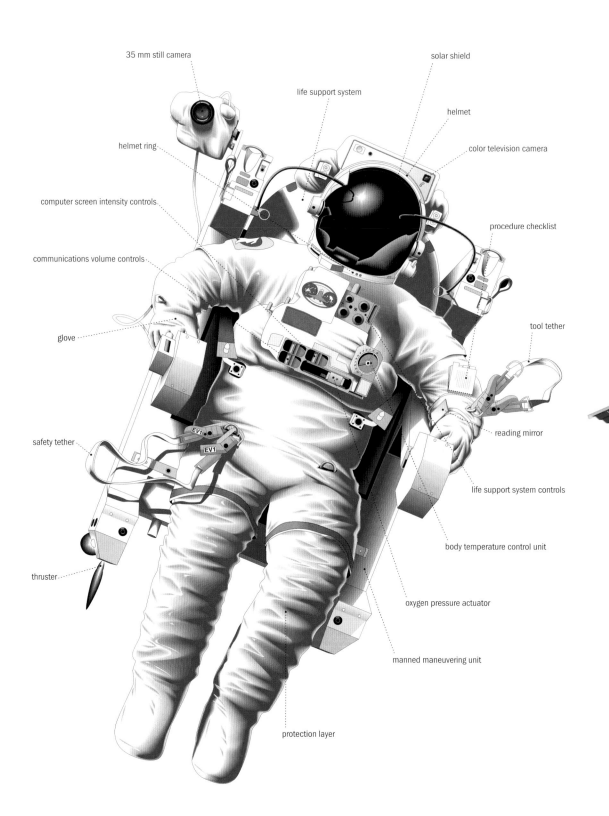

35 mm still camera

solar shield

life support system

helmet

helmet ring

color television camera

computer screen intensity controls

procedure checklist

communications volume controls

tool tether

glove

reading mirror

safety tether

life support system controls

body temperature control unit

thruster

oxygen pressure actuator

manned maneuvering unit

protection layer

international space station

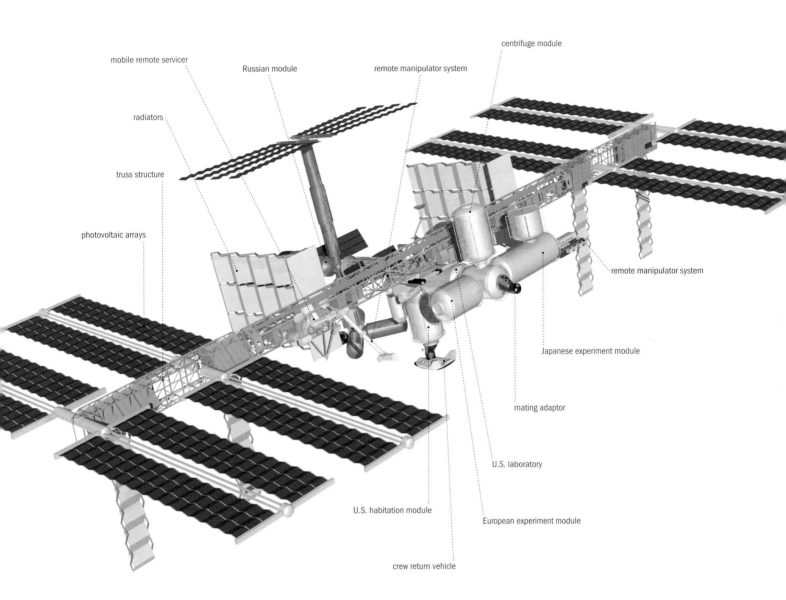

centrifuge module

mobile remote servicer

Russian module

remote manipulator system

radiators

truss structure

photovoltaic arrays

remote manipulator system

Japanese experiment module

mating adaptor

U.S. laboratory

U.S. habitation module

European experiment module

crew return vehicle

space shuttle

space shuttle at takeoff

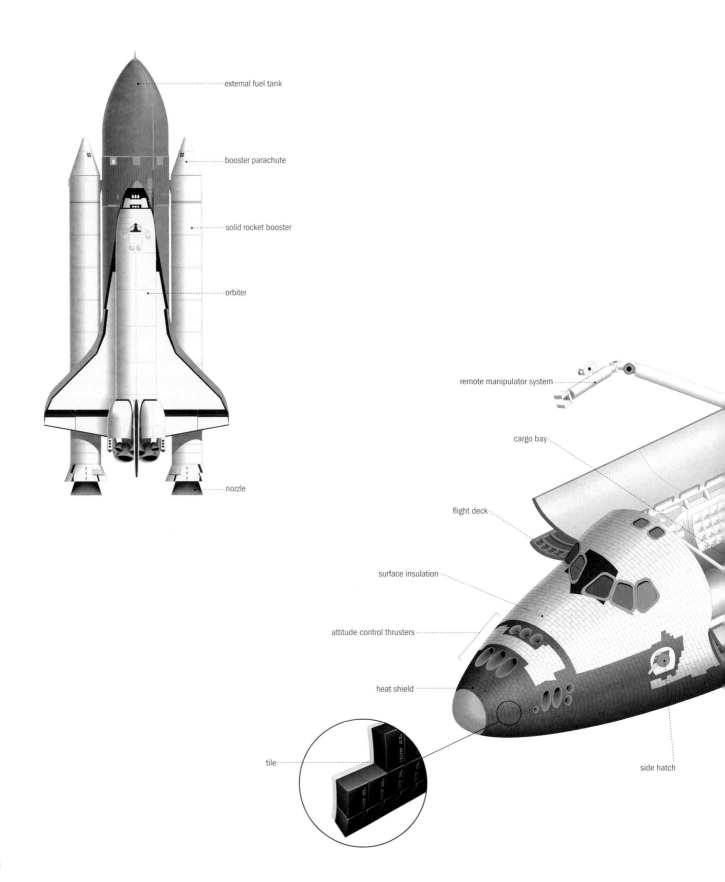

external fuel tank

booster parachute

solid rocket booster

orbiter

nozzle

remote manipulator system

cargo bay

flight deck

surface insulation

attitude control thrusters

heat shield

tile

side hatch

orbiter

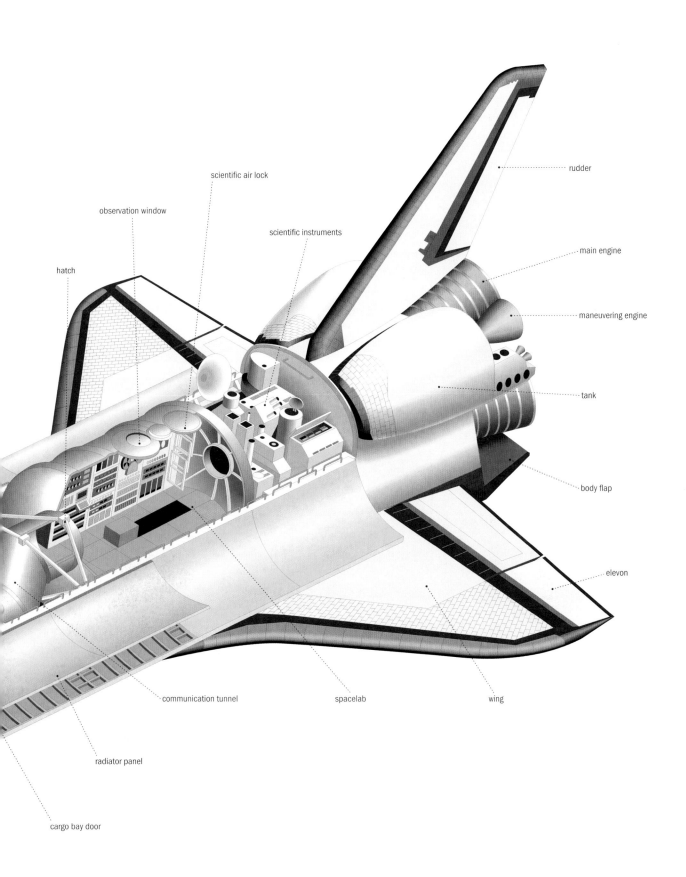

scientific air lock

observation window

scientific instruments

hatch

rudder

main engine

maneuvering engine

tank

body flap

elevon

communication tunnel

spacelab

wing

radiator panel

cargo bay door

space launcher

cross section of a space launcher (Ariane V)

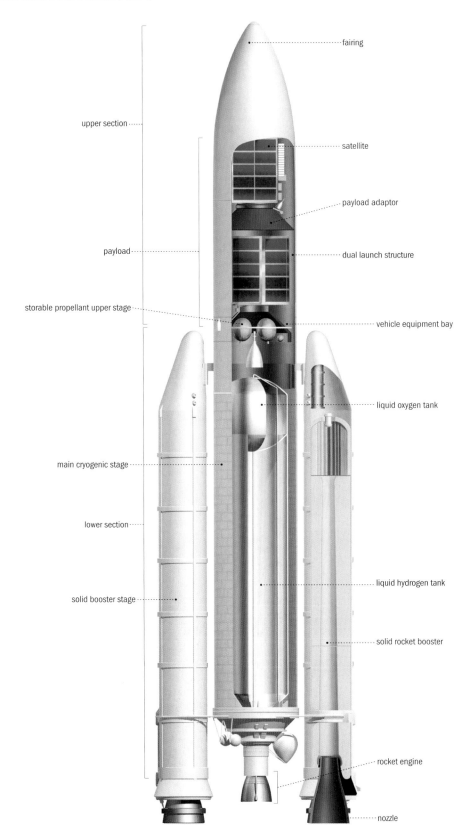

fairing

upper section

satellite

payload adaptor

payload

dual launch structure

storable propellant upper stage

vehicle equipment bay

liquid oxygen tank

main cryogenic stage

lower section

liquid hydrogen tank

solid booster stage

solid rocket booster

rocket engine

nozzle

examples of space launchers

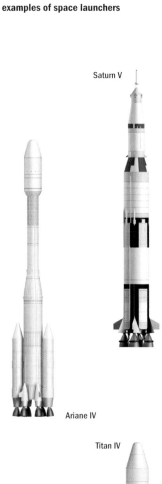

Saturn V

Ariane IV

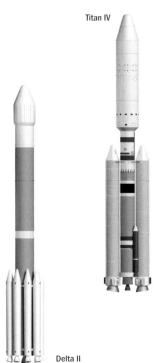

Titan IV

Delta II

cross section of a space launcher (Saturn V)

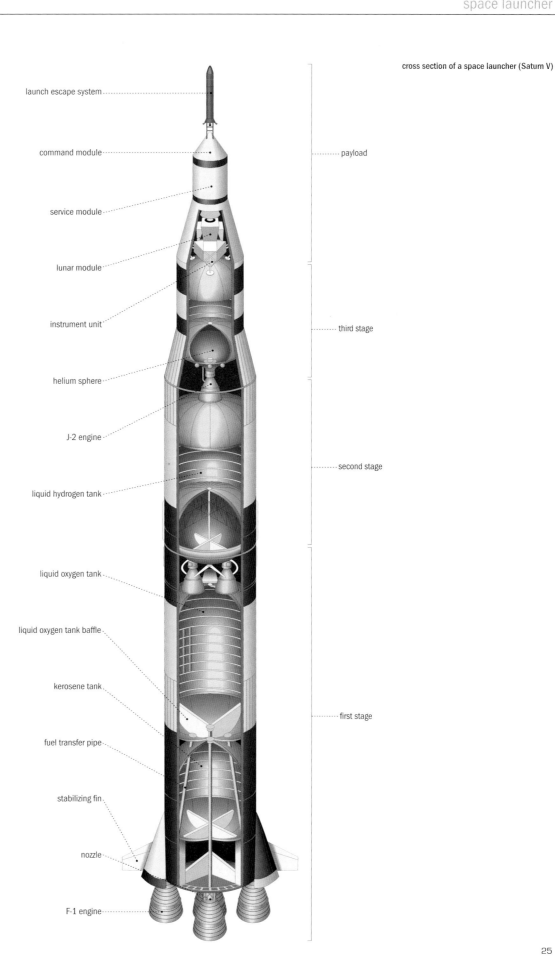

launch escape system

command module

service module

lunar module

instrument unit

helium sphere

J-2 engine

liquid hydrogen tank

liquid oxygen tank

liquid oxygen tank baffle

kerosene tank

fuel transfer pipe

stabilizing fin

nozzle

F-1 engine

payload

third stage

second stage

first stage

EARTH

configuration of the continents

planisphere

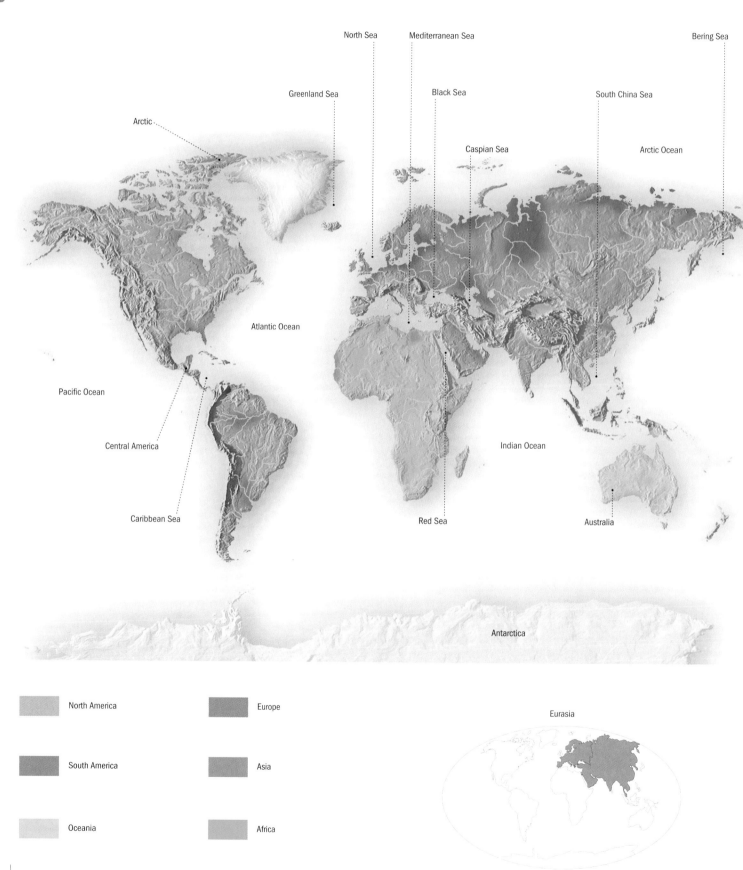

North Sea
Mediterranean Sea
Bering Sea
Greenland Sea
Black Sea
South China Sea
Arctic
Caspian Sea
Arctic Ocean
Atlantic Ocean
Pacific Ocean
Central America
Indian Ocean
Caribbean Sea
Red Sea
Australia
Antarctica

North America

South America

Oceania

Europe

Asia

Africa

Eurasia

Antarctica

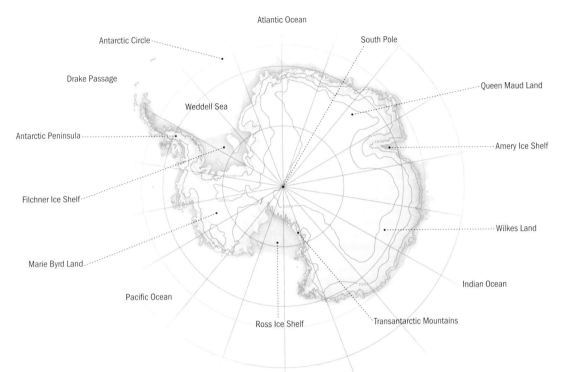

Atlantic Ocean

Antarctic Circle

South Pole

Drake Passage

Queen Maud Land

Weddell Sea

Antarctic Peninsula

Amery Ice Shelf

Filchner Ice Shelf

Wilkes Land

Marie Byrd Land

Indian Ocean

Pacific Ocean

Ross Ice Shelf

Transantarctic Mountains

Oceania

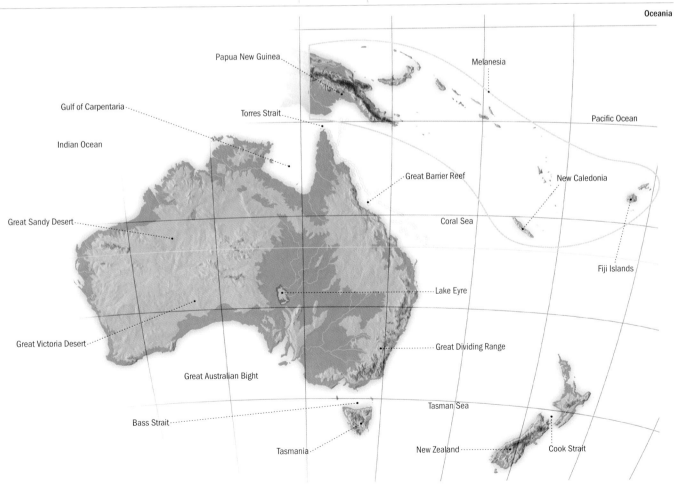

Papua New Guinea

Melanesia

Gulf of Carpentaria

Torres Strait

Pacific Ocean

Indian Ocean

Great Barrier Reef

New Caledonia

Great Sandy Desert

Coral Sea

Fiji Islands

Lake Eyre

Great Victoria Desert

Great Dividing Range

Great Australian Bight

Tasman Sea

Bass Strait

New Zealand

Cook Strait

Tasmania

configuration of the continents

EARTH

North America

Beaufort Sea

Mackenzie River

Hudson Bay

Baffin Island

Bering Strait

Greenland

Gulf of Alaska

Great Lakes

Aleutian Islands

Newfoundland Island

Rocky Mountains

Saint Lawrence River

Grand Canyon

Appalachian Mountains

Mississippi River

Gulf of California

Gulf of Mexico

West Indies

Yucatan Peninsula

Caribbean Sea

Central America

Isthmus of Panama

Orinoco River

Amazon River

Gulf of Panama

Equator

Andes Cordillera

Lake Titicaca

Atacama Desert

Paraná River

Patagonia

Falkland Islands

Tierra del Fuego

Cape Horn

Drake Passage

configuration of the continents

Barents Sea

Ural Mountains

Lake Ladoga

Kola Peninsula

Volga River

Gulf of Bothnia

Norwegian Sea

Dnieper River

Iceland

North Sea

Scandinavian Peninsula

Baltic Sea

Irish Sea

Atlantic Ocean

English Channel

Vistula River

Alps

Black Sea

Iberian Peninsula

Strait of Gibraltar

Pyrenees

Danube River

Balkan Peninsula

Carpathian Mountains

Mediterranean Sea

Adriatic Sea

Aegean Sea

Aral Sea

Lake Baikal   Gobi Desert

Caspian Sea

Kamchatka Peninsula

Black Sea

Sea of Japan

Red Sea

Pacific Ocean

Japan

Korean Peninsula

East China Sea

Philippines

Gulf of Aden   Himalayas

Arabian Peninsula   Gulf of Oman

South China Sea

Persian Gulf   Arabian Sea

Indonesia

Indian Ocean   Bay of Bengal

Africa

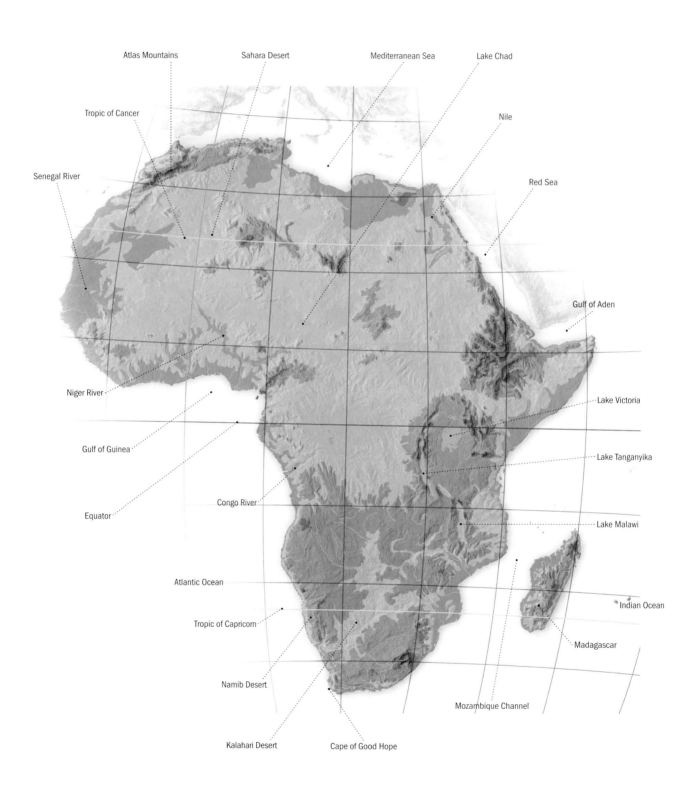

Atlas Mountains

Sahara Desert

Mediterranean Sea

Lake Chad

Tropic of Cancer

Nile

Senegal River

Red Sea

Gulf of Aden

Niger River

Lake Victoria

Gulf of Guinea

Lake Tanganyika

Equator

Congo River

Lake Malawi

Atlantic Ocean

Indian Ocean

Tropic of Capricorn

Madagascar

Namib Desert

Mozambique Channel

Kalahari Desert

Cape of Good Hope

cartography

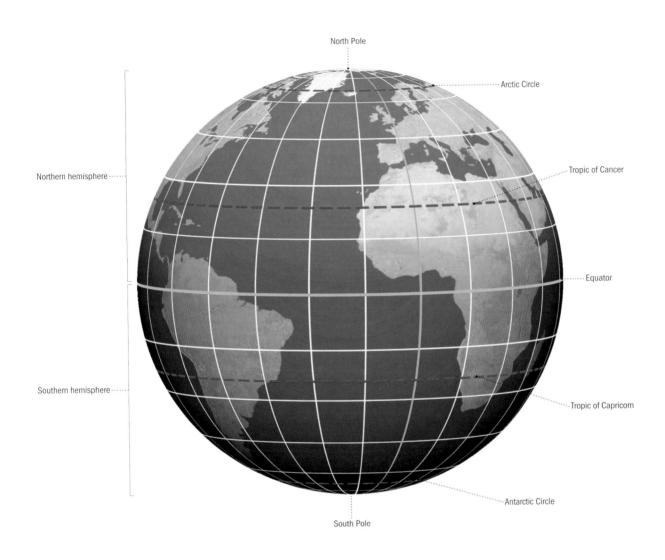

North Pole

Arctic Circle

Tropic of Cancer

Northern hemisphere

Equator

Southern hemisphere

Tropic of Capricorn

Antarctic Circle

South Pole

hemispheres

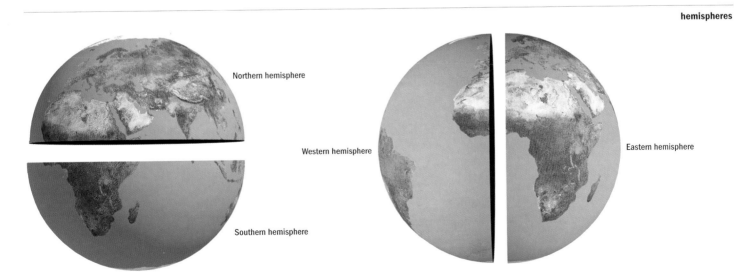

Northern hemisphere

Southern hemisphere

Western hemisphere

Eastern hemisphere

cartography

grid system

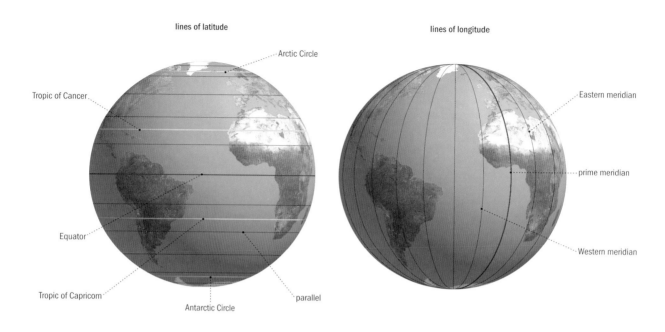

lines of latitude

lines of longitude

Arctic Circle

Tropic of Cancer

Eastern meridian

prime meridian

Equator

Western meridian

Tropic of Capricorn

Antarctic Circle

parallel

map projections

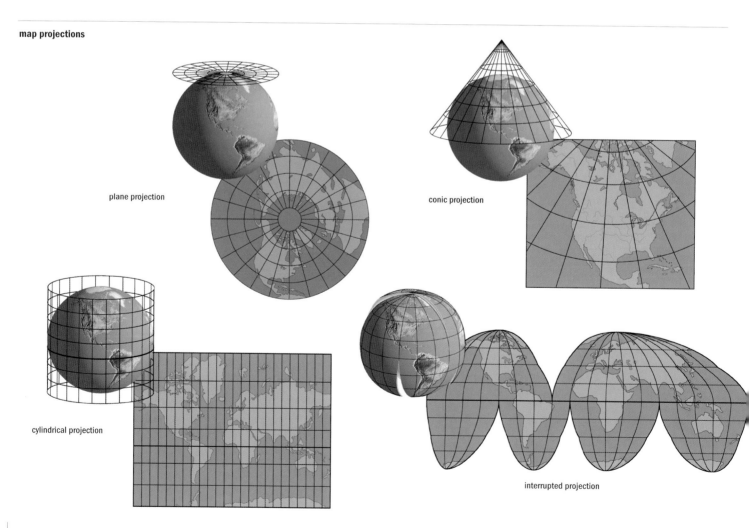

plane projection

conic projection

cylindrical projection

interrupted projection

compass card

North

North-Northwest

North-Northeast

Northwest

Northeast

West-Northwest

East-Northeast

West

East

West-Southwest

East-Southeast

Southwest

Southeast

South-Southwest

South-Southeast

South

political map

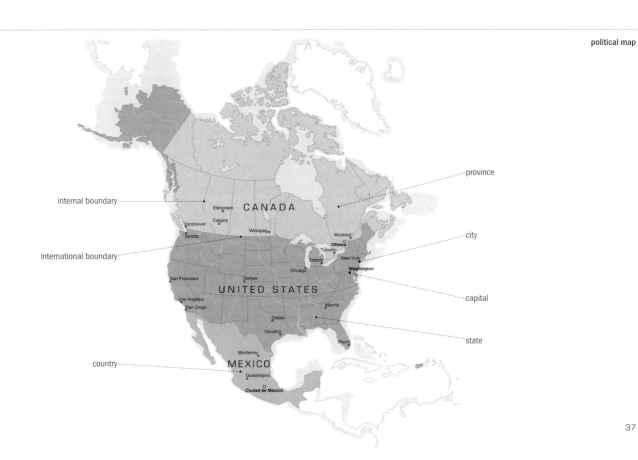

internal boundary

province

CANADA

Edmonton

Calgary

Vancouver

Winnipeg

Seattle

Montréal

Ottawa

Toronto

city

international boundary

Detroit

New York

Chicago

Washington

San Francisco

Denver

capital

UNITED STATES

Los Angeles

San Diego

Atlanta

Dallas

state

Houston

Miami

Monterrey

country

MEXICO

Guadalajara

Ciudad de México

physical map

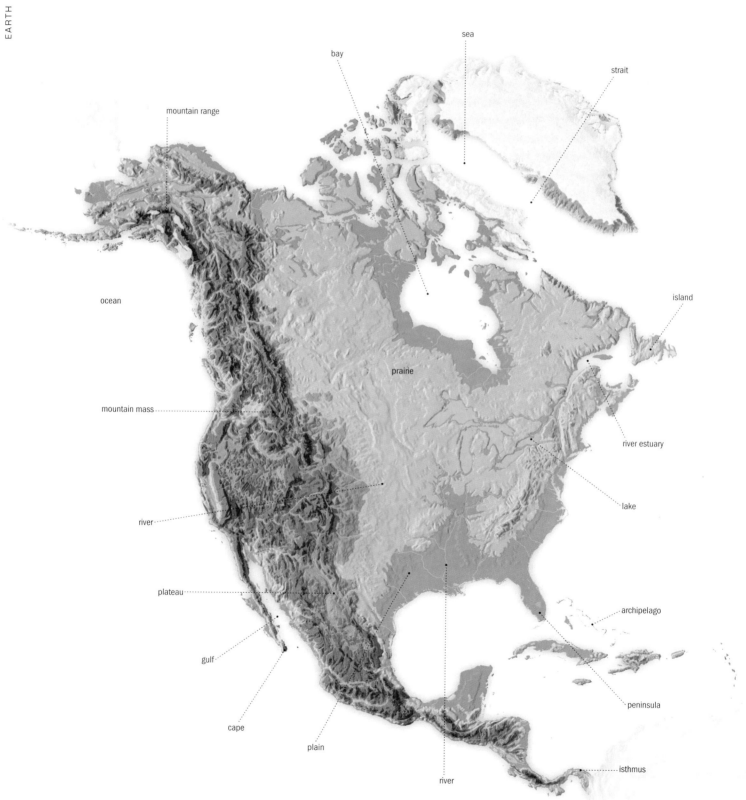

mountain range

sea

bay

strait

ocean

prairie

mountain mass

island

river estuary

lake

river

plateau

archipelago

gulf

peninsula

cape

isthmus

plain

river

railroad line

railroad station

bridge

park

suburbs

cemetery

river

monument

woods

circular route

traffic circle

highway

district

street

avenue

public building

boulevard

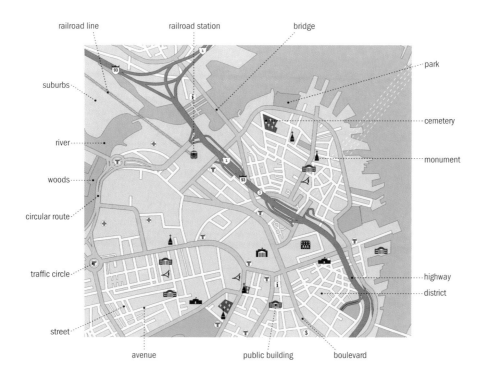

road map

highway number

road

highway

road number

rest area

service area

airport

national park

belt highway

scenic route

secondary road

point of interest

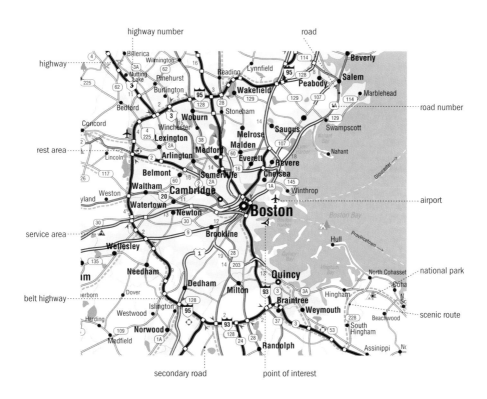

remote sensing

radar

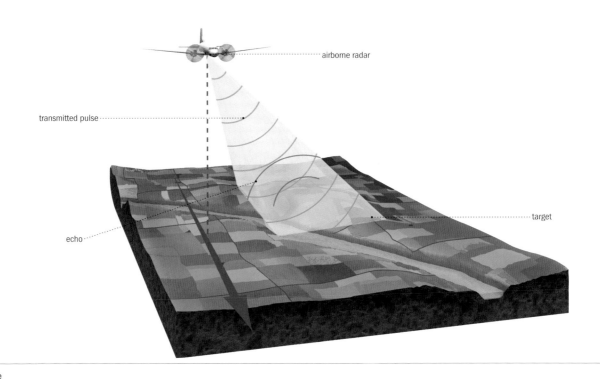

airborne radar

transmitted pulse

target

echo

Radarsat satellite

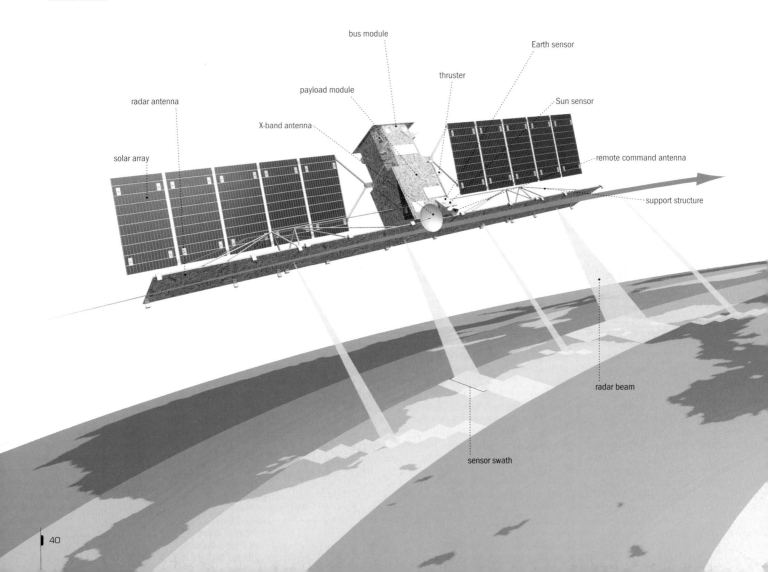

bus module

Earth sensor

thruster

payload module

Sun sensor

radar antenna

X-band antenna

remote command antenna

solar array

support structure

radar beam

sensor swath

sonar

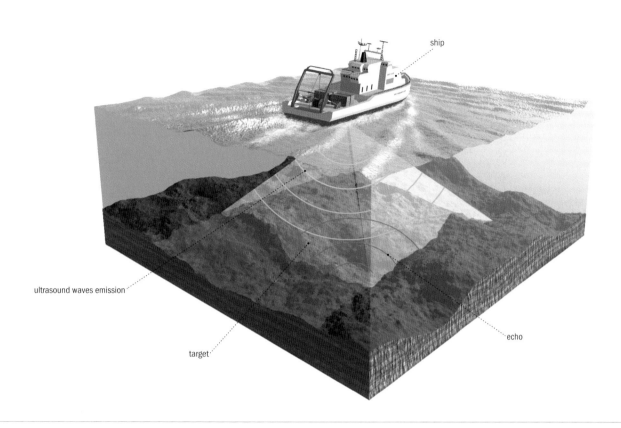

ship

ultrasound waves emission

target

echo

satellite remote sensing

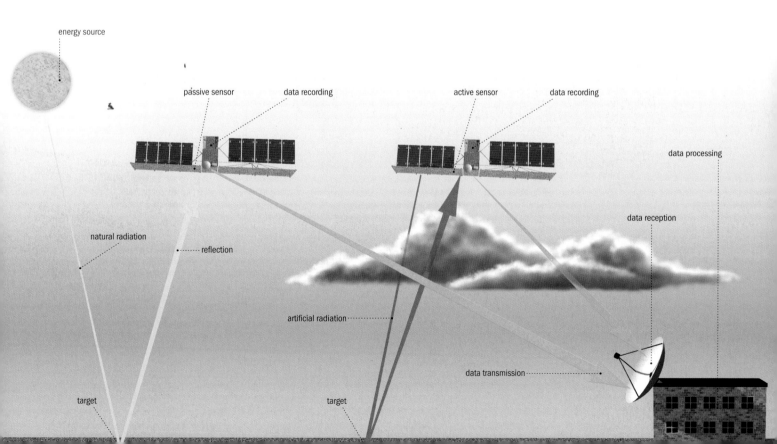

energy source

passive sensor

data recording

active sensor

data recording

data processing

data reception

natural radiation

reflection

artificial radiation

data transmission

target

target

EARTH

structure of the Earth

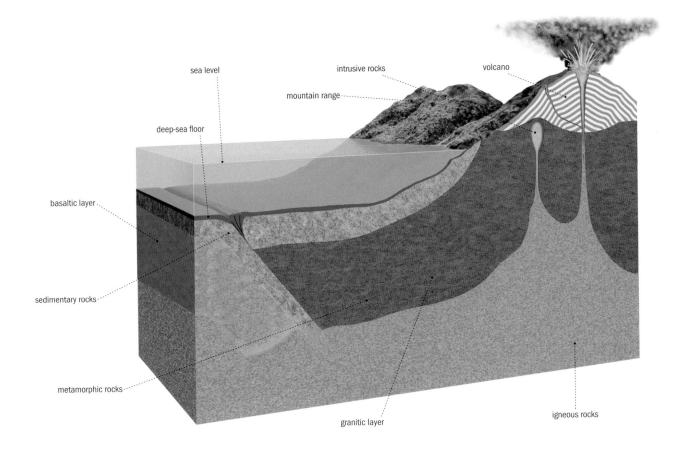

sea level

intrusive rocks

volcano

mountain range

deep-sea floor

basaltic layer

sedimentary rocks

metamorphic rocks

granitic layer

igneous rocks

section of the Earth's crust

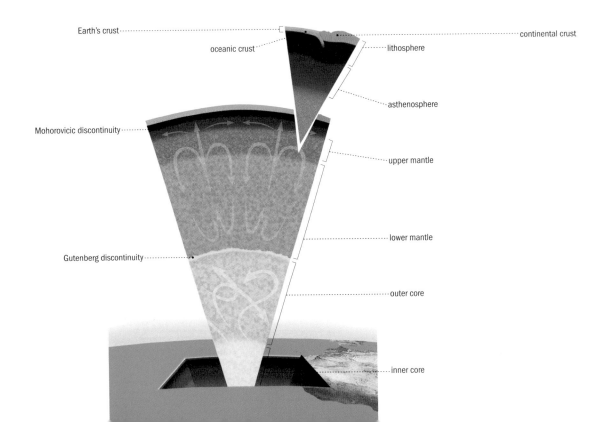

Earth's crust

oceanic crust

continental crust

lithosphere

asthenosphere

Mohorovicic discontinuity

upper mantle

lower mantle

Gutenberg discontinuity

outer core

inner core

tectonic plates

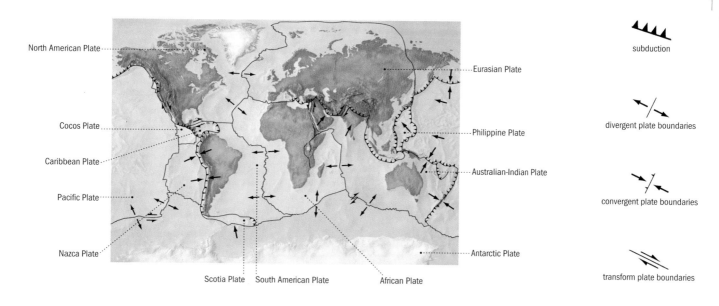

North American Plate

Eurasian Plate

Cocos Plate

Philippine Plate

Caribbean Plate

Australian-Indian Plate

Pacific Plate

Antarctic Plate

Nazca Plate

Scotia Plate   South American Plate   African Plate

subduction

divergent plate boundaries

convergent plate boundaries

transform plate boundaries

earthquake

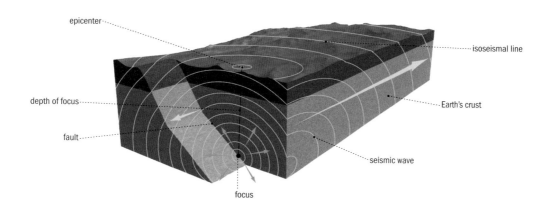

epicenter

isoseismal line

depth of focus

Earth's crust

fault

seismic wave

focus

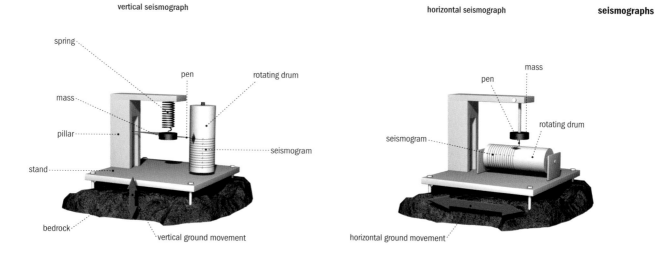

vertical seismograph

horizontal seismograph

seismographs

spring

mass

pen

pen

mass

rotating drum

rotating drum

seismogram

pillar

seismogram

stand

bedrock

vertical ground movement

horizontal ground movement

volcano

volcano during eruption

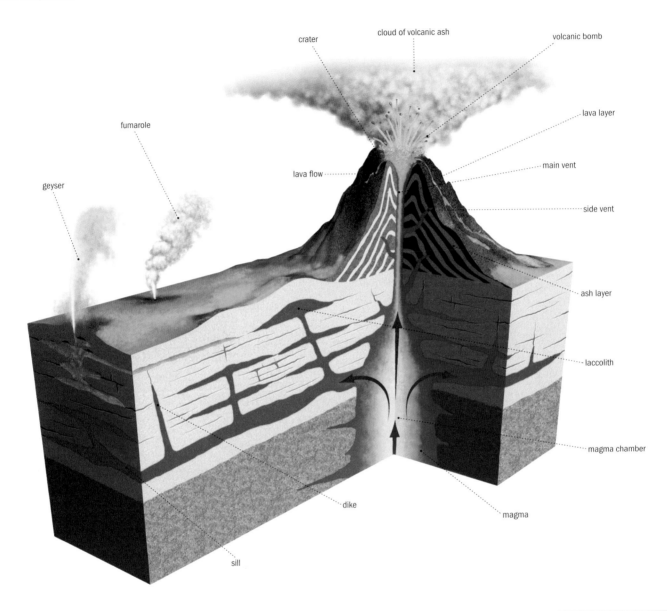

crater

cloud of volcanic ash

volcanic bomb

fumarole

lava layer

main vent

geyser

lava flow

side vent

ash layer

laccolith

magma chamber

dike

magma

sill

examples of volcanoes

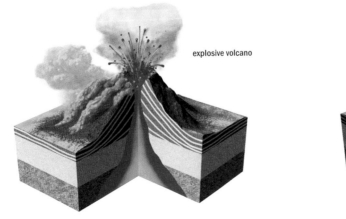

explosive volcano

effusive volcano

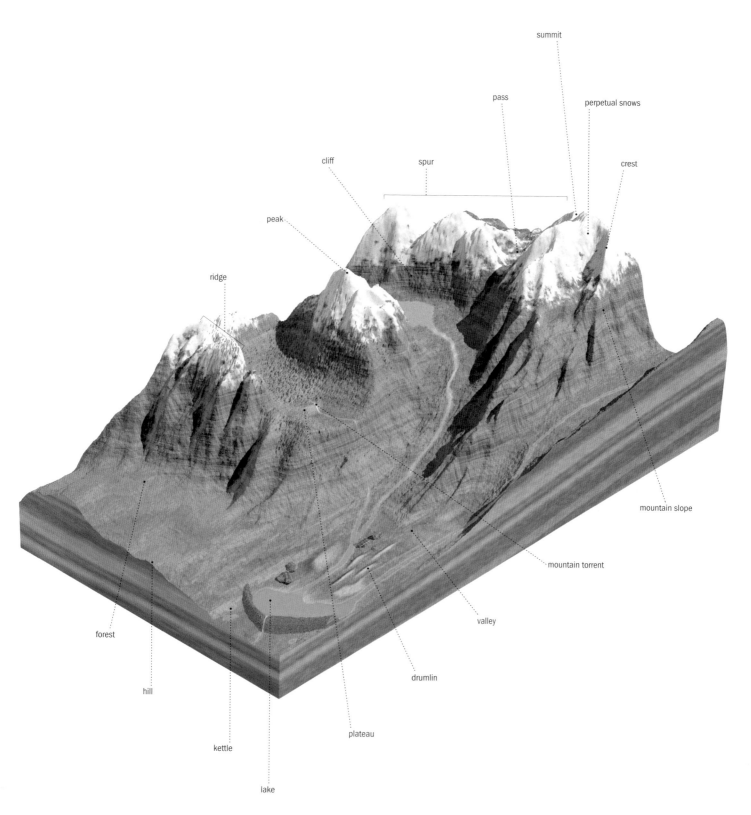

summit

pass

perpetual snows

cliff

spur

crest

peak

ridge

forest

hill

kettle

lake

plateau

drumlin

valley

mountain torrent

mountain slope

glacier

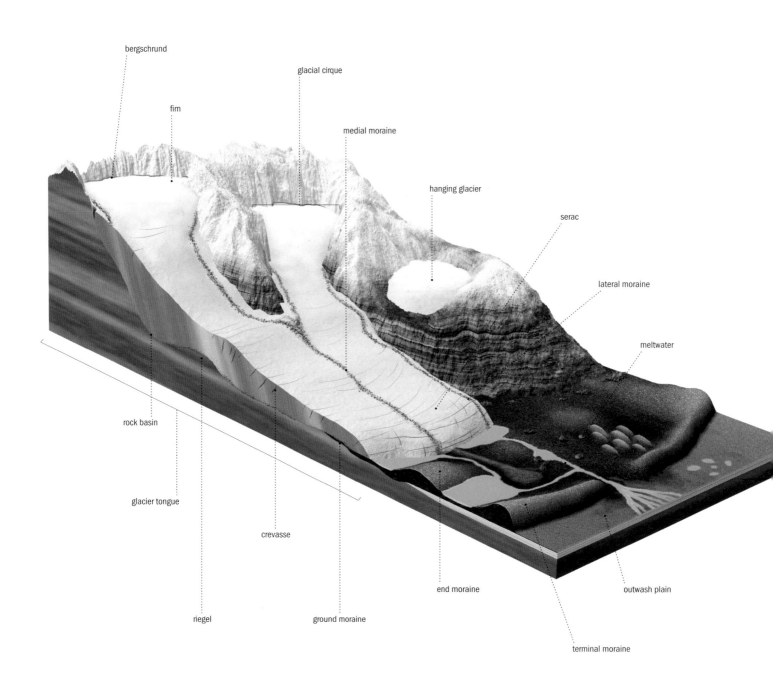

bergschrund

glacial cirque

firn

medial moraine

hanging glacier

serac

lateral moraine

meltwater

rock basin

glacier tongue

crevasse

end moraine

outwash plain

riegel

ground moraine

terminal moraine

cave

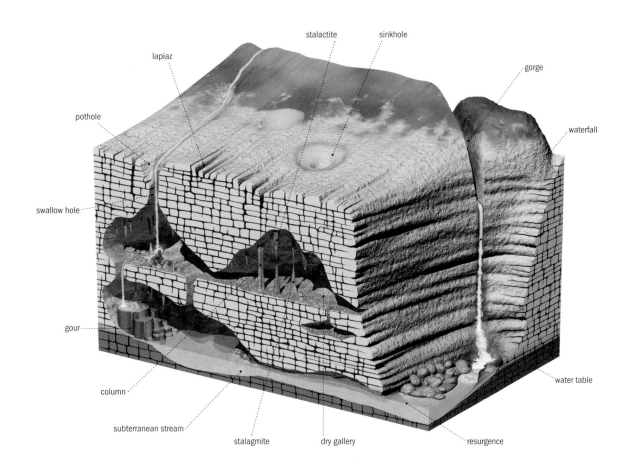

lapiaz

stalactite

sinkhole

gorge

pothole

waterfall

swallow hole

gour

column

water table

subterranean stream

stalagmite

dry gallery

resurgence

landslides

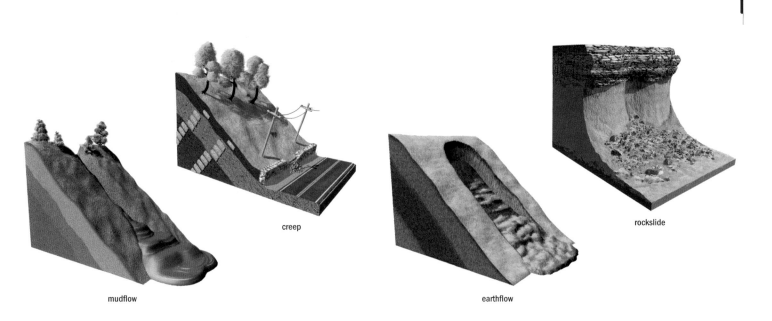

mudflow

creep

earthflow

rockslide

watercourse

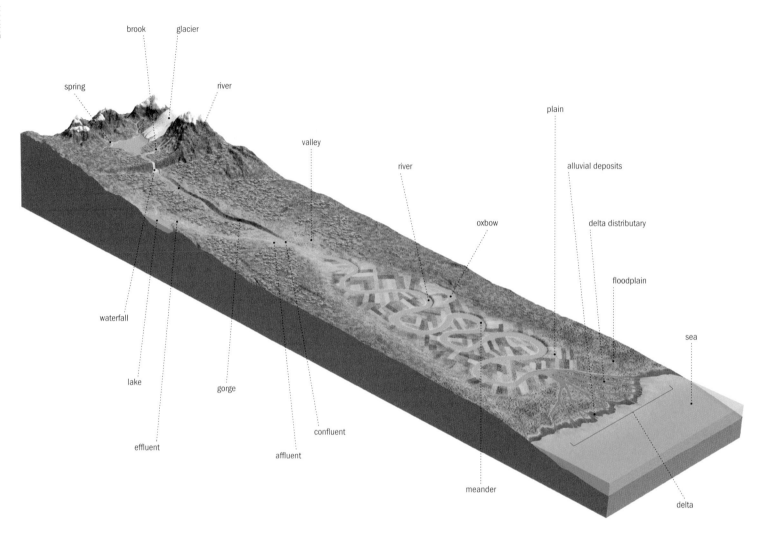

brook

glacier

spring

river

plain

valley

alluvial deposits

river

oxbow

delta distributary

floodplain

waterfall

sea

lake

gorge

effluent

confluent

affluent

meander

delta

lakes

glacial lake

volcanic lake

tectonic lake

oxbow lake

oasis

artificial lake

wave

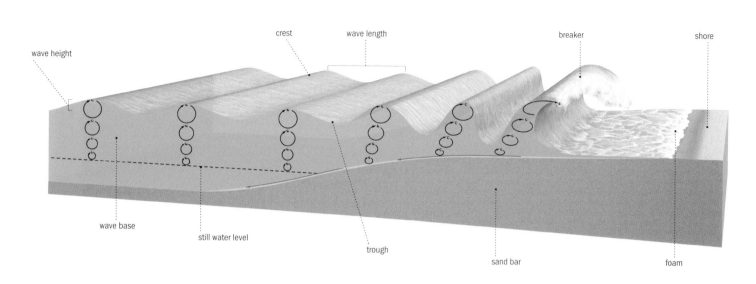

wave height

crest wave length breaker shore

wave base

still water level

trough

sand bar

foam

ocean floor

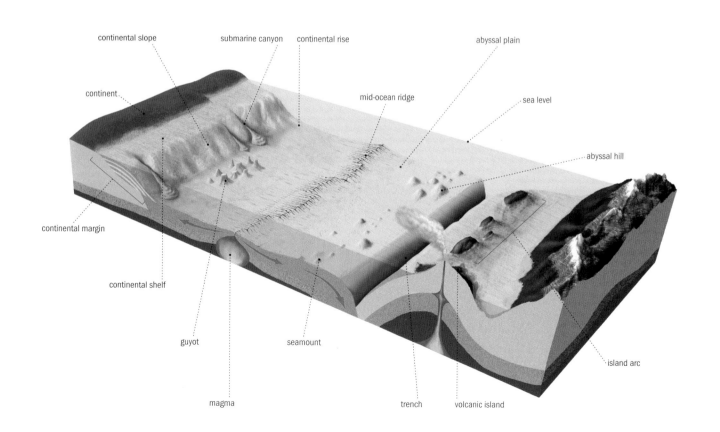

continental slope submarine canyon continental rise abyssal plain

continent mid-ocean ridge sea level

abyssal hill

continental margin

continental shelf

guyot seamount

island arc

magma trench volcanic island

ocean trenches and ridges

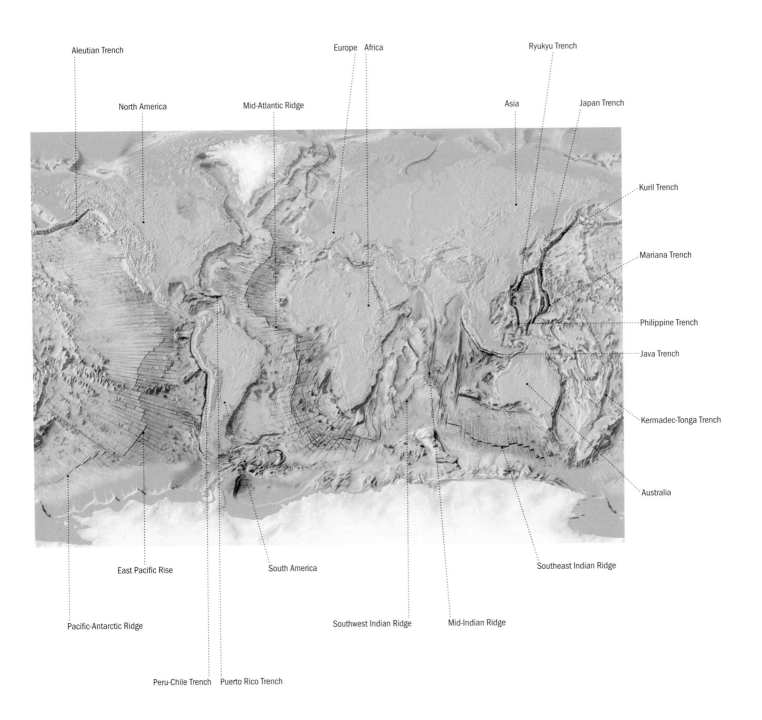

Aleutian Trench

Europe Africa

Ryukyu Trench

North America

Mid-Atlantic Ridge

Asia

Japan Trench

Kuril Trench

Mariana Trench

Philippine Trench

Java Trench

Kermadec-Tonga Trench

Australia

East Pacific Rise

South America

Southeast Indian Ridge

Pacific-Antarctic Ridge

Southwest Indian Ridge

Mid-Indian Ridge

Peru-Chile Trench Puerto Rico Trench

common coastal features

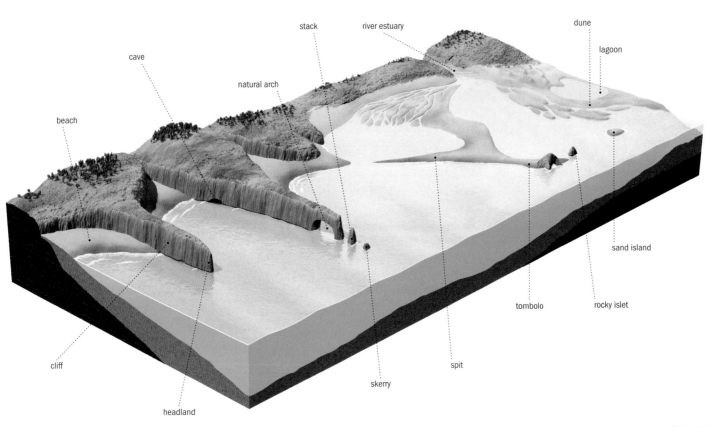

stack

river estuary

dune

cave

lagoon

natural arch

beach

sand island

cliff

tombolo

rocky islet

headland

skerry

spit

examples of shorelines

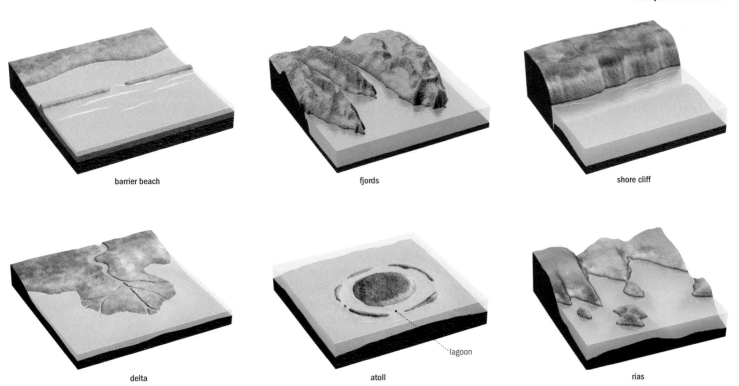

barrier beach

fjords

shore cliff

delta

atoll

lagoon

rias

desert

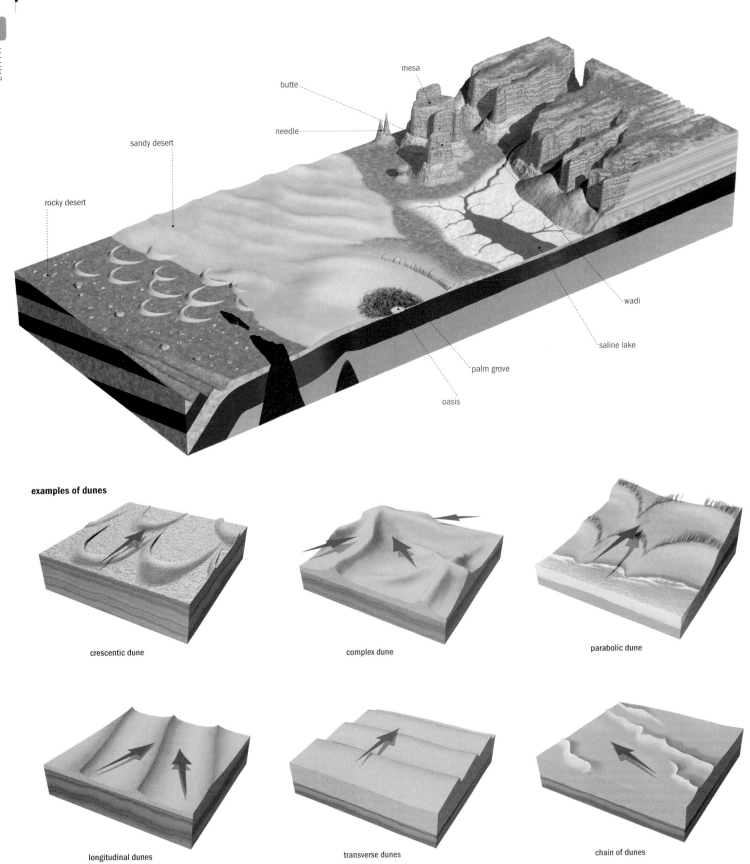

mesa

butte

needle

sandy desert

rocky desert

wadi

saline lake

palm grove

oasis

examples of dunes

crescentic dune

complex dune

parabolic dune

longitudinal dunes

transverse dunes

chain of dunes

profile of the Earth's atmosphere

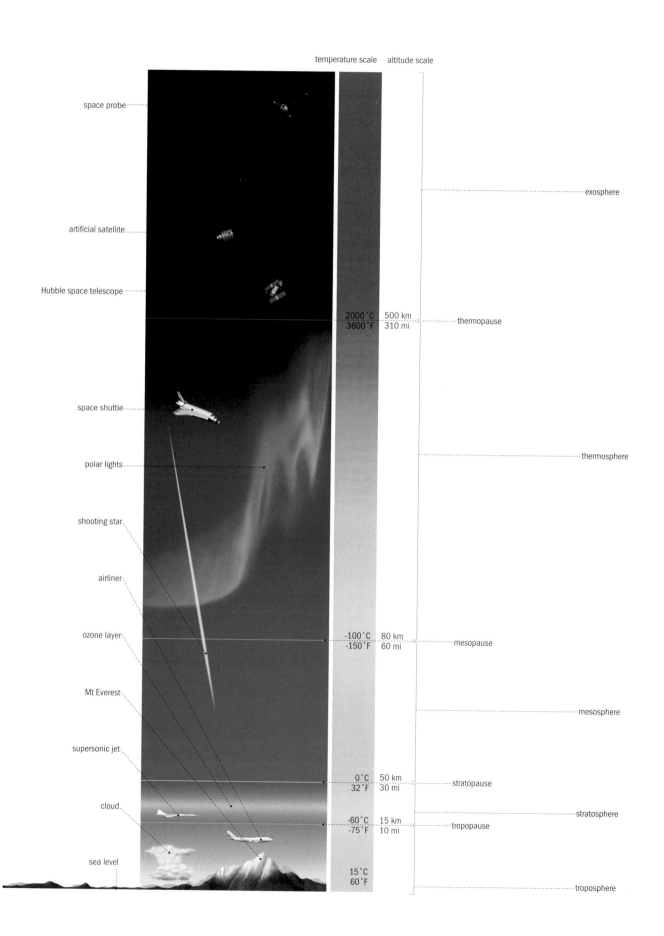

temperature scale   altitude scale

space probe

artificial satellite

Hubble space telescope

2000°C   500 km   thermopause
3600°F   310 mi

space shuttle

polar lights .... thermosphere

shooting star

airliner

ozone layer   -100°C   80 km   mesopause
-150°F   60 mi

Mt Everest   mesosphere

supersonic jet

0°C   50 km   stratopause
32°F   30 mi

cloud   stratosphere

-60°C   15 km   tropopause
-75°F   10 mi

sea level   15°C
60°F   troposphere

exosphere

EARTH

seasons of the year

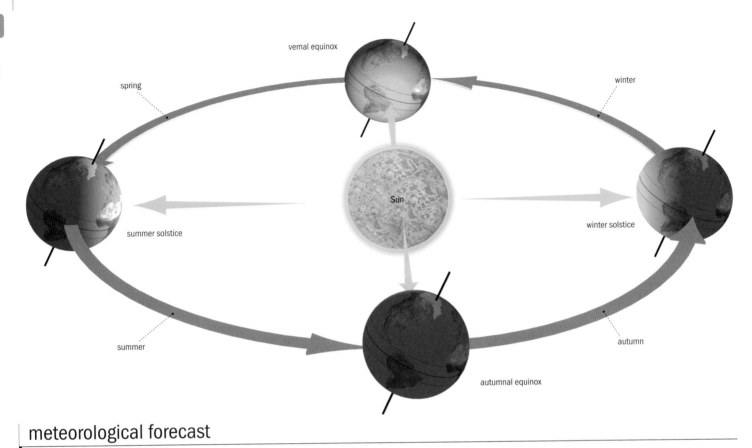

vernal equinox

spring

winter

summer solstice

Sun

winter solstice

summer

autumn

autumnal equinox

meteorological forecast

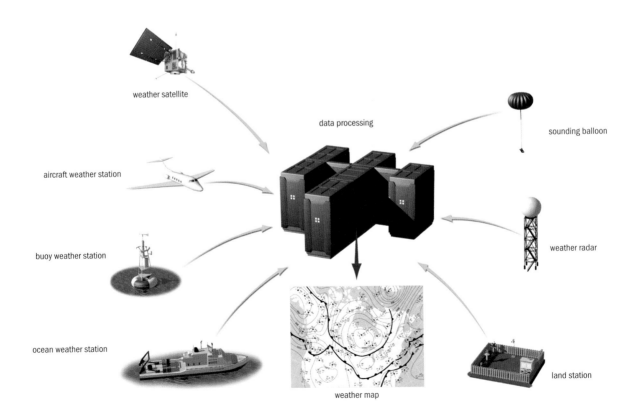

weather satellite

data processing

sounding balloon

aircraft weather station

buoy weather station

weather radar

ocean weather station

land station

weather map

weather map

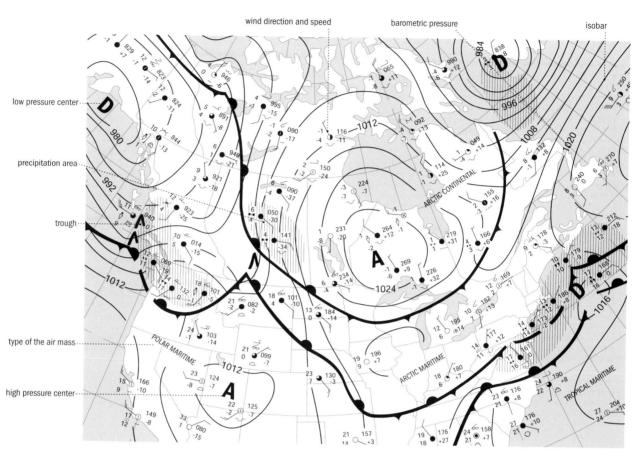

wind direction and speed

barometric pressure

isobar

low pressure center

precipitation area

trough

type of the air mass

high pressure center

station model

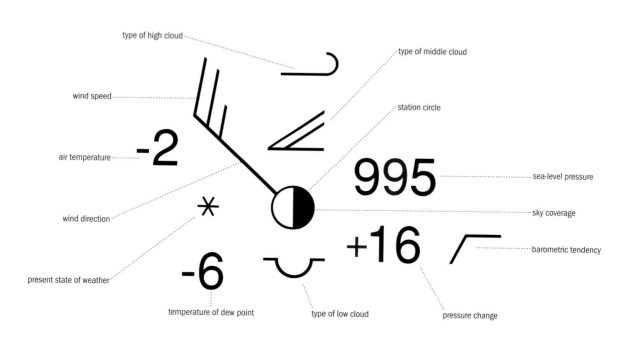

type of high cloud

type of middle cloud

wind speed

station circle

air temperature

sea-level pressure

wind direction

sky coverage

barometric tendency

present state of weather

temperature of dew point

type of low cloud

pressure change

international weather symbols

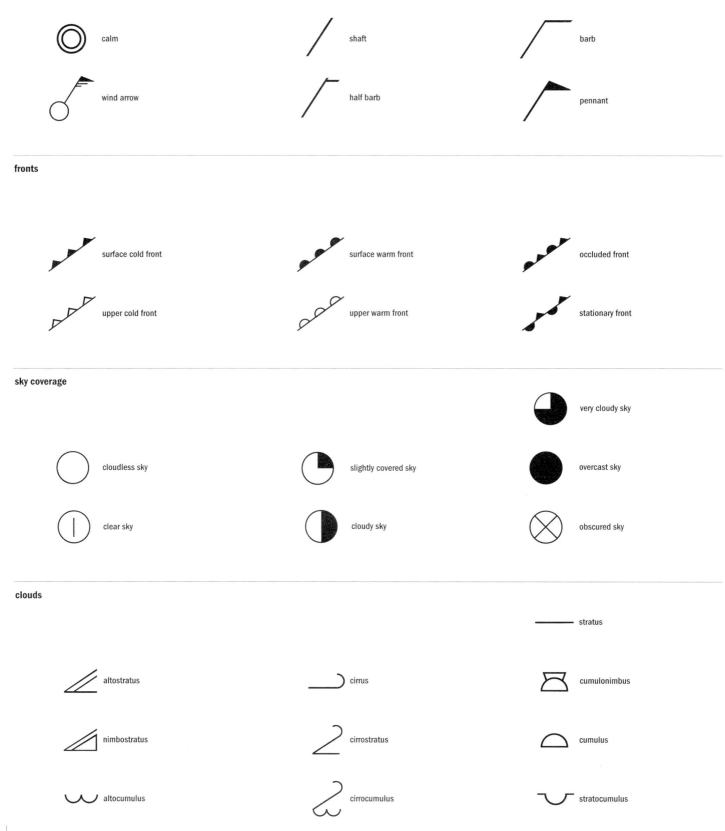

wind

calm

shaft

barb

wind arrow

half barb

pennant

fronts

surface cold front

surface warm front

occluded front

upper cold front

upper warm front

stationary front

sky coverage

very cloudy sky

cloudless sky

slightly covered sky

overcast sky

clear sky

cloudy sky

obscured sky

clouds

stratus

altostratus

cirrus

cumulonimbus

nimbostratus

cirrostratus

cumulus

altocumulus

cirrocumulus

stratocumulus

present weather

 sandstorm or dust storm

 thunderstorm

 heavy thunderstorm

 lightning

 tropical storm

hurricane

tornado

light intermittent rain

 light intermittent drizzle

 light intermittent snow

moderate intermittent rain

 moderate intermittent drizzle

moderate intermittent snow

 heavy intermittent rain

 thick intermittent drizzle

heavy intermittent snow

 light continuous rain

 light continuous drizzle

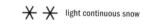 light continuous snow

 moderate continuous rain

 moderate continuous drizzle

 moderate continuous snow

 heavy continuous rain

 thick continuous drizzle

 heavy continuous snow

 sleet

 mist

 snow shower

 drifting snow low

 fog

 rain shower

 drifting snow high

 haze

 hail shower

 freezing rain

 smoke

 squall

57

meteorological station

EARTH

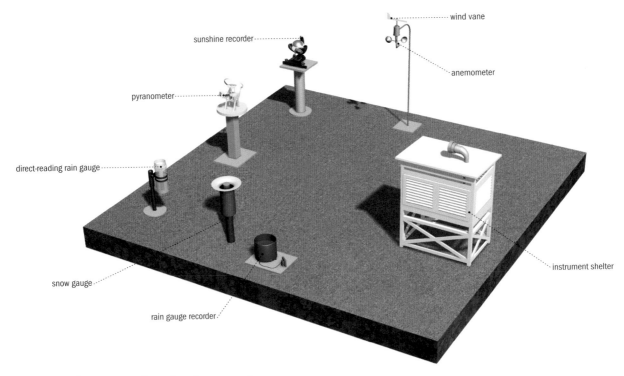

sunshine recorder

wind vane

anemometer

pyranometer

direct-reading rain gauge

instrument shelter

snow gauge

rain gauge recorder

meteorological measuring instruments

measure of sunshine

measure of sky radiation

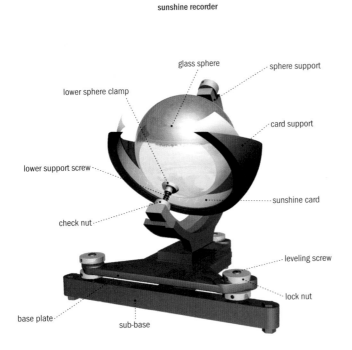

sunshine recorder

glass sphere

sphere support

lower sphere clamp

card support

lower support screw

sunshine card

check nut

leveling screw

lock nut

base plate

sub-base

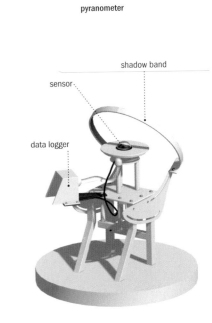

pyranometer

shadow band

sensor

data logger

meteorological measuring instruments

measure of rainfall

direct-reading rain gauge

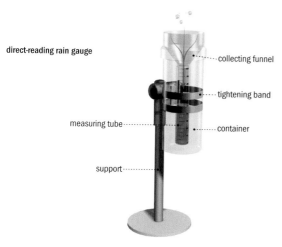

collecting funnel

tightening band

measuring tube

container

support

rain gauge recorder

collecting vessel

recording unit

upper-air sounding

sounding balloon

radiosonde

measure of air pressure

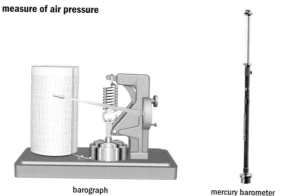

barograph

mercury barometer

measure of snowfall

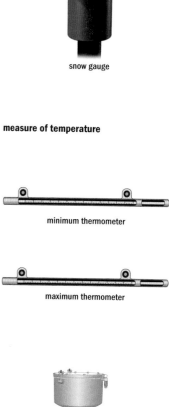

snow gauge

measure of humidity

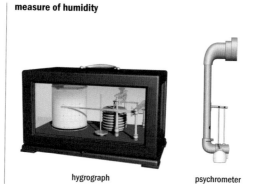

hygrograph

psychrometer

measure of temperature

minimum thermometer

maximum thermometer

measure of wind direction

wind vane

measure of cloud ceiling

alidade

theodolite

ceiling projector

measure of wind strength

anemometer

weather satellites

polar-orbiting satellite

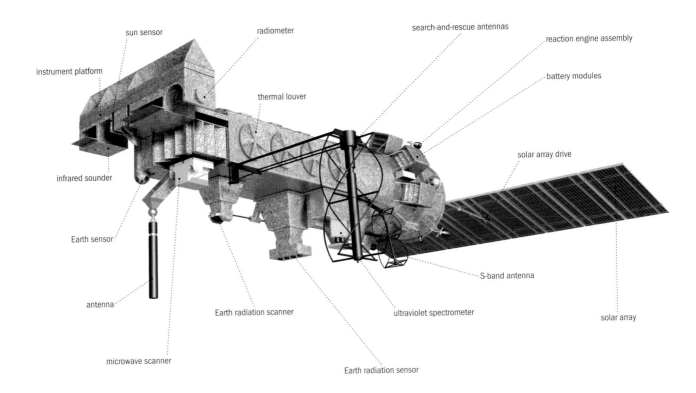

sun sensor

radiometer

search-and-rescue antennas

reaction engine assembly

instrument platform

battery modules

thermal louver

solar array drive

infrared sounder

Earth sensor

S-band antenna

antenna

Earth radiation scanner

ultraviolet spectrometer

solar array

microwave scanner

Earth radiation sensor

geostationary satellite

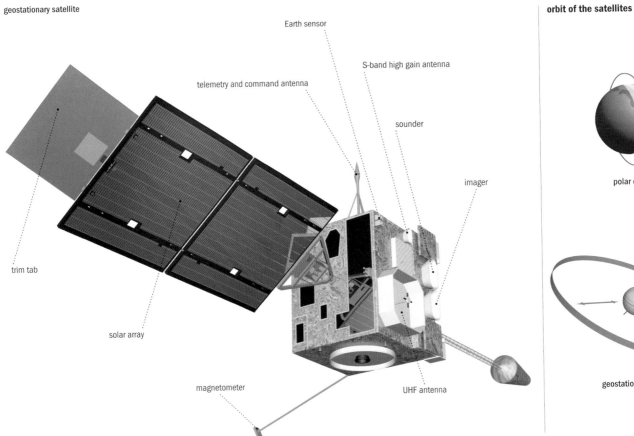

Earth sensor

S-band high gain antenna

telemetry and command antenna

sounder

imager

trim tab

solar array

magnetometer

UHF antenna

orbit of the satellites

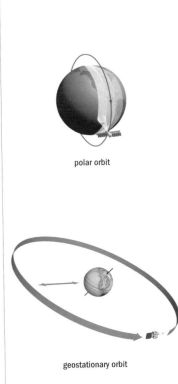

polar orbit

geostationary orbit

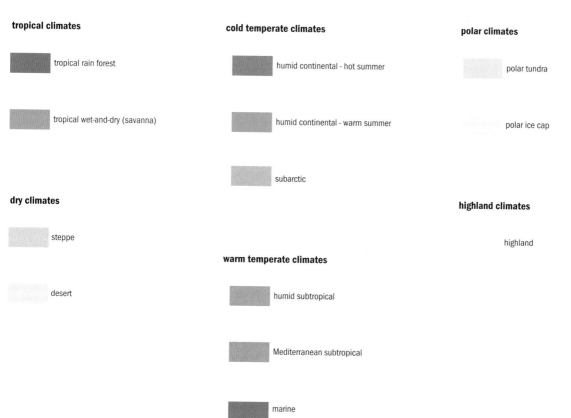

tropical climates

    tropical rain forest

    tropical wet-and-dry (savanna)

dry climates

    steppe

    desert

cold temperate climates

    humid continental - hot summer

    humid continental - warm summer

    subarctic

warm temperate climates

    humid subtropical

    Mediterranean subtropical

    marine

polar climates

    polar tundra

    polar ice cap

highland climates

    highland

clouds

EARTH

high clouds

middle clouds

low clouds

cirrostratus

cirrocumulus

cirrus

altostratus

altocumulus

stratocumulus

nimbostratus

cumulus

stratus

clouds of vertical development

cumulonimbus

tornado and waterspout

waterspout

wall cloud

funnel cloud

debris

tornado

tropical cyclone

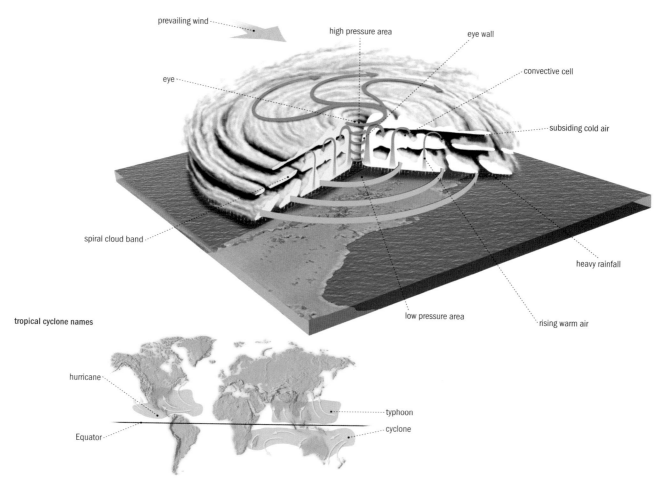

prevailing wind

high pressure area

eye wall

eye

convective cell

subsiding cold air

spiral cloud band

heavy rainfall

low pressure area

rising warm air

tropical cyclone names

hurricane

typhoon

Equator

cyclone

precipitations

EARTH

rain forms

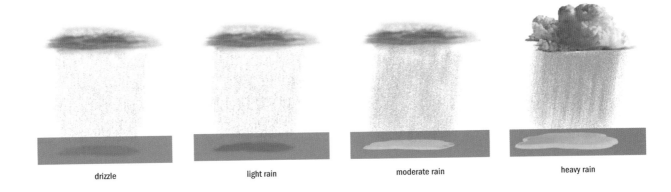

drizzle   light rain   moderate rain   heavy rain

winter precipitations

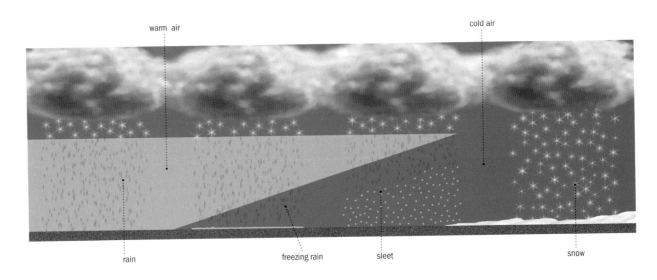

warm air   cold air

rain   freezing rain   sleet   snow

snow crystals

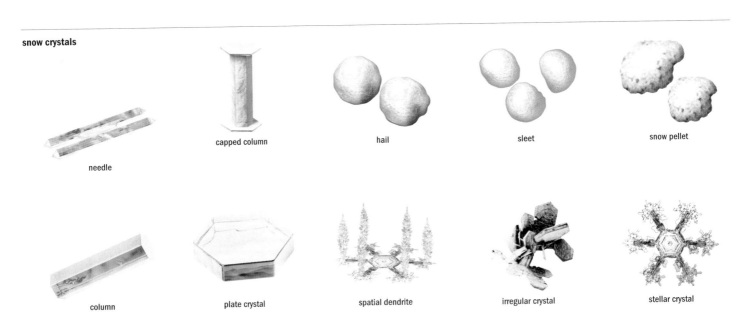

needle   capped column   hail   sleet   snow pellet

column   plate crystal   spatial dendrite   irregular crystal   stellar crystal

stormy sky

cloud

lightning

rainbow

rain

dew

rime

mist

fog

frost

vegetation and biosphere

vegetation regions

	tundra		temperate forest		tropical rain forest		desert
	boreal forest		grassland		savanna		maquis

elevation zones and vegetation

structure of the biosphere

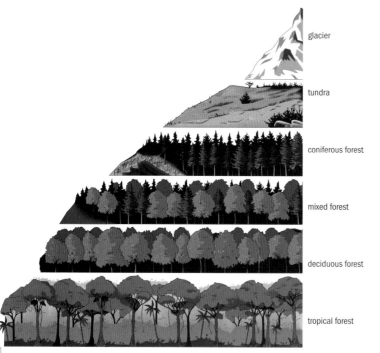

glacier

tundra

coniferous forest

mixed forest

deciduous forest

tropical forest

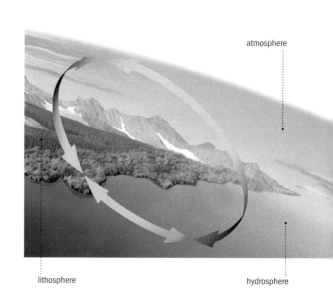

atmosphere

lithosphere

hydrosphere

food chain

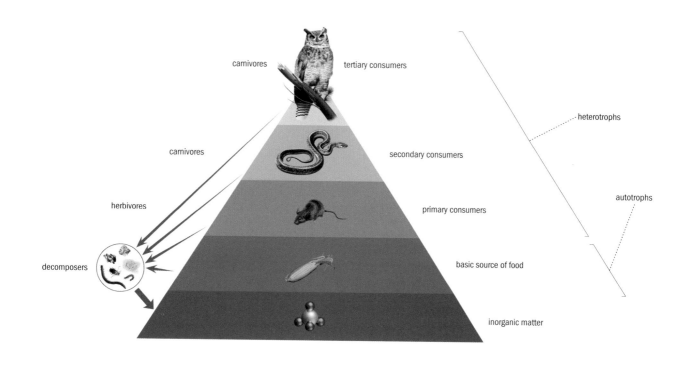

carnivores · tertiary consumers

carnivores · secondary consumers

herbivores · primary consumers

decomposers · basic source of food

inorganic matter

heterotrophs

autotrophs

hydrologic cycle

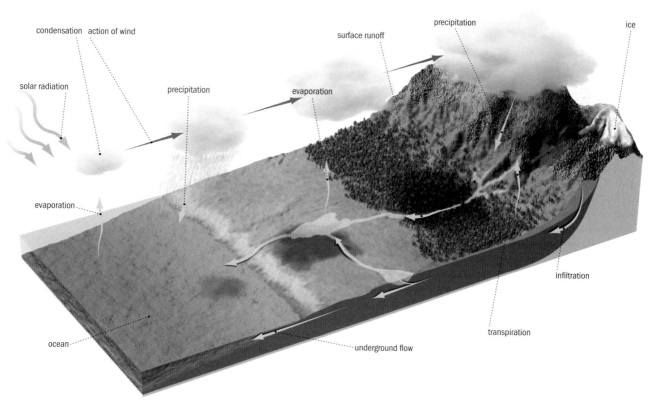

condensation   action of wind

precipitation

surface runoff

precipitation

ice

solar radiation

precipitation

evaporation

evaporation

infiltration

transpiration

ocean

underground flow

greenhouse effect

natural greenhouse effect

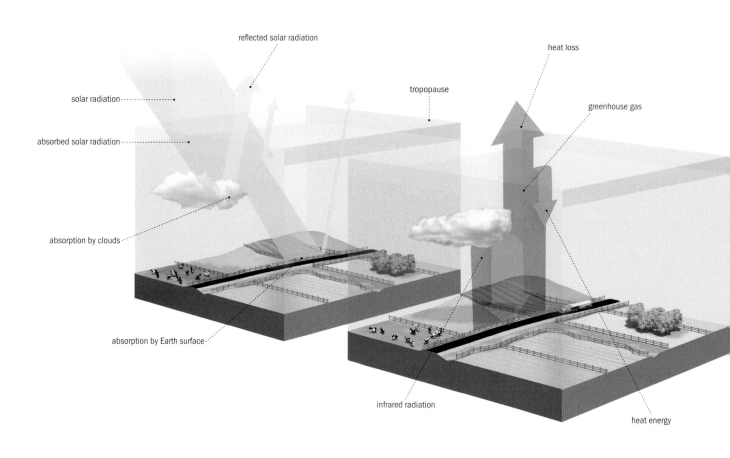

reflected solar radiation

solar radiation

absorbed solar radiation

absorption by clouds

absorption by Earth surface

heat loss

tropopause

greenhouse gas

infrared radiation

heat energy

enhanced greenhouse effect

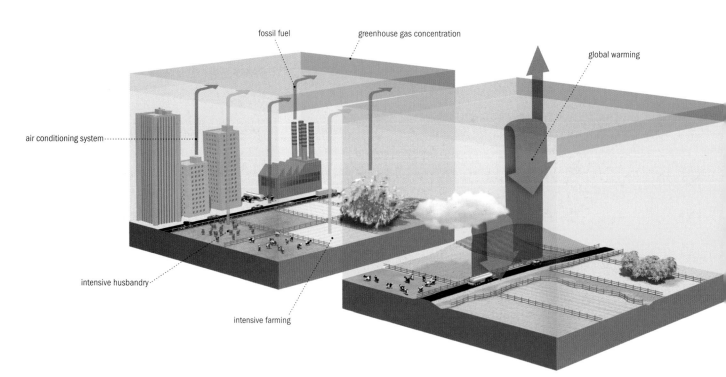

fossil fuel

greenhouse gas concentration

global warming

air conditioning system

intensive husbandry

intensive farming

air pollution

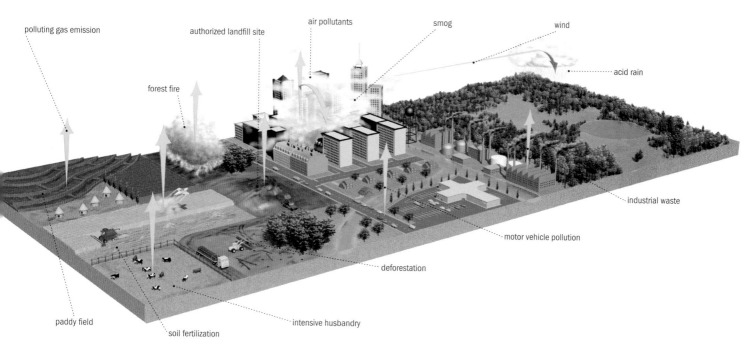

polluting gas emission

authorized landfill site

air pollutants

smog

wind

acid rain

forest fire

industrial waste

motor vehicle pollution

deforestation

paddy field

soil fertilization

intensive husbandry

land pollution

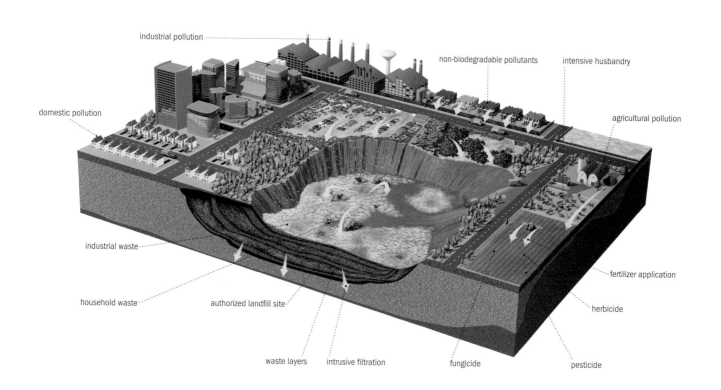

industrial pollution

non-biodegradable pollutants

intensive husbandry

domestic pollution

agricultural pollution

industrial waste

fertilizer application

household waste

authorized landfill site

herbicide

waste layers

intrusive filtration

fungicide

pesticide

EARTH

water pollution

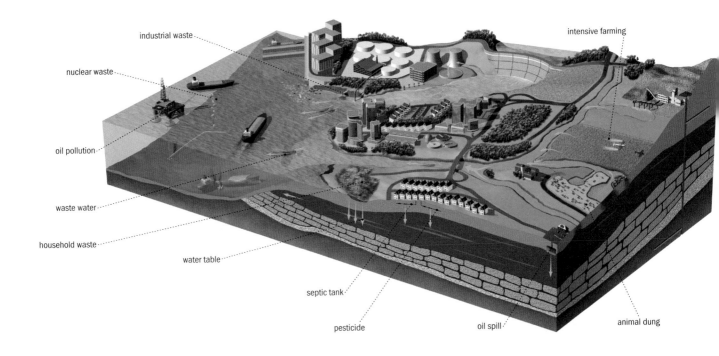

industrial waste

nuclear waste

intensive farming

oil pollution

waste water

household waste

water table

septic tank

pesticide

oil spill

animal dung

acid rain

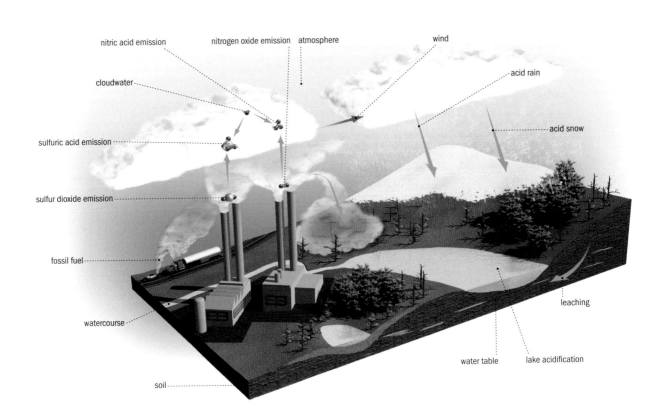

nitric acid emission

nitrogen oxide emission   atmosphere

wind

acid rain

cloudwater

acid snow

sulfuric acid emission

sulfur dioxide emission

fossil fuel

watercourse

leaching

soil

water table

lake acidification

selective sorting of waste

sorting plant

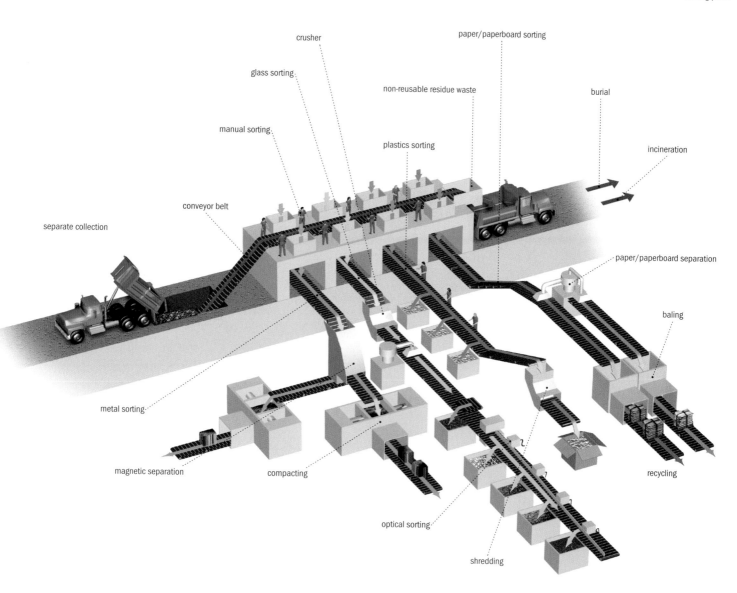

crusher

glass sorting

paper/paperboard sorting

non-reusable residue waste

burial

manual sorting

plastics sorting

incineration

conveyor belt

separate collection

paper/paperboard separation

baling

metal sorting

magnetic separation

compacting

recycling

optical sorting

shredding

recycling containers

paper recycling container

glass recycling container

aluminum recycling container

paper collection unit

glass collection unit

recycling bin

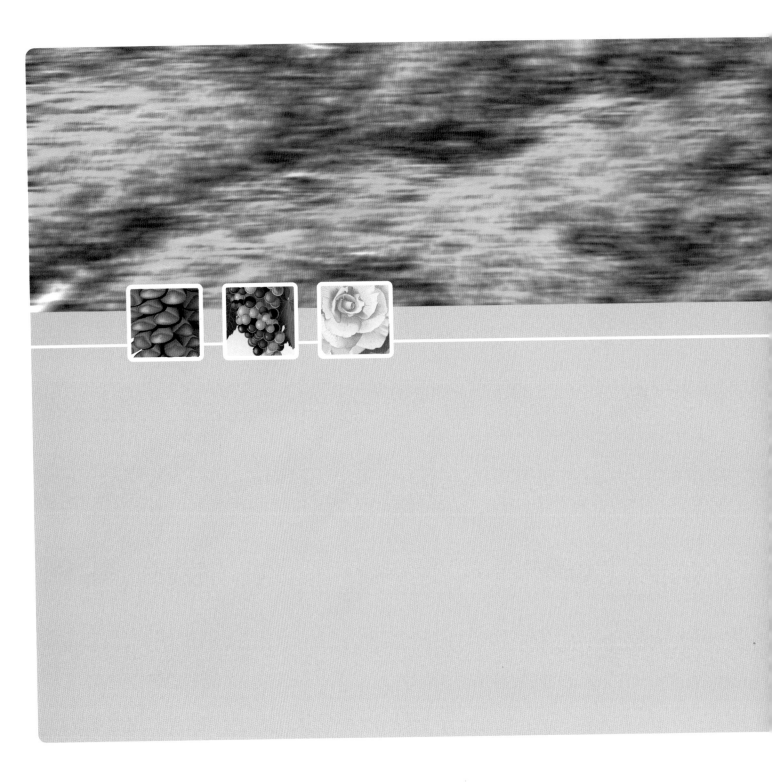

VEGETABLE KINGDOM

74

plant cell

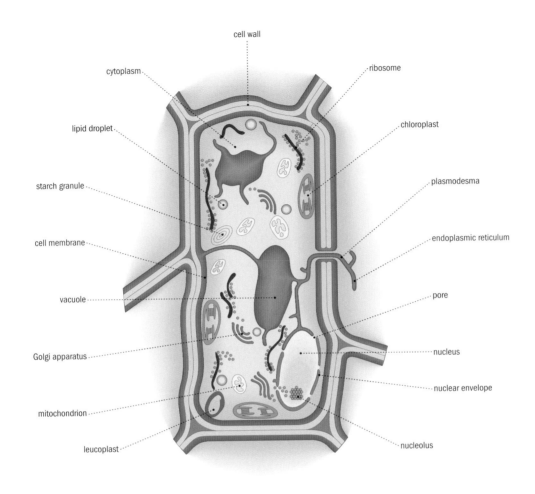

cell wall

cytoplasm

ribosome

lipid droplet

chloroplast

starch granule

plasmodesma

cell membrane

endoplasmic reticulum

vacuole

pore

Golgi apparatus

nucleus

nuclear envelope

mitochondrion

leucoplast

nucleolus

lichen

structure of a lichen

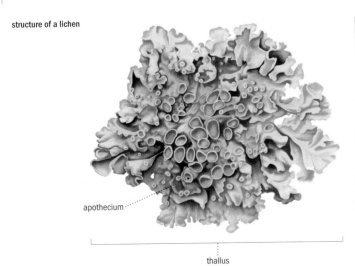

apothecium

thallus

examples of lichens

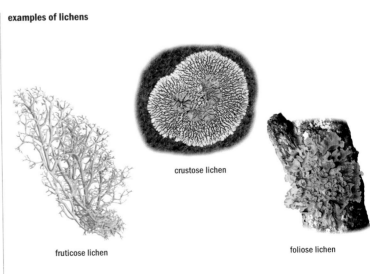

crustose lichen

fruticose lichen

foliose lichen

structure of a moss

examples of mosses

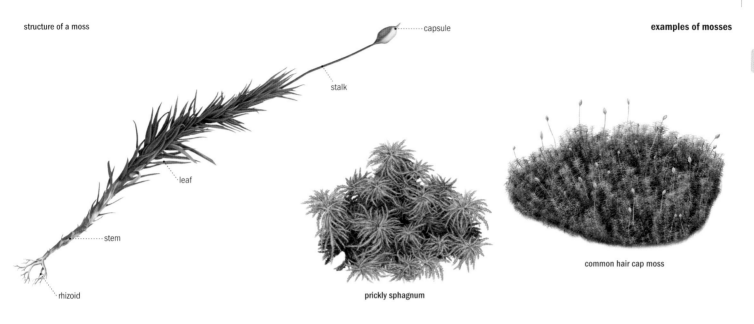

capsule

stalk

leaf

stem

rhizoid

prickly sphagnum

common hair cap moss

alga

structure of an alga

examples of algae

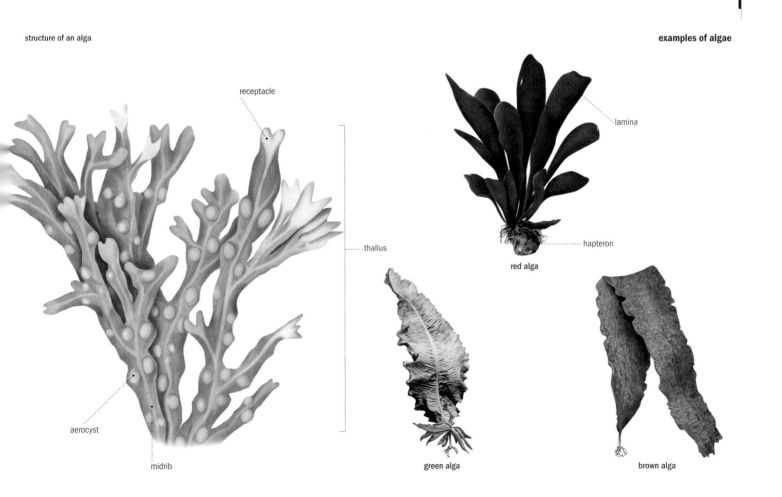

receptacle

thallus

aerocyst

midrib

lamina

hapteron

red alga

green alga

brown alga

mushroom

structure of a mushroom

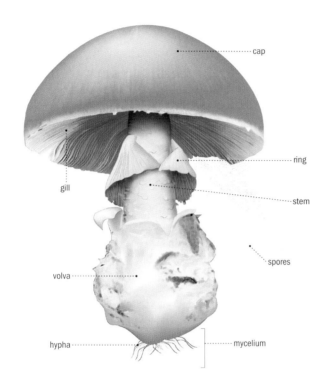

cap

ring

gill

stem

spores

volva

hypha

mycelium

deadly poisonous mushroom

poisonous mushroom

destroying angel

fly agaric

fern

structure of a fern

examples of ferns

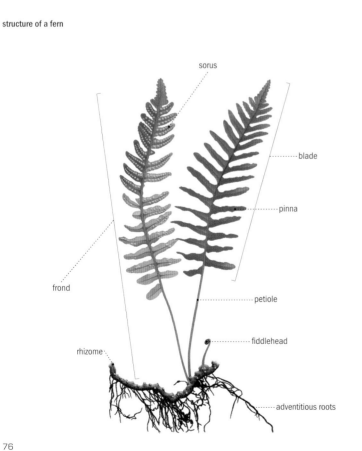

sorus

blade

pinna

frond

petiole

fiddlehead

rhizome

adventitious roots

tree fern

trunk

common polypody

bird's nest fern

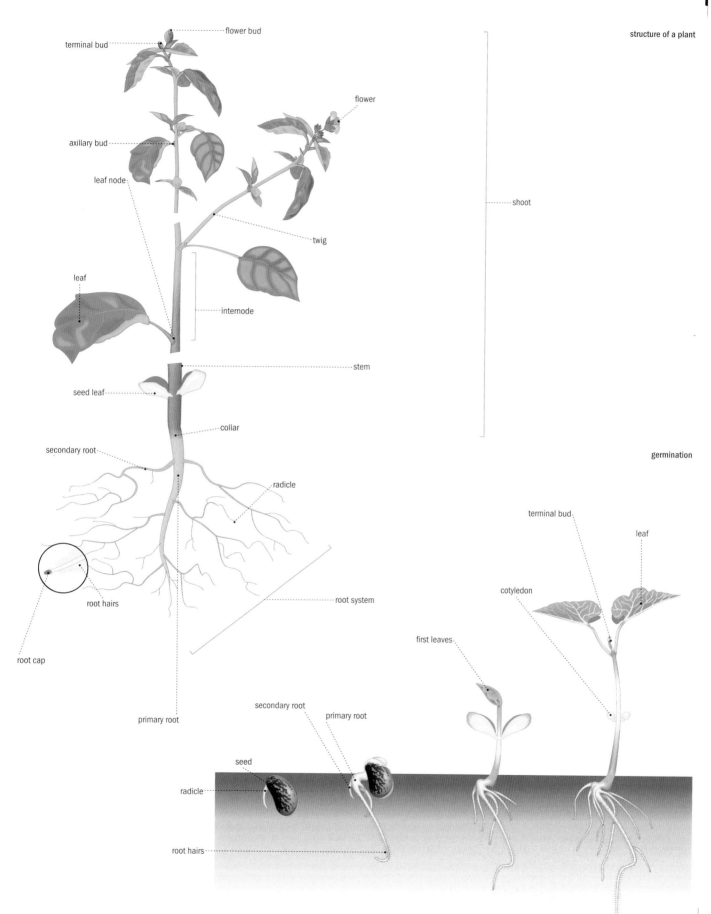

structure of a plant

flower bud

terminal bud

flower

axillary bud

leaf node

shoot

twig

leaf

internode

stem

seed leaf

collar

secondary root

radicle

root hairs

root cap

root system

primary root

germination

terminal bud

leaf

cotyledon

first leaves

secondary root

primary root

seed

radicle

root hairs

photosynthesis

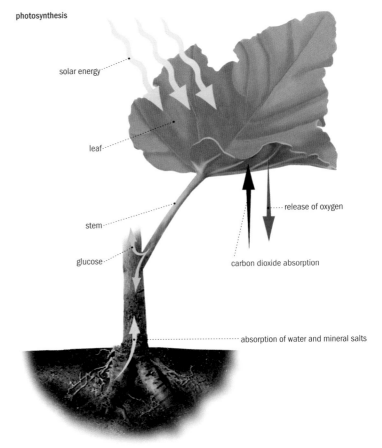

solar energy

leaf

stem

glucose

release of oxygen

carbon dioxide absorption

absorption of water and mineral salts

soil profile

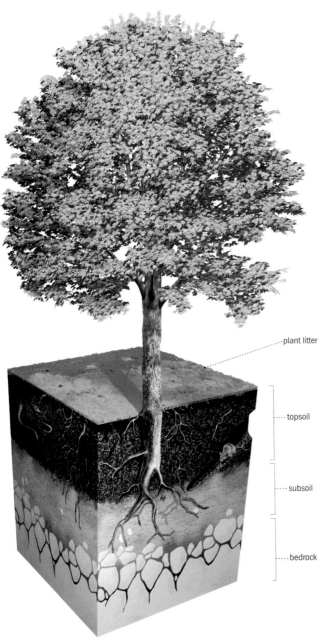

plant litter

topsoil

subsoil

bedrock

section of a bulb

scale leaf

bud

fleshy leaf

bulbil

underground stem

base

root

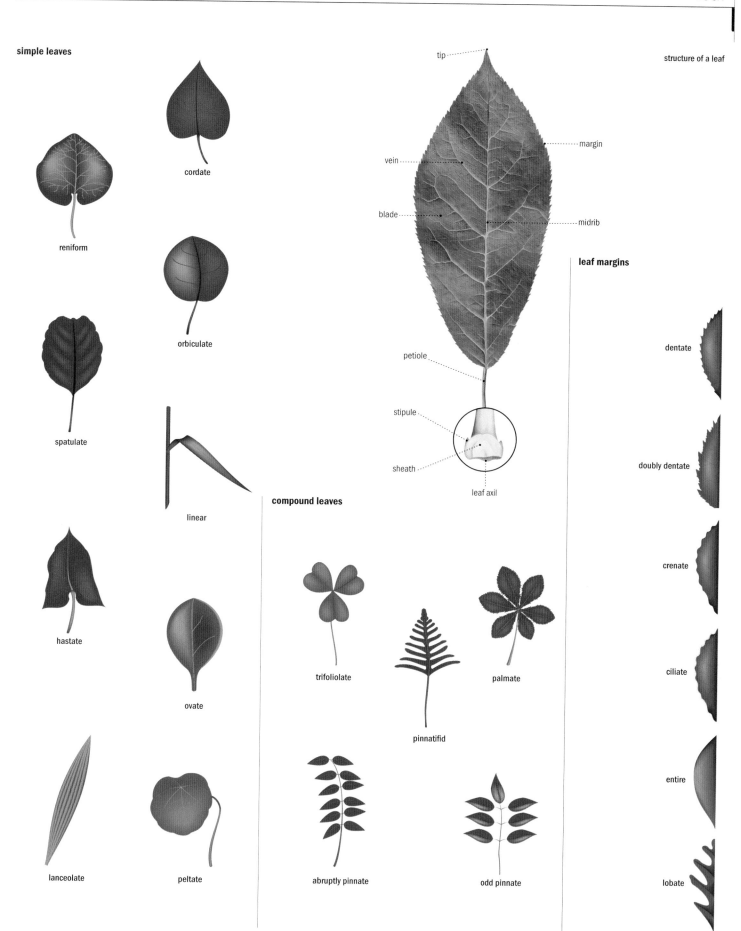

simple leaves

reniform

cordate

orbiculate

spatulate

linear

hastate

ovate

lanceolate

peltate

structure of a leaf

tip

margin

vein

blade

midrib

petiole

stipule

sheath

leaf axil

compound leaves

trifoliolate

palmate

pinnatifid

abruptly pinnate

odd pinnate

leaf margins

dentate

doubly dentate

crenate

ciliate

entire

lobate

flower

structure of a flower

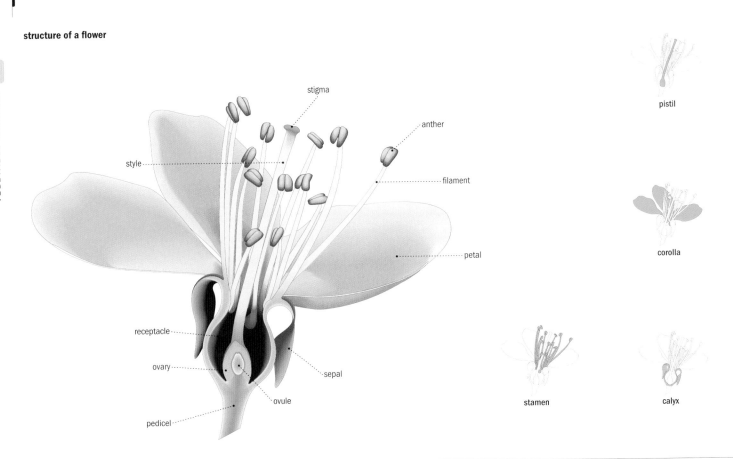

stigma

anther

style

filament

pistil

corolla

petal

receptacle

ovary

sepal

stamen

calyx

ovule

pedicel

examples of flowers

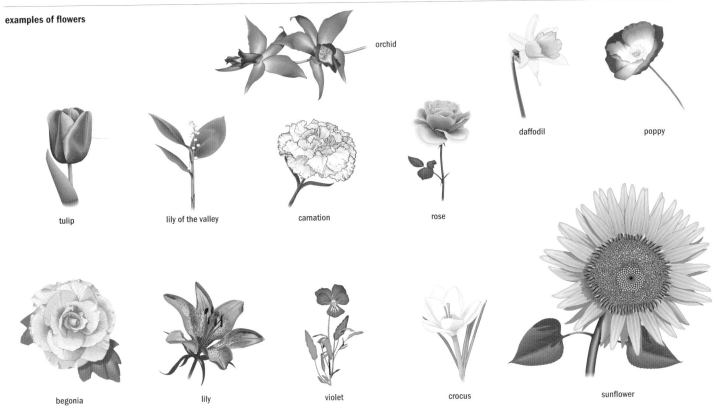

orchid

daffodil

poppy

tulip

lily of the valley

carnation

rose

begonia

lily

violet

crocus

sunflower

types of inflorescences

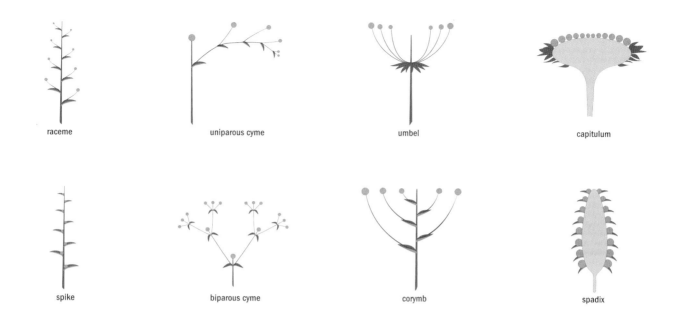

raceme

uniparous cyme

umbel

capitulum

spike

biparous cyme

corymb

spadix

fruit

stone fleshy fruit

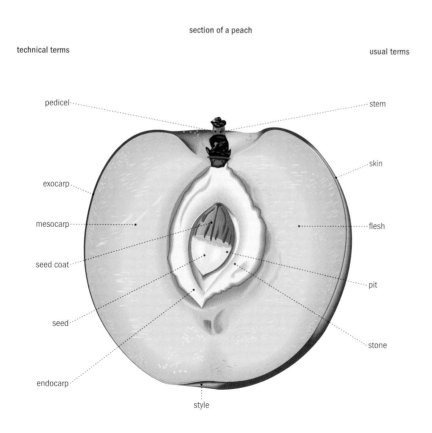

section of a peach

technical terms

usual terms

pedicel

exocarp

mesocarp

seed coat

seed

endocarp

style

stem

skin

flesh

pit

stone

pome fleshy fruit

VEGETABLE KINGDOM

section of an apple

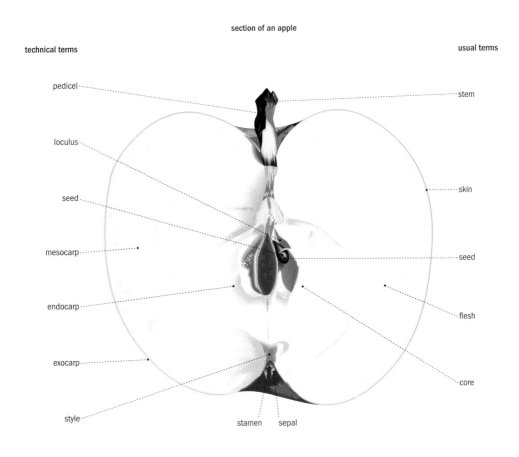

technical terms

usual terms

- pedicel
- loculus
- seed
- mesocarp
- endocarp
- exocarp
- style
- stamen
- sepal

- stem
- skin
- seed
- flesh
- core

fleshy fruit: citrus fruit

section of an orange

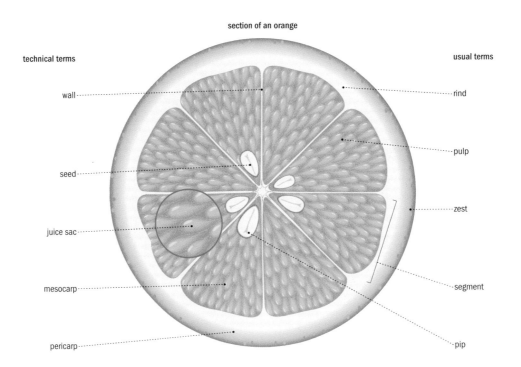

technical terms

usual terms

- wall
- seed
- juice sac
- mesocarp
- pericarp

- rind
- pulp
- zest
- segment
- pip

fleshy fruit: berry fruit

section of a grape

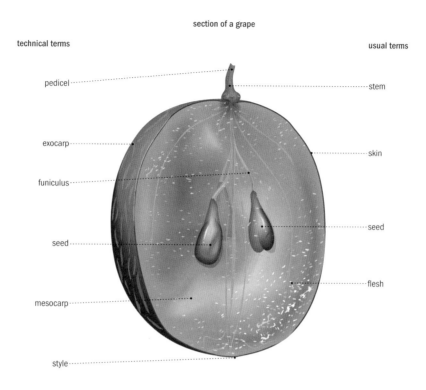

technical terms

usual terms

pedicel

stem

exocarp

skin

funiculus

seed

seed

flesh

mesocarp

style

section of a strawberry

pedicel

calyx

epicalyx

achene

flesh

receptacle

section of a raspberry

pedicel

sepal

seed

receptacle

drupelet

VEGETABLE KINGDOM

dry fruits

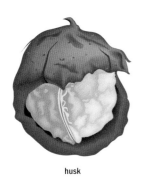

husk

section of a hazelnut

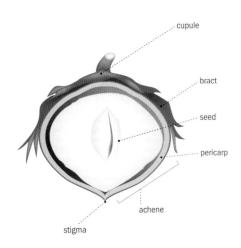

cupule

bract

seed

pericarp

achene

stigma

section of a follicle: star anise

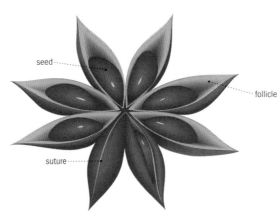

seed

follicle

suture

section of a silique: mustard

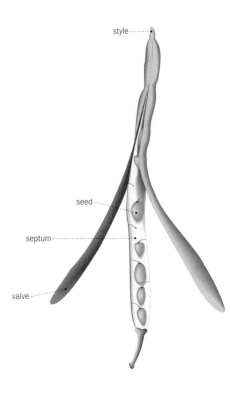

style

seed

septum

valve

section of a legume: pea

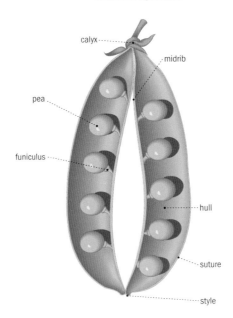

calyx

midrib

pea

funiculus

hull

suture

style

section of a walnut

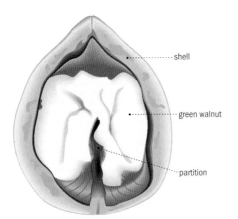

shell

green walnut

partition

section of a capsule: poppy

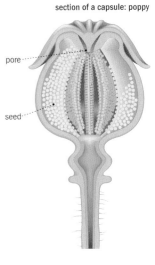

pore

seed

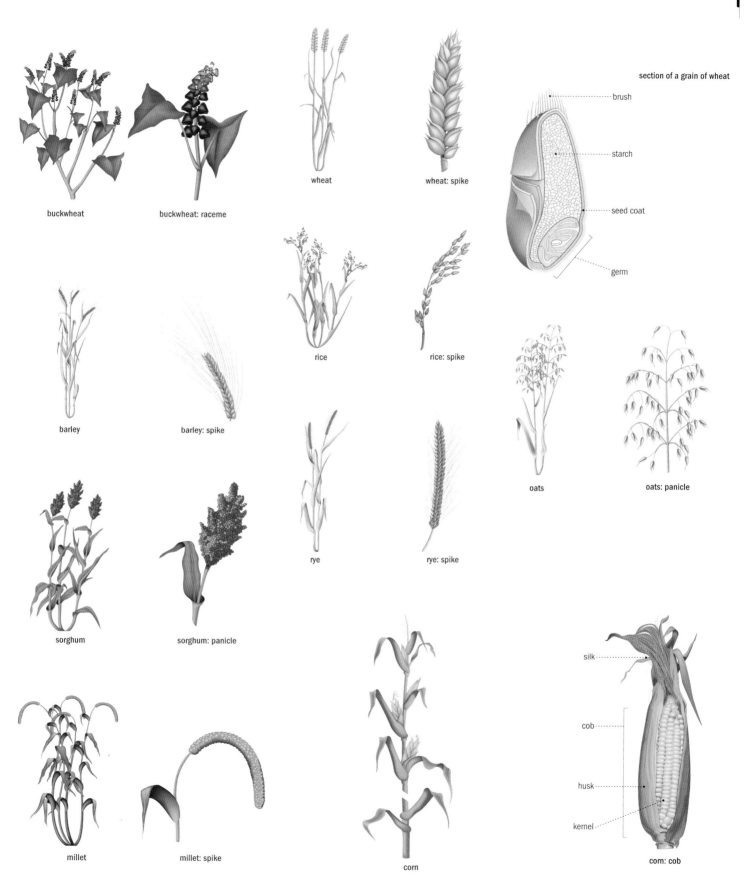

buckwheat

buckwheat: raceme

wheat

wheat: spike

section of a grain of wheat

brush

starch

seed coat

germ

rice

rice: spike

barley

barley: spike

oats

oats: panicle

sorghum

sorghum: panicle

rye

rye: spike

millet

millet: spike

corn

silk

cob

husk

kernel

corn: cob

grape

VEGETABLE KINGDOM

bunch of grapes

vine stock

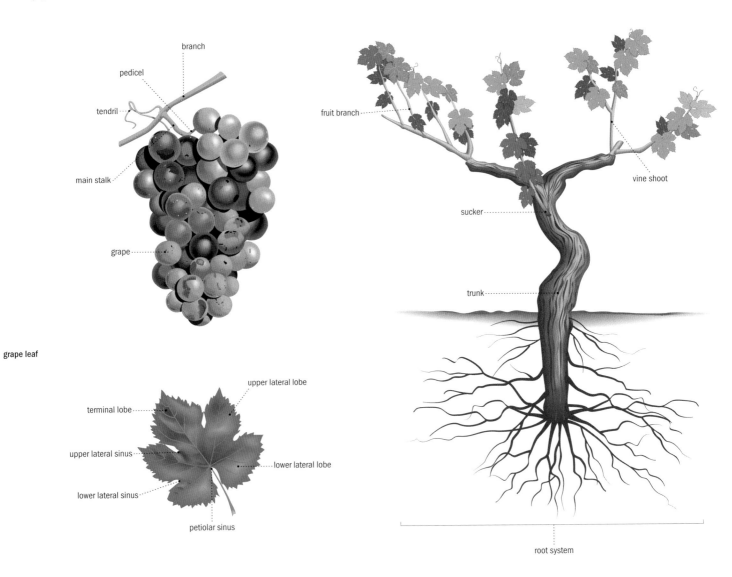

branch

pedicel

tendril

main stalk

grape

fruit branch

vine shoot

sucker

trunk

root system

grape leaf

terminal lobe

upper lateral lobe

upper lateral sinus

lower lateral lobe

lower lateral sinus

petiolar sinus

maturing steps

flowering

fruition

ripening

ripeness

structure of a tree

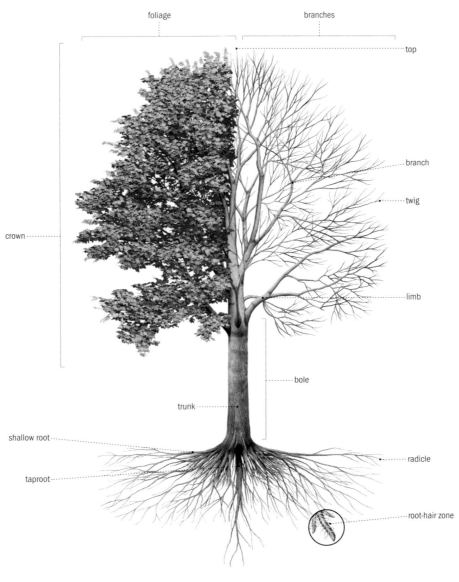

foliage

branches

top

branch

twig

crown

limb

bole

trunk

shallow root

radicle

taproot

root-hair zone

cross section of a trunk

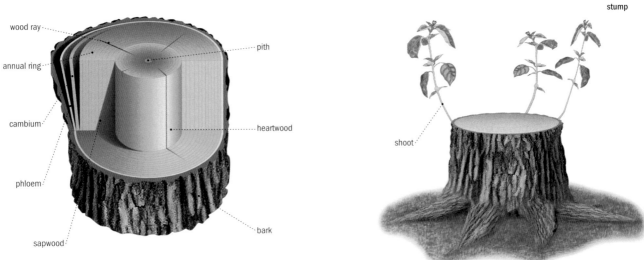

wood ray

pith

annual ring

cambium

heartwood

phloem

sapwood

bark

stump

shoot

examples of broadleaved trees

oak

birch

weeping willow

poplar

palm tree

maple

beech

walnut

VEGETABLE KINGDOM

branch

cone

pine seed

male cone

female cone

examples of leaves

fir needles

pine needles

cypress scalelike leaves

examples of conifers

umbrella pine

cedar of Lebanon

fir

spruce

larch

ANIMAL KINGDOM

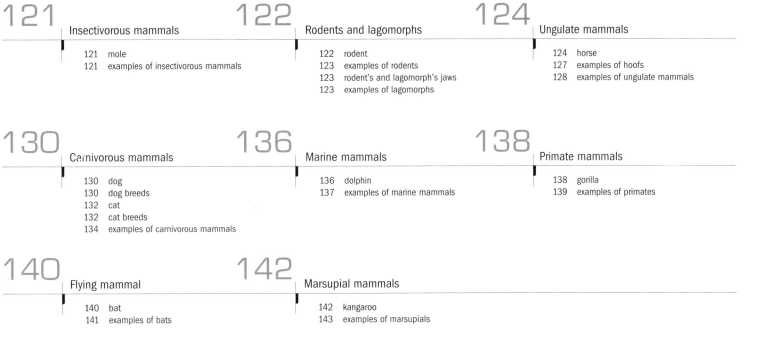

origin and evolution of species

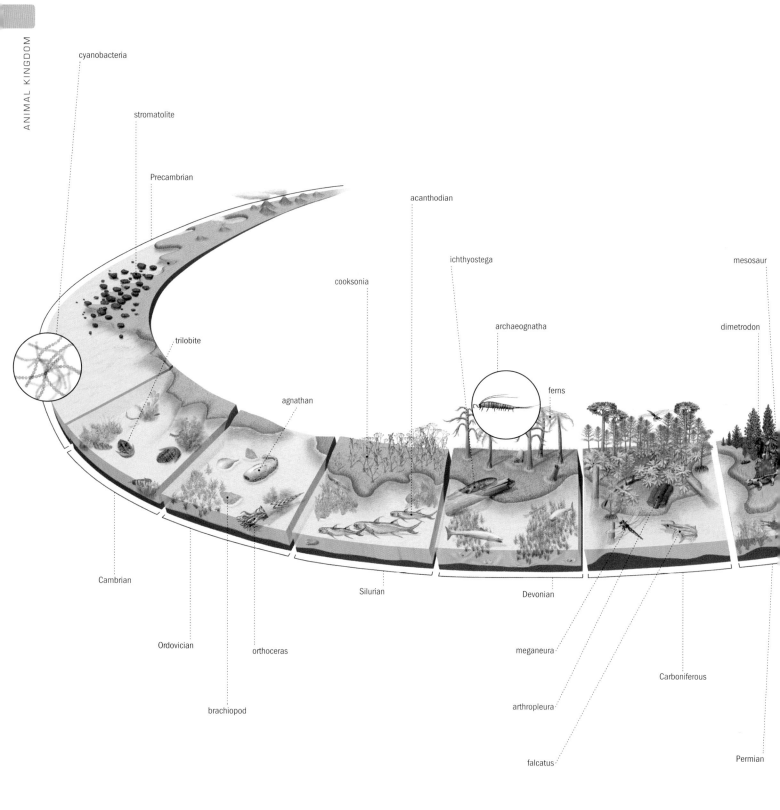

ANIMAL KINGDOM

cyanobacteria

stromatolite

Precambrian

acanthodian

ichthyostega

mesosaur

cooksonia

archaeognatha

dimetrodon

trilobite

ferns

agnathan

Cambrian

Silurian

Devonian

Ordovician

meganeura

orthoceras

Carboniferous

arthropleura

brachiopod

falcatus

Permian

ANIMAL KINGDOM

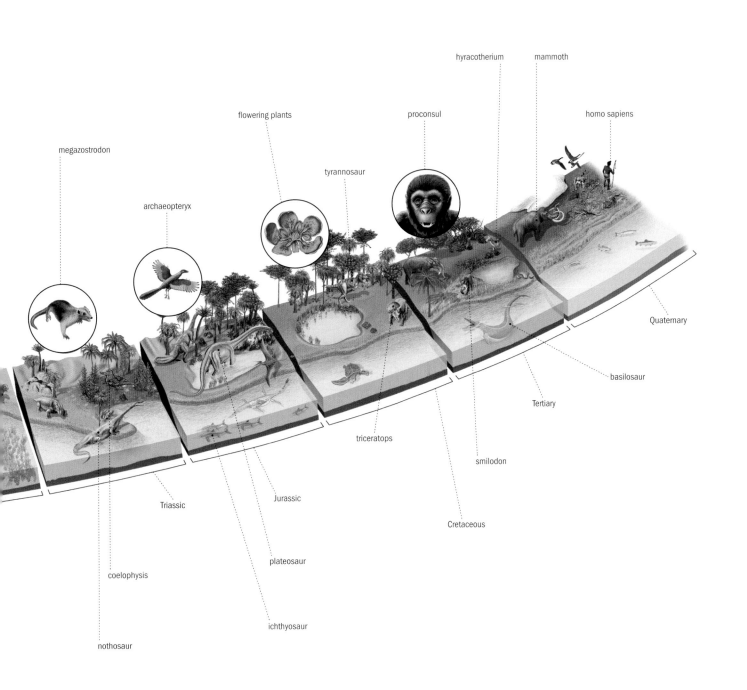

megazostrodon

archaeopteryx

flowering plants

tyrannosaur

proconsul

hyracotherium

mammoth

homo sapiens

Quaternary

basilosaur

Tertiary

smilodon

triceratops

Cretaceous

Jurassic

Triassic

plateosaur

coelophysis

ichthyosaur

nothosaur

animal cell

ANIMAL KINGDOM

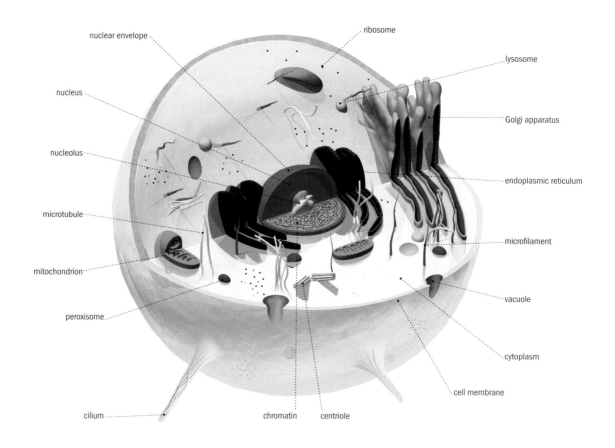

nuclear envelope
ribosome
lysosome
nucleus
Golgi apparatus
nucleolus
endoplasmic reticulum
microtubule
microfilament
mitochondrion
vacuole
peroxisome
cytoplasm
cell membrane
cilium
chromatin
centriole
cytoplasm

unicellulars

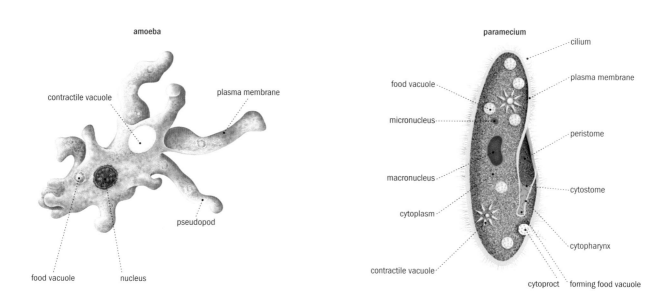

amoeba

contractile vacuole
plasma membrane
food vacuole
nucleus
pseudopod

paramecium

food vacuole
cilium
plasma membrane
micronucleus
peristome
macronucleus
cytostome
cytoplasm
cytopharynx
contractile vacuole
cytoproct
forming food vacuole

sponge

calcareous sponge

anatomy of a sponge

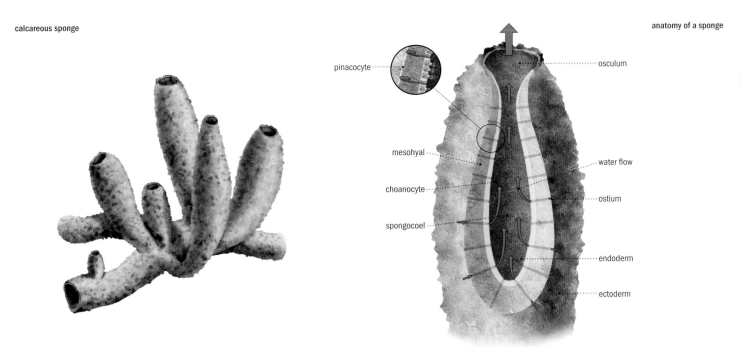

pinacocyte

osculum

mesohyal

water flow

choanocyte

ostium

spongocoel

endoderm

ectoderm

echinoderms

morphology of a starfish

anatomy of a starfish

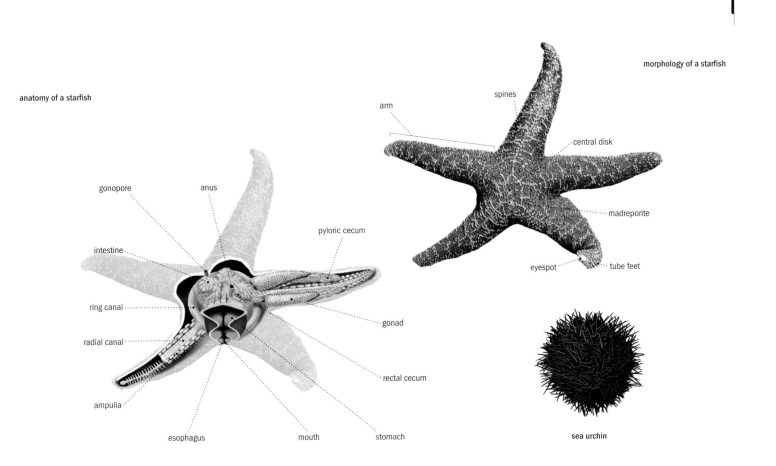

spines

arm

central disk

gonopore

anus

pyloric cecum

intestine

madreporite

ring canal

radial canal

gonad

eyespot

tube feet

ampulla

rectal cecum

esophagus

mouth

stomach

sea urchin

butterfly

morphology of a butterfly

cell

forewing

wing vein

head

compound eye

hind wing

labial palp

antenna

proboscis

thorax

foreleg

spiracle

middle leg

hind leg

abdomen

hind leg

coxa

trochanter

femur

tibia

tarsus

claw

anatomy of a female butterfly

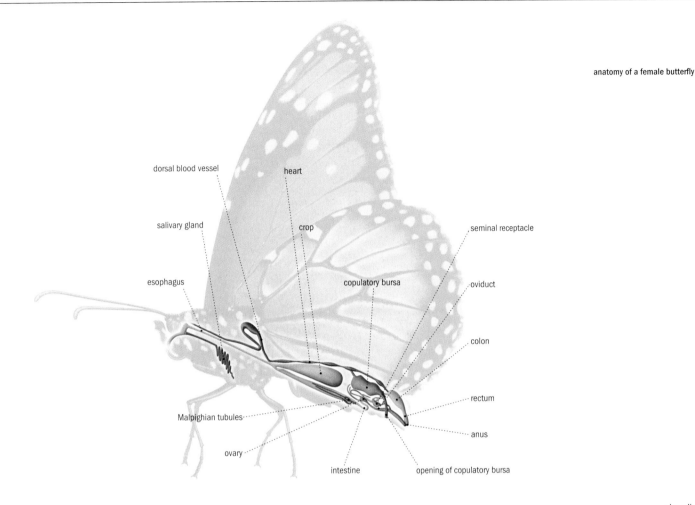

dorsal blood vessel

heart

salivary gland

crop

seminal receptacle

esophagus

copulatory bursa

oviduct

colon

rectum

Malpighian tubules

anus

ovary

intestine

opening of copulatory bursa

chrysalis

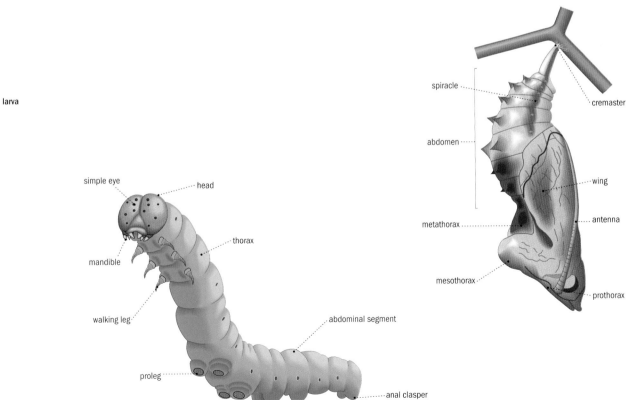

larva

spiracle

cremaster

abdomen

wing

simple eye

head

antenna

thorax

metathorax

mandible

mesothorax

walking leg

prothorax

abdominal segment

proleg

anal clasper

honeybee

ANIMAL KINGDOM

morphology of a honeybee: worker

wing

thorax

abdomen

compound eye

pollen basket

mouthparts

sting

antenna

hind leg

middle leg

foreleg

foreleg (outer surface)

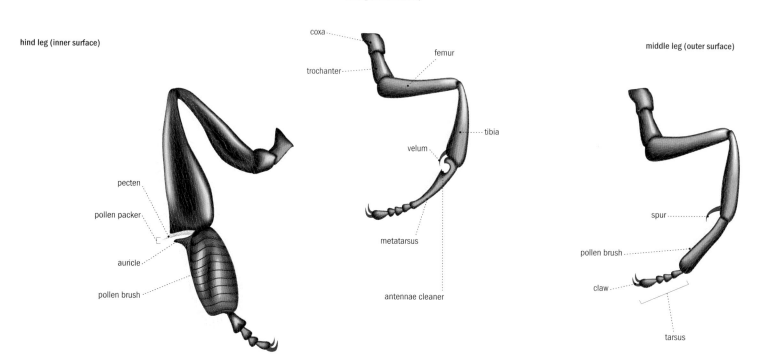

hind leg (inner surface)

middle leg (outer surface)

coxa

femur

trochanter

tibia

velum

pecten

pollen packer

spur

metatarsus

pollen brush

auricle

claw

pollen brush

antennae cleaner

tarsus

anatomy of a honeybee

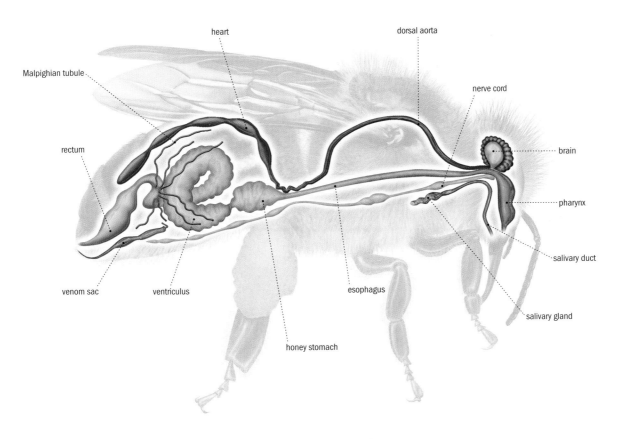

heart

dorsal aorta

Malpighian tubule

nerve cord

rectum

brain

venom sac

pharynx

ventriculus

esophagus

salivary duct

salivary gland

honey stomach

head

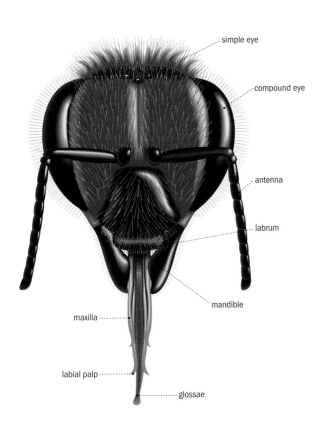

simple eye

compound eye

antenna

labrum

mandible

maxilla

labial palp

glossae

castes

queen

worker

drone

honeybee

hive

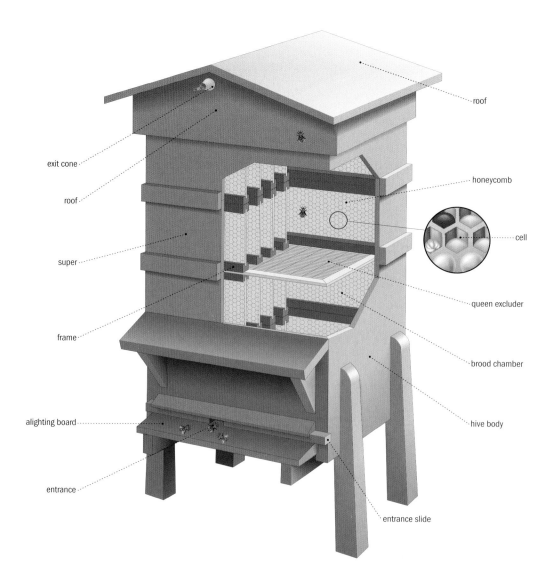

roof

exit cone

honeycomb

roof

cell

super

queen excluder

frame

brood chamber

alighting board

hive body

entrance

entrance slide

honeycomb section

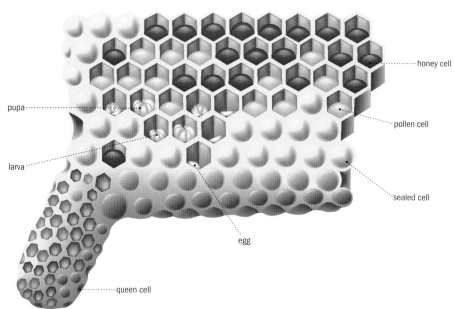

honey cell

pupa

pollen cell

larva

sealed cell

egg

queen cell

examples of insects

flea

louse

mosquito

tsetse fly

termite

furniture beetle

ant

fly

ladybird beetle

shield bug

sexton beetle

yellowjacket

hornet

horsefly

bumblebee

oriental cockroach

peppered moth

giant water bug (with eggs)

cockchafer

monarch butterfly

great green bush-cricket

cicada

examples of insects

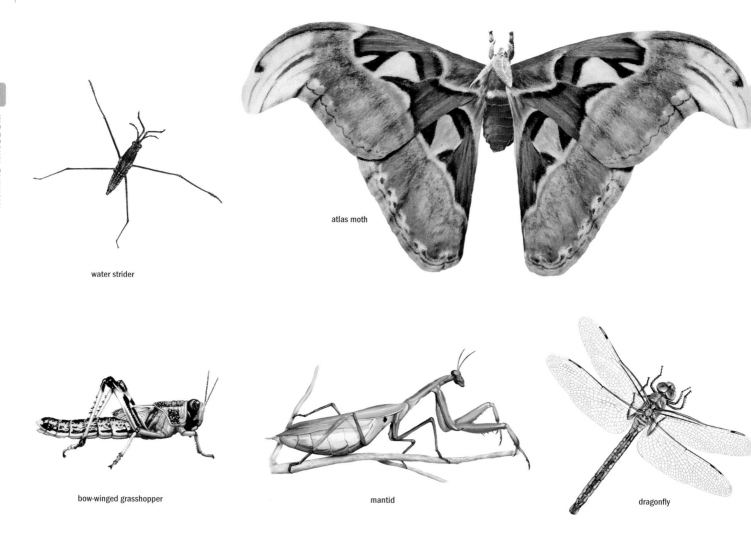

water strider

atlas moth

bow-winged grasshopper

mantid

dragonfly

examples of arachnids

crab spider

garden spider

scorpion

tick

water spider

red-kneed tarantula

spider web

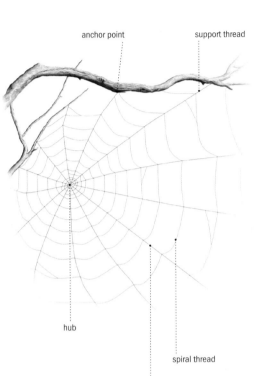

anchor point

support thread

hub

spiral thread

radial thread

spinneret

abdomen

cephalothorax

leg

eye

pedipalp

fang

anatomy of a female spider

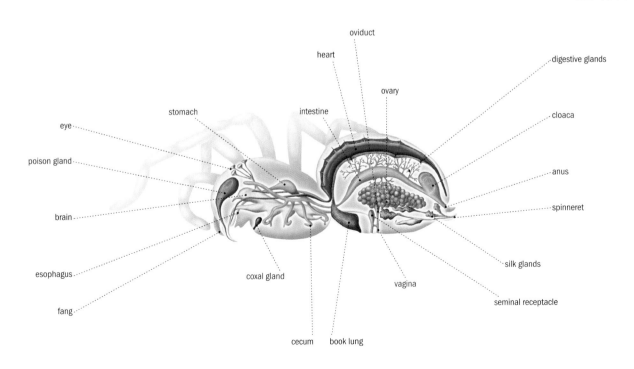

oviduct

heart

ovary

digestive glands

stomach

intestine

cloaca

eye

poison gland

anus

brain

spinneret

esophagus

silk glands

coxal gland

vagina

seminal receptacle

fang

cecum

book lung

snail

morphology of a snail

anatomy of a snail

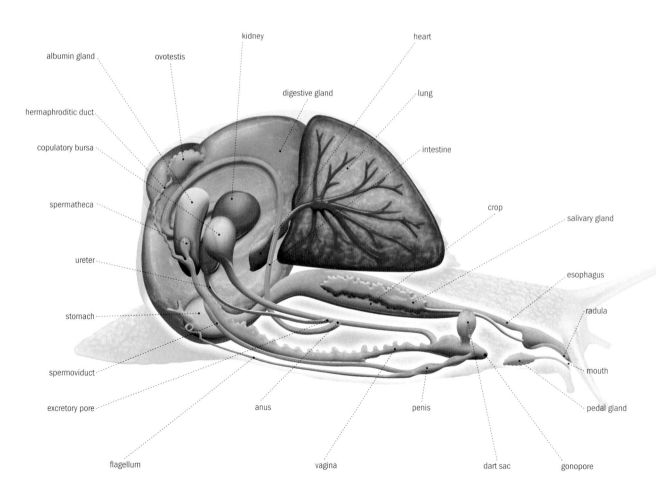

univalve shell

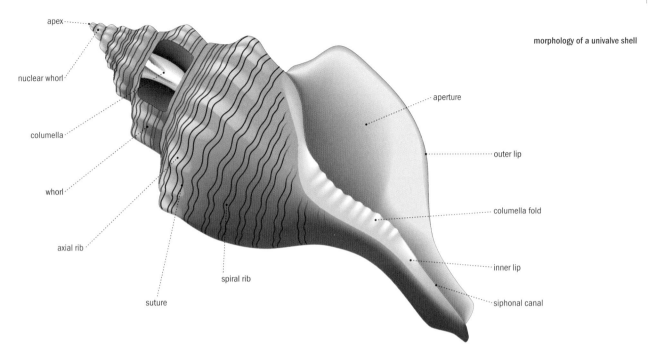

morphology of a univalve shell

apex

nuclear whorl

columella

whorl

axial rib

spiral rib

suture

aperture

outer lip

columella fold

inner lip

siphonal canal

bivalve shell

anatomy of a bivalve shell

morphology of a bivalve shell

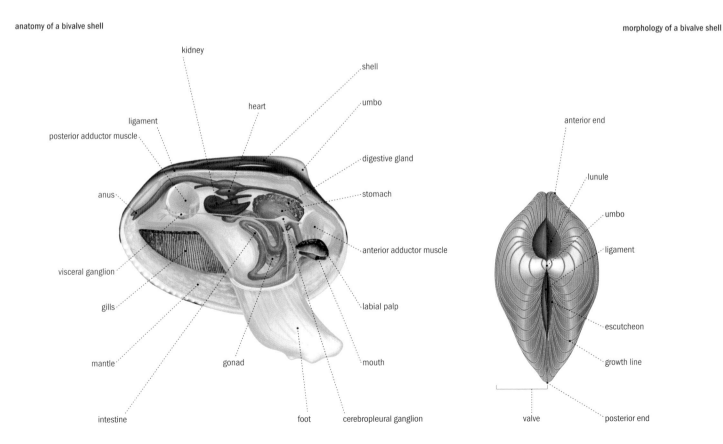

kidney

ligament

posterior adductor muscle

anus

visceral ganglion

gills

mantle

intestine

heart

gonad

foot

shell

umbo

digestive gland

stomach

anterior adductor muscle

labial palp

mouth

cerebropleural ganglion

anterior end

lunule

umbo

ligament

escutcheon

growth line

valve

posterior end

octopus

ANIMAL KINGDOM

morphology of an octopus

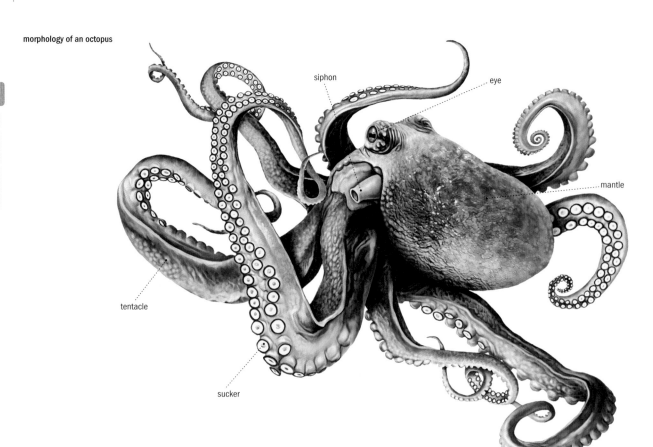

siphon

eye

mantle

tentacle

sucker

anatomy of an octopus

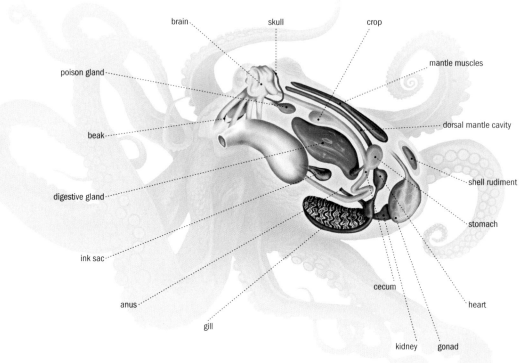

brain

skull

crop

poison gland

mantle muscles

beak

dorsal mantle cavity

digestive gland

shell rudiment

stomach

ink sac

anus

gill

cecum

kidney

gonad

heart

lobster

morphology of a lobster

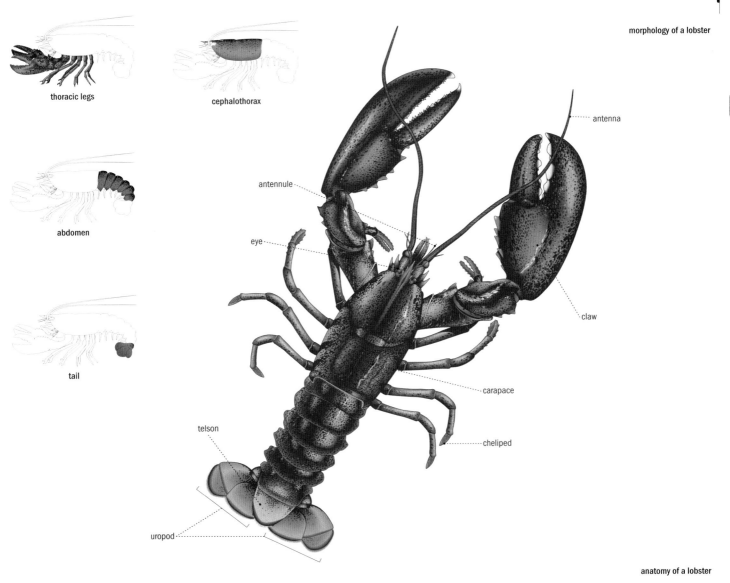

thoracic legs

cephalothorax

abdomen

tail

antenna

antennule

eye

claw

carapace

telson

cheliped

uropod

anatomy of a lobster

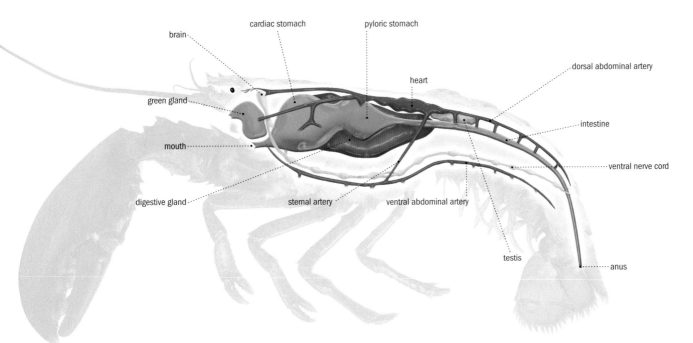

brain

cardiac stomach

pyloric stomach

heart

dorsal abdominal artery

green gland

intestine

mouth

ventral nerve cord

digestive gland

sternal artery

ventral abdominal artery

testis

anus

cartilaginous fish

morphology of a female shark

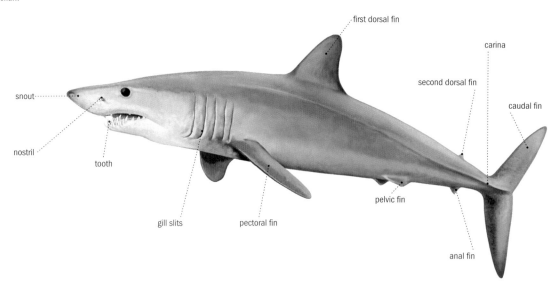

first dorsal fin

carina

second dorsal fin

caudal fin

snout

nostril

tooth

gill slits

pectoral fin

pelvic fin

anal fin

bony fish

morphology of a perch

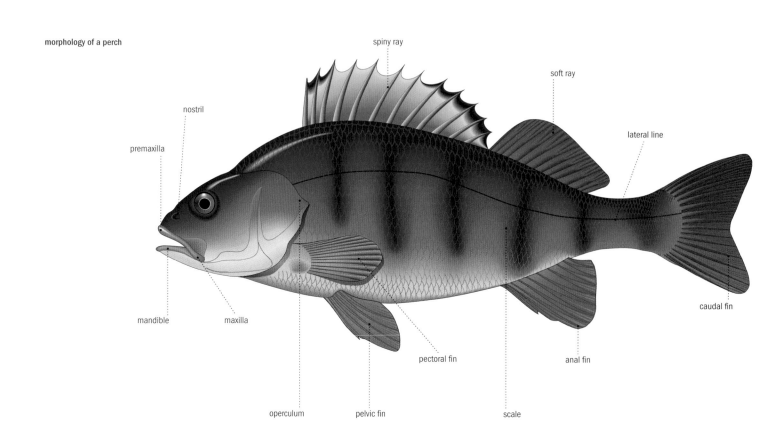

spiny ray

soft ray

lateral line

nostril

premaxilla

mandible

maxilla

caudal fin

anal fin

pectoral fin

operculum

pelvic fin

scale

anatomy of a female perch

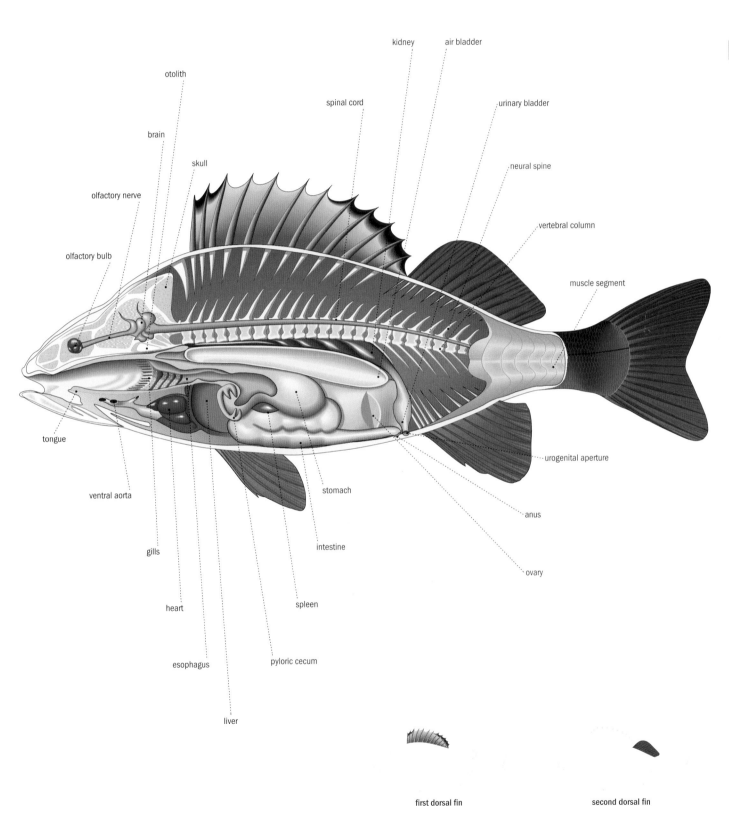

kidney

air bladder

otolith

spinal cord

urinary bladder

brain

skull

neural spine

olfactory nerve

vertebral column

olfactory bulb

muscle segment

tongue

urogenital aperture

ventral aorta

anus

ovary

gills

heart

spleen

stomach

intestine

esophagus

pyloric cecum

liver

first dorsal fin

second dorsal fin

frog

morphology of a frog

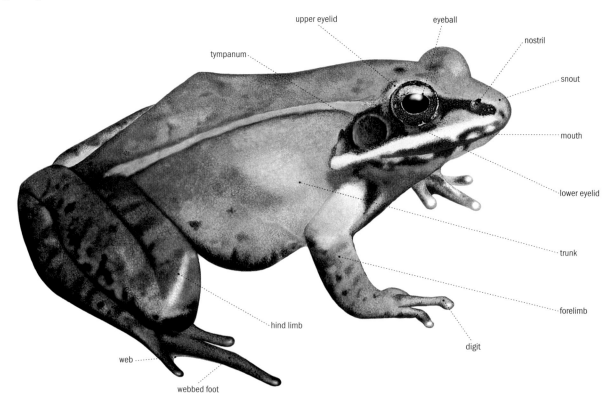

upper eyelid · eyeball · nostril · tympanum · snout · mouth · lower eyelid · trunk · forelimb · digit · hind limb · web · webbed foot

anatomy of a male frog

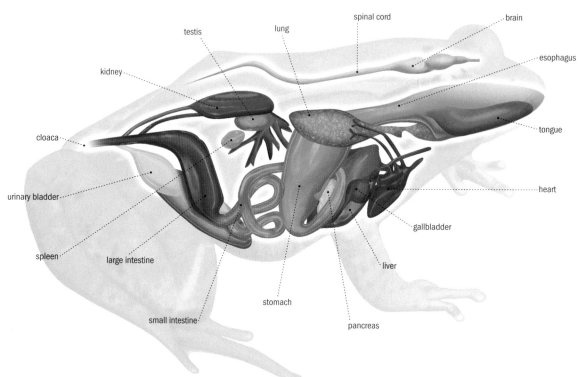

testis · lung · spinal cord · brain · kidney · esophagus · tongue · cloaca · heart · urinary bladder · gallbladder · spleen · large intestine · liver · small intestine · stomach · pancreas

skeleton of a frog

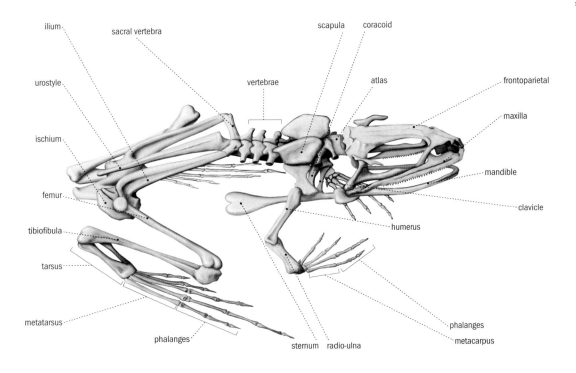

ilium

sacral vertebra

scapula

coracoid

urostyle

vertebrae

atlas

frontoparietal

ischium

maxilla

femur

mandible

tibiofibula

clavicle

tarsus

humerus

metatarsus

phalanges

phalanges

sternum   radio-ulna

metacarpus

life cycle of the tadpole

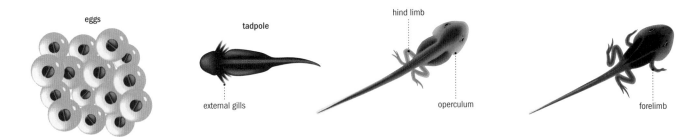

eggs

tadpole

hind limb

external gills

operculum

forelimb

examples of amphibians

salamander

wood frog

common frog

tree frog

common toad

Northern leopard frog

adhesive disk

newt

snake

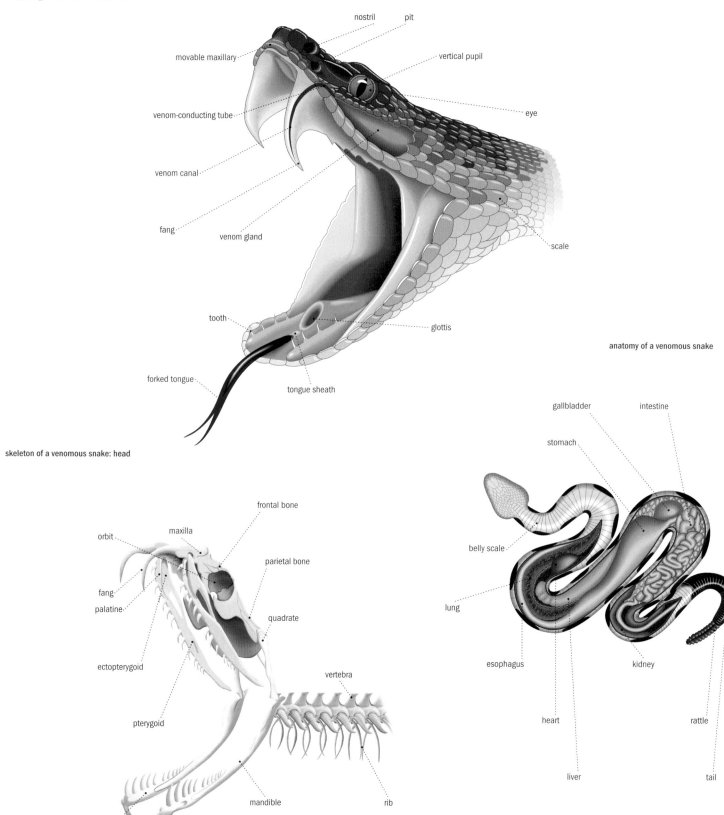

morphology of a venomous snake: head

nostril

pit

movable maxillary

vertical pupil

venom-conducting tube

eye

venom canal

fang

venom gland

scale

tooth

glottis

anatomy of a venomous snake

forked tongue

tongue sheath

gallbladder

intestine

stomach

skeleton of a venomous snake: head

belly scale

frontal bone

maxilla

orbit

parietal bone

fang

palatine

quadrate

lung

ectopterygoid

vertebra

esophagus

kidney

pterygoid

heart

rattle

mandible

rib

liver

tail

dentary bone

turtle

morphology of a turtle

vertebral shield
costal shield
carapace
eyelid
pygal shield
eye
tail
horny beak
leg
neck
scale
claw
plastron
marginal shield

turtle: digestive system

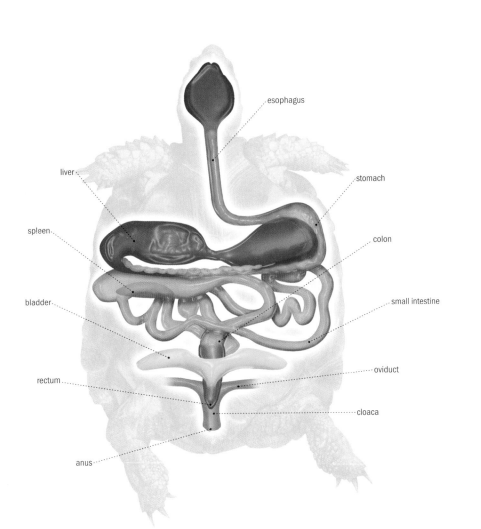

esophagus
liver
stomach
spleen
colon
bladder
small intestine
rectum
oviduct
anus
cloaca

113

examples of reptiles

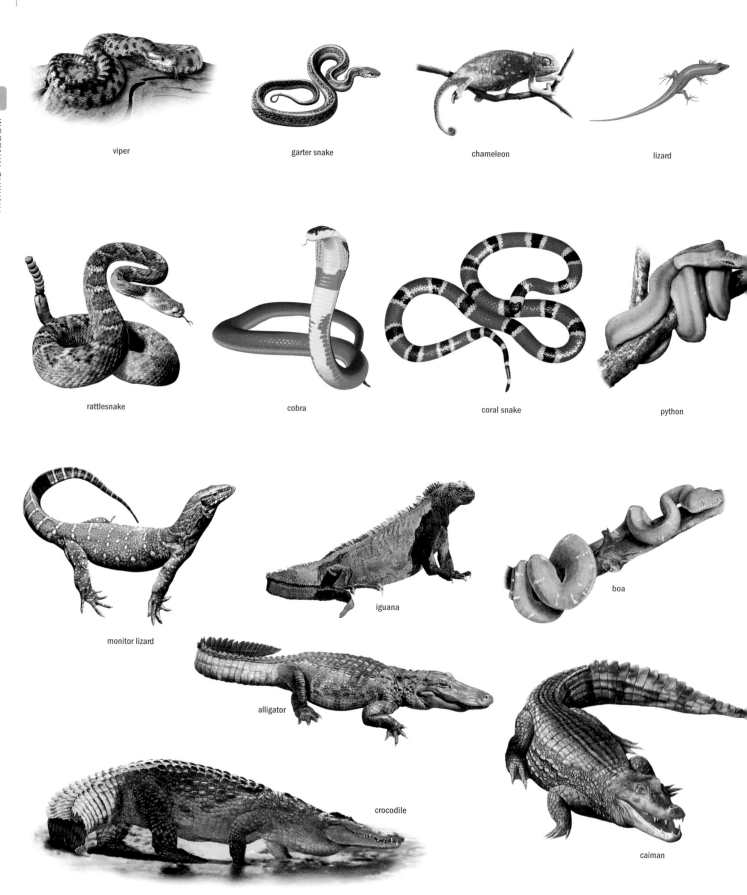

viper

garter snake

chameleon

lizard

rattlesnake

cobra

coral snake

python

monitor lizard

iguana

boa

alligator

crocodile

caiman

morphology of a bird

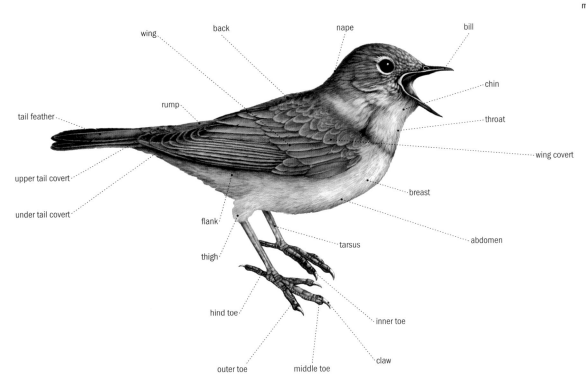

wing

back

nape

bill

chin

rump

throat

tail feather

wing covert

upper tail covert

breast

under tail covert

abdomen

flank

tarsus

thigh

hind toe

inner toe

outer toe

middle toe

claw

contour feather

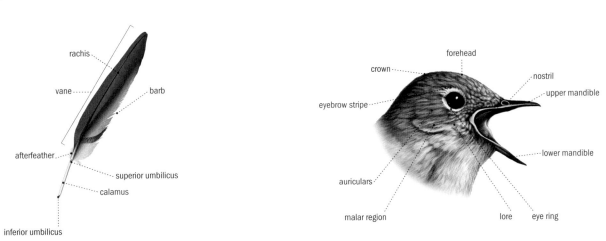

rachis

vane

barb

afterfeather

superior umbilicus

calamus

inferior umbilicus

head

forehead

crown

nostril

eyebrow stripe

upper mandible

auriculars

lower mandible

malar region

lore

eye ring

wing

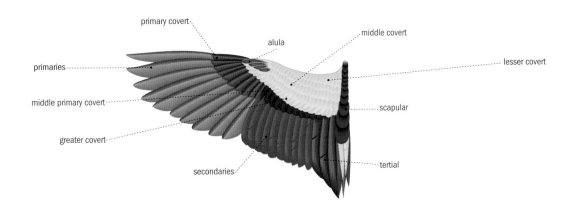

primary covert

alula

middle covert

lesser covert

primaries

middle primary covert

scapular

greater covert

secondaries

tertial

bird

ANIMAL KINGDOM

skeleton of a bird

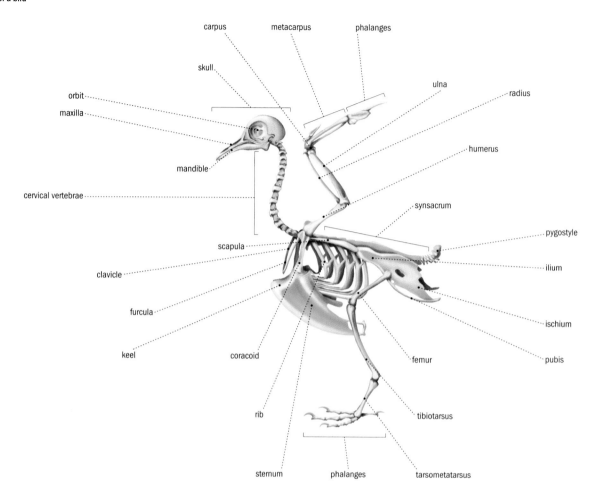

carpus metacarpus phalanges
skull
orbit ulna radius
maxilla
humerus
mandible
synsacrum
cervical vertebrae
pygostyle
scapula
ilium
clavicle
ischium
furcula
pubis
keel coracoid femur
tibiotarsus
rib
sternum phalanges tarsometatarsus

anatomy of a bird

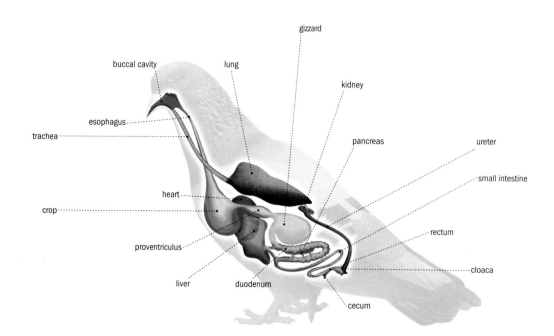

gizzard
buccal cavity lung
kidney
esophagus
trachea pancreas ureter
small intestine
heart
crop rectum
proventriculus cloaca
liver duodenum cecum

egg

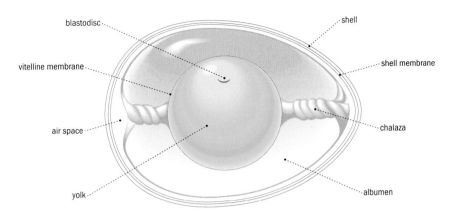

blastodisc
shell
vitelline membrane
shell membrane
air space
chalaza
yolk
albumen

examples of bills

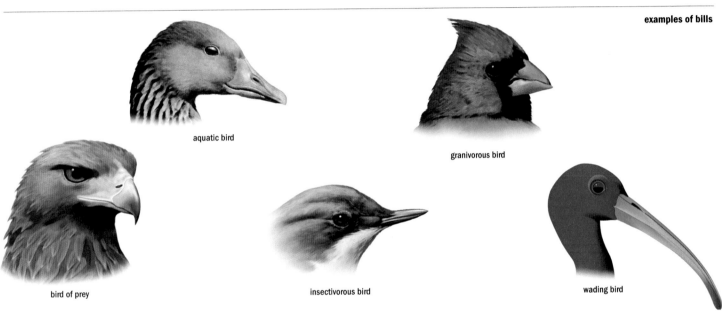

aquatic bird

granivorous bird

bird of prey

insectivorous bird

wading bird

examples of feet

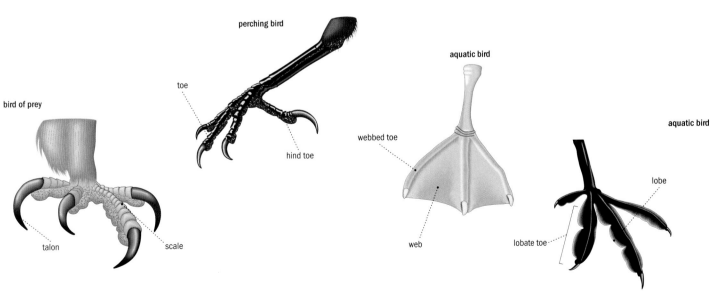

perching bird

aquatic bird

bird of prey

aquatic bird

toe

hind toe

webbed toe

lobe

talon

scale

web

lobate toe

examples of birds

hummingbird

European robin

finch

goldfinch

bullfinch

sparrow

nightingale

swallow

kingfisher

magpie

cardinal

jay

starling

swift

northern saw-whet owl

partridge

lapwing

oystercatcher

woodpecker

raven

macaw

cockatoo

tern

ANIMAL KINGDOM

albatross

toucan

falcon

great horned owl

heron

condor

eagle

penguin

pelican

stork

vulture

ostrich

peacock

flamingo

examples of birds

ANIMAL KINGDOM

chick

quail

pigeon

duck

hen

rooster

pheasant

guinea fowl

goose

turkey

mole

morphology of a mole

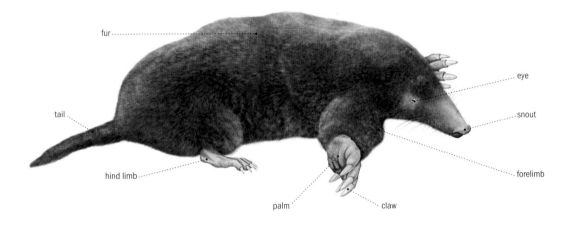

fur

eye

snout

tail

hind limb

forelimb

palm

claw

skeleton of a mole

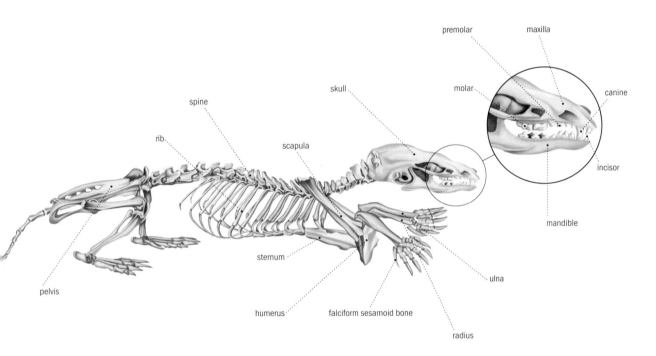

premolar

maxilla

skull

molar

canine

spine

rib

scapula

incisor

pelvis

mandible

sternum

ulna

humerus

falciform sesamoid bone

radius

examples of insectivorous mammals

mole

hedgehog

shrew

rodent

morphology of a rat

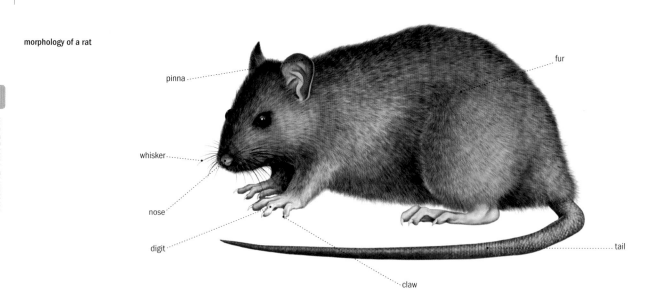

pinna

fur

whisker

nose

digit

claw

tail

skeleton of a rat

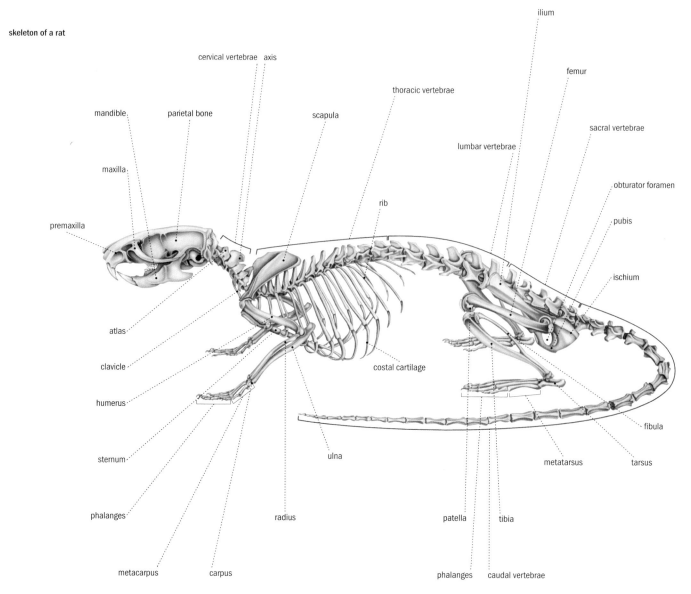

cervical vertebrae   axis

ilium

thoracic vertebrae

femur

mandible

parietal bone

scapula

sacral vertebrae

maxilla

lumbar vertebrae

obturator foramen

rib

premaxilla

pubis

ischium

atlas

clavicle

costal cartilage

humerus

fibula

sternum

ulna

metatarsus

tarsus

phalanges

radius

patella

tibia

metacarpus

carpus

phalanges

caudal vertebrae

examples of rodents

field mouse

chipmunk

jerboa

hamster

squirrel

rat

guinea pig

groundhog

porcupine

beaver

rodent's and lagomorph's jaws

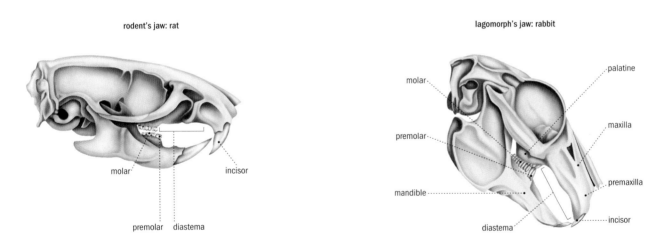

rodent's jaw: rat

molar

incisor

premolar   diastema

lagomorph's jaw: rabbit

molar

palatine

premolar

maxilla

mandible

premaxilla

incisor

diastema

examples of lagomorphs

pika

rabbit

hare

horse

morphology of a horse

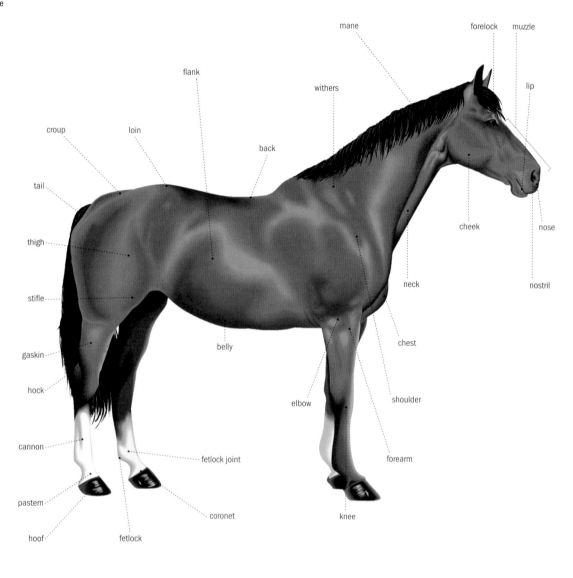

gaits

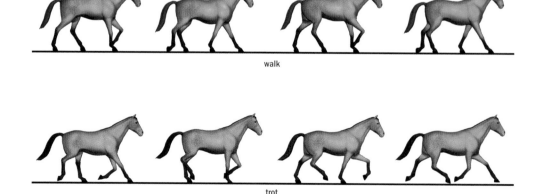

walk

trot

anatomy of a horse

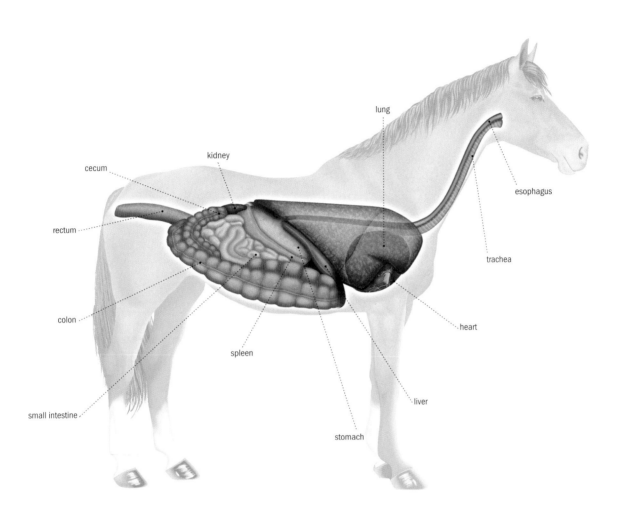

lung

kidney

cecum

rectum

colon

small intestine

spleen

stomach

liver

heart

trachea

esophagus

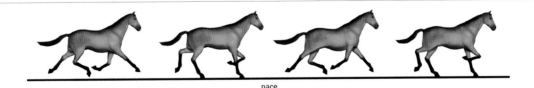

pace

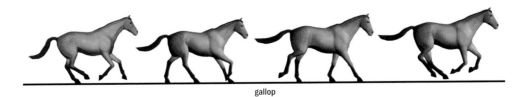

gallop

skeleton of a horse

ANIMAL KINGDOM

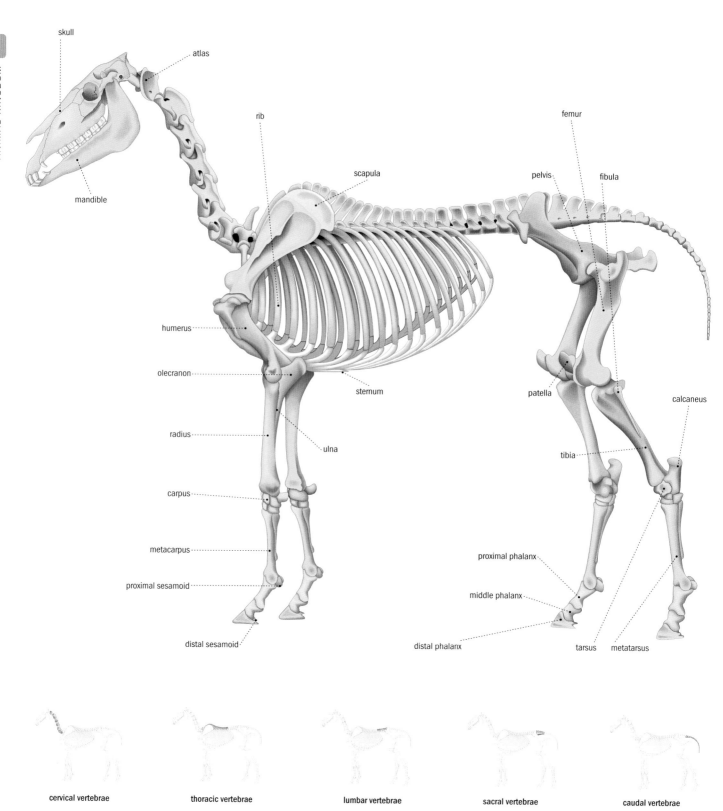

skull

atlas

mandible

rib

femur

scapula

pelvis

fibula

humerus

olecranon

patella

calcaneus

radius

ulna

sternum

tibia

carpus

metacarpus

proximal phalanx

proximal sesamoid

middle phalanx

distal sesamoid

distal phalanx

tarsus

metatarsus

cervical vertebrae

thoracic vertebrae

lumbar vertebrae

sacral vertebrae

caudal vertebrae

ANIMAL KINGDOM

plantar surface of the hoof

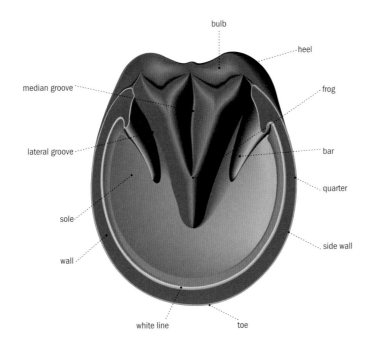

bulb

heel

median groove

frog

lateral groove

bar

quarter

sole

side wall

wall

white line   toe

horseshoe

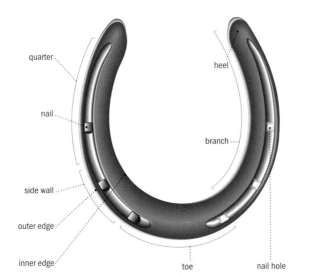

quarter

nail

heel

branch

side wall

outer edge

inner edge

toe   nail hole

hoof

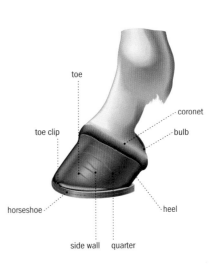

toe

coronet

bulb

toe clip

horseshoe

heel

side wall   quarter

examples of hoofs

one-toe hoof

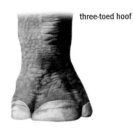

two-toed hoof

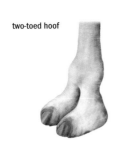

three-toed hoof

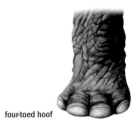

four-toed hoof

examples of ungulate mammals

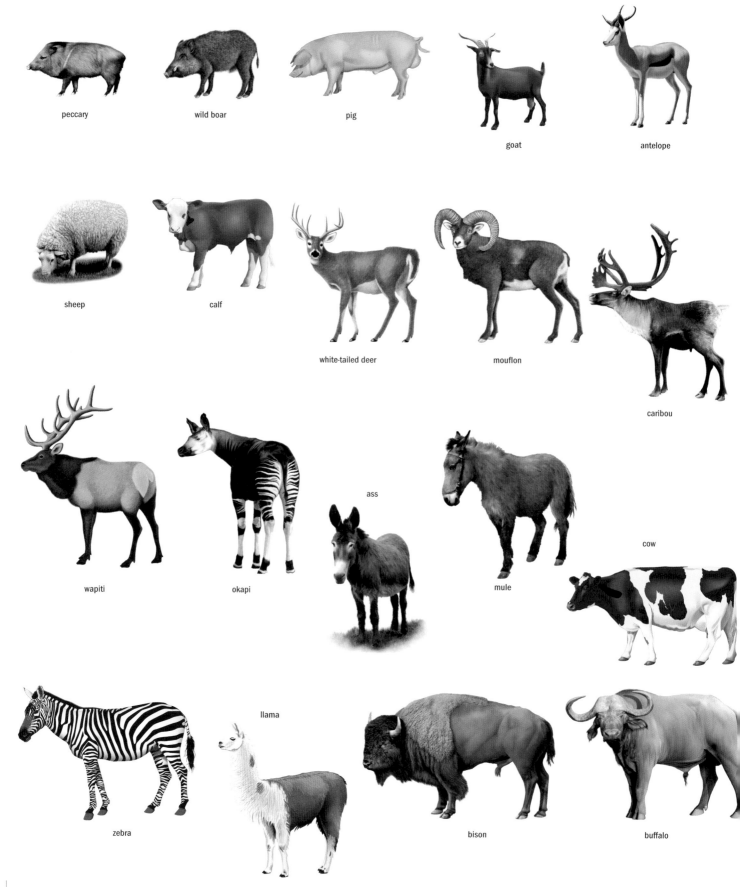

peccary

wild boar

pig

goat

antelope

sheep

calf

white-tailed deer

mouflon

caribou

wapiti

okapi

ass

mule

cow

zebra

llama

bison

buffalo

ANIMAL KINGDOM

ox

yak

horse

moose

bactrian camel

dromedary camel

rhinoceros

hippopotamus

giraffe

elephant

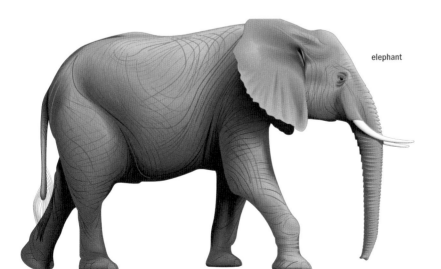

dog

morphology of a dog

dog's forepaw

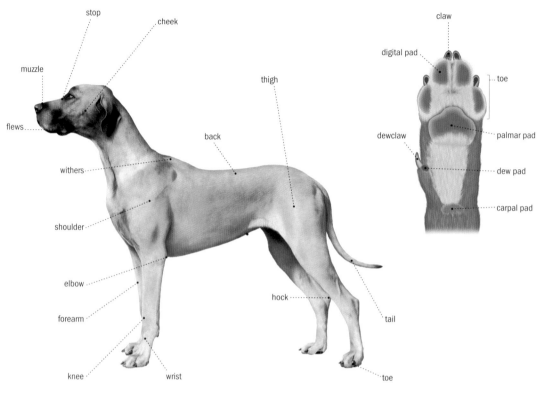

stop

cheek

muzzle

thigh

flews

back

withers

shoulder

elbow

hock

forearm

tail

knee

wrist

toe

claw

digital pad

toe

dewclaw

palmar pad

dew pad

carpal pad

dog breeds

bulldog

schnauzer

poodle

German shepherd

chow chow

collie

skeleton of a dog

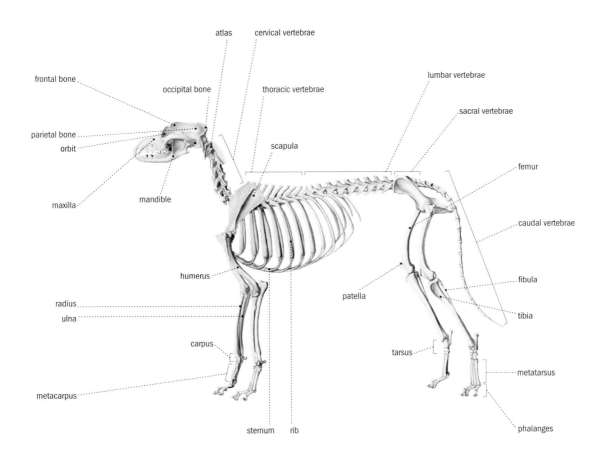

atlas

cervical vertebrae

lumbar vertebrae

frontal bone

occipital bone

thoracic vertebrae

sacral vertebrae

parietal bone

orbit

scapula

femur

maxilla

mandible

caudal vertebrae

humerus

fibula

radius

patella

ulna

tibia

carpus

tarsus

metatarsus

metacarpus

sternum   rib

phalanges

dog breeds

dalmatian

greyhound

Saint Bernard

Great Dane

cat

ANIMAL KINGDOM

cat's head

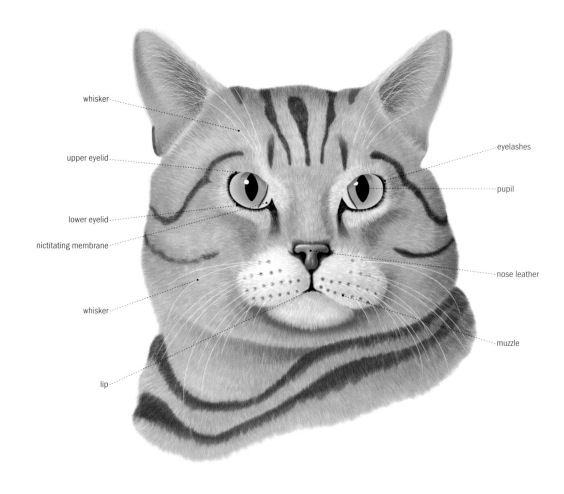

whisker

upper eyelid

lower eyelid

nictitating membrane

whisker

lip

eyelashes

pupil

nose leather

muzzle

cat breeds

American shorthair

Persian

Maine coon

morphology of a cat

ear

eye

fur

tail

retracted claw

extended claw

claw

metacarpus

tendon

distal phalanx

middle phalanx

proximal phalanx

elastic ligament

tendon

digital pad

plantar pad

cat breeds

Siamese

Abyssinian

Manx

examples of carnivorous mammals

ANIMAL KINGDOM

weasel

mink

stone marten

marten

mongoose

fennec

fox

raccoon

river otter

badger

skunk

hyena

lynx

wolf

cougar

examples of carnivorous mammals

ANIMAL KINGDOM

cheetah

leopard

lion

jaguar

tiger

polar bear

black bear

dolphin

morphology of a dolphin

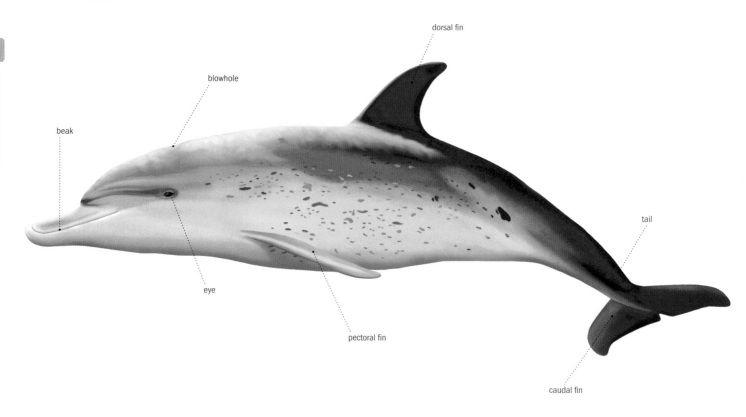

dorsal fin

blowhole

beak

tail

eye

pectoral fin

caudal fin

skeleton of a dolphin

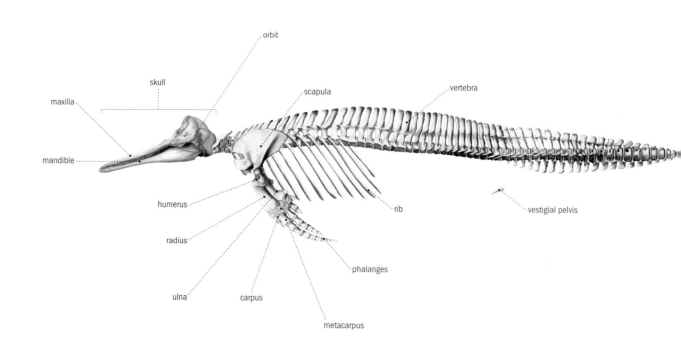

orbit

skull

scapula

vertebra

maxilla

mandible

humerus

rib

vestigial pelvis

radius

ulna

carpus

metacarpus

phalanges

examples of marine mammals

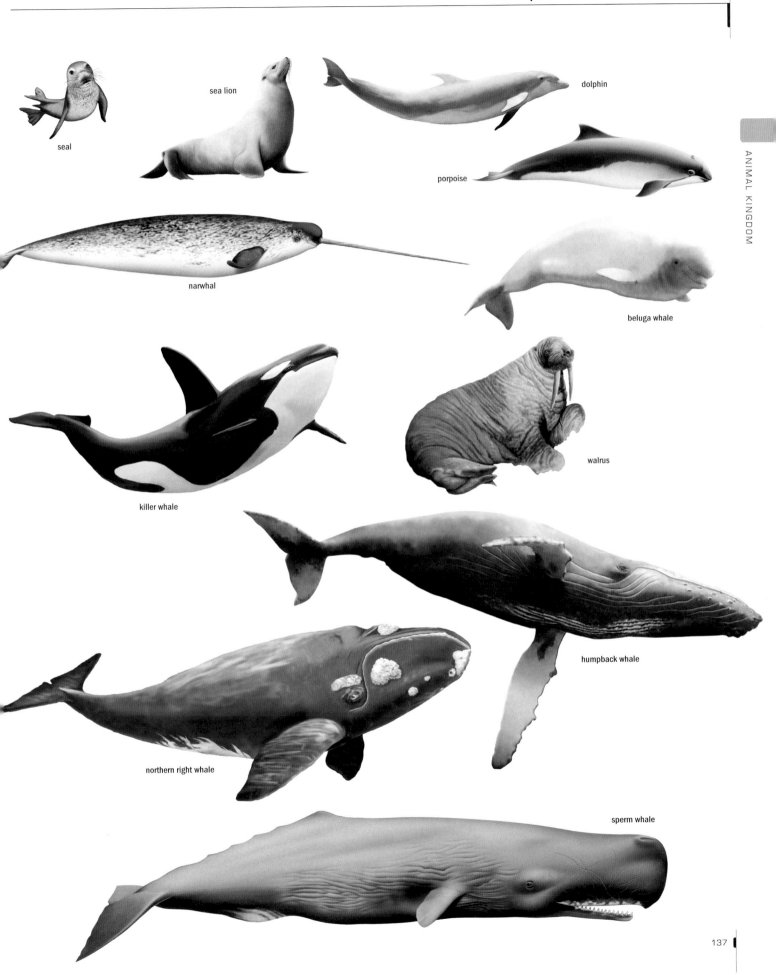

seal

sea lion

dolphin

porpoise

narwhal

beluga whale

killer whale

walrus

humpback whale

northern right whale

sperm whale

gorilla

skeleton of a gorilla

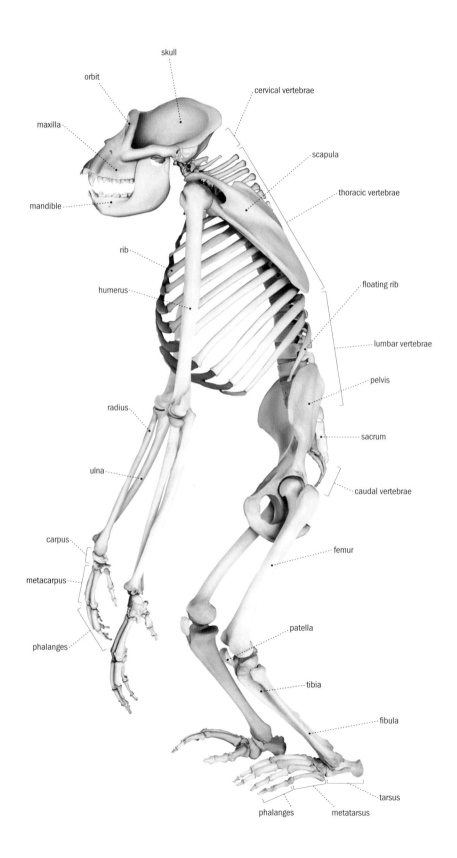

skull

orbit

cervical vertebrae

maxilla

scapula

thoracic vertebrae

mandible

rib

floating rib

humerus

lumbar vertebrae

pelvis

radius

sacrum

ulna

caudal vertebrae

carpus

femur

metacarpus

phalanges

patella

tibia

fibula

tarsus

phalanges

metatarsus

morphology of a gorilla

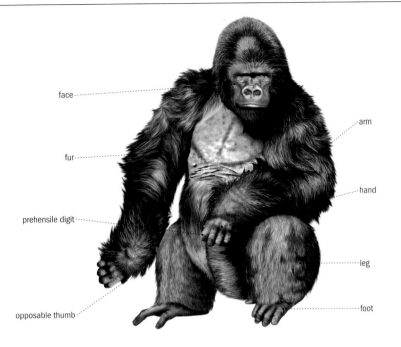

face

fur

prehensile digit

opposable thumb

arm

hand

leg

foot

examples of primates

tamarin

marmoset

baboon

macaque

orangutan

chimpanzee

lemur

gibbon

bat

ANIMAL KINGDOM

morphology of a bat

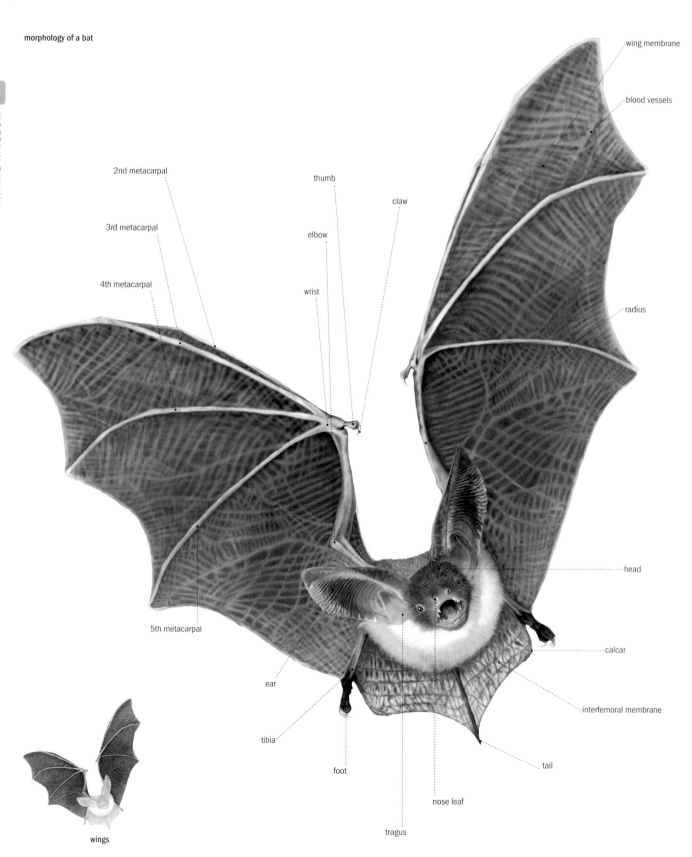

wing membrane

blood vessels

2nd metacarpal

3rd metacarpal

4th metacarpal

thumb

elbow

claw

wrist

radius

head

calcar

interfemoral membrane

5th metacarpal

ear

tail

tibia

foot

nose leaf

tragus

wings

skeleton of a bat

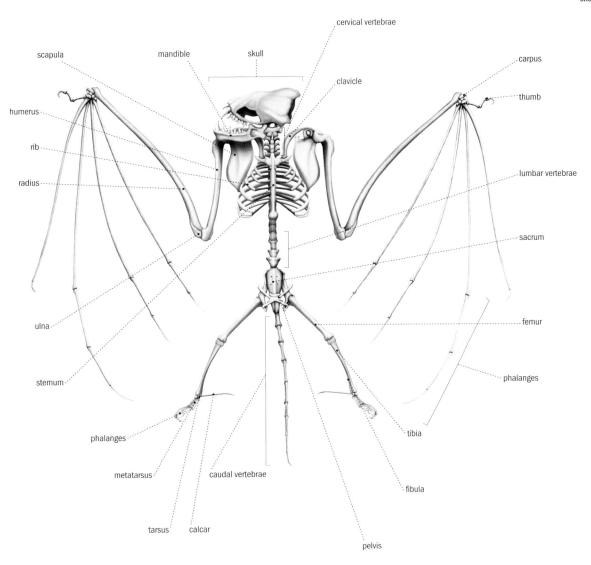

cervical vertebrae

scapula   mandible   skull

clavicle

carpus

thumb

humerus

rib

radius

lumbar vertebrae

sacrum

ulna

femur

sternum

phalanges

phalanges

tibia

metatarsus   caudal vertebrae

fibula

tarsus   calcar

pelvis

examples of bats

vampire bat

black flying fox

spear-nosed bat

kangaroo

skeleton of a kangaroo

ANIMAL KINGDOM

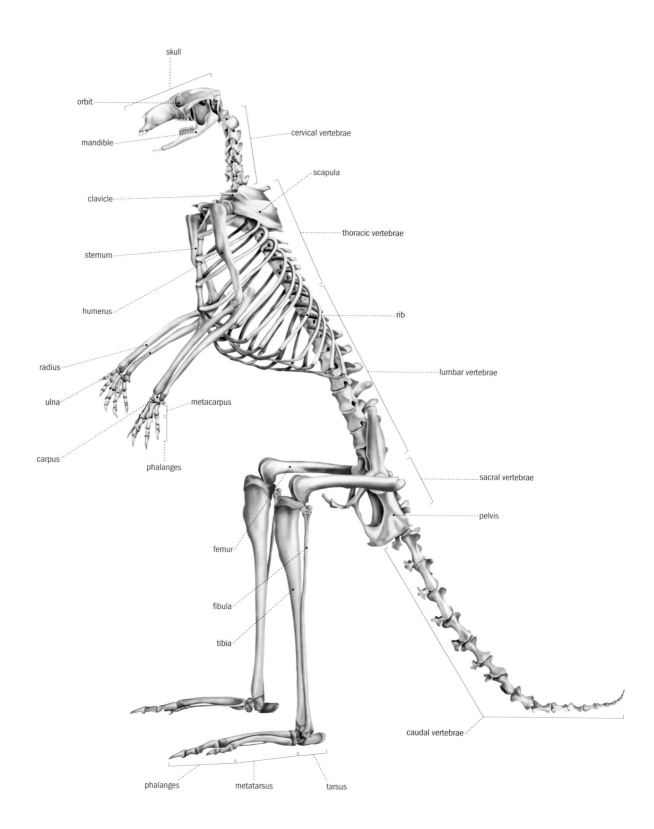

skull

orbit

mandible

cervical vertebrae

scapula

clavicle

thoracic vertebrae

sternum

humerus

rib

radius

lumbar vertebrae

ulna

metacarpus

carpus

phalanges

sacral vertebrae

pelvis

femur

fibula

tibia

caudal vertebrae

phalanges

metatarsus

tarsus

ANIMAL KINGDOM

morphology of a female kangaroo

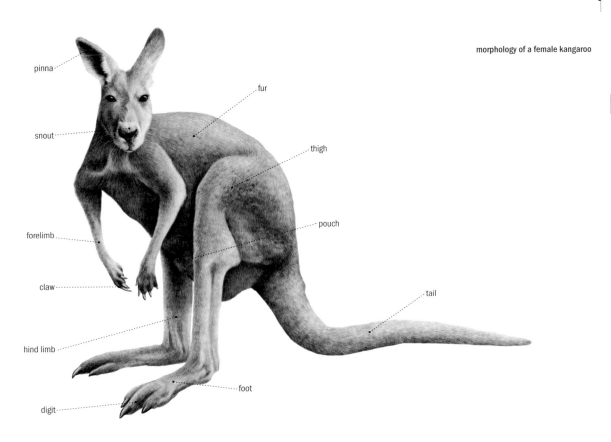

pinna

fur

snout

thigh

forelimb

pouch

claw

tail

hind limb

foot

digit

examples of marsupials

Tasmanian devil

koala

wallaby

opossum

kangaroo

HUMAN BEING

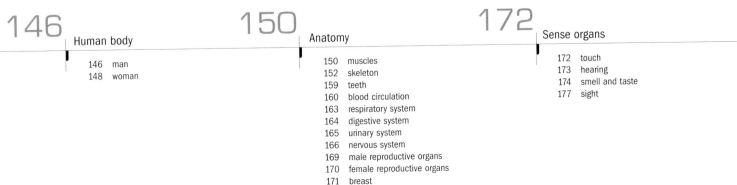

man

anterior view

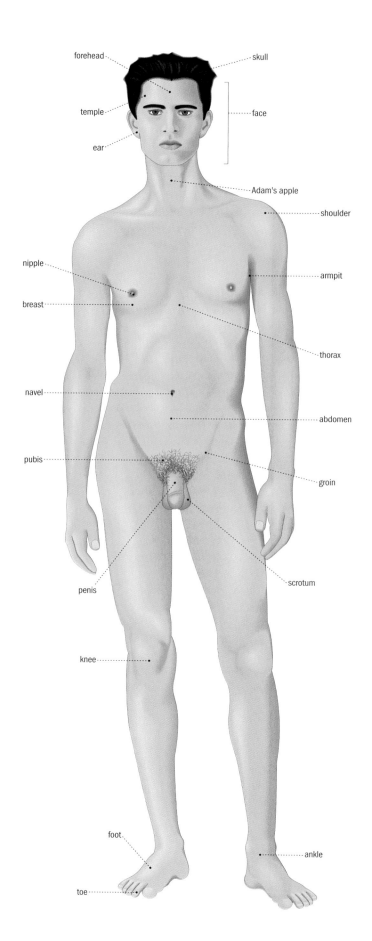

forehead

skull

temple

face

ear

Adam's apple

shoulder

nipple

armpit

breast

thorax

navel

abdomen

pubis

groin

penis

scrotum

knee

foot

ankle

toe

posterior view

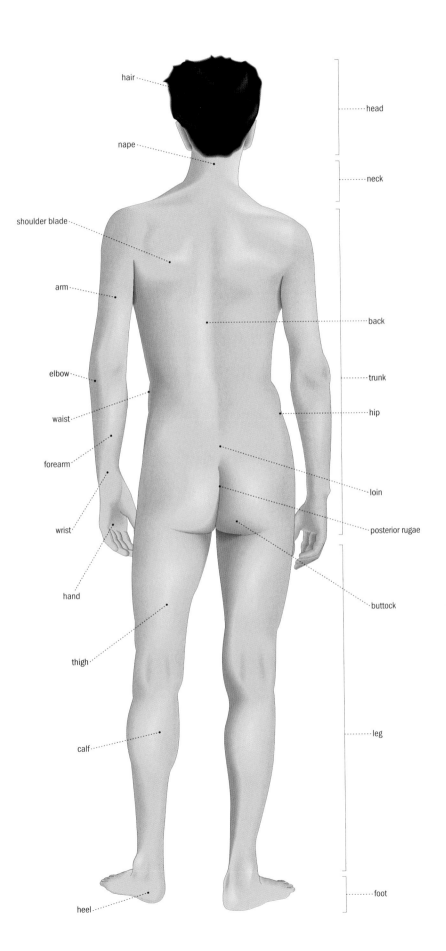

hair

head

nape

neck

shoulder blade

back

arm

trunk

elbow

hip

waist

forearm

loin

wrist

posterior rugae

hand

buttock

thigh

leg

calf

foot

heel

woman

anterior view

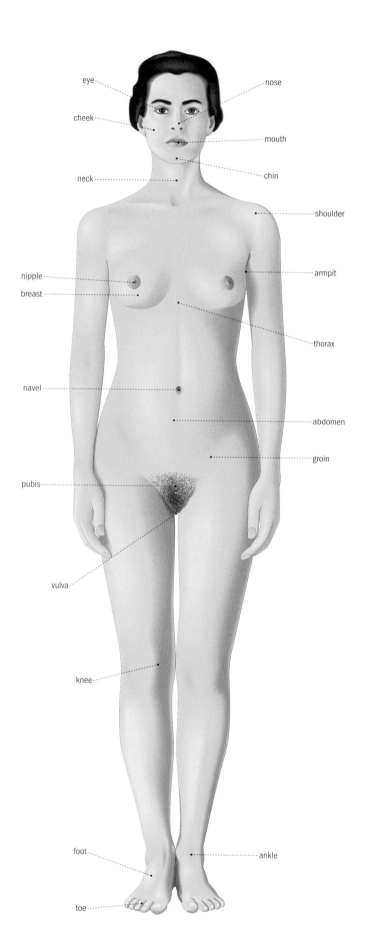

eye

nose

cheek

mouth

chin

neck

shoulder

nipple

armpit

breast

thorax

navel

abdomen

groin

pubis

vulva

knee

foot

ankle

toe

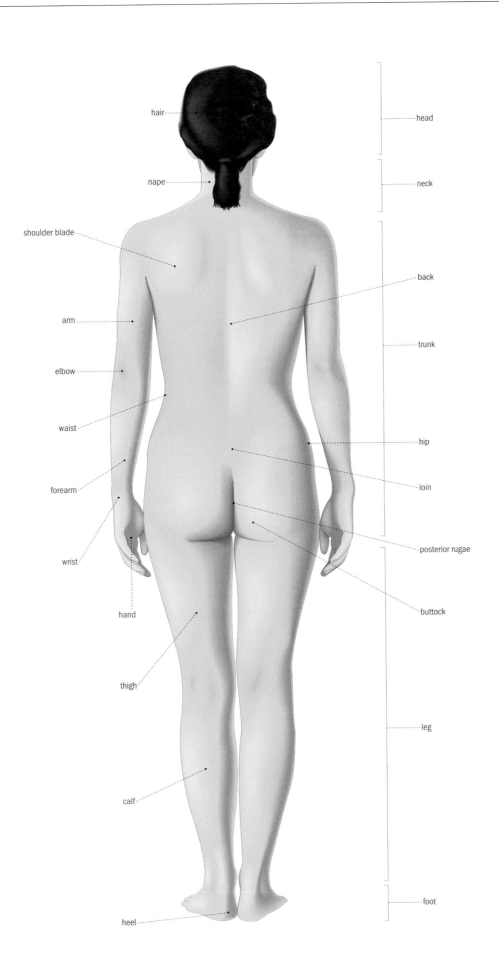

hair

nape

shoulder blade

arm

elbow

waist

forearm

wrist

hand

thigh

calf

heel

head

neck

back

trunk

hip

loin

posterior rugae

buttock

leg

foot

muscles

anterior view

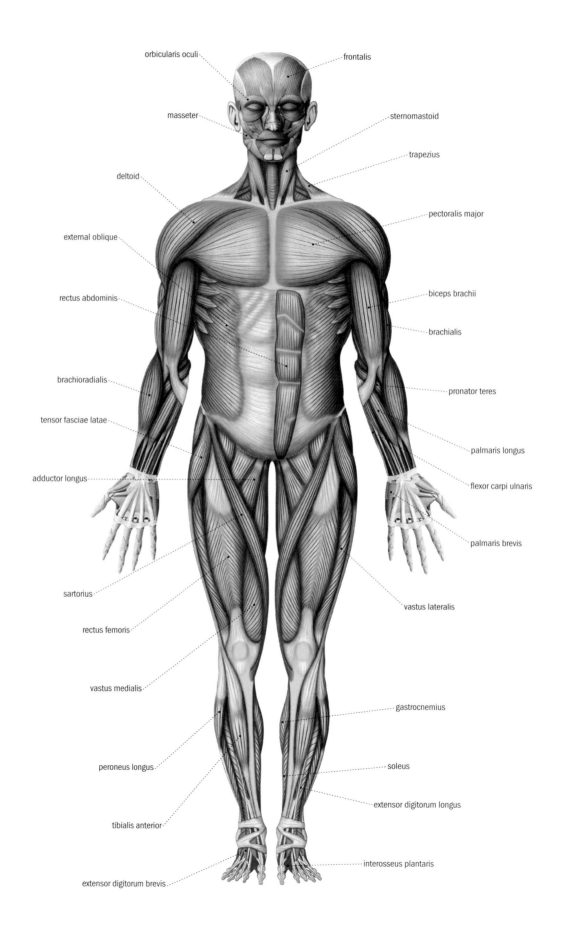

orbicularis oculi

frontalis

masseter

sternomastoid

trapezius

deltoid

pectoralis major

external oblique

rectus abdominis

biceps brachii

brachialis

brachioradialis

pronator teres

tensor fasciae latae

palmaris longus

adductor longus

flexor carpi ulnaris

palmaris brevis

sartorius

vastus lateralis

rectus femoris

vastus medialis

gastrocnemius

peroneus longus

soleus

extensor digitorum longus

tibialis anterior

interosseus plantaris

extensor digitorum brevis

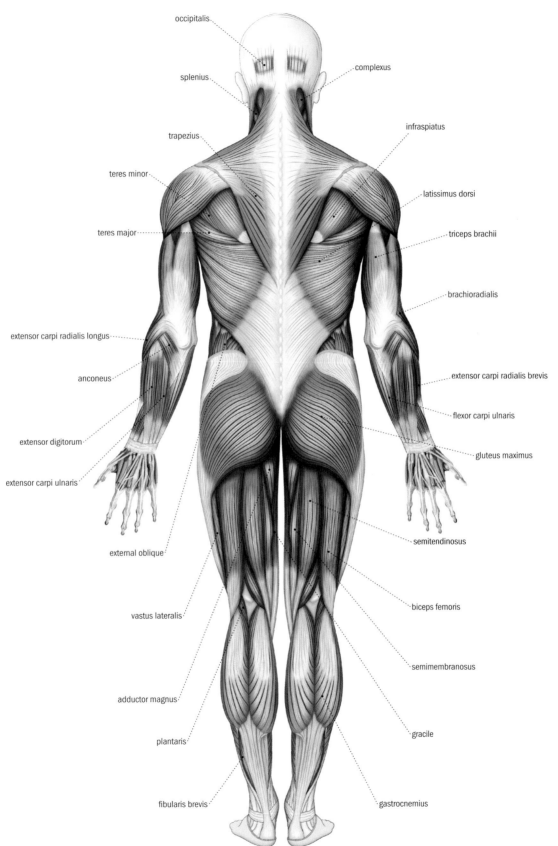

occipitalis

complexus

splenius

trapezius

infraspiatus

teres minor

latissimus dorsi

teres major

triceps brachii

brachioradialis

extensor carpi radialis longus

extensor carpi radialis brevis

anconeus

flexor carpi ulnaris

extensor digitorum

gluteus maximus

extensor carpi ulnaris

semitendinosus

external oblique

biceps femoris

vastus lateralis

semimembranosus

adductor magnus

gracile

plantaris

fibularis brevis

gastrocnemius

skeleton

anterior view

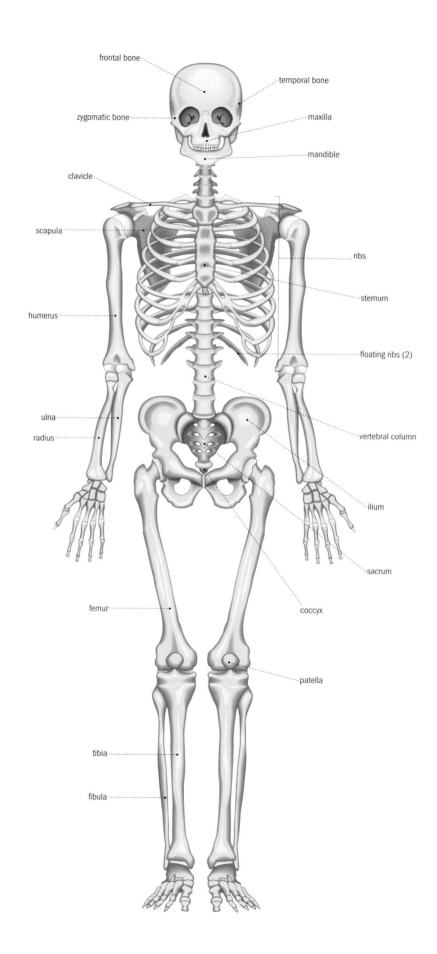

frontal bone

temporal bone

zygomatic bone

maxilla

mandible

clavicle

scapula

ribs

sternum

humerus

floating ribs (2)

ulna

radius

vertebral column

ilium

sacrum

coccyx

femur

patella

tibia

fibula

posterior view

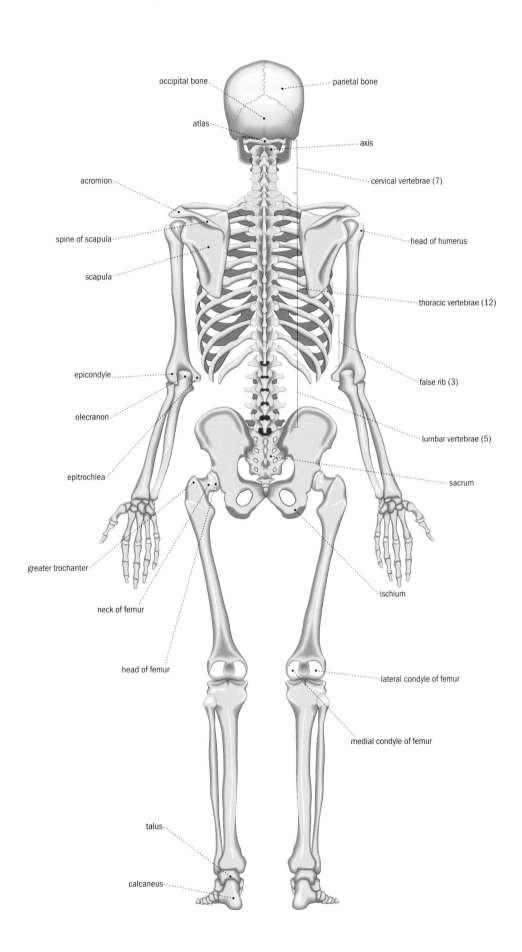

occipital bone

parietal bone

atlas

axis

cervical vertebrae (7)

acromion

head of humerus

spine of scapula

scapula

thoracic vertebrae (12)

epicondyle

false rib (3)

olecranon

lumbar vertebrae (5)

epitrochlea

sacrum

greater trochanter

ischium

neck of femur

head of femur

lateral condyle of femur

medial condyle of femur

talus

calcaneus

skeleton

hand

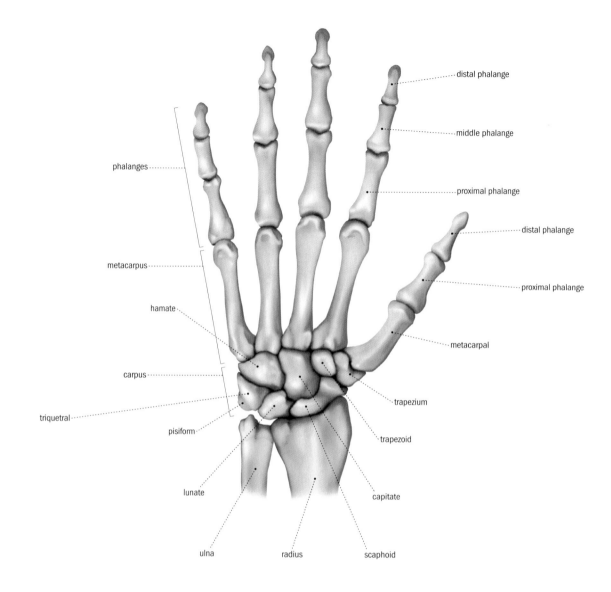

phalanges

distal phalange

middle phalange

proximal phalange

distal phalange

proximal phalange

metacarpus

hamate

metacarpal

carpus

triquetral

trapezium

pisiform

trapezoid

lunate

capitate

ulna

radius

scaphoid

structure of a long bone

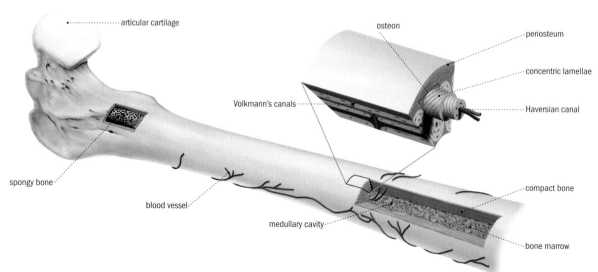

articular cartilage

osteon

periosteum

concentric lamellae

Volkmann's canals

Haversian canal

spongy bone

compact bone

blood vessel

medullary cavity

bone marrow

foot

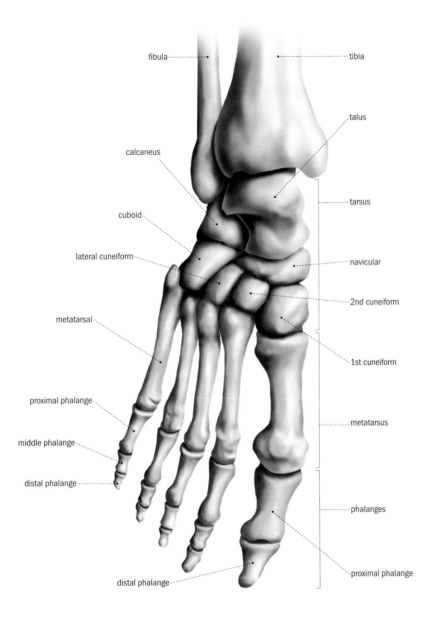

fibula

tibia

talus

calcaneus

tarsus

cuboid

lateral cuneiform

navicular

2nd cuneiform

metatarsal

1st cuneiform

proximal phalange

metatarsus

middle phalange

distal phalange

phalanges

distal phalange

proximal phalange

parts of a long bone

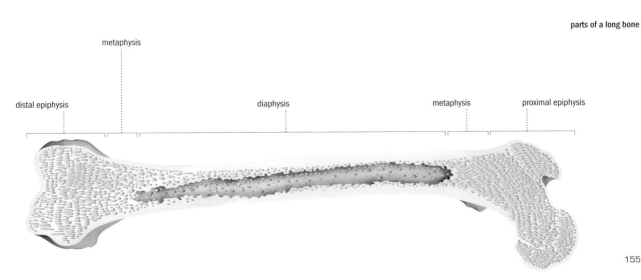

metaphysis

distal epiphysis

diaphysis

metaphysis

proximal epiphysis

155

skeleton

HUMAN BEING

types of synovial joints

hinge joint

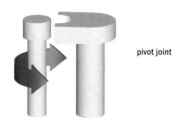

pivot joint

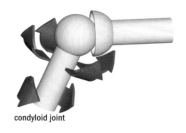

condyloid joint

leg

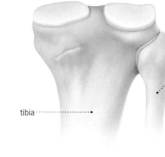

shoulder

elbow

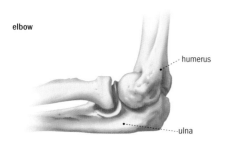

humerus

ulna

tibia

fibula

scapula

humerus

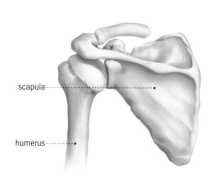

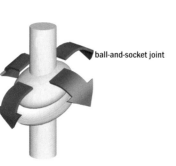

ball-and-socket joint

gliding joint

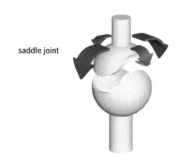

saddle joint

wrist

tarsus

thumb

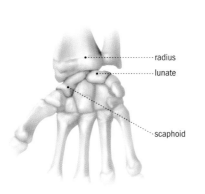

radius

lunate

scaphoid

navicular

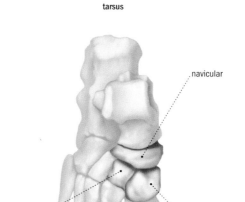

2nd cuneiform

1st cuneiform

trapezium

metacarpal

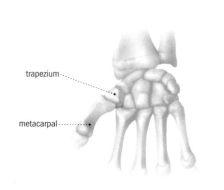

vertebral column

types of bones

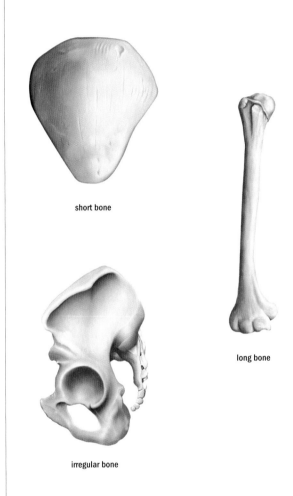

short bone

long bone

irregular bone

flat bone

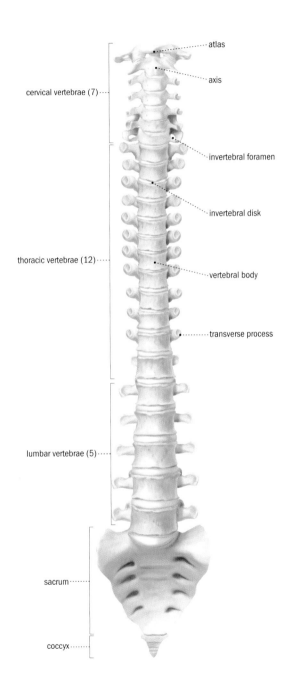

atlas

axis

cervical vertebrae (7)

invertebral foramen

invertebral disk

vertebral body

thoracic vertebrae (12)

transverse process

lumbar vertebrae (5)

sacrum

coccyx

skeleton

lateral view of adult skull

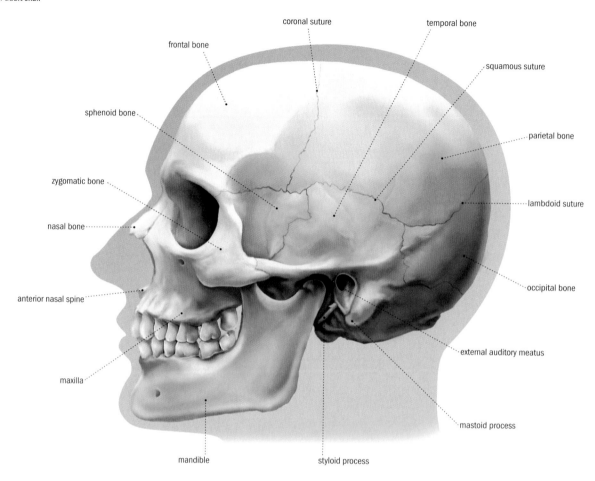

coronal suture

temporal bone

frontal bone

squamous suture

sphenoid bone

parietal bone

zygomatic bone

lambdoid suture

nasal bone

anterior nasal spine

occipital bone

maxilla

external auditory meatus

mastoid process

mandible

styloid process

lateral view of child's skull

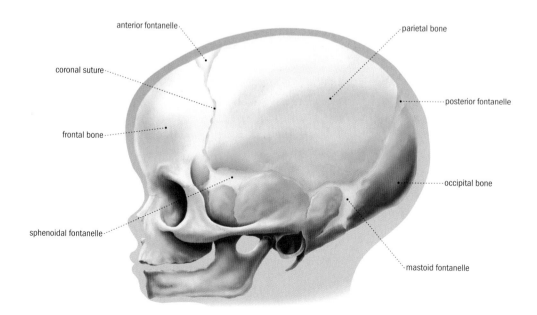

anterior fontanelle

parietal bone

coronal suture

posterior fontanelle

frontal bone

sphenoidal fontanelle

occipital bone

mastoid fontanelle

teeth

human denture

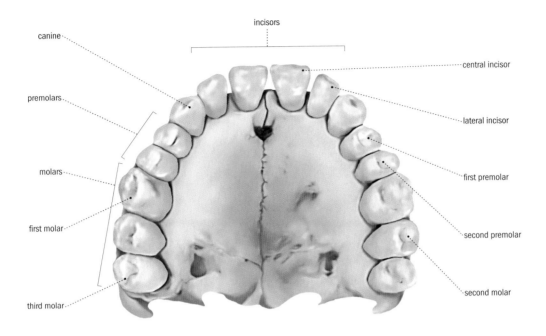

incisors

canine

central incisor

premolars

lateral incisor

molars

first premolar

first molar

second premolar

third molar

second molar

cross section of a molar

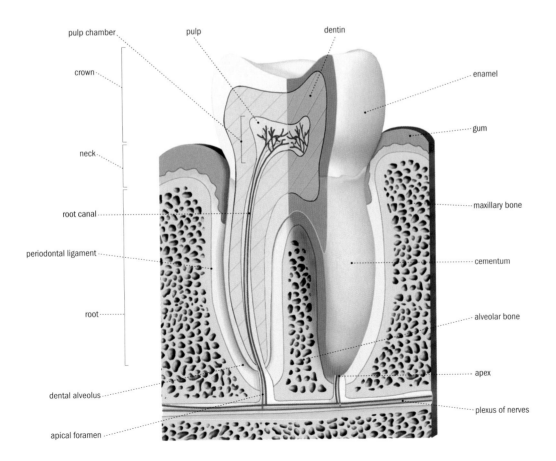

pulp chamber

pulp

dentin

crown

enamel

neck

gum

root canal

maxillary bone

periodontal ligament

cementum

root

alveolar bone

dental alveolus

apex

apical foramen

plexus of nerves

blood circulation

HUMAN BEING

principal veins and arteries

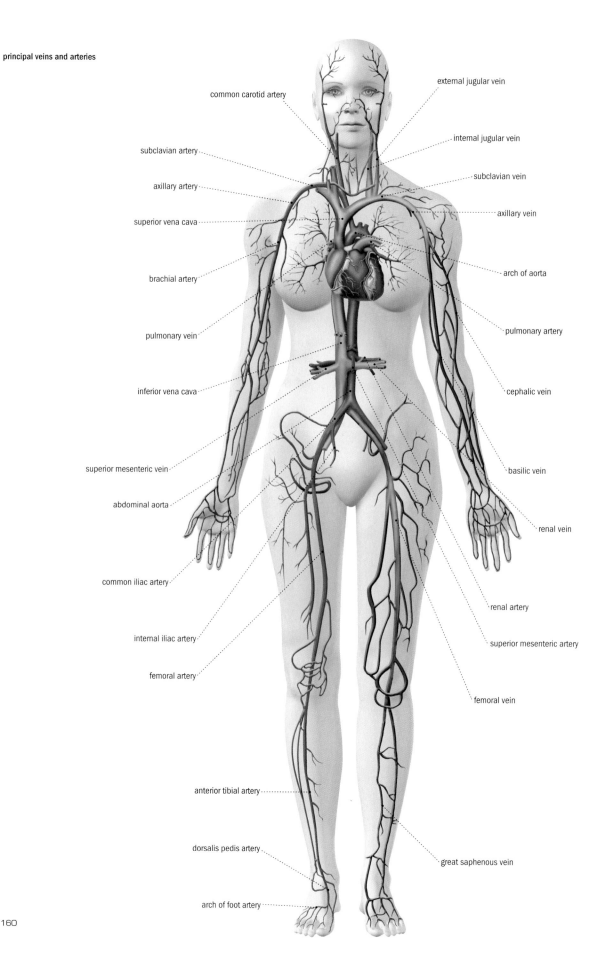

common carotid artery

subclavian artery

axillary artery

superior vena cava

brachial artery

pulmonary vein

inferior vena cava

superior mesenteric vein

abdominal aorta

common iliac artery

internal iliac artery

femoral artery

anterior tibial artery

dorsalis pedis artery

arch of foot artery

external jugular vein

internal jugular vein

subclavian vein

axillary vein

arch of aorta

pulmonary artery

cephalic vein

basilic vein

renal vein

renal artery

superior mesenteric artery

femoral vein

great saphenous vein

schema of circulation

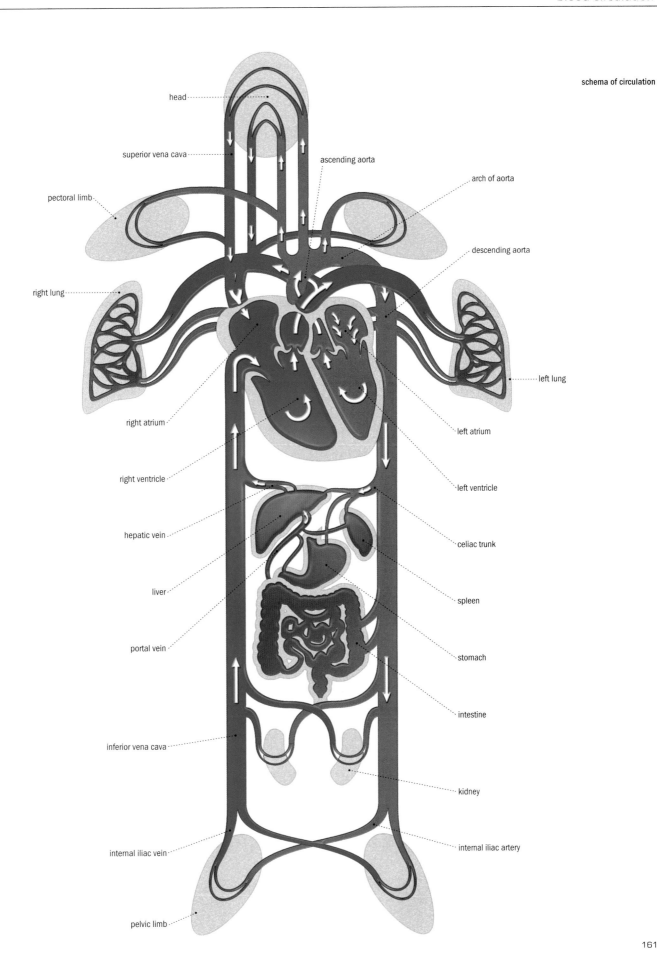

head

superior vena cava

ascending aorta

arch of aorta

pectoral limb

descending aorta

right lung

left lung

right atrium

left atrium

right ventricle

left ventricle

hepatic vein

celiac trunk

liver

spleen

portal vein

stomach

inferior vena cava

intestine

kidney

internal iliac vein

internal iliac artery

pelvic limb

blood circulation

composition of the blood

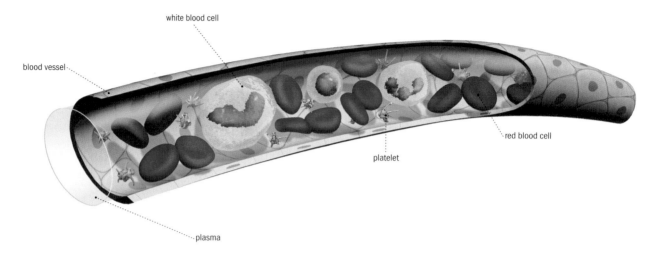

white blood cell

blood vessel

red blood cell

platelet

plasma

heart

oxygenated blood

deoxygenated blood

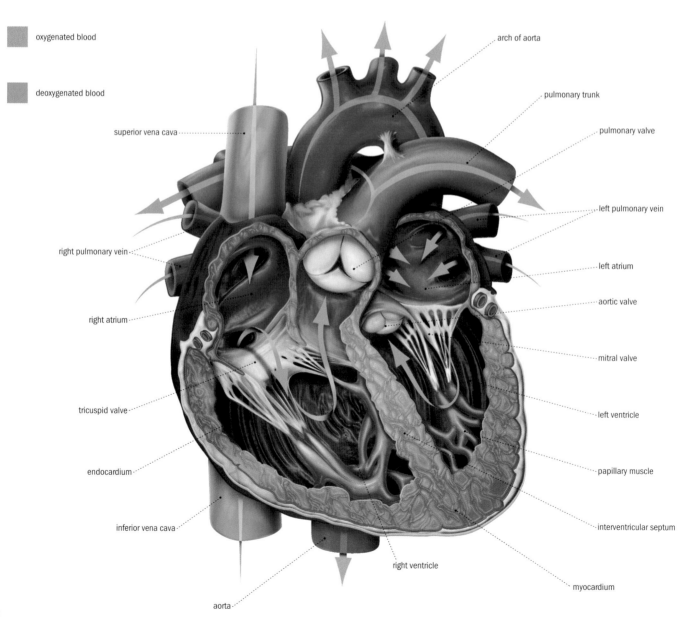

arch of aorta

pulmonary trunk

pulmonary valve

superior vena cava

left pulmonary vein

right pulmonary vein

left atrium

aortic valve

right atrium

mitral valve

tricuspid valve

left ventricle

endocardium

papillary muscle

inferior vena cava

interventricular septum

right ventricle

myocardium

aorta

respiratory system

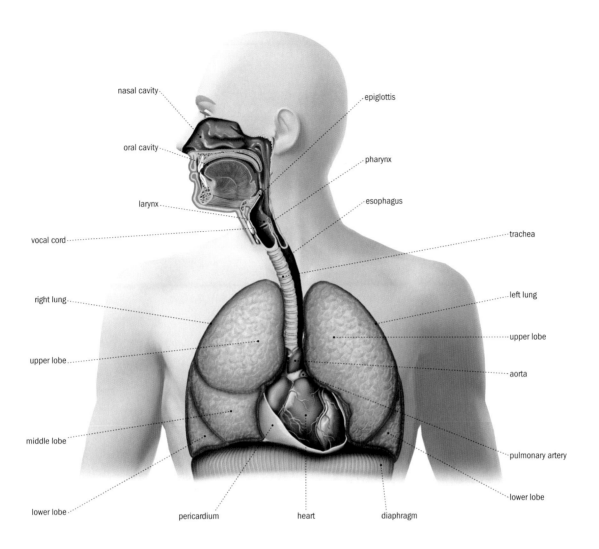

nasal cavity

oral cavity

larynx

vocal cord

right lung

upper lobe

middle lobe

lower lobe

pericardium

heart

diaphragm

epiglottis

pharynx

esophagus

trachea

left lung

upper lobe

aorta

pulmonary artery

lower lobe

lungs

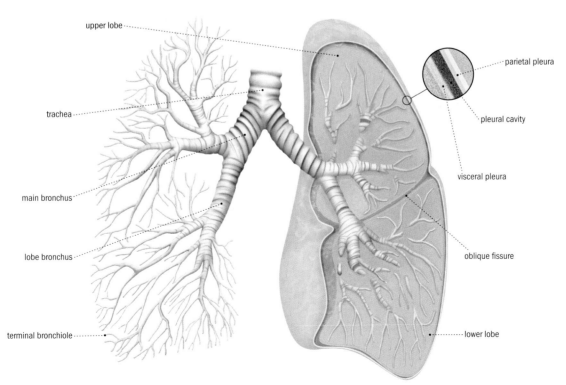

upper lobe

trachea

main bronchus

lobe bronchus

terminal bronchiole

parietal pleura

pleural cavity

visceral pleura

oblique fissure

lower lobe

digestive system

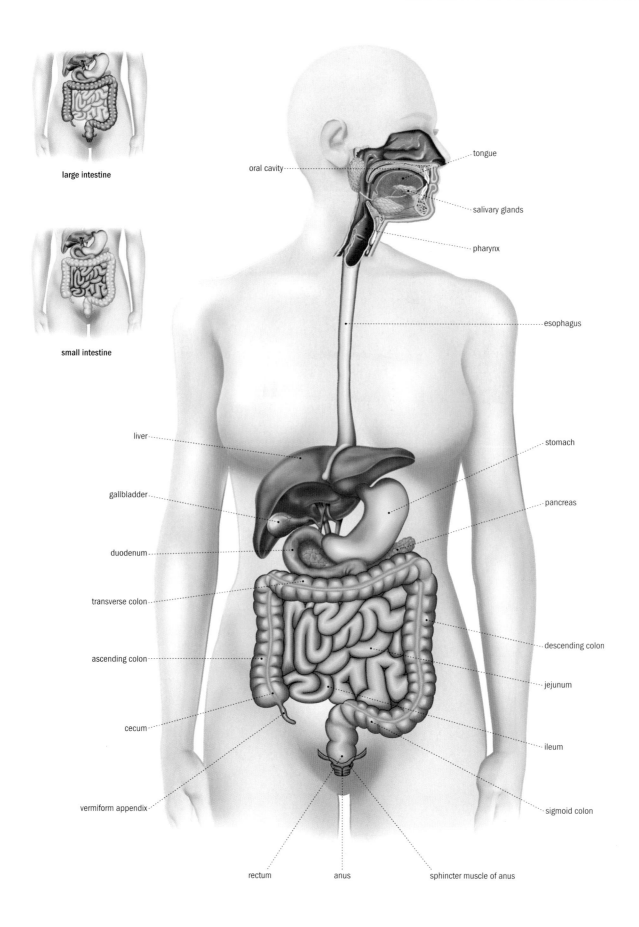

large intestine

small intestine

oral cavity

tongue

salivary glands

pharynx

esophagus

liver

stomach

gallbladder

pancreas

duodenum

transverse colon

descending colon

ascending colon

jejunum

cecum

ileum

vermiform appendix

sigmoid colon

rectum

anus

sphincter muscle of anus

urinary system

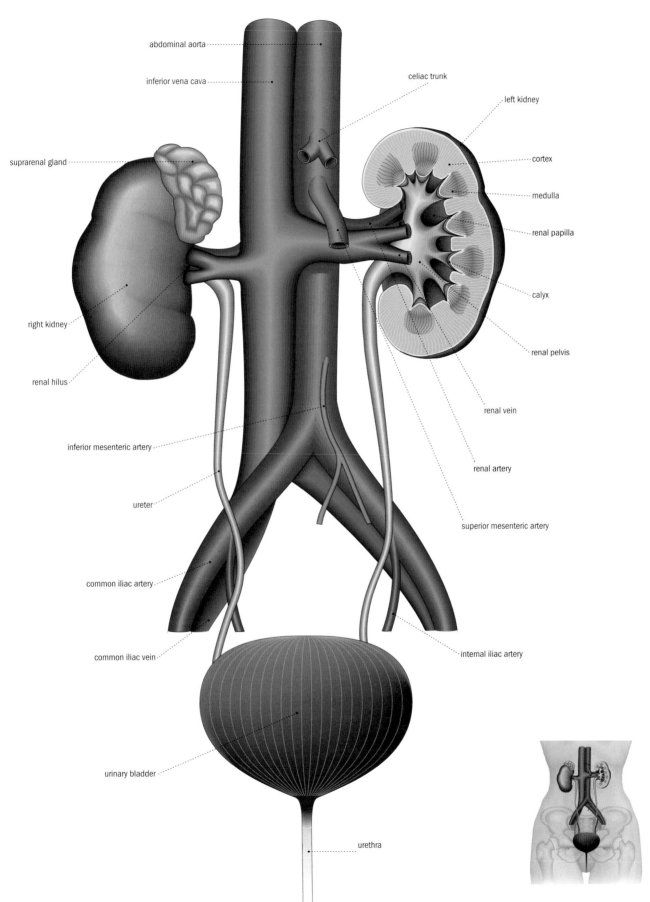

abdominal aorta

inferior vena cava

celiac trunk

left kidney

cortex

medulla

renal papilla

suprarenal gland

calyx

renal pelvis

right kidney

renal hilus

renal vein

renal artery

inferior mesenteric artery

ureter

superior mesenteric artery

common iliac artery

common iliac vein

internal iliac artery

urinary bladder

urethra

nervous system

peripheral nervous system

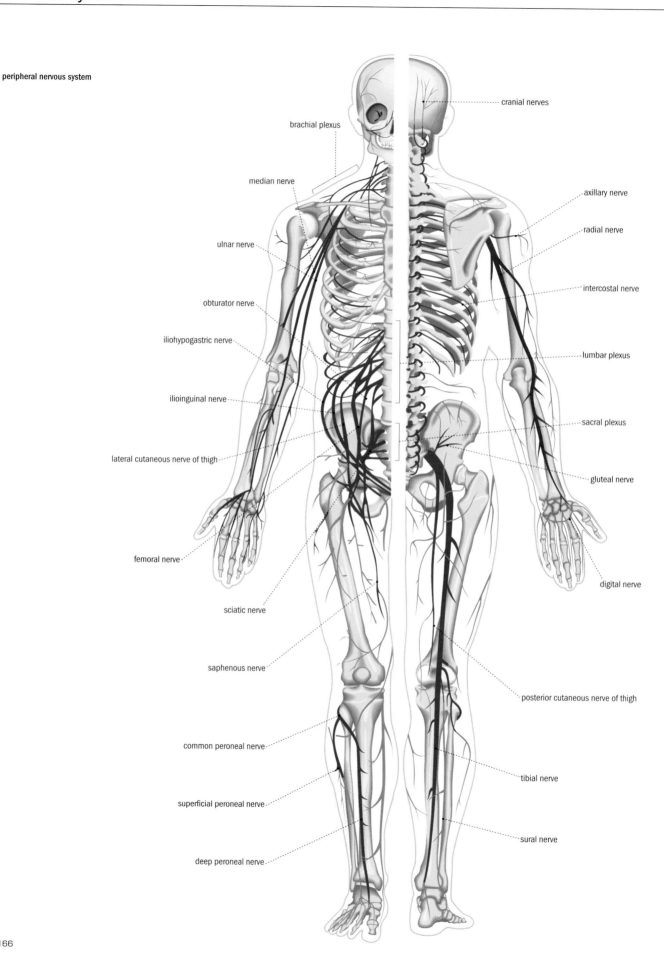

cranial nerves

brachial plexus

median nerve

axillary nerve

radial nerve

ulnar nerve

intercostal nerve

obturator nerve

iliohypogastric nerve

lumbar plexus

ilioinguinal nerve

sacral plexus

lateral cutaneous nerve of thigh

gluteal nerve

femoral nerve

digital nerve

sciatic nerve

saphenous nerve

posterior cutaneous nerve of thigh

common peroneal nerve

tibial nerve

superficial peroneal nerve

sural nerve

deep peroneal nerve

central nervous system

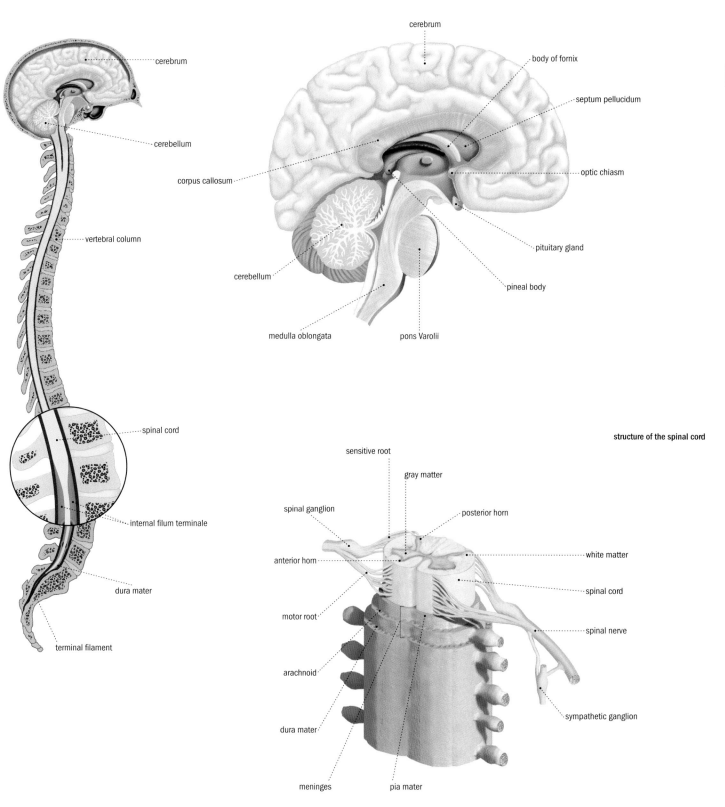

cerebrum

cerebellum

corpus callosum

vertebral column

cerebrum

body of fornix

septum pellucidum

optic chiasm

pituitary gland

pineal body

cerebellum

medulla oblongata

pons Varolii

spinal cord

internal filum terminale

dura mater

terminal filament

structure of the spinal cord

sensitive root

gray matter

spinal ganglion

posterior horn

anterior horn

white matter

motor root

spinal cord

arachnoid

spinal nerve

dura mater

sympathetic ganglion

meninges

pia mater

nervous system

chain of neurons

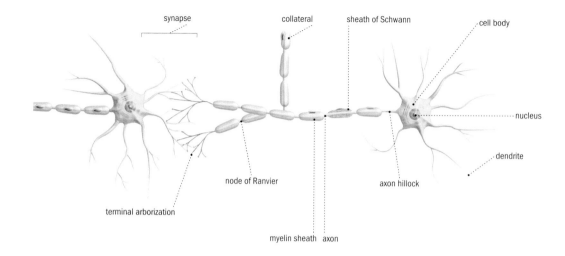

synapse

collateral

sheath of Schwann

cell body

nucleus

dendrite

node of Ranvier

axon hillock

terminal arborization

myelin sheath   axon

sensory impulse

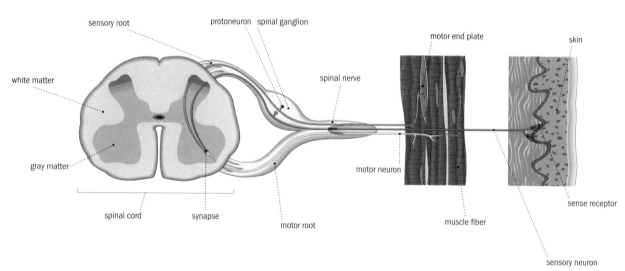

sensory root

protoneuron   spinal ganglion

motor end plate

skin

white matter

spinal nerve

gray matter

spinal cord

synapse

motor root

motor neuron

muscle fiber

sense receptor

sensory neuron

lumbar vertebra

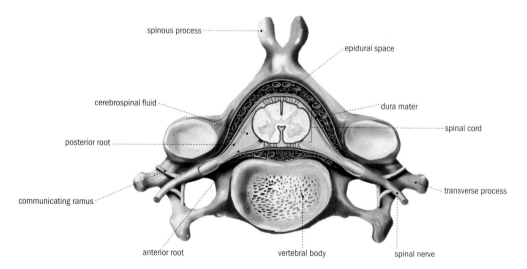

spinous process

epidural space

cerebrospinal fluid

dura mater

posterior root

spinal cord

communicating ramus

transverse process

anterior root

vertebral body

spinal nerve

male reproductive organs

sagittal section

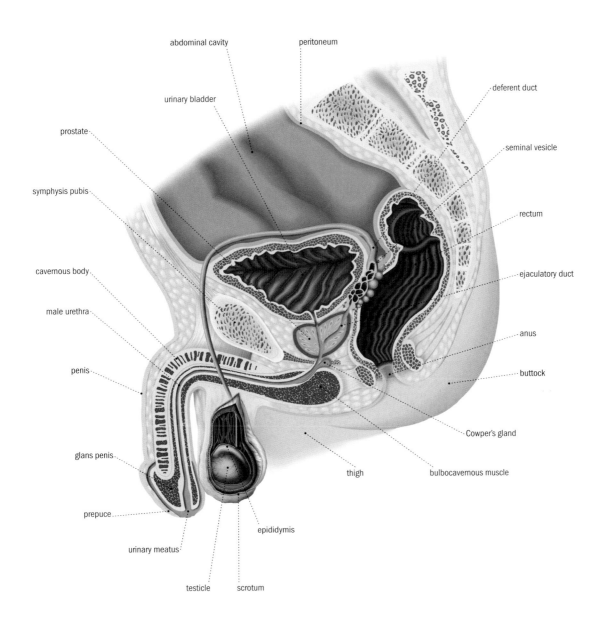

abdominal cavity

peritoneum

urinary bladder

deferent duct

prostate

seminal vesicle

symphysis pubis

rectum

cavernous body

ejaculatory duct

male urethra

anus

penis

buttock

Cowper's gland

glans penis

bulbocavernous muscle

prepuce

thigh

epididymis

urinary meatus

testicle

scrotum

spermatozoon

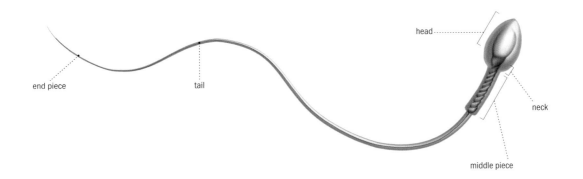

head

end piece

tail

neck

middle piece

female reproductive organs

sagittal section

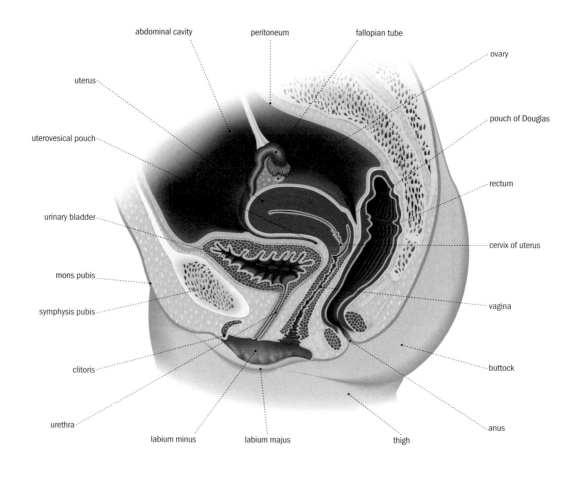

abdominal cavity

peritoneum

fallopian tube

ovary

uterus

pouch of Douglas

uterovesical pouch

rectum

urinary bladder

cervix of uterus

mons pubis

vagina

symphysis pubis

clitoris

buttock

urethra

anus

labium minus

labium majus

thigh

egg

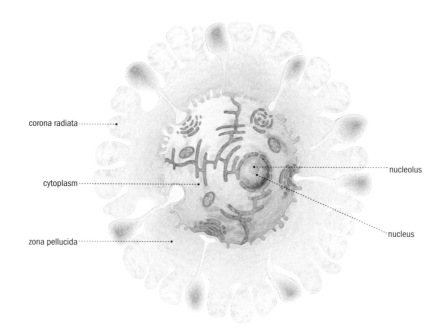

corona radiata

nucleolus

cytoplasm

nucleus

zona pellucida

posterior view

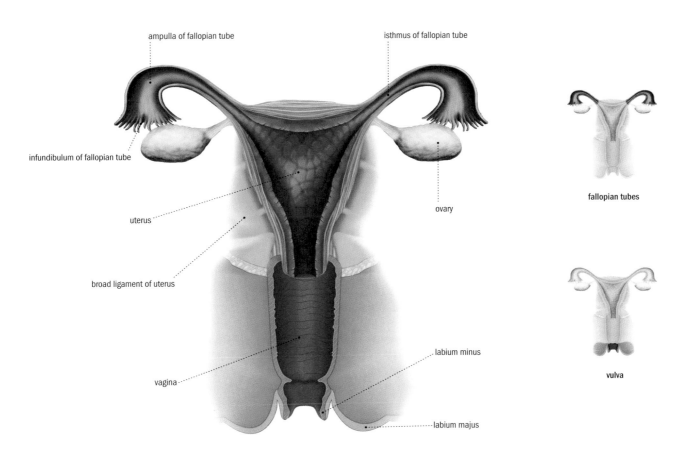

ampulla of fallopian tube

isthmus of fallopian tube

infundibulum of fallopian tube

ovary

uterus

broad ligament of uterus

vagina

labium minus

labium majus

fallopian tubes

vulva

HUMAN BEING

breast

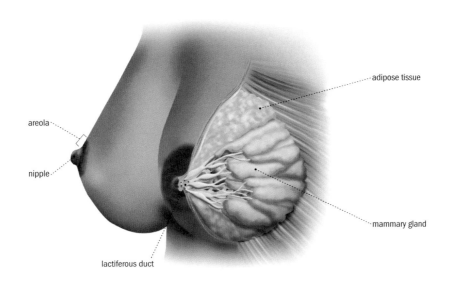

adipose tissue

areola

nipple

mammary gland

lactiferous duct

touch

skin

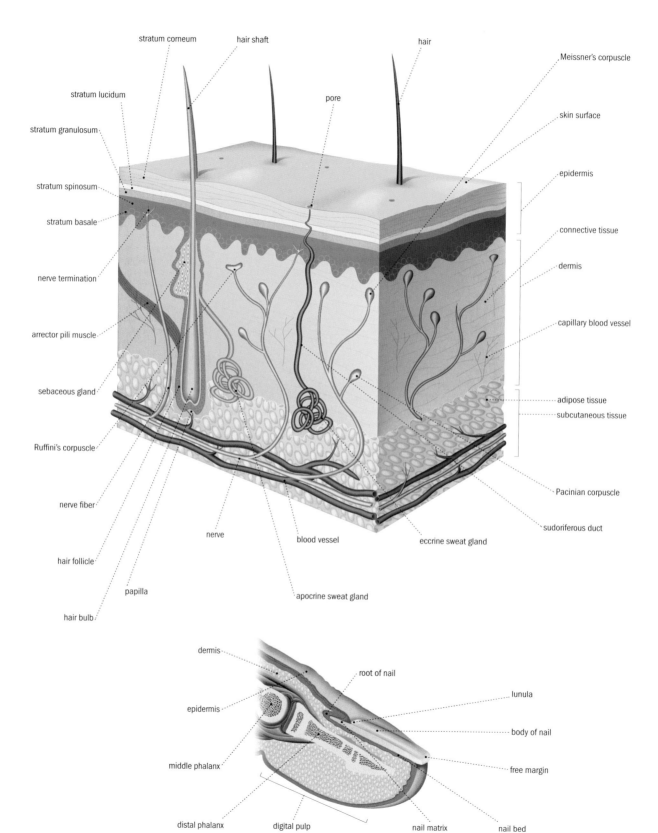

stratum corneum   hair shaft   hair   Meissner's corpuscle

stratum lucidum   pore   skin surface

stratum granulosum   epidermis

stratum spinosum   connective tissue

stratum basale   dermis

nerve termination   capillary blood vessel

arrector pili muscle

sebaceous gland   adipose tissue

subcutaneous tissue

Ruffini's corpuscle   Pacinian corpuscle

nerve fiber   sudoriferous duct

nerve   blood vessel   eccrine sweat gland

hair follicle

papilla   apocrine sweat gland

hair bulb

finger

dermis   root of nail   lunula

epidermis   body of nail

middle phalanx   free margin

distal phalanx   digital pulp   nail matrix   nail bed

touch

hand

palm

back

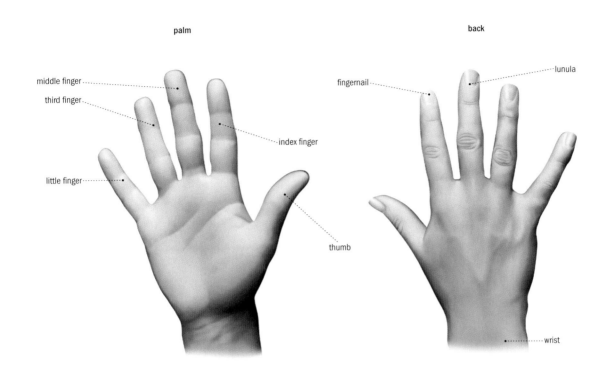

middle finger

third finger

index finger

little finger

thumb

fingernail

lunula

wrist

HUMAN BEING

hearing

auricle

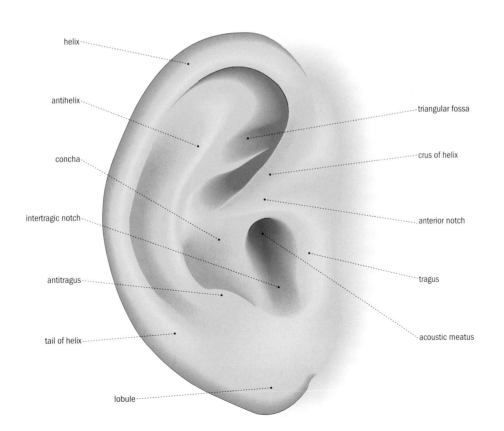

helix

antihelix

concha

intertragic notch

antitragus

tail of helix

lobule

triangular fossa

crus of helix

anterior notch

tragus

acoustic meatus

hearing

HUMAN BEING

structure of the ear

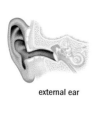

external ear

middle ear

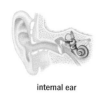

internal ear

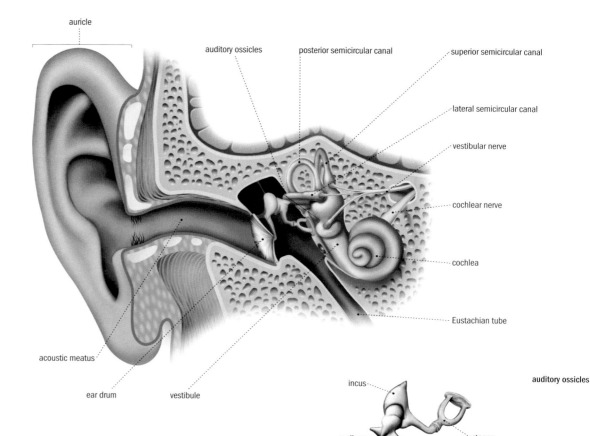

auricle

auditory ossicles

posterior semicircular canal

superior semicircular canal

lateral semicircular canal

vestibular nerve

cochlear nerve

cochlea

Eustachian tube

acoustic meatus

ear drum

vestibule

incus

malleus

stapes

auditory ossicles

smell and taste

mouth

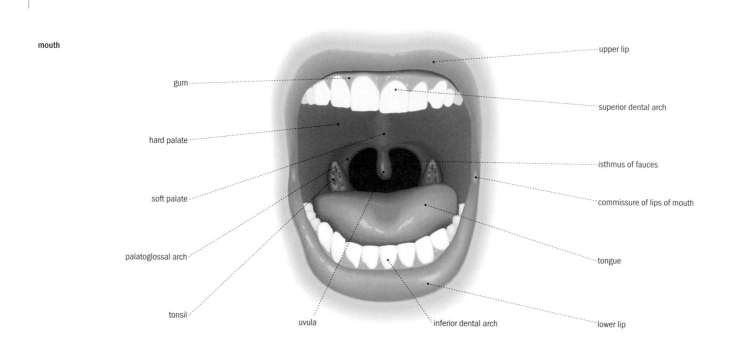

upper lip

gum

superior dental arch

hard palate

isthmus of fauces

soft palate

commissure of lips of mouth

palatoglossal arch

tongue

tonsil

uvula

inferior dental arch

lower lip

external nose

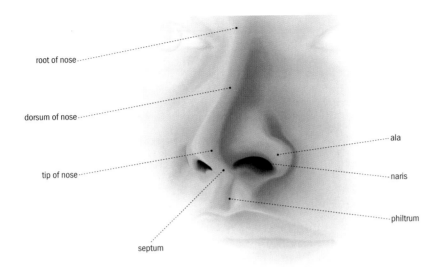

root of nose

dorsum of nose

ala

tip of nose

naris

philtrum

septum

nasal fossae

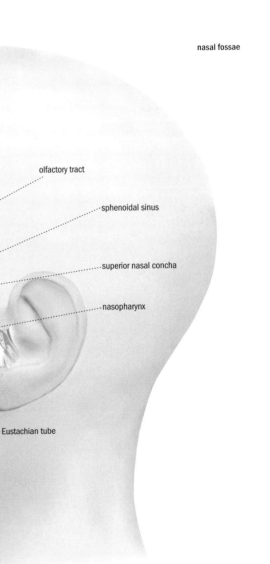

middle nasal concha

cribriform plate of ethmoid

olfactory bulb

frontal sinus

olfactory nerve

olfactory tract

nasal bone

sphenoidal sinus

inferior nasal concha

superior nasal concha

septal cartilage of nose

nasopharynx

greater alar cartilage

maxilla

Eustachian tube

olfactory mucosa

uvula

hard palate

tongue

soft palate

smell and taste

dorsum of tongue

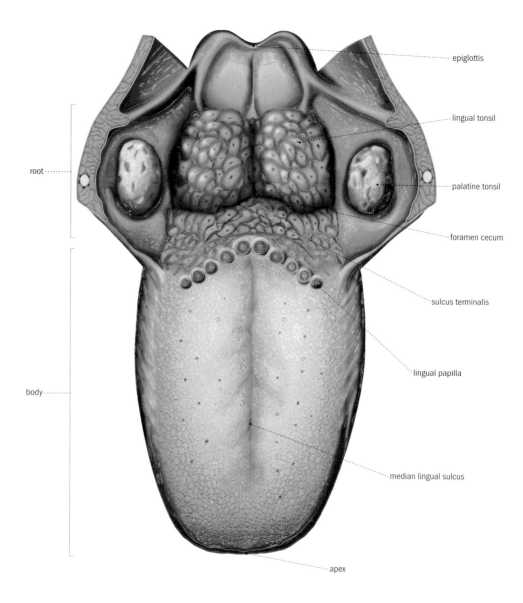

epiglottis

lingual tonsil

root

palatine tonsil

foramen cecum

sulcus terminalis

lingual papilla

body

median lingual sulcus

apex

taste receptors

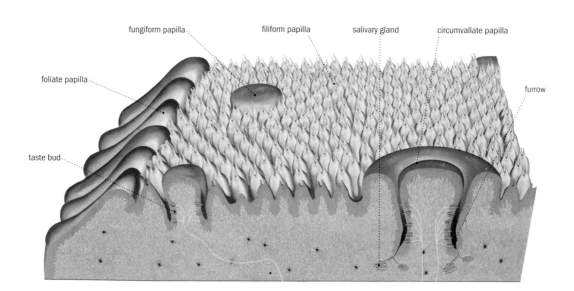

fungiform papilla

filiform papilla

salivary gland

circumvallate papilla

foliate papilla

furrow

taste bud

sight

eye

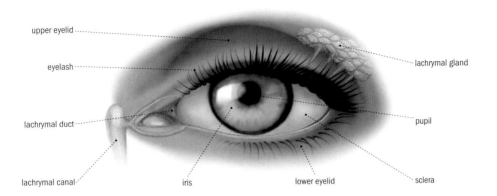

upper eyelid

eyelash

lachrymal duct

lachrymal canal

lachrymal gland

pupil

sclera

iris

lower eyelid

eyeball

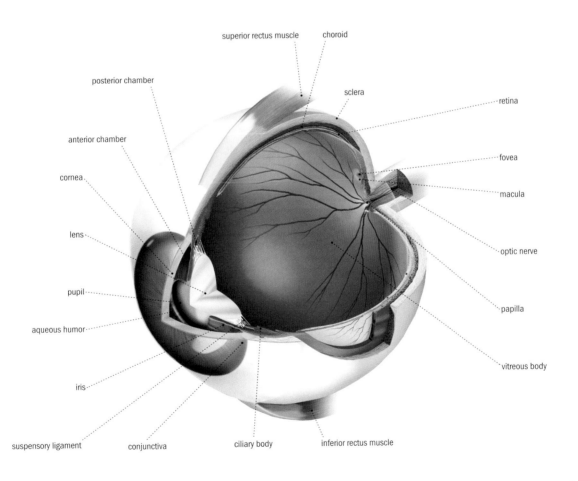

superior rectus muscle

choroid

posterior chamber

sclera

retina

anterior chamber

fovea

cornea

macula

lens

optic nerve

pupil

aqueous humor

papilla

iris

vitreous body

suspensory ligament

conjunctiva

ciliary body

inferior rectus muscle

photoreceptors

cone

rod

FOOD AND KITCHEN

supermarket

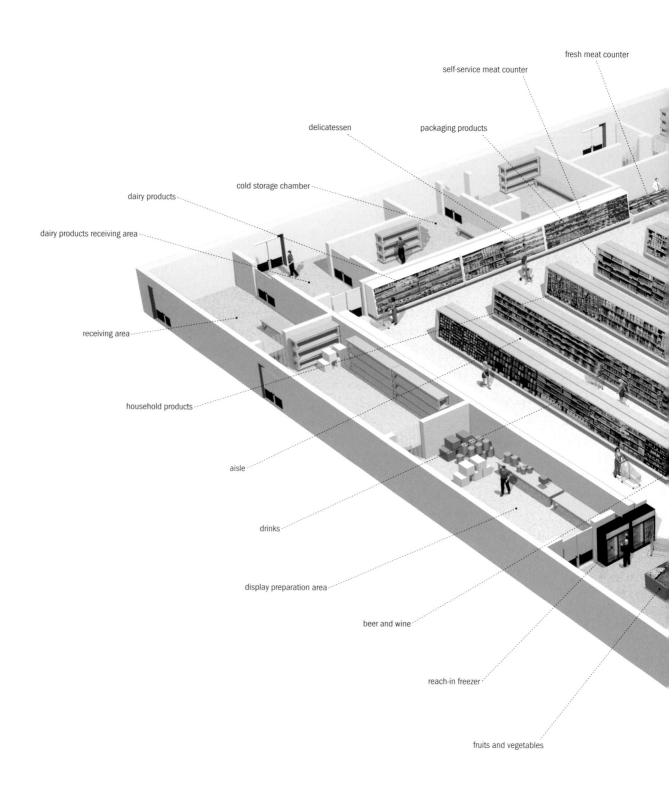

fresh meat counter

self-service meat counter

delicatessen

packaging products

cold storage chamber

dairy products

dairy products receiving area

receiving area

household products

aisle

drinks

display preparation area

beer and wine

reach-in freezer

fruits and vegetables

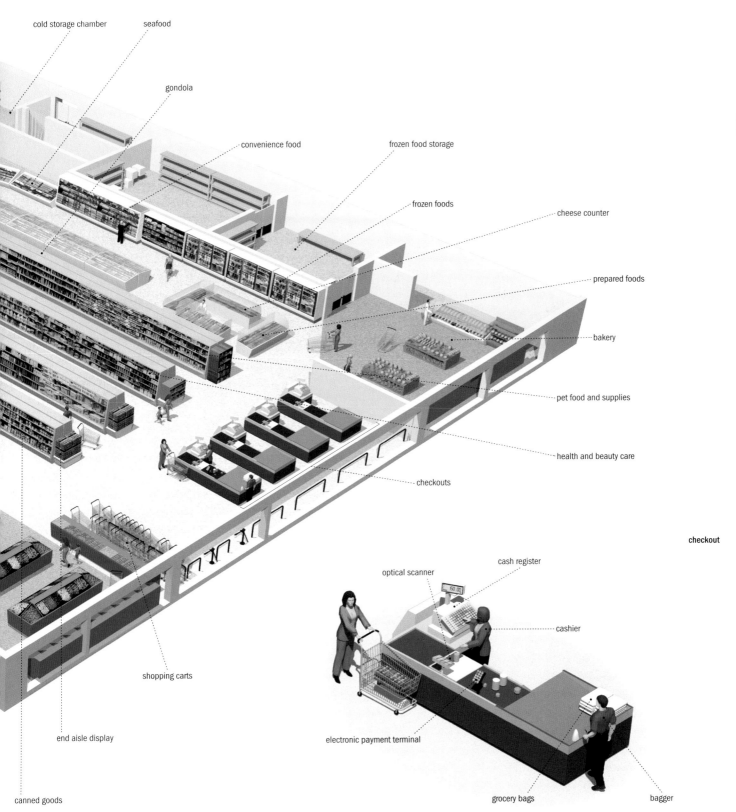

cold storage chamber

seafood

gondola

convenience food

frozen food storage

frozen foods

cheese counter

prepared foods

bakery

pet food and supplies

health and beauty care

checkouts

checkout

cash register

optical scanner

cashier

electronic payment terminal

grocery bags

bagger

shopping carts

end aisle display

canned goods

farmstead

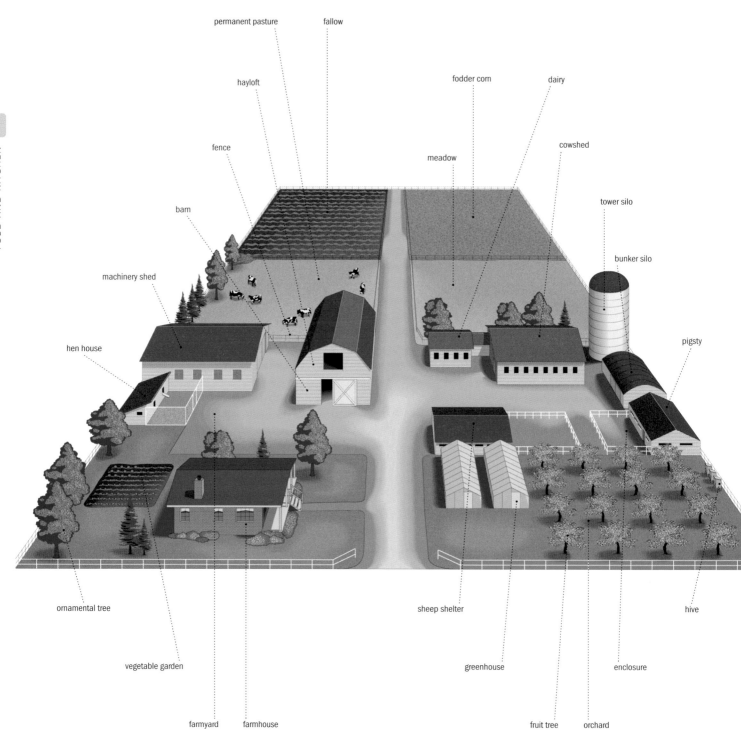

permanent pasture

fallow

hayloft

fodder corn

dairy

fence

meadow

cowshed

barn

tower silo

machinery shed

bunker silo

hen house

pigsty

ornamental tree

sheep shelter

hive

vegetable garden

greenhouse

enclosure

farmyard farmhouse

fruit tree orchard

mushrooms

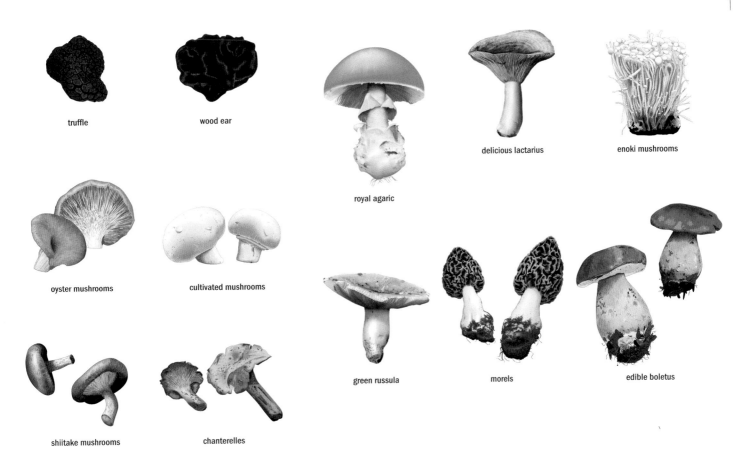

truffle

wood ear

royal agaric

delicious lactarius

enoki mushrooms

oyster mushrooms

cultivated mushrooms

green russula

morels

edible boletus

shiitake mushrooms

chanterelles

seaweed

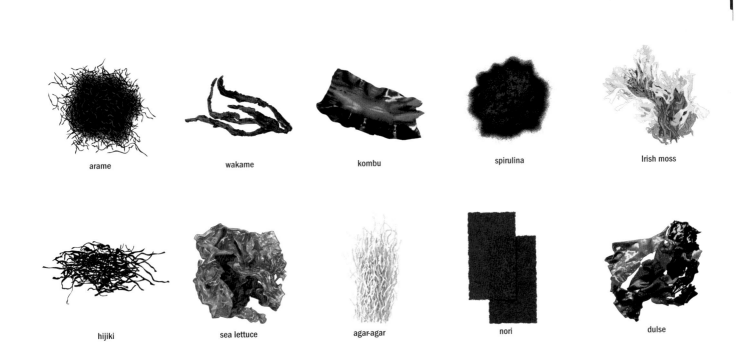

arame

wakame

kombu

spirulina

Irish moss

hijiki

sea lettuce

agar-agar

nori

dulse

vegetables

FOOD AND KITCHEN

bulb vegetables

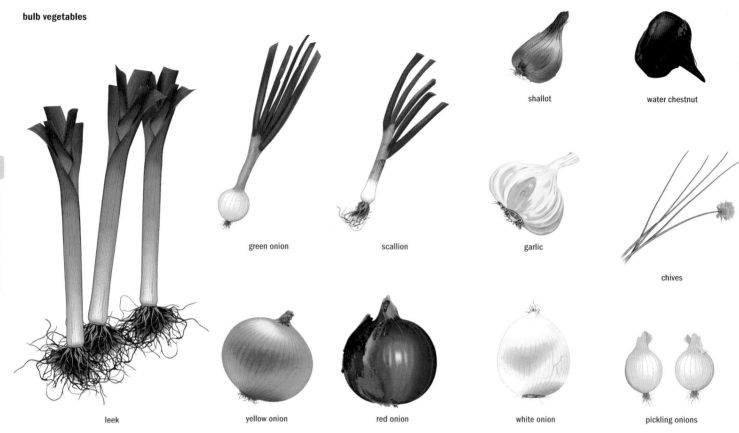

shallot

water chestnut

green onion

scallion

garlic

chives

leek

yellow onion

red onion

white onion

pickling onions

tuber vegetables

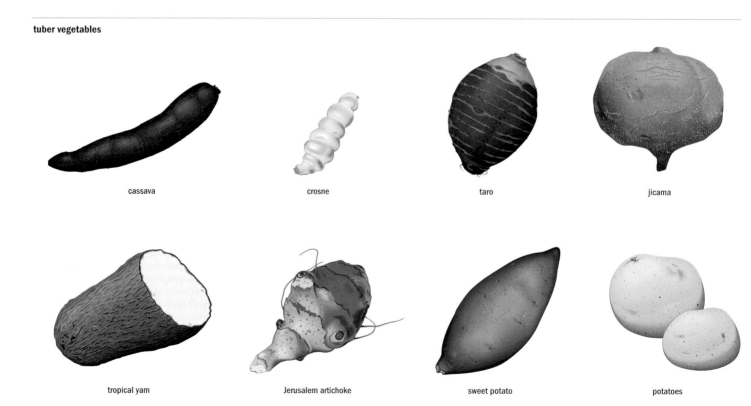

cassava

crosne

taro

jicama

tropical yam

Jerusalem artichoke

sweet potato

potatoes

stalk vegetables

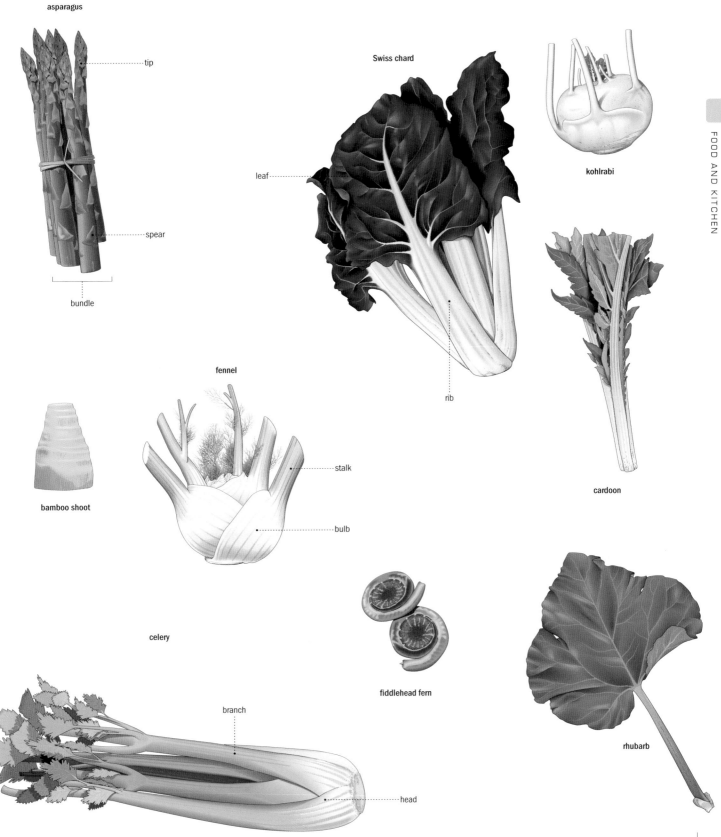

asparagus

tip

spear

bundle

Swiss chard

leaf

rib

kohlrabi

cardoon

fennel

stalk

bulb

bamboo shoot

fiddlehead fern

celery

branch

head

rhubarb

leaf vegetables

leaf lettuce

romaine lettuce

celtuce

sea kale

collards

escarole

butterhead lettuce

iceberg lettuce

radicchio

ornamental kale

curled kale

grape leaves

brussels sprouts

red cabbage

white cabbage

savoy cabbage

green cabbage

pe-tsai

bok choy

FOOD AND KITCHEN

purslane

nettle

watercress

dandelion

corn salad

arugula

spinach

garden cress

garden sorrel

curled endive

Belgian endive

inflorescent vegetables

cauliflower

broccoli

Gai-lohn

broccoli rabe

artichoke

vegetables

fruit vegetables

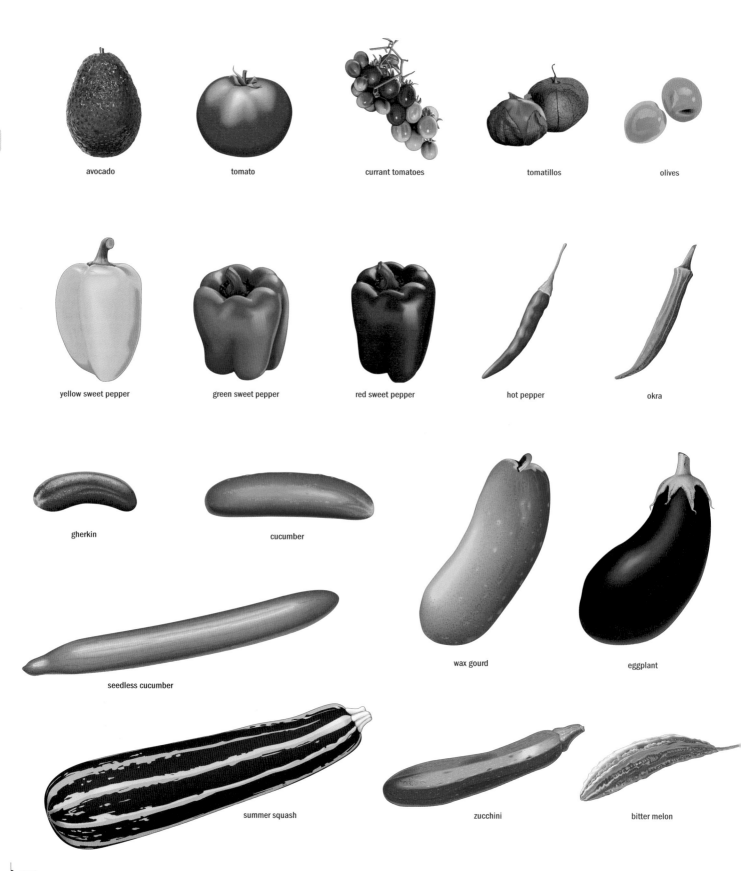

avocado

tomato

currant tomatoes

tomatillos

olives

yellow sweet pepper

green sweet pepper

red sweet pepper

hot pepper

okra

gherkin

cucumber

wax gourd

eggplant

seedless cucumber

summer squash

zucchini

bitter melon

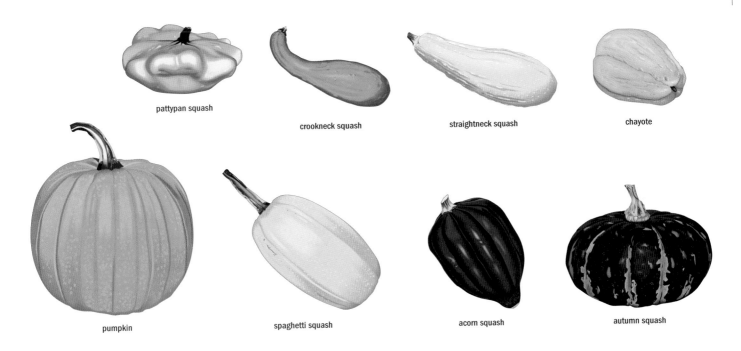

pattypan squash

crookneck squash

straightneck squash

chayote

pumpkin

spaghetti squash

acorn squash

autumn squash

root vegetables

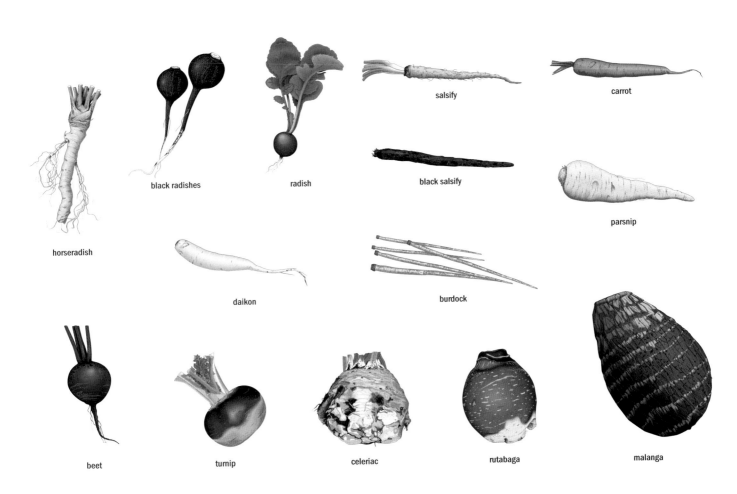

salsify

carrot

black radishes

radish

black salsify

parsnip

horseradish

daikon

burdock

beet

turnip

celeriac

rutabaga

malanga

legumes

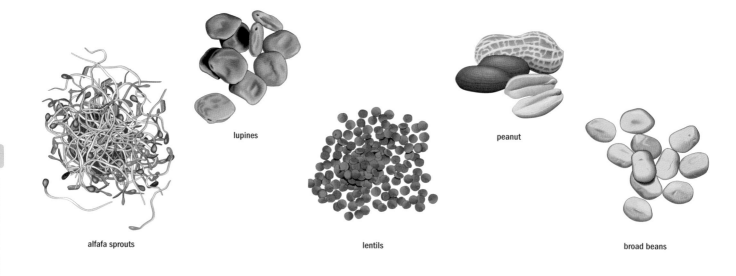

alfafa sprouts

lupines

lentils

peanut

broad beans

peas

dolichos beans

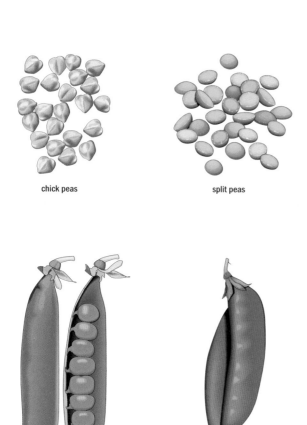

chick peas

split peas

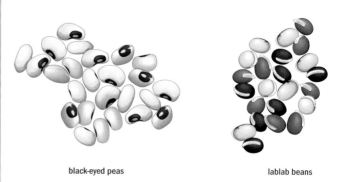

black-eyed peas

lablab beans

green peas

sweet peas

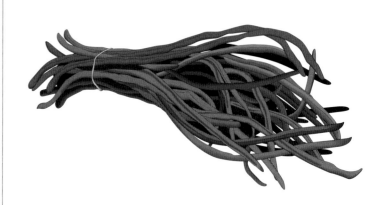

yard-long beans

beans

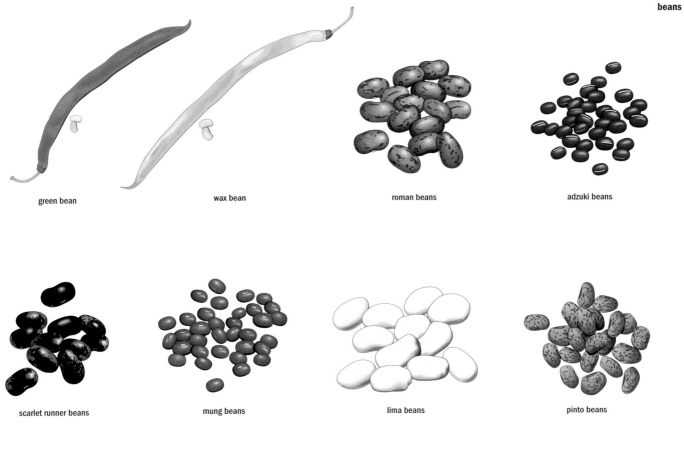

green bean

wax bean

roman beans

adzuki beans

scarlet runner beans

mung beans

lima beans

pinto beans

red kidney beans

black gram

black beans

soybeans

soybean sprouts

flageolets

fruits

berries

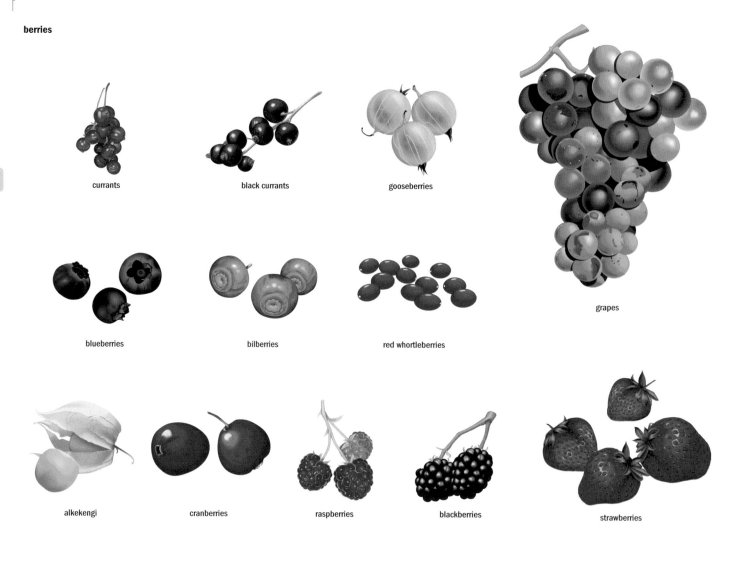

currants

black currants

gooseberries

grapes

blueberries

bilberries

red whortleberries

alkekengi

cranberries

raspberries

blackberries

strawberries

stone fruits

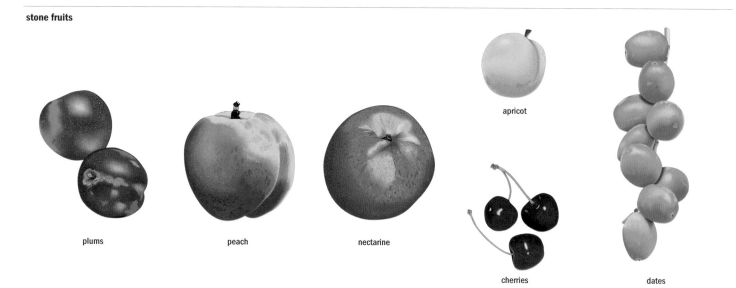

apricot

plums

peach

nectarine

cherries

dates

dry fruits

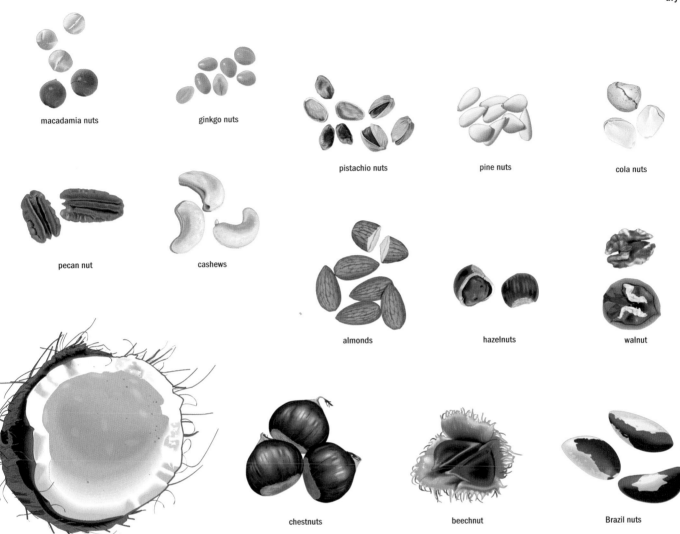

macadamia nuts

ginkgo nuts

pistachio nuts

pine nuts

cola nuts

pecan nut

cashews

almonds

hazelnuts

walnut

coconut

chestnuts

beechnut

Brazil nuts

pome fruits

pear

quince

apple

Japanese plums

fruits

citrus fruits

lemon

kumquat

lime

orange

mandarin

bergamot

grapefruit

pomelo

citron

cantaloupe

casaba melon

honeydew melon

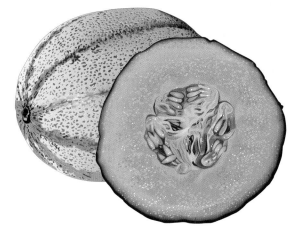

muskmelon

canary melon

watermelon

Ogen melon

tropical fruits

FOOD AND KITCHEN

plantain

banana

longan

tamarillo

passion fruit

horned melon

mangosteen

kiwi

pomegranate

cherimoya

jackfruit

pineapple

jaboticabas

litchi

fig

jujubes

sapodilla

guava

rambutan

Japanese persimmon

prickly pear

carambola

Asian pear

mango

durian

papaya

pepino

feijoa

spices

juniper berries

cloves

allspice

white mustard

black mustard

black pepper

white pepper

pink pepper

green pepper

nutmeg

caraway

cardamom

cinnamon

saffron

cumin

curry

turmeric

fenugreek

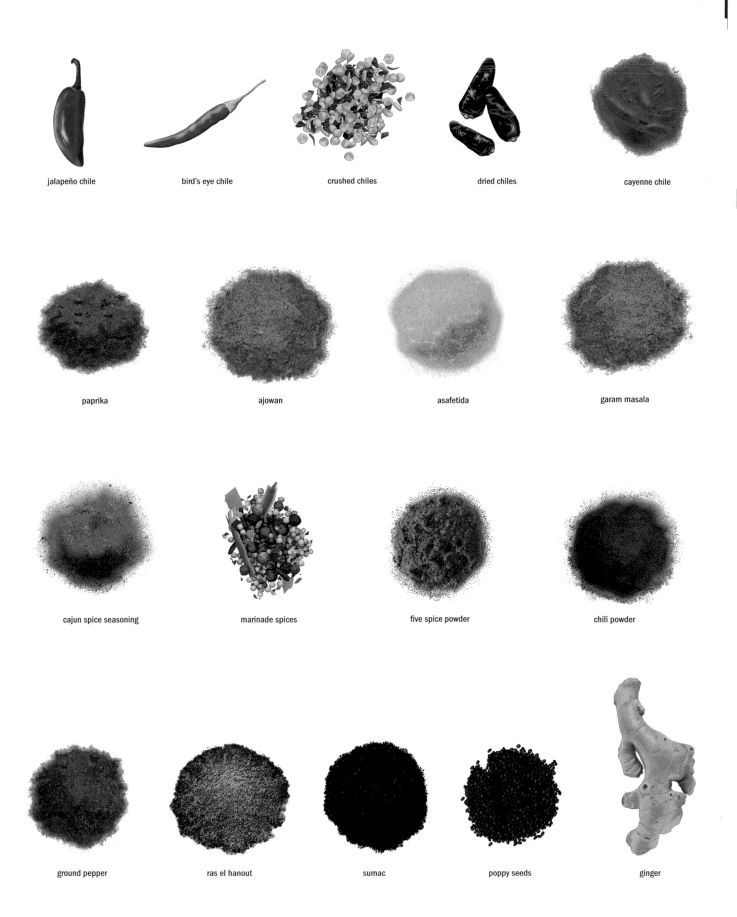

jalapeño chile

bird's eye chile

crushed chiles

dried chiles

cayenne chile

paprika

ajowan

asafetida

garam masala

cajun spice seasoning

marinade spices

five spice powder

chili powder

ground pepper

ras el hanout

sumac

poppy seeds

ginger

condiments

Tabasco® sauce

Worcestershire sauce

tamarind paste

vanilla extract

tomato paste

tomato coulis

hummus

tahini

hoisin sauce

soy sauce

powdered mustard

wholegrain mustard

Dijon mustard

German mustard

English mustard

American mustard

plum sauce

mango chutney

harissa

sambal oelek

ketchup

wasabi

table salt

coarse salt

sea salt

balsamic vinegar

rice vinegar

apple cider vinegar

malt vinegar

wine vinegar

herbs

dill

anise

sweet bay

oregano

tarragon

basil

sage

thyme

mint

parsley

chervil

coriander

rosemary

hyssop

borage

lovage

savory

lemon balm

cereal

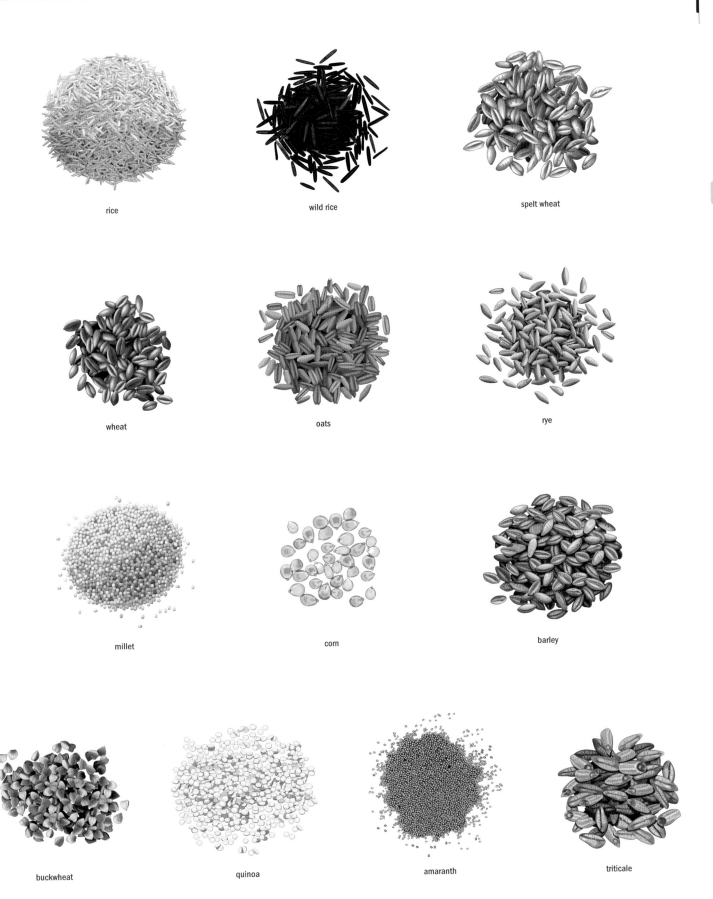

rice

wild rice

spelt wheat

wheat

oats

rye

millet

corn

barley

buckwheat

quinoa

amaranth

triticale

cereal products

flour and semolina

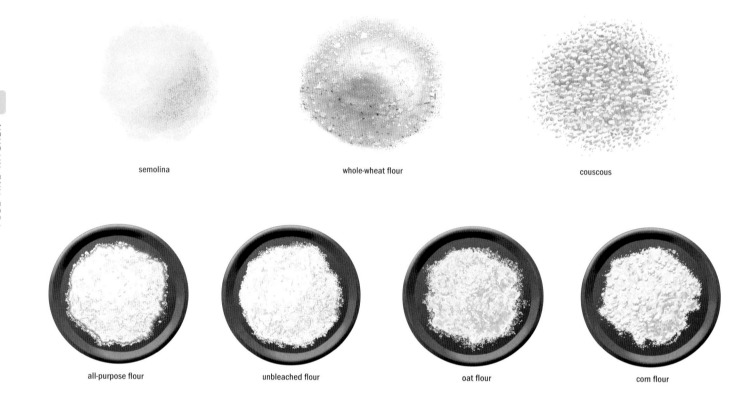

semolina

whole-wheat flour

couscous

all-purpose flour

unbleached flour

oat flour

corn flour

bread

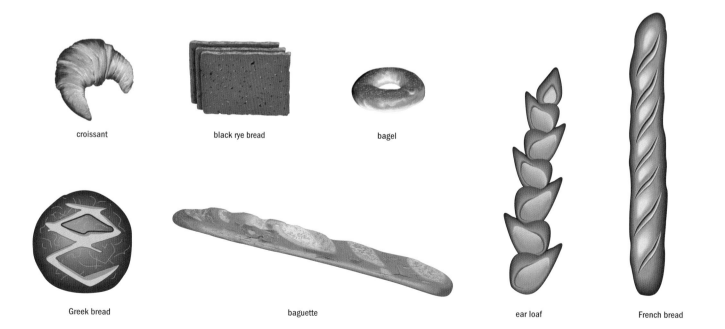

croissant

black rye bread

bagel

Greek bread

baguette

ear loaf

French bread

Indian chapati bread

tortillas

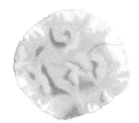

pita bread

Indian naan bread

cracked rye bread

phyllo dough

unleavened bread

Danish rye bread

white bread

multigrain bread

Scandinavian cracked bread

Jewish hallah

American corn bread

German rye bread

Russian pumpernickel

farmhouse bread

wholemeal bread

Irish bread

English loaf

pasta

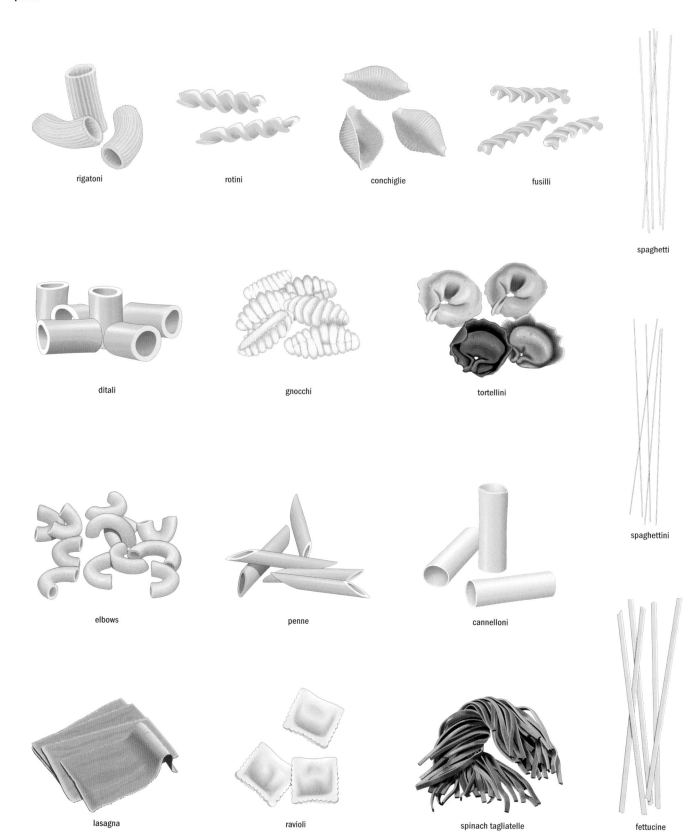

rigatoni

rotini

conchiglie

fusilli

spaghetti

ditali

gnocchi

tortellini

spaghettini

elbows

penne

cannelloni

lasagna

ravioli

spinach tagliatelle

fettucine

FOOD AND KITCHEN

Asian noodles

soba noodles

somen noodles

udon noodles

rice papers

rice noodles

bean thread cellophane noodles

egg noodles

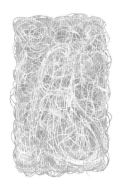

rice vermicelli

won ton skins

rice

white rice

brown rice

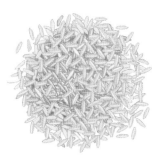

parboiled rice

basmati rice

coffee and infusions

coffee

herbal teas

green coffee beans   roasted coffee beans

linden   chamomile   verbena

tea

green tea

black tea

oolong tea

tea bag

chocolate

dark chocolate

milk chocolate

cocoa

white chocolate

sugar

granulated sugar

powdered sugar

brown sugar

rock candy

molasses

corn syrup

maple syrup

honey

fats and oils

corn oil

olive oil

sunflower-seed oil

peanut oil

sesame oil

shortening

lard

margarine

dairy products

cream

yogurt   ghee   butter

whipping cream   sour cream

milk

homogenized milk   goat's milk   evaporated milk   buttermilk   powdered milk

fresh cheeses

goat's-milk cheeses

cottage cheese   mozzarella

ricotta   cream cheese

chèvre cheese

Crottin de Chavignol

pressed cheeses

Jarlsberg

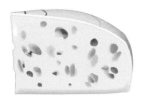

Emmenthal

raclette

Gruyère

Romano

Parmesan

blue-veined cheeses

Roquefort

Stilton

Gorgonzola

Danish Blue

soft cheeses

Pont-l'Évêque

Coulommiers

Camembert

Brie

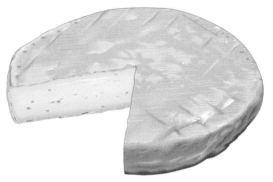

Munster

FOOD AND KITCHEN

variety meat

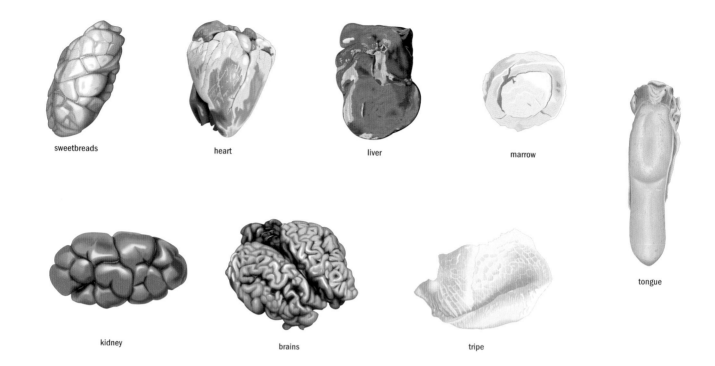

sweetbreads

heart

liver

marrow

tongue

kidney

brains

tripe

game

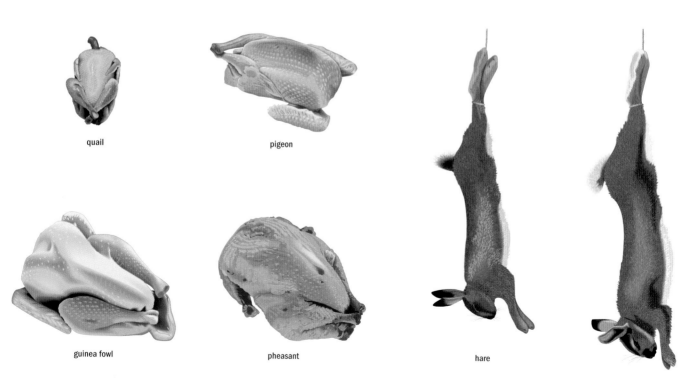

quail

pigeon

guinea fowl

pheasant

hare

rabbit

poultry

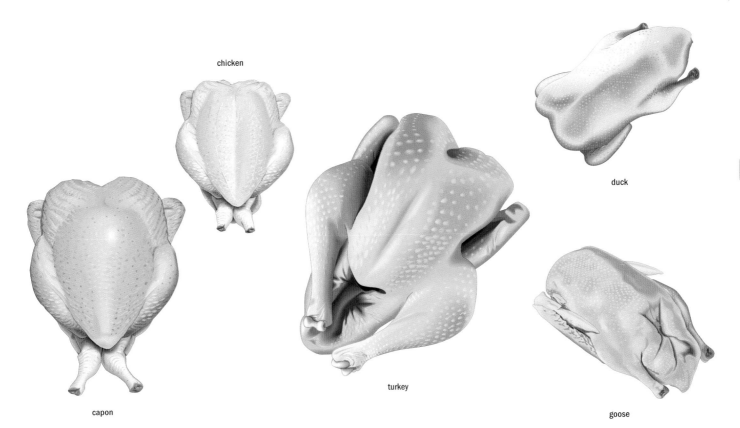

chicken

duck

capon

turkey

goose

eggs

ostrich egg

goose egg

quail egg

pheasant egg

duck egg

hen egg

meat

FOOD AND KITCHEN

cuts of beef

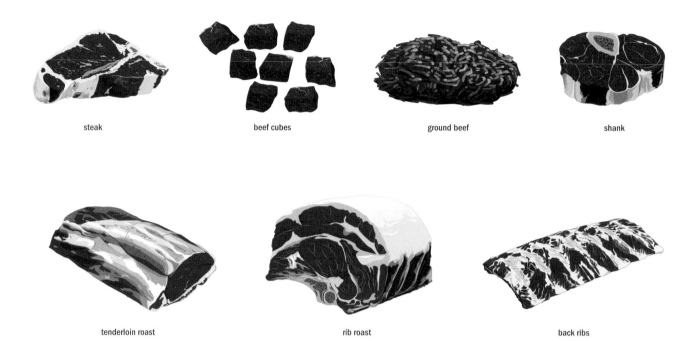

steak beef cubes ground beef shank

tenderloin roast rib roast back ribs

cuts of veal

veal cubes ground veal shank

roast steak chop

cuts of lamb

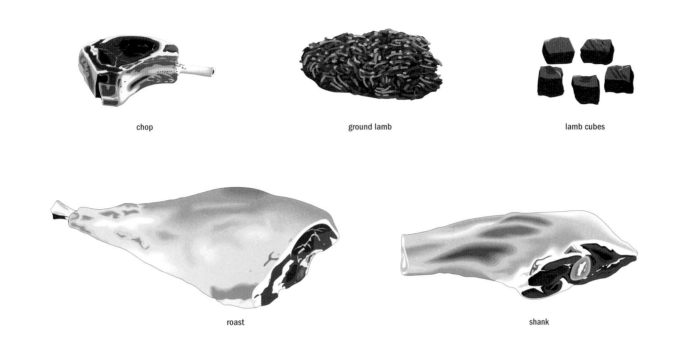

chop

ground lamb

lamb cubes

roast

shank

cuts of pork

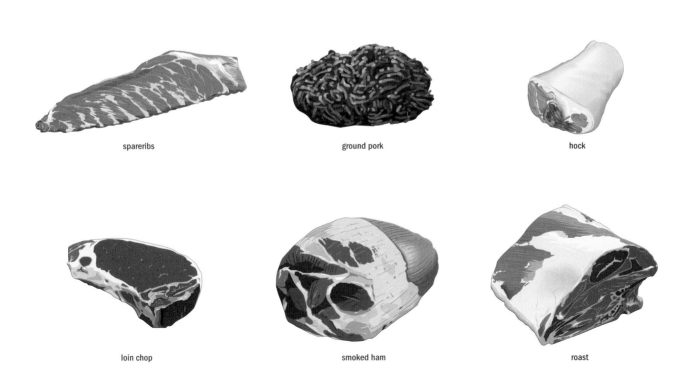

spareribs

ground pork

hock

loin chop

smoked ham

roast

delicatessen

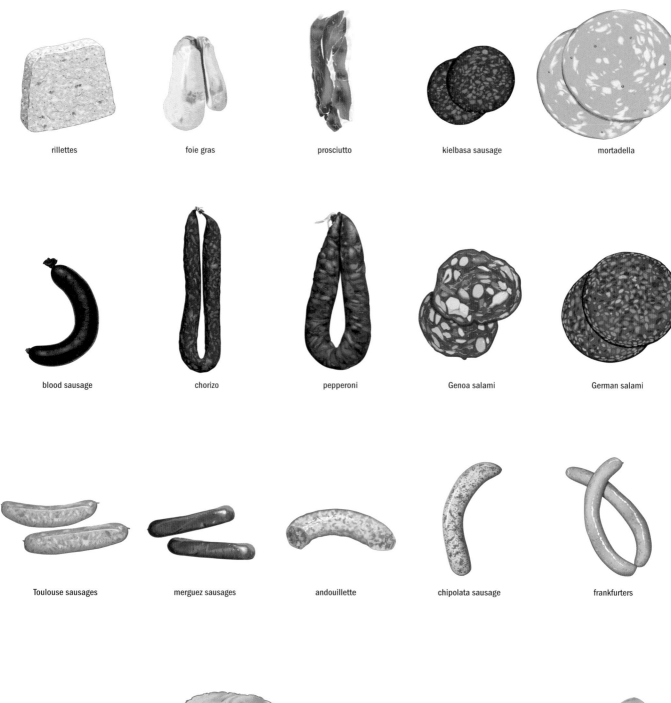

rillettes

foie gras

prosciutto

kielbasa sausage

mortadella

blood sausage

chorizo

pepperoni

Genoa salami

German salami

Toulouse sausages

merguez sausages

andouillette

chipolata sausage

frankfurters

pancetta

cooked ham

American bacon

Canadian bacon

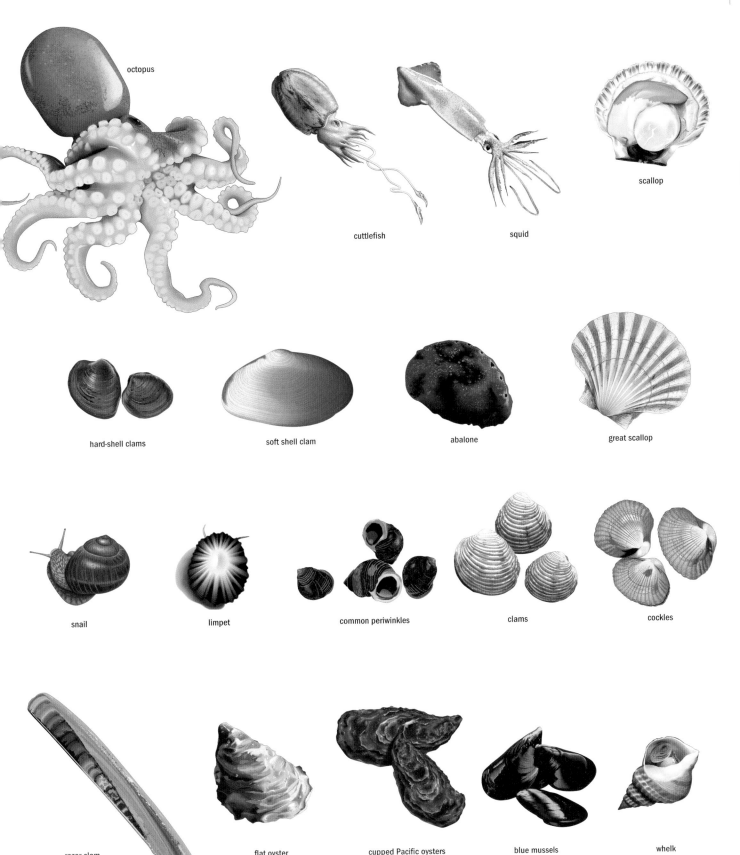

octopus

cuttlefish

squid

scallop

hard-shell clams

soft shell clam

abalone

great scallop

snail

limpet

common periwinkles

clams

cockles

razor clam

flat oyster

cupped Pacific oysters

blue mussels

whelk

FOOD AND KITCHEN

217

crustaceans

crayfish

spiny lobster

lobster

shrimp

scampi

crab

cartilaginous fishes

larger spotted dogfish

skate

smooth hound

sturgeon

bony fishes

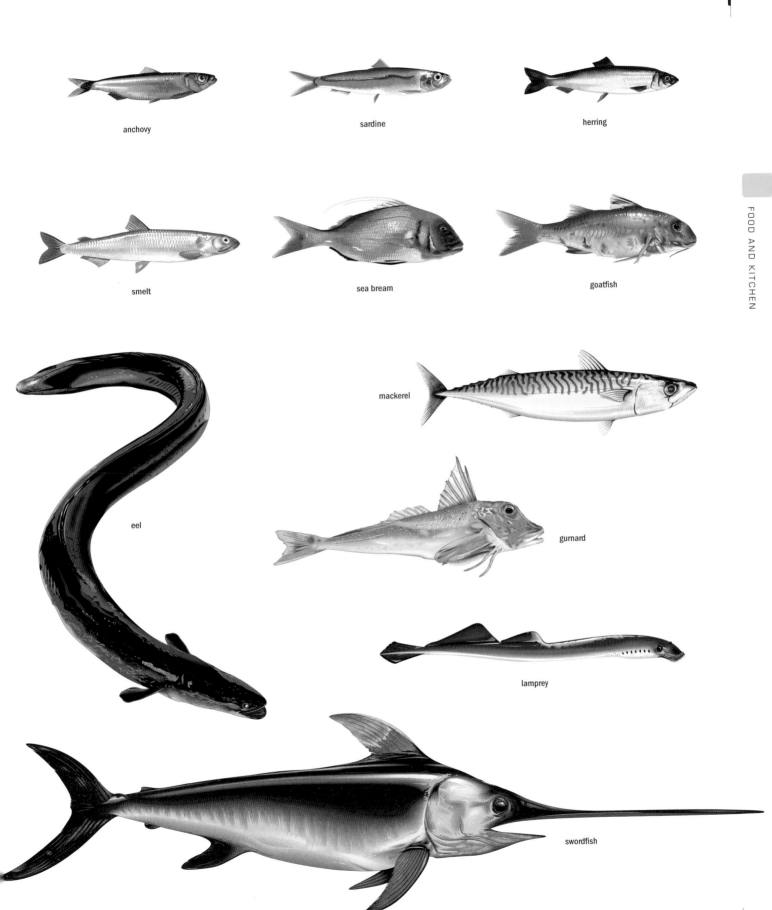

anchovy

sardine

herring

smelt

sea bream

goatfish

eel

mackerel

gurnard

lamprey

swordfish

bass

mullet

carp

perch

shad

pike

pike perch

bluefish

sea bass

monkfish

tuna

redfish

whiting

haddock

black pollock

Atlantic cod

trout

Pacific salmon

Atlantic salmon

brook trout

John Dory

halibut

turbot

common plaice

sole

packaging

pouch

parchment paper

aluminum foil

freezer bag

waxed paper

plastic film

mesh bag

canisters

egg carton

food tray

small crate

small open crate

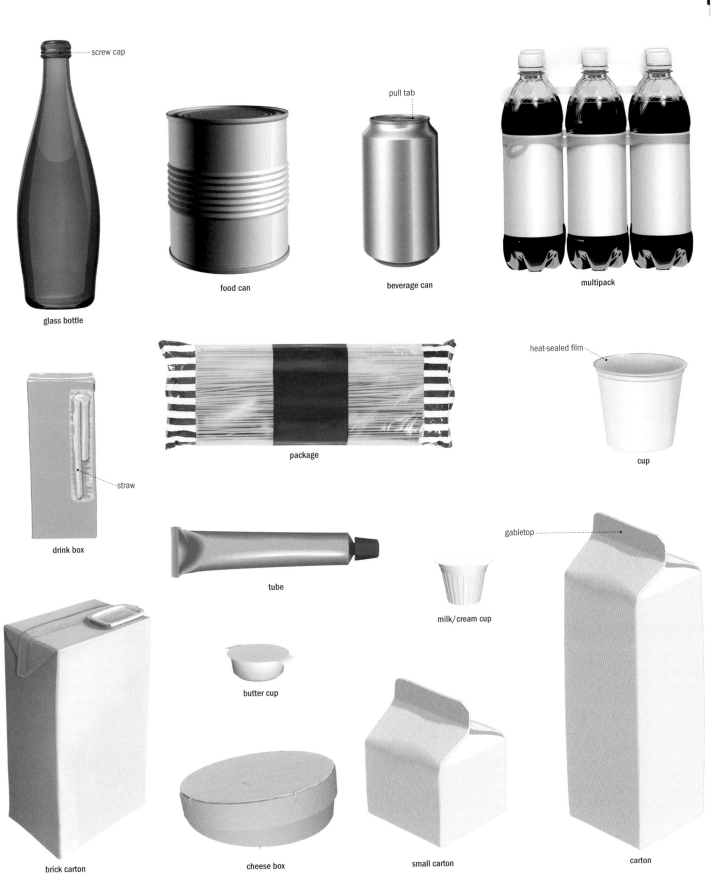

screw cap

glass bottle

food can

pull tab

beverage can

multipack

FOOD AND KITCHEN

heat-sealed film

package

cup

straw

drink box

tube

milk/cream cup

gabletop

butter cup

brick carton

cheese box

small carton

carton

kitchen

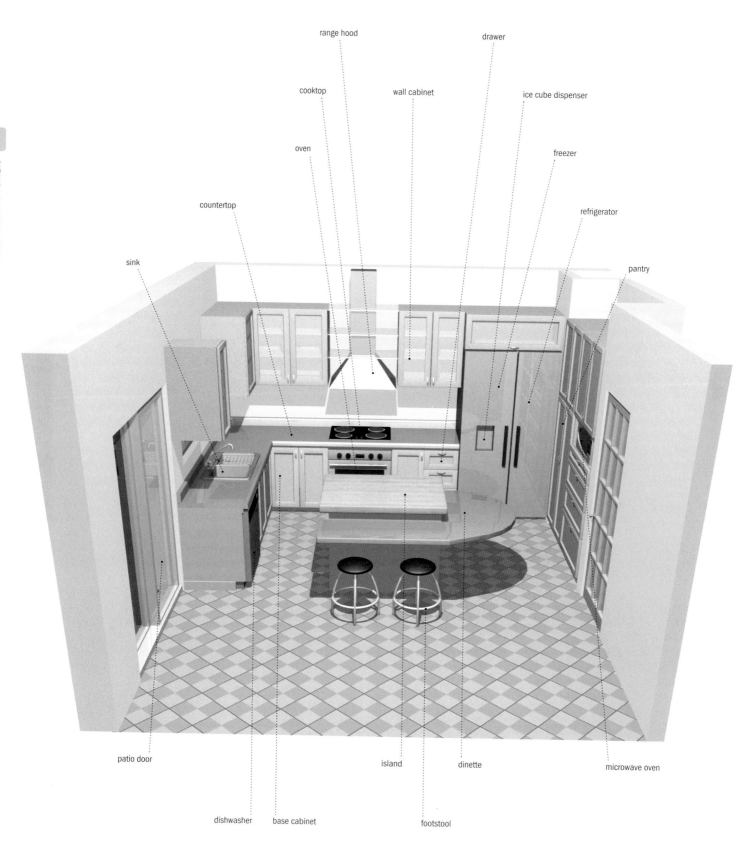

range hood

drawer

cooktop

wall cabinet

ice cube dispenser

oven

freezer

countertop

refrigerator

sink

pantry

patio door

island

dinette

microwave oven

dishwasher

base cabinet

footstool

glassware

liqueur glass

port glass

sparkling wine glass

brandy snifter

Alsace glass

burgundy glass

bordeaux glass

white wine glass

water goblet

cocktail glass

highball glass

old-fashioned glass

beer mug

champagne flute

small decanter

decanter

dinnerware

demitasse

cup

coffee mug

creamer

sugar bowl

salt shaker

pepper shaker

gravy boat

butter dish

ramekin

soup bowl

rim soup bowl

dinner plate

salad plate

bread and butter plate

teapot

platter

vegetable bowl

fish platter

hors d'oeuvre dish

water pitcher

salad bowl

salad dish

soup tureen

silverware

knife

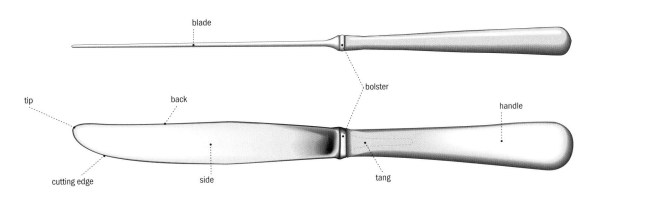

blade

bolster

tip   back   handle

cutting edge   side   tang

fork

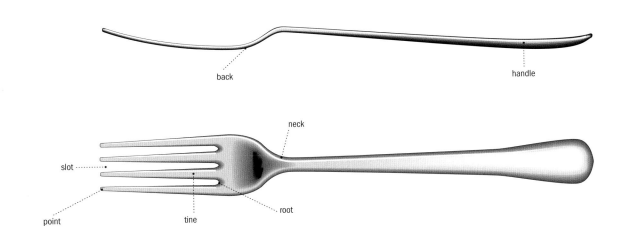

back   handle

neck

slot   root

point   tine

spoon

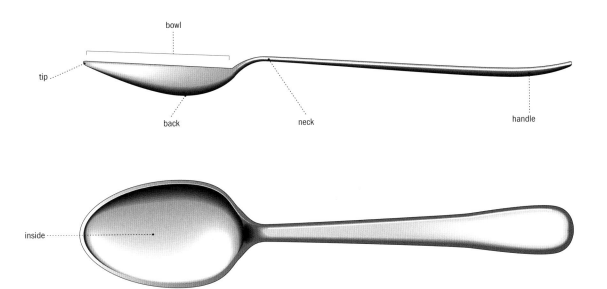

bowl

tip

back   neck   handle

inside

silverware

examples of forks

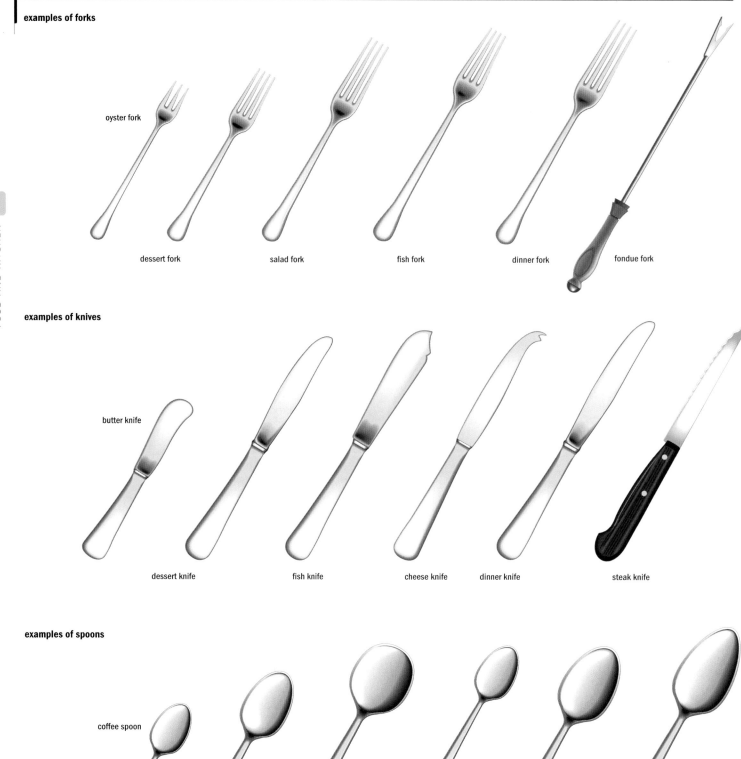

oyster fork

dessert fork

salad fork

fish fork

dinner fork

fondue fork

examples of knives

butter knife

dessert knife

fish knife

cheese knife

dinner knife

steak knife

examples of spoons

coffee spoon

teaspoon

soup spoon

sundae spoon

dessert spoon

tablespoon

kitchen utensils

kitchen knife

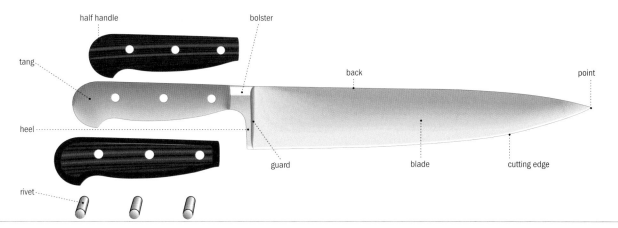

half handle

bolster

tang

back

point

heel

guard

blade

cutting edge

rivet

examples of utensils for cutting

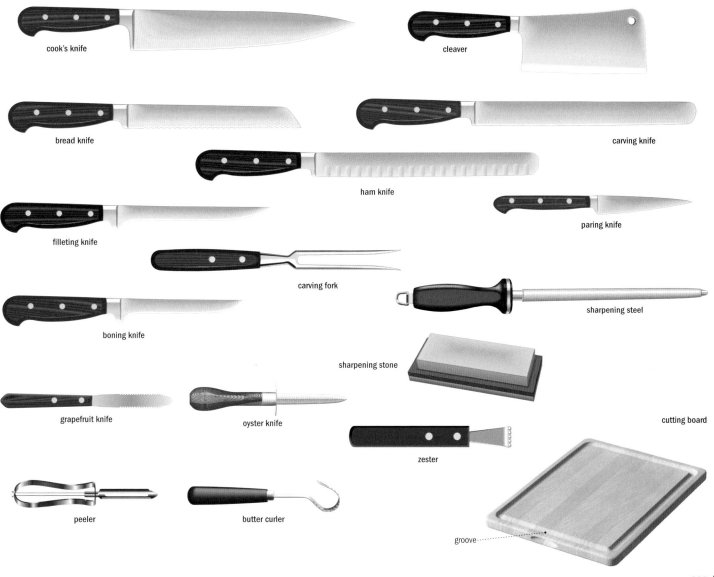

cook's knife

cleaver

bread knife

carving knife

ham knife

paring knife

filleting knife

carving fork

sharpening steel

boning knife

sharpening stone

grapefruit knife

oyster knife

zester

cutting board

peeler

butter curler

groove

for opening

can opener

bottle opener

waiter's corkscrew

lever corkscrew

for grinding and grating

mortar

pestle

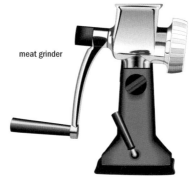

meat grinder

nutcracker

garlic press

citrus juicer

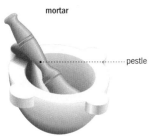

nutmeg grater

grater

rotary cheese grater

pusher

crank

drum

handle

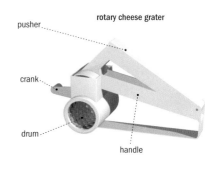

pasta maker

food mill

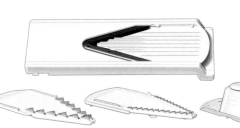

mandoline

for measuring

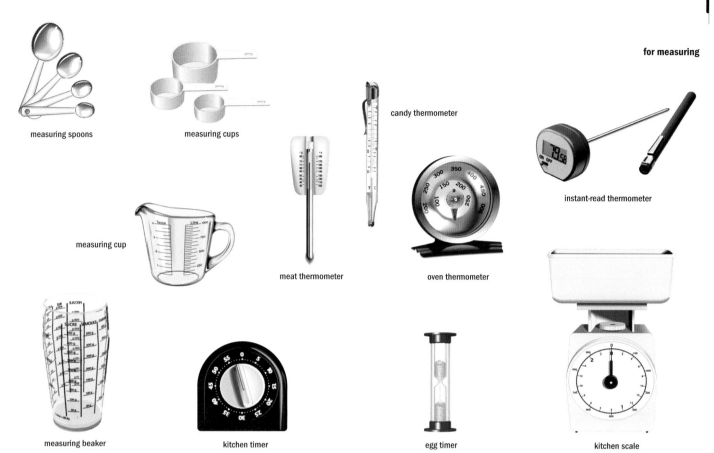

measuring spoons

measuring cups

candy thermometer

measuring cup

meat thermometer

oven thermometer

instant-read thermometer

measuring beaker

kitchen timer

egg timer

kitchen scale

FOOD AND KITCHEN

for straining and draining

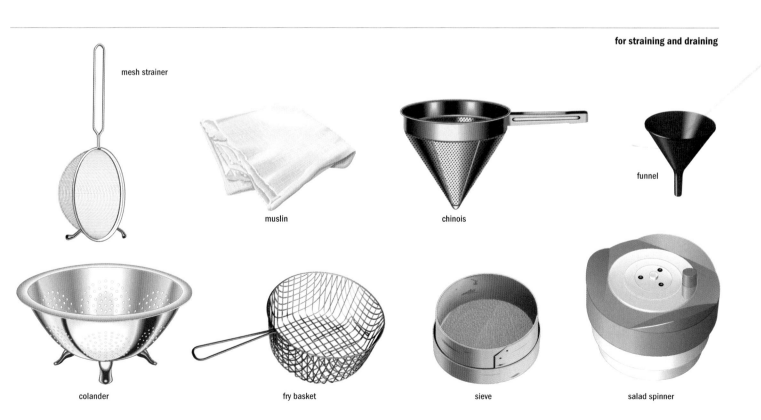

mesh strainer

muslin

chinois

funnel

colander

fry basket

sieve

salad spinner

kitchen utensils

baking utensils

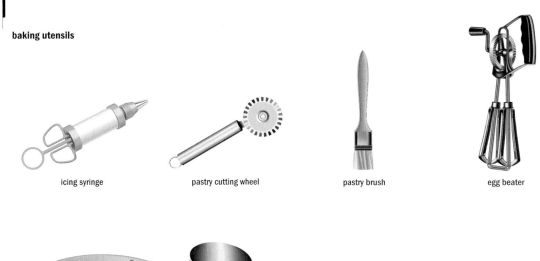

icing syringe

pastry cutting wheel

pastry brush

egg beater

whisk

pastry bag and nozzles

sifter

cookie cutters

dredger

pastry blender

mixing bowls

rolling pin

baking sheet

muffin pan

soufflé dish

charlotte mold

removable-bottomed pan

pie pan

quiche plate

cake pan

set of utensils

skimmer

draining spoon

spatula

turner

ladle

potato masher

miscellaneous utensils

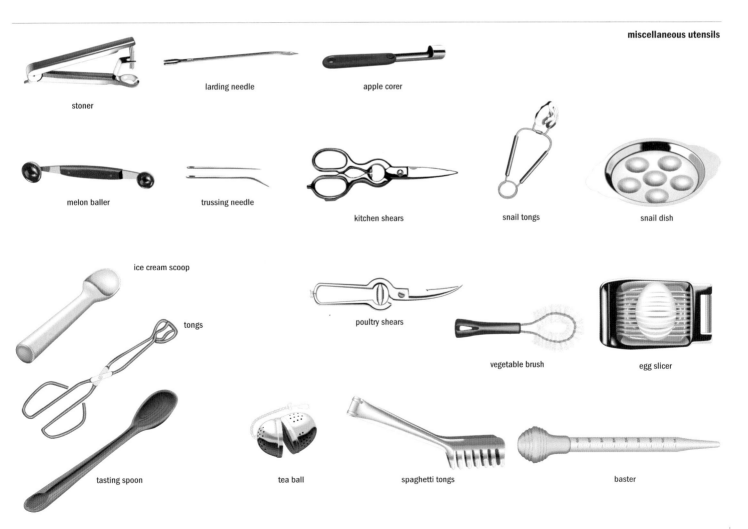

stoner

larding needle

apple corer

melon baller

trussing needle

kitchen shears

snail tongs

snail dish

ice cream scoop

tongs

poultry shears

vegetable brush

egg slicer

tasting spoon

tea ball

spaghetti tongs

baster

FOOD AND KITCHEN

cooking utensils

wok set

lid

rack

wok

burner ring

tagine

fish poacher

rack

lid

fondue set

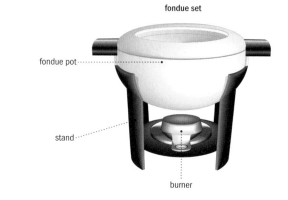

fondue pot

stand

burner

dripping pan

terrine

roasting pans

pressure cooker

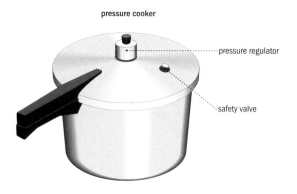

pressure regulator

safety valve

Dutch oven

stock pot

couscous kettle

frying pan

steamer

egg poacher

sauté pan

small saucepan

diable

pancake pan

steamer basket

double boiler

saucepan

domestic appliances

for mixing and blending

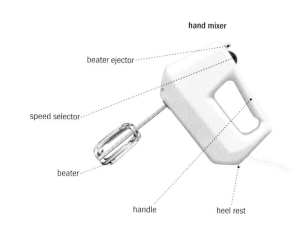

hand mixer

beater ejector

speed selector

beater

handle · heel rest

blender

cap

container

cutting blade

motor unit

push button

table mixer

beater ejector

beater

tilt-back head

speed control

mixing bowl

turntable

stand

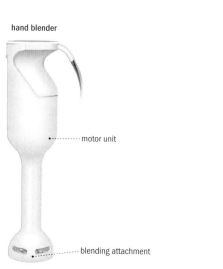

hand blender

motor unit

blending attachment

beaters

four blade beater

spiral beater

wire beater

dough hook

FOOD AND KITCHEN

for cutting

food processor

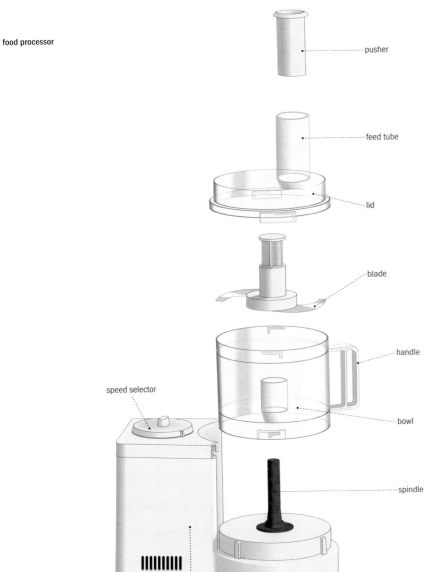

pusher

feed tube

disks

lid

blade

handle

speed selector

bowl

spindle

motor unit

for juicing

citrus juicer

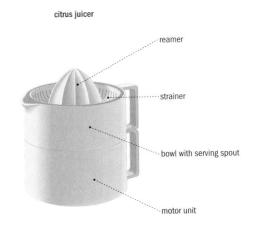

reamer

strainer

bowl with serving spout

motor unit

electric knife

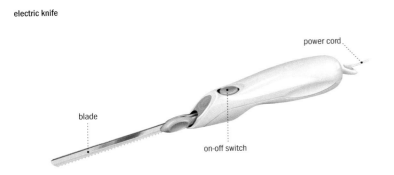

power cord

blade

on-off switch

domestic appliances

for cooking

FOOD AND KITCHEN

microwave oven

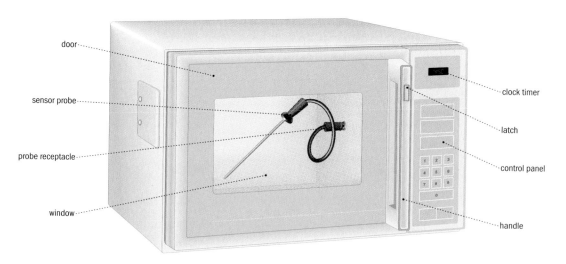

door

sensor probe

probe receptacle

window

clock timer

latch

control panel

handle

waffle iron

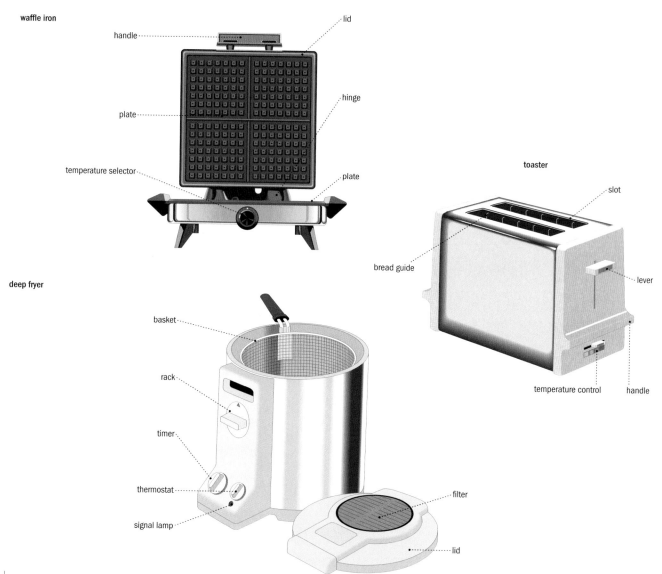

lid

handle

hinge

plate

temperature selector

plate

toaster

slot

bread guide

lever

deep fryer

basket

rack

timer

thermostat

signal lamp

temperature control

handle

filter

lid

FOOD AND KITCHEN

raclette with grill

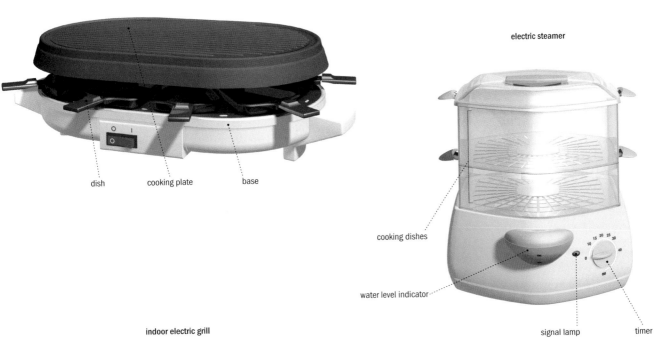

dish

cooking plate

base

electric steamer

cooking dishes

water level indicator

signal lamp

timer

indoor electric grill

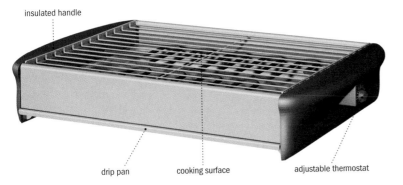

insulated handle

drip pan

cooking surface

adjustable thermostat

bread machine

lid

control panel

window

loaf pan

griddle

cooking surface

handle

detachable control

grease well

miscellaneous domestic appliances

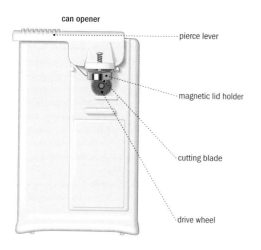

can opener

pierce lever

magnetic lid holder

cutting blade

drive wheel

coffee mill

lid

blade

on-off button

motor unit

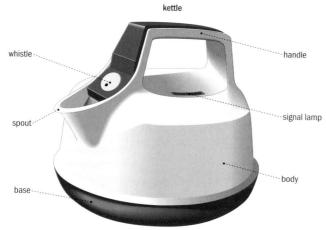

kettle

whistle

handle

signal lamp

spout

body

base

ice cream freezer

motor unit

cover

handle

freezer bucket

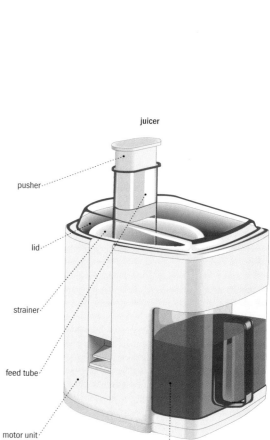

juicer

pusher

lid

strainer

feed tube

motor unit

bowl

automatic drip coffee maker

reservoir

water level

signal lamp

on-off switch

lid

basket

carafe

warming plate

Neapolitan coffee maker

espresso machine

on-off switch

tamper

drip tray

steam nozzle

steam control knob

filter holder

water tank

vacuum coffee maker

upper bowl

stem

lower bowl

plunger

espresso coffee maker

percolator

spout

signal light

HOUSE

exterior of a house

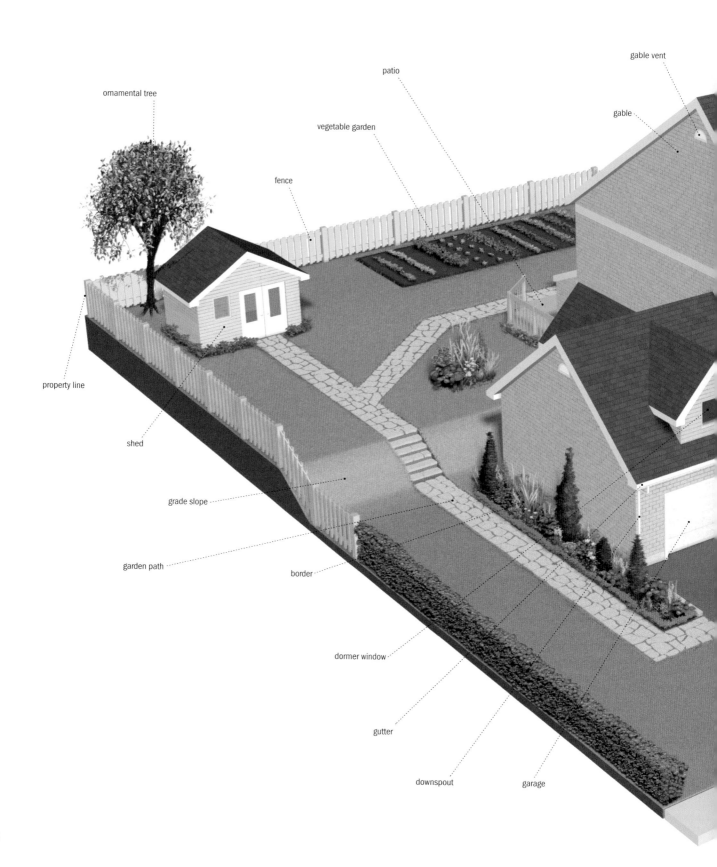

gable vent

patio

gable

ornamental tree

vegetable garden

fence

property line

shed

grade slope

garden path

border

dormer window

gutter

downspout

garage

HOUSE

kylight

lightning rod

chimney pot

chimney

roof

cornice

steps

basement window

hedge

lawn

flower bed

sidewalk

porch

driveway

site plan

pool

above ground swimming pool

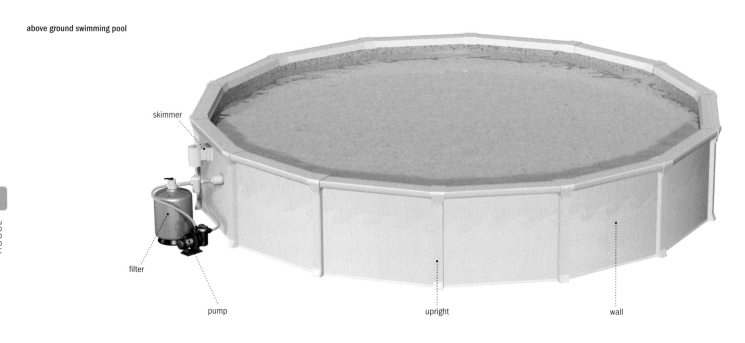

skimmer

filter

pump

upright

wall

in-ground swimming pool

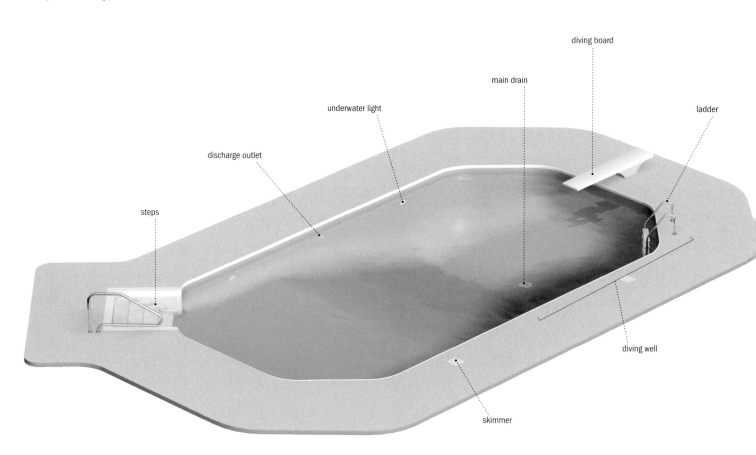

diving board

main drain

underwater light

ladder

discharge outlet

steps

diving well

skimmer

exterior door

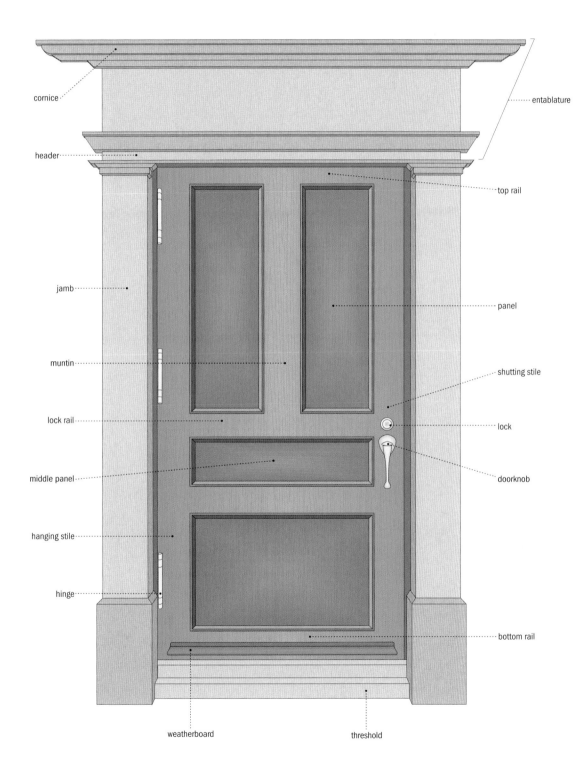

cornice

entablature

header

top rail

jamb

panel

muntin

shutting stile

lock rail

lock

middle panel

doorknob

hanging stile

hinge

bottom rail

weatherboard

threshold

lock

HOUSE

general view

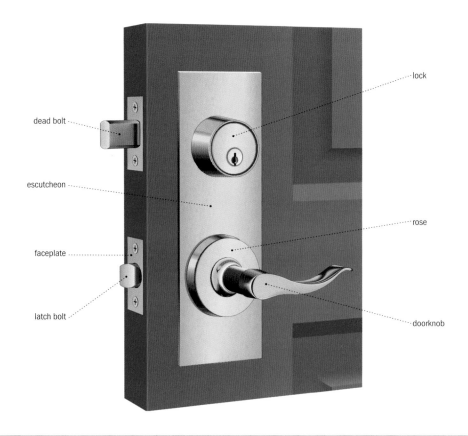

lock

dead bolt

escutcheon

rose

faceplate

doorknob

latch bolt

tubular lock

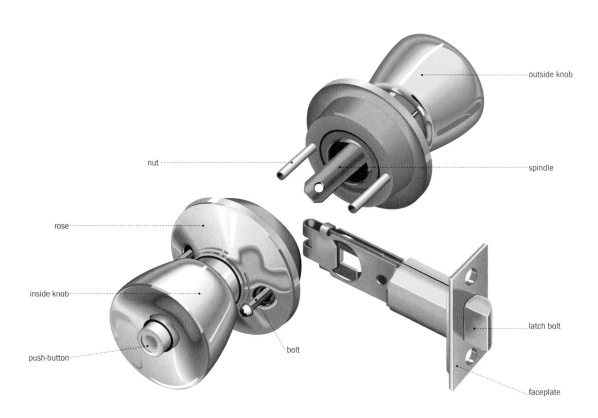

outside knob

nut

spindle

rose

inside knob

latch bolt

push-button

bolt

faceplate

mortise lock

HOUSE

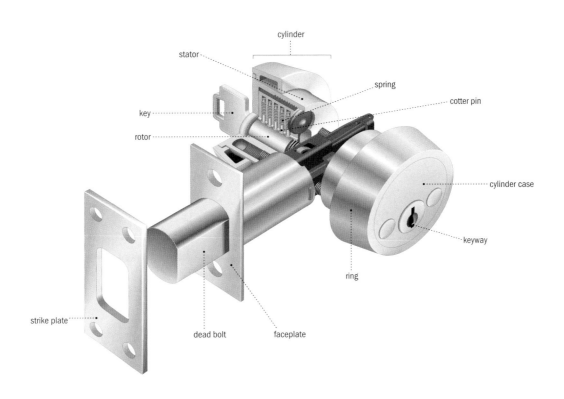

cylinder

stator

spring

key

cotter pin

rotor

cylinder case

keyway

ring

strike plate

dead bolt

faceplate

window

structure

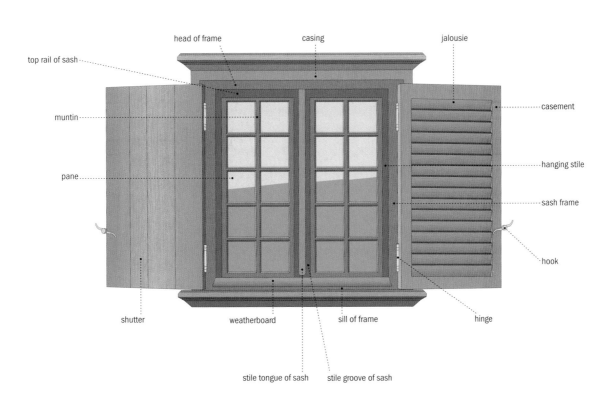

head of frame

casing

jalousie

top rail of sash

muntin

casement

pane

hanging stile

sash frame

hook

shutter

weatherboard

sill of frame

hinge

stile tongue of sash

stile groove of sash

main rooms

elevation

third floor

second floor

first floor

basement

first floor

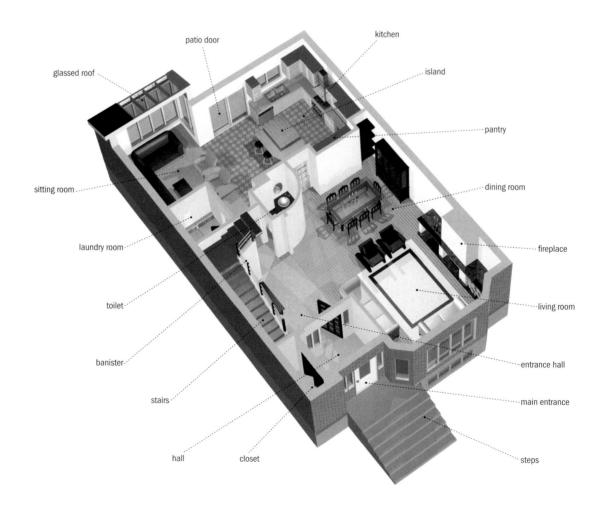

patio door

kitchen

glassed roof

island

pantry

sitting room

dining room

laundry room

fireplace

toilet

living room

banister

entrance hall

stairs

main entrance

hall

closet

steps

third floor

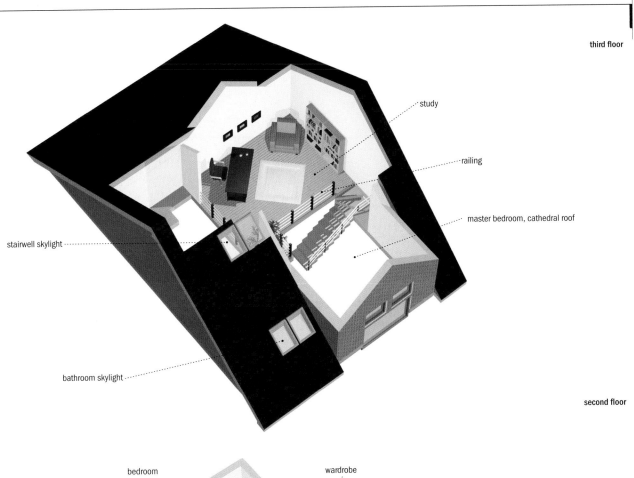

study

railing

master bedroom, cathedral roof

stairwell skylight

bathroom skylight

second floor

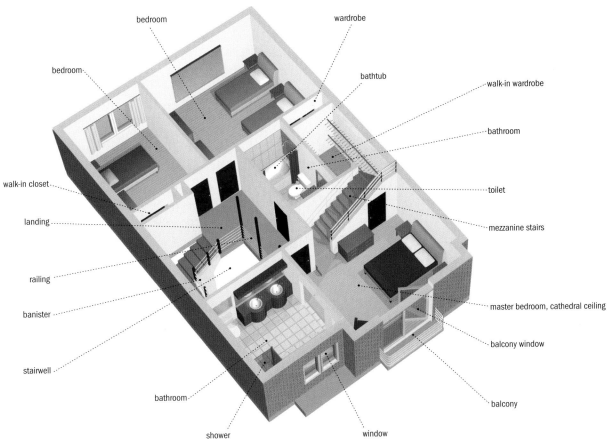

bedroom

wardrobe

bedroom

bathtub

walk-in wardrobe

bathroom

walk-in closet

toilet

landing

mezzanine stairs

railing

banister

master bedroom, cathedral ceiling

balcony window

stairwell

balcony

bathroom

shower

window

frame

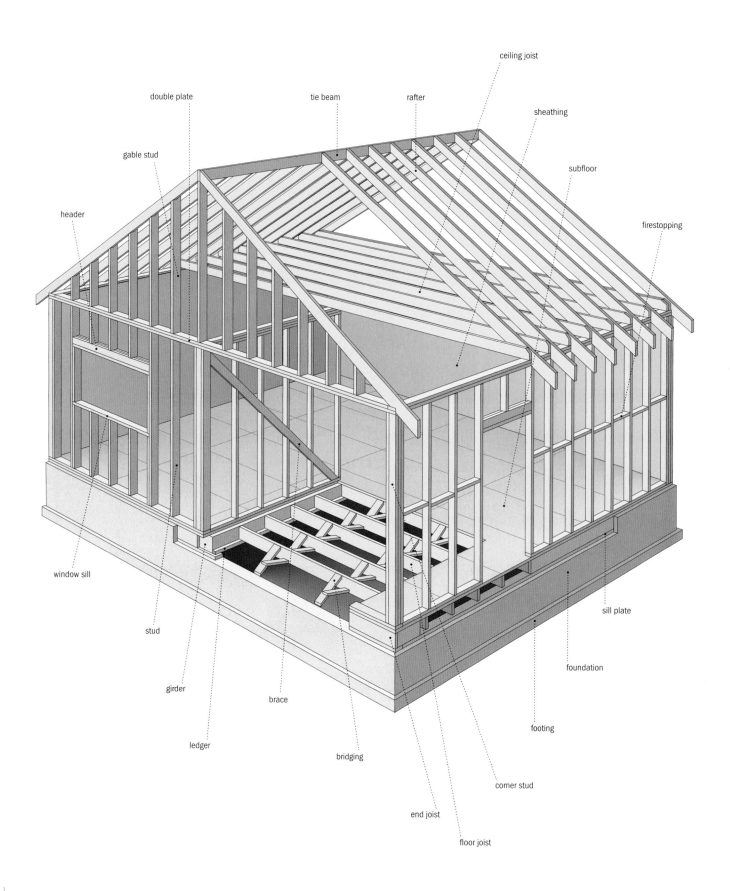

ceiling joist

double plate

tie beam

rafter

sheathing

gable stud

subfloor

header

firestopping

window sill

stud

girder

brace

ledger

bridging

end joist

floor joist

corner stud

footing

foundation

sill plate

roof truss

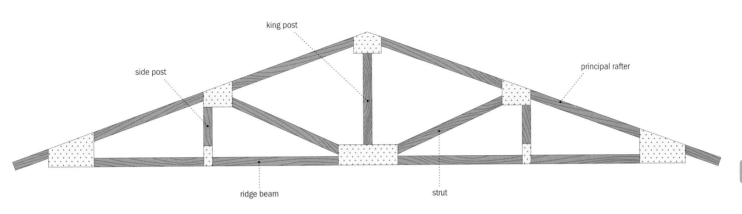

king post

side post

principal rafter

ridge beam

strut

foundation

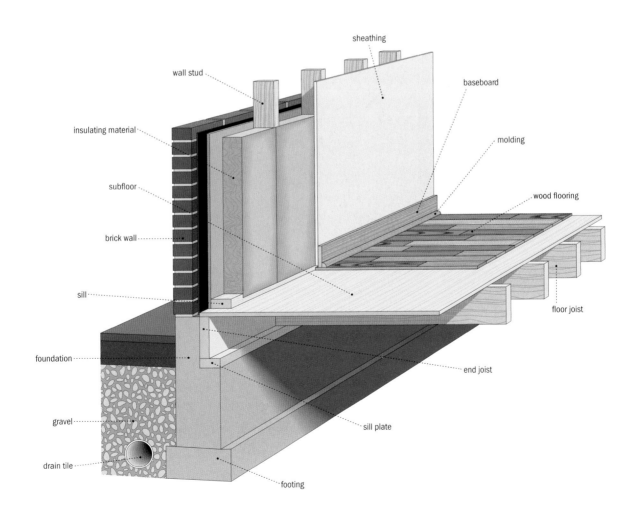

sheathing

wall stud

baseboard

insulating material

molding

subfloor

wood flooring

brick wall

sill

floor joist

foundation

end joist

gravel

sill plate

drain tile

footing

wood flooring

wood flooring on cement screed

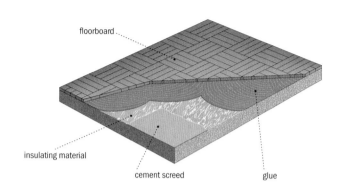

floorboard

insulating material

cement screed

glue

wood flooring on wooden structure

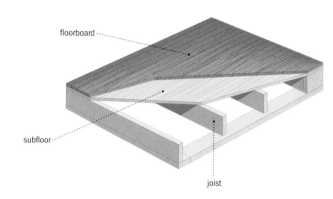

floorboard

subfloor

joist

wood flooring arrangements

overlay flooring

strip flooring with alternate joints

herringbone parquet

herringbone pattern

inlaid parquet

basket weave pattern

Arenberg parquet

Chantilly parquet

Versailles parquet

textile floor coverings

rug

pile carpet

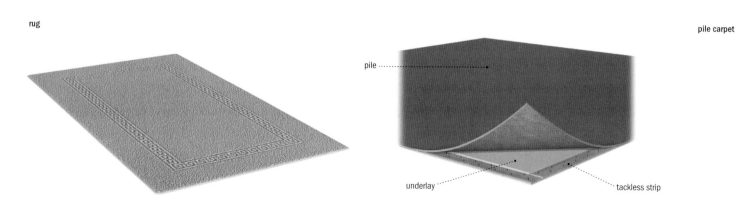

pile

underlay

tackless strip

stairs

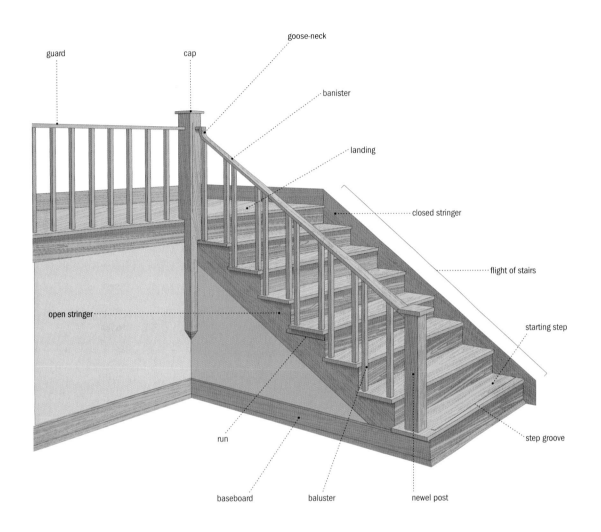

guard

cap

goose-neck

banister

landing

closed stringer

flight of stairs

open stringer

starting step

step groove

run

baseboard

baluster

newel post

step

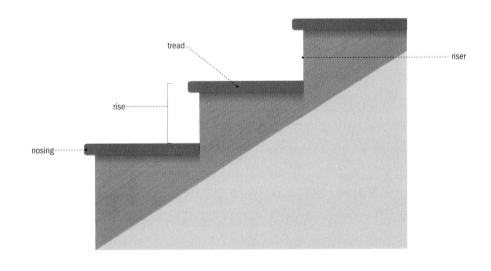

tread

riser

rise

nosing

wood firing

fireplace

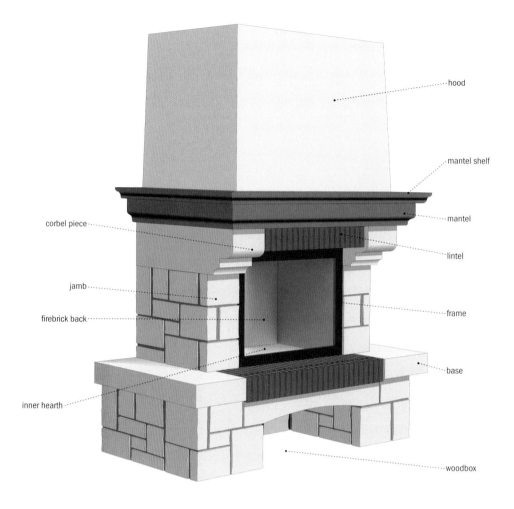

hood

mantel shelf

corbel piece

mantel

lintel

jamb

firebrick back

frame

base

inner hearth

woodbox

slow-burning stove

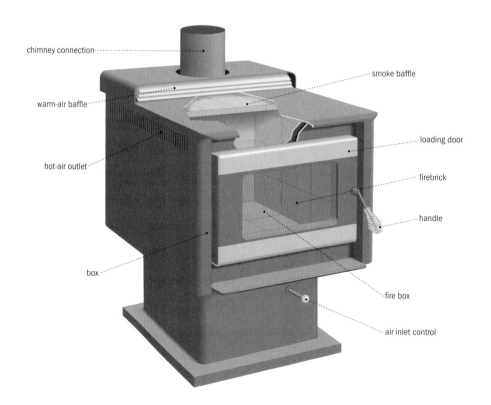

chimney connection

smoke baffle

warm-air baffle

loading door

hot-air outlet

firebrick

handle

box

fire box

air inlet control

HOUSE

chimney

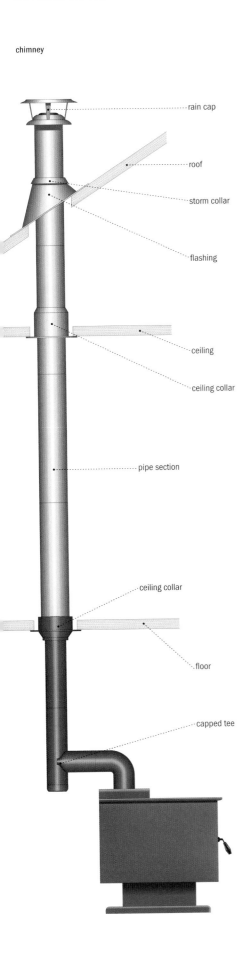

rain cap

roof

storm collar

flashing

ceiling

ceiling collar

pipe section

ceiling collar

floor

capped tee

fire irons

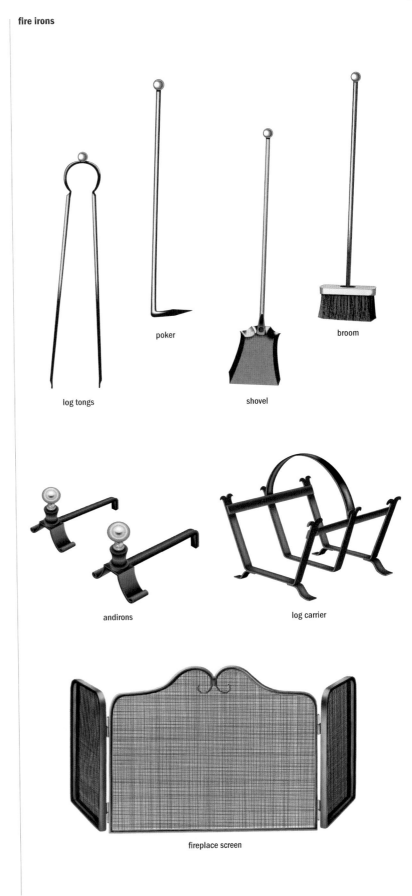

log tongs

poker

shovel

broom

andirons

log carrier

fireplace screen

forced warm-air system

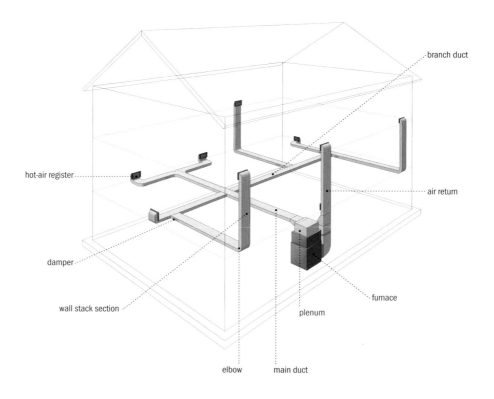

branch duct

hot-air register

air return

damper

furnace

wall stack section

plenum

elbow   main duct

electric furnace

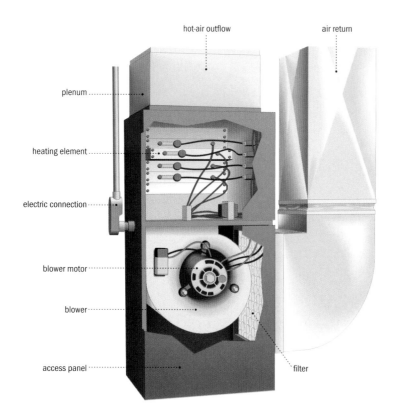

hot-air outflow

air return

plenum

heating element

electric connection

blower motor

blower

access panel

filter

types of registers

baseboard register

wall register

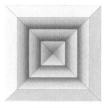

ceiling register

forced hot-water system

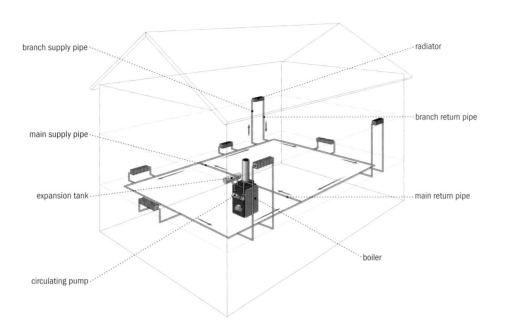

branch supply pipe

radiator

main supply pipe

branch return pipe

expansion tank

main return pipe

circulating pump

boiler

oil burner

boiler

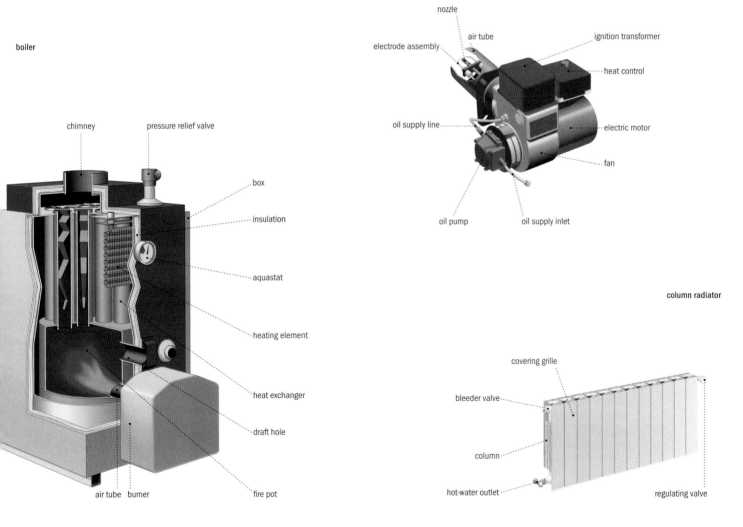

chimney

pressure relief valve

box

insulation

aquastat

heating element

heat exchanger

draft hole

air tube   burner

fire pot

nozzle

air tube

electrode assembly

ignition transformer

heat control

oil supply line

electric motor

fan

oil pump

oil supply inlet

column radiator

covering grille

bleeder valve

column

hot-water outlet

regulating valve

heat pump

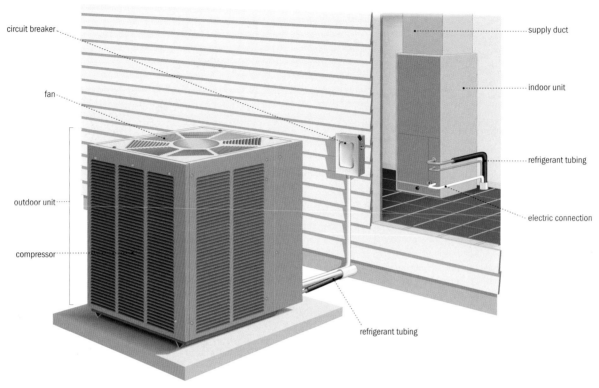

circuit breaker

fan

outdoor unit

compressor

supply duct

indoor unit

refrigerant tubing

electric connection

refrigerant tubing

auxiliary heating

electric baseboard radiator

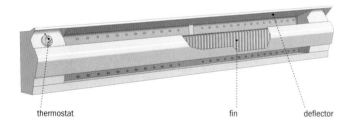

thermostat

fin

deflector

fan heater

convector

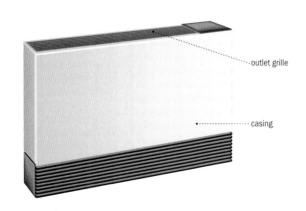

outlet grille

casing

radiant heater

oil-filled heater

air conditioning appliances

dehumidifier

humidistat

front grille

water level

bucket

ceiling fan

rod

motor

blade

programmable thermostat

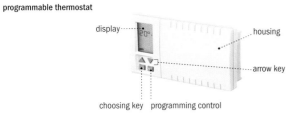

display

housing

arrow key

choosing key   programming control

room thermostat

cover

desired temperature

temperature control

pointer

actual temperature

air purifier

humidifier

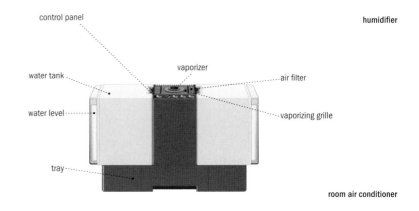

control panel

water tank

vaporizer

air filter

water level

vaporizing grille

tray

room air conditioner

hygrometer

humidity

temperature

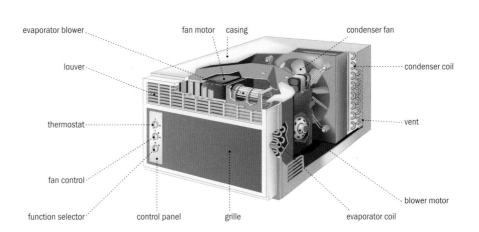

evaporator blower

fan motor   casing

condenser fan

louver

condenser coil

thermostat

vent

fan control

blower motor

function selector   control panel   grille   evaporator coil

plumbing system

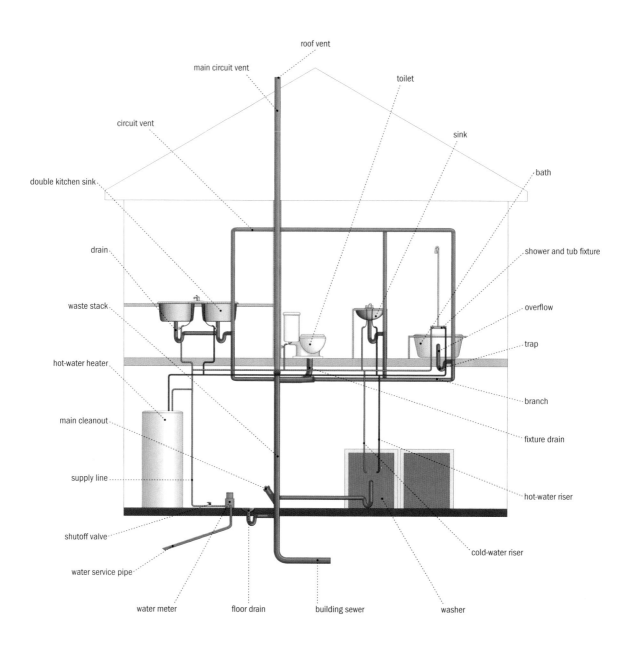

roof vent

main circuit vent

toilet

circuit vent

sink

bath

double kitchen sink

drain

shower and tub fixture

waste stack

overflow

hot-water heater

trap

main cleanout

branch

fixture drain

supply line

hot-water riser

shutoff valve

cold-water riser

water service pipe

water meter   floor drain   building sewer   washer

ventilating circuit   draining circuit   cold-water circuit   hot-water circuit

pedestal-type sump pump

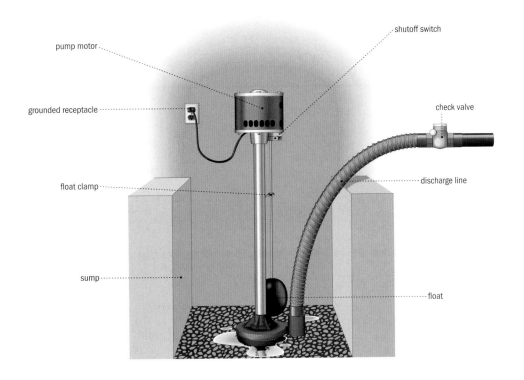

pump motor

shutoff switch

grounded receptacle

check valve

float clamp

discharge line

sump

float

HOUSE

septic tank

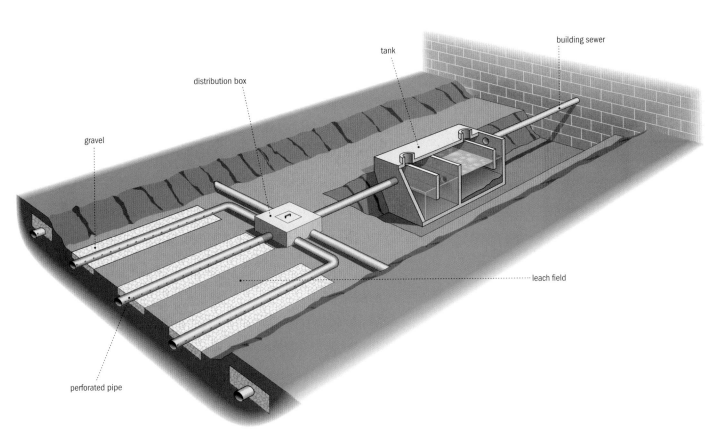

building sewer

tank

distribution box

gravel

leach field

perforated pipe

bathroom

sliding door

shower head

portable shower head

overflow

spray hose

shower stall

faucet

mirror

tissue holder

tub platform

sink

towel bar

toilet tank

bidet

bathtub

soap dish

toilet

seat

vanity cabinet

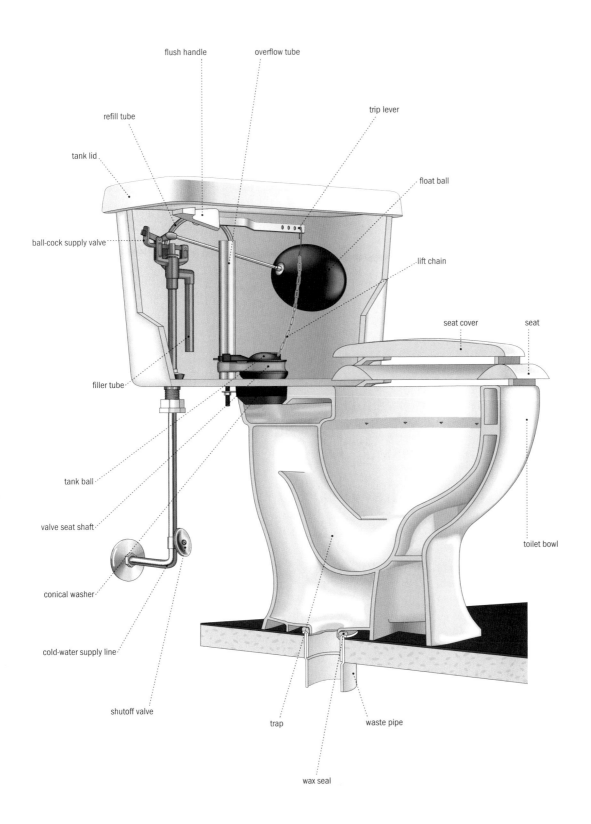

flush handle

overflow tube

trip lever

refill tube

float ball

tank lid

ball-cock supply valve

lift chain

seat cover

seat

filler tube

tank ball

toilet bowl

valve seat shaft

conical washer

cold-water supply line

shutoff valve

trap

waste pipe

wax seal

water-heater tank

electric water-heater tank

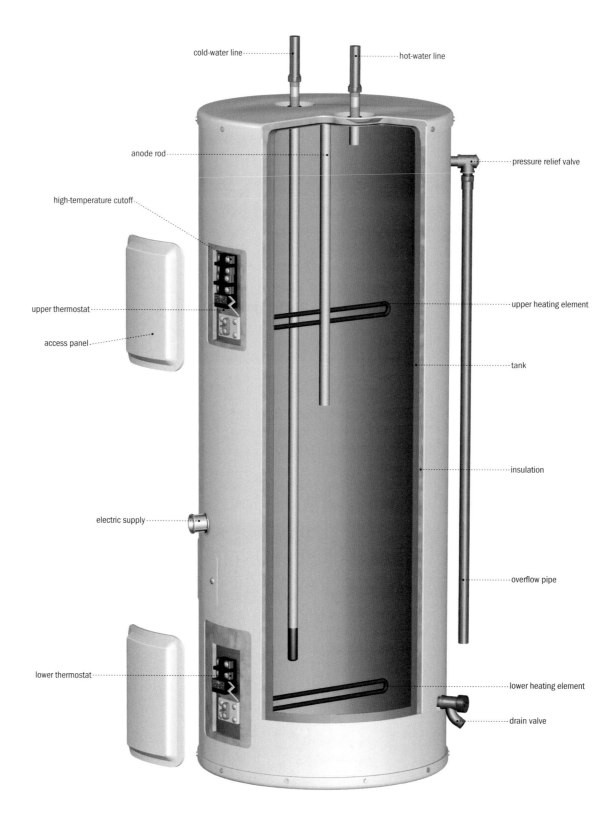

cold-water line

hot-water line

anode rod

pressure relief valve

high-temperature cutoff

upper thermostat

upper heating element

access panel

tank

insulation

electric supply

overflow pipe

lower thermostat

lower heating element

drain valve

gas water-heater tank

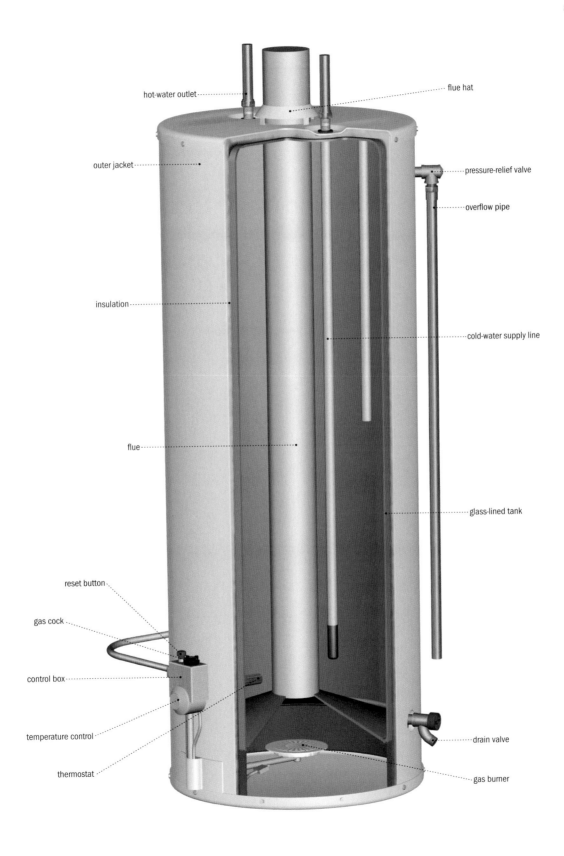

hot-water outlet

flue hat

outer jacket

pressure-relief valve

overflow pipe

insulation

cold-water supply line

flue

glass-lined tank

reset button

gas cock

control box

temperature control

thermostat

drain valve

gas burner

faucets

stem faucet

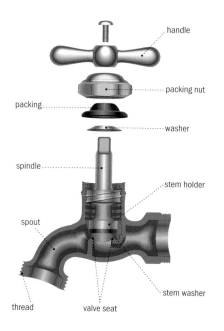

handle

packing nut

packing

washer

spindle

stem holder

spout

thread

valve seat

stem washer

disc faucet

handle

bonnet

cylinder

spout

seal

water inlet

aerator

escutcheon

ball-type faucet

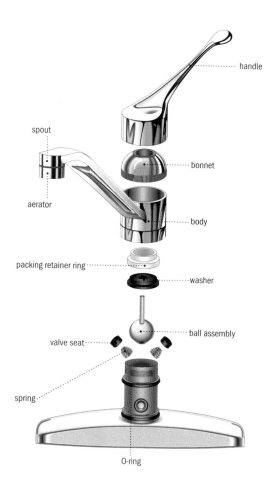

handle

spout

bonnet

aerator

body

packing retainer ring

washer

valve seat

ball assembly

spring

O-ring

cartridge faucet

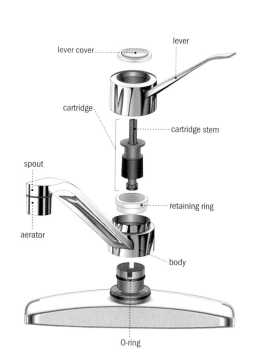

lever cover

lever

cartridge

cartridge stem

spout

retaining ring

aerator

body

O-ring

fittings

examples of transition fittings

steel to plastic

copper to plastic

copper to steel

examples of fittings

offset

tee

Y-branch

trap

cap

U-bend

threaded cap

elbow

45° elbow

pipe coupling

hexagon bushing

flush bushing

nipple

reducing coupling

square head plug

mechanical connectors

union

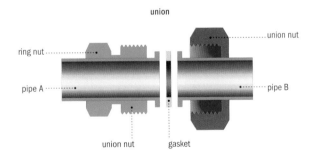

ring nut

union nut

pipe A

pipe B

union nut

gasket

compression fitting

flare joint

pipe A

pipe B

nut

connector

gasket

pipe A

pipe B

nut

connector

tube end

examples of branching

garbage disposal sink

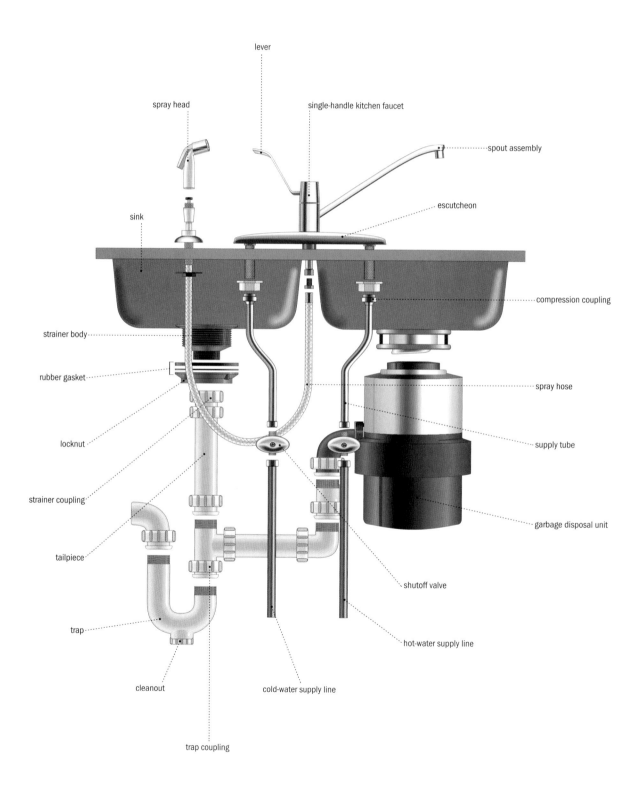

lever

spray head

single-handle kitchen faucet

spout assembly

escutcheon

sink

compression coupling

strainer body

rubber gasket

spray hose

locknut

supply tube

strainer coupling

garbage disposal unit

tailpiece

shutoff valve

trap

hot-water supply line

cleanout

cold-water supply line

trap coupling

washer

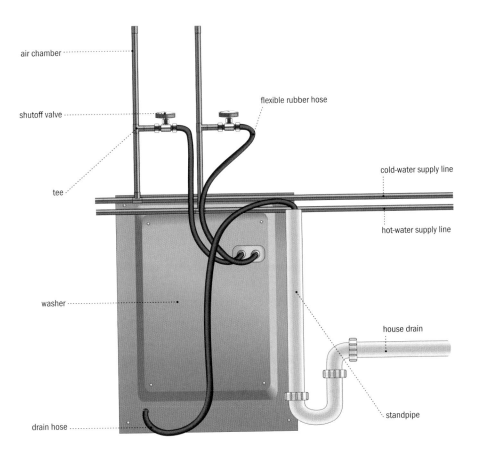

air chamber

shutoff valve

tee

flexible rubber hose

cold-water supply line

hot-water supply line

washer

house drain

drain hose

standpipe

HOUSE

dishwasher

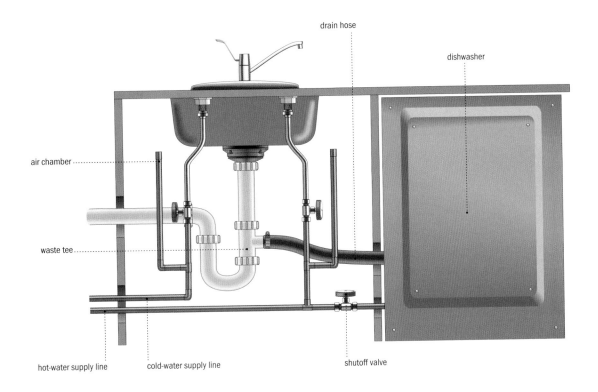

drain hose

dishwasher

air chamber

waste tee

hot-water supply line

cold-water supply line

shutoff valve

distribution panel

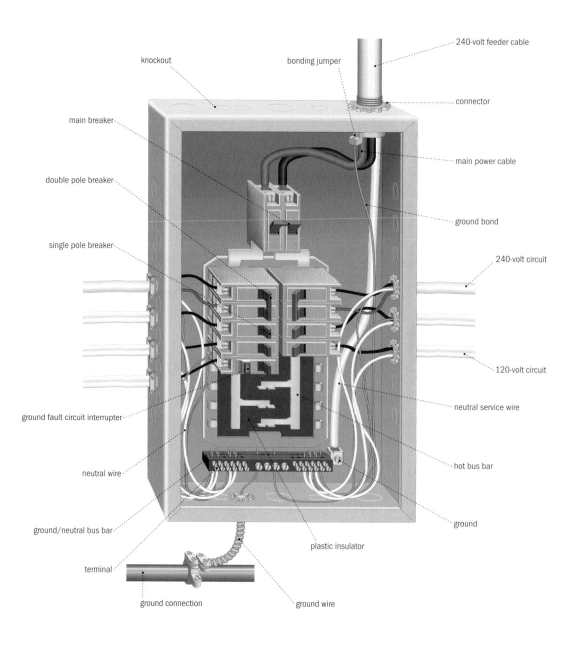

knockout

bonding jumper

240-volt feeder cable

connector

main breaker

main power cable

double pole breaker

ground bond

single pole breaker

240-volt circuit

120-volt circuit

neutral service wire

ground fault circuit interrupter

neutral wire

hot bus bar

ground/neutral bus bar

ground

plastic insulator

terminal

ground connection

ground wire

examples of fuses

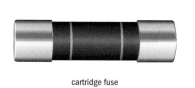

cartridge fuse

plug fuse

knife-blade cartridge fuse

network connection

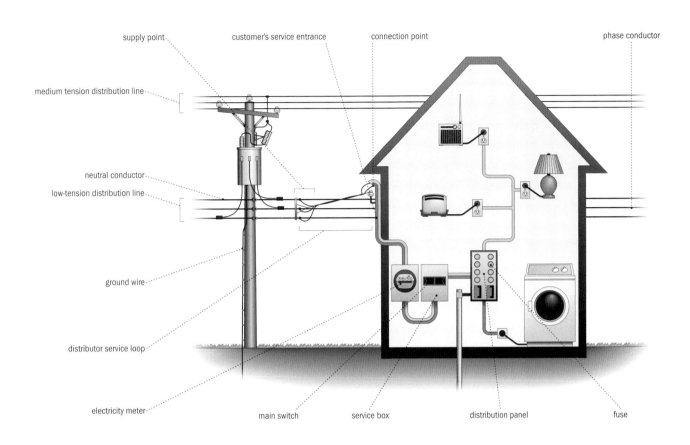

supply point

customer's service entrance

connection point

phase conductor

medium tension distribution line

neutral conductor

low-tension distribution line

ground wire

distributor service loop

electricity meter

main switch

service box

distribution panel

fuse

electricity meter

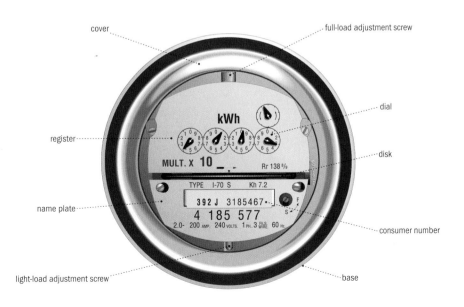

cover

full-load adjustment screw

dial

register

kWh

MULT. X **10**

Rr 138 ⁸/₉

TYPE I-70 S   Kh 7.2

disk

name plate

392 J 3185467

4 185 577

2.0- 200 AMP. 240 VOLTS. 1 PH. 3 WIRE 60 Hz.

consumer number

light-load adjustment screw

base

contact devices

European plug

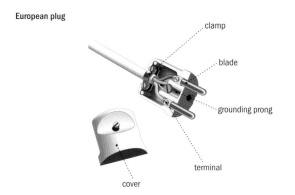

clamp

blade

grounding prong

terminal

cover

American plug

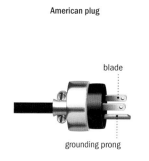

blade

grounding prong

switch

switch plate

European outlet

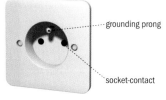

grounding prong

socket-contact

plug adapter

outlet

electrical box

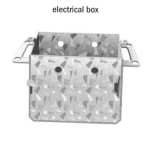

dimmer switch

lighting

incandescent lamp

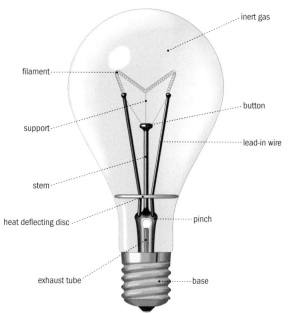

inert gas

filament

button

support

lead-in wire

stem

heat deflecting disc

pinch

exhaust tube

base

tungsten-halogen lamp

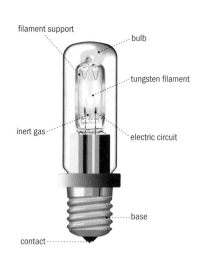

filament support

bulb

tungsten filament

inert gas

electric circuit

base

contact

HOUSE

parts of a lamp socket

lamp socket

bayonet base

bulb

screw base

energy saving bulb

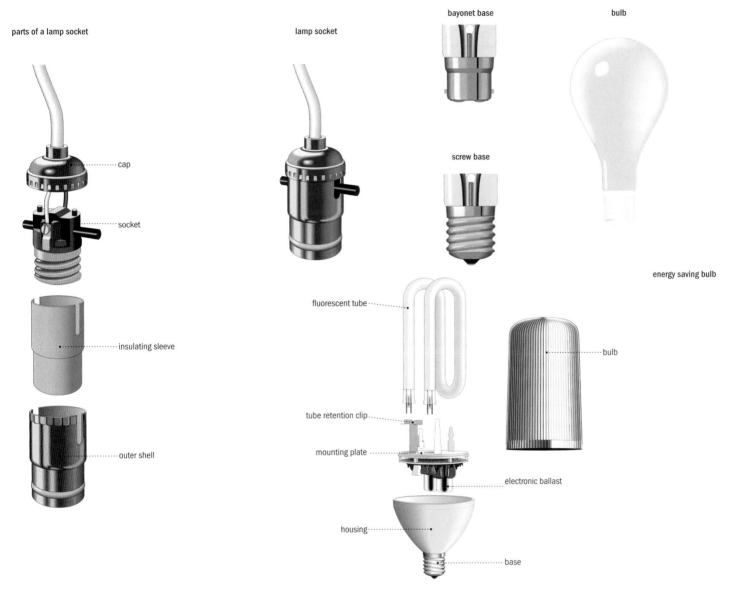

- cap
- socket
- insulating sleeve
- outer shell

fluorescent tube
tube retention clip
mounting plate
electronic ballast
housing
base
bulb

fluorescent tube

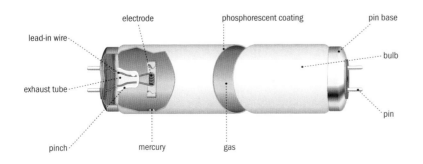

electrode
lead-in wire
exhaust tube
phosphorescent coating
pin base
bulb
pin
pinch
mercury
gas

tungsten-halogen lamp

pin

armchair

parts

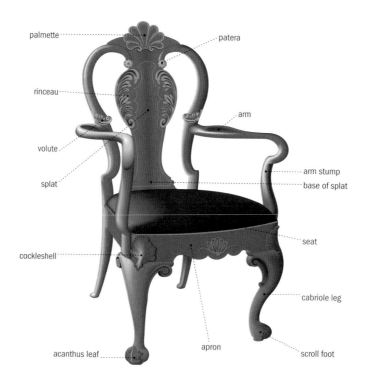

palmette

patera

rinceau

arm

volute

arm stump

splat

base of splat

cockleshell

seat

cabriole leg

acanthus leaf

apron

scroll foot

examples of armchairs

Wassily chair

director's chair

rocking chair

cabriolet

méridienne

récamier

club chair

bergère

sofa

love seat

chesterfield

side chair

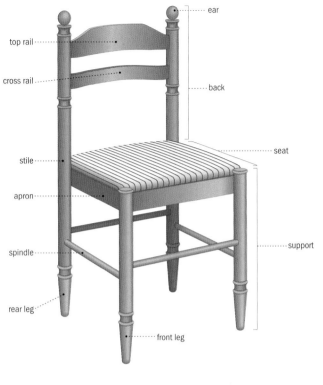

ear

top rail

cross rail

back

seat

stile

apron

support

spindle

rear leg

front leg

examples of chairs

rocking chair

stacking chairs

folding chairs

chaise longue

seats

ottoman

bench

banquette

bean bag chair

step chair

footstool

bar stool

table

gate-leg table

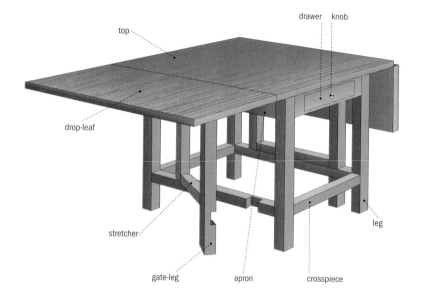

top
drop-leaf
stretcher
gate-leg
apron
crosspiece
drawer
knob
leg

examples of tables

extension table

top
extension

nest of tables

serving cart

storage furniture

armoire

frame

door

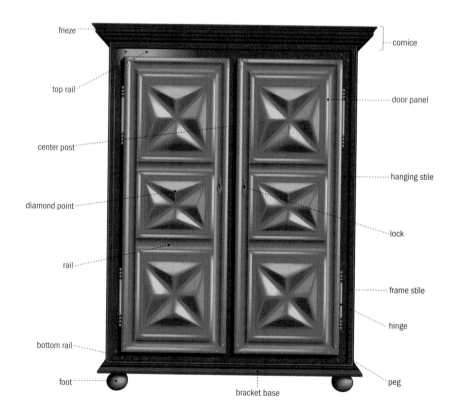

frieze
top rail
center post
diamond point
rail
bottom rail
foot
cornice
door panel
hanging stile
lock
frame stile
hinge
peg
bracket base

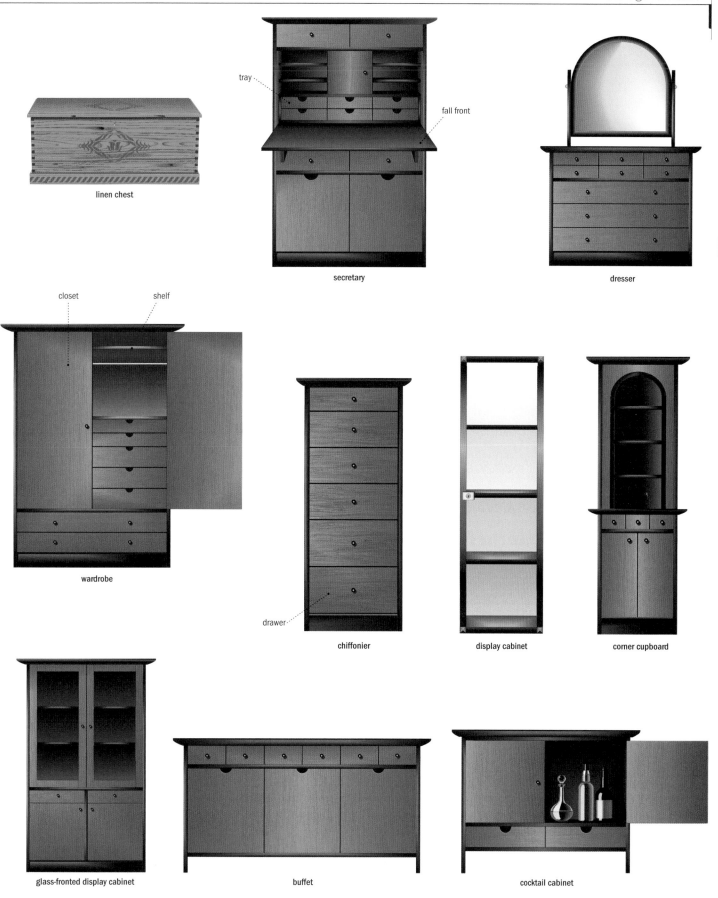

linen chest

tray

fall front

secretary

dresser

HOUSE

closet   shelf

wardrobe

drawer

chiffonier

display cabinet

corner cupboard

glass-fronted display cabinet

buffet

cocktail cabinet

bed

HOUSE

sofa bed

futon

frame

parts

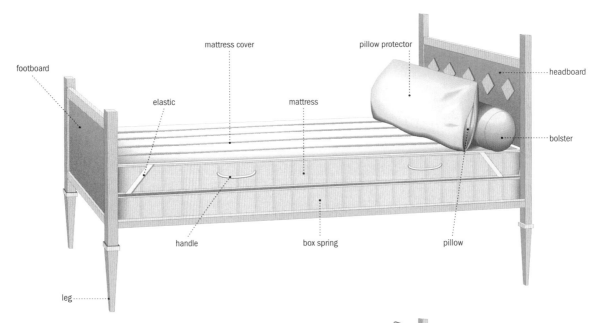

mattress cover

pillow protector

footboard

elastic

mattress

headboard

bolster

handle

box spring

pillow

leg

linen

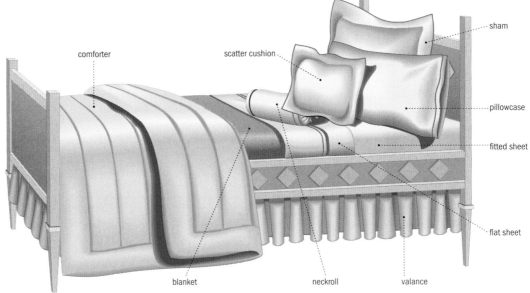

comforter

scatter cushion

sham

pillowcase

fitted sheet

flat sheet

blanket

neckroll

valance

children's furniture

playpen

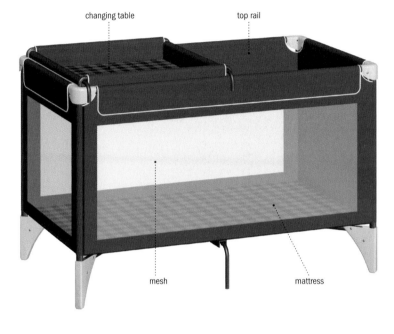

changing table

top rail

mesh

mattress

booster seat

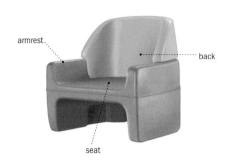

armrest

back

seat

changing table

high chair

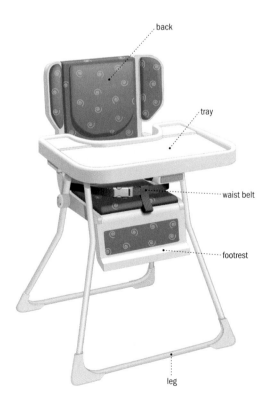

back

tray

waist belt

footrest

leg

crib

headboard

barrier

slat

caster

drawer

mattress

window accessories

HOUSE

indoor shutters

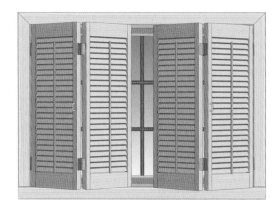

window curtain

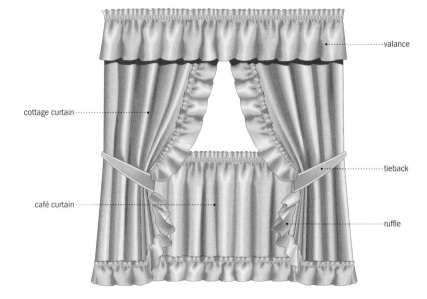

valance

cottage curtain

tieback

café curtain

ruffle

curtain

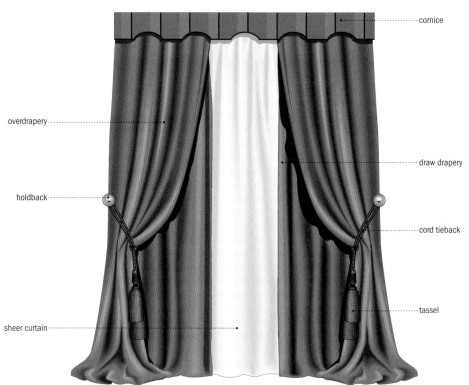

cornice

overdrapery

draw drapery

holdback

cord tieback

tassel

sheer curtain

examples of pleats

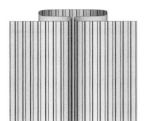

box pleat

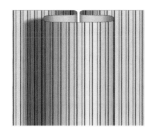

inverted pleat

pinch pleat

examples of headings

HOUSE

pleated heading

pencil pleat heading

shirred heading

draped swag

examples of curtains

attached curtain

crisscross curtains

loose curtain

balloon curtain

window accessories

poles

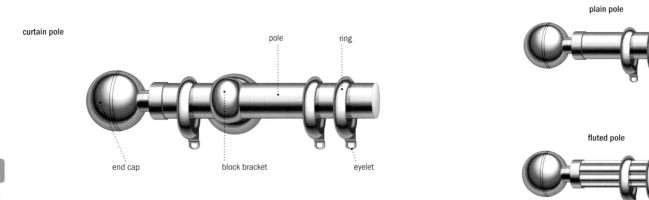

curtain pole

plain pole

fluted pole

pole

ring

end cap

block bracket

eyelet

single curtain rod

double curtain rod

curtain track

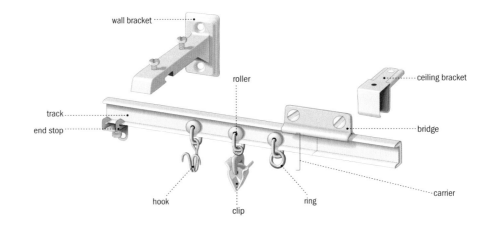

wall bracket

roller

ceiling bracket

track

bridge

end stop

carrier

hook

ring

clip

traverse rod

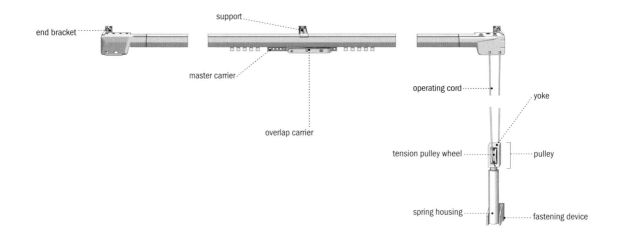

end bracket

support

master carrier

overlap carrier

operating cord

yoke

tension pulley wheel

pulley

spring housing

fastening device

blinds

HOUSE

roller shade

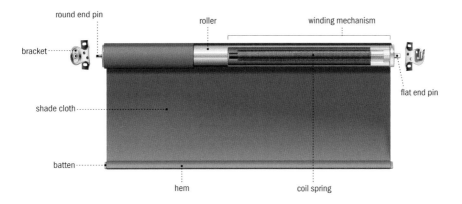

round end pin

roller

winding mechanism

bracket

flat end pin

shade cloth

batten

hem

coil spring

venetian blind

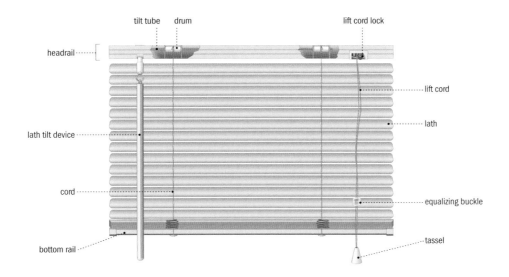

tilt tube   drum

lift cord lock

headrail

lift cord

lath

lath tilt device

cord

equalizing buckle

bottom rail

tassel

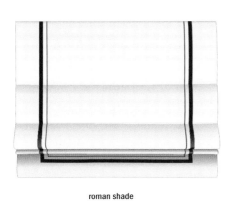

roman shade

roll-up blind

lights

ceiling fitting

hanging pendant

clamp spotlight

halogen desk lamp

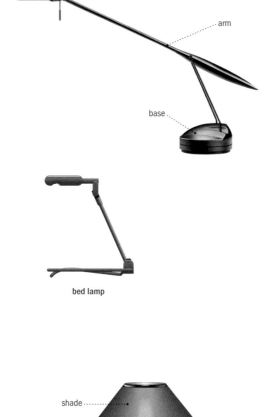
arm

base

base

floor lamp

bed lamp

shade

stand

table lamp

adjustable lamp

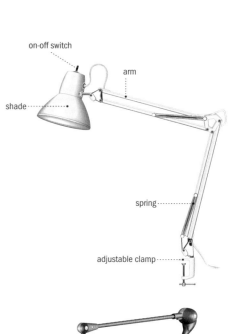
on-off switch

arm

shade

spring

adjustable clamp

desk lamp

chandelier

bobeche

crystal drop

crystal button

column

track lighting

bar frame

transformer

contact lever

spot

wall lantern

swivel wall lamp

wall sconce

strip light

post lantern

domestic appliances

steam iron

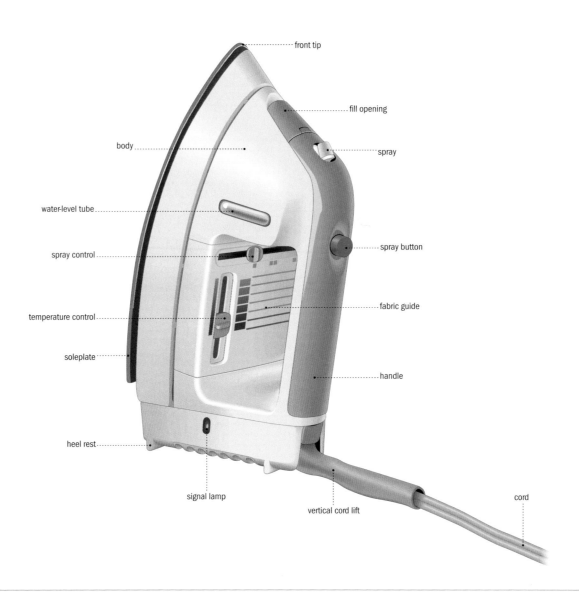

front tip

fill opening

body

spray

water-level tube

spray button

spray control

fabric guide

temperature control

soleplate

handle

heel rest

signal lamp

vertical cord lift

cord

hand vacuum cleaner

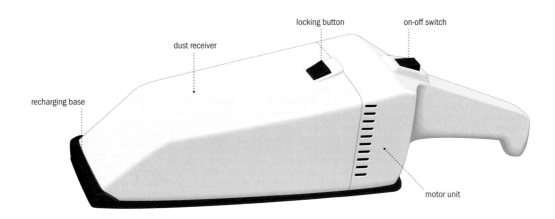

locking button

on-off switch

dust receiver

recharging base

motor unit

HOUSE

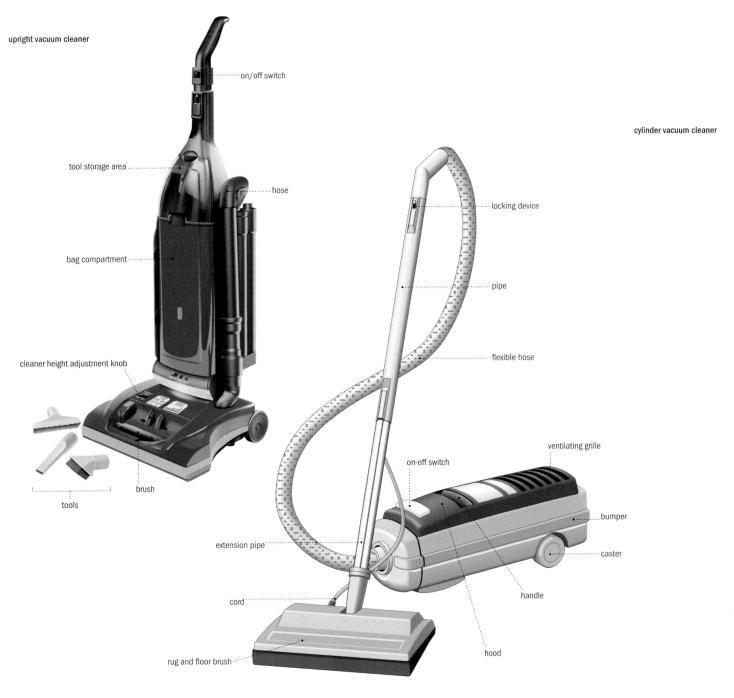

upright vacuum cleaner

on/off switch

tool storage area

hose

bag compartment

cleaner height adjustment knob

tools

brush

cylinder vacuum cleaner

locking device

pipe

flexible hose

ventilating grille

on-off switch

bumper

extension pipe

caster

cord

handle

rug and floor brush

hood

cleaning tools

upholstery nozzle

dusting brush

crevice tool

floor brush

domestic appliances

range hood

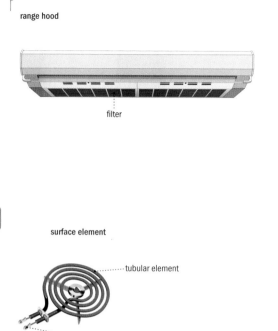

filter

gas range

grate

burner

lid

burner control knobs

cooktop

handle

control panel

window

door

rack

oven

drawer

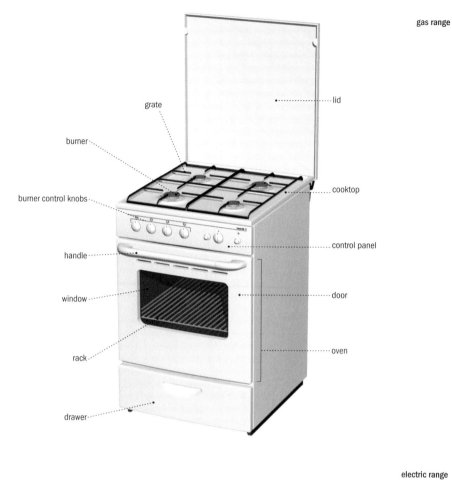

surface element

tubular element

terminal

drip bowl

trim ring

electric range

oven control knobs

clock timer

signal lamp

backguard

control knob

timed outlet

control panel

cooktop

surface element

cooktop edge

rack

handle

oven

window

drawer

chest freezer

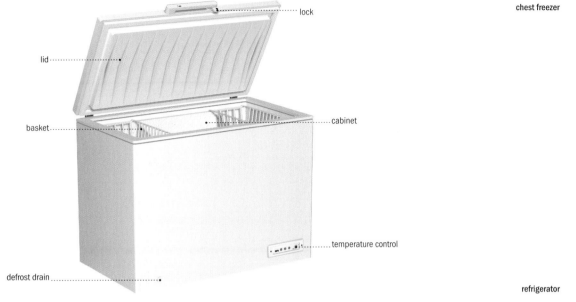

lock

lid

basket

cabinet

temperature control

defrost drain

refrigerator

HOUSE

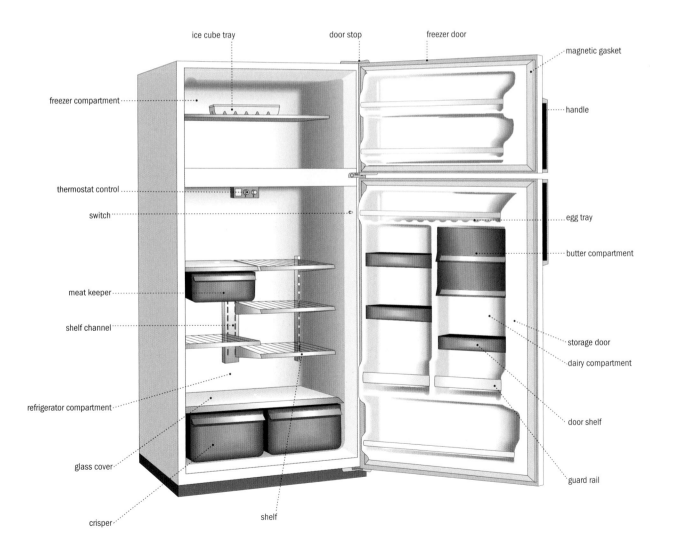

ice cube tray

door stop

freezer door

magnetic gasket

freezer compartment

handle

thermostat control

switch

egg tray

butter compartment

meat keeper

shelf channel

storage door

dairy compartment

refrigerator compartment

door shelf

glass cover

guard rail

crisper

shelf

domestic appliances

washer

water-level selector

temperature selector

control knob

control panel

backguard

lid

tub rim

agitator

cabinet

basket

tub

lint filter

suspension arm

transmission

drain hose

motor

emptying hose

torque converter

leveling foot

drive belt

spring

pump

dryer

HOUSE

temperature selector

control panel

control knob

start switch

backguard

door switch

heating duct

door

vane

drum

lint trap

fan

cabinet

leveling foot

motor

safety thermostat

heating element

domestic appliances

control panel: dishwasher

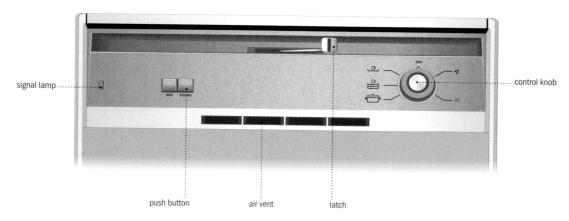

signal lamp

control knob

push button

air vent

latch

dishwasher

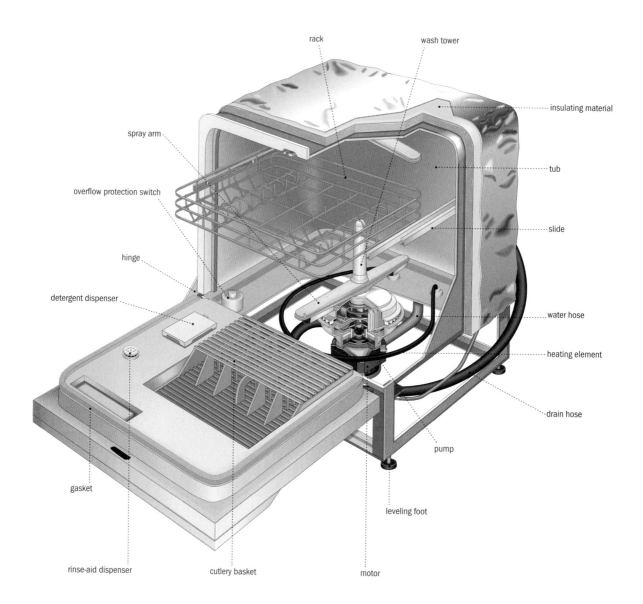

rack

wash tower

insulating material

spray arm

overflow protection switch

tub

slide

hinge

detergent dispenser

water hose

heating element

drain hose

pump

gasket

leveling foot

rinse-aid dispenser

cutlery basket

motor

household equipment

kitchen towel

dustpan

broom

mop

scouring pad

brush

block

fibers

handle

garbage can

lid

handle

fibers

pail

pouring spout

handle

DO-IT-YOURSELF AND GARDENING

basic building materials

brick

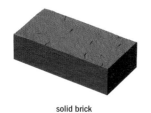
solid brick

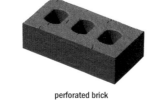
perforated brick

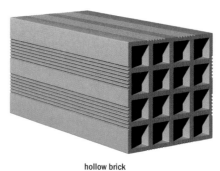
hollow brick

partition tile

brick wall

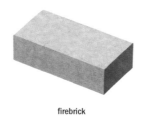
firebrick

mortar

stone

flagstone

rubble

cut stone

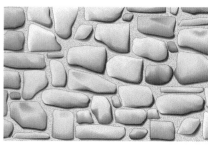
stone wall

concrete

concrete block

prestressed concrete

reinforced concrete

steel

covering materials

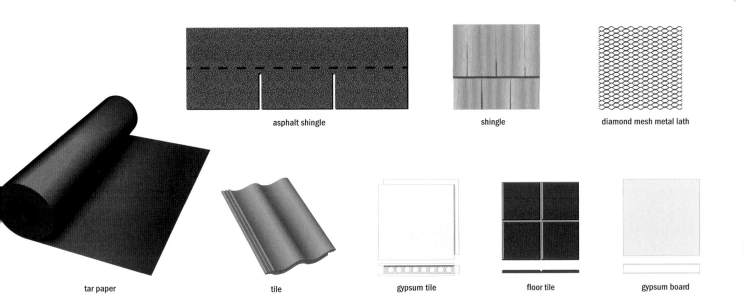

asphalt shingle

shingle

diamond mesh metal lath

tar paper

tile

gypsum tile

floor tile

gypsum board

insulating materials

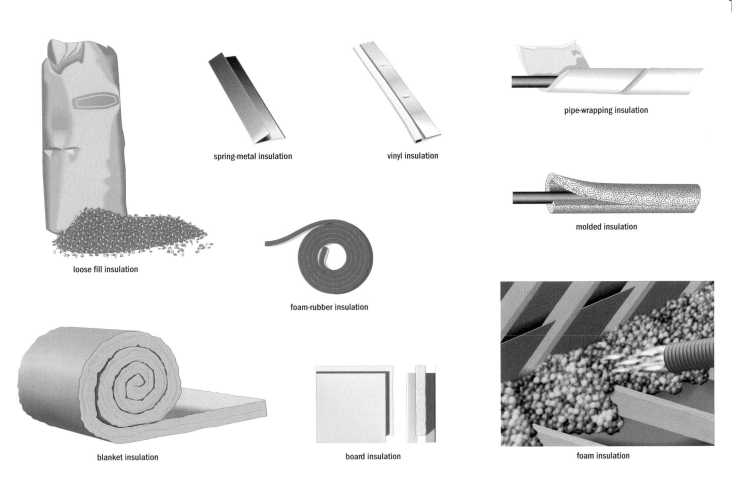

spring-metal insulation

vinyl insulation

pipe-wrapping insulation

molded insulation

loose fill insulation

foam-rubber insulation

blanket insulation

board insulation

foam insulation

wood

section of a log

board

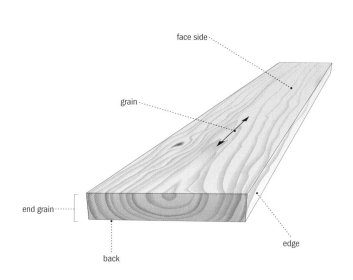

wood-based materials

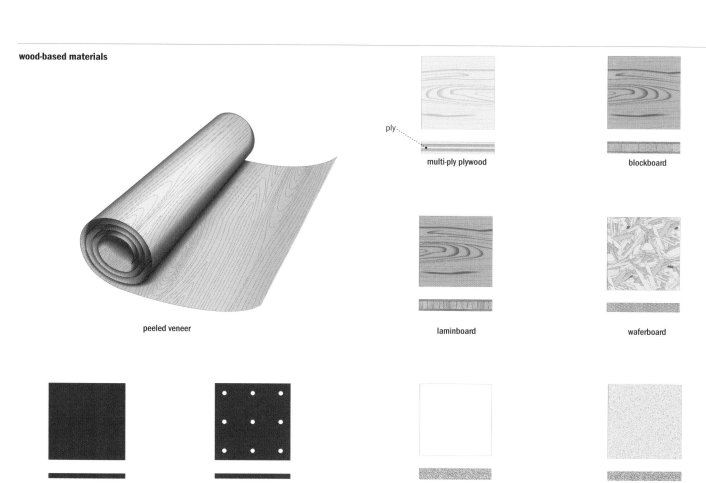

peeled veneer

multi-ply plywood

blockboard

laminboard

waferboard

hardboard

perforated hardboard

plastic-laminated particle board

particle board

carpentry: nailing tools

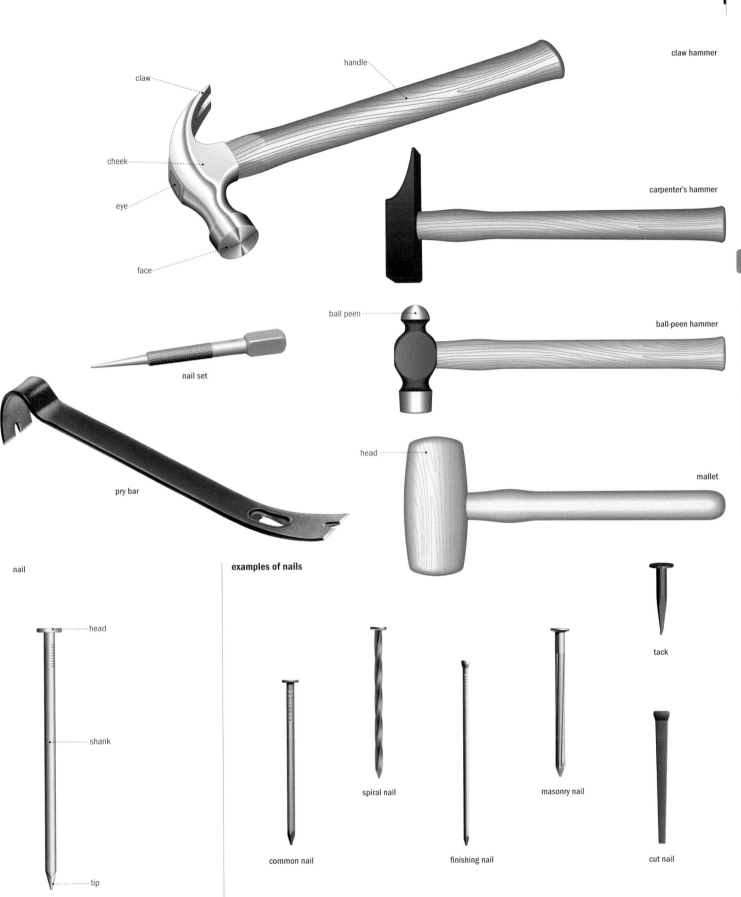

claw hammer

handle

claw

cheek

eye

face

carpenter's hammer

nail set

ball peen

ball-peen hammer

pry bar

head

mallet

nail

examples of nails

head

shank

tip

tack

spiral nail

masonry nail

common nail

finishing nail

cut nail

carpentry: screwing tools

screwdriver

spiral screwdriver

cordless screwdriver

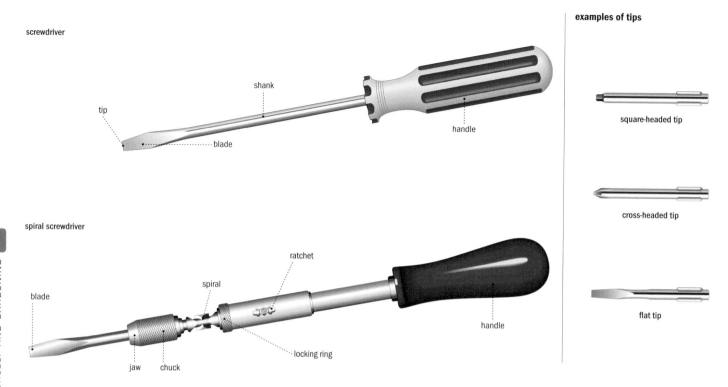

examples of tips

square-headed tip

cross-headed tip

flat tip

toggle bolt

expansion bolt

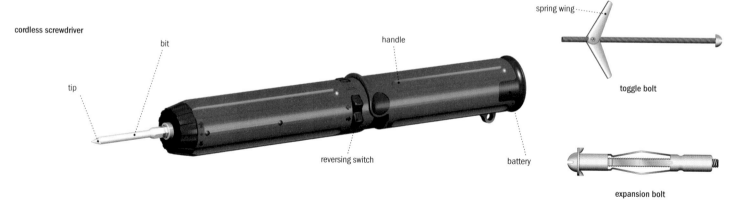

screw

examples of heads

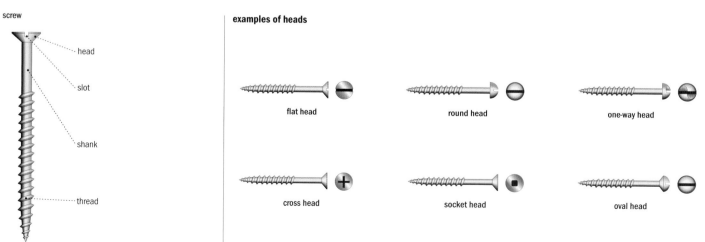

flat head

round head

one-way head

cross head

socket head

oval head

carpentry: sawing tools

hacksaw

coping saw

frame

grip handle

adjustable frame

handle

blade

blade

handsaw

handle

back

blade

compass saw

blade

heel

tooth

toe

handle

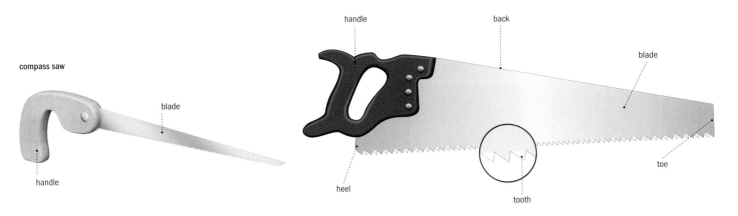

hand miter saw

blade

handle

fence

miter box

end stop

miter latch

clamp

miter scale

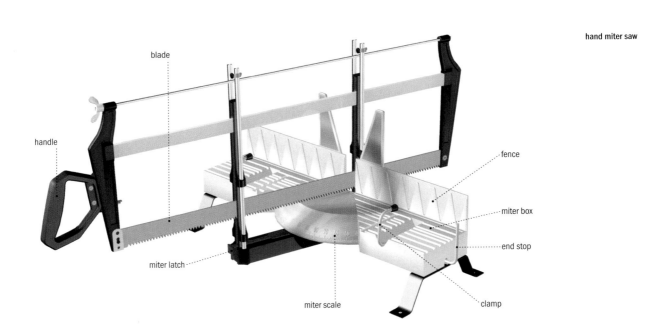

carpentry: sawing tools

electric miter saw

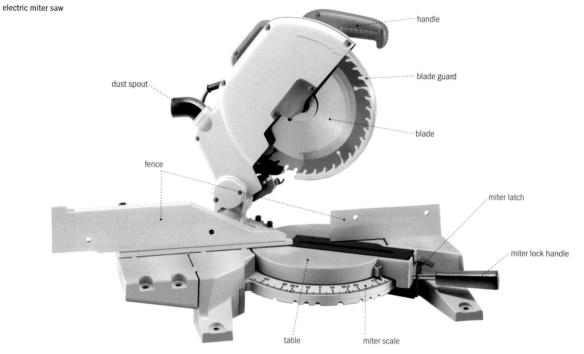

handle

blade guard

dust spout

blade

fence

miter latch

miter lock handle

table

miter scale

circular saw blade

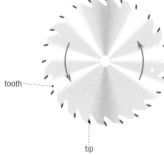

tooth

tip

circular saw

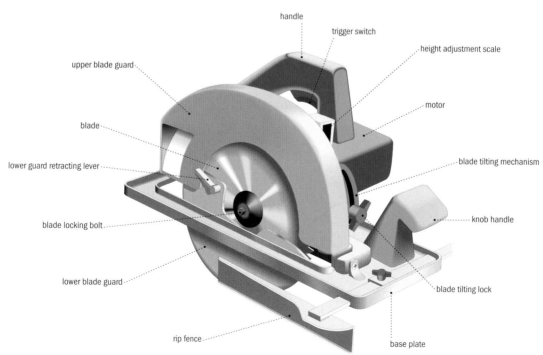

handle

trigger switch

height adjustment scale

upper blade guard

motor

blade

blade tilting mechanism

lower guard retracting lever

knob handle

blade locking bolt

lower blade guard

blade tilting lock

rip fence

base plate

jig saw

speed selector switch

lock-on button

trigger switch

handle

orbital-action selector

chip cover

power cord

blade

base

table saw

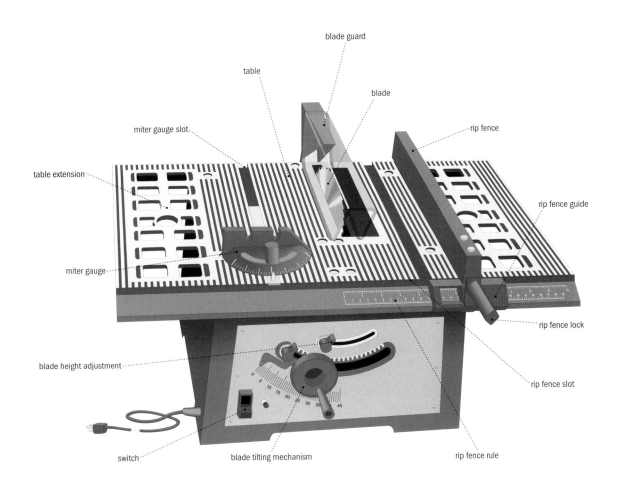

blade guard

table

blade

miter gauge slot

rip fence

table extension

rip fence guide

miter gauge

rip fence lock

blade height adjustment

rip fence slot

switch

blade tilting mechanism

rip fence rule

carpentry: drilling tools

cordless drill

speed selector switch

screwdriver bit

keyless chuck

torque adjustment collar

trigger switch

reversing switch

battery pack

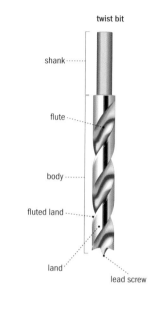

battery pack

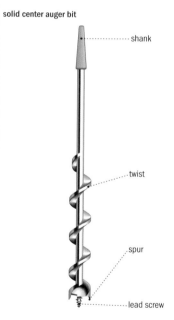

charger

chuck key

electric drill

name plate

warning plate

switch lock

housing

chuck

trigger switch

pistol grip handle

jaw

cable sleeve

auxiliary handle

plug

cable

examples of bits and drills

twist bit

shank

flute

body

fluted land

land

lead screw

solid center auger bit

shank

twist

spur

lead screw

masonry drill

twist drill

spade bit

double-twist auger bit

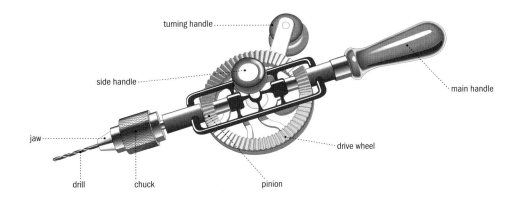

turning handle

side handle

main handle

jaw

drive wheel

drill

chuck

pinion

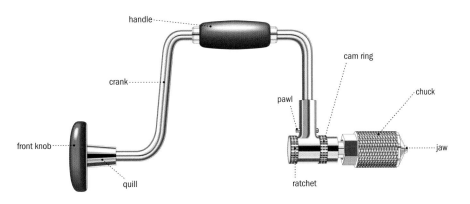

handle

cam ring

crank

chuck

pawl

front knob

jaw

quill

ratchet

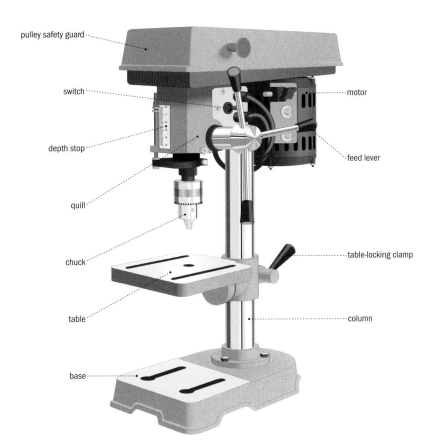

pulley safety guard

switch

motor

depth stop

feed lever

quill

chuck

table-locking clamp

table

column

base

DO-IT-YOURSELF AND GARDENING

carpentry: shaping tools

angle grinder

random orbit sander

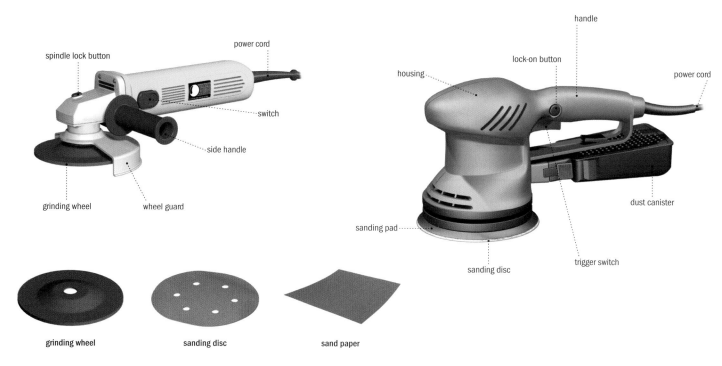

spindle lock button

power cord

switch

side handle

grinding wheel

wheel guard

handle

lock-on button

housing

power cord

dust canister

sanding pad

sanding disc

trigger switch

grinding wheel

sanding disc

sand paper

examples of bits

router

motor

head

switch

cord sleeve

depth adjustment

guide handle

collet

base

tool holder

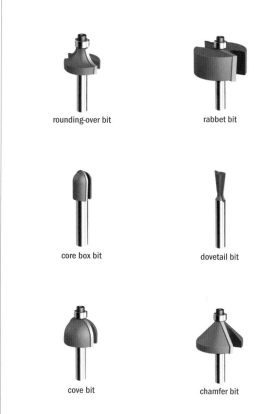

rounding-over bit

rabbet bit

core box bit

dovetail bit

cove bit

chamfer bit

plane

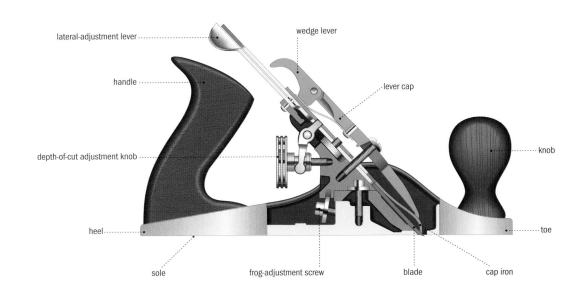

lateral-adjustment lever

wedge lever

handle

lever cap

depth-of-cut adjustment knob

knob

heel

toe

sole

frog-adjustment screw

blade

cap iron

jointer plane

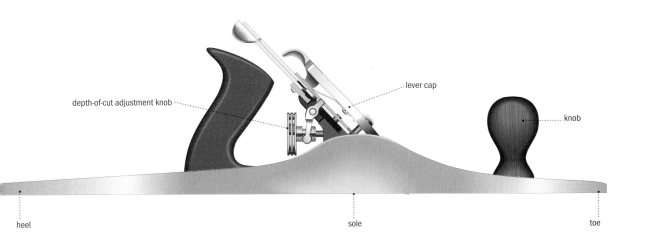

depth-of-cut adjustment knob

lever cap

knob

heel

sole

toe

rasp

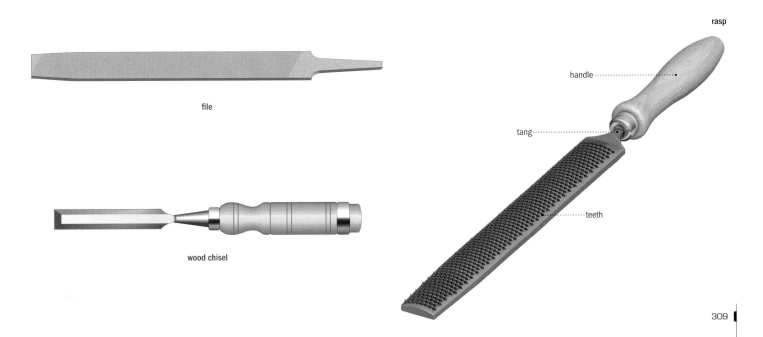

file

handle

tang

wood chisel

teeth

carpentry: gripping and tightening tools

pliers

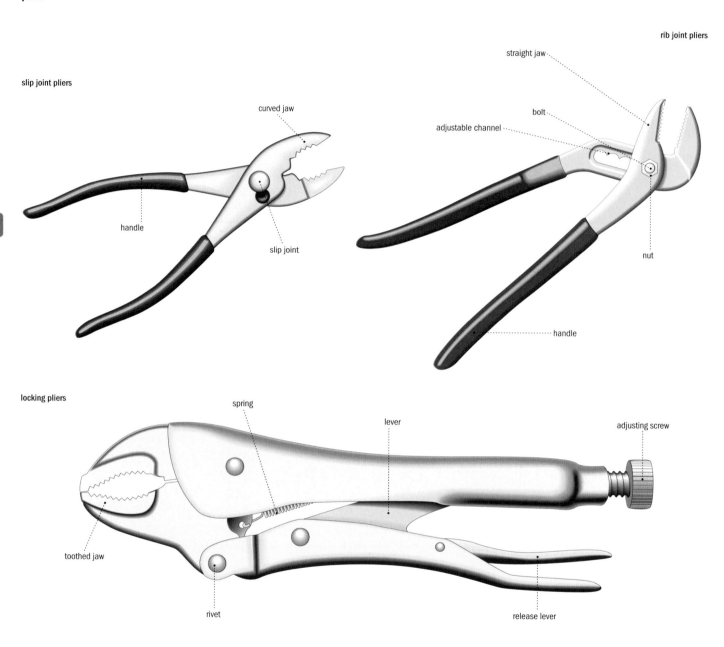

slip joint pliers

curved jaw

handle

slip joint

rib joint pliers

straight jaw

bolt

adjustable channel

nut

handle

locking pliers

spring

lever

adjusting screw

toothed jaw

rivet

release lever

washers

flat washer

lock washer

external tooth lock washer

internal tooth lock washer

wrenches

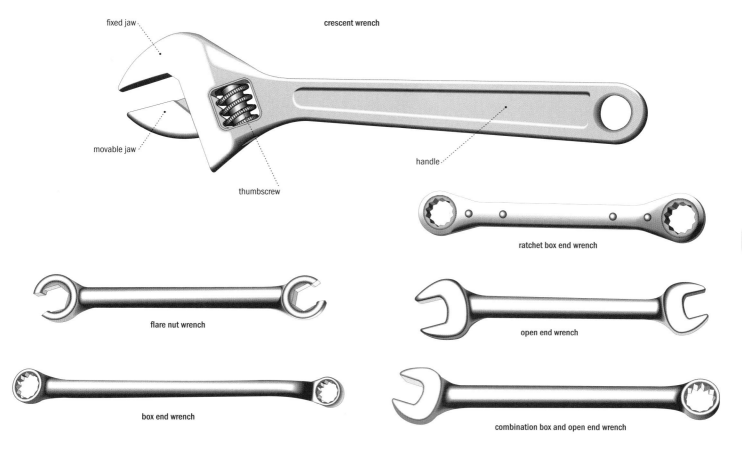

fixed jaw

crescent wrench

movable jaw

thumbscrew

handle

ratchet box end wrench

flare nut wrench

open end wrench

box end wrench

combination box and open end wrench

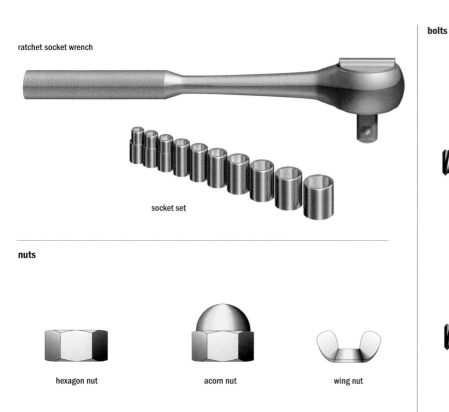

ratchet socket wrench

socket set

bolts

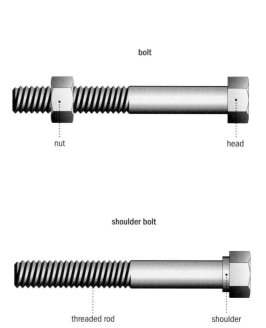

bolt

nut

head

nuts

shoulder bolt

hexagon nut

acorn nut

wing nut

threaded rod

shoulder

carpentry: gripping and tightening tools

DO-IT-YOURSELF AND GARDENING

C-clamp

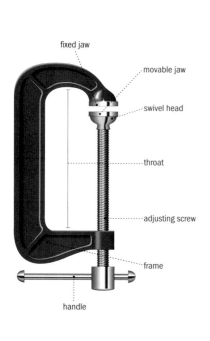

fixed jaw

movable jaw

swivel head

throat

adjusting screw

frame

handle

vise

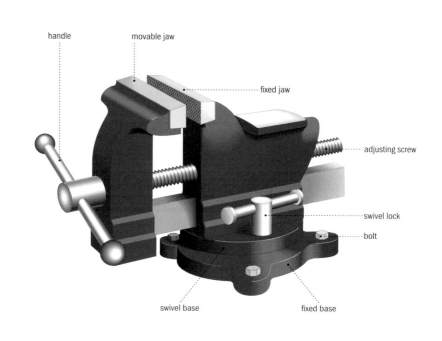

handle

movable jaw

fixed jaw

adjusting screw

swivel lock

bolt

swivel base

fixed base

pipe clamp

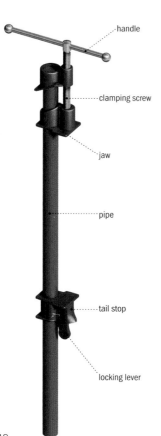

handle

clamping screw

jaw

pipe

tail stop

locking lever

work bench and vise

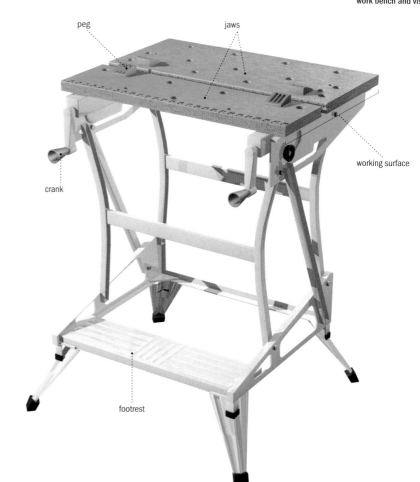

peg

jaws

crank

working surface

footrest

carpentry: measuring and marking tools

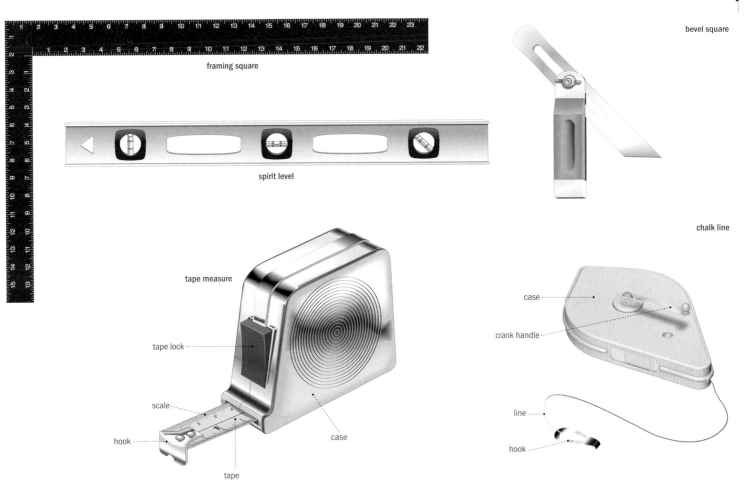

framing square

bevel square

spirit level

chalk line

tape measure

tape lock

scale

hook

tape

case

case

crank handle

line

hook

carpentry: miscellaneous material

tool box

tool belt

handle

lid

tray

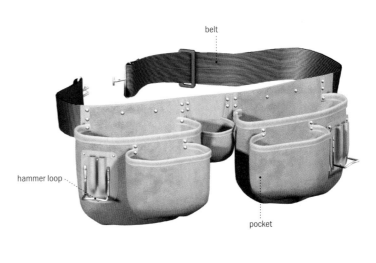

belt

hammer loop

pocket

plumbing tools

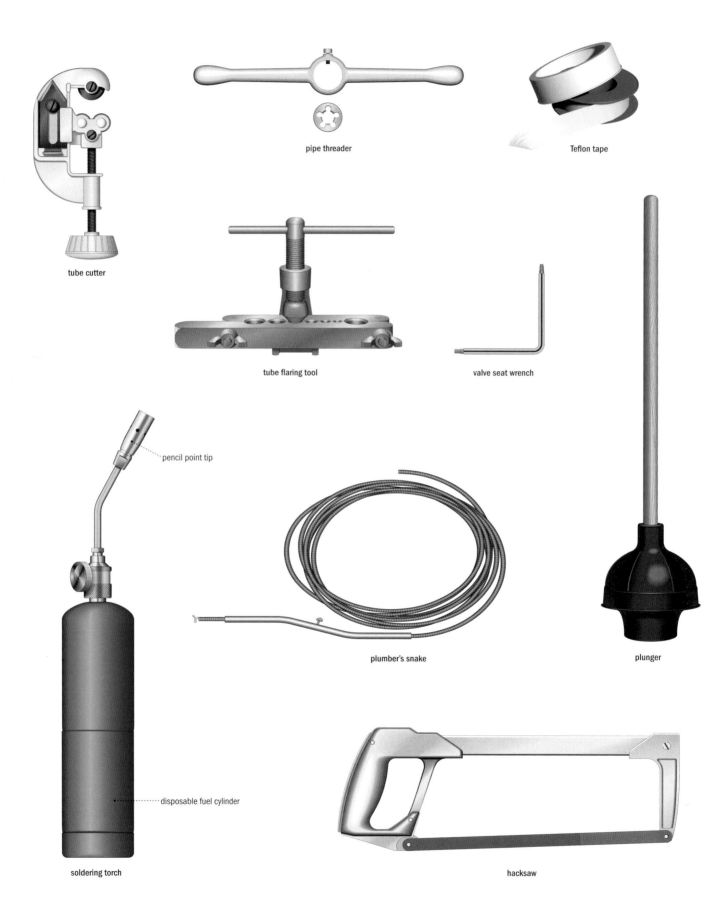

pipe threader

Teflon tape

tube cutter

tube flaring tool

valve seat wrench

pencil point tip

plumber's snake

plunger

disposable fuel cylinder

soldering torch

hacksaw

wrenches

adjustable spud wrench

basin wrench

pipe wrench

strap wrench

chain pipe wrench

masonry tools

caulking gun

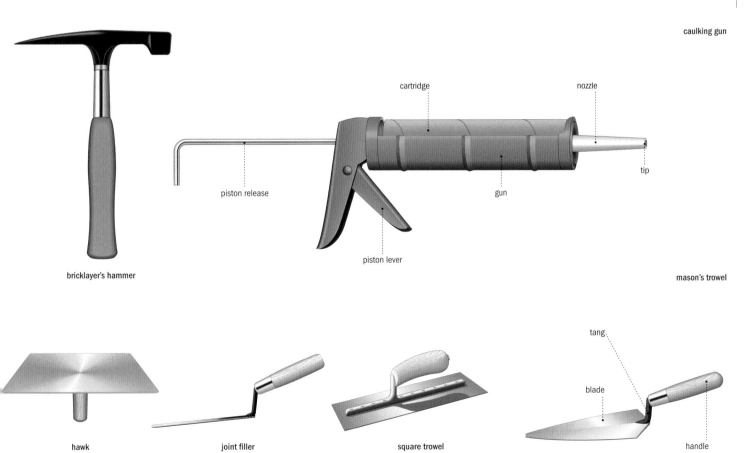

bricklayer's hammer

piston release

cartridge

nozzle

tip

gun

piston lever

mason's trowel

hawk

joint filler

square trowel

tang

blade

handle

electricity tools

multimeter

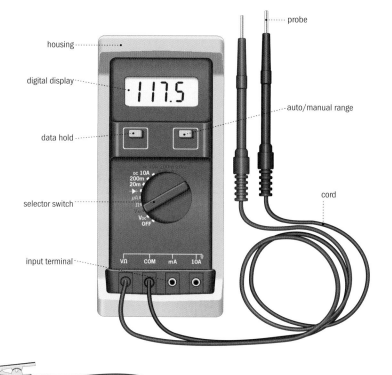

housing

digital display

data hold

selector switch

input terminal

probe

auto/manual range

cord

VΩ   COM   mA   10A

continuity tester

neon tester

receptacle analyzer

high-voltage tester

voltage tester

insulated blade

insulated handle

neon lamp

drop light

hook

reflector

bulb

guard

convenience outlet

handle

cord

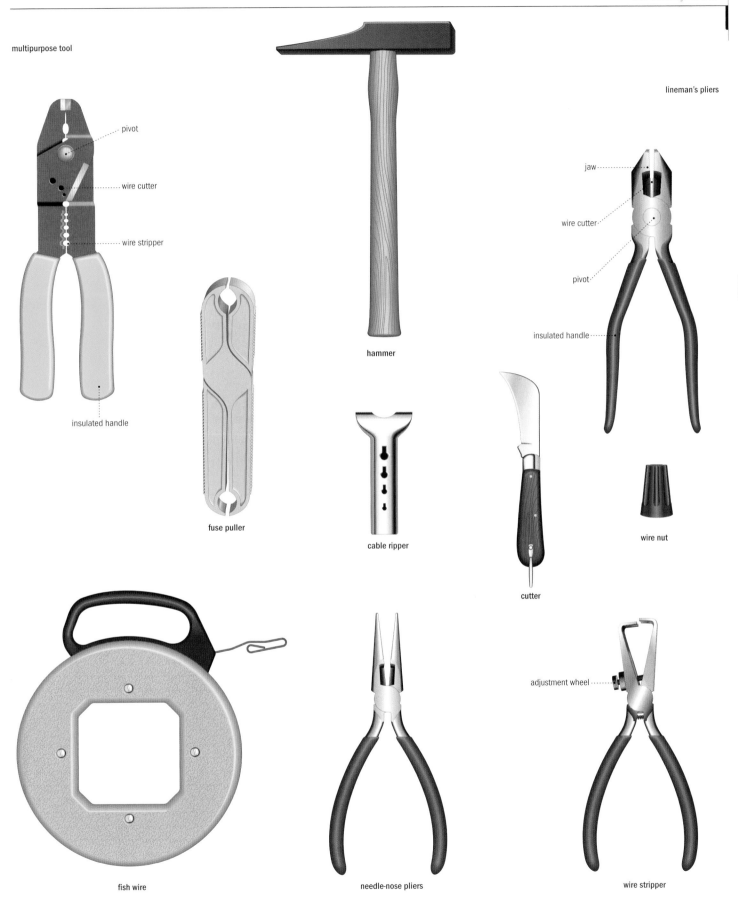

multipurpose tool

pivot

wire cutter

wire stripper

insulated handle

fuse puller

hammer

cable ripper

cutter

lineman's pliers

jaw

wire cutter

pivot

insulated handle

wire nut

fish wire

needle-nose pliers

adjustment wheel

wire stripper

soldering and welding tools

soldering gun

tip

heating element

housing

on-off switch

pistol grip handle

cord sleeve

soldering iron

solder

tip cleaners

welding curtain

striker

friction strip

flint

electrode holder

electrode lead

electrode

ground clamp

work lead

arc welding

arc welding machine

protective clothing

goggles

face shield

hand shield

gauntlets

mittens

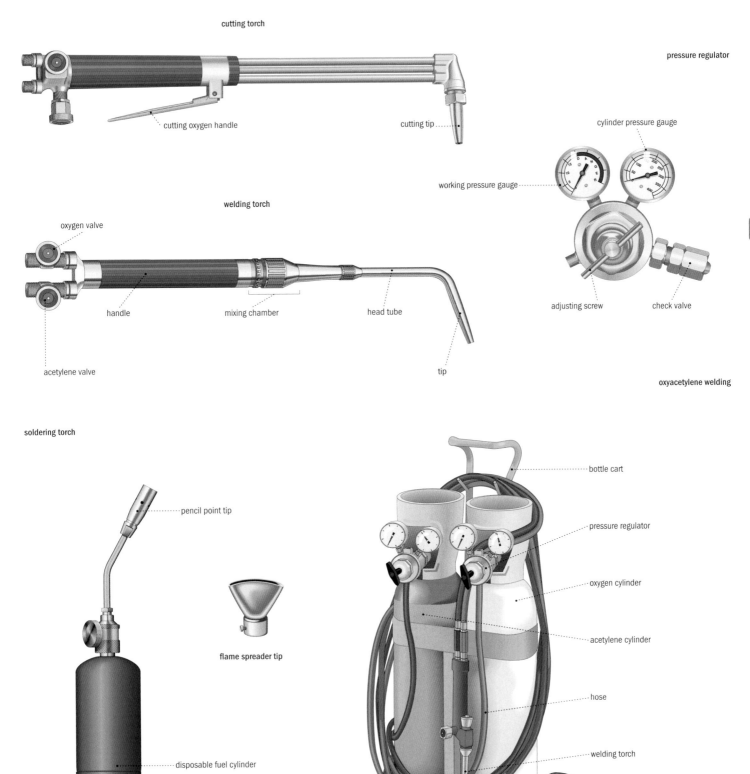

cutting torch

pressure regulator

cutting oxygen handle

cutting tip

cylinder pressure gauge

working pressure gauge

welding torch

oxygen valve

handle

mixing chamber

head tube

adjusting screw

check valve

acetylene valve

tip

oxyacetylene welding

soldering torch

pencil point tip

bottle cart

pressure regulator

oxygen cylinder

flame spreader tip

acetylene cylinder

hose

disposable fuel cylinder

welding torch

painting

spray paint gun

spreader adjustment screw

fluid adjustment screw

nozzle

air cap

air valve

trigger

gun body

vent hole

air hose connection

container

brush

handle

ferrule

bristles

scraper

knurled bolt

blade

handle

air compressor

pump

motor

handle

air tank

wheel

heat gun

nozzle

switch

tray

paint roller

handle

roller frame

roller cover

ladders and stepladders

foldaway ladder

straight ladder

hook ladder

extension ladder

rung

side rail

pulley

locking device

hoisting rope

antislip shoe

ladder scaffold

rope ladder

fruit-picking ladder

multipurpose ladder

rolling ladder

stepladder

top

tool shelf

brace

step

step stool

platform ladder

safety rail

shelf

frame

platform

rubber tip

step

pleasure garden

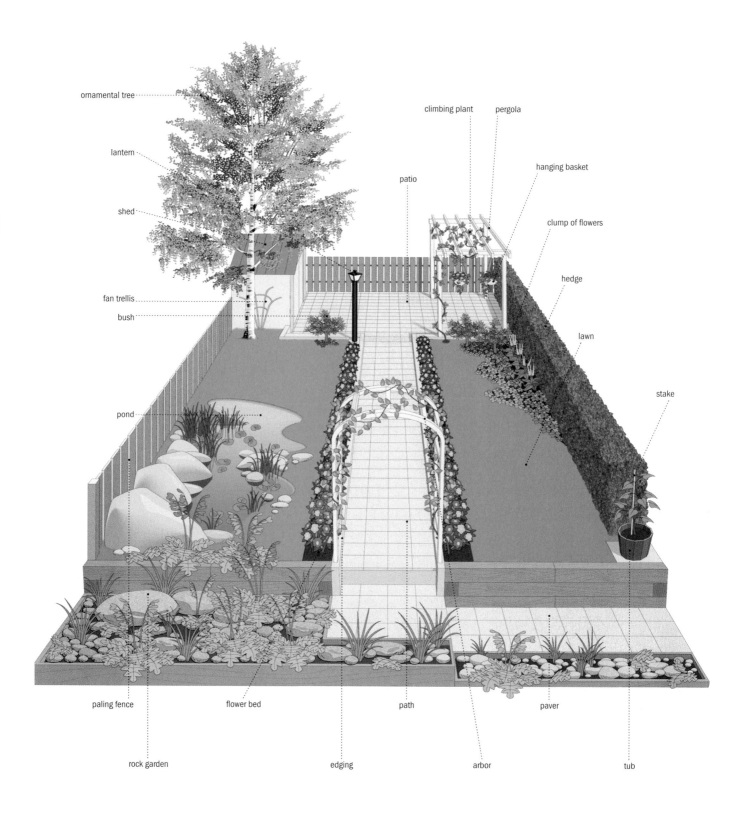

ornamental tree

climbing plant

pergola

lantern

hanging basket

shed

patio

clump of flowers

hedge

fan trellis

lawn

bush

stake

pond

paling fence

flower bed

path

paver

rock garden

edging

arbor

tub

miscellaneous equipment

motorized earth auger

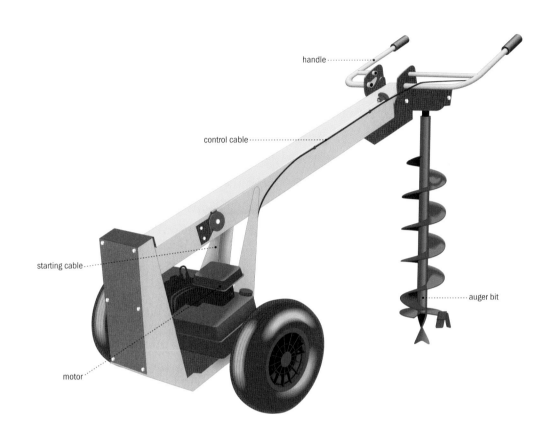

handle

control cable

starting cable

motor

auger bit

wheelbarrow

compost bin

tray

handle

leg

wheel

seeding and planting tools

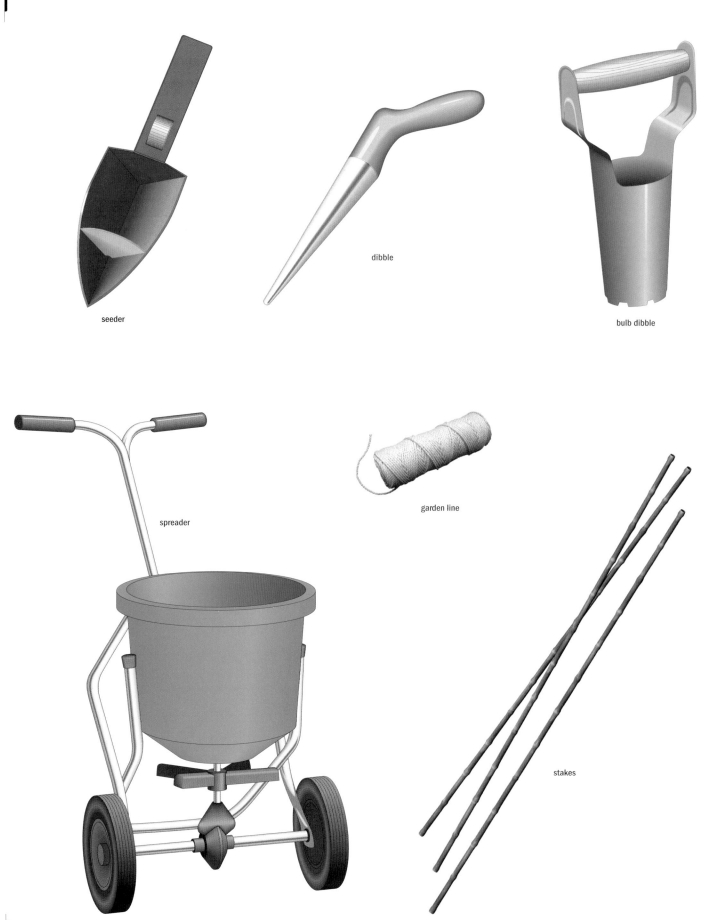

seeder

dibble

bulb dibble

spreader

garden line

stakes

small hand cultivator

trowel

weeder

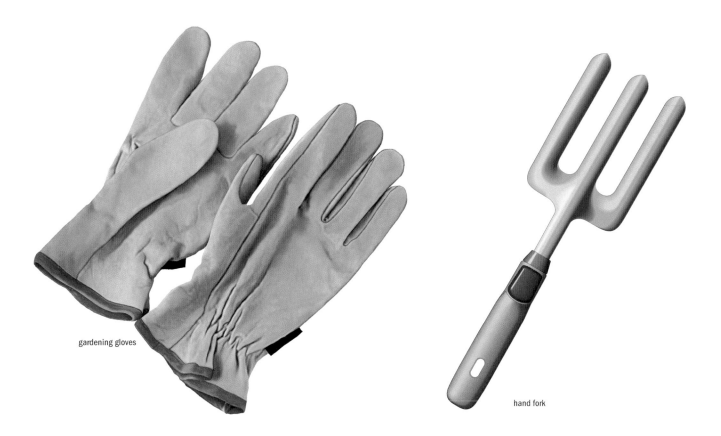

gardening gloves

hand fork

DO-IT-YOURSELF AND GARDENING

tools for loosening the earth

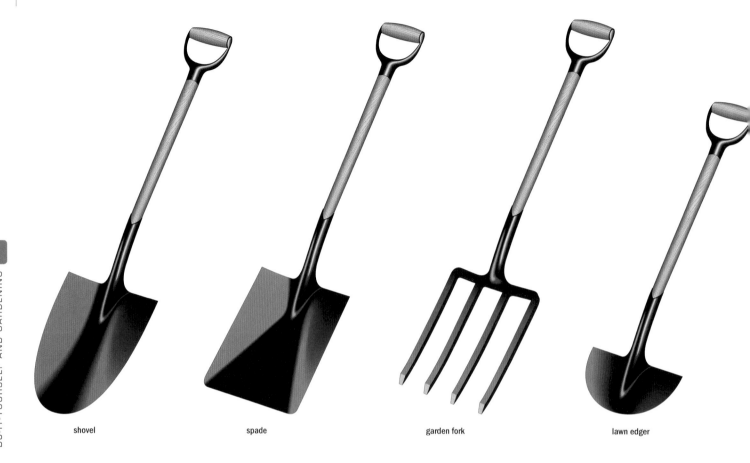

shovel

spade

garden fork

lawn edger

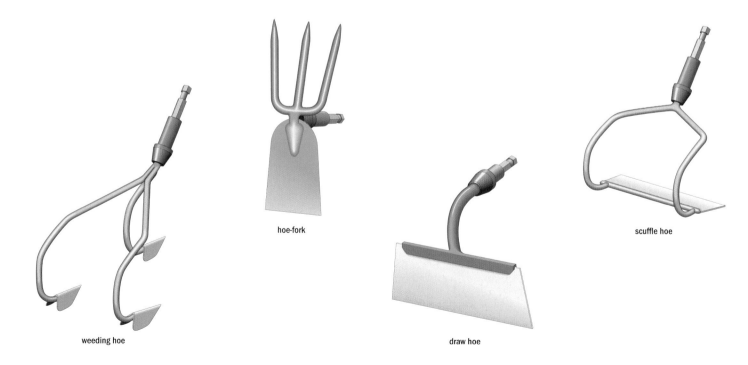

weeding hoe

hoe-fork

draw hoe

scuffle hoe

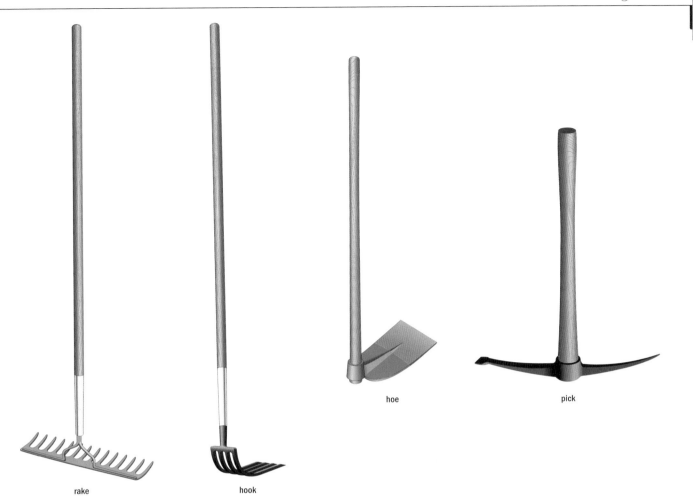

hoe

pick

rake

hook

tiller

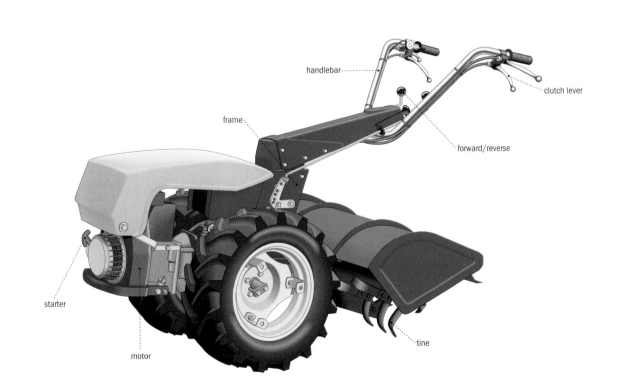

handlebar

clutch lever

frame

forward/reverse

starter

motor

tine

watering tools

hose trolley

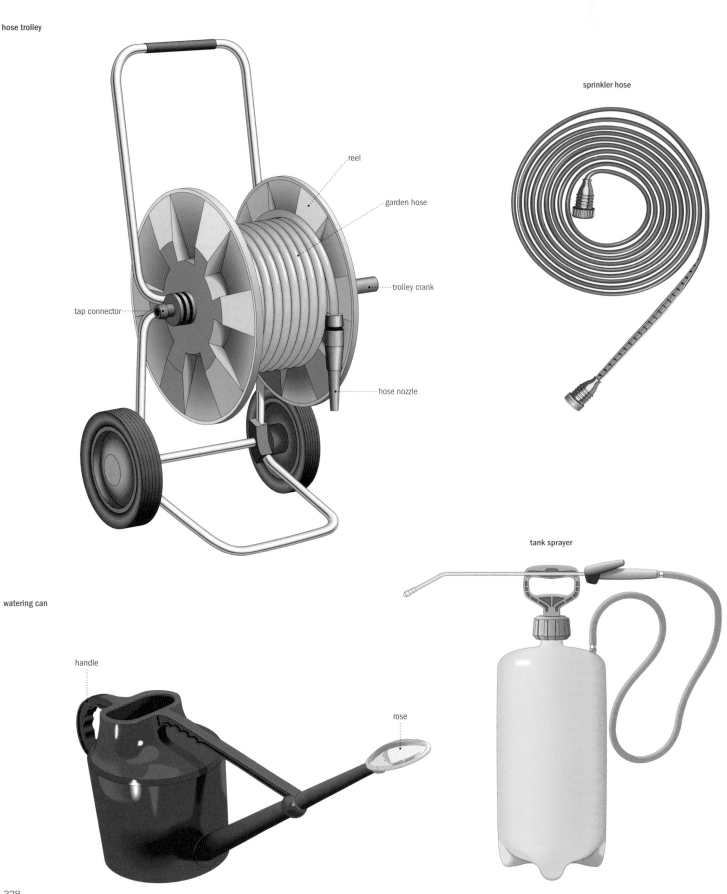

reel

garden hose

trolley crank

tap connector

hose nozzle

sprinkler hose

tank sprayer

watering can

handle

rose

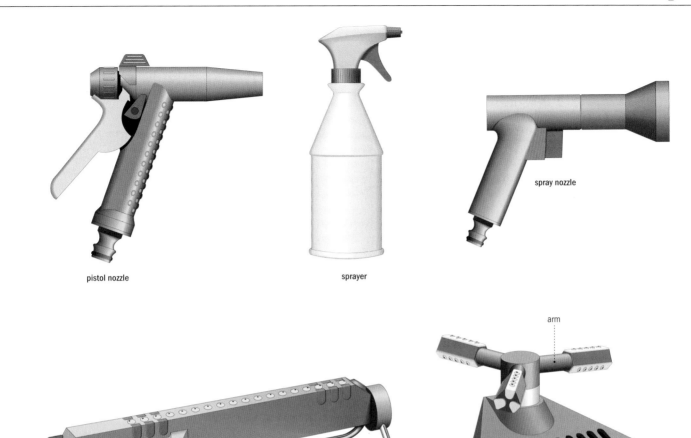

pistol nozzle

sprayer

spray nozzle

oscillating sprinkler

arm

revolving sprinkler

impulse sprinkler

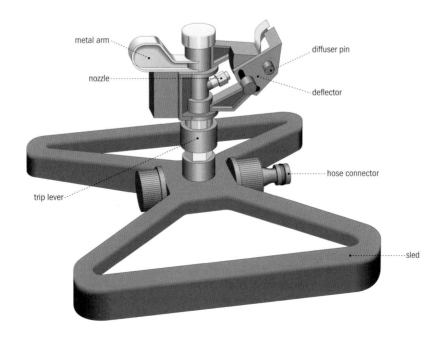

metal arm

nozzle

trip lever

diffuser pin

deflector

hose connector

sled

pruning and cutting tools

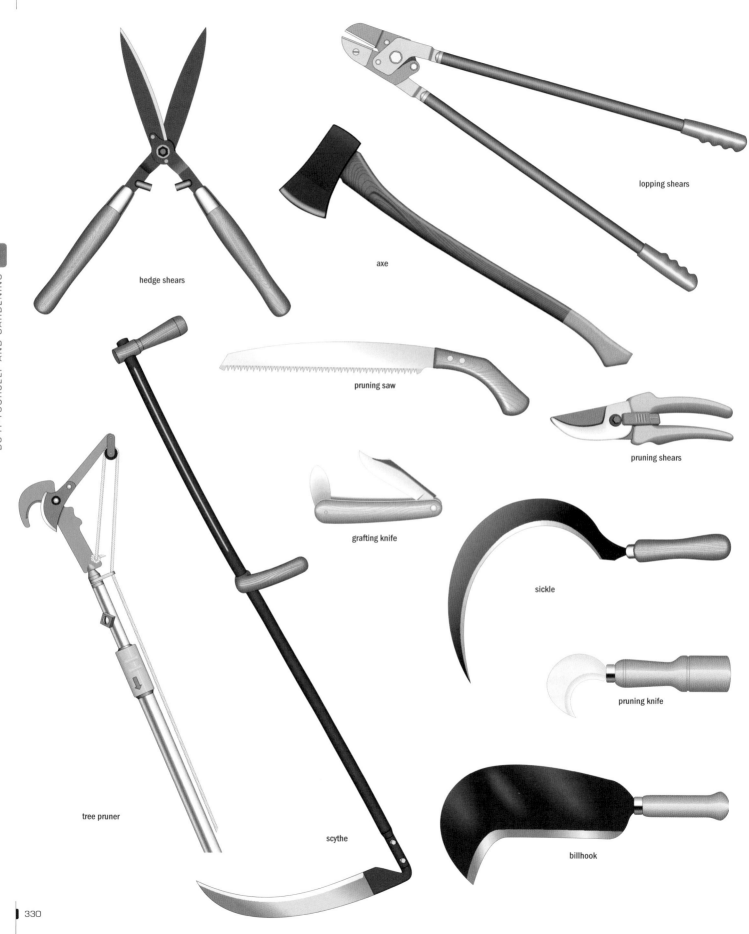

hedge shears

axe

lopping shears

pruning saw

pruning shears

grafting knife

sickle

pruning knife

tree pruner

scythe

billhook

hedge trimmer

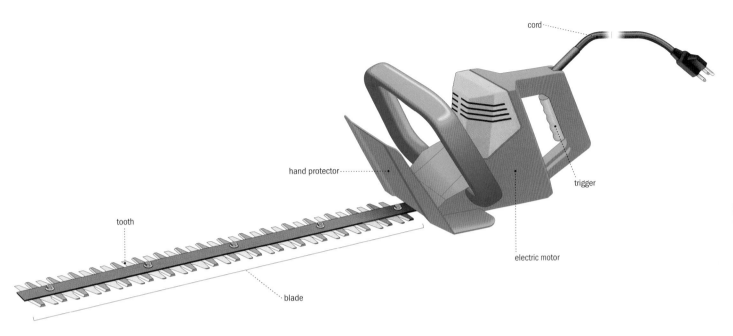

cord

hand protector

tooth

blade

trigger

electric motor

chainsaw

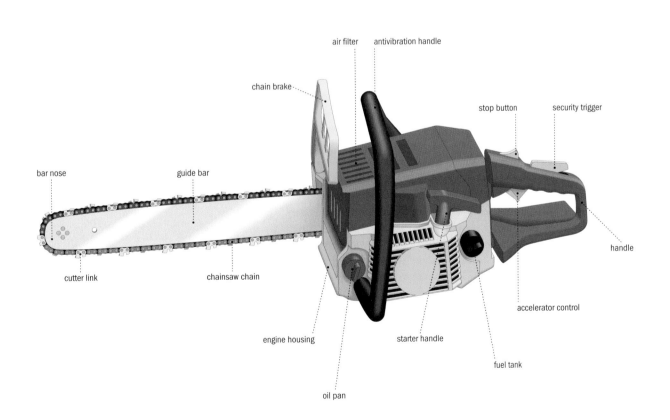

air filter

antivibration handle

chain brake

stop button

security trigger

bar nose

guide bar

handle

cutter link

chainsaw chain

accelerator control

engine housing

starter handle

fuel tank

oil pan

lawn care

edger

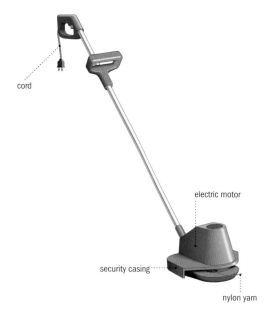

cord

electric motor

security casing

nylon yarn

hand mower

blade

cutting cylinder

power mower

handle

ignition key

speed control

safety handle

grassbox

starter

filler cap

motor

accelerator cable

spark plug

deflector

casing

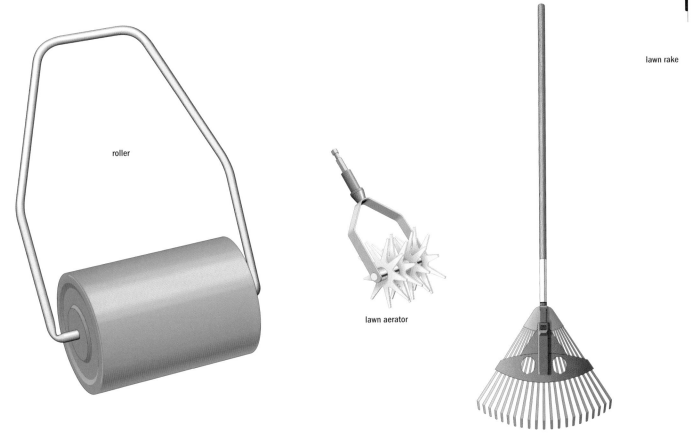

roller

lawn rake

lawn aerator

lawn tractor

seat

ignition key

steering wheel

cruise control lever

mower deck lift lever

hood

brake pedal

rear wheel

forward travel pedal

headlight

reverse travel pedal

deflector

mower deck

gauge wheel

front wheel

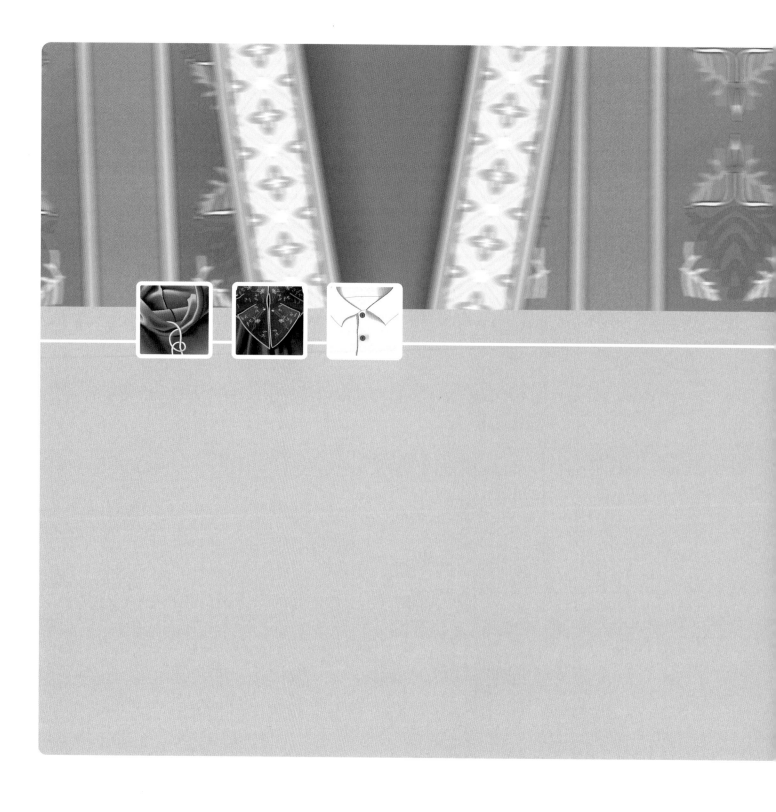

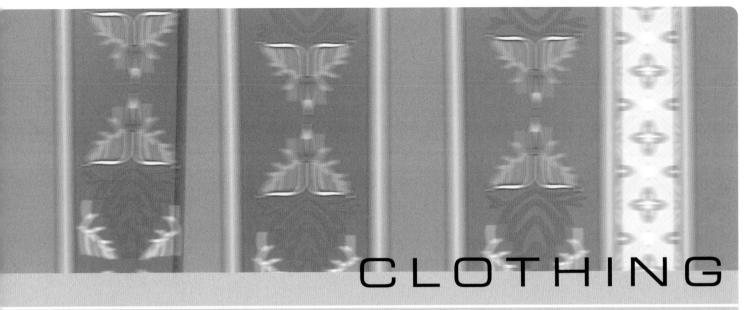

CLOTHING

peplos

fibula

fold

toga

sinus

purple border

stola

palla

chlamys

chiton

floating sleeve

vertical pocket

cotehardie

short sleeve

sleeve

fringe

dress with crinoline

corset

underskirt

shawl

caraco jacket

ruffle

stomacher

bustle

surcoat

dress with panniers

dress with bustle

CLOTHING

frock coat

waistcoat

breeches

justaucorps

vest

cuff

breeches

cape

jacket

houppelande

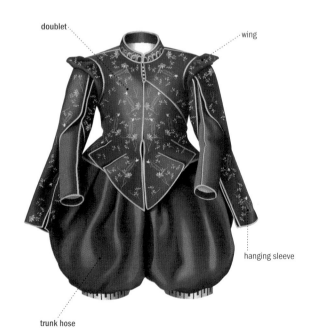

doublet

wing

hanging sleeve

trunk hose

braies

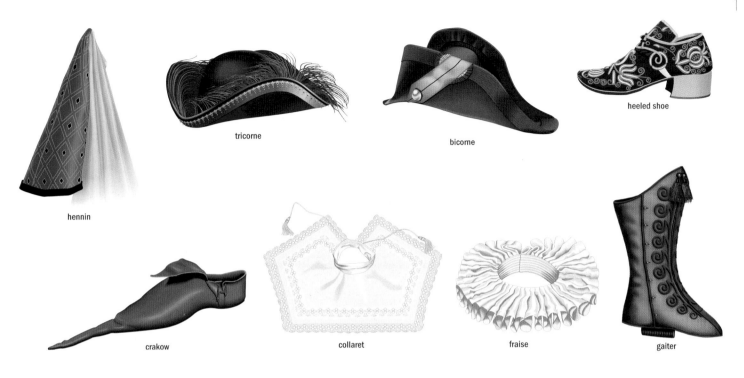

hennin

tricorne

bicorne

heeled shoe

crakow

collaret

fraise

gaiter

CLOTHING

traditional clothing

turban

boubou

caftan

loincloth

fez

headgear

men's headgear

felt hat

hatband

binding

crown

brim

bow

boater

skullcap

derby

garrison cap

top hat

shapka

hunting cap

ear flap

peak

cap

panama

CLOTHING

women's headgear

pillbox hat

cartwheel hat

cloche

toque

gob hat

—————— crown

—— brim

turban

sou'wester

unisex headgear

beret

balaclava

···· peak

stocking cap

felt hat

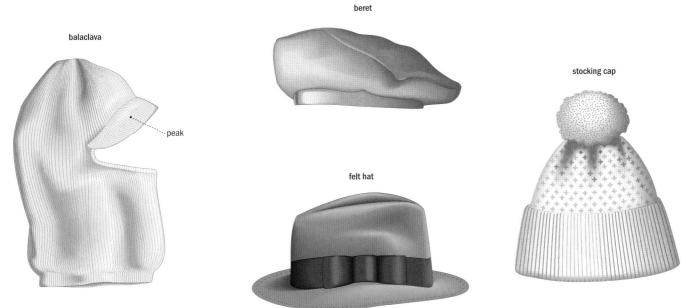

shoes

men's shoes

parts of a shoe

lining

shoelace

cuff

tongue

vamp

heel grip

stitch

quarter

punch hole

outside counter

heel

top lift

waist

nose of the quarter

eyelet tab

tag

perforated toe cap

outsole

eyelet

welt

heavy duty boot

chukka

rubber

bootee

oxford shoe

blucher oxford

342

sandal

ballerina

pump

sling back shoe

one-bar shoe

T-strap shoe

casual shoe

thigh-boot

boot

ankle boot

unisex shoes

mule

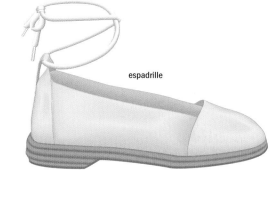

espadrille

tennis shoe

loafer

sandal

moccasin

thong

clog

sandal

hiking boot

CLOTHING

CLOTHING

shoeshine kit

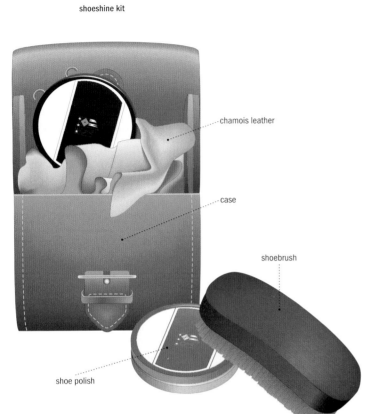

chamois leather

case

shoebrush

shoe polish

shoe polisher

shoehorn

insole

climbing iron

shoetree

shoe rack

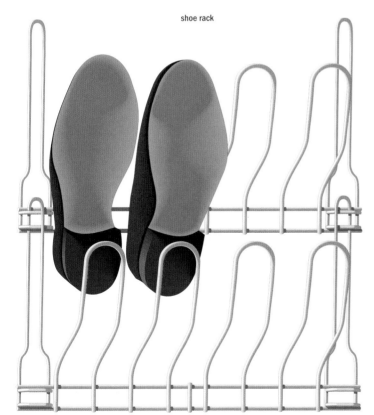

boot jack

gloves

men's gloves

back of a glove   palm of a glove

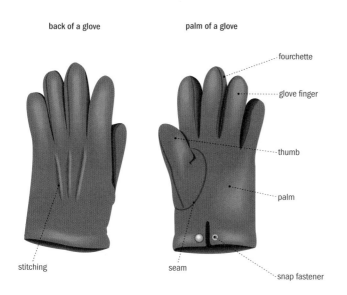

fourchette

glove finger

thumb

palm

stitching

seam

snap fastener

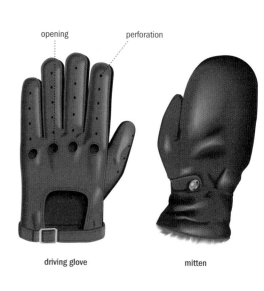

opening   perforation

driving glove   mitten

women's gloves

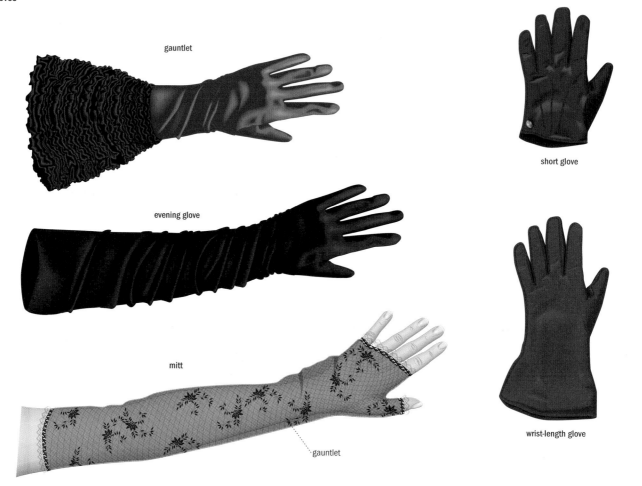

gauntlet

evening glove

mitt

gauntlet

short glove

wrist-length glove

do not wash

hand wash in lukewarm water

machine wash in lukewarm water at a gentle setting/reduced agitation

machine wash in warm water at a gentle setting/reduced agitation

machine wash in warm water at a normal setting

machine wash in hot water at a normal setting

do not use chlorine bleach

use chlorine bleach as directed

CLOTHING

hang to dry

dry flat

do not tumble dry

tumble dry at medium temperature

tumble dry at low temperature

drip dry

do not iron

iron at low setting

iron at medium setting

iron at high setting

left: American symbols   right: European symbols

men's clothing

jackets

double-breasted jacket

collar

peaked lapel

lining

breast welt pocket

sleeve

flap

outside ticket pocket

patch pocket

side back vent

vest

V-neck

lining

welt

front

seam

welt pocket

adjustable waist tab

single-breasted jacket

lapel

notch

lining

front

pocket handkerchief

flap pocket

back

sleeve

center back vent

CLOTHING

shirt

yoke

collar

set-in sleeve

collar point

breast pocket

buttoned placket

front

pointed tab end

button

cuff

shirttail

collar stay

buttondown collar

ascot tie

bow tie

spread collar

necktie

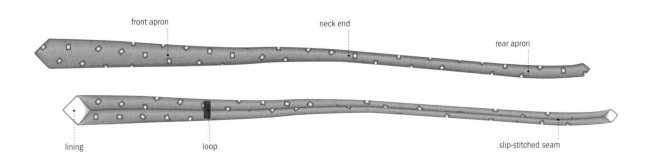

front apron

neck end

rear apron

lining

loop

slip-stitched seam

CLOTHING

pants

belt loop

waistband

front top pocket

knife pleat

waistband extension

fly

crease

cuff

back pocket

suspender clip

suspenders

elastic webbing

adjustment slide

leather end

button loop

belt

top stitching

panel

tip

punch hole

belt loop

tongue

buckle

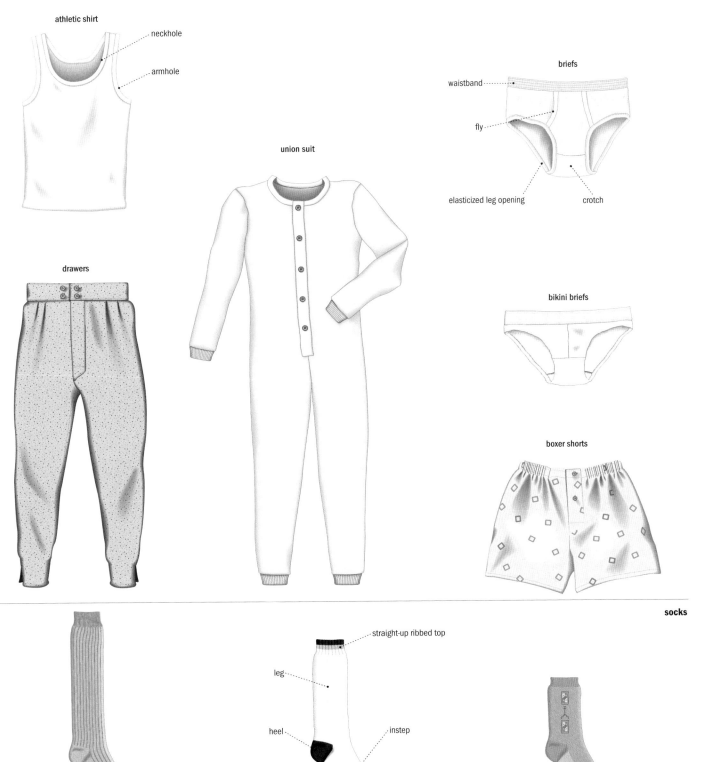

athletic shirt

neckhole

armhole

briefs

waistband

fly

elasticized leg opening

crotch

union suit

drawers

bikini briefs

boxer shorts

socks

straight-up ribbed top

leg

heel

instep

sole

toe

executive length

mid-calf length

ankle length

coats

raincoat

collar

raglan sleeve

notched lapel

tab

broad welt side pocket

buttonhole

side panel

overcoat

notched lapel

breast pocket

breast dart

flap pocket

trench coat

two-way collar

epaulet

raglan sleeve

gun flap

sleeve strap loop

double-breasted buttoning

belt

sleeve strap

belt loop

broad welt side pocket

frame

three-quarter coat

parka

sheepskin jacket

snap-fastening tab

zipper

duffle coat

hood

yoke

frog

patch pocket

toggle fastening

jacket

windbreaker

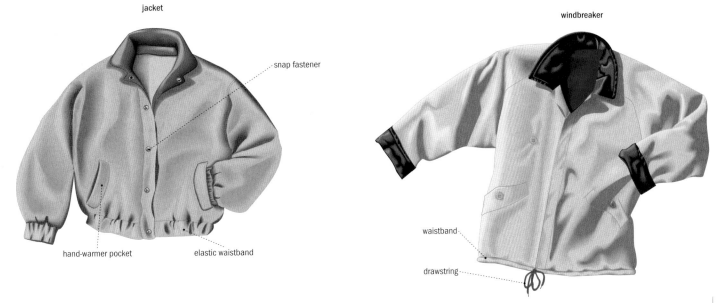

snap fastener

hand-warmer pocket

elastic waistband

waistband

drawstring

sweaters

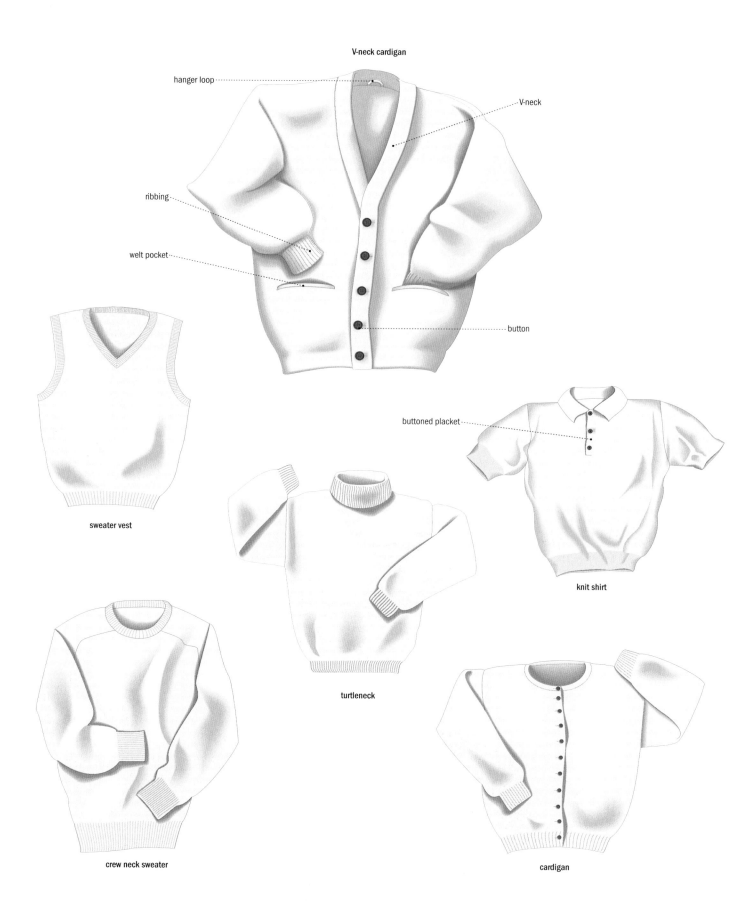

V-neck cardigan

hanger loop

V-neck

ribbing

welt pocket

button

buttoned placket

sweater vest

turtleneck

knit shirt

crew neck sweater

cardigan

coats

suit

jacket

skirt

raglan

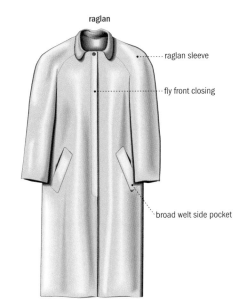

raglan sleeve

fly front closing

broad welt side pocket

top coat

pelerine

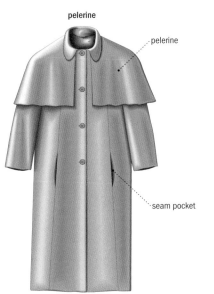

pelerine

seam pocket

cape

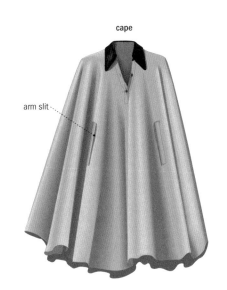

arm slit

pea jacket

tailored collar

hand-warmer pocket

mock pocket

overcoat

car coat

jacket

poncho

CLOTHING

examples of dresses

CLOTHING

sheath dress

princess dress

coat dress

polo dress

house dress

shirtwaist dress

drop waist dress

trapeze dress

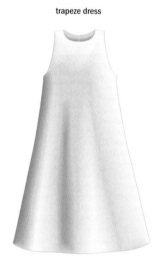

sundress

wraparound dress

tunic dress

jumper

examples of skirts

gored skirt

kilt

sarong

wraparound skirt

sheath skirt

ruffled skirt

straight skirt

yoke skirt

gather skirt

culottes

examples of pleats

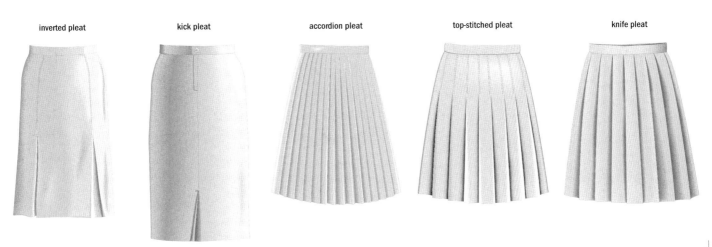

inverted pleat

kick pleat

accordion pleat

top-stitched pleat

knife pleat

CLOTHING

examples of pants

shorts

Bermuda shorts

knickers

pedal pushers

jeans

ski pants

footstrap

jumpsuit

overalls

bell bottoms

jackets, vest and sweaters

bolero

spencer

blazer

safari jacket

gusset pocket

vest

twin-set

crew neck sweater

cardigan

examples of blouses

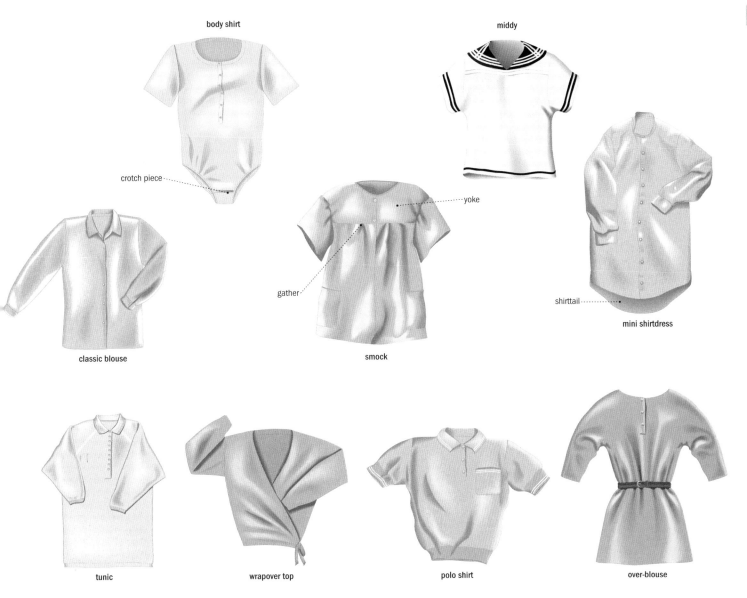

body shirt

crotch piece

middy

classic blouse

yoke

gather

smock

shirttail

mini shirtdress

tunic

wrapover top

polo shirt

over-blouse

CLOTHING

examples of pockets

gusset pocket

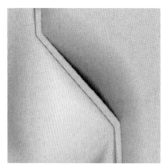

inset pocket

welt pocket

seam pocket

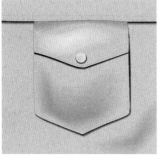

flap pocket

broad welt side pocket

patch pocket

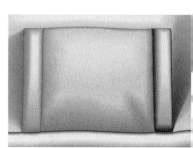

hand-warmer pouch

examples of sleeves

puff sleeve

cap sleeve

three-quarter sleeve

epaulet sleeve

French cuff

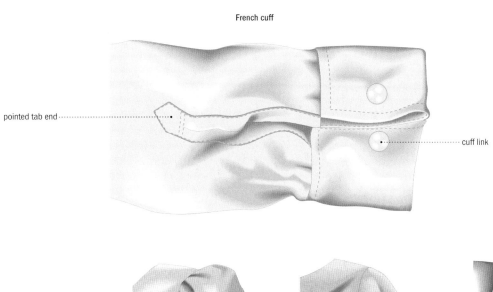

pointed tab end

cuff link

batwing sleeve

leg-of-mutton sleeve

bishop sleeve

kimono sleeve

raglan sleeve

pagoda sleeve

shirt sleeve

tailored sleeve

examples of collars

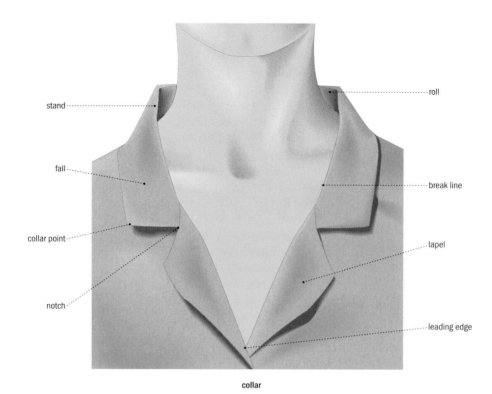

stand ··········· roll
fall ··· break line
collar point ··· lapel
notch ··· leading edge

collar

dog ear collar

shawl collar

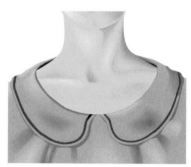

Peter Pan collar

shirt collar

tailored collar

bow collar

jabot

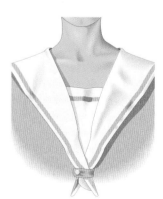

sailor collar

CLOTHING

CLOTHING

mandarin collar

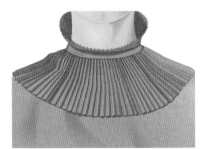

collaret

bertha collar

turtleneck

cowl neck

polo collar

stand-up collar

necklines and necks

plunging neckline

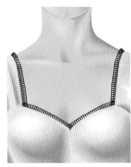

sweetheart neckline

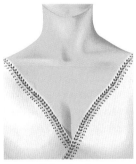

V-shaped neck

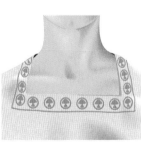

square neck

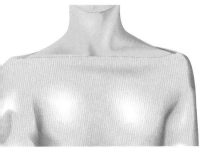

bateau neck

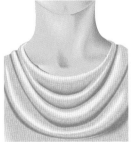

draped neck

draped neckline

round neck

nightwear

nightgown

baby doll

kimono

bathrobe

pajamas

negligee

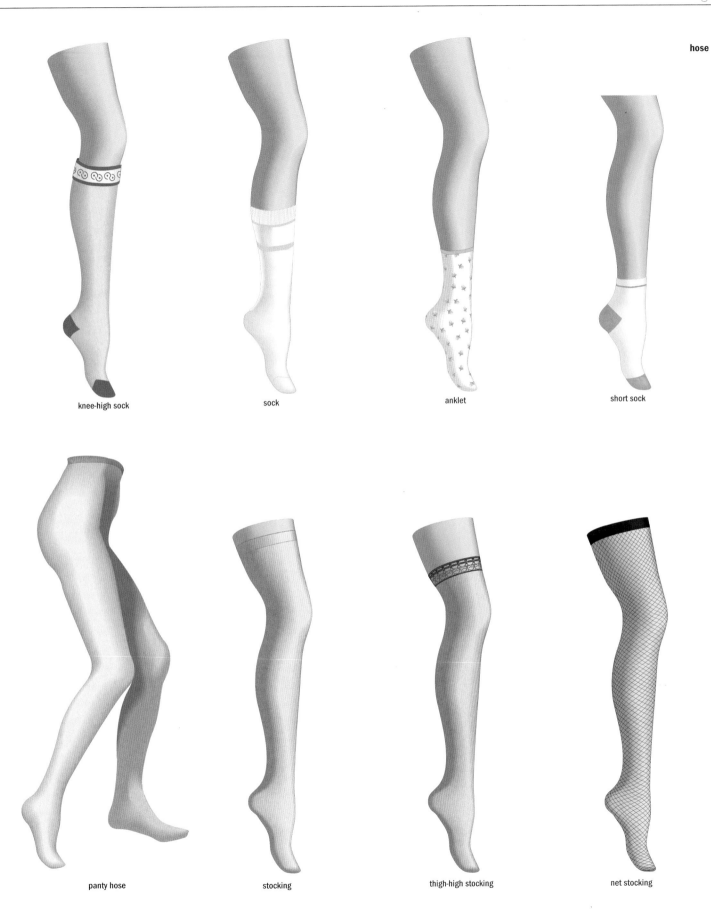

knee-high sock

sock

anklet

short sock

panty hose

stocking

thigh-high stocking

net stocking

underwear

CLOTHING

corselette

camisole

teddy

body suit

panty corselette

half-slip

princess seaming

foundation slip

slip

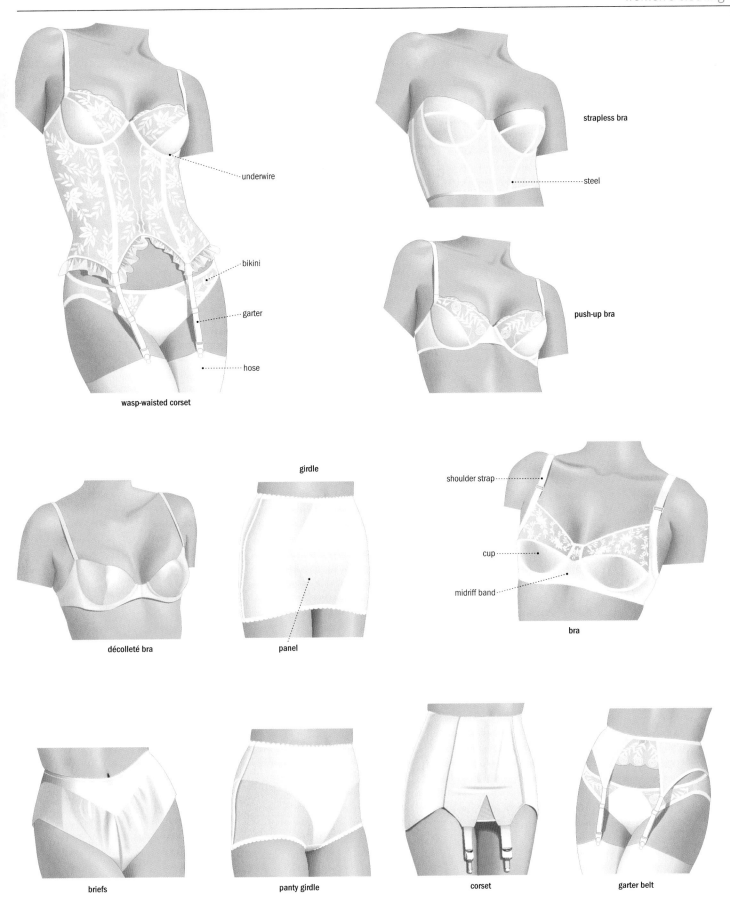

underwire

strapless bra

steel

bikini

garter

push-up bra

hose

wasp-waisted corset

girdle

shoulder strap

décolleté bra

panel

cup

midriff band

bra

briefs

panty girdle

corset

garter belt

newborn children's clothing

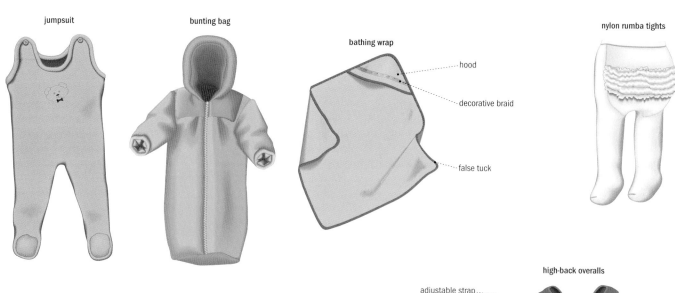

jumpsuit

bunting bag

bathing wrap
- hood
- decorative braid
- false tuck

nylon rumba tights

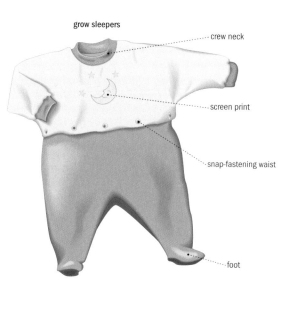

grow sleepers
- crew neck
- screen print
- snap-fastening waist
- foot

high-back overalls
- adjustable strap
- bib
- patch pocket
- top stitching
- fly
- inside-leg snap-fastening

shirt

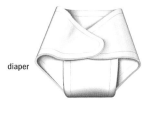

diaper

bib

ruffled rumba pants
- ruching

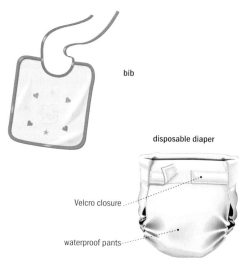

disposable diaper
- Velcro closure
- waterproof pants

blanket sleepers

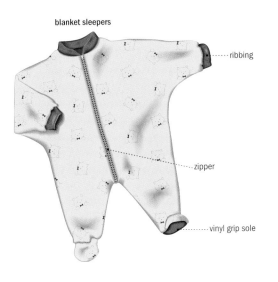

ribbing

zipper

vinyl grip sole

sleepers

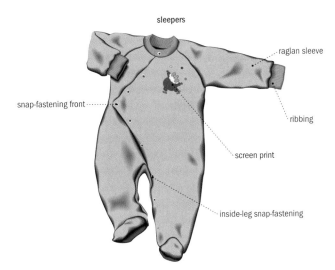

raglan sleeve

snap-fastening front

ribbing

screen print

inside-leg snap-fastening

children's clothing

overalls

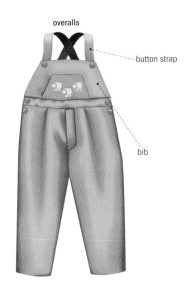

button strap

bib

snowsuit

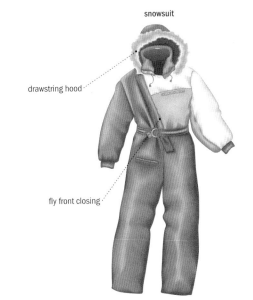

drawstring hood

fly front closing

pajama

T-shirt dress

rompers

training set

tank top

shorts

jumpsuit

sportswear

running shoe

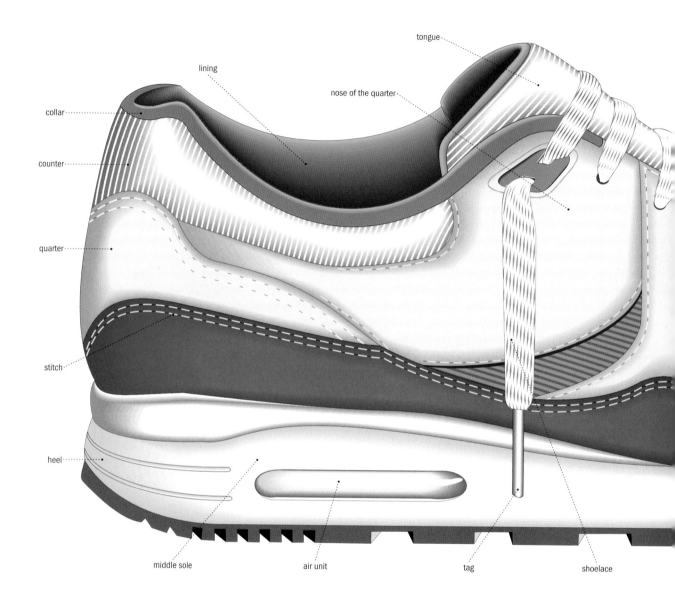

tongue

lining

nose of the quarter

collar

counter

quarter

stitch

heel

middle sole   air unit   tag   shoelace

training suit

sweat pants

hooded sweat shirt

sweat shirt

swimming trunks

swimsuit

leotard

eyelet

vamp

punch hole

footless tights

leg-warmer

stud

outsole

pants

anorak

boxer shorts

tank top

CLOTHING

PERSONAL ADORNMENT AND ARTICLES

jewelry

earrings

clip earrings

screw earring

pierced earrings

drop earrings

hoop earrings

necklaces

rope necklace

opera-length necklace

matinee-length necklace

velvet-band choker

pendant

bib necklace

choker

locket

brilliant cut facets

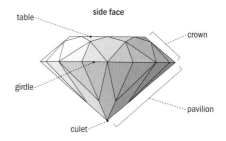

side face

table
crown
girdle
pavilion
culet

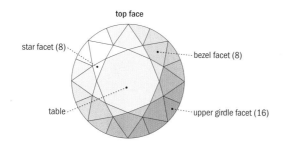

top face

star facet (8)
bezel facet (8)
table
upper girdle facet (16)

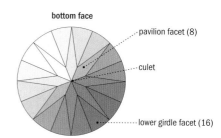

bottom face

pavilion facet (8)
culet
lower girdle facet (16)

cuts for gemstones

step cut

rose cut

table cut

cabochon cut

pear-shaped cut

emerald cut

brilliant full cut

eight cut

scissors cut

briolette cut

baguette cut

French cut

oval cut

navette cut

semiprecious stones

amethyst

lapis lazuli

aquamarine

topaz

tourmaline

opal

turquoise

garnet

precious stones

emerald

sapphire

diamond

ruby

jewelry

rings

parts of a ring

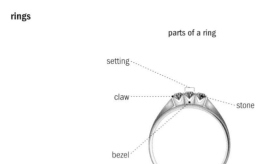

setting

claw

stone

bezel

signet ring

class ring

band ring

engagement ring

wedding ring

solitaire ring

bracelets

charms

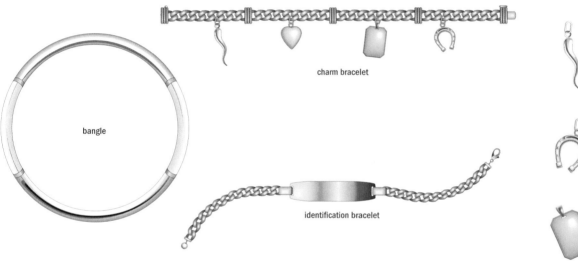

charm bracelet

bangle

identification bracelet

horn

horseshoe

nameplate

pins

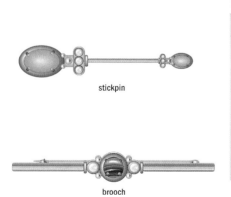

stickpin

brooch

tie bar

tiepin

collar bar

nail care

manicure set

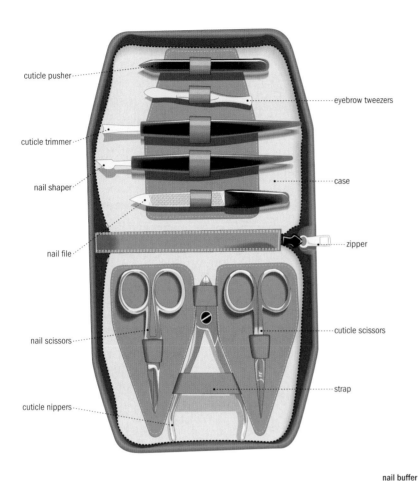

cuticle pusher

eyebrow tweezers

cuticle trimmer

nail shaper

case

nail file

zipper

nail scissors

cuticle scissors

cuticle nippers

strap

nail enamel

safety scissors

nail buffer

chamois leather

nail clippers

lever

jaw

nail cleaner

folding nail file

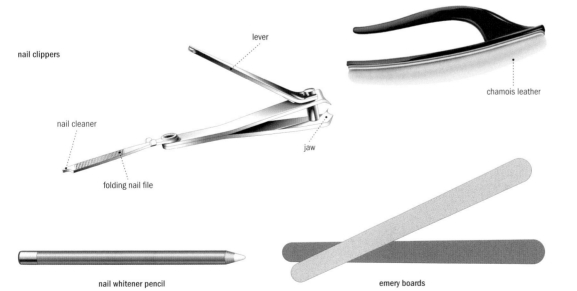

nail whitener pencil

emery boards

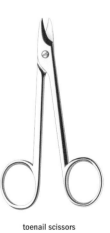

toenail scissors

makeup

facial makeup

compact

blusher brush

pressed powder

powder puff

powder blusher

synthetic sponge

loose powder

loose powder brush

liquid foundation

fan brush

eye makeup

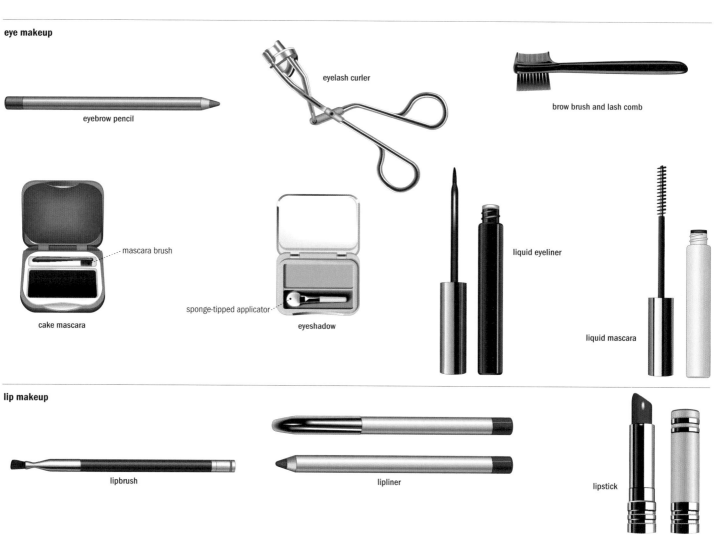

eyelash curler

brow brush and lash comb

eyebrow pencil

mascara brush

liquid eyeliner

sponge-tipped applicator

cake mascara

eyeshadow

liquid mascara

lip makeup

lipbrush

lipliner

lipstick

body care

stopper

bottle

eau de parfum

eau de toilette

bubble bath

haircolor

toilet soap

deodorant

hair conditioner

shampoo

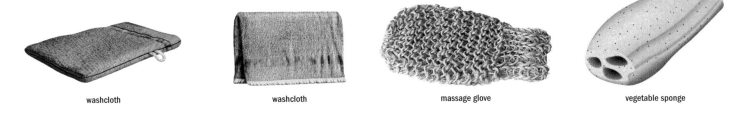

washcloth

washcloth

massage glove

vegetable sponge

bath sheet

bath towel

bath brush

natural sponge

back brush

hairdressing

hairbrushes

flat-back brush

round brush

quill brush

vent brush

combs

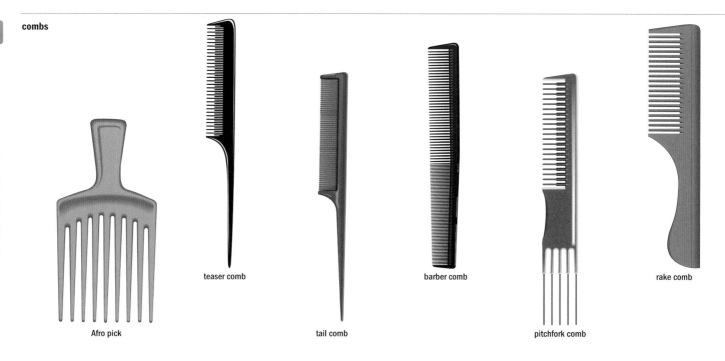

Afro pick

teaser comb

tail comb

barber comb

pitchfork comb

rake comb

hair roller

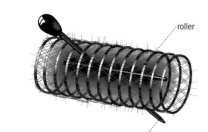

roller

hair roller pin

wave clip

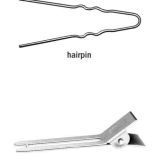

hairpin

hair clip

bobby pin

barrette

lighted mirror

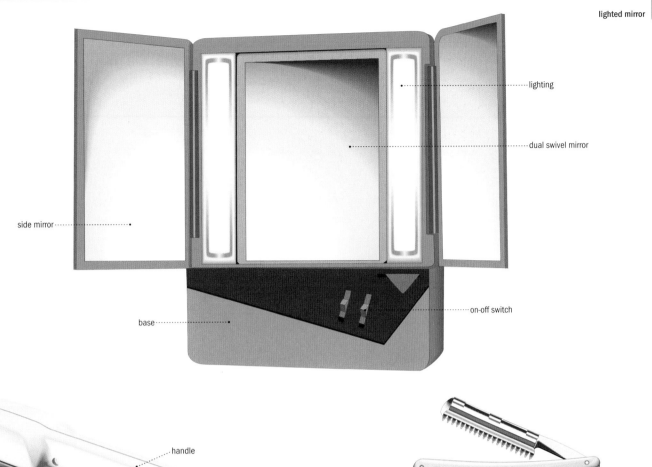

lighting

dual swivel mirror

side mirror

on-off switch

base

straightening iron

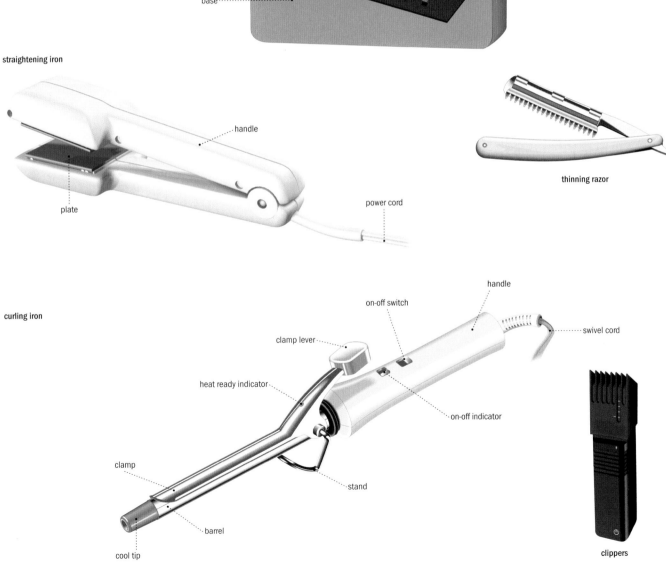

handle

plate

power cord

thinning razor

curling iron

handle

on-off switch

clamp lever

swivel cord

heat ready indicator

on-off indicator

clamp

stand

cool tip

barrel

clippers

hairdressing

haircutting scissors

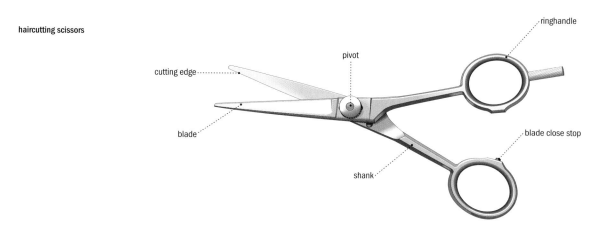

cutting edge

pivot

ringhandle

blade

blade close stop

shank

notched single-edged thinning scissors

notched double-edged thinning scissors

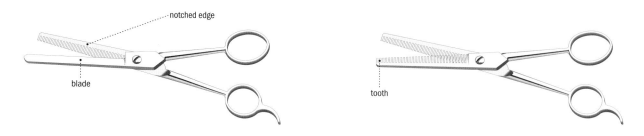

notched edge

blade

tooth

hair dryer

barrel

fan housing

air-inlet grille

air-outlet grille

speed selector switch

on-off switch

heat selector switch

air concentrator

handle

hang-up ring

power supply cord

shaving

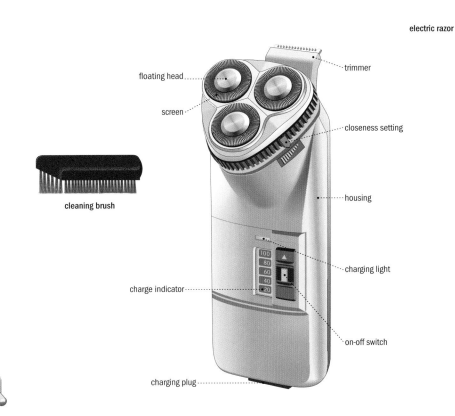

electric razor

floating head

screen

trimmer

closeness setting

housing

charging light

charge indicator

on-off switch

charging plug

shaving foam

power cord

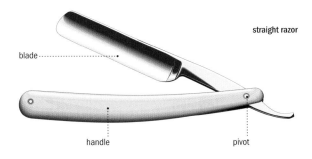

cleaning brush

shaving brush

plug adapter

bristle

after shave

straight razor

blade

handle

pivot

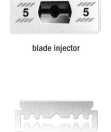

shaving mug

blade injector

double-edged blade

double-edged razor

disposable razor

head

collar

handle

dental care

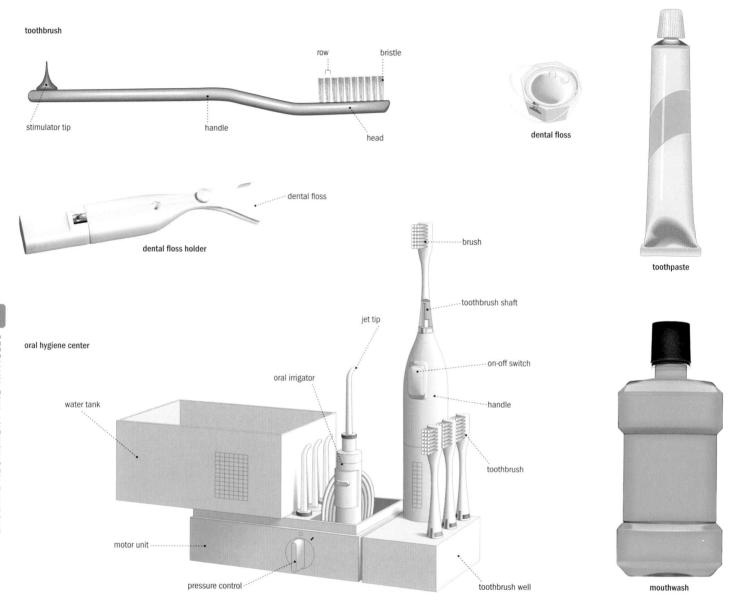

toothbrush

row

bristle

stimulator tip

handle

head

dental floss

toothpaste

dental floss holder

dental floss

brush

jet tip

toothbrush shaft

oral hygiene center

oral irrigator

on-off switch

water tank

handle

toothbrush

motor unit

pressure control

toothbrush well

mouthwash

contact lenses

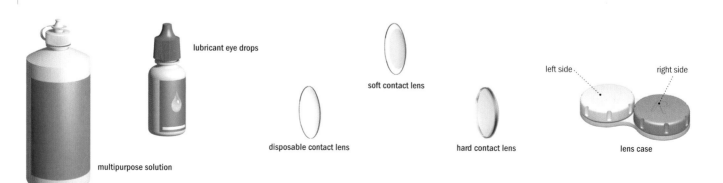

lubricant eye drops

soft contact lens

left side

right side

multipurpose solution

disposable contact lens

hard contact lens

lens case

eyeglasses

eyeglasses parts

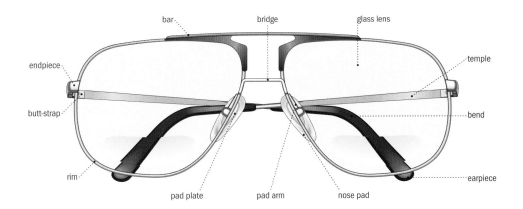

bar · bridge · glass lens

endpiece · temple

butt-strap · bend

rim · earpiece

pad plate · pad arm · nose pad

frames

distance · bifocal lens

reading

rim

examples of eyeglasses

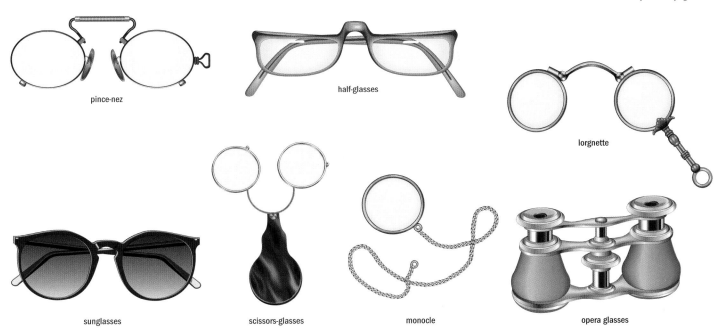

pince-nez

half-glasses

lorgnette

sunglasses

scissors-glasses

monocle

opera glasses

leather goods

attaché case

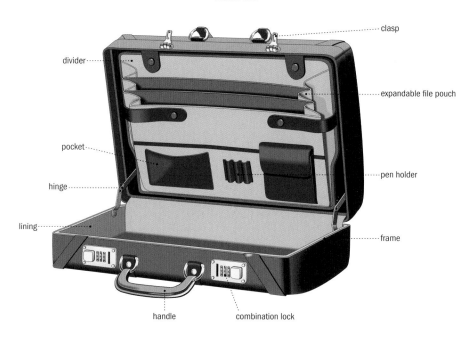

clasp

divider

expandable file pouch

pocket

pen holder

hinge

lining

frame

handle

combination lock

bottom-fold portfolio

briefcase

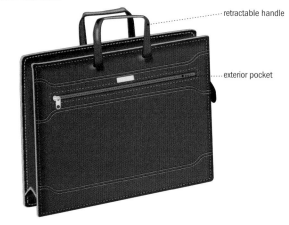

retractable handle

exterior pocket

tab

key lock

gusset

checkbook/secretary clutch

card case

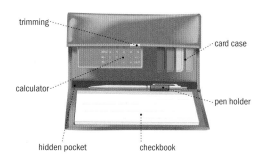

trimming

card case

calculator

pen holder

hidden pocket

checkbook

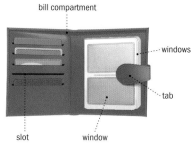

bill compartment

windows

tab

slot

window

wallet

coin purse

key case

purse

passport case

billfold

writing case

checkbook

eyeglasses case

underarm portfolio

handbags

drawstring bag

eyelet

drawstring

front pocket

satchel bag

handle

flap

clasp

lock

handbags

PERSONAL ADORNMENT AND ARTICLES

box bag

drawstring bag

shoulder bag

buckle

shoulder strap

muff

hobo bag

accordion bag

gusset

tote bag

men's bag

sea bag

duffel bag

carrier bag

shopping bag

luggage

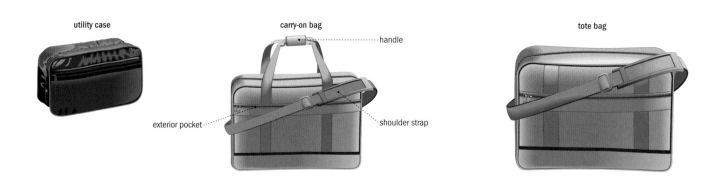

utility case

carry-on bag

handle

exterior pocket

shoulder strap

tote bag

luggage

garment bag

zipper

Pullman case

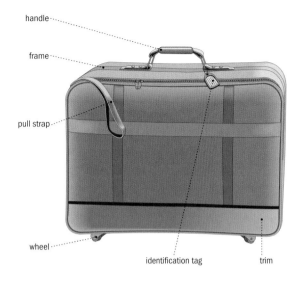

handle

frame

pull strap

wheel

identification tag

trim

vanity case

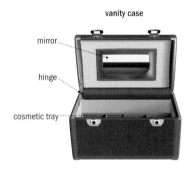

mirror

hinge

cosmetic tray

weekender

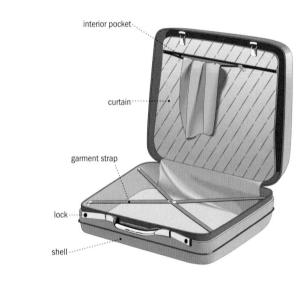

interior pocket

curtain

garment strap

lock

shell

luggage carrier

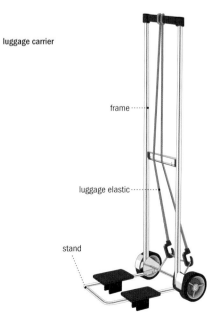

frame

luggage elastic

stand

trunk

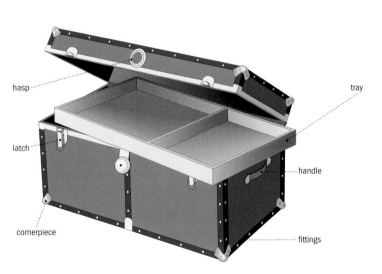

hasp

latch

cornerpiece

tray

handle

fittings

smoking accessories

pipe

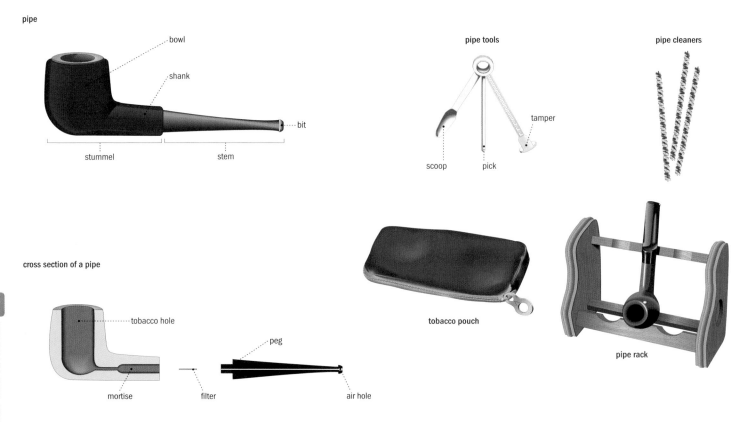

bowl

shank

bit

stummel

stem

pipe tools

scoop

pick

tamper

pipe cleaners

cross section of a pipe

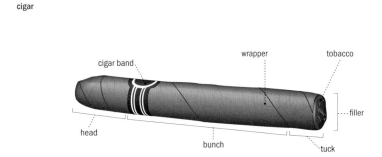

tobacco hole

peg

mortise

filter

air hole

tobacco pouch

pipe rack

cigar cutter

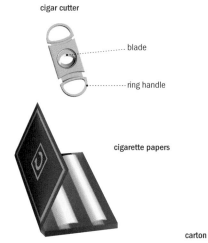

blade

ring handle

cigar

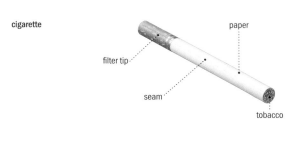

cigar band

wrapper

tobacco

filler

head

bunch

tuck

cigarette papers

carton

cigarette

paper

filter tip

seam

tobacco

cigarette pack

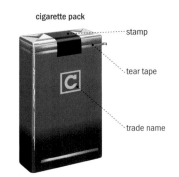

stamp

tear tape

trade name

smoking accessories

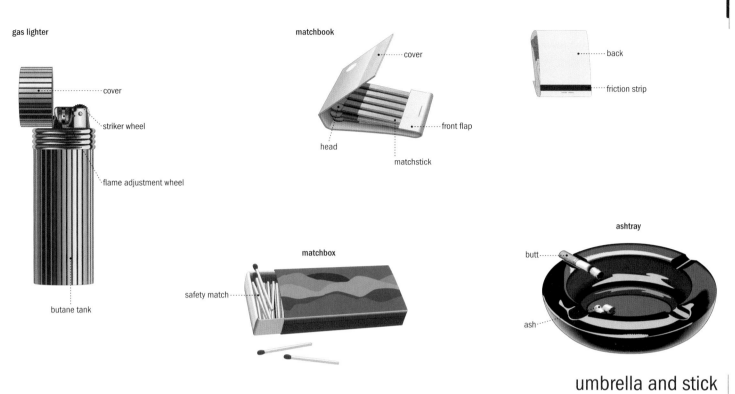

gas lighter
- cover
- striker wheel
- flame adjustment wheel
- butane tank

matchbook
- cover
- head
- front flap
- matchstick

- back
- friction strip

matchbox
- safety match

ashtray
- butt
- ash

umbrella and stick

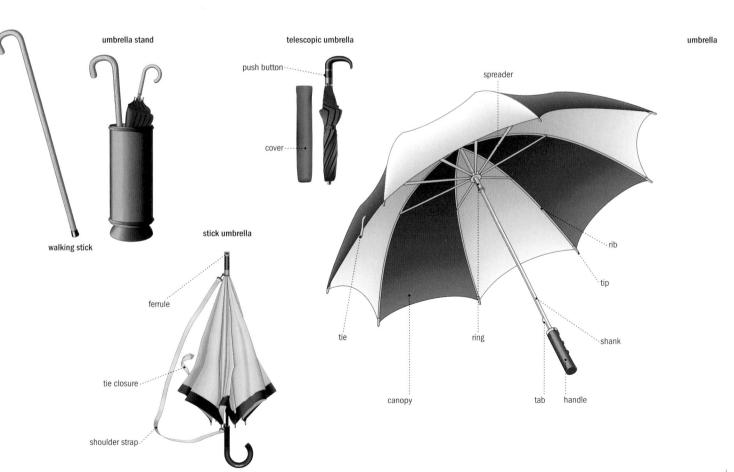

umbrella stand

telescopic umbrella
- push button
- cover

umbrella
- spreader
- rib
- tip
- shank
- tie
- ring
- canopy
- tab
- handle

walking stick

stick umbrella
- ferrule
- tie closure
- shoulder strap

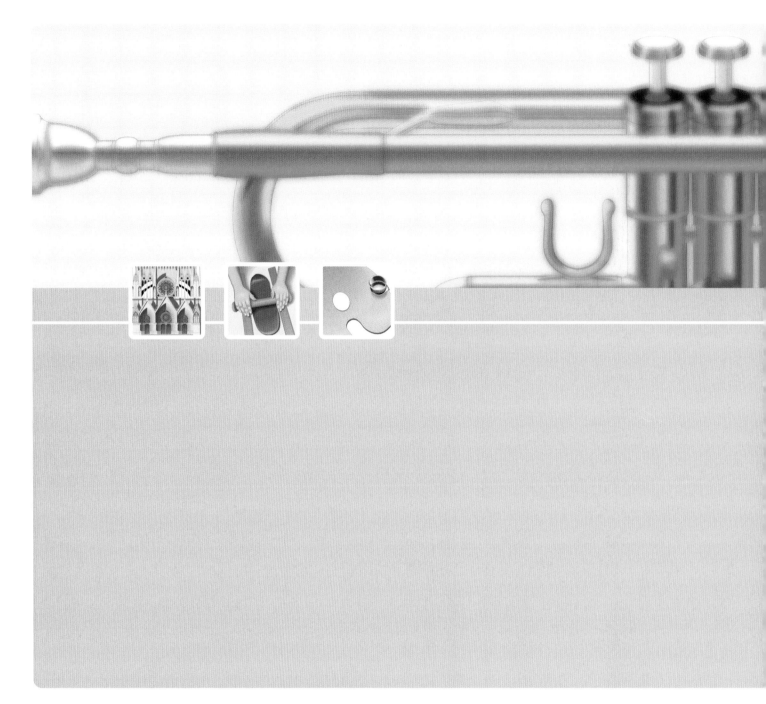

ARTS AND ARCHITECTURE

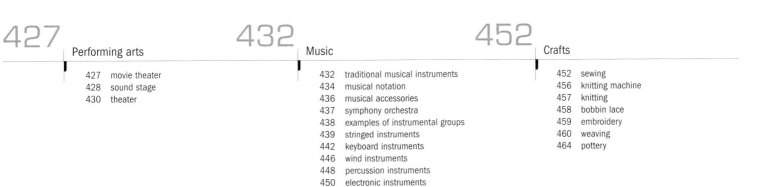

museum

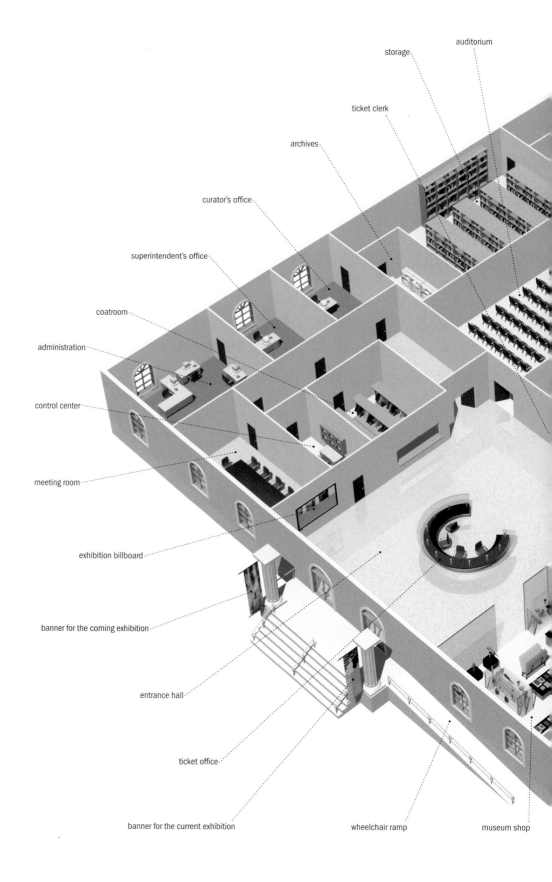

storage
auditorium
ticket clerk
archives
curator's office
superintendent's office
coatroom
administration
control center
meeting room
exhibition billboard
banner for the coming exhibition
entrance hall
ticket office
banner for the current exhibition
wheelchair ramp
museum shop

audioguide

ARTS AND ARCHITECTURE

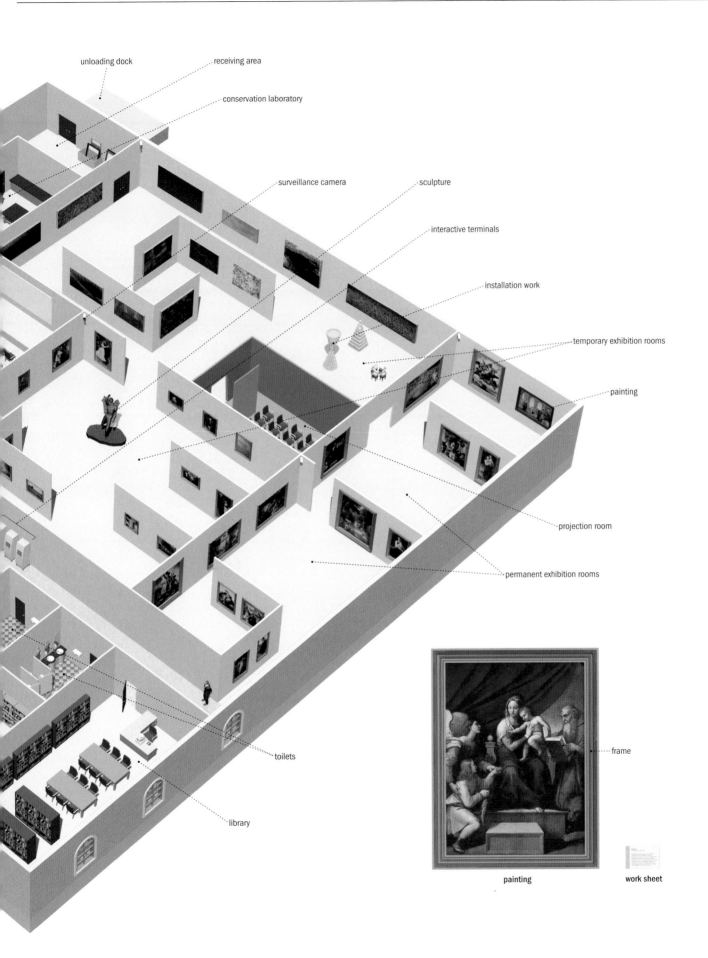

unloading dock

receiving area

conservation laboratory

surveillance camera

sculpture

interactive terminals

installation work

temporary exhibition rooms

painting

projection room

permanent exhibition rooms

toilets

library

frame

painting

work sheet

painting and drawing

major techniques

ink drawing

charcoal drawing

oil painting

watercolor

gouache

felt tip pen drawing

dry pastel drawing

oil pastel drawing

colored pencil drawing

wax crayon drawing

equipment

oil pastel

wax crayons

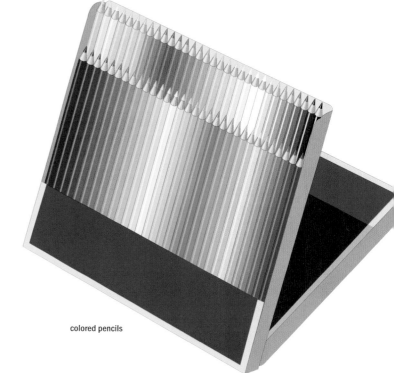
colored pencils

soft pastel

felt tip pen

ink

oil paint

watercolor/gouache tube

marker pen

charcoal

watercolor/gouache cakes

spatula

painting knife

reservoir-nib pen

flat brush

sumi-e brush

fan brush

brush

painting and drawing

color chart

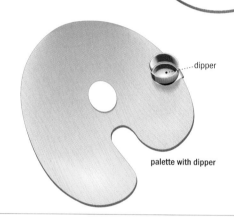

palette with hollows

dipper

palette with dipper

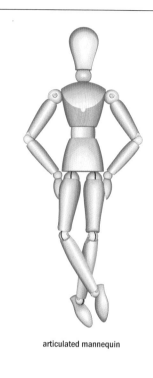

articulated mannequin

airbrush

cross section of an airbrush

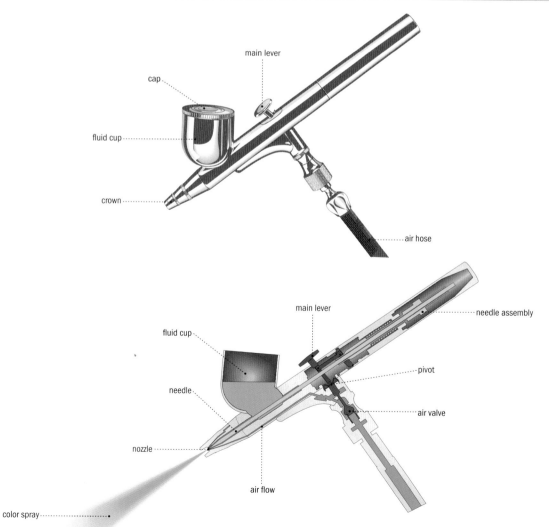

main lever

cap

fluid cup

crown

air hose

main lever

fluid cup

needle assembly

needle

pivot

air valve

nozzle

air flow

color spray

drafting table

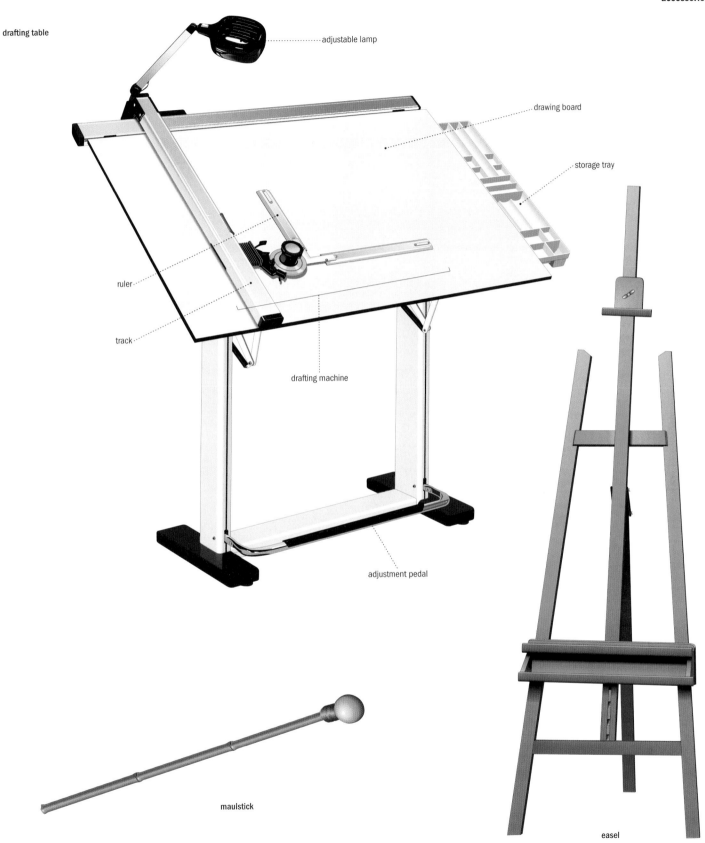

adjustable lamp

drawing board

storage tray

ruler

track

drafting machine

adjustment pedal

maulstick

easel

painting and drawing

color circle

primary colors

secondary colors

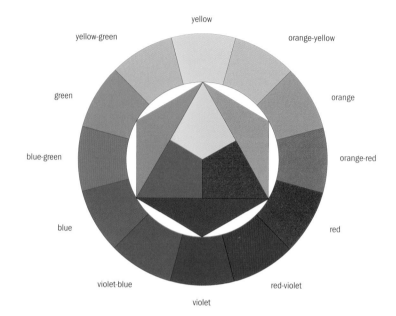

yellow

yellow-green

orange-yellow

green

orange

blue-green

orange-red

blue

red

violet-blue

red-violet

violet

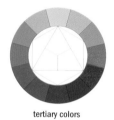

tertiary colors

utility liquids

fixative

turpentine

linseed oil

varnish

supports

paper

cardboard

canvas

panel

steps

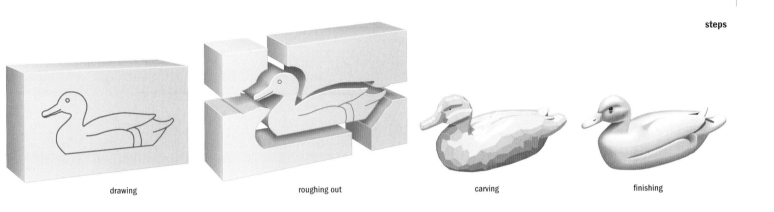

drawing

roughing out

carving

finishing

examples of tools

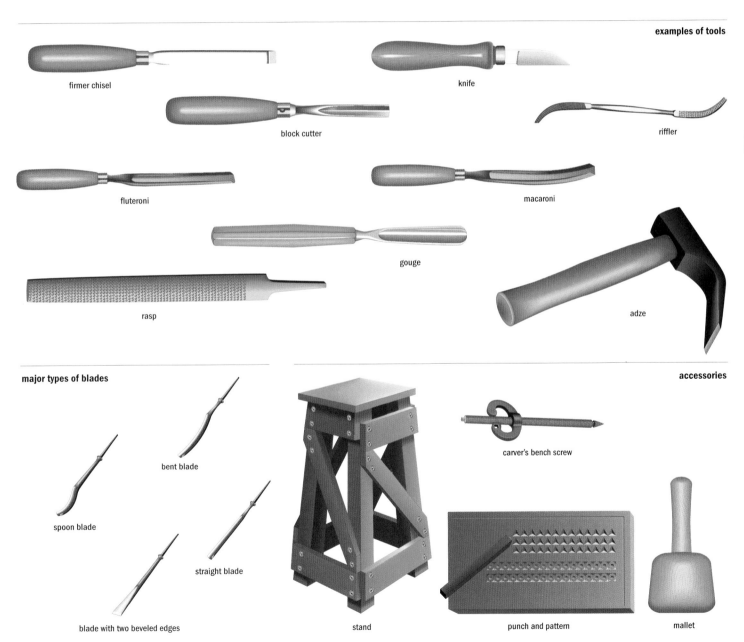

firmer chisel

knife

block cutter

riffler

fluteroni

macaroni

gouge

rasp

adze

major types of blades

accessories

bent blade

spoon blade

straight blade

carver's bench screw

blade with two beveled edges

stand

punch and pattern

mallet

ARTS AND ARCHITECTURE

pyramid

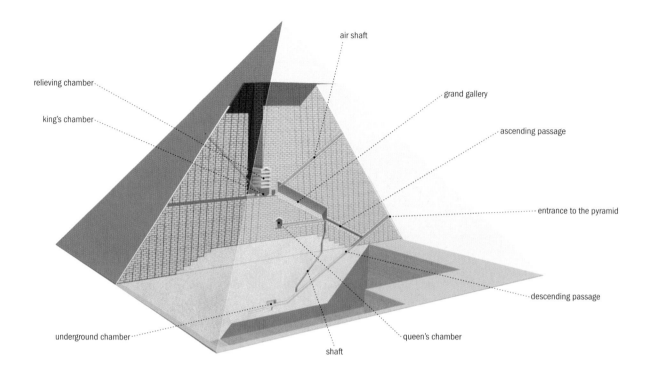

relieving chamber

king's chamber

air shaft

grand gallery

ascending passage

entrance to the pyramid

descending passage

underground chamber

queen's chamber

shaft

Greek theater

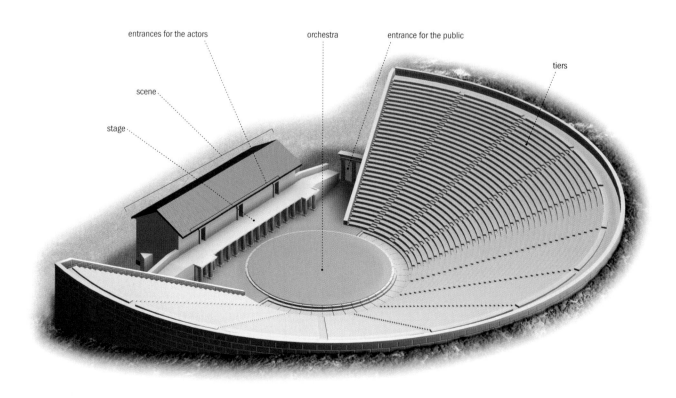

entrances for the actors

orchestra

entrance for the public

tiers

scene

stage

Greek temple

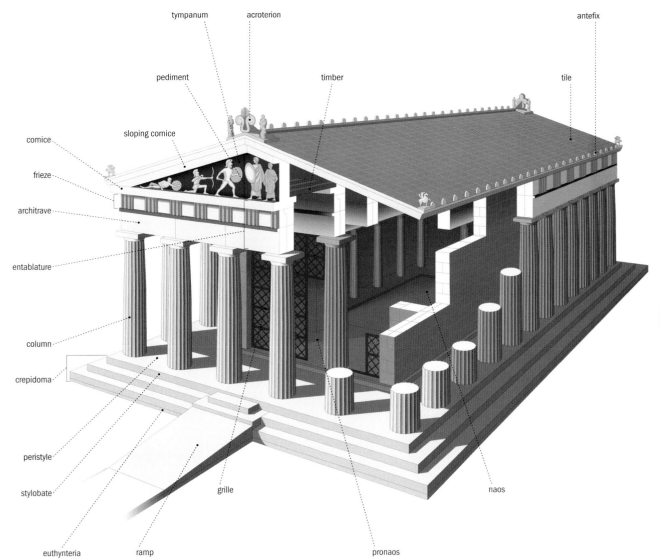

tympanum

acroterion

antefix

pediment

timber

tile

sloping cornice

cornice

frieze

architrave

entablature

column

crepidoma

peristyle

stylobate

euthynteria

ramp

grille

pronaos

naos

plan

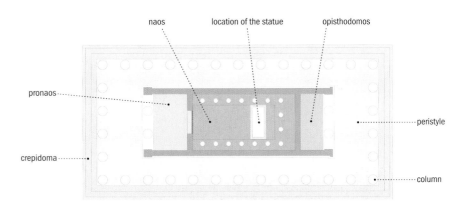

naos

location of the statue

opisthodomos

pronaos

peristyle

crepidoma

column

architectural styles

Doric order

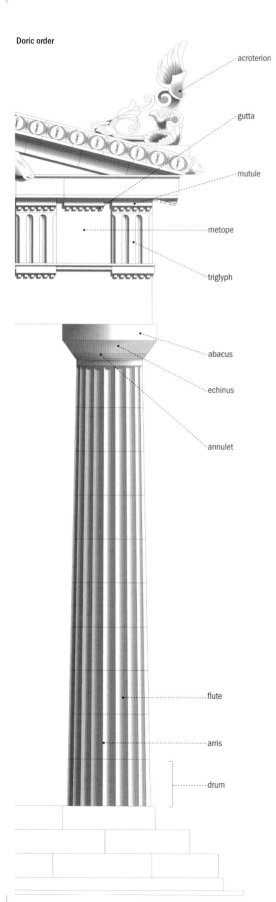

acroterion

gutta

mutule

metope

triglyph

abacus

echinus

annulet

flute

arris

drum

Ionic order

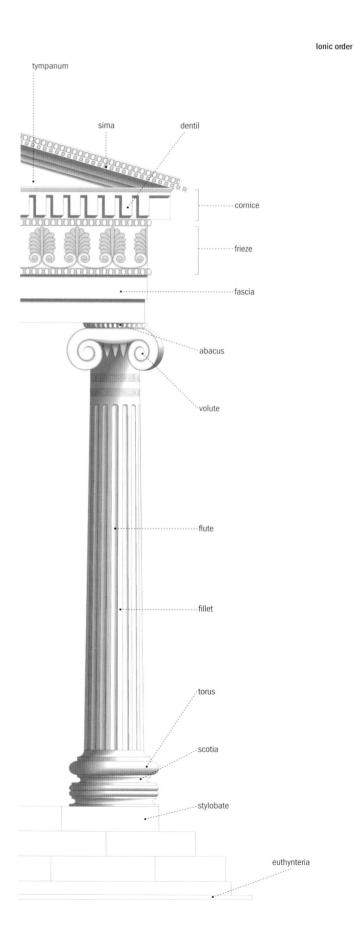

tympanum

sima

dentil

cornice

frieze

fascia

abacus

volute

flute

fillet

torus

scotia

stylobate

euthynteria

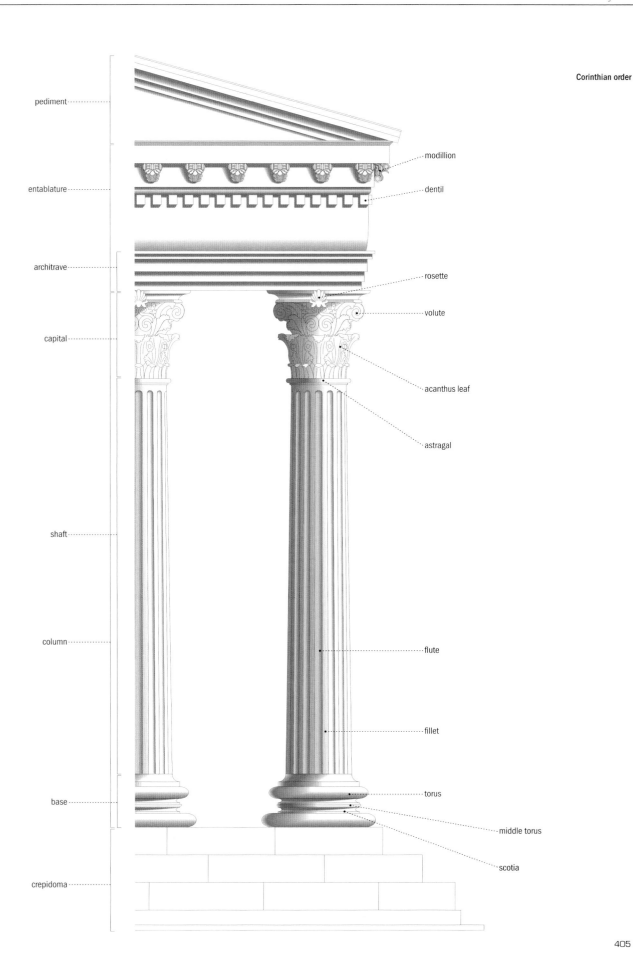

Corinthian order

pediment

entablature

modillion

dentil

architrave

capital

rosette

volute

acanthus leaf

astragal

shaft

column

flute

fillet

base

torus

middle torus

scotia

crepidoma

Roman house

ARTS AND ARCHITECTURE

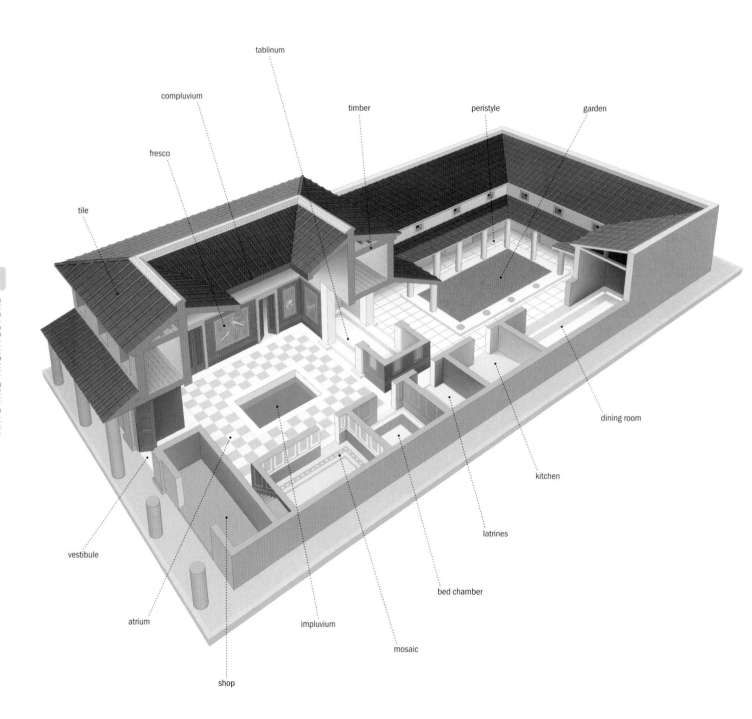

tablinum

compluvium

timber

peristyle

garden

fresco

tile

dining room

kitchen

latrines

vestibule

bed chamber

atrium

impluvium

mosaic

shop

Roman amphitheater

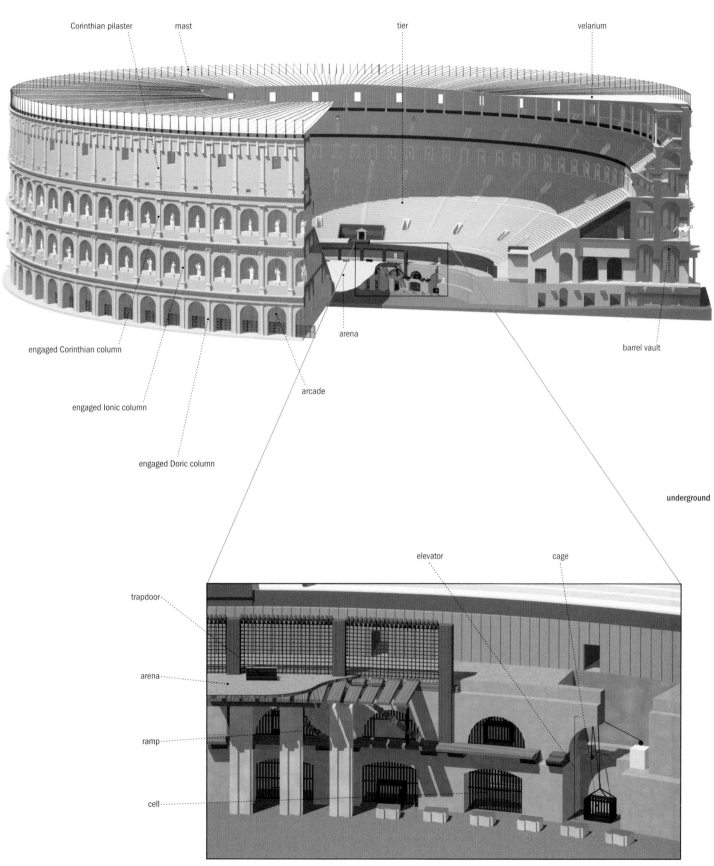

Corinthian pilaster

mast

tier

velarium

engaged Corinthian column

arena

barrel vault

engaged Ionic column

arcade

engaged Doric column

underground

elevator

cage

trapdoor

arena

ramp

cell

castle

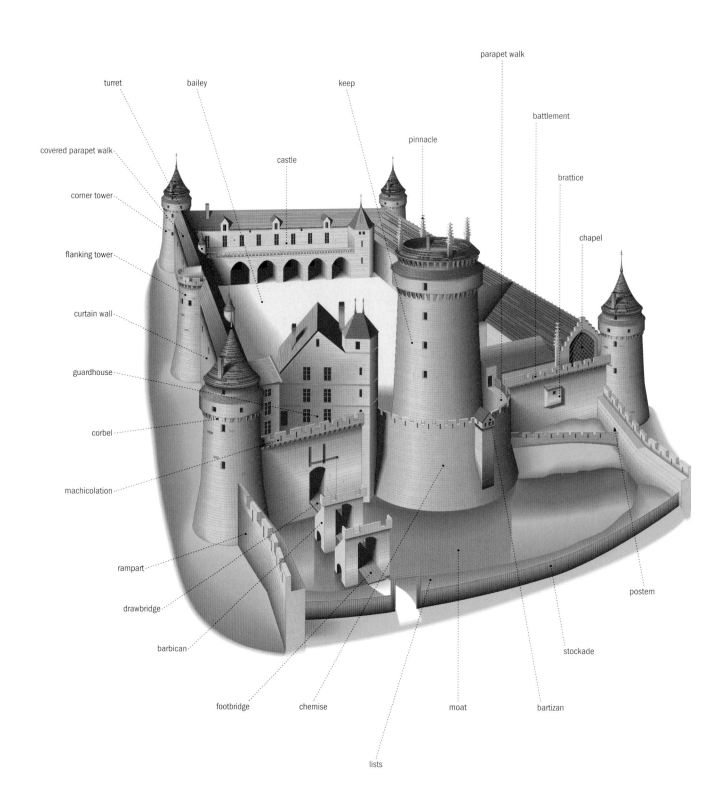

turret

bailey

keep

parapet walk

battlement

pinnacle

covered parapet walk

castle

brattice

corner tower

chapel

flanking tower

curtain wall

guardhouse

corbel

machicolation

rampart

postern

drawbridge

barbican

stockade

footbridge

chemise

moat

bartizan

lists

Vauban fortification

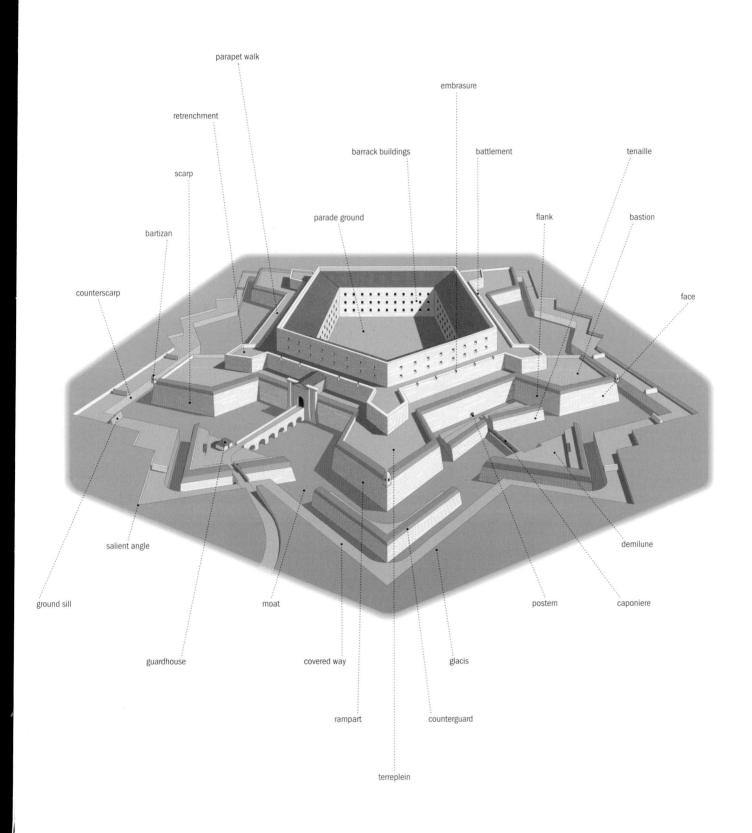

parapet walk

embrasure

retrenchment

barrack buildings

battlement

tenaille

scarp

flank

bastion

parade ground

bartizan

counterscarp

face

salient angle

demilune

ground sill

moat

postern

caponiere

guardhouse

covered way

glacis

rampart

counterguard

terreplein

cathedral

Gothic cathedral

vault

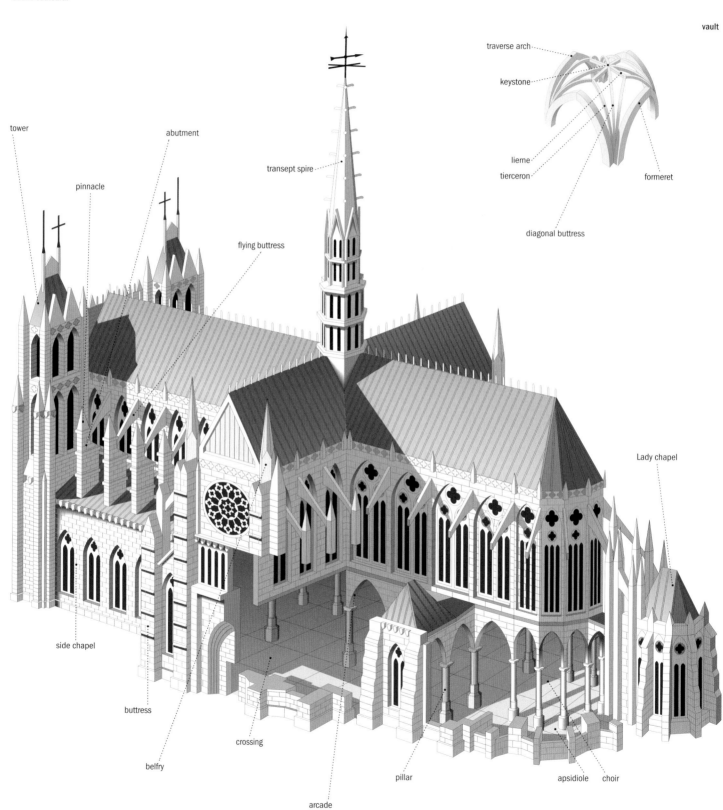

traverse arch

keystone

lierne

tierceron

formeret

diagonal buttress

tower

abutment

pinnacle

transept spire

flying buttress

Lady chapel

side chapel

buttress

crossing

belfry

pillar

apsidiole   choir

arcade

façade

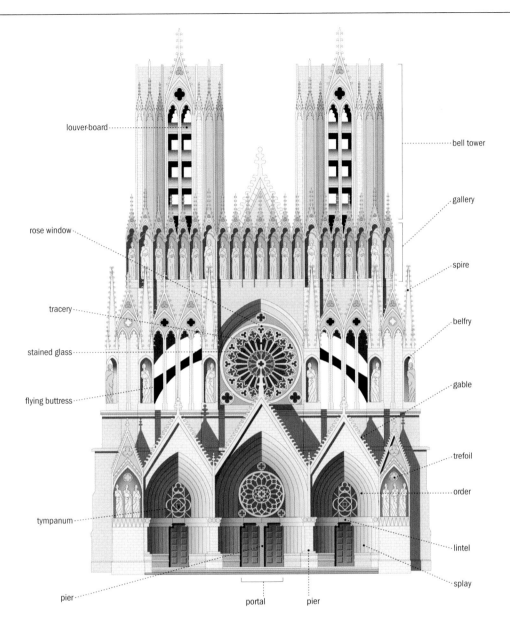

louver-board

rose window

tracery

stained glass

flying buttress

tympanum

pier

portal

pier

bell tower

gallery

spire

belfry

gable

trefoil

order

lintel

splay

plan

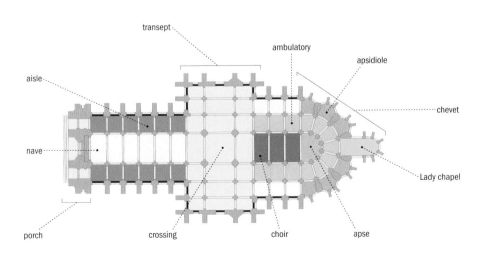

transept

ambulatory

apsidiole

aisle

nave

chevet

Lady chapel

porch

crossing

choir

apse

pagoda

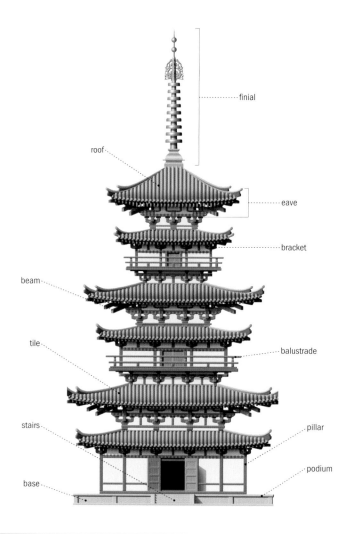

finial

roof

eave

bracket

beam

balustrade

tile

stairs

pillar

base

podium

Aztec temple

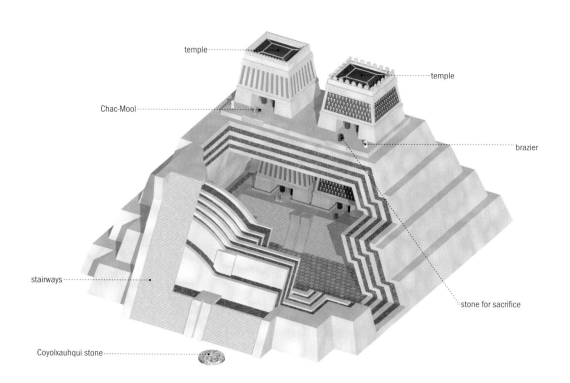

temple

temple

Chac-Mool

brazier

stairways

stone for sacrifice

Coyolxauhqui stone

elements of architecture

semicircular arch

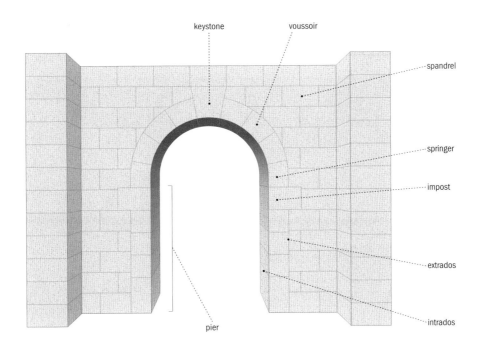

keystone

voussoir

spandrel

springer

impost

extrados

intrados

pier

examples of arches

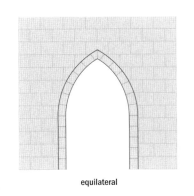

equilateral

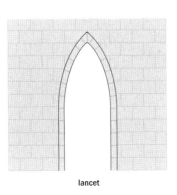

lancet

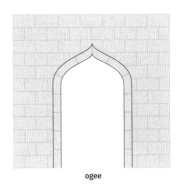

ogee

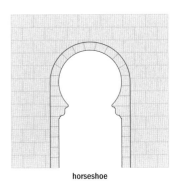

horseshoe

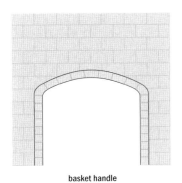

basket handle

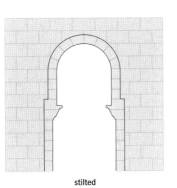

stilted

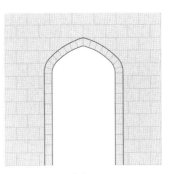

Tudor

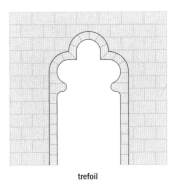

trefoil

elements of architecture

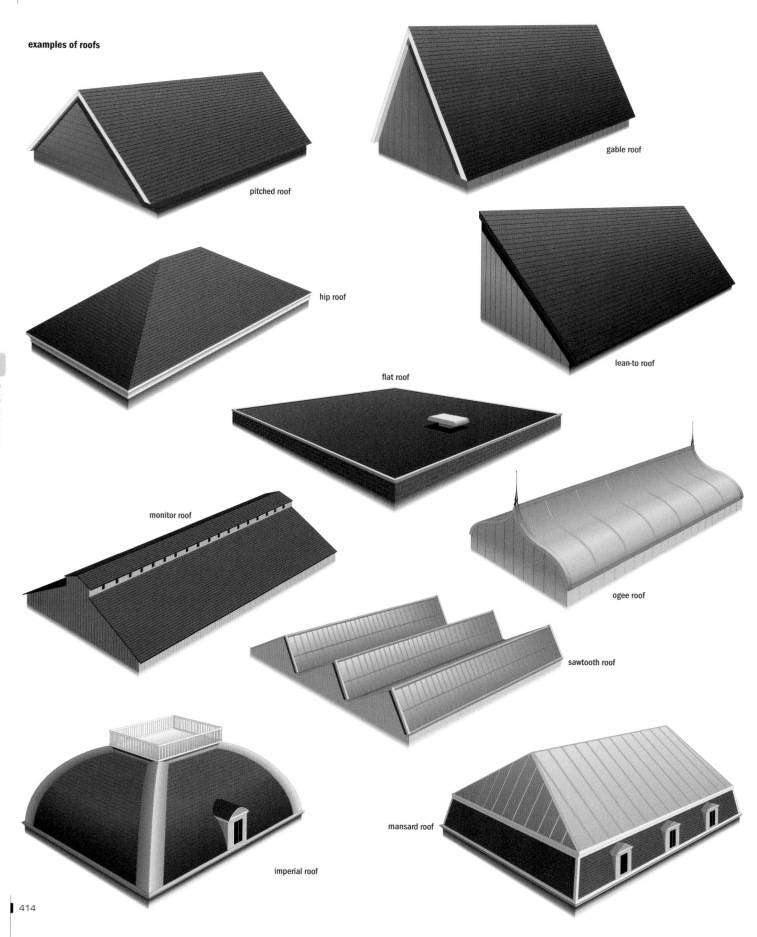

examples of roofs

pitched roof

gable roof

hip roof

lean-to roof

flat roof

monitor roof

ogee roof

sawtooth roof

imperial roof

mansard roof

ARTS AND ARCHITECTURE

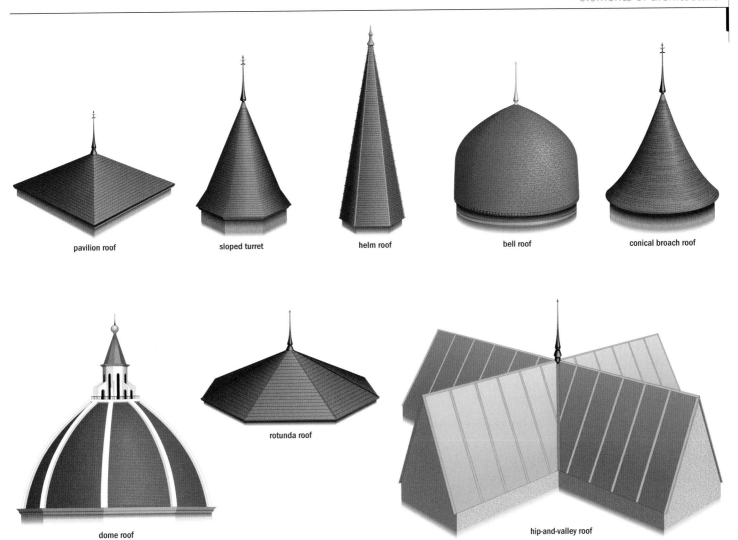

pavilion roof

sloped turret

helm roof

bell roof

conical broach roof

dome roof

rotunda roof

hip-and-valley roof

examples of windows

sliding folding window

French window

casement window

louvered window

sliding window

sash window

horizontal pivoting window

vertical pivoting window

examples of doors

manual revolving door

automatic sliding door

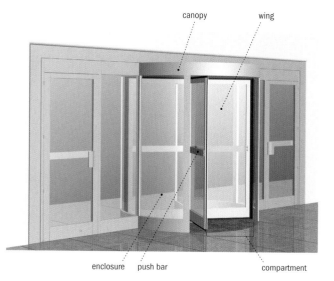

canopy

wing

enclosure   push bar

compartment

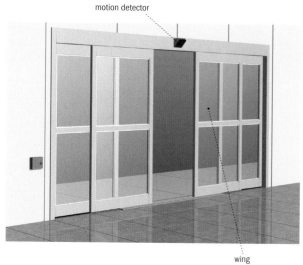

motion detector

wing

ARTS AND ARCHITECTURE

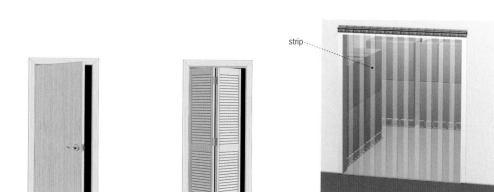

strip

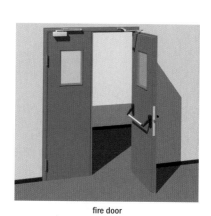

conventional door

folding door

strip door

fire door

sliding folding door

sliding door

sectional garage door

up and over garage door

escalator

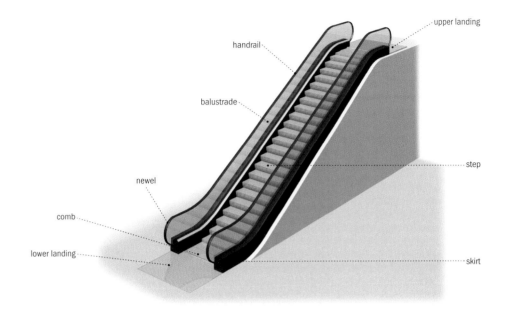

handrail

upper landing

balustrade

step

newel

comb

lower landing

skirt

elevator

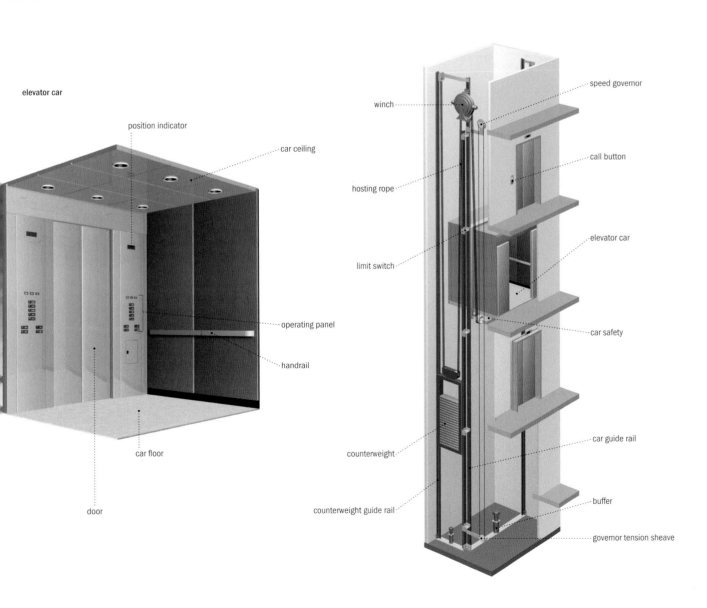

elevator car

position indicator

car ceiling

winch

speed governor

hosting rope

call button

limit switch

elevator car

operating panel

car safety

handrail

car floor

counterweight

car guide rail

door

counterweight guide rail

buffer

governor tension sheave

traditional houses

igloo

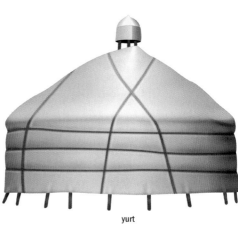

yurt

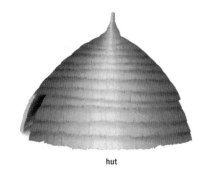

hut

wigwam

hut

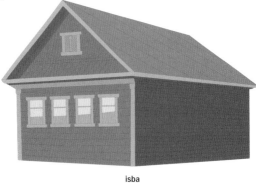

isba

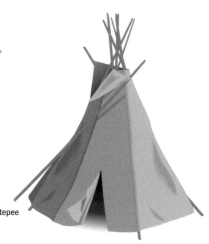

tepee

pile dwelling

adobe house

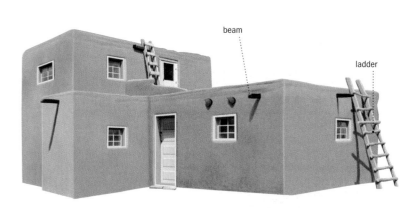

beam

ladder

ARTS AND ARCHITECTURE

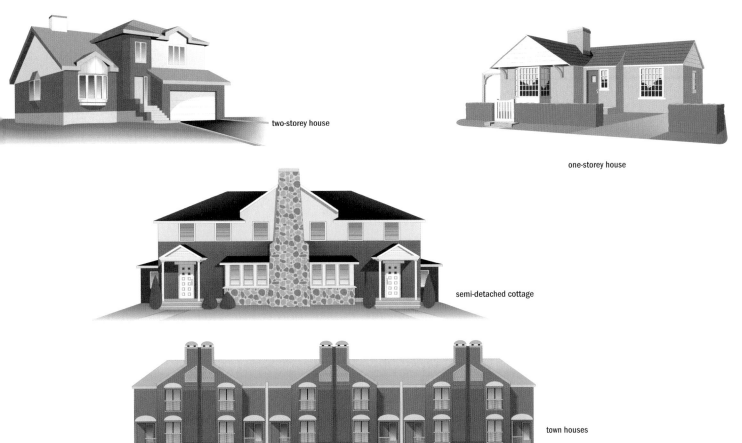

two-storey house

one-storey house

semi-detached cottage

town houses

condominiums

high-rise apartment

printing

relief printing

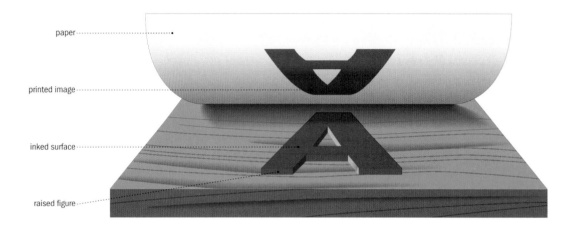

paper

printed image

inked surface

raised figure

intaglio printing

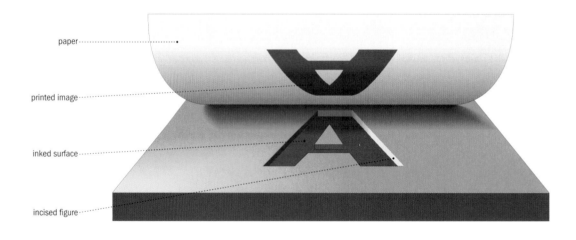

paper

printed image

inked surface

incised figure

lithographic printing

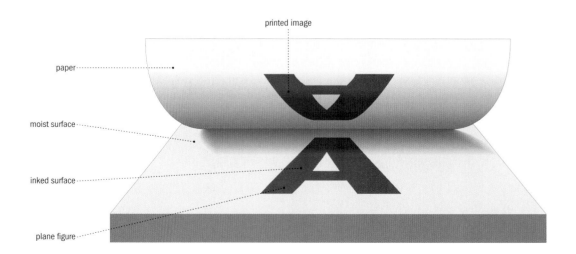

printed image

paper

moist surface

inked surface

plane figure

relief printing process

equipment

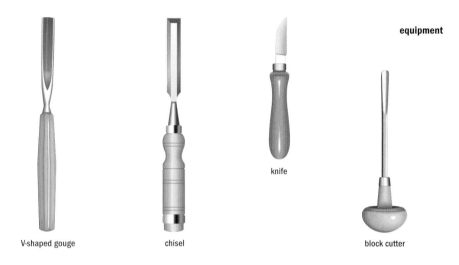

mallet

U-shaped gouge

V-shaped gouge

chisel

knife

block cutter

ink

spatula

inking slab

ink

brayer

baren

woodcut

wood engraving

etching press

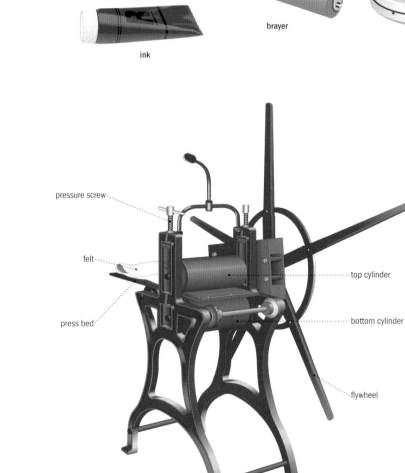

pressure screw

felt

press bed

top cylinder

bottom cylinder

flywheel

intaglio printing process

equipment

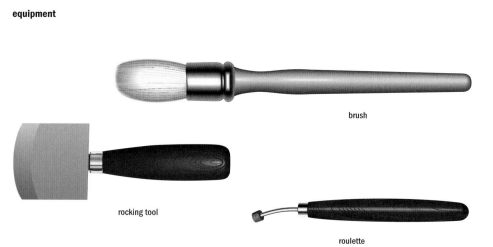

brush

rocking tool

roulette

copper plate

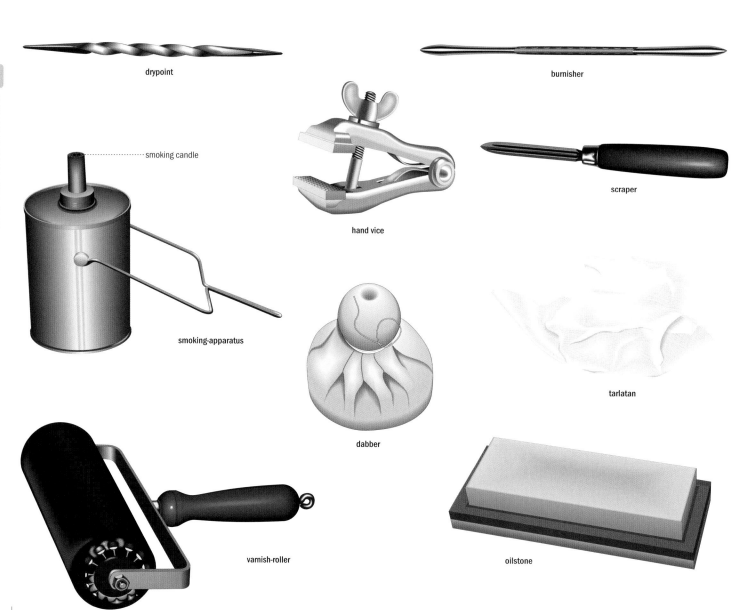

drypoint

burnisher

smoking candle

smoking-apparatus

hand vice

scraper

tarlatan

dabber

varnish-roller

oilstone

lithography

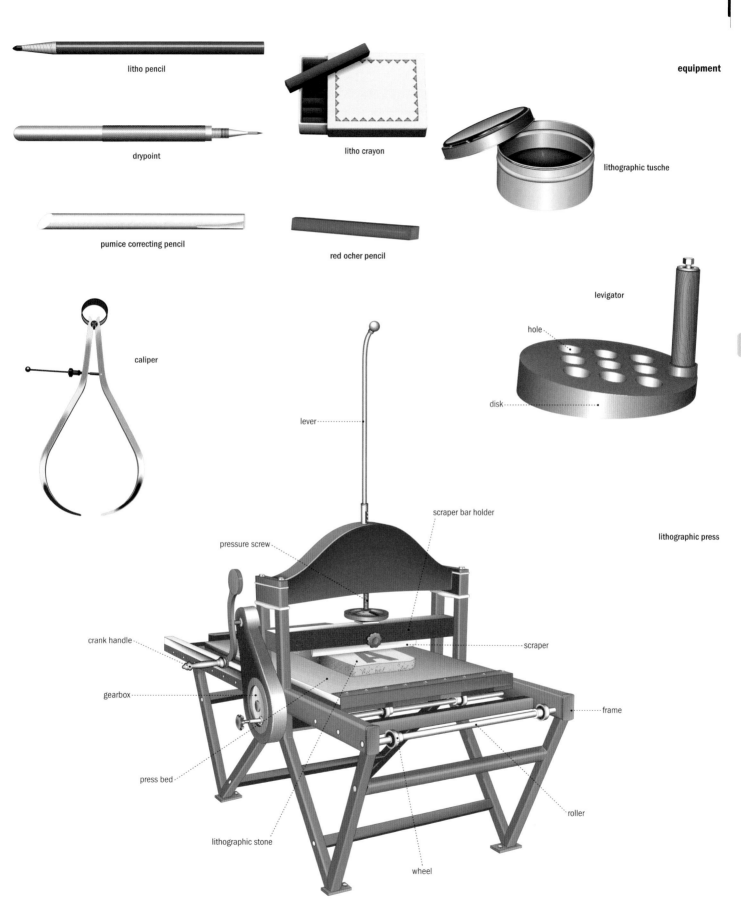

litho pencil

drypoint

litho crayon

lithographic tusche

equipment

pumice correcting pencil

red ocher pencil

levigator

hole

disk

caliper

lever

scraper bar holder

lithographic press

pressure screw

scraper

crank handle

gearbox

frame

press bed

roller

lithographic stone

wheel

ARTS AND ARCHITECTURE

fine bookbinding

sawing-in

sewing

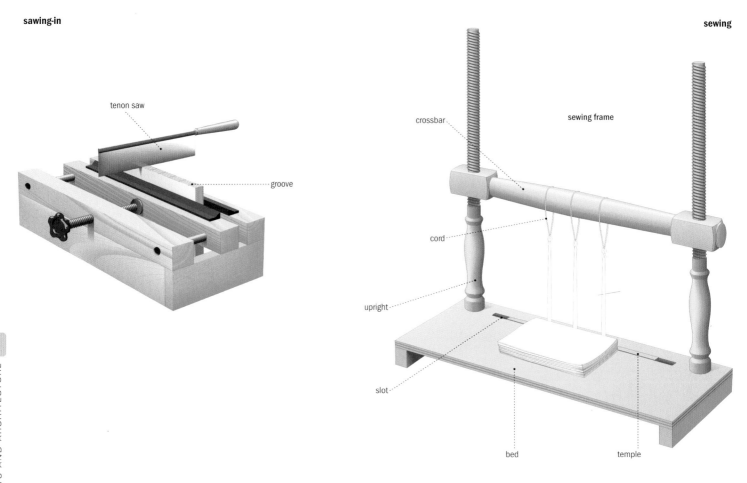

tenon saw

groove

crossbar

sewing frame

cord

upright

slot

bed

temple

trimming

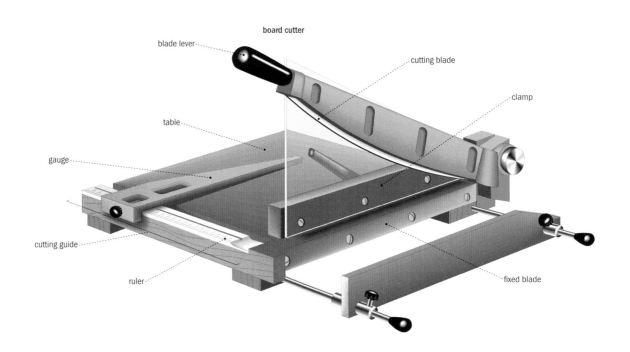

board cutter

blade lever

cutting blade

clamp

table

gauge

cutting guide

ruler

fixed blade

backing

pressing

backing press

spine of the book

backing board

standing press

upright

central screw

hand-wheel

platen

pressing board

base

backing hammer

claw

face

handle

covering

bookbinding leather

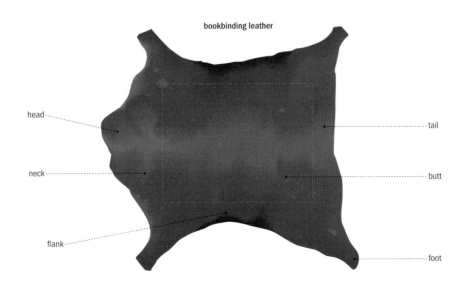

head

neck

flank

tail

butt

foot

fine bookbinding

ARTS AND ARCHITECTURE

bound book

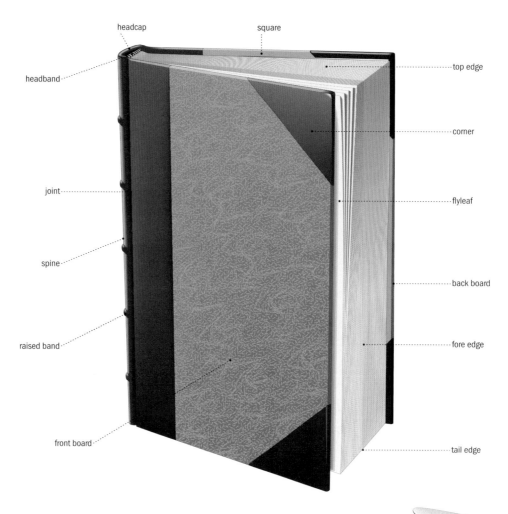

headcap

square

headband

top edge

corner

joint

flyleaf

spine

back board

raised band

fore edge

front board

tail edge

gathering

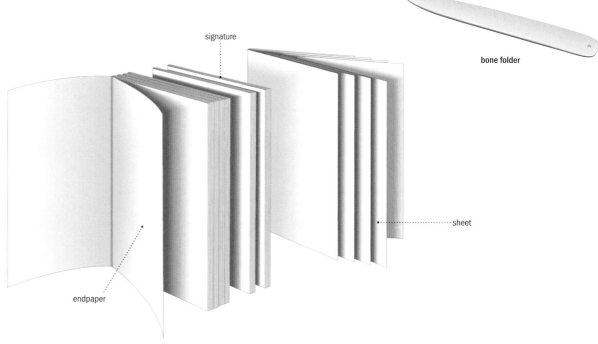

signature

bone folder

sheet

endpaper

movie theater

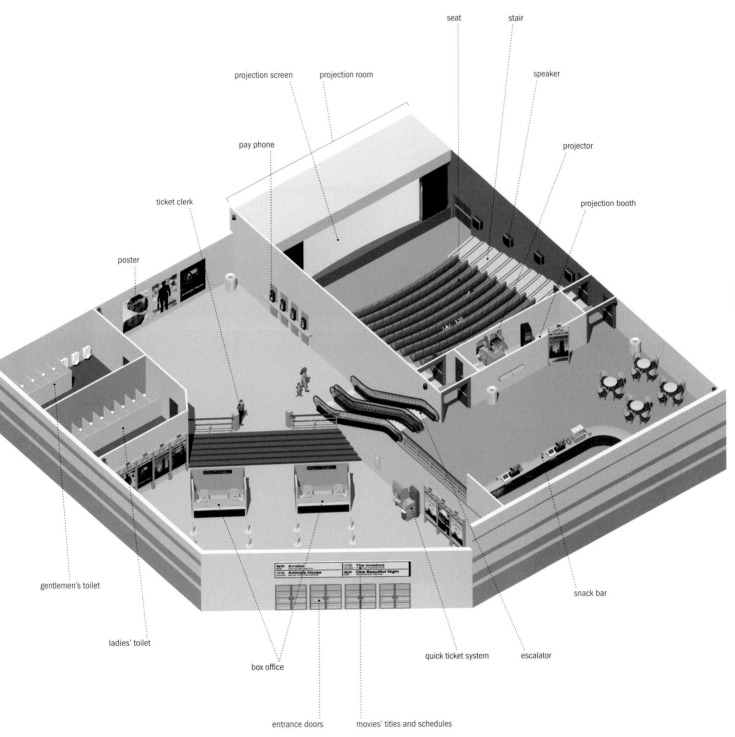

seat

stair

projection screen

projection room

speaker

pay phone

projector

ticket clerk

projection booth

poster

gentlemen's toilet

snack bar

ladies' toilet

quick ticket system

escalator

box office

entrance doors

movies' titles and schedules

sound stage

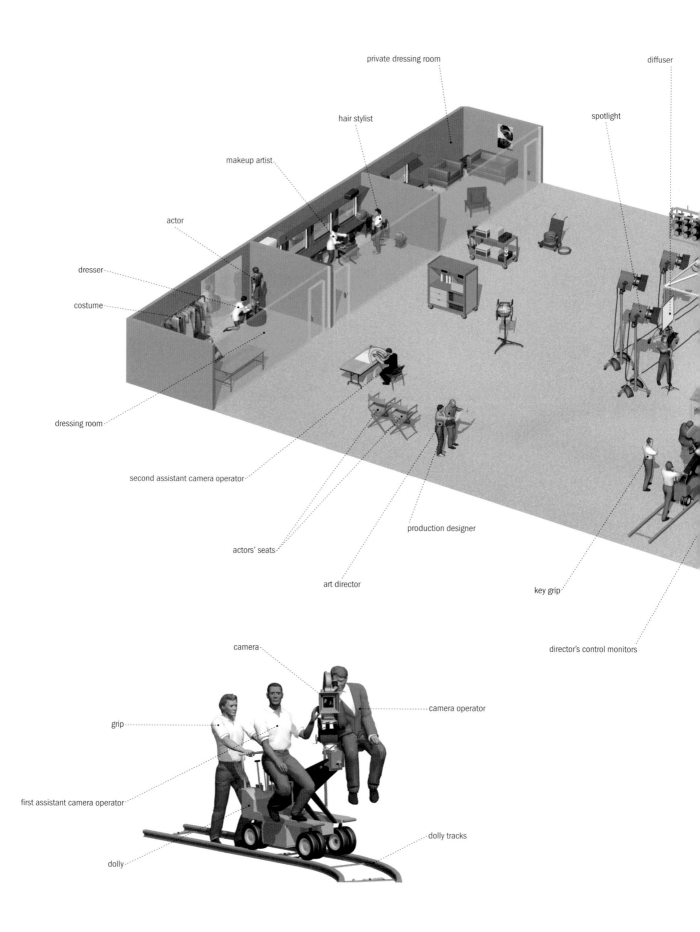

private dressing room

diffuser

hair stylist

spotlight

makeup artist

actor

dresser

costume

dressing room

second assistant camera operator

actors' seats

production designer

art director

key grip

director's control monitors

camera

camera operator

grip

first assistant camera operator

dolly tracks

dolly

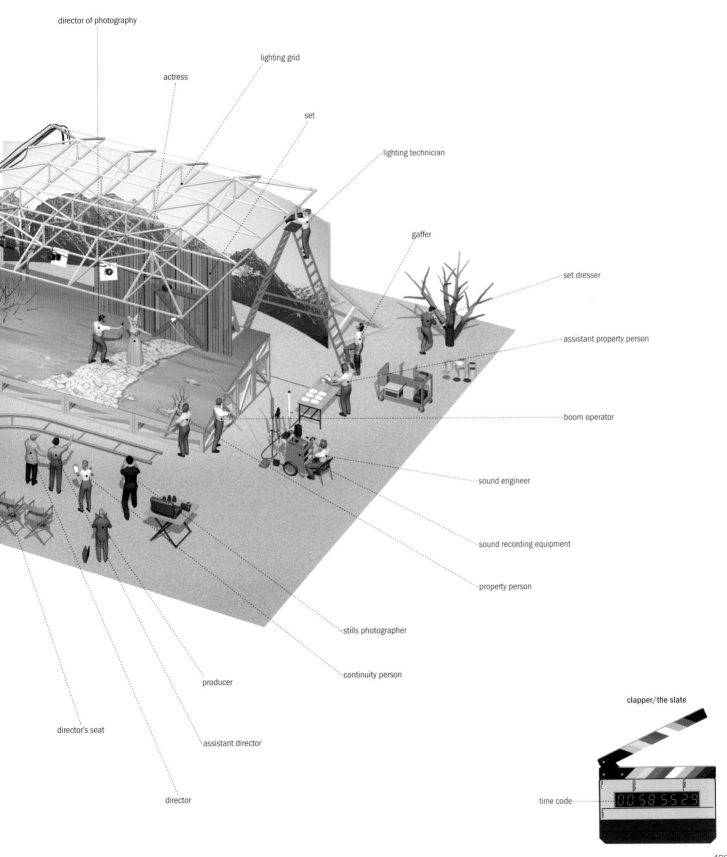

director of photography

lighting grid

actress

set

lighting technician

gaffer

set dresser

assistant property person

boom operator

sound engineer

sound recording equipment

property person

stills photographer

continuity person

producer

director's seat

assistant director

director

clapper/the slate

time code

00 58 55 29

theater

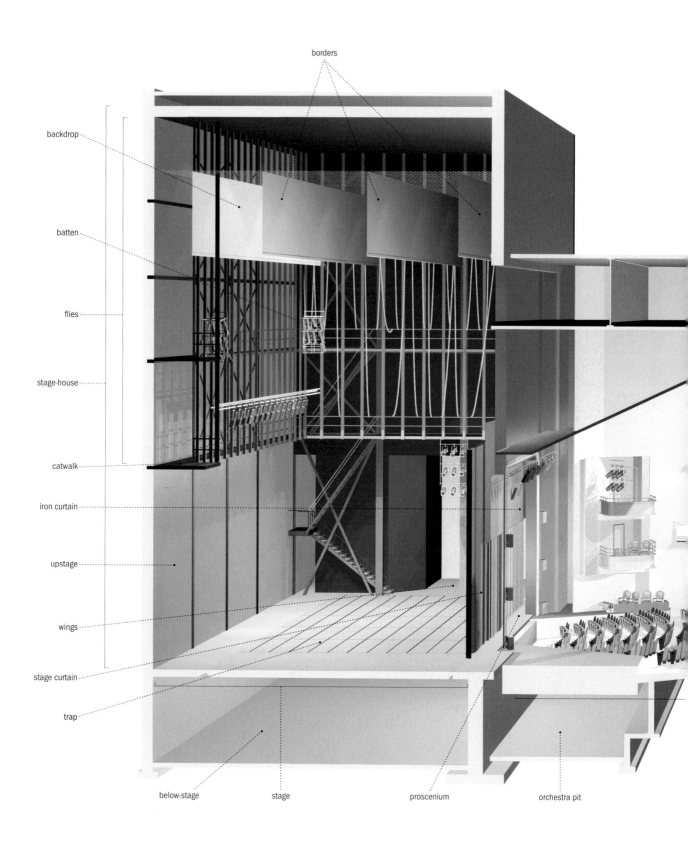

borders

backdrop

batten

flies

stage-house

catwalk

iron curtain

upstage

wings

stage curtain

trap

below-stage

stage

proscenium

orchestra pit

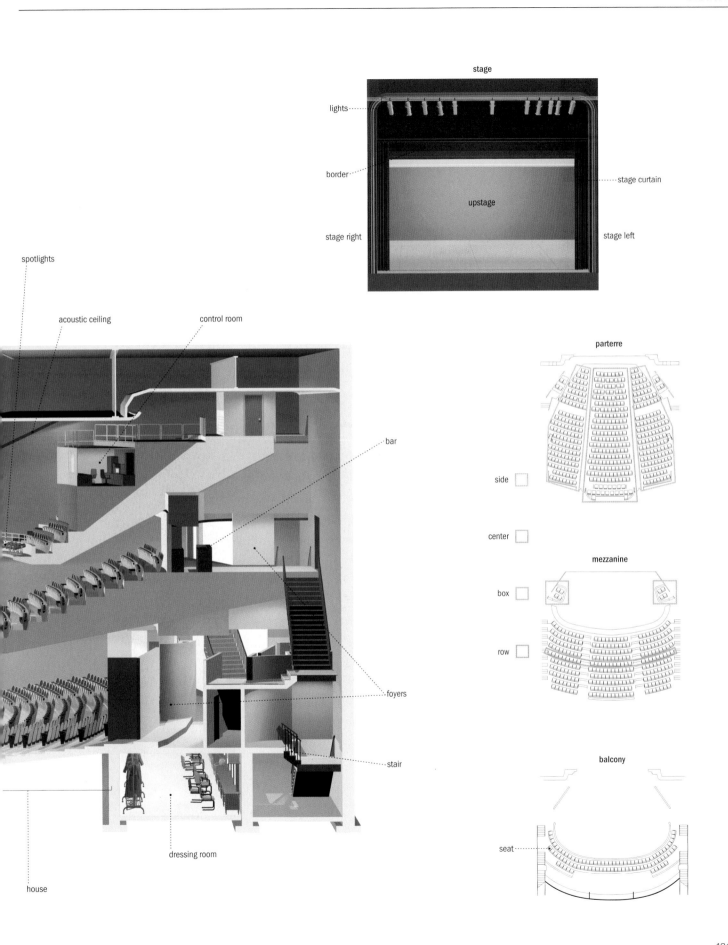

stage

lights

border

stage curtain

upstage

stage right

stage left

spotlights

acoustic ceiling

control room

bar

foyers

stair

dressing room

house

parterre

side

center

mezzanine

box

row

balcony

seat

traditional musical instruments

accordion

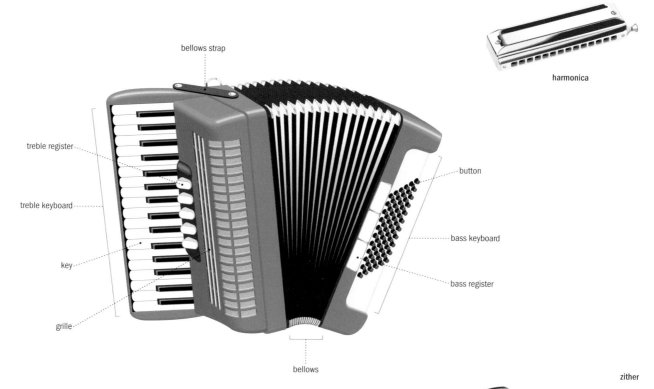

bellows strap

treble register

treble keyboard

key

grille

bellows

harmonica

button

bass keyboard

bass register

zither

bagpipes

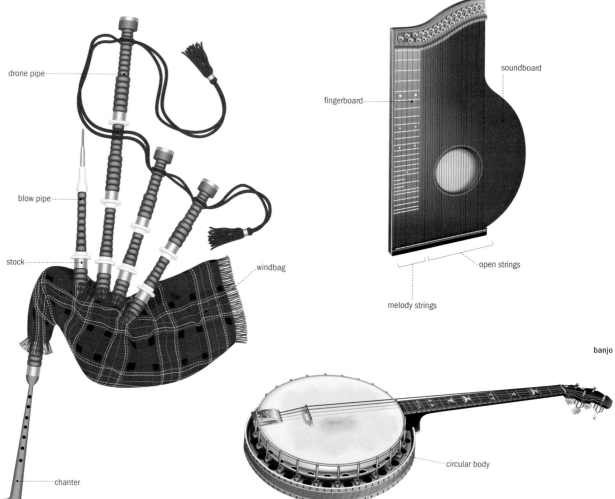

drone pipe

blow pipe

stock

windbag

chanter

soundboard

fingerboard

open strings

melody strings

banjo

circular body

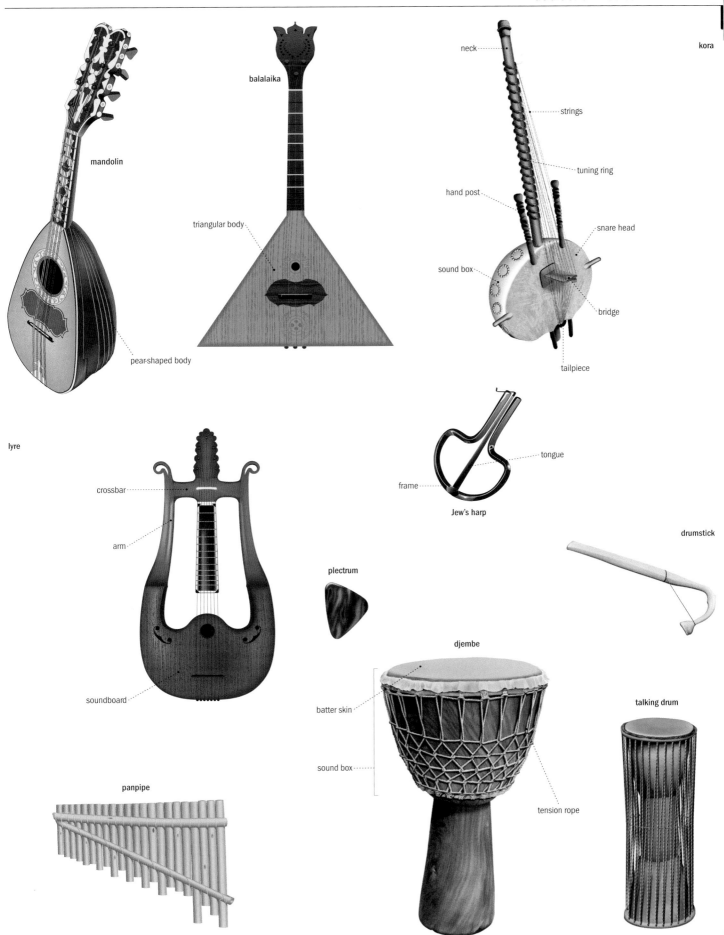

mandolin

pear-shaped body

balalaika

triangular body

neck

kora

strings

tuning ring

hand post

snare head

sound box

bridge

tailpiece

lyre

crossbar

arm

frame

tongue

Jew's harp

drumstick

plectrum

soundboard

djembe

talking drum

batter skin

sound box

tension rope

panpipe

musical notation

staff

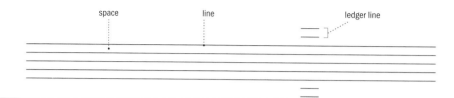

space line ledger line

clefs

treble clef · bass clef · C clef

time signatures

two-two time

three-four time

four-four time

bar line

repeat mark

intervals

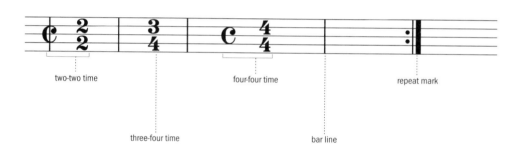

unison · second · third · fourth · fifth · sixth · seventh · octave

scale

C   D   E   F   G   A   B   C

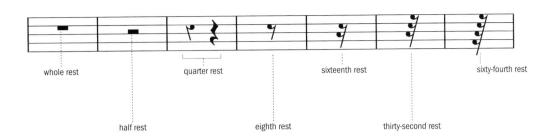

whole rest

quarter rest

sixteenth rest

sixty-fourth rest

half rest

eighth rest

thirty-second rest

ornaments

appoggiatura

trill

turn

mordent

note symbols

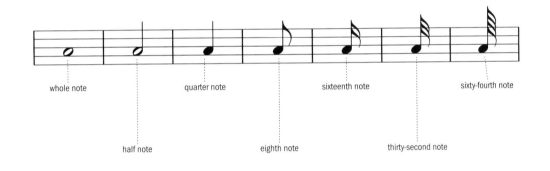

whole note

quarter note

sixteenth note

sixty-fourth note

half note

eighth note

thirty-second note

ARTS AND ARCHITECTURE

accidentals

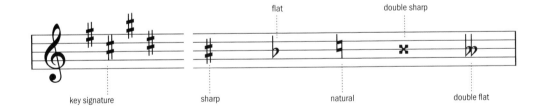

flat

double sharp

key signature

sharp

natural

double flat

other signs

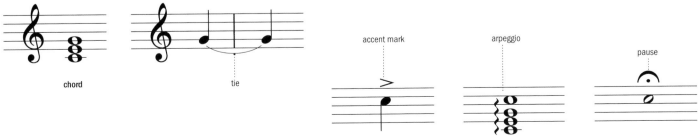

chord

tie

accent mark

arpeggio

pause

435

musical accessories

metronome

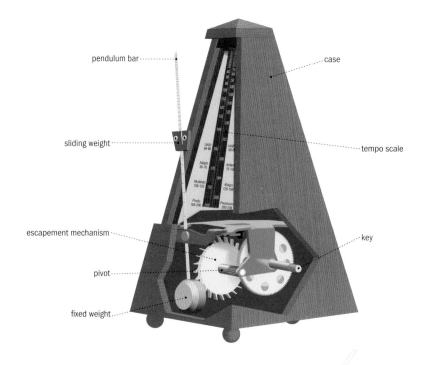

pendulum bar

case

sliding weight

tempo scale

escapement mechanism

key

pivot

fixed weight

music stand

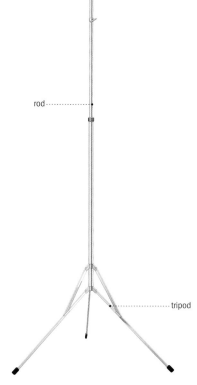

music rest

adjusting lever

rod

tripod

tuning fork

quartz metronome

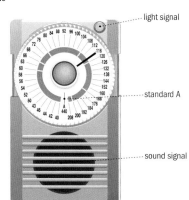

light signal

standard A

sound signal

symphony orchestra

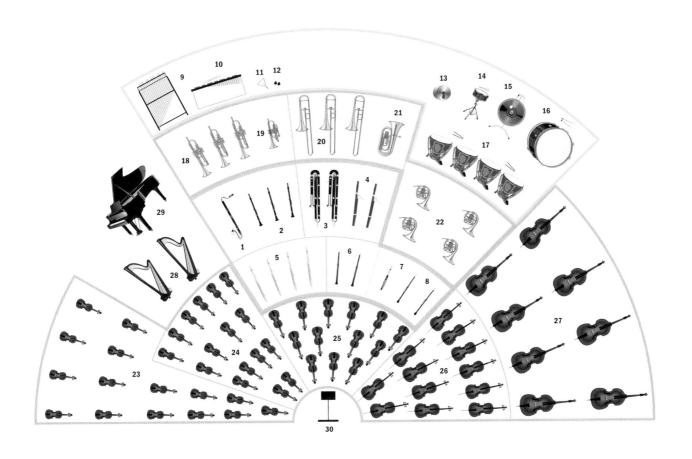

woodwind family

1 bass clarinet

2 clarinets

3 contrabassoons

4 bassoons

5 flutes

6 oboes

7 piccolo

8 English horns

percussion instruments

9 tubular bells

10 xylophone

11 triangle

12 castanets

13 cymbals

14 snare drum

15 gong

16 bass drum

17 timpani

28 harps

brass family

18 trumpets

19 cornet

20 trombones

21 tuba

22 French horns

29 piano

violin family

23 first violins

24 second violins

25 violas

26 cellos

27 double basses

30 conductor's podium

examples of instrumental groups

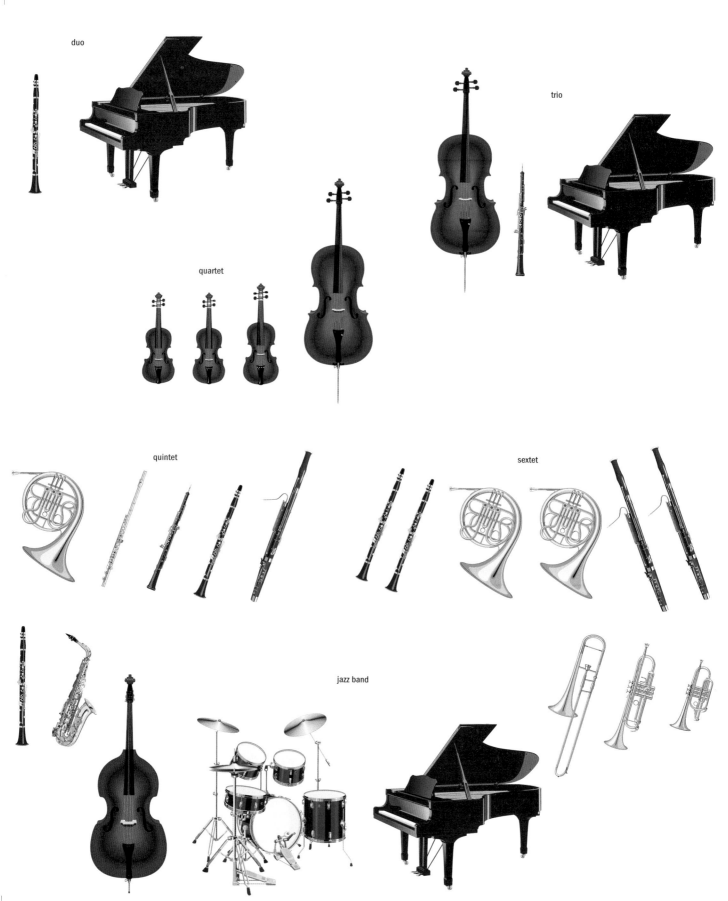

duo

trio

quartet

quintet

sextet

jazz band

bow

violin

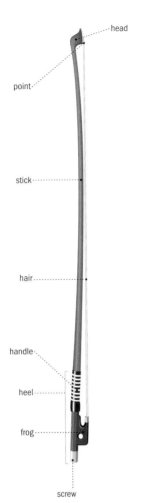

head

point

peg

scroll

peg box

nut

neck

fingerboard

stick

soundboard

string

purfling

hair

waist

rib

handle

bridge

sound hole

heel

frog

tailpiece

chin rest

end button

screw

violin family

double bass

cello

viola

violin

stringed instruments

harp

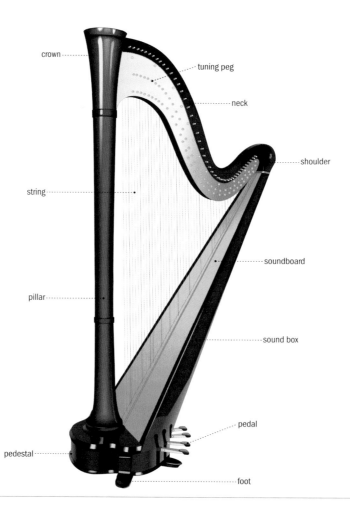

crown

tuning peg

neck

shoulder

string

soundboard

pillar

sound box

pedal

pedestal

foot

acoustic guitar

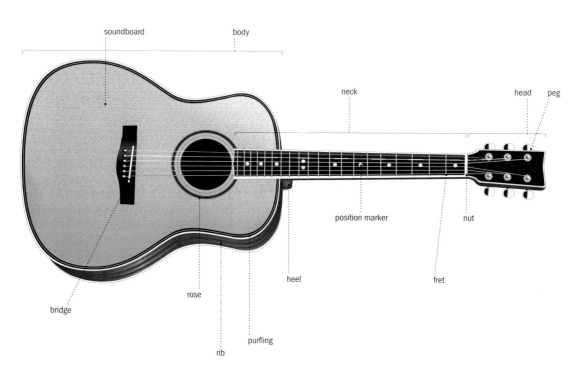

soundboard

body

neck

head

peg

rose

position marker

nut

heel

fret

bridge

rib

purfling

ARTS AND ARCHITECTURE

electric guitar

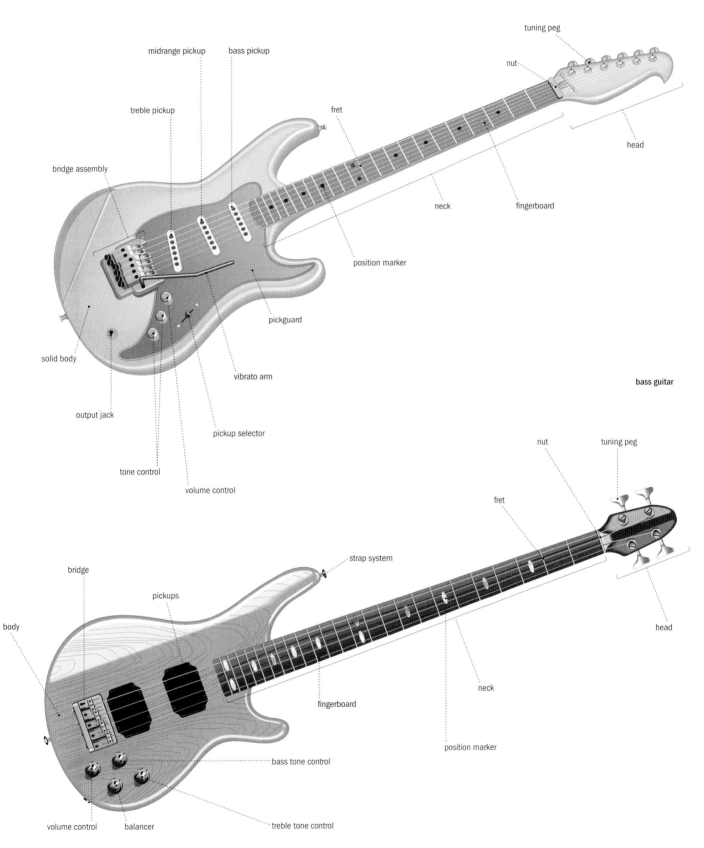

tuning peg

nut

midrange pickup   bass pickup

treble pickup   fret   head

bridge assembly   neck   fingerboard

position marker

pickguard

solid body   vibrato arm   bass guitar

output jack   pickup selector

tone control   nut   tuning peg

volume control   fret   head

strap system

bridge   pickups   neck

body   fingerboard   position marker

bass tone control

volume control   balancer   treble tone control

keyboard instruments

upright piano

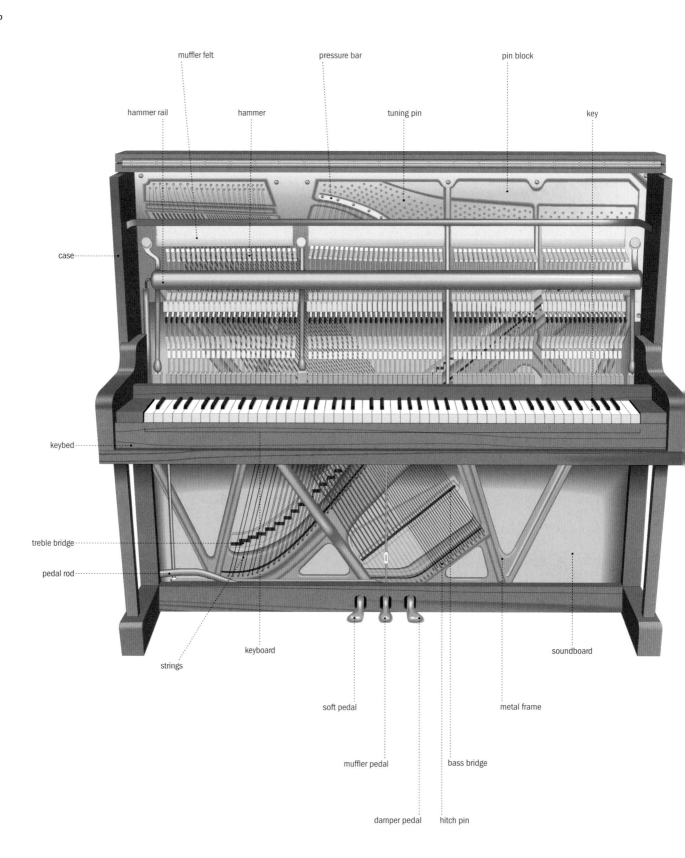

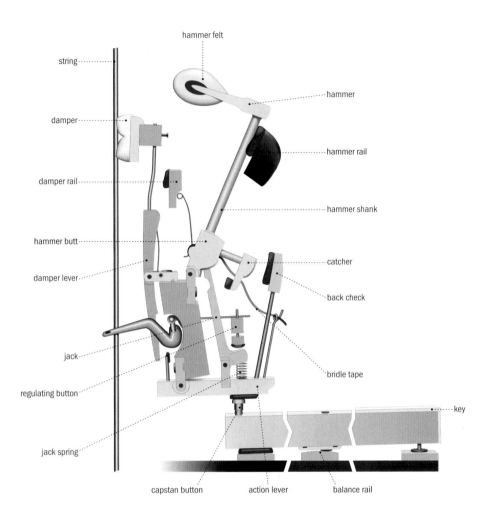

hammer felt

string

hammer

damper

hammer rail

damper rail

hammer shank

hammer butt

catcher

damper lever

back check

jack

bridle tape

regulating button

key

jack spring

capstan button   action lever   balance rail

examples of keyboard instruments

concert grand

baby grand

boudoir grand

harpsichord

keyboard instruments

organ

organ console

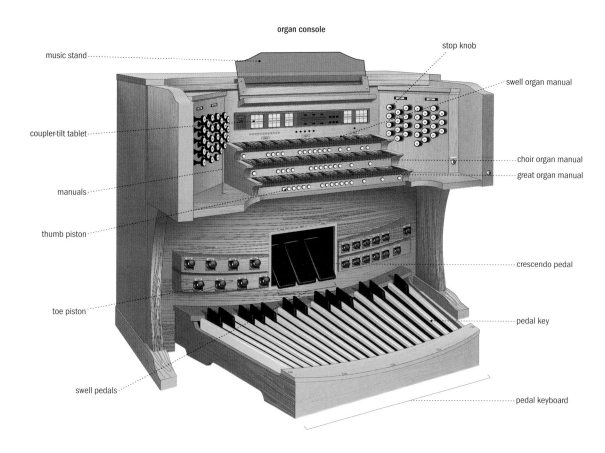

music stand

stop knob

swell organ manual

coupler-tilt tablet

choir organ manual

great organ manual

manuals

thumb piston

crescendo pedal

toe piston

pedal key

swell pedals

pedal keyboard

reed pipe

flue pipe

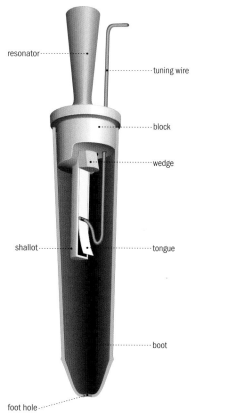

resonator

tuning wire

block

wedge

shallot

tongue

boot

foot hole

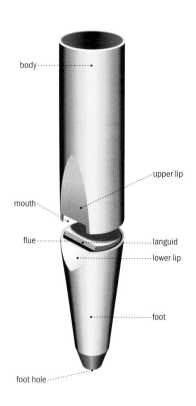

body

upper lip

mouth

flue

languid

lower lip

foot

foot hole

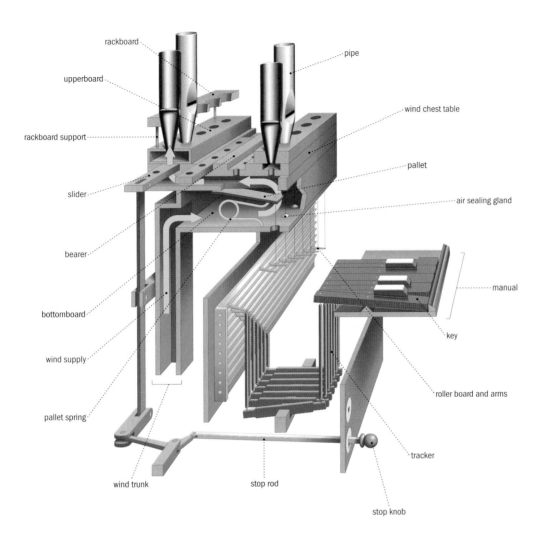

rackboard

upperboard

pipe

rackboard support

wind chest table

slider

pallet

air sealing gland

bearer

manual

bottomboard

key

wind supply

roller board and arms

pallet spring

tracker

wind trunk

stop rod

stop knob

production of sound

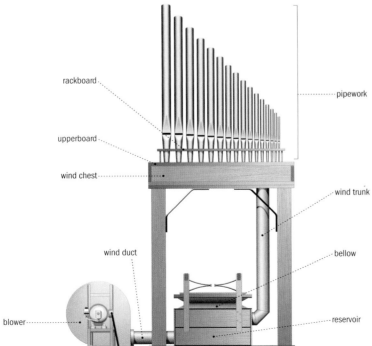

rackboard

pipework

upperboard

wind chest

wind trunk

wind duct

bellow

blower

reservoir

ARTS AND ARCHITECTURE

wind instruments

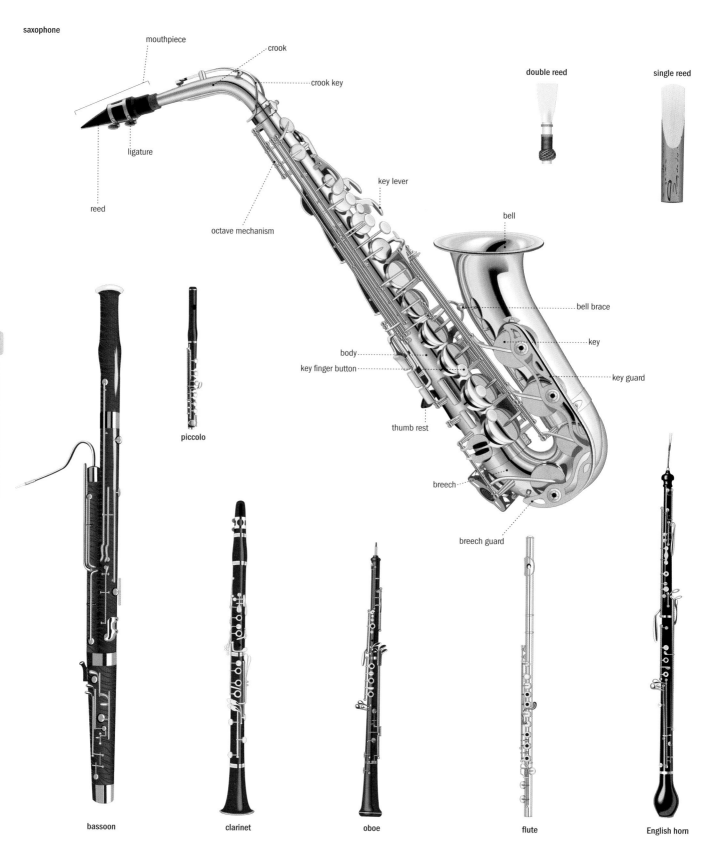

saxophone

mouthpiece

crook

crook key

double reed

single reed

ligature

key lever

bell

reed

octave mechanism

bell brace

key

body

key guard

key finger button

thumb rest

breech

breech guard

piccolo

bassoon

clarinet

oboe

flute

English horn

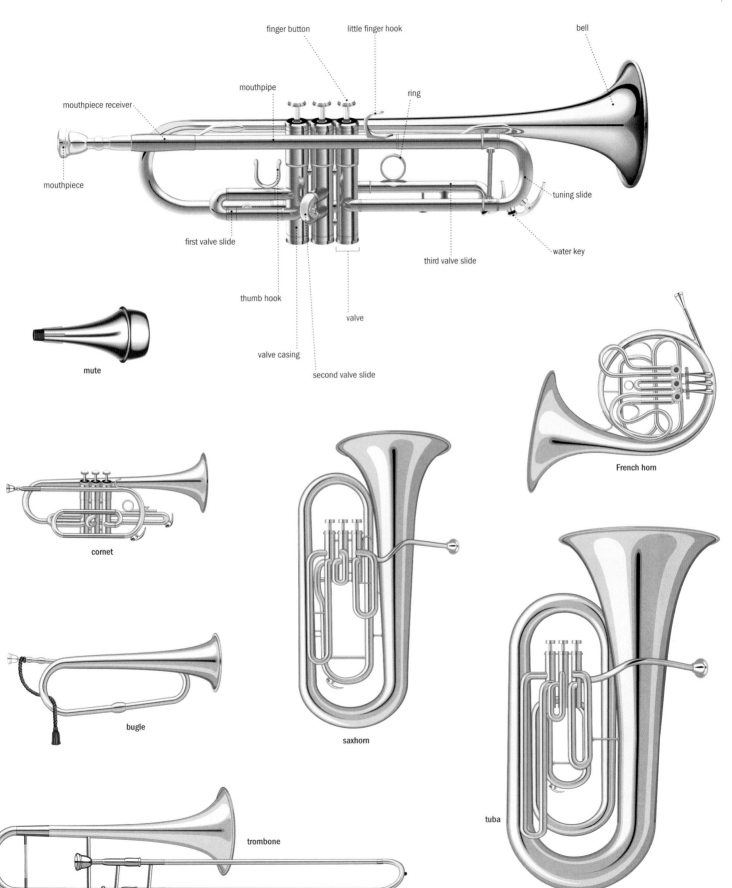

finger button

little finger hook

bell

mouthpipe

ring

mouthpiece receiver

mouthpiece

first valve slide

tuning slide

water key

third valve slide

thumb hook

valve

valve casing

second valve slide

mute

cornet

French horn

bugle

saxhorn

tuba

trombone

percussion instruments

drums

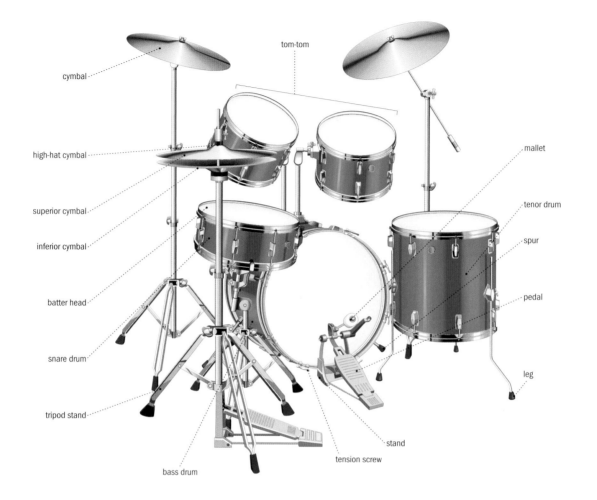

cymbal

high-hat cymbal

superior cymbal

inferior cymbal

batter head

snare drum

tripod stand

bass drum

tom-tom

mallet

tenor drum

spur

pedal

leg

stand

tension screw

kettledrum

snare drum

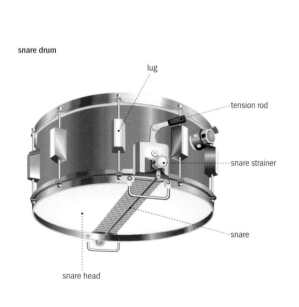

lug

tension rod

snare strainer

snare

snare head

tie rod

batter head

metal counterhoop

tuning gauge

shell

strut

tension rod

caster

foot

crown

pedal

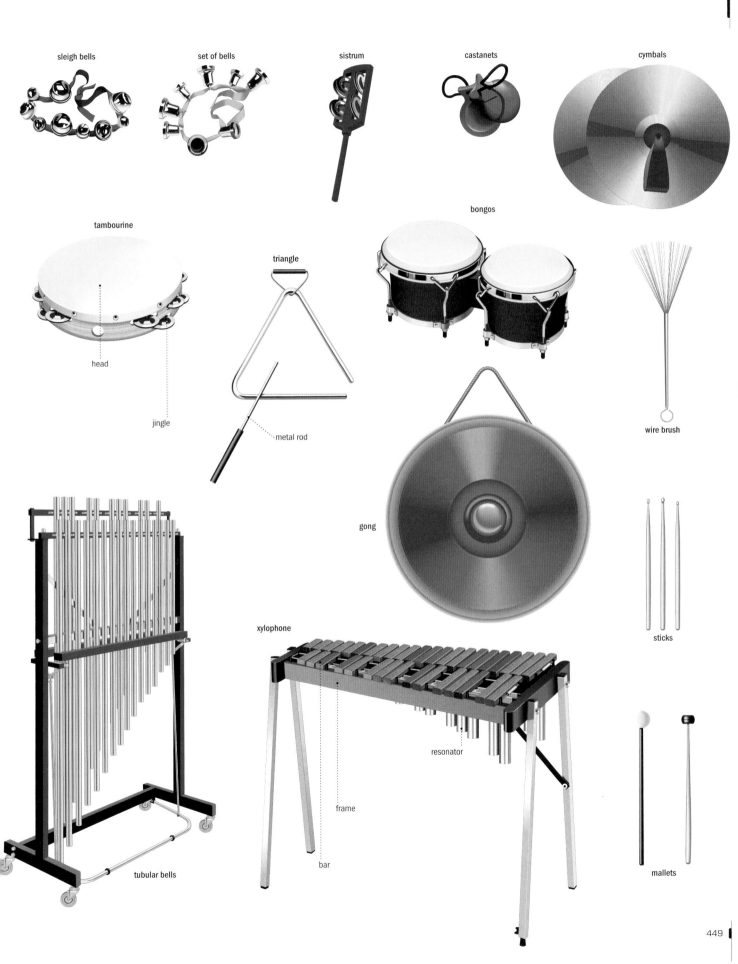

sleigh bells

set of bells

sistrum

castanets

cymbals

bongos

tambourine

triangle

wire brush

head

jingle

metal rod

gong

sticks

tubular bells

xylophone

resonator

frame

bar

mallets

electronic instruments

sequencer

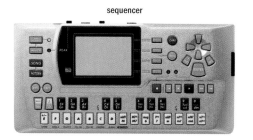

sampler

headphone jack ·········

function display

disk drive

expander

synthesizer

disk drive   system buttons

volume control

function display

fine data entry control

sequencer control

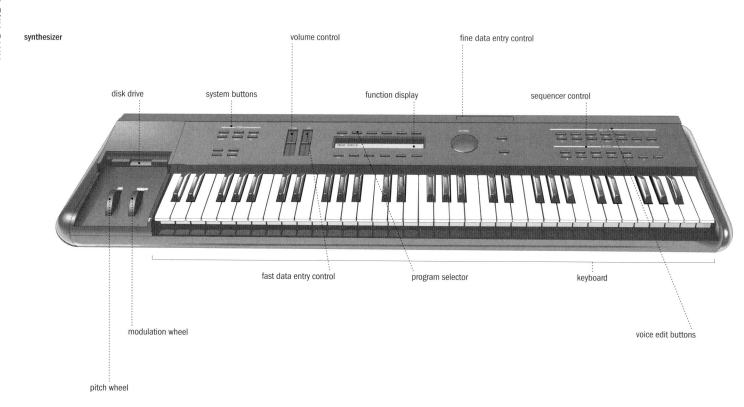

fast data entry control

program selector

keyboard

voice edit buttons

modulation wheel

pitch wheel

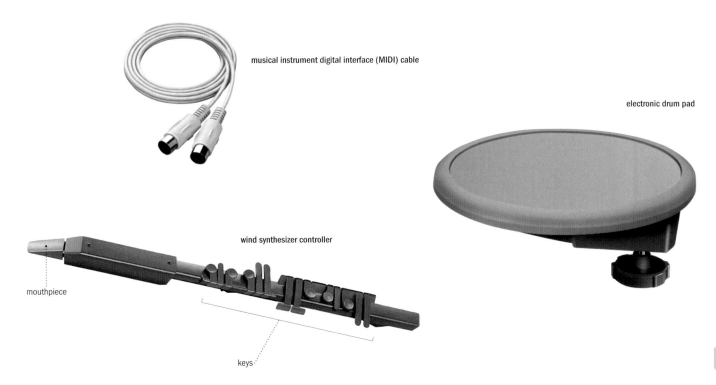

musical instrument digital interface (MIDI) cable

electronic drum pad

wind synthesizer controller

mouthpiece

keys

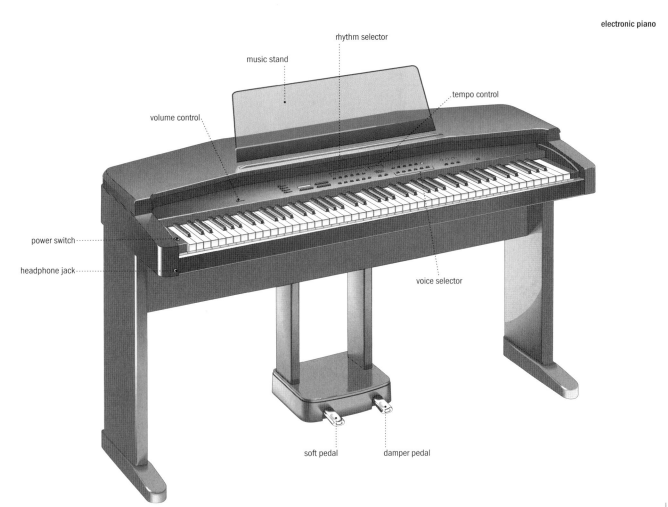

electronic piano

rhythm selector

music stand

tempo control

volume control

power switch

headphone jack

voice selector

soft pedal

damper pedal

sewing

ARTS AND ARCHITECTURE

sewing machine

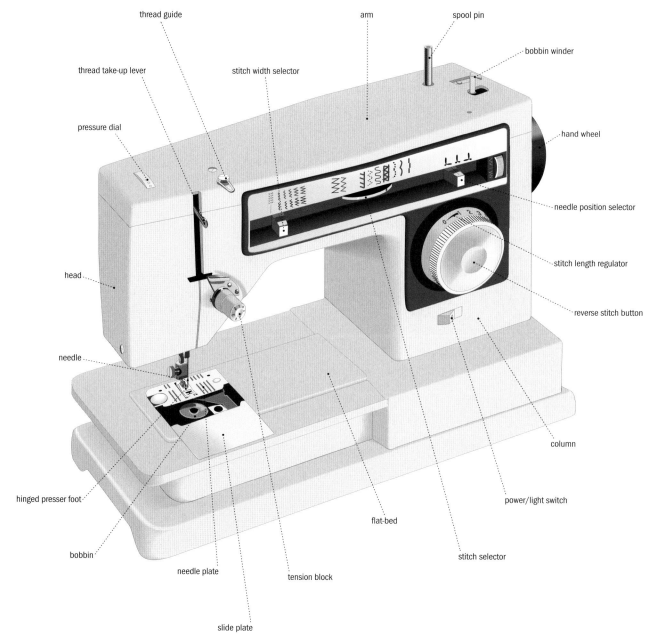

thread guide

arm

spool pin

bobbin winder

thread take-up lever

stitch width selector

pressure dial

hand wheel

needle position selector

head

stitch length regulator

reverse stitch button

needle

column

hinged presser foot

power/light switch

bobbin

flat-bed

stitch selector

needle plate

tension block

slide plate

foot control

bobbin case

connecting terminal

speed controller

bobbin

latch lever

hook

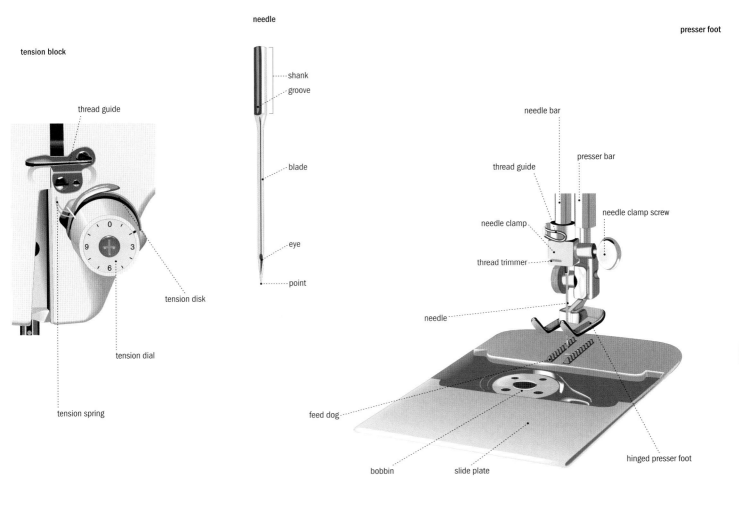

tension block

thread guide

0
9 · · 3
6

tension disk

tension dial

tension spring

needle

shank
groove

blade

eye

point

presser foot

needle bar

presser bar

thread guide

needle clamp screw

needle clamp

thread trimmer

needle

feed dog

bobbin

slide plate

hinged presser foot

fasteners

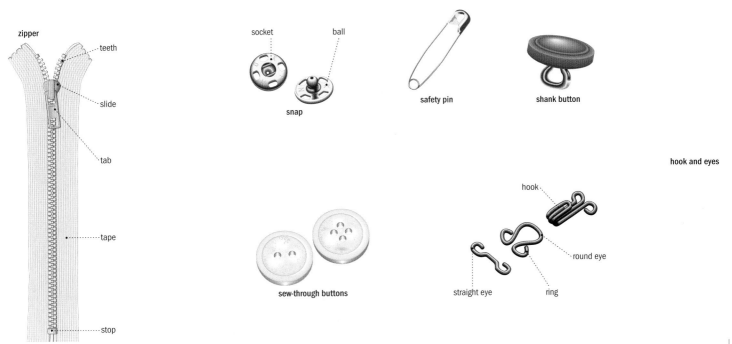

zipper

teeth

slide

tab

tape

stop

socket

ball

snap

safety pin

shank button

hook and eyes

hook

round eye

sew-through buttons

straight eye

ring

sewing

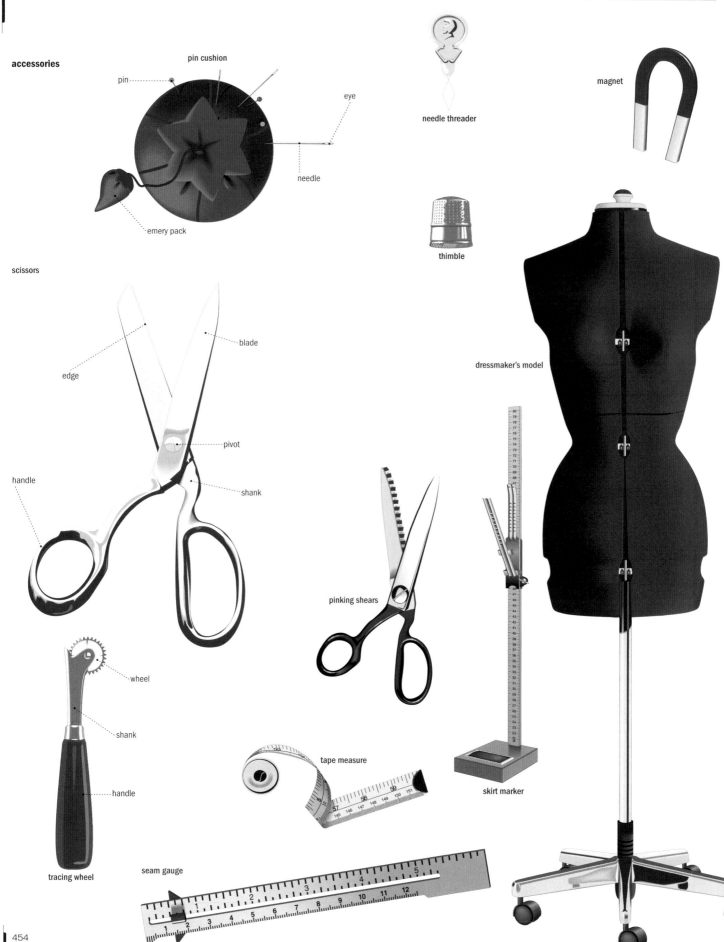

accessories

pin cushion

pin

eye

needle

emery pack

needle threader

magnet

thimble

scissors

blade

edge

pivot

handle

shank

dressmaker's model

pinking shears

wheel

shank

handle

tape measure

skirt marker

tracing wheel

seam gauge

underlying fabrics

pattern

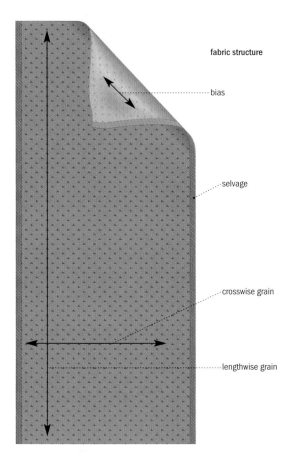

garment fabric

interfacing

underlining

lining

interlining

cutting line

notch

seam line

fold line

marking dot

seam allowance

alteration line

dart

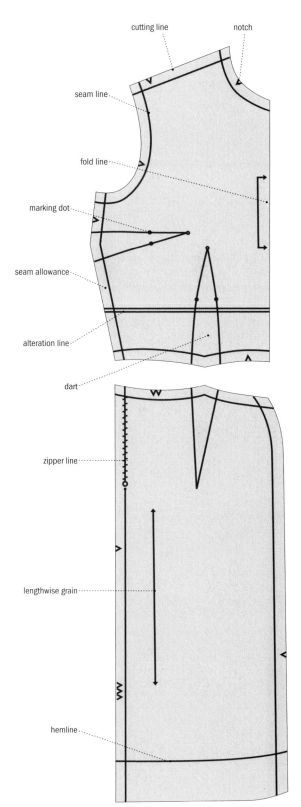

fabric structure

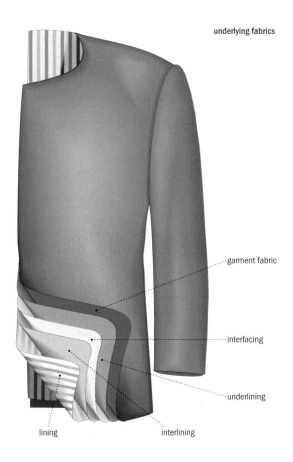

bias

selvage

crosswise grain

lengthwise grain

zipper line

lengthwise grain

hemline

ARTS AND ARCHITECTURE

knitting machine

needle bed and carriages

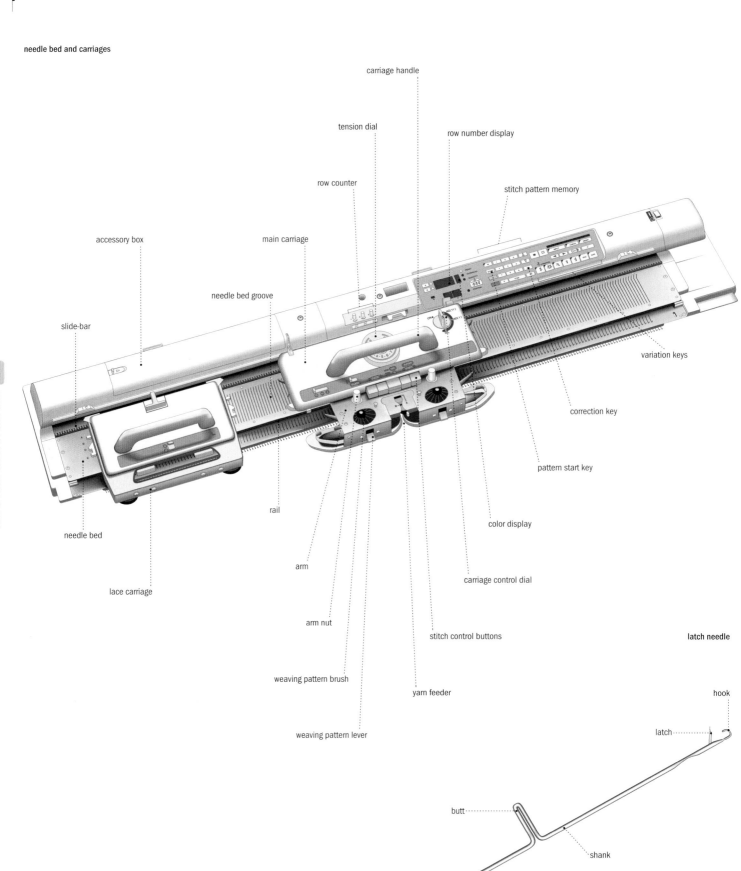

carriage handle

tension dial

row number display

row counter

stitch pattern memory

accessory box

main carriage

needle bed groove

slide-bar

variation keys

correction key

pattern start key

rail

color display

needle bed

arm

carriage control dial

lace carriage

arm nut

stitch control buttons

latch needle

weaving pattern brush

yarn feeder

hook

latch

weaving pattern lever

butt

shank

tension block

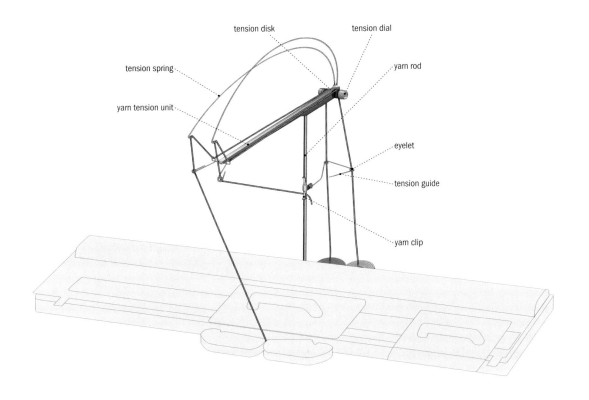

tension disk   tension dial

tension spring

yarn rod

yarn tension unit

eyelet

tension guide

yarn clip

knitting

knitting needle

head   shank   point

crochet hook

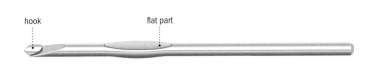

hook   flat part

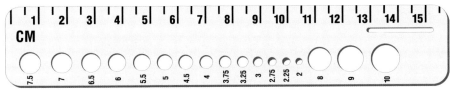

CM

7.5   7   6.5   6   5.5   5   4.5   4   3.75   3.25   3   2.75   2.25   2   8   9   10

circular needle   cast-on stitches   knitting measure

stitch patterns

moss stitch

sample

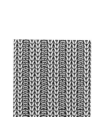

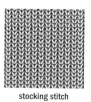

rib stitch

stocking stitch

basket stitch

garter stitch

cable stitch

bobbin lace

pillow

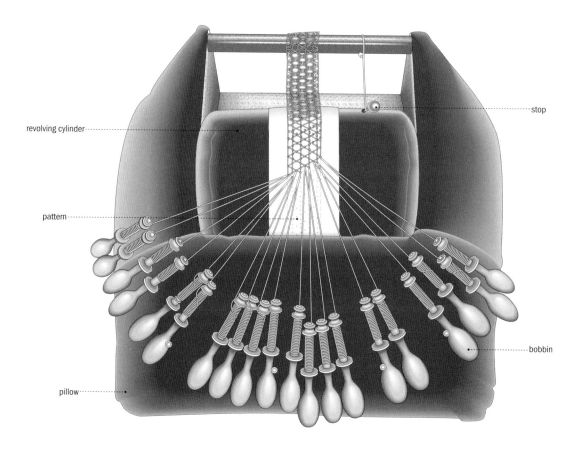

revolving cylinder

stop

pattern

bobbin

pillow

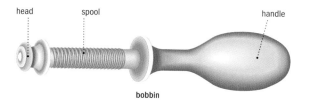

head   spool   handle

bobbin

pricker

hoops

frame

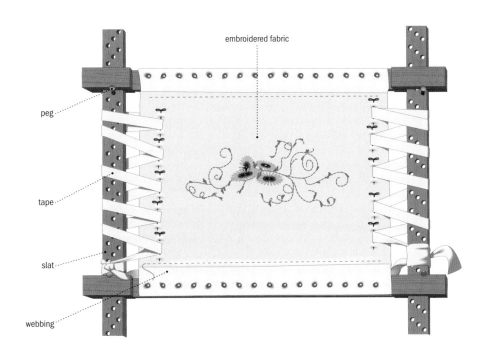

embroidered fabric

peg

tape

slat

webbing

stitches

cross stitches

herringbone stitch

chevron stitch

loop stitches

chain stitch

feather stitch

knot stitches

bullion stitch

French knot stitch

flat stitches

fishbone stitch

long and short stitch

couched stitches

Romanian couching stitch

Oriental couching stitch

weaving

low warp loom

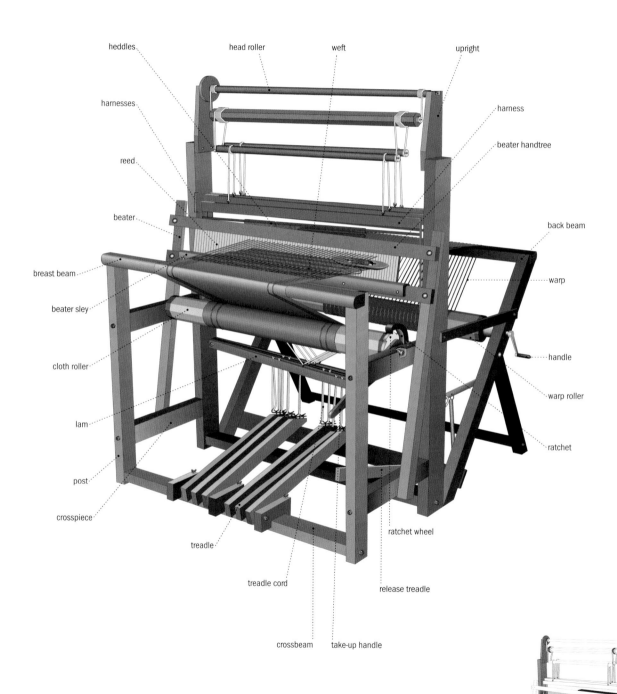

heddles

head roller

weft

upright

harnesses

harness

beater handtree

reed

beater

back beam

breast beam

warp

beater sley

cloth roller

handle

warp roller

lam

ratchet

post

crosspiece

ratchet wheel

treadle

treadle cord

release treadle

crossbeam

take-up handle

frame

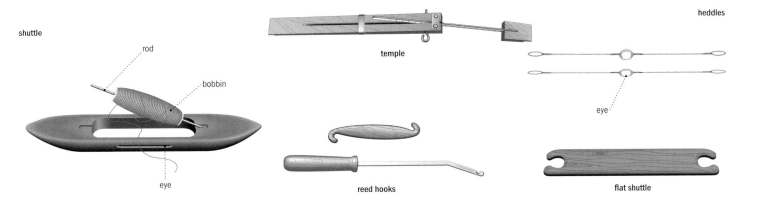

shuttle

rod

bobbin

eye

temple

reed hooks

heddles

eye

flat shuttle

high warp loom

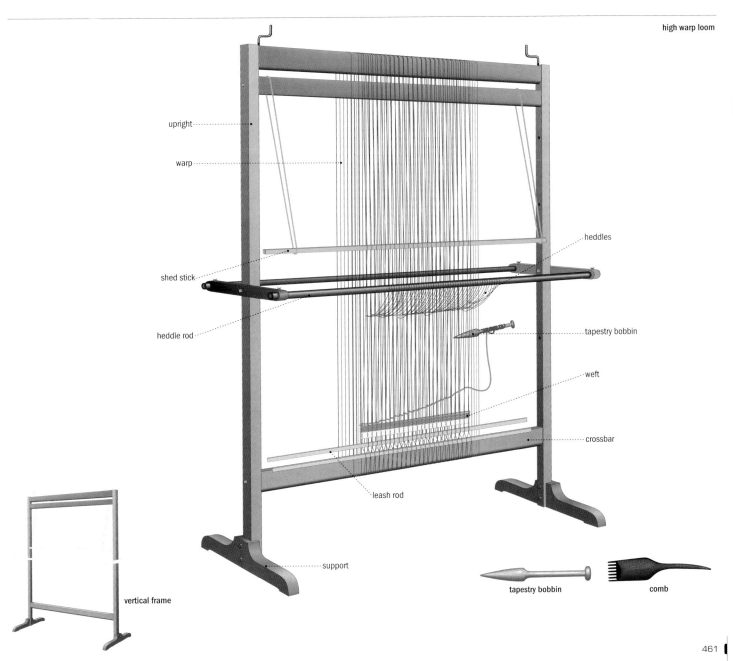

upright

warp

shed stick

heddle rod

heddles

tapestry bobbin

weft

crossbar

leash rod

support

vertical frame

tapestry bobbin

comb

accessories

bobbin winder

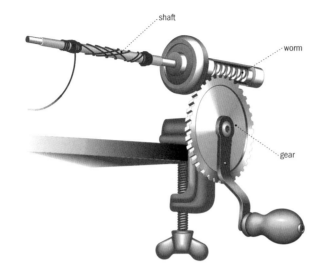

shaft

worm

gear

swift

ball winder

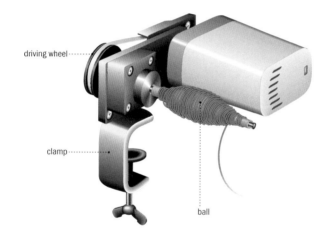

driving wheel

clamp

ball

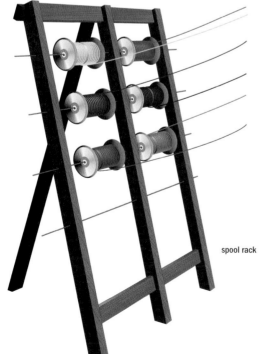

spool rack

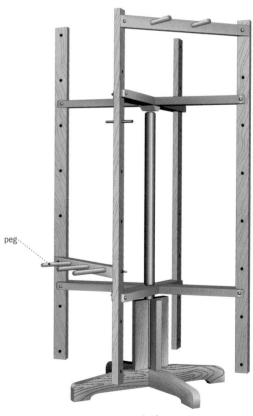

peg

warping frame

diagram of weaving principle

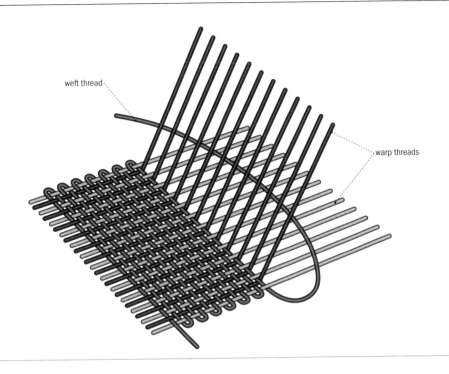

weft thread

warp threads

basic weaves

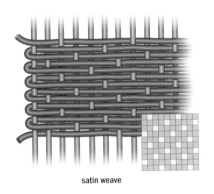

satin weave

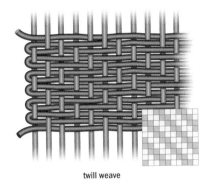

twill weave

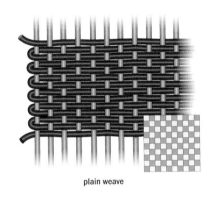

plain weave

other techniques

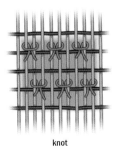

knot

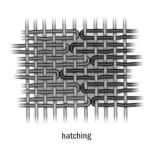

hatching

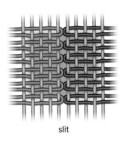

slit

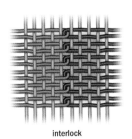

interlock

ARTS AND ARCHITECTURE

pottery

turning

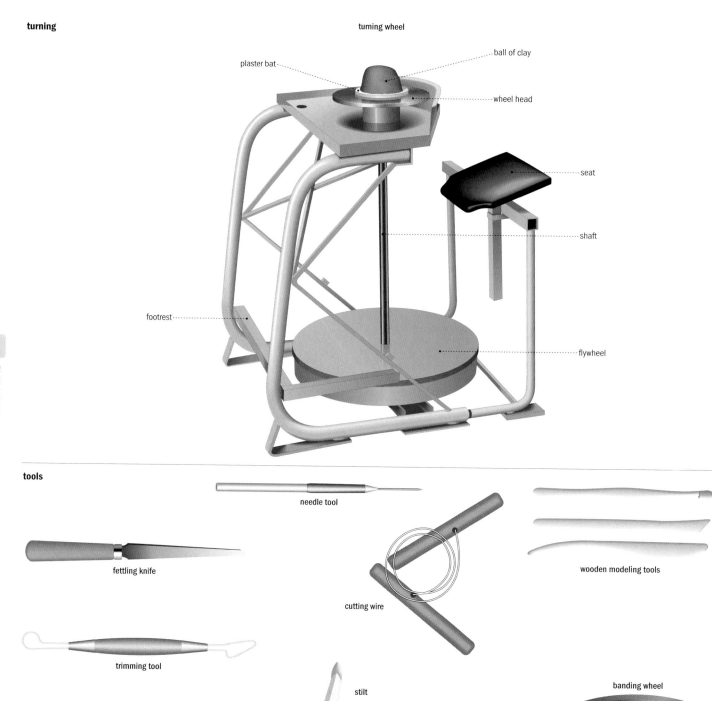

turning wheel

plaster bat

ball of clay

wheel head

seat

shaft

footrest

flywheel

tools

needle tool

fettling knife

cutting wire

wooden modeling tools

trimming tool

stilt

banding wheel

pyrometric cone

ribs

slab building

coiling

firing

electric kiln

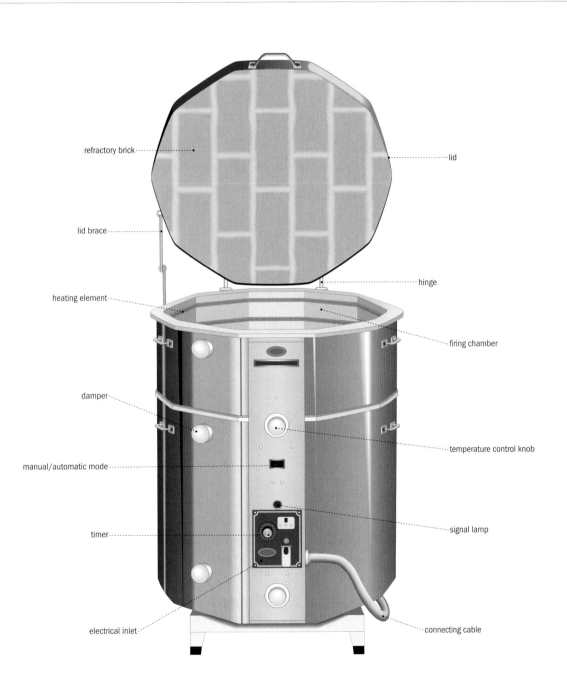

refractory brick

lid

lid brace

heating element

hinge

firing chamber

damper

temperature control knob

manual/automatic mode

signal lamp

timer

electrical inlet

connecting cable

ARTS AND ARCHITECTURE

COMMUNICATIONS AND
OFFICE AUTOMATION

languages of the world

the origin of major language families

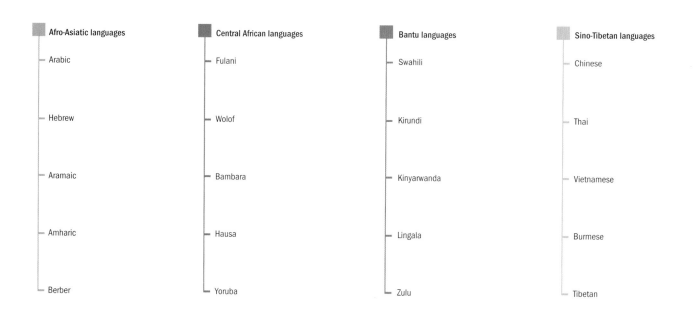

Afro-Asiatic languages

- Arabic
- Hebrew
- Aramaic
- Amharic
- Berber

Central African languages

- Fulani
- Wolof
- Bambara
- Hausa
- Yoruba

Bantu languages

- Swahili
- Kirundi
- Kinyarwanda
- Lingala
- Zulu

Sino-Tibetan languages

- Chinese
- Thai
- Vietnamese
- Burmese
- Tibetan

Indo-European languages

Romance languages	Germanic languages	Celtic languages	Slavic languages	Indo-Iranian languages
French	English	Breton	Czech	Persian
Spanish	German	Welsh	Slovak	Urdu
Catalan	Dutch	Scottish	Polish	Hindi
Portuguese	Danish	Irish	Russian	
Italian	Swedish		Ukrainian	
Romanian	Norwegian	isolated languages	Bulgarian	
	Icelandic	Greek	Slovene	
	Yiddish	Albanian	Serbo-Croatian	
		Armenian		

Amerindian languages

Inuktitut
Cree
Montagnais
Navajo
Nahuatl
Maya
Quechua
Aymara
Guarani

Ural-Altaic languages

Japanese
Korean
Mongolian
Turkish

Malayo-Polynesian languages

Indonesian	Tahitian
Tagalog	Hawaiian
Malagasy	Maori
Samoan	

Oceanian languages

Melanesian
Papuan languages
Australian aboriginal languages

COMMUNICATIONS AND OFFICE AUTOMATION

writing instruments

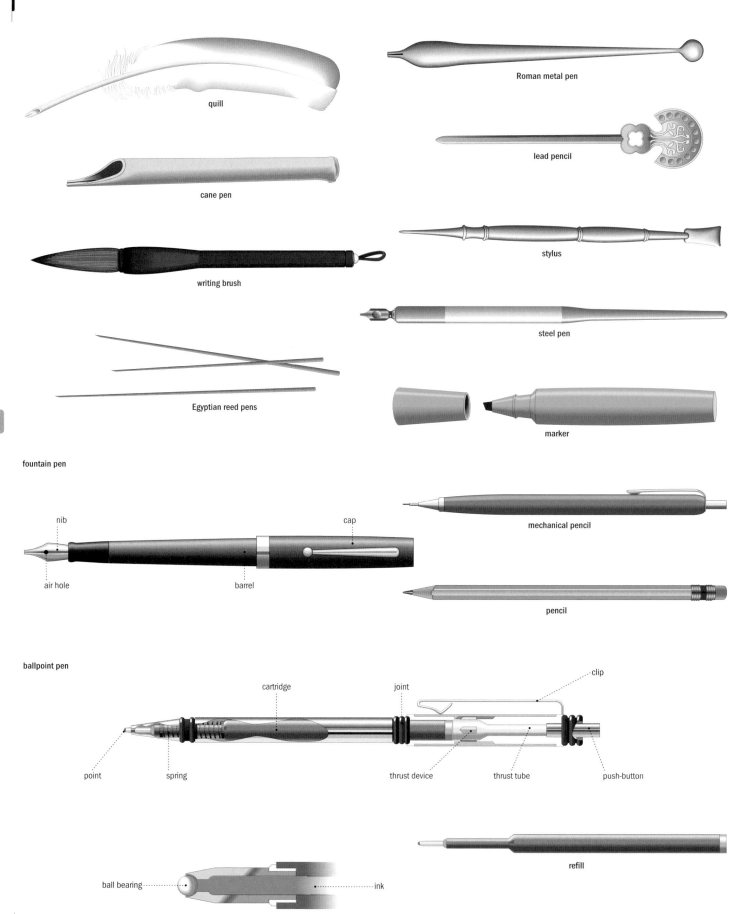

quill

Roman metal pen

cane pen

lead pencil

writing brush

stylus

Egyptian reed pens

steel pen

marker

fountain pen

nib

cap

mechanical pencil

air hole

barrel

pencil

ballpoint pen

cartridge

joint

clip

point

spring

thrust device

thrust tube

push-button

refill

ball bearing

ink

newspaper

heading

section

article

literary supplement

tabloid

color supplement

magazine

front page

nameplate

banner

front picture

caption

kicker

headline

deck

index

subhead

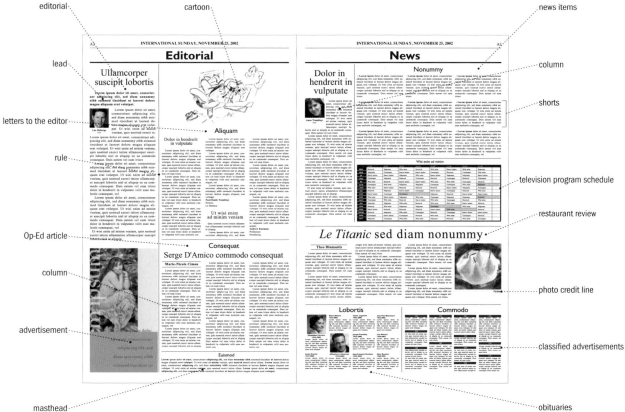

editorial

lead

letters to the editor

rule

Op-Ed article

column

advertisement

masthead

cartoon

news items

column

shorts

television program schedule

restaurant review

photo credit line

classified advertisements

obituaries

typography

characters of a font

sans serif type

abcdefghijklmnopqrstuvwxyz 0123456789

letters · figures

serif type

abcdefghijklmnopqrstuvwxyz 0123456789

shape of characters

ABCDEF
uppercase

ABCDEF
small capital

abcdef
lowercase

abcdef
italic

weight

extra-light

light

medium

semi-bold

bold

black

extra-bold

set width

condensed

narrow

normal

wide

extended

leading

Lorem ipsum dolor sit amet, consectetuer adipiscing elit, sed
simple spacing

Lorem ipsum dolor sit amet, consectetuer adipiscing elit, sed
1.5 spacing

Lorem ipsum dolor sit amet, consectetuer adipiscing elit, sed
double spacing

position of a character

H_2SO_4
inferior

XXe
superior

diacritic symbols

grave accent

umlaut

acute accent

circumflex accent

cedilla

tilde

miscellaneous symbols

registered trademark

copyright

ampersand

apostrophe

punctuation marks

period

semicolon

comma

ellipses

colon

asterisk

dash

parentheses

square brackets

virgule

exclamation point

question mark

single quotation marks

quotation marks

quotation marks (French)

COMMUNICATIONS AND OFFICE AUTOMATION

public postal network

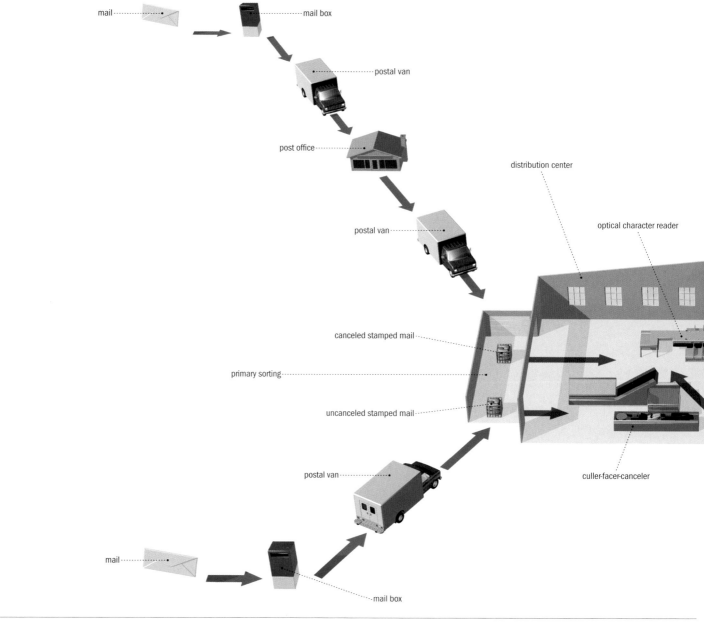

mail

mail box

postal van

post office

postal van

distribution center

optical character reader

canceled stamped mail

primary sorting

uncanceled stamped mail

culler-facer-canceler

postal van

mail

mail box

mail

.50 EURO

B Thompson
bracostrasse 35
3052 ES Rotterdam
Netherlands

Phillip Schuman
2002 Euro avenue
Montreal, Canada
H0H 1H1

postage stamp

letter

postcard

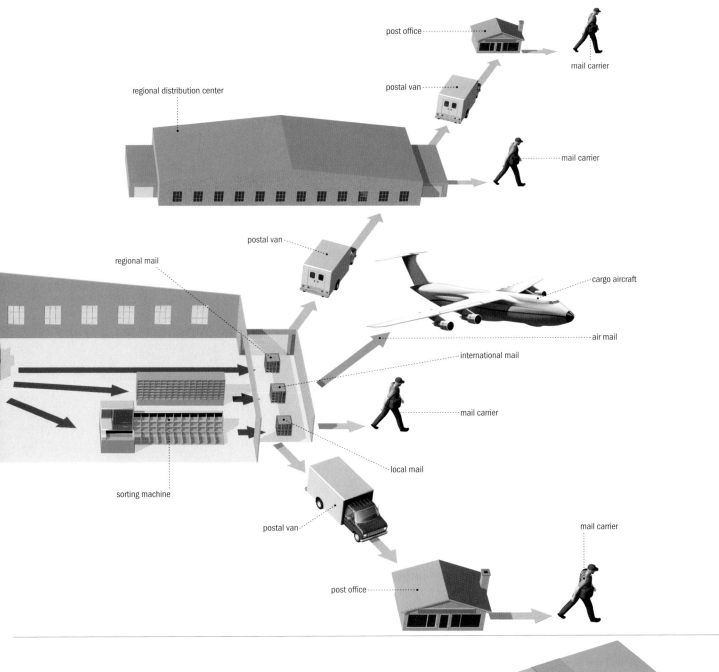

post office

mail carrier

postal van

mail carrier

regional distribution center

postal van

cargo aircraft

regional mail

air mail

international mail

mail carrier

sorting machine

local mail

mail carrier

postal van

post office

bulk mail letter

postal order

postal parcel

photography

single-lens reflex (SLR) camera: front view

film rewind knob

accessory shoe

exposure adjustment knob

hot-shoe contact

film advance mode

control panel

exposure mode

command control dial

multiple exposure mode

on-off switch

film speed

shutter release button

remote control terminal

self-timer indicator

focus mode selector

camera body

depth-of-field preview button

lens release button

objective lens

single-lens reflex (SLR) camera: camera back

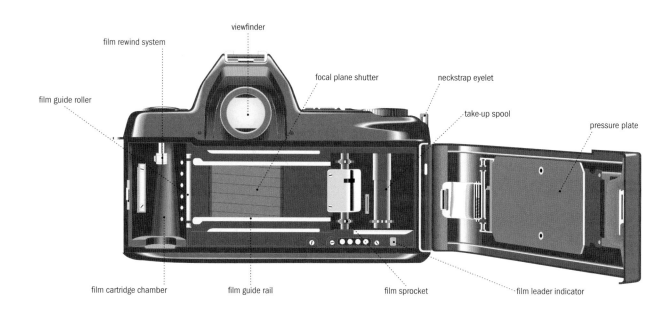

viewfinder

film rewind system

focal plane shutter

neckstrap eyelet

film guide roller

take-up spool

pressure plate

film cartridge chamber

film guide rail

film sprocket

film leader indicator

cross section of a reflex camera

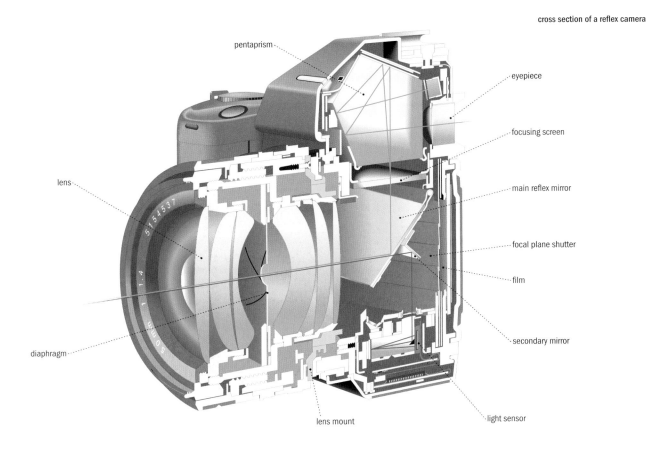

pentaprism

eyepiece

focusing screen

lens

main reflex mirror

focal plane shutter

film

diaphragm

secondary mirror

lens mount

light sensor

digital reflex camera: camera back

menu button

power switch

settings display button

viewfinder

strap eyelet

cover

multi-image jump button

MENU

INFO.

video and digital terminals

JUMP

MB

64

index/enlarge button

remote control terminal

compact memory card

image review button

liquid crystal display

erase button

four-way selector

eject button

photography

lenses

standard lens

lens

distance scale

focus setting ring

depth-of-field scale

lens aperture scale

bayonet mount

zoom lens

lens accessories

wide-angle lens

macro lens

telephoto lens

lens cap

lens hood

color filter

close-up lens

polarizing filter

objective lens

tele-converter

fisheye lens

semi-fisheye lens

exposure meter

diffuser

light-reading scale

indicator needle

exposure value

cine scale

exposure-time scale

aperture scale

film speed

calculator dial

transfer scale

spotmeter

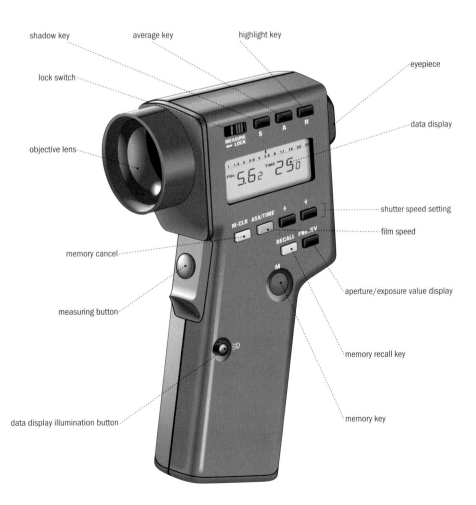

shadow key

average key

highlight key

eyepiece

lock switch

data display

objective lens

shutter speed setting

film speed

memory cancel

aperture/exposure value display

measuring button

memory recall key

data display illumination button

memory key

photography

still cameras

rangefinder

Polaroid® camera

underwater camera

single-lens reflex (SLR) camera

pocket camera

disposable camera

twin-lens reflex camera

view camera

medium format SLR (6 x 6)

stereo camera

digital camera

disk camera

---

film and digital storage

roll film

sheet film

film pack

64 ......MB

compact flash memory card

film disk

still video film disk

cartridge film

photographic accessories

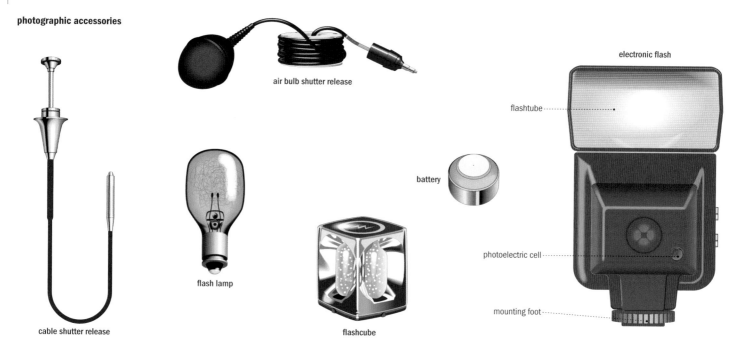

air bulb shutter release

electronic flash

flashtube

battery

flash lamp

photoelectric cell

flashcube

mounting foot

cable shutter release

tripod

camera platform

camera screw

panoramic head

plate

quick release system

camera platform lock

side-tilt lock

column lock

horizontal motion lock

column

column crank

collet

telescoping leg

slide projector

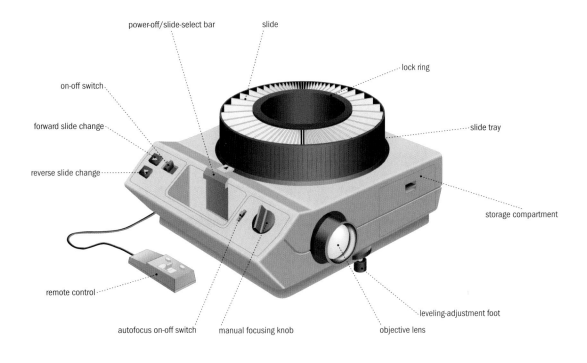

power-off/slide-select bar

slide

lock ring

on-off switch

forward slide change

reverse slide change

slide tray

storage compartment

remote control

leveling-adjustment foot

autofocus on-off switch

manual focusing knob

objective lens

transparency slide

projection screen

hanger

saddle

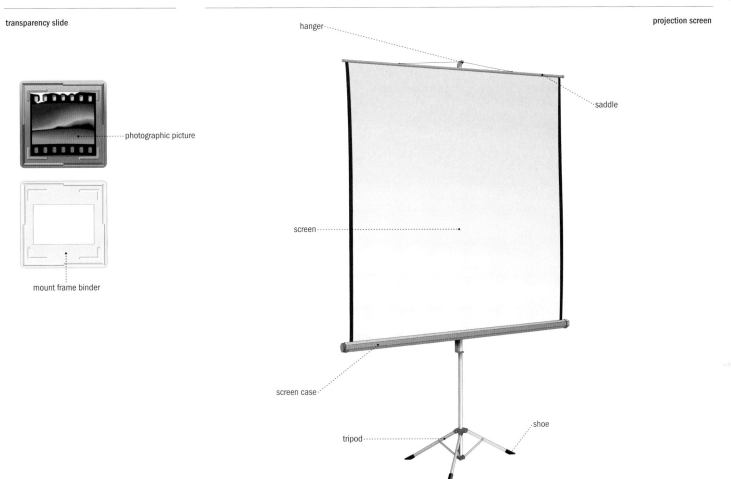

photographic picture

screen

mount frame binder

screen case

tripod

shoe

photography

darkroom

developing tank

cap

lid

reel

tank

lightbox

timer

safelight

guillotine trimmer

film drying cabinet

easel

contact printer

telecommunications by satellite

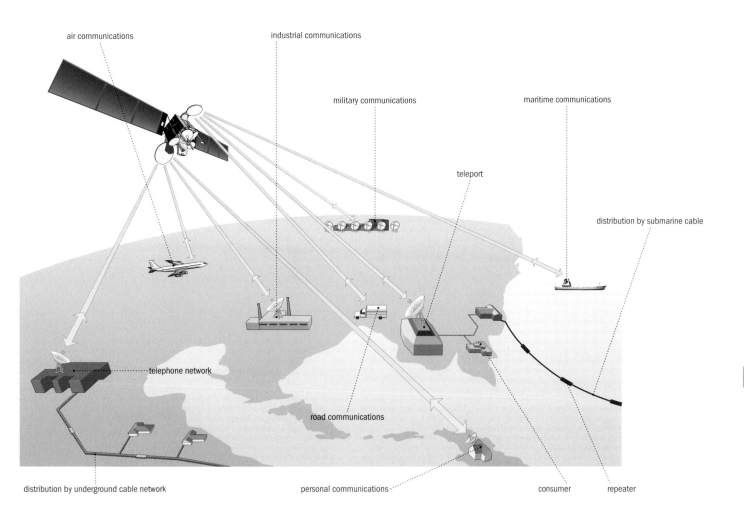

air communications

industrial communications

military communications

maritime communications

teleport

distribution by submarine cable

telephone network

road communications

distribution by underground cable network

personal communications

consumer

repeater

telecommunication satellites

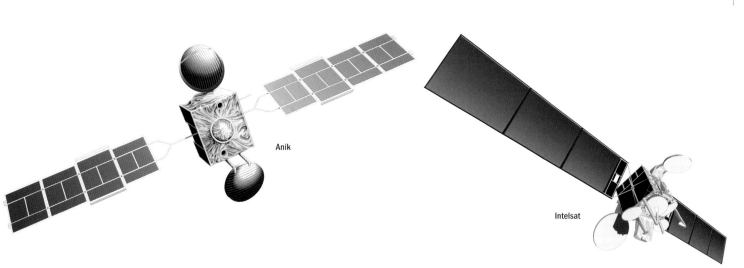

Anik

Intelsat

dynamic microphone

windscreen

moving coil

diaphragm

on-off switch

magnet

connector

housing

plug

cable

radio: studio and control room

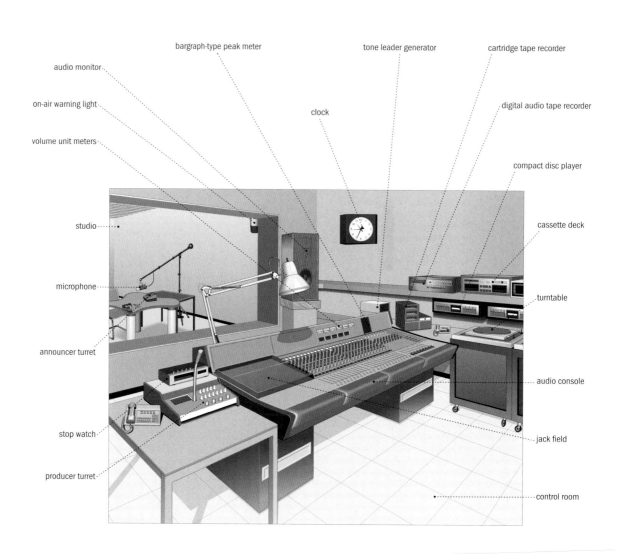

bargraph-type peak meter

tone leader generator

cartridge tape recorder

audio monitor

on-air warning light

clock

digital audio tape recorder

volume unit meters

compact disc player

studio

cassette deck

microphone

turntable

announcer turret

audio console

stop watch

jack field

producer turret

control room

television

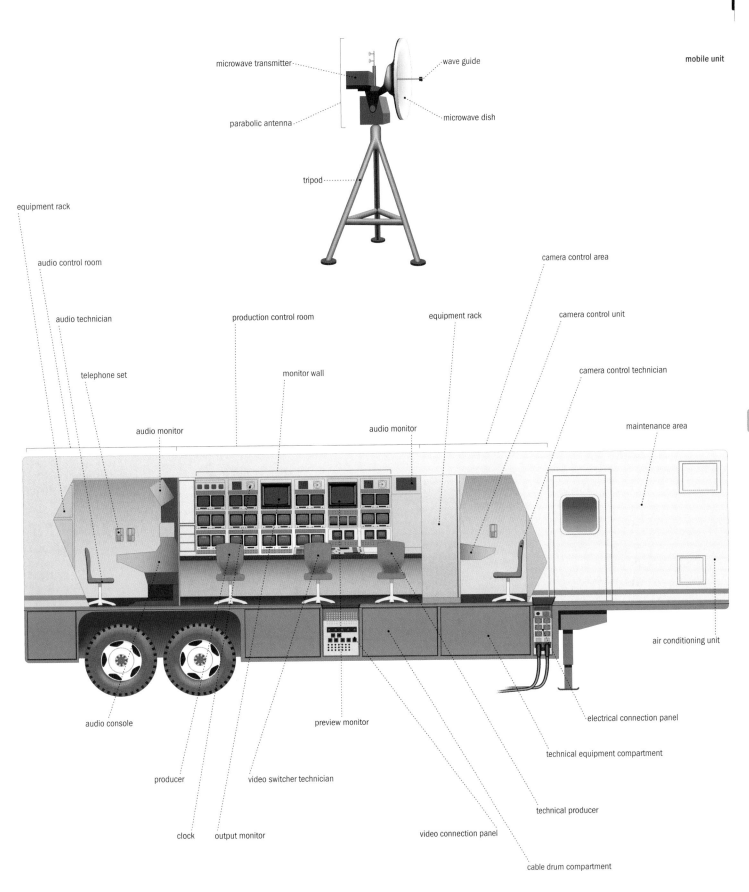

mobile unit

microwave transmitter

wave guide

parabolic antenna

microwave dish

tripod

equipment rack

audio control room

camera control area

audio technician

production control room

equipment rack

camera control unit

telephone set

monitor wall

camera control technician

audio monitor

audio monitor

maintenance area

audio console

producer

video switcher technician

clock

output monitor

preview monitor

video connection panel

technical producer

cable drum compartment

technical equipment compartment

electrical connection panel

air conditioning unit

television

studio and control rooms

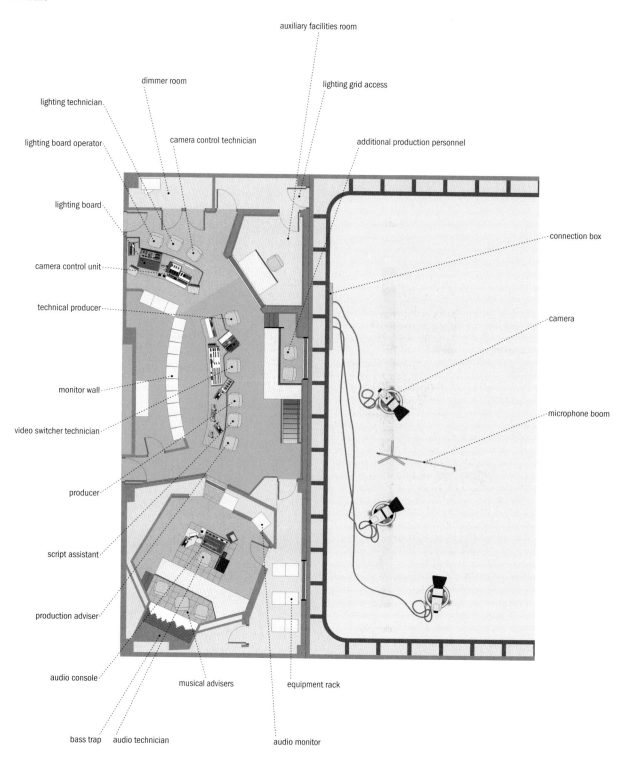

auxiliary facilities room

dimmer room

lighting grid access

lighting technician

camera control technician

lighting board operator

additional production personnel

lighting board

connection box

camera control unit

technical producer

camera

monitor wall

microphone boom

video switcher technician

producer

script assistant

production adviser

audio console

musical advisers

equipment rack

bass trap   audio technician

audio monitor

 studio floor

 lighting/camera control area

audio control room

 production control room

COMMUNICATIONS AND OFFICE AUTOMATION

production control room

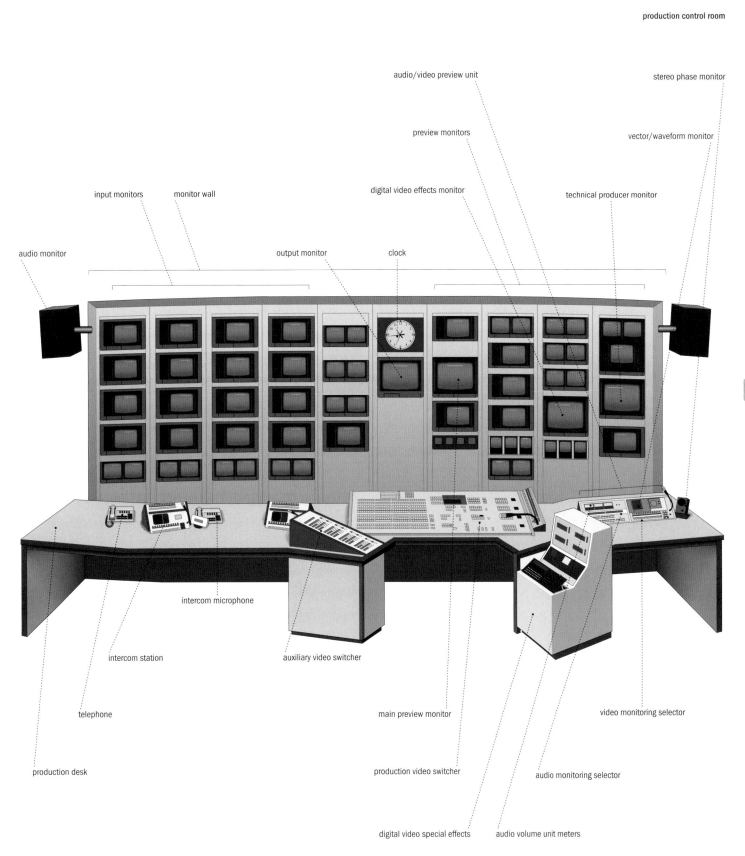

audio/video preview unit

stereo phase monitor

preview monitors

vector/waveform monitor

input monitors   monitor wall

digital video effects monitor

technical producer monitor

audio monitor

output monitor   clock

intercom microphone

intercom station   auxiliary video switcher

telephone

main preview monitor   video monitoring selector

production desk

production video switcher   audio monitoring selector

digital video special effects   audio volume unit meters

television

COMMUNICATIONS AND OFFICE AUTOMATION

studio floor

floodlight

test pattern

floodlight on pantograph

lighting grid

spotlight

curtain

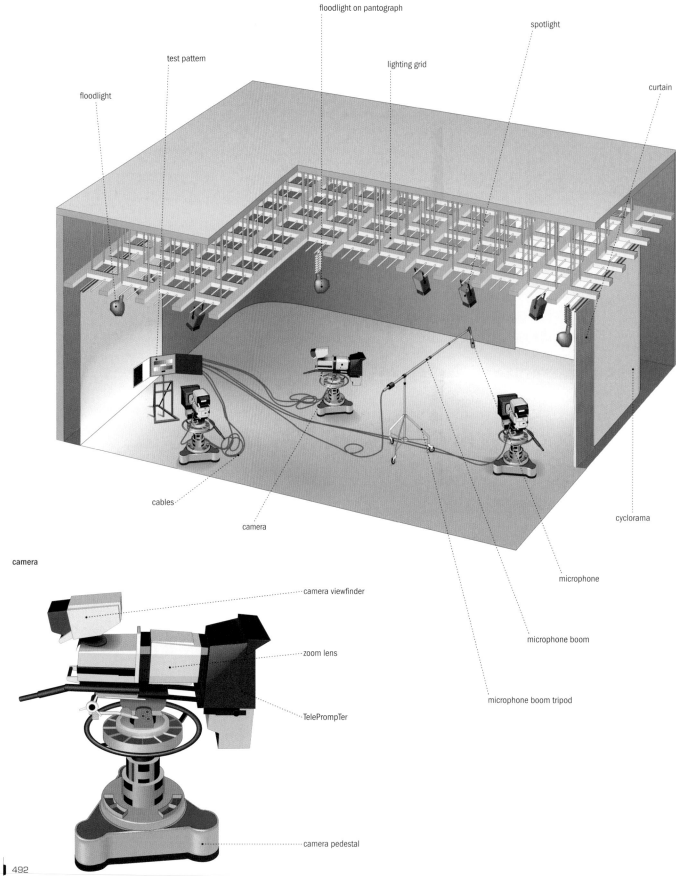

cables

camera

camera

cyclorama

microphone

microphone boom

microphone boom tripod

camera viewfinder

zoom lens

TelePrompTer

camera pedestal

dish antenna

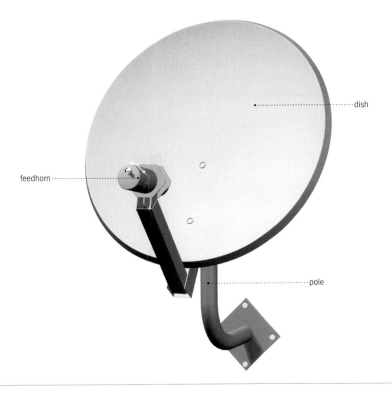

dish

feedhorn

pole

receiver

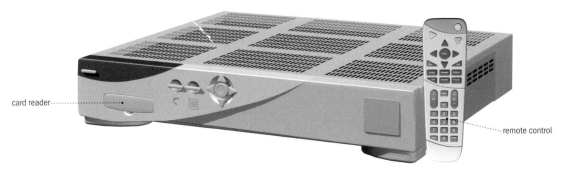

card reader

remote control

home theater

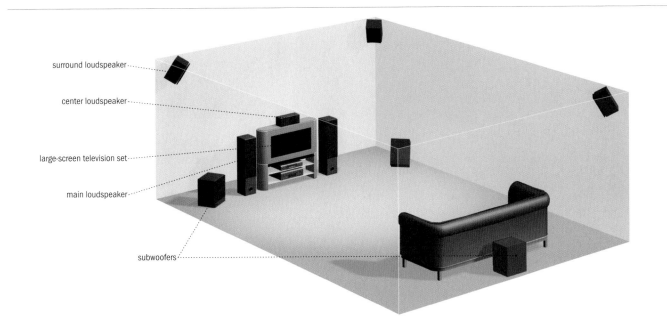

surround loudspeaker

center loudspeaker

large-screen television set

main loudspeaker

subwoofers

television

television set

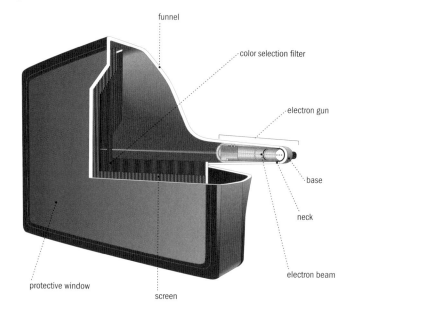

cabinet

screen

indicators

remote control sensor

tuning controls

power button

picture tube

funnel

color selection filter

electron gun

base

neck

electron beam

protective window

screen

electron gun

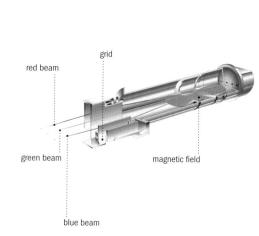

grid

red beam

green beam

magnetic field

blue beam

DVD player

power button

disc tray

display

digital versatile disc (DVD)

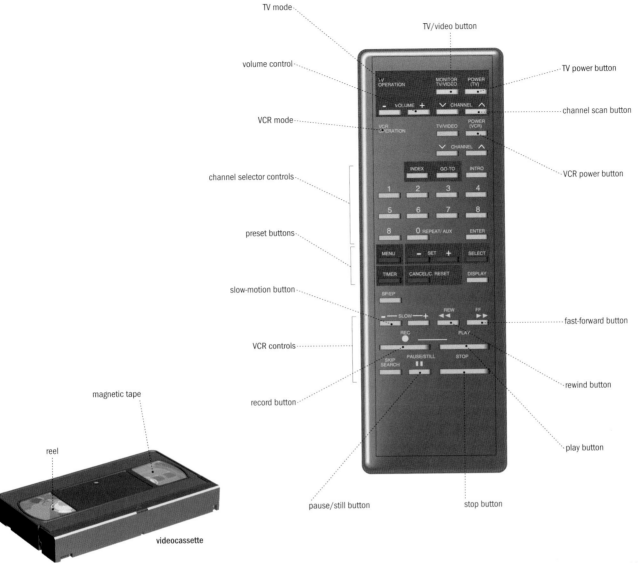

TV mode
TV/video button
volume control
TV power button
channel scan button
VCR mode
VCR power button
channel selector controls
preset buttons
slow-motion button
fast-forward button
VCR controls
rewind button
record button
play button
pause/still button
stop button

reel
magnetic tape
videocassette

videocassette recorder

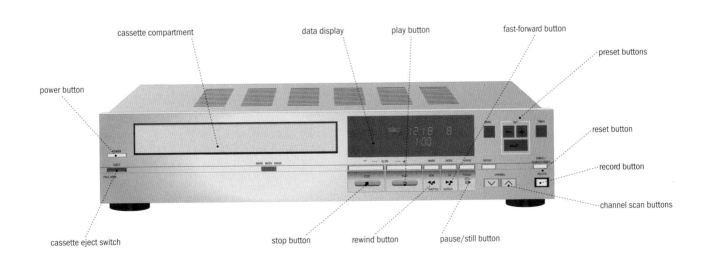

cassette compartment
data display
play button
fast-forward button
preset buttons
power button
reset button
record button
channel scan buttons
cassette eject switch
stop button
rewind button
pause/still button

television

analog camcorder: front view

electronic viewfinder

eyecup

edit search button

videotape operation controls

display panel

zoom lens

nightshot switch

power/functions switch

microphone

focus selector

near/far dial

cassette compartment

compact videocassette adapter

analog camcorder: back view

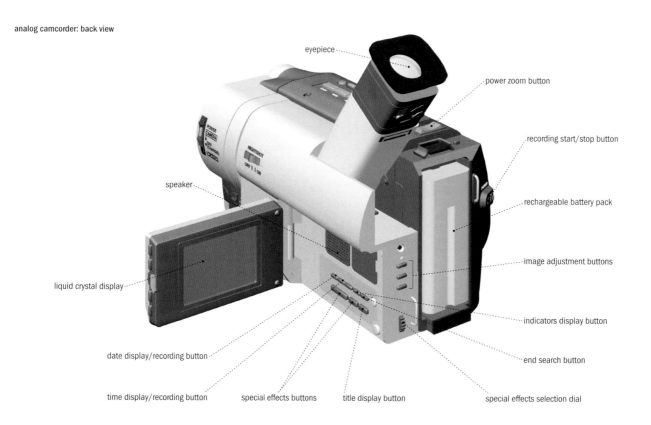

eyepiece

power zoom button

recording start/stop button

rechargeable battery pack

speaker

image adjustment buttons

liquid crystal display

indicators display button

date display/recording button

end search button

time display/recording button

special effects buttons

title display button

special effects selection dial

sound reproducing system

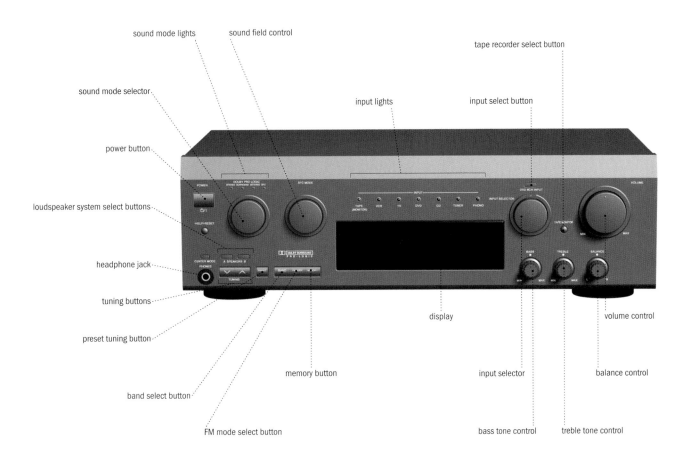

sound mode lights

sound field control

tape recorder select button

sound mode selector

input lights

input select button

power button

loudspeaker system select buttons

headphone jack

tuning buttons

preset tuning button

display

volume control

memory button

input selector

balance control

band select button

FM mode select button

bass tone control

treble tone control

power cord

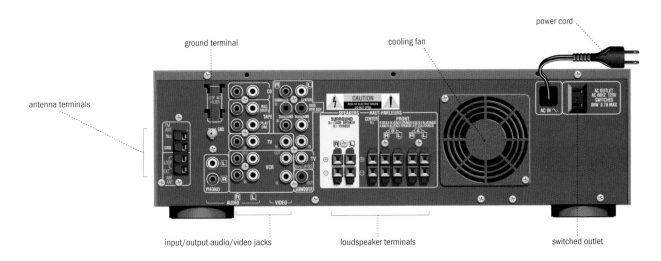

ground terminal

cooling fan

antenna terminals

input/output audio/video jacks

loudspeaker terminals

switched outlet

sound reproducing system

tuner

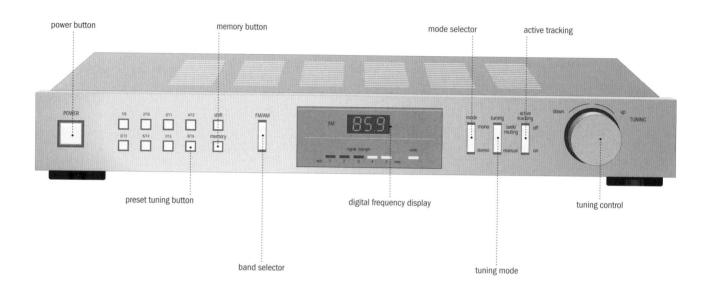

power button   memory button   mode selector   active tracking

POWER

1/9 2/10 3/11 4/12 shift   FM/AM

5/13 6/14 7/15 8/16 memory

FM   85.9

signal strength

min   1   2   3   4   5   max   tuned

mode   tuning   active tracking   down   up   TUNING

mono   seek/muting   off

stereo   manual   on

preset tuning button   digital frequency display   tuning control

band selector   tuning mode

graphic equalizer

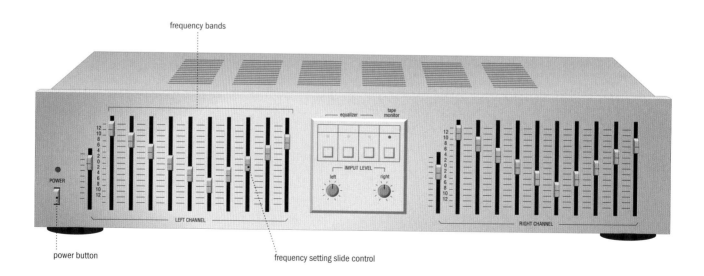

frequency bands

equalizer   tape monitor

INPUT LEVEL

left   right

POWER

12 10 8 6 4 2 0 2 4 6 8 10 12

LEFT CHANNEL

12 10 8 6 4 2 0 2 4 6 8 10 12

RIGHT CHANNEL

power button   frequency setting slide control

cassette

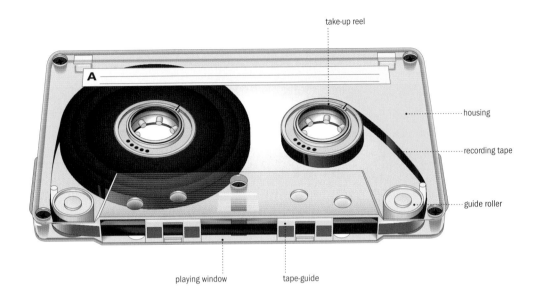

take-up reel

housing

recording tape

guide roller

playing window

tape-guide

cassette tape deck

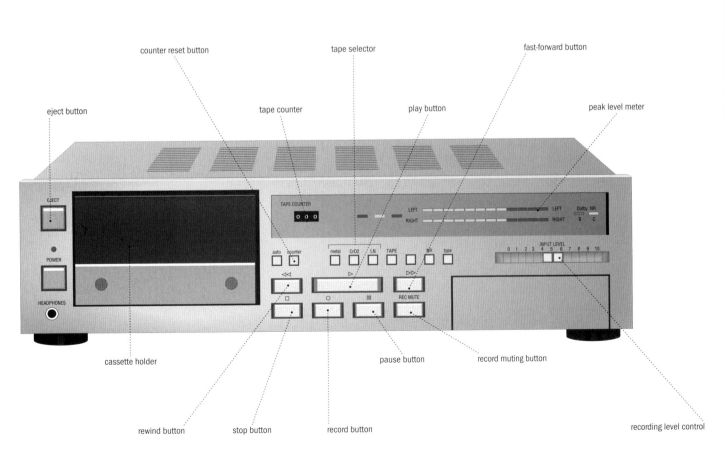

counter reset button

tape selector

fast-forward button

eject button

tape counter

play button

peak level meter

cassette holder

pause button

record muting button

rewind button

stop button

record button

recording level control

sound reproducing system

record

spiral

spiral-in groove

tail-out groove

center hole

locked groove

band

label

record player

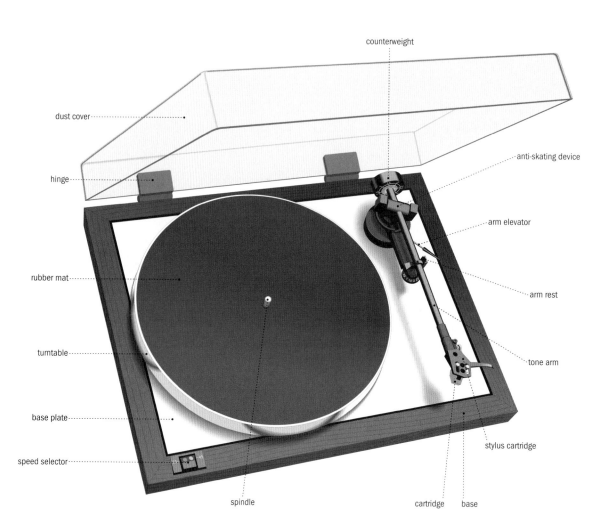

counterweight

dust cover

anti-skating device

hinge

arm elevator

arm rest

rubber mat

turntable

tone arm

base plate

stylus cartridge

speed selector

spindle

cartridge

base

compact disc

technical identification band

pressed area

reading start

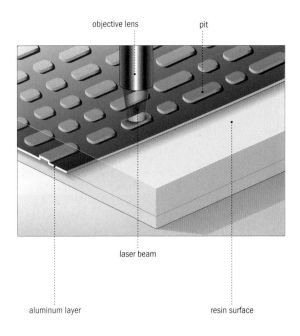

objective lens

pit

laser beam

aluminum layer

resin surface

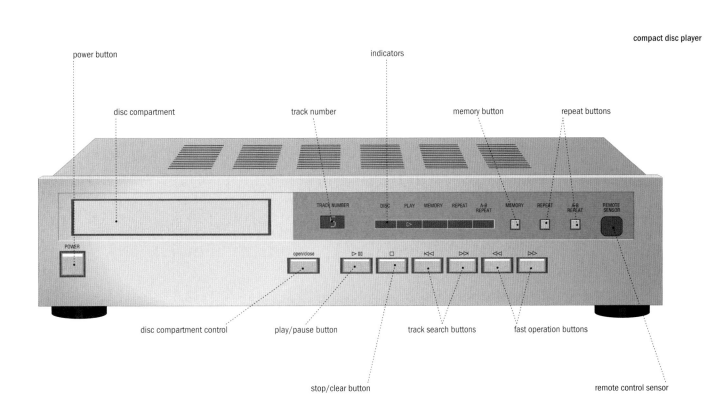

power button

indicators

disc compartment

track number

memory button

repeat buttons

TRACK NUMBER

DISC   PLAY   MEMORY   REPEAT   A-B REPEAT

MEMORY   REPEAT   A-B REPEAT   REMOTE SENSOR

POWER

open/close

disc compartment control

play/pause button

track search buttons

fast operation buttons

stop/clear button

remote control sensor

sound reproducing system

headphones

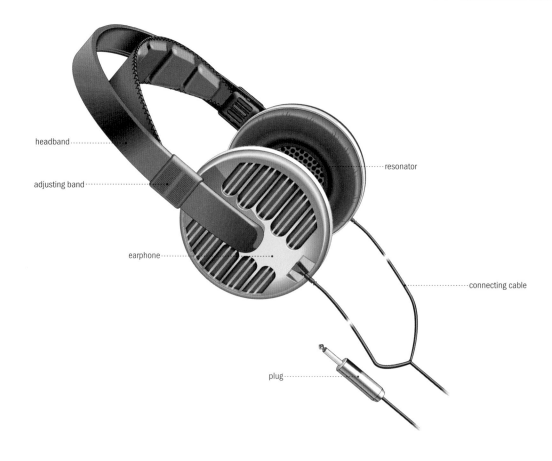

headband

adjusting band

earphone

resonator

connecting cable

plug

loudspeakers

right channel

left channel

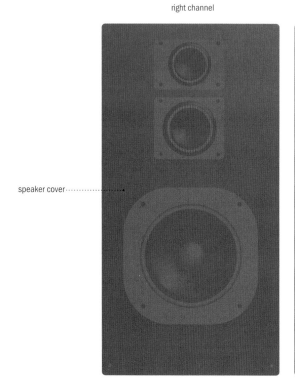

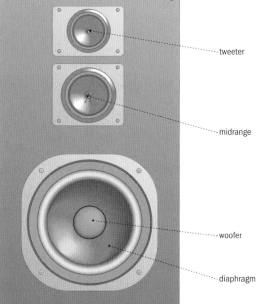

tweeter

midrange

speaker cover

woofer

diaphragm

mini stereo sound system

compact disc player

ampli-tuner

loudspeaker

compact disc recorder

dual cassette deck

portable sound systems

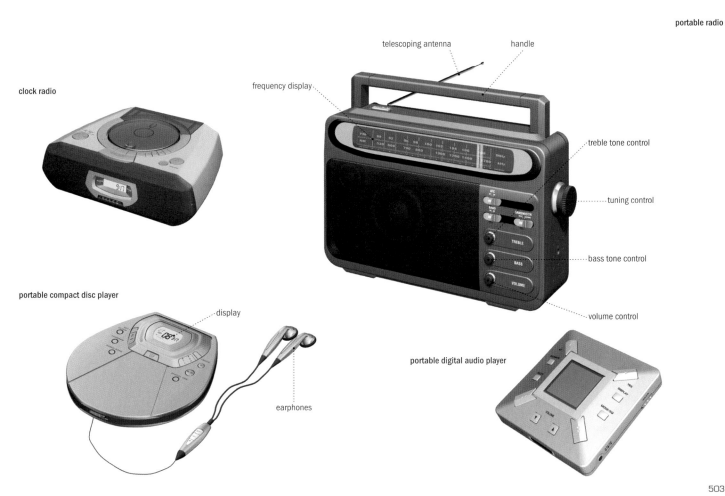

clock radio

portable compact disc player

portable radio

telescoping antenna

handle

frequency display

treble tone control

tuning control

bass tone control

volume control

display

earphones

portable digital audio player

portable sound systems

personal radio cassette player

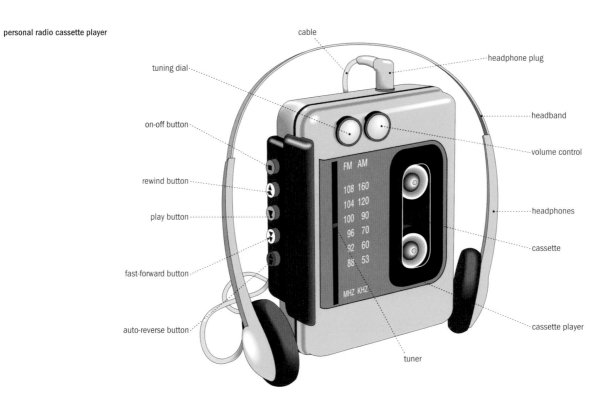

cable

headphone plug

tuning dial

on-off button

rewind button

play button

fast-forward button

auto-reverse button

headband

volume control

headphones

cassette

cassette player

tuner

FM AM
108 160
104 120
100 90
96 70
92 60
88 53
MHZ KHZ

portable CD radio cassette recorder

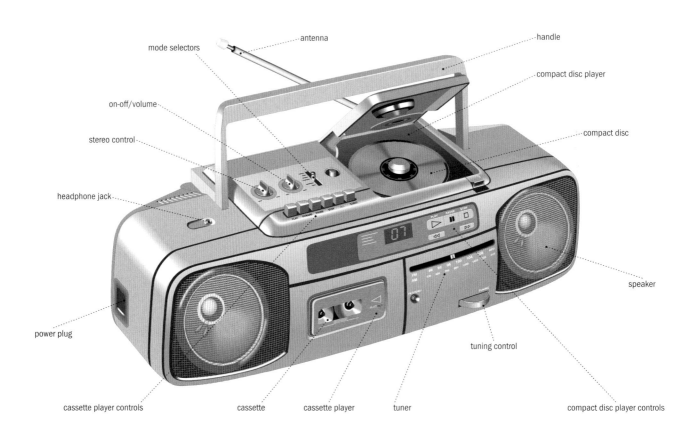

mode selectors

antenna

handle

on-off/volume

compact disc player

stereo control

compact disc

headphone jack

speaker

power plug

cassette player controls

cassette

cassette player

tuner

tuning control

compact disc player controls

wireless communication

walkie-talkie

volume control
display
antenna
call button
power button
scroll button
light button
menu button
microphone
lock button
monitor button
push-to-talk switch
speaker

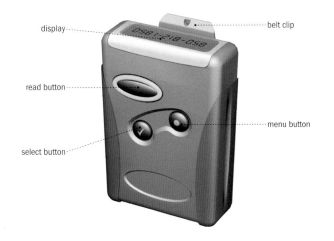

numeric pager

display
belt clip
read button
menu button
select button

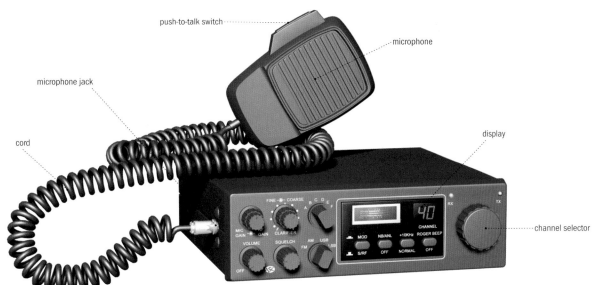

CB radio

push-to-talk switch
microphone
microphone jack
cord
display
channel selector

communication by telephone

portable cellular telephone

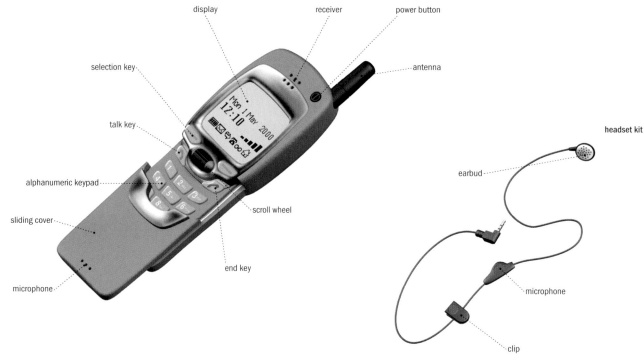

display

receiver

power button

selection key

antenna

talk key

headset kit

earbud

alphanumeric keypad

scroll wheel

sliding cover

microphone

end key

microphone

clip

telephone set

receiver

display

handset

on-off light

receiver volume control

transmitter

display setting

ringing volume control

handset cord

push buttons

telephone index

automatic dialer index

memory button

function selectors

examples of telephones

pay phone

coin slot

volume control

handset

armored cord

display

next call

language display button

push button

card reader

coin return bucket

cordless telephone

telecommunication terminal

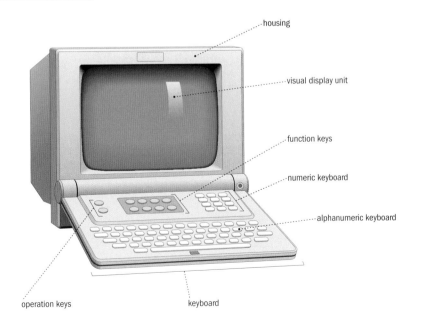

housing

visual display unit

function keys

numeric keyboard

alphanumeric keyboard

operation keys

keyboard

push-button telephone

call director telephone

communication by telephone

telephone answering machine

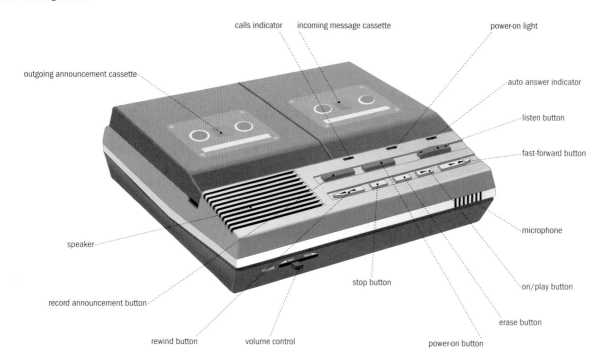

calls indicator
incoming message cassette
power-on light
outgoing announcement cassette
auto answer indicator
listen button
fast-forward button
microphone
speaker
on/play button
stop button
erase button
record announcement button
power-on button
rewind button
volume control

facsimile machine

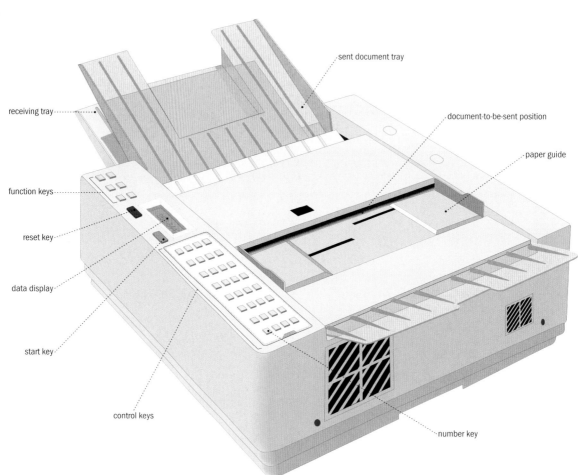

sent document tray
document-to-be-sent position
receiving tray
paper guide
function keys
reset key
data display
start key
control keys
number key

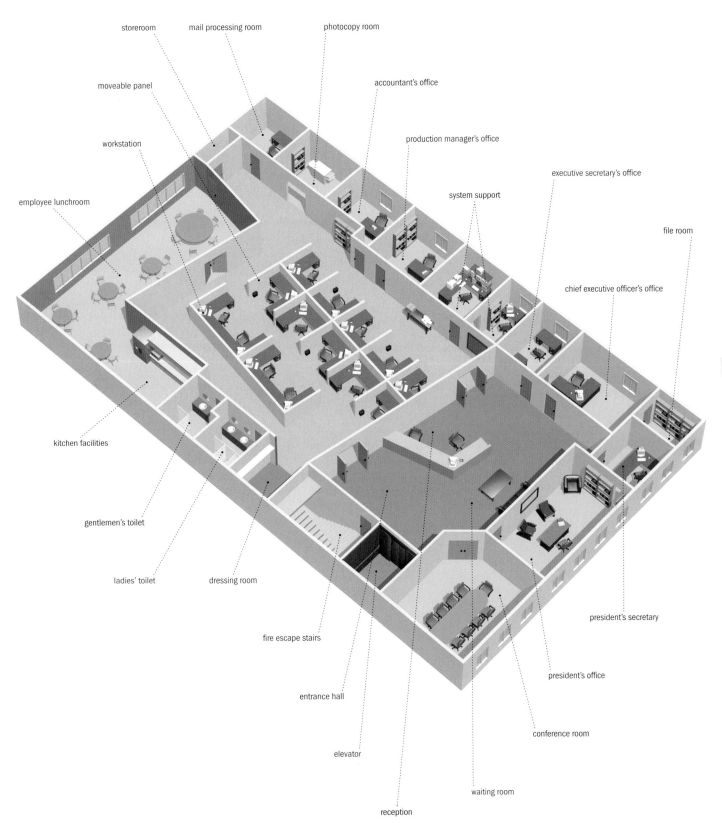

storeroom

mail processing room

photocopy room

moveable panel

accountant's office

production manager's office

workstation

executive secretary's office

system support

employee lunchroom

file room

chief executive officer's office

kitchen facilities

gentlemen's toilet

ladies' toilet

dressing room

president's secretary

fire escape stairs

president's office

entrance hall

conference room

elevator

waiting room

reception

office furniture

filing furniture

mobile filing unit

mobile drawer unit

lateral filing cabinet

storage furniture

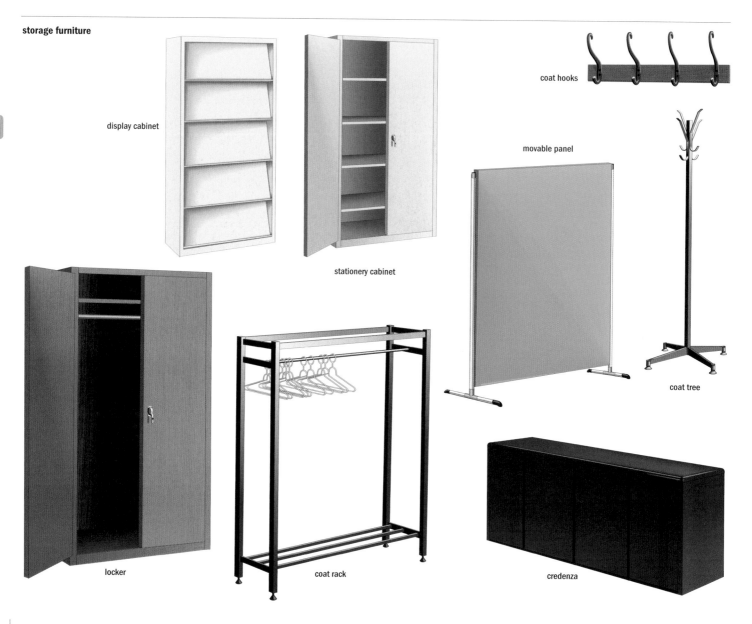

display cabinet

stationery cabinet

coat hooks

movable panel

coat tree

locker

coat rack

credenza

work furniture

computer table

adjustable platen

panel

printer table

paper feed channel

paper catcher

paper tray

typist's chair

executive desk

desk mat

swivel-tilter armchair

return

secretarial desk

office furniture

COMMUNICATIONS AND OFFICE AUTOMATION

photocopier

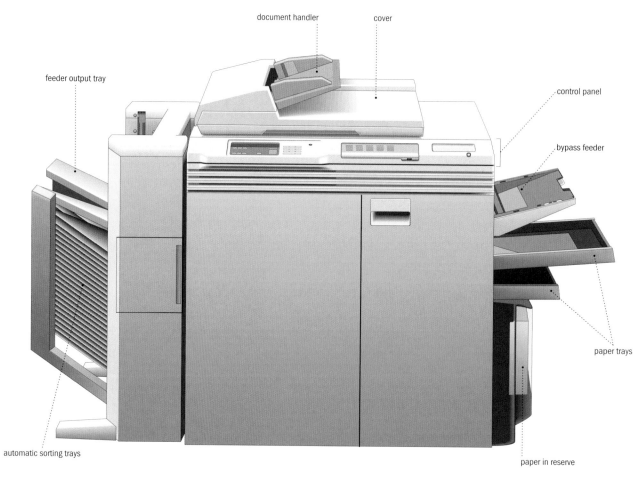

document handler

cover

feeder output tray

control panel

bypass feeder

paper trays

automatic sorting trays

paper in reserve

control panel

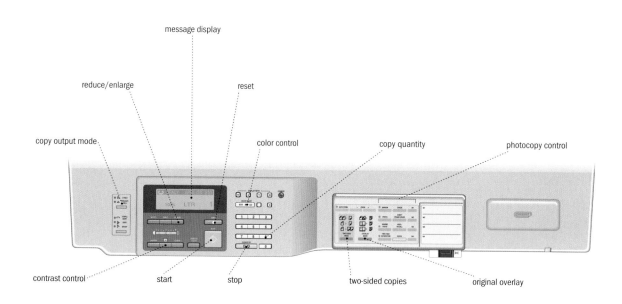

message display

reduce/enlarge

reset

copy output mode

color control

copy quantity

photocopy control

contrast control

start

stop

two-sided copies

original overlay

personal computer

tower case: back view

tower case: front view

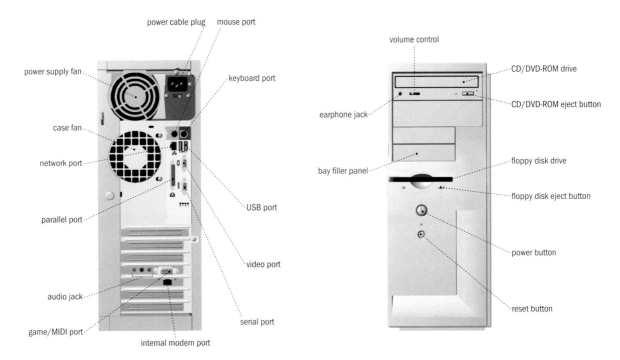

power cable plug   mouse port

power supply fan

keyboard port

case fan

network port

parallel port

USB port

video port

audio jack

game/MIDI port

internal modem port

serial port

volume control

CD/DVD-ROM drive

CD/DVD-ROM eject button

earphone jack

floppy disk drive

bay filler panel

floppy disk eject button

power button

reset button

tower case: interior view

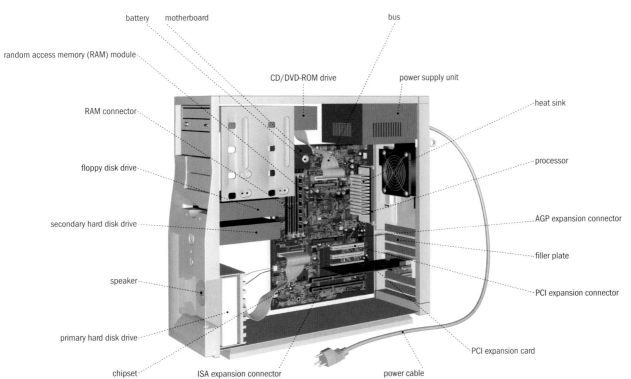

battery   motherboard

bus

random access memory (RAM) module

RAM connector

floppy disk drive

secondary hard disk drive

speaker

primary hard disk drive

chipset

ISA expansion connector

CD/DVD-ROM drive

power supply unit

power cable

heat sink

processor

AGP expansion connector

filler plate

PCI expansion connector

PCI expansion card

input devices

keyboard and pictograms

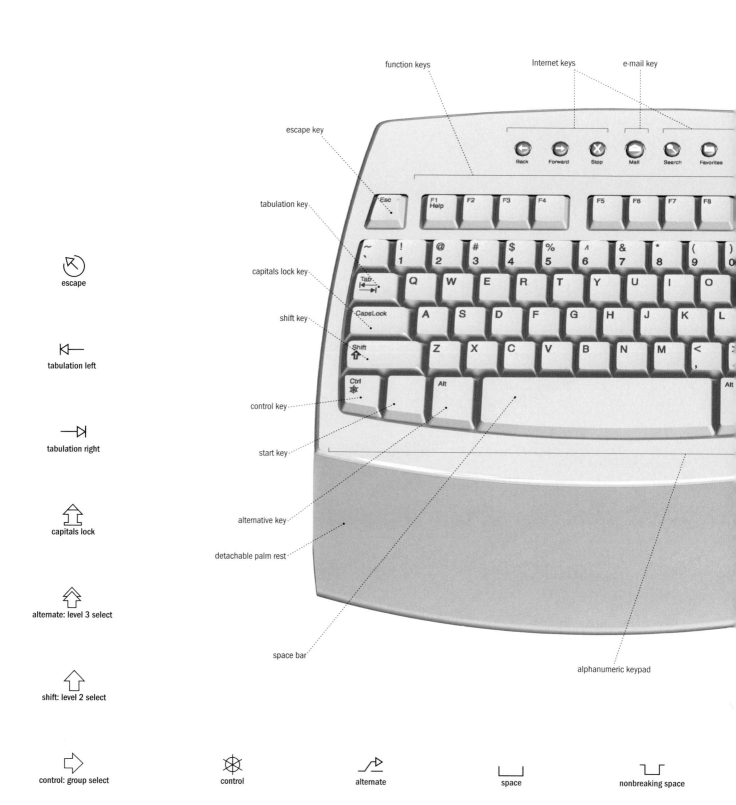

function keys

Internet keys

e-mail key

escape key

tabulation key

capitals lock key

shift key

control key

start key

alternative key

detachable palm rest

space bar

alphanumeric keypad

Back   Forward   Stop   Mail   Search   Favorites

Esc   F1 Help   F2   F3   F4   F5   F6   F7   F8

~   !   @   # $ %   ^   &   *   (   )
     1   2   3   4   5   6   7   8   9   0

Tab   Q   W   E   R   T   Y   U   I   O

CapsLock   A   S   D   F   G   H   J   K   L

Shift   Z   X   C   V   B   N   M   <   ,

Ctrl   Alt   Alt

escape

tabulation left

tabulation right

capitals lock

alternate: level 3 select

shift: level 2 select

control: group select

control

alternate

space

nonbreaking space

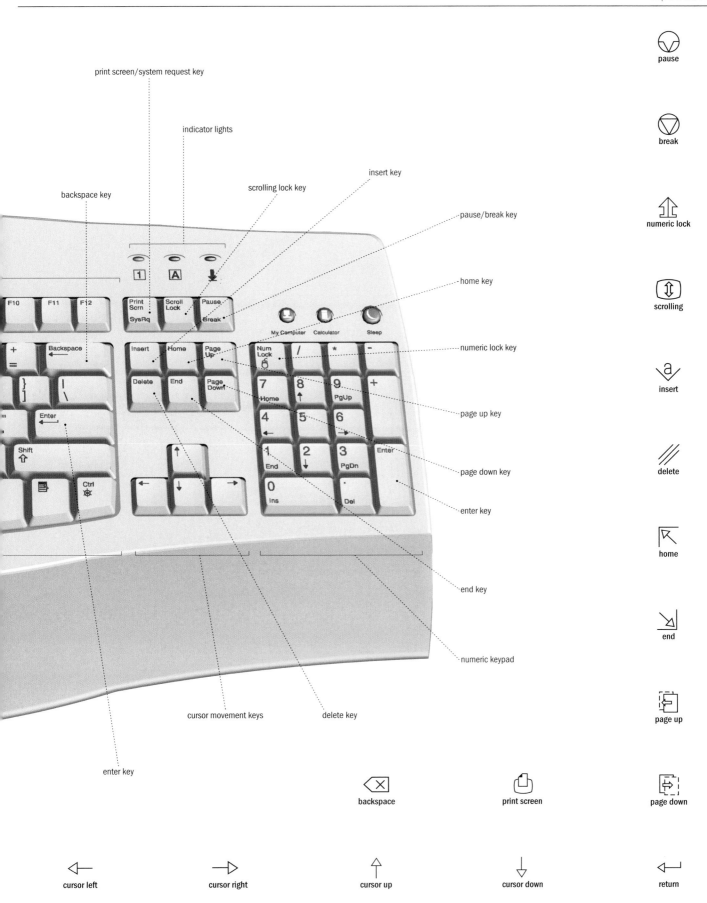

print screen/system request key

indicator lights

insert key

scrolling lock key

pause/break key

backspace key

home key

numeric lock key

page up key

page down key

enter key

end key

numeric keypad

cursor movement keys

delete key

enter key

pause

break

numeric lock

scrolling

insert

delete

home

end

page up

backspace

print screen

page down

cursor left

cursor right

cursor up

cursor down

return

input devices

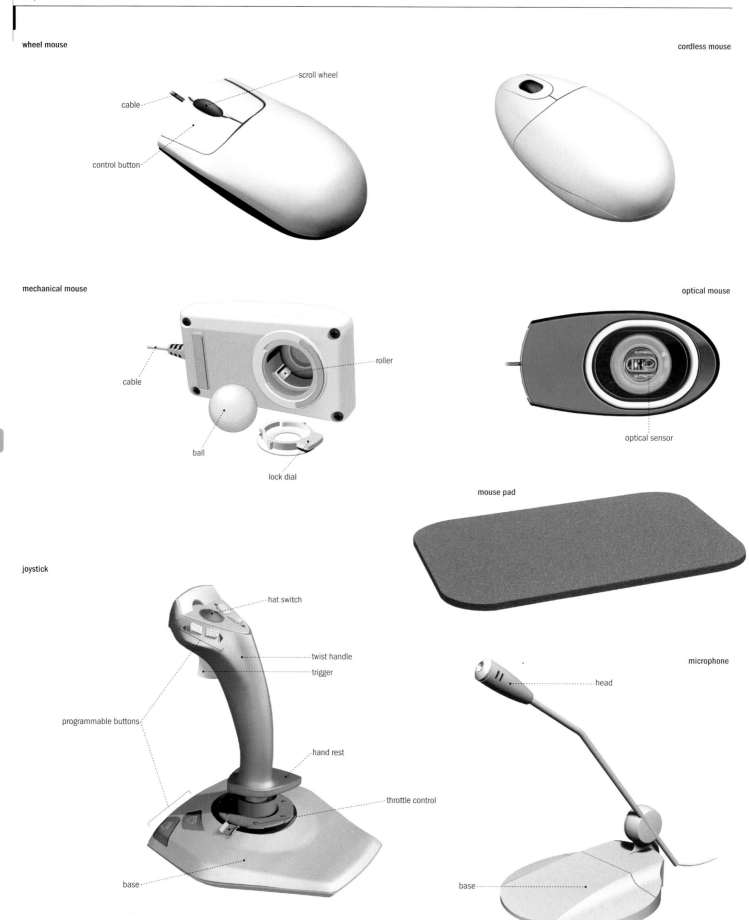

wheel mouse

scroll wheel

cable

control button

cordless mouse

mechanical mouse

cable

roller

ball

lock dial

optical mouse

optical sensor

mouse pad

joystick

hat switch

twist handle

trigger

programmable buttons

hand rest

throttle control

base

microphone

head

base

trackball

digitizing pad

stylus holder

stylus

CD/ROM player

Webcam

cable

lens

microphone

base

bar code reader

digital camera

digital camcorder

optical scanner

output devices

flat screen monitor

video monitor

vertical control

horizontal control

centering control

contrast control

power indicator

power switch

brightness control

projector

control panel

lens

remote sensor

power switch

connector panel

computer connector

mouse port

inkjet printer

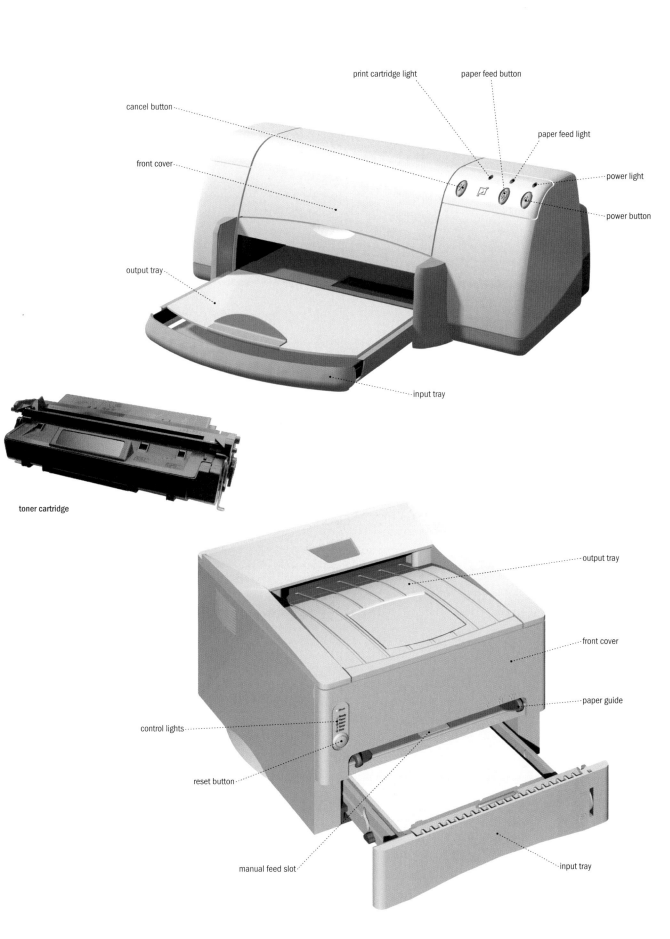

print cartridge light

paper feed button

cancel button

paper feed light

front cover

power light

power button

output tray

input tray

toner cartridge

laser printer

output tray

front cover

paper guide

control lights

reset button

manual feed slot

input tray

desktop video unit

film recorder

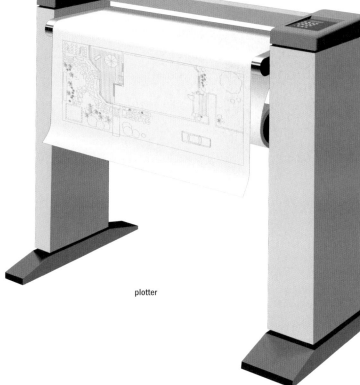

plotter

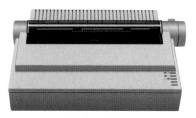

dot matrix printer

uninterruptible power supply (UPS)

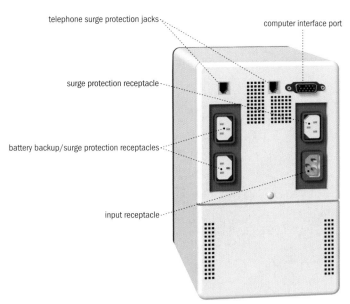

telephone surge protection jacks

computer interface port

control lights

surge protection receptacle

battery backup/surge protection receptacles

input receptacle

on/off/test button

data storage devices

hard disk drive

removable hard disk drive

disk eject button

removable hard disk

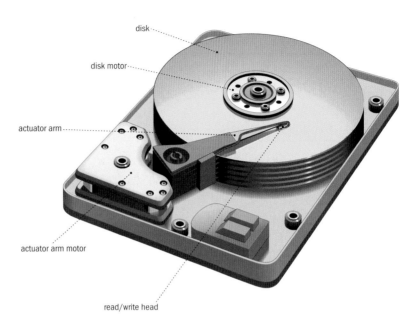

disk

disk motor

actuator arm

actuator arm motor

read/write head

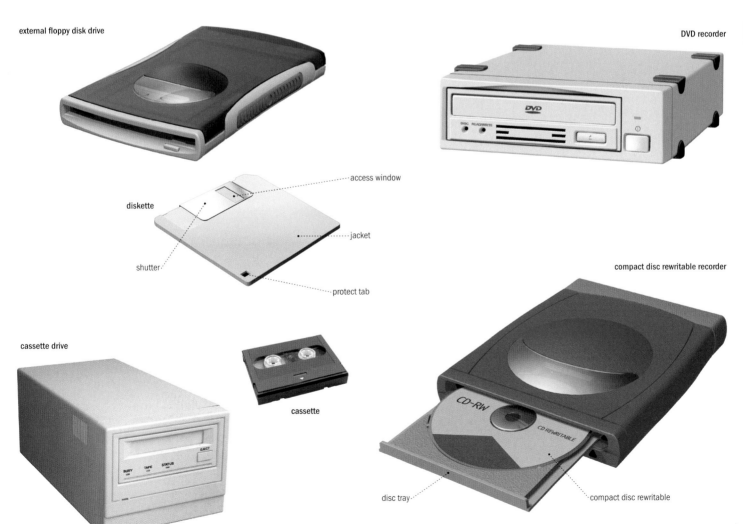

external floppy disk drive

DVD recorder

diskette

access window

jacket

shutter

protect tab

compact disc rewritable recorder

cassette drive

cassette

disc tray

compact disc rewritable

CD-RW

CD REWRITABLE

communication devices

network interface card

network access point transceiver

wireless network interface card

modem

examples of networks

ring network

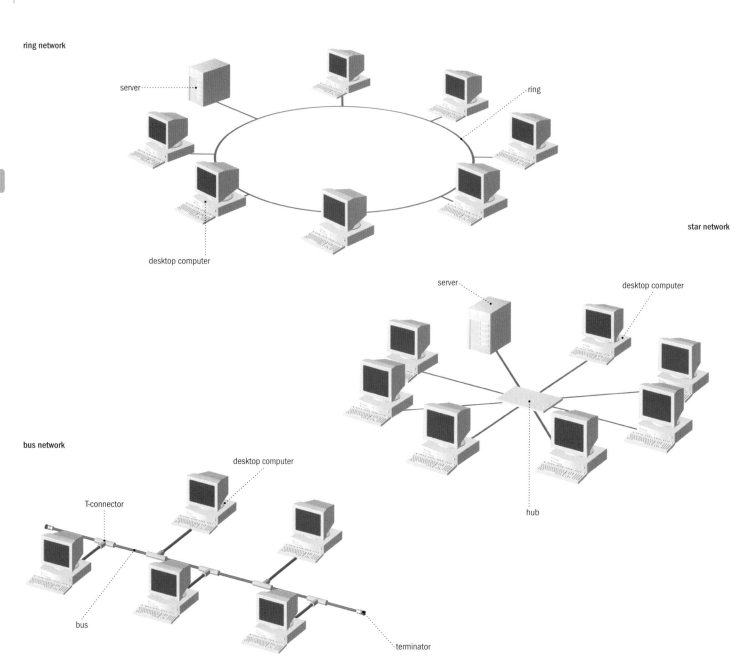

server

ring

desktop computer

star network

server

desktop computer

hub

bus network

desktop computer

T-connector

bus

terminator

computer network

wide area network

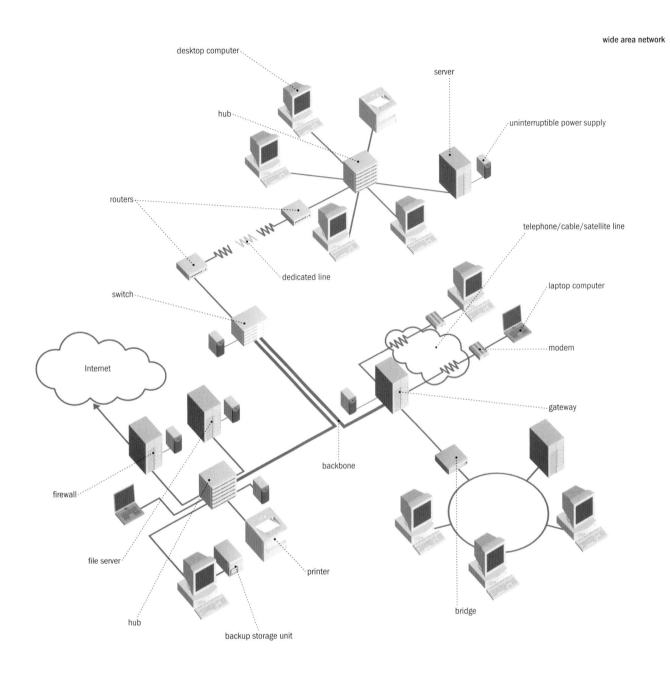

desktop computer

server

hub

uninterruptible power supply

routers

telephone/cable/satellite line

laptop computer

dedicated line

switch

modem

Internet

gateway

backbone

firewall

file server

printer

bridge

hub

backup storage unit

cables

coaxial cable

twisted-pair cable

fiber optic cable

Internet

URL (uniform resource locator)

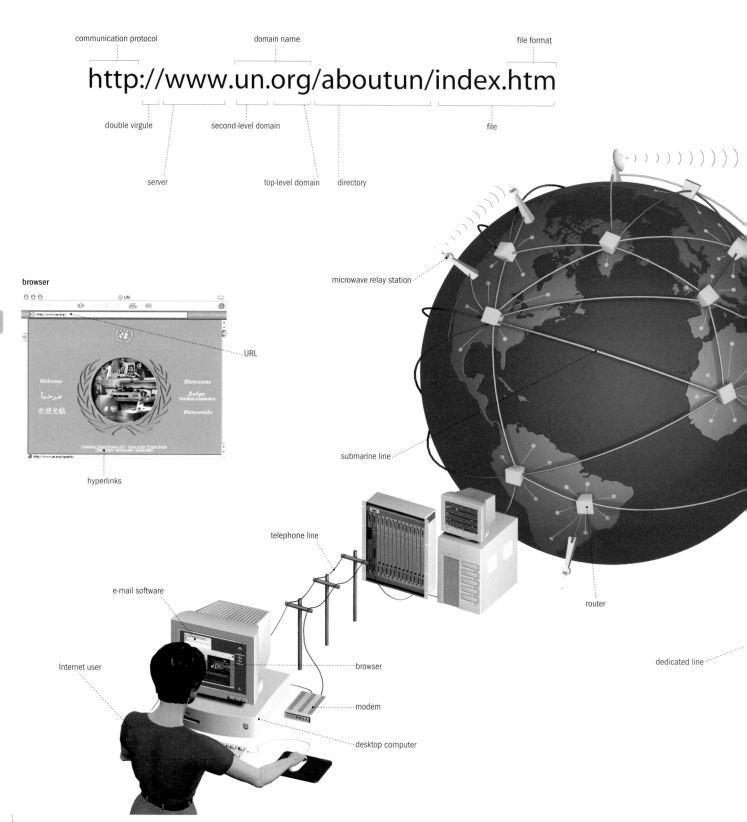

communication protocol

domain name

file format

http://www.un.org/aboutun/index.htm

double virgule

second-level domain

file

server

top-level domain

directory

browser

URL

hyperlinks

microwave relay station

submarine line

router

telephone line

e-mail software

Internet user

browser

modem

desktop computer

dedicated line

Internet uses

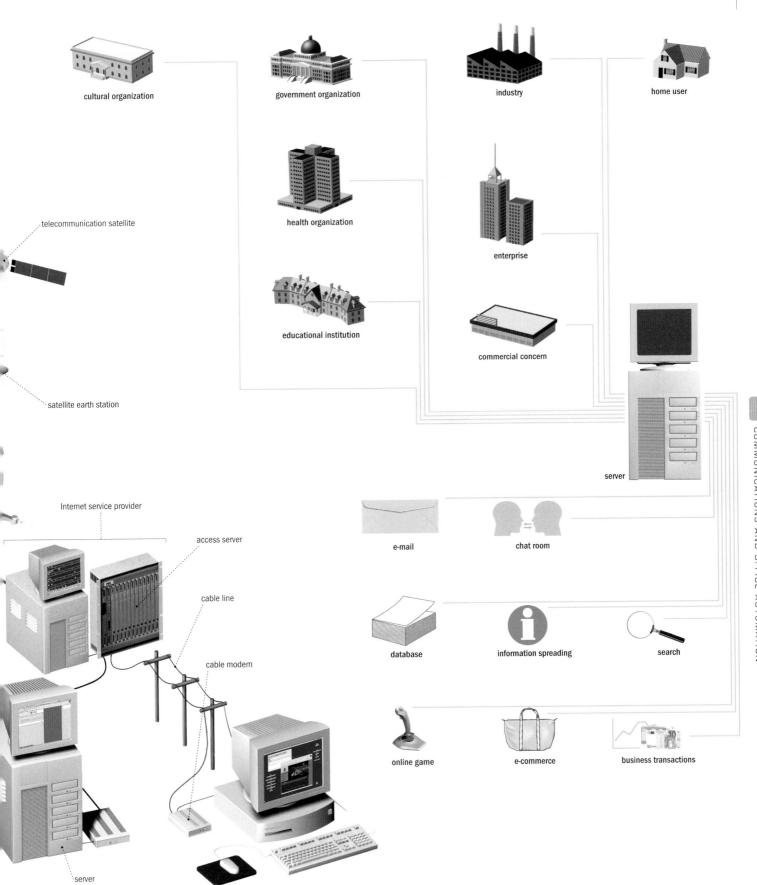

cultural organization

government organization

industry

home user

telecommunication satellite

health organization

enterprise

satellite earth station

educational institution

commercial concern

server

Internet service provider

access server

e-mail

chat room

cable line

database

information spreading

search

cable modem

online game

e-commerce

business transactions

server

laptop computer

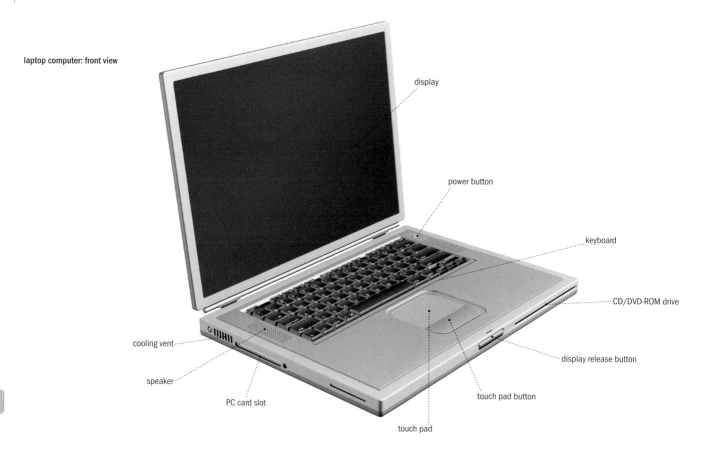

laptop computer: front view

display

power button

keyboard

CD/DVD-ROM drive

display release button

touch pad button

cooling vent

speaker

PC card slot

touch pad

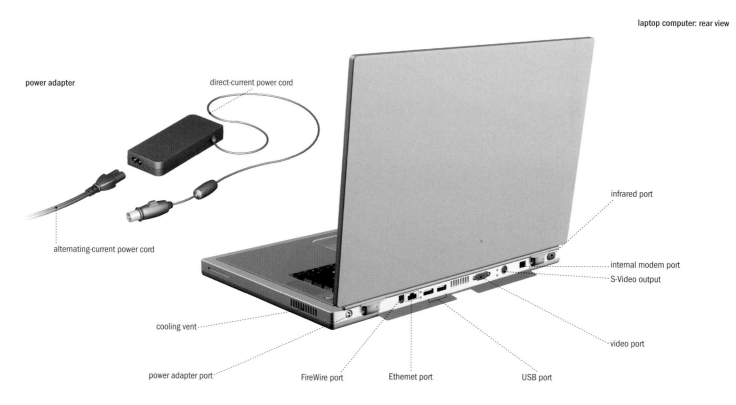

laptop computer: rear view

power adapter

direct-current power cord

infrared port

alternating-current power cord

internal modem port

S-Video output

video port

cooling vent

power adapter port

FireWire port

Ethernet port

USB port

laptop computer briefcase

computer compartment

document compartment

shoulder strap

electronic book

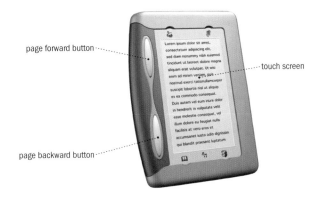

page forward button

touch screen

page backward button

handheld computer

audio input/output jack

microphone

infrared port

voice recorder button

alarm/charge indicator light

dial/action button

touch screen

exit button

application launch buttons

sync cable

power and backlight button

power plug

docking cradle

stylus

COMMUNICATIONS AND OFFICE AUTOMATION

stationery

electronic typewriter

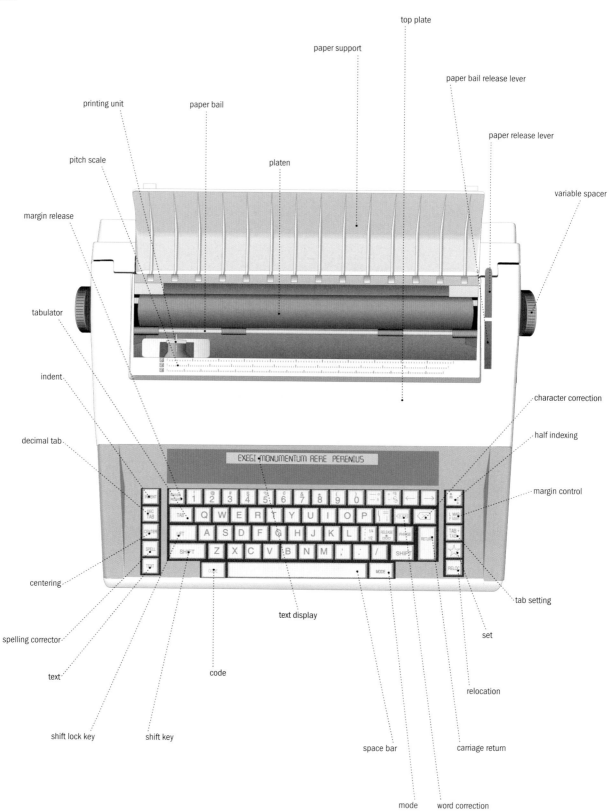

top plate

paper support

paper bail release lever

printing unit

paper bail

paper release lever

pitch scale

platen

variable spacer

margin release

tabulator

indent

decimal tab

character correction

half indexing

margin control

centering

tab setting

spelling corrector

set

text

code

relocation

shift lock key

shift key

space bar

carriage return

mode

word correction

text display

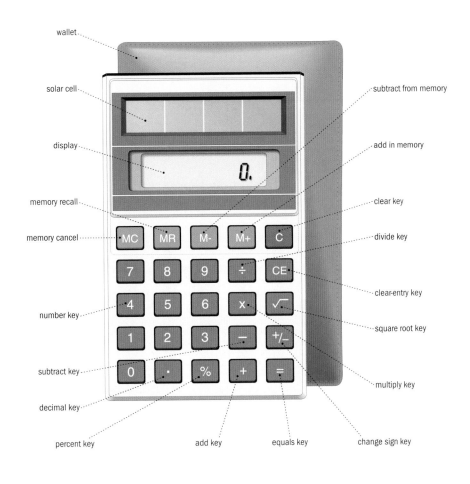

wallet

solar cell

display

memory recall

memory cancel

number key

subtract key

decimal key

percent key

add key

equals key

change sign key

subtract from memory

add in memory

clear key

divide key

clear-entry key

square root key

multiply key

MC   MR   M-   M+   C

7   8   9   ÷   CE

4   5   6   ×   √

1   2   3   —   +/−

0   ·   %   +   =

0.

scientific calculator

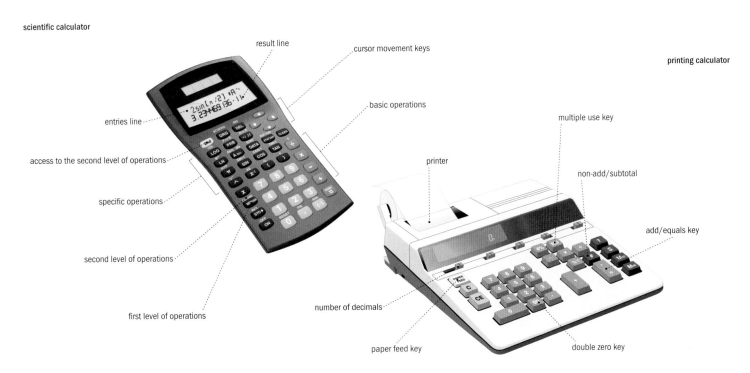

result line

cursor movement keys

entries line

basic operations

access to the second level of operations

specific operations

second level of operations

first level of operations

printing calculator

multiple use key

non-add/subtotal

printer

add/equals key

number of decimals

paper feed key

double zero key

stationery

for time management

tear-off calendar

calendar pad

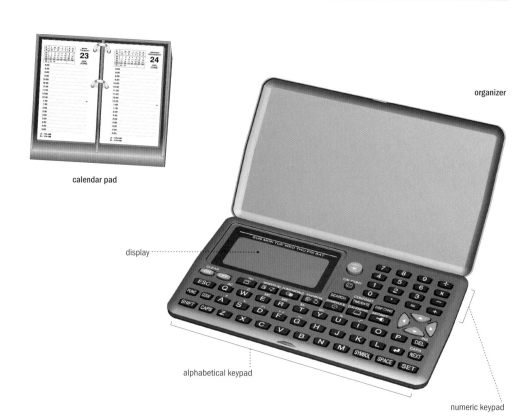

organizer

display

alphabetical keypad

numeric keypad

appointment book

time clock

display

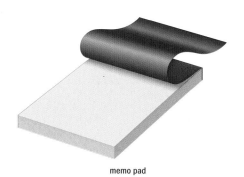

memo pad

time card

stationery

for correspondence

padded envelope

self-sealing flap

air bubbles

letter opener

numbering machine

dater

finger tip

letter scale

steno book

moistener

stamp rack

stamp pad

rubber stamp

signature book

blotting paper

telephone index

rotary file

postage meter

postmarking module

desk tray

feed deck

base

COMMUNICATIONS AND OFFICE AUTOMATION

stationery

for filing

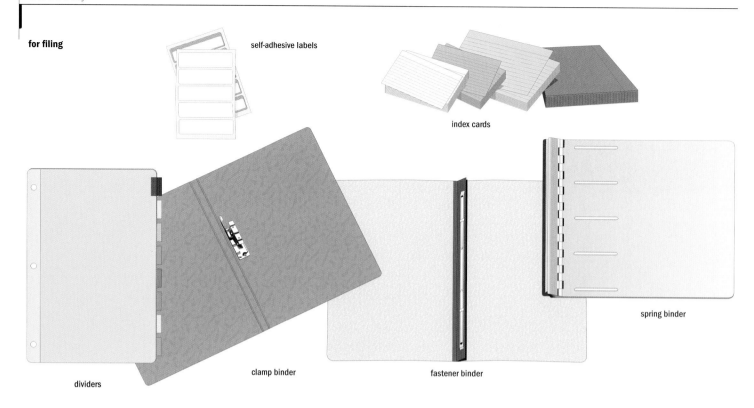

self-adhesive labels

index cards

dividers

clamp binder

fastener binder

spring binder

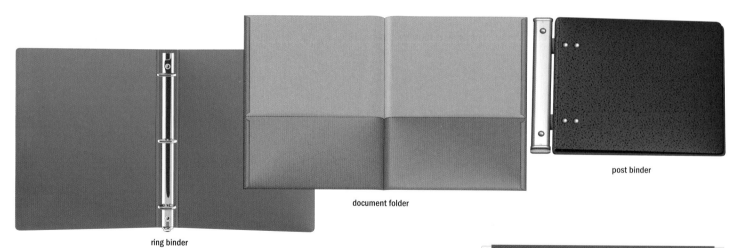

ring binder

document folder

post binder

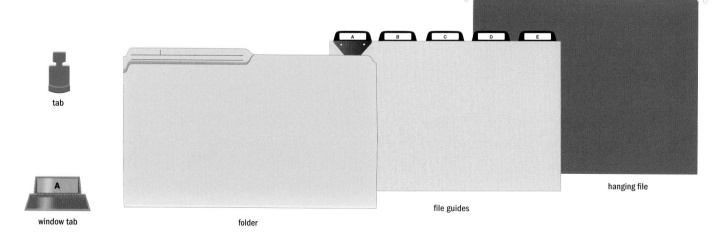

tab

window tab

folder

file guides

hanging file

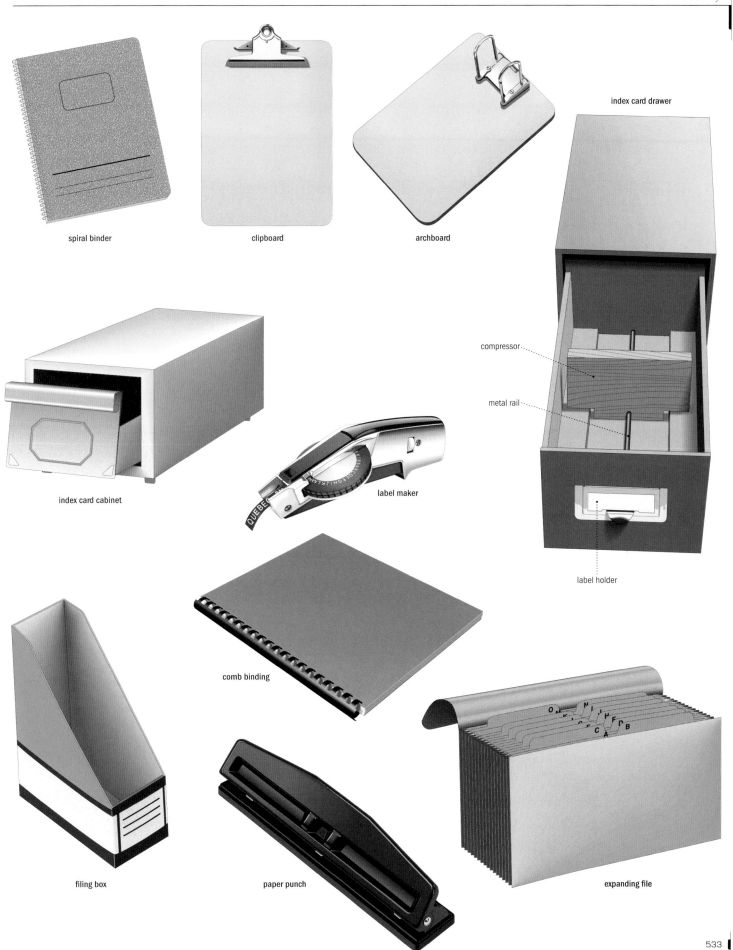

spiral binder

clipboard

archboard

index card drawer

index card cabinet

label maker

compressor

metal rail

label holder

comb binding

filing box

paper punch

expanding file

stationery

miscellaneous articles

paper clips

thumb tacks

paper fasteners

box sealing tape dispenser

tape guide

hub

cutting blade

tension adjusting screw

handle

pencil sharpener

eraser

correction fluid

paper clip holder

magnet

clip

glue stick

tape dispenser

staple remover

digital voice recorder

pencil sharpener

correction paper

bill-file

staples

stapler

overhead projector

projection head

mirror

optical lens

optical stage

cutting head

account book

waste basket

waste basket

paper shredder

bulletin board

book ends

lightbox

posting surface

slotted box

paper cutter

flap

hand hole

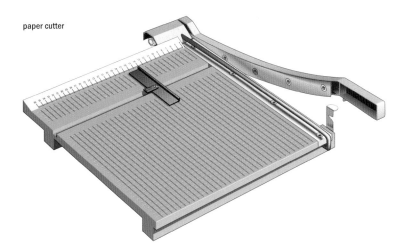
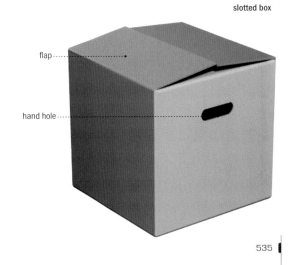

TRANSPORT AND MACHINERY

road system

TRANSPORT AND MACHINERY

cross section of a road

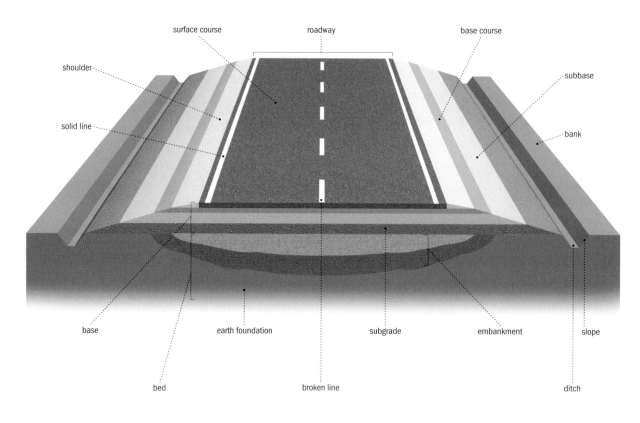

examples of interchanges

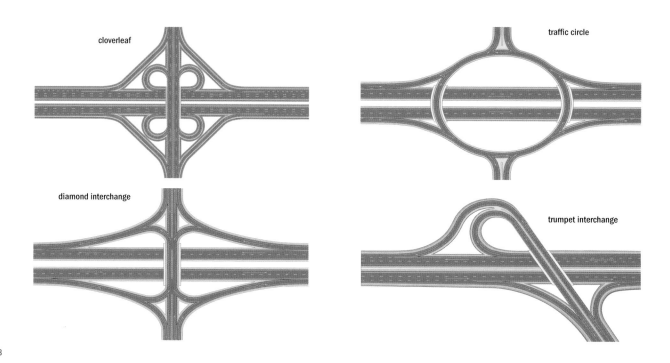

cloverleaf

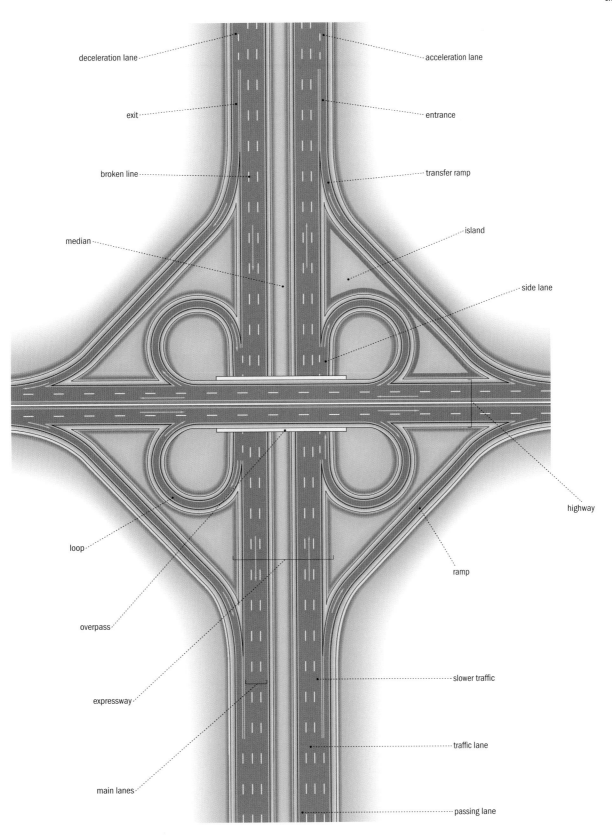

deceleration lane

acceleration lane

exit

entrance

broken line

transfer ramp

median

island

side lane

loop

highway

overpass

ramp

expressway

slower traffic

main lanes

traffic lane

passing lane

fixed bridges

TRANSPORT AND MACHINERY

beam bridge

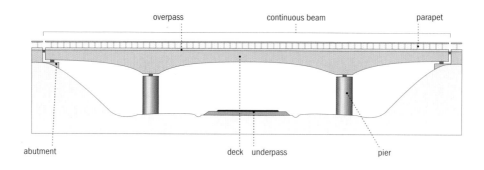

overpass · continuous beam · parapet · abutment · deck · underpass · pier

arch bridge

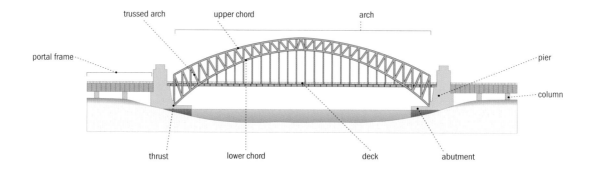

trussed arch · upper chord · arch · portal frame · pier · column · thrust · lower chord · deck · abutment

suspension bridge

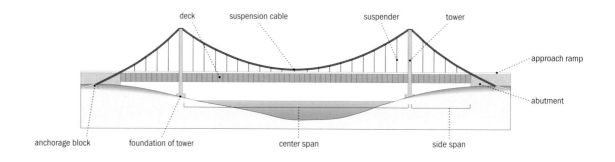

deck · suspension cable · suspender · tower · approach ramp · abutment · anchorage block · foundation of tower · center span · side span

cantilever bridge

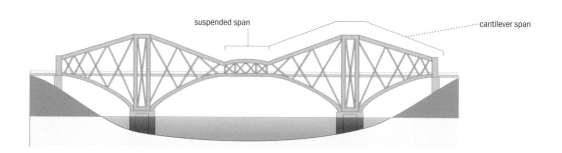

suspended span · cantilever span

cable-stayed bridges

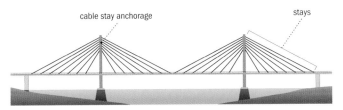

fan cable stays

harp cable stays

examples of arch bridges

deck arch bridge

through arch bridge

portal bridge

half-through arch bridge

examples of arches

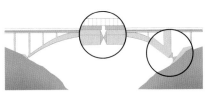

three-hinged arch

two-hinged arch

fixed arch

examples of beam bridges

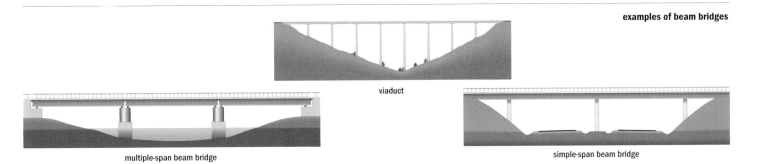

viaduct

multiple-span beam bridge

simple-span beam bridge

TRANSPORT AND MACHINERY

movable bridges

swing bridge

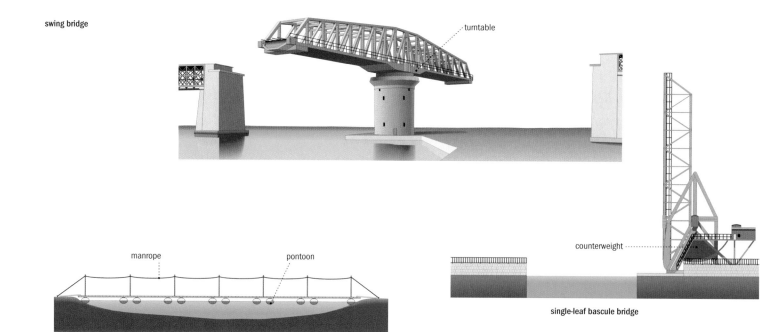

turntable

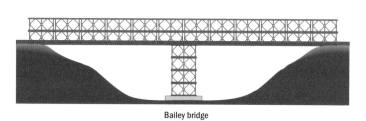

manrope   pontoon

floating bridge

counterweight

single-leaf bascule bridge

Bailey bridge

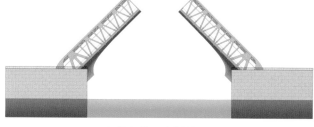

double-leaf bascule bridge

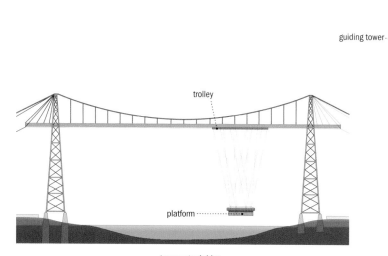

trolley

platform

transporter bridge

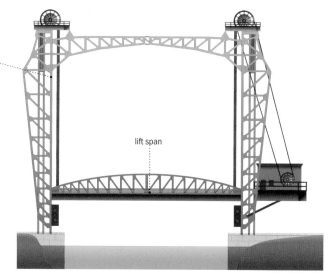

guiding tower

lift span

lift bridge

road tunnel

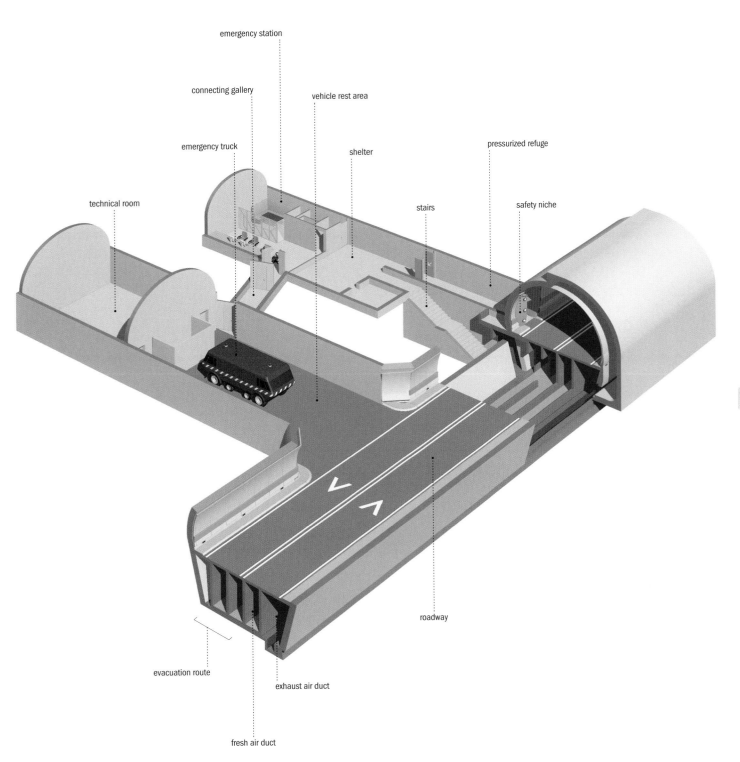

emergency station

connecting gallery

vehicle rest area

emergency truck

shelter

pressurized refuge

technical room

stairs

safety niche

roadway

evacuation route

exhaust air duct

fresh air duct

road signs

major international road signs

right bend

double bend

roadway narrows

stop at intersection

no entry

no U-turn

passing prohibited

direction to be followed

direction to be followed

direction to be followed

direction to be followed

one-way traffic

two-way traffic

yield

priority intersection

falling rocks

overhead clearance

signal ahead

school zone

pedestrian crossing

road works ahead

slippery road

railroad crossing

deer crossing

steep hill

bumps

closed to bicycles

closed to motorcycles

closed to trucks

closed to pedestrians

road signs

major North American road signs

stop at intersection

no entry

yield

closed to motorcycles

closed to pedestrians

closed to bicycles

closed to trucks

direction to be followed

direction to be followed

direction to be followed

direction to be followed

no U-turn

passing prohibited

one-way traffic

two-way traffic

double bend

merging traffic

right bend

roadway narrows

slippery road

deer crossing

road works ahead

bumps

steep hill

falling rocks

railroad crossing

overhead clearance

signal ahead

school zone

pedestrian crossing

TRANSPORT AND MACHINERY

service station

gasoline pump

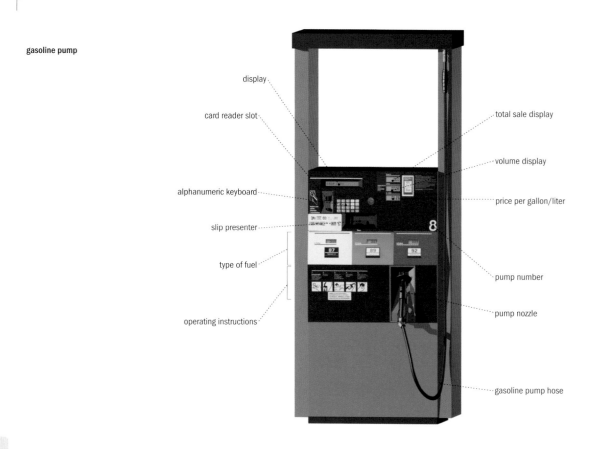

display

card reader slot

alphanumeric keyboard

slip presenter

type of fuel

operating instructions

total sale display

volume display

price per gallon/liter

pump number

pump nozzle

gasoline pump hose

service station

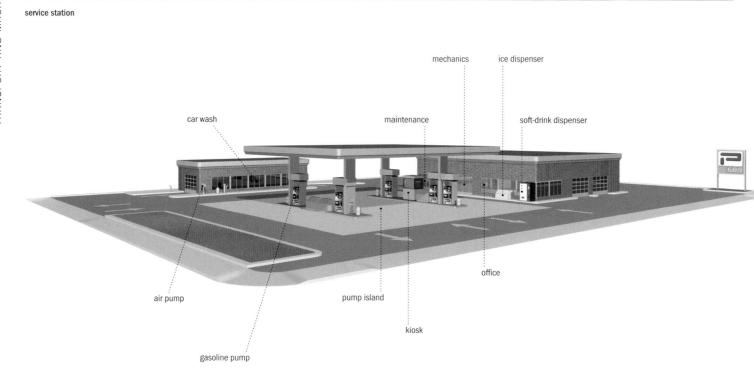

mechanics

ice dispenser

car wash

maintenance

soft-drink dispenser

office

air pump

pump island

gasoline pump

kiosk

automobile

examples of bodies

sports car

micro compact car

hatchback

two-door sedan

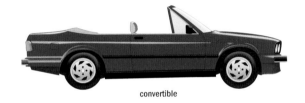

convertible

four-door sedan

station wagon

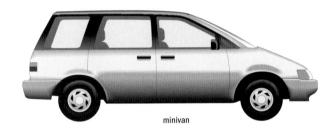

minivan

sport-utility vehicle

pickup truck

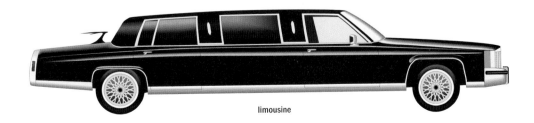

limousine

automobile

body

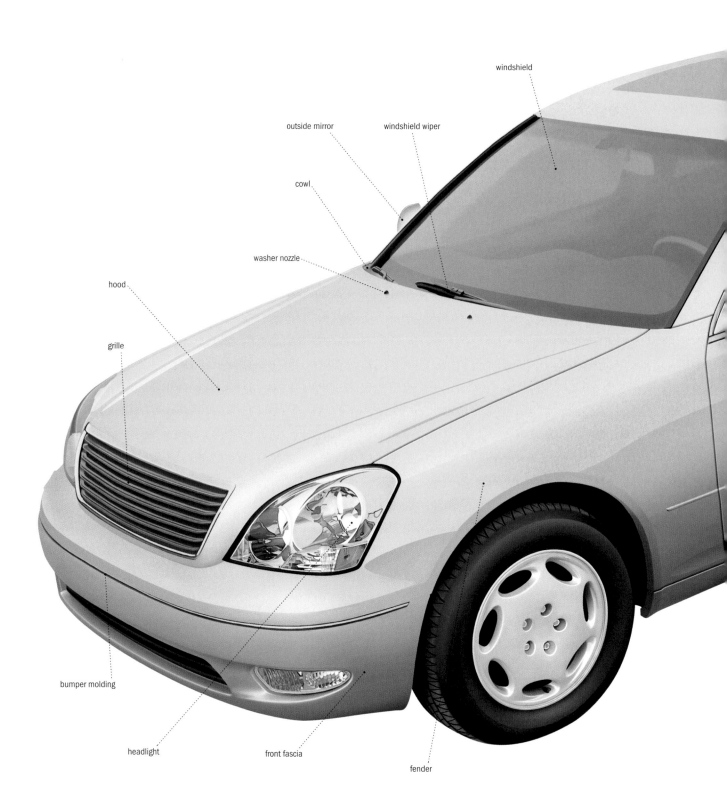

windshield

outside mirror

windshield wiper

cowl

washer nozzle

hood

grille

bumper molding

headlight

front fascia

fender

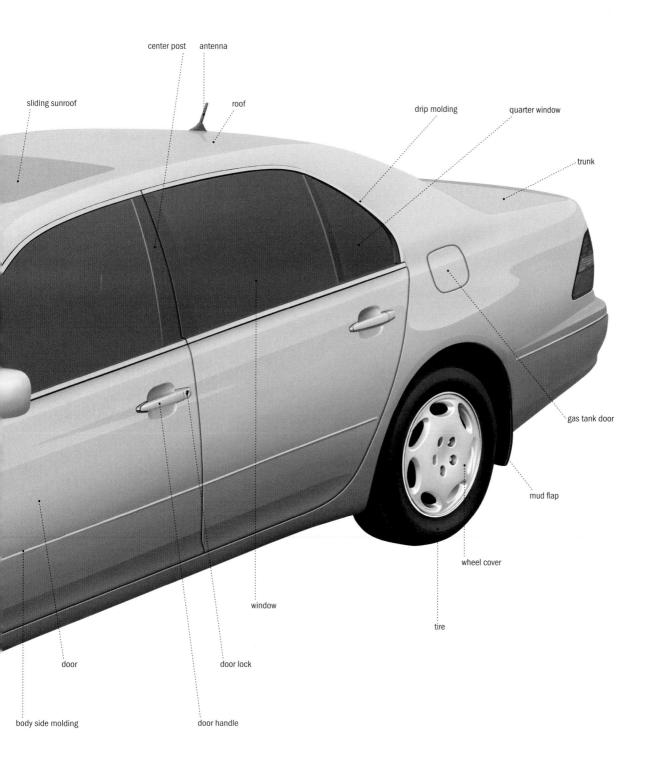

center post   antenna

sliding sunroof

roof

drip molding

quarter window

trunk

gas tank door

mud flap

wheel cover

window

tire

door

door lock

body side molding

door handle

automobile

automobile systems: main parts

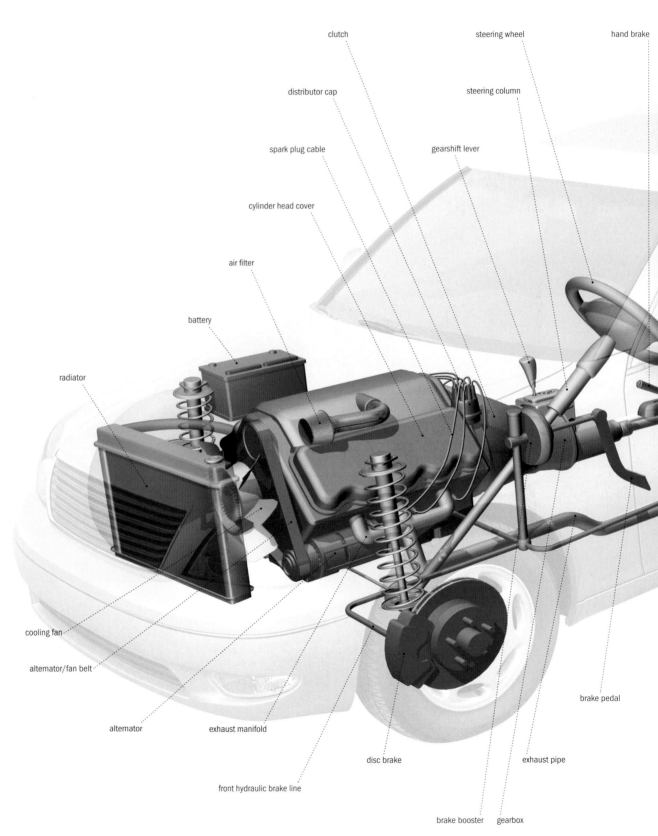

clutch

steering wheel

hand brake

distributor cap

steering column

spark plug cable

gearshift lever

cylinder head cover

air filter

battery

radiator

cooling fan

alternator/fan belt

alternator

exhaust manifold

disc brake

brake pedal

exhaust pipe

front hydraulic brake line

brake booster

gearbox

TRANSPORT AND MACHINERY

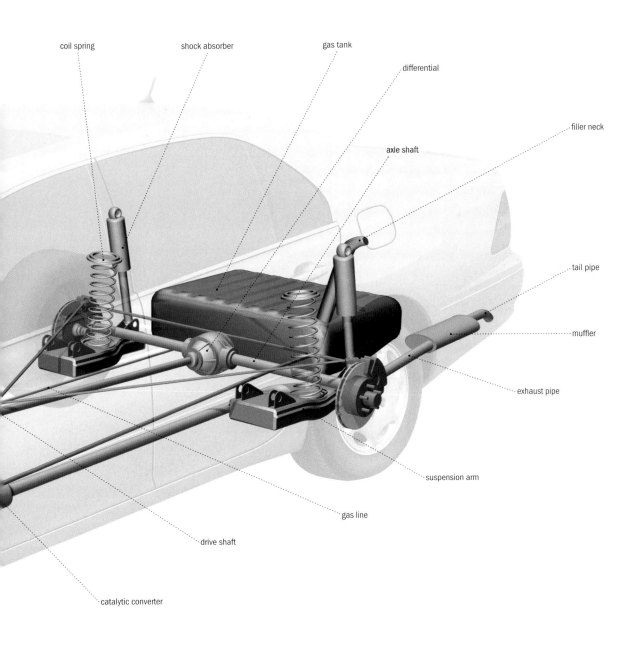

coil spring

shock absorber

gas tank

differential

axle shaft

filler neck

tail pipe

muffler

exhaust pipe

suspension arm

gas line

drive shaft

catalytic converter

automobile systems

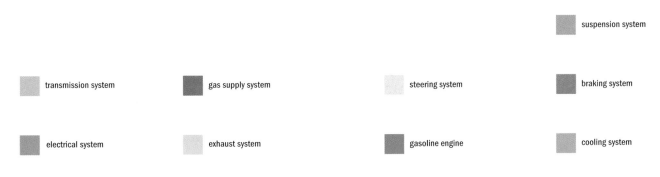

suspension system

transmission system

gas supply system

steering system

braking system

electrical system

exhaust system

gasoline engine

cooling system

automobile

headlights

high beam

low beam

turn signal

side-marker light

fog light

taillights

brake light

turn signal

reverse light

taillight

brake light

side-marker light

license plate light

door

interior door handle

window

assist grip

interior door lock button

outside mirror control

armrest

window regulator handle

lock

trim panel

hinge

inner door shell

accessory pocket

bucket seat: front view

bucket seat: side view

shoulder belt

sliding rail

sliding lever

headrest

backrest

seat

adjustment knob

seat belt

rear seat

armrest

webbing

buckle

bench seat

automobile

TRANSPORT AND MACHINERY

dashboard

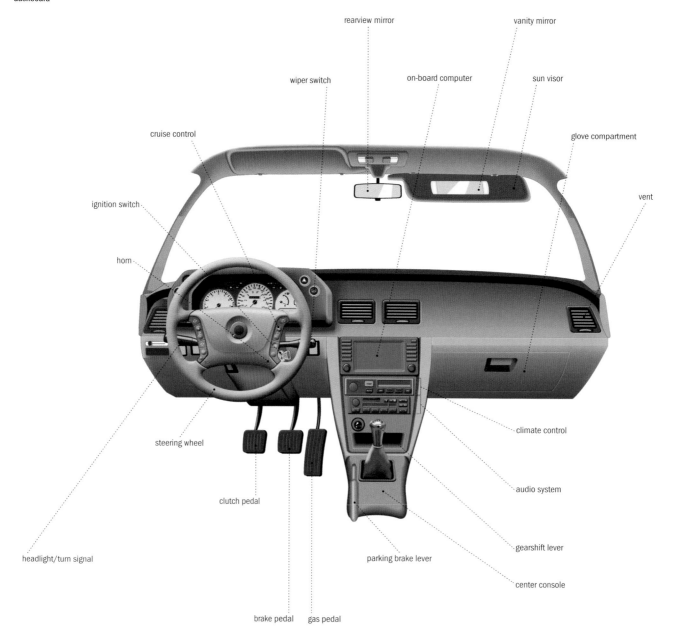

rearview mirror

vanity mirror

wiper switch

on-board computer

sun visor

cruise control

glove compartment

ignition switch

vent

horn

steering wheel

clutch pedal

climate control

audio system

gearshift lever

headlight/turn signal

parking brake lever

center console

brake pedal   gas pedal

air bag restraint system

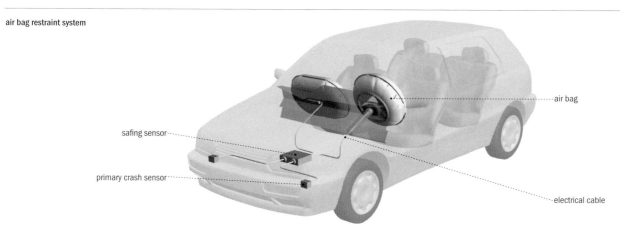

air bag

safing sensor

primary crash sensor

electrical cable

instrument panel

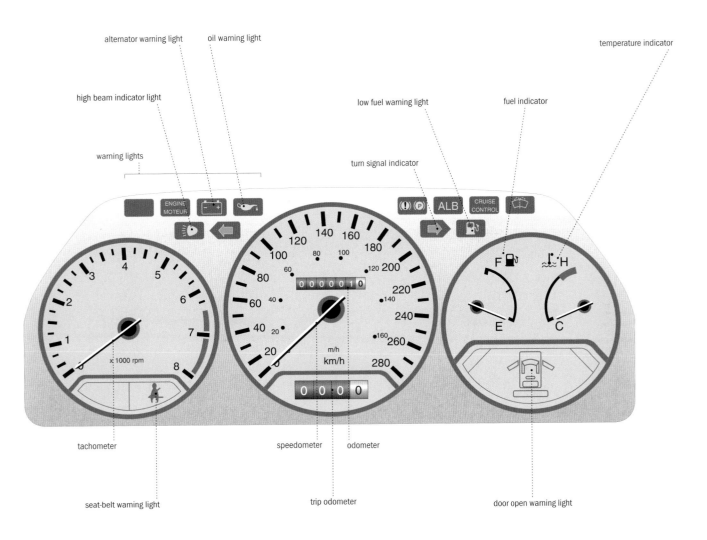

alternator warning light

oil warning light

temperature indicator

high beam indicator light

low fuel warning light

fuel indicator

warning lights

turn signal indicator

tachometer

speedometer   odometer

seat-belt warning light

trip odometer

door open warning light

windshield wiper

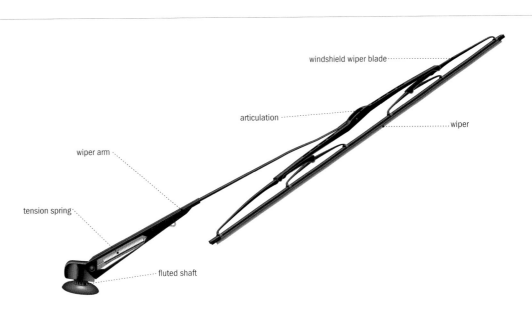

windshield wiper blade

articulation

wiper

wiper arm

tension spring

fluted shaft

automobile

accessories

roller shade

jumper cables

black clamp

red clamp

cable

floor mat

ball mount

hitch ball

snow brush with scraper

four-way lug wrench

bike carrier

ski rack

sun visor

vehicle jack

handle

car cover

child safety seat

TRANSPORT AND MACHINERY

brakes

disc brake

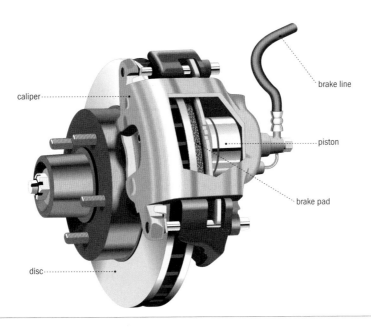

caliper

brake line

piston

brake pad

disc

drum brake

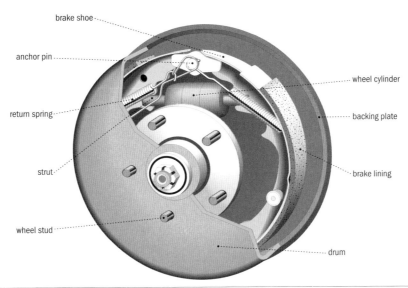

brake shoe

anchor pin

wheel cylinder

return spring

backing plate

strut

brake lining

wheel stud

drum

antilock braking system (ABS)

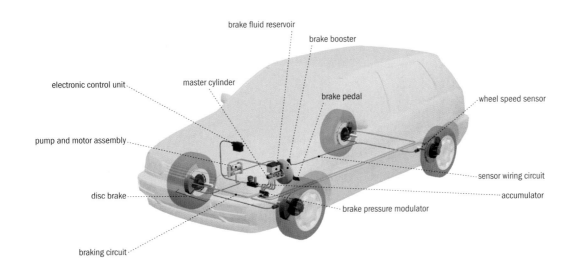

brake fluid reservoir

brake booster

electronic control unit

master cylinder

brake pedal

wheel speed sensor

pump and motor assembly

sensor wiring circuit

disc brake

accumulator

brake pressure modulator

braking circuit

tire

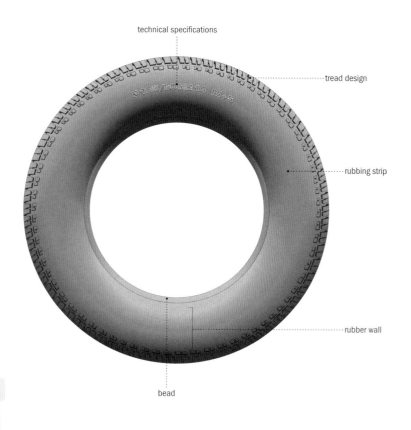

technical specifications

tread design

rubbing strip

rubber wall

bead

wheel

disk

rim

rim flange

examples of tires

performance tire

all-season tire

winter tire

touring tire

studded tire

steel belted radial tire

bias-ply tire

radial tire

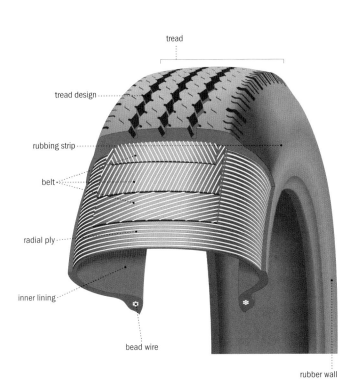

tread

tread design

rubbing strip

belt

radial ply

inner lining

bead wire

rubber wall

radiator

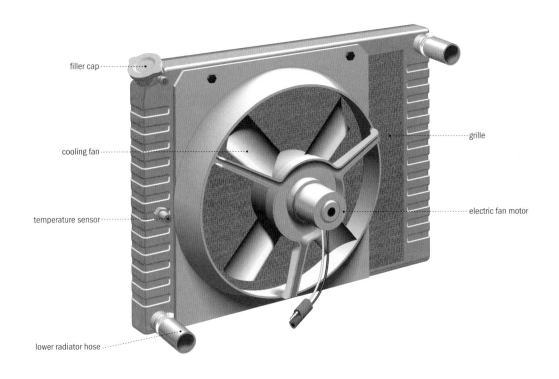

filler cap

cooling fan

temperature sensor

grille

electric fan motor

lower radiator hose

spark plug

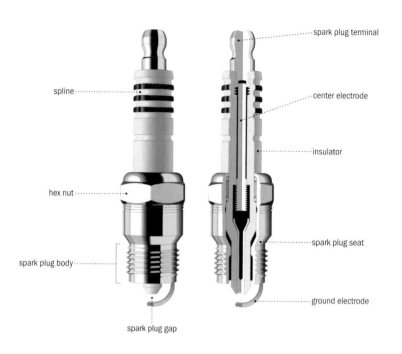

spline

hex nut

spark plug body

spark plug gap

spark plug terminal

center electrode

insulator

spark plug seat

ground electrode

battery

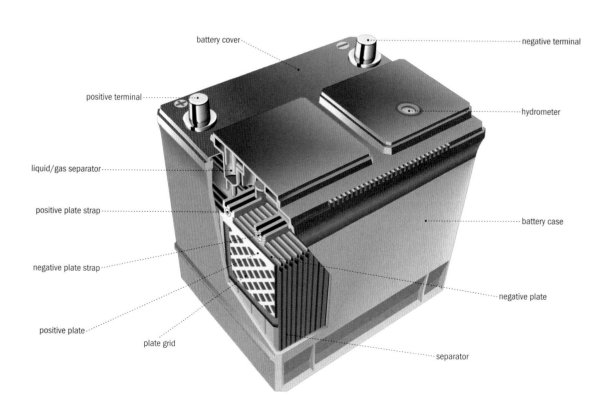

battery cover

positive terminal

liquid/gas separator

positive plate strap

negative plate strap

positive plate

plate grid

negative terminal

hydrometer

battery case

negative plate

separator

electric automobile

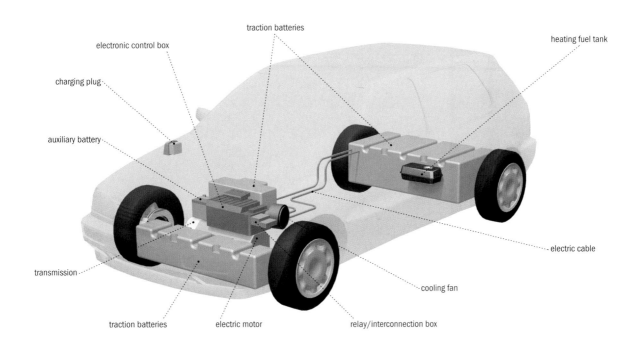

traction batteries

electronic control box

heating fuel tank

charging plug

auxiliary battery

electric cable

transmission

cooling fan

traction batteries

electric motor

relay/interconnection box

hybrid automobile

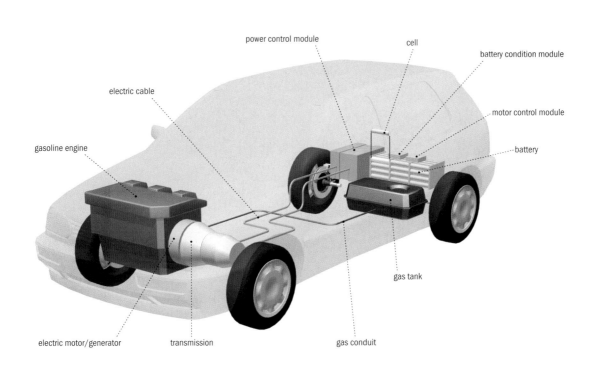

power control module

cell

battery condition module

electric cable

motor control module

gasoline engine

battery

gas tank

electric motor/generator

transmission

gas conduit

types of engines

turbo-compressor engine

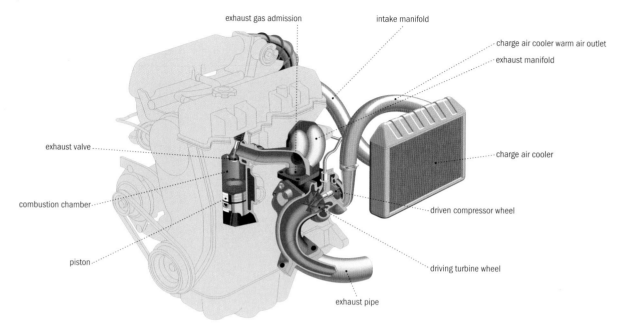

exhaust gas admission
intake manifold
charge air cooler warm air outlet
exhaust manifold
exhaust valve
charge air cooler
combustion chamber
driven compressor wheel
piston
driving turbine wheel
exhaust pipe

four-stroke-cycle engine

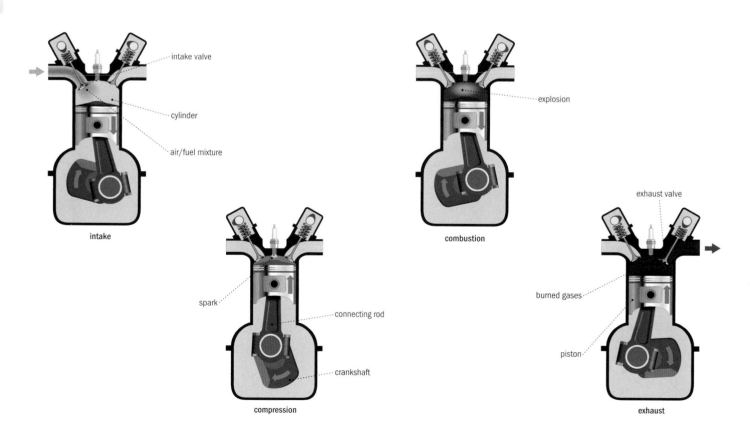

intake valve
cylinder
air/fuel mixture

explosion

intake

combustion

exhaust valve

spark
burned gases
connecting rod
piston
crankshaft

compression

exhaust

two-stroke-cycle engine cycle

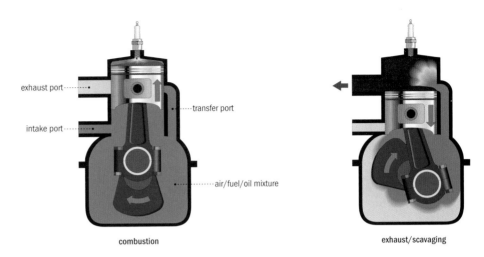

spark plug

exhaust port

transfer port

intake port

air/fuel/oil mixture

compression/intake

combustion

exhaust/scavaging

rotary engine cycle

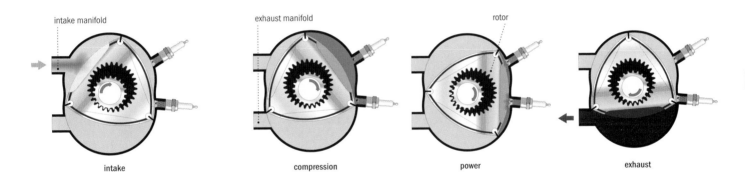

intake manifold

exhaust manifold

rotor

intake

compression

power

exhaust

diesel engine cycle

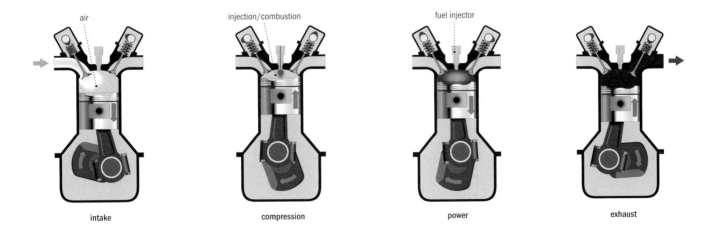

air

injection/combustion

fuel injector

intake

compression

power

exhaust

TRANSPORT AND MACHINERY

types of engines

gasoline engine

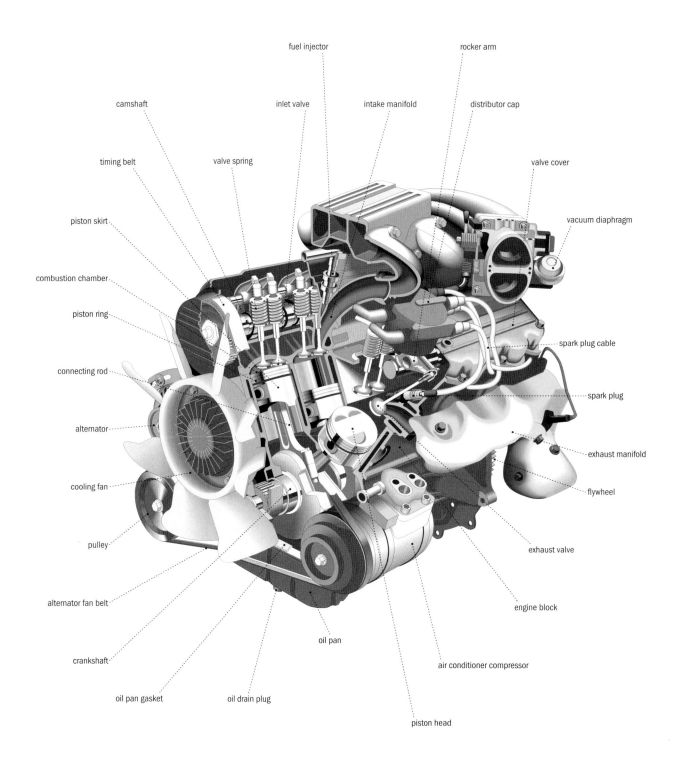

fuel injector

rocker arm

camshaft

inlet valve

intake manifold

distributor cap

timing belt

valve spring

valve cover

piston skirt

vacuum diaphragm

combustion chamber

piston ring

spark plug cable

connecting rod

spark plug

alternator

exhaust manifold

cooling fan

flywheel

pulley

exhaust valve

alternator fan belt

engine block

crankshaft

air conditioner compressor

oil pan

oil pan gasket

oil drain plug

piston head

camping trailers

trailer

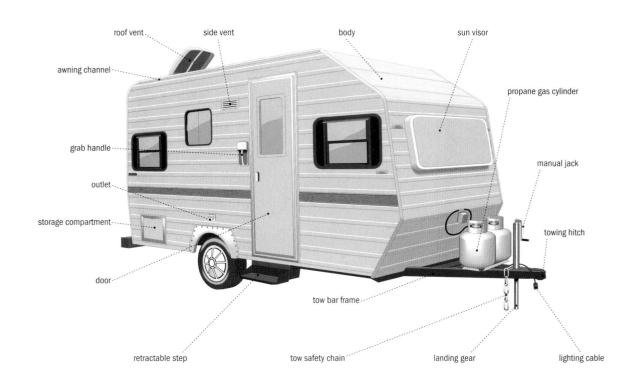

roof vent

side vent

body

sun visor

awning channel

propane gas cylinder

grab handle

manual jack

outlet

storage compartment

towing hitch

door

tow bar frame

retractable step

tow safety chain

landing gear

lighting cable

tent trailer

roof

canopy

window

bunk

spare tire

body

stabilizer jack

screen door

motor home

air conditioner

luggage rack

ladder

bus

school bus

outside mirror

blind spot mirror

blinking lights

crossover mirror

crossing arm

city bus

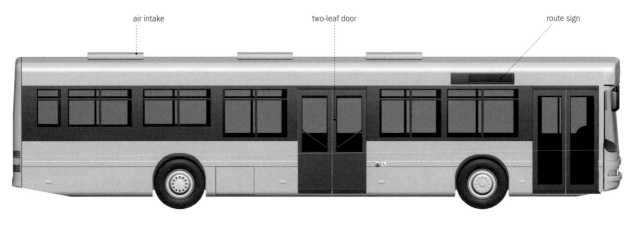

air intake

two-leaf door

route sign

coach

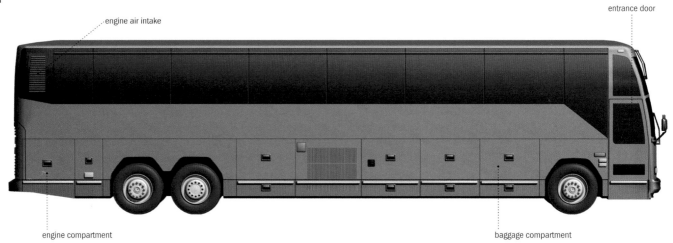

engine air intake

entrance door

engine compartment

baggage compartment

double-deck bus

upper deck

route sign

minibus

lift door

blind spot mirror

West Coast mirror

handrail

wheelchair lift

platform

entrance door

articulated bus

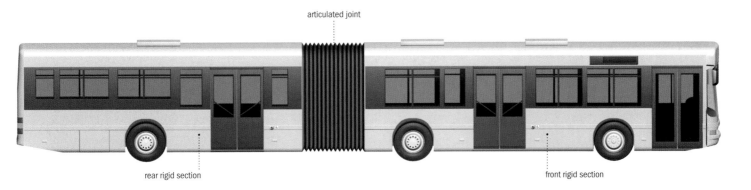

articulated joint

rear rigid section

front rigid section

trucking

truck tractor

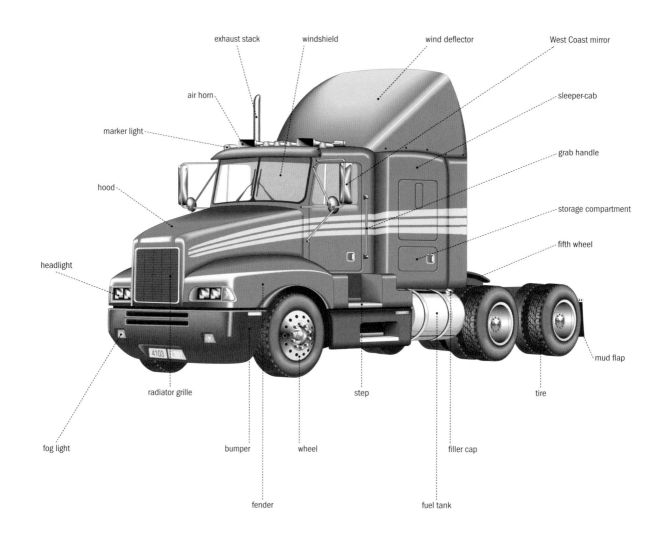

exhaust stack   windshield   wind deflector   West Coast mirror

air horn

sleeper-cab

marker light

grab handle

hood

storage compartment

fifth wheel

headlight

mud flap

radiator grille   step   tire

fog light   bumper   wheel   filler cap

fender   fuel tank

tandem tractor trailer

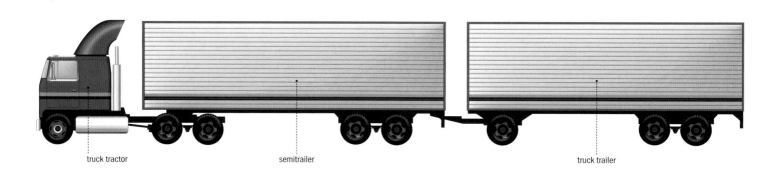

truck tractor   semitrailer   truck trailer

TRANSPORT AND MACHINERY

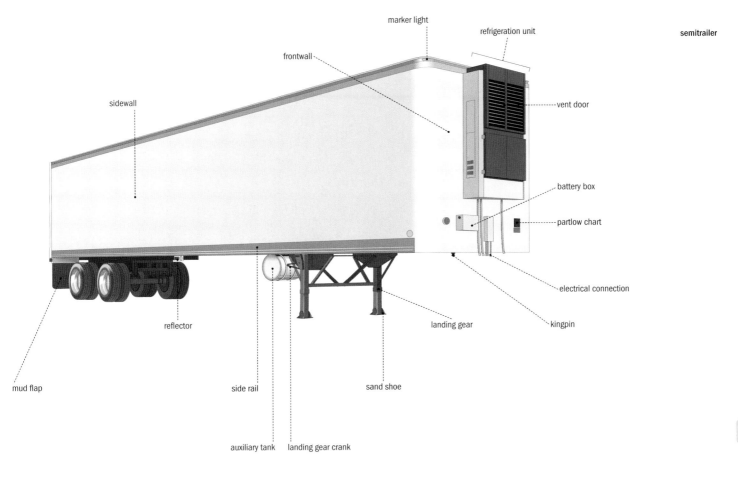

marker light

refrigeration unit

frontwall

sidewall

vent door

battery box

partlow chart

electrical connection

reflector

landing gear

kingpin

mud flap

side rail

sand shoe

auxiliary tank

landing gear crank

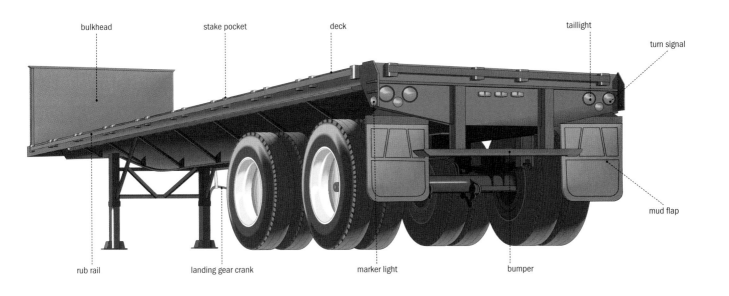

bulkhead

stake pocket

deck

taillight

turn signal

mud flap

rub rail

landing gear crank

marker light

bumper

trucking

examples of semitrailers

tank trailer

tank body

automobile transport semitrailer

dump body

dump semitrailer

twist lock

container semitrailer

chip van

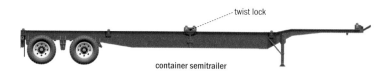

double drop lowbed semitrailer

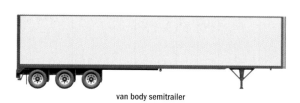

van body semitrailer

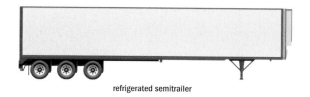

refrigerated semitrailer

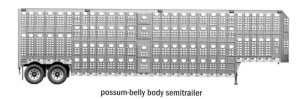

possum-belly body semitrailer

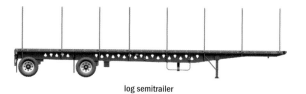

log semitrailer

TRANSPORT AND MACHINERY

tow truck

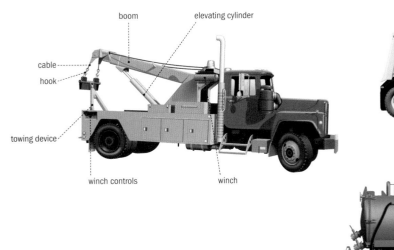

boom

elevating cylinder

cable

hook

towing device

winch controls

winch

dump body

dump truck

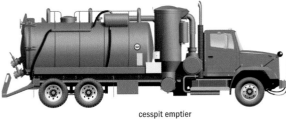

cesspit emptier

loading hopper

packer body

collection truck

concrete mixer truck

van straight truck

detachable body

tank truck

tank body

street sweeper

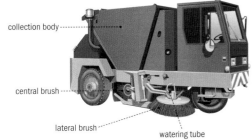

collection body

central brush

lateral brush

watering tube

snowblower

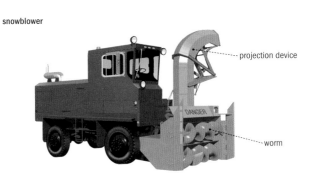

projection device

worm

motorcycle

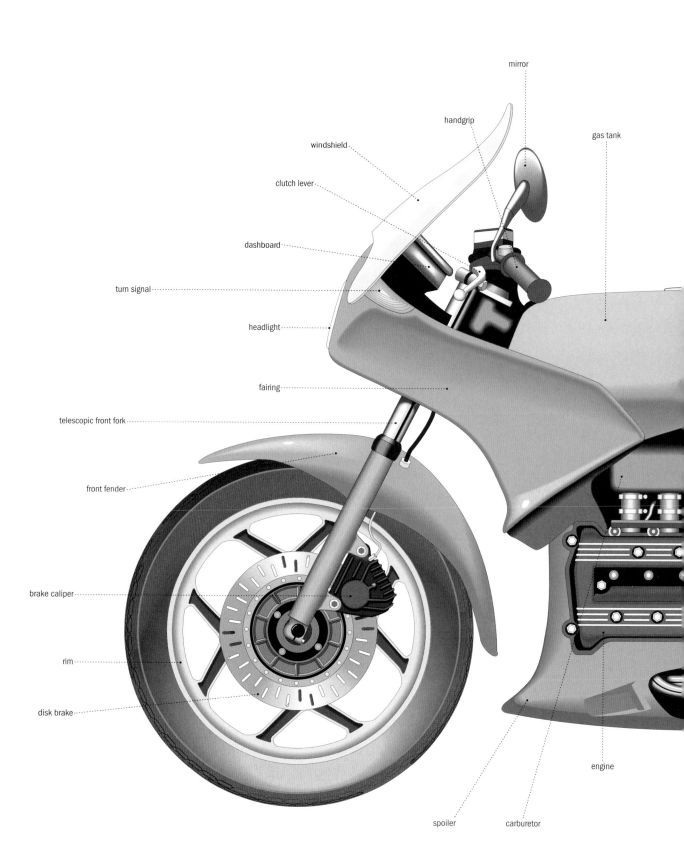

mirror

handgrip

windshield

gas tank

clutch lever

dashboard

turn signal

headlight

fairing

telescopic front fork

front fender

brake caliper

rim

disk brake

spoiler

carburetor

engine

protective helmet

bubble

visor

air inlet

chin protector

visor hinge

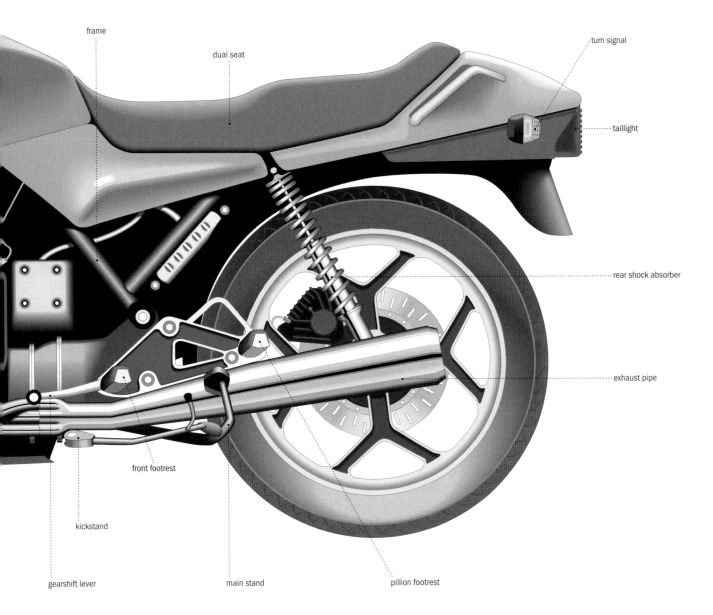

frame

dual seat

turn signal

taillight

rear shock absorber

exhaust pipe

front footrest

kickstand

gearshift lever

main stand

pillion footrest

motorcycle

motorcycle dashboard

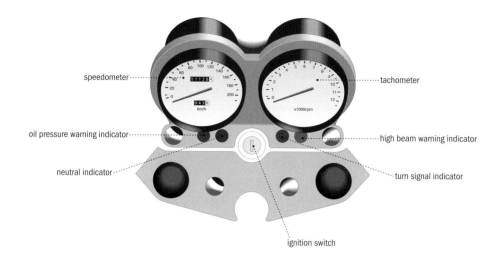

speedometer

tachometer

oil pressure warning indicator

high beam warning indicator

neutral indicator

turn signal indicator

ignition switch

motorcycle: view from above

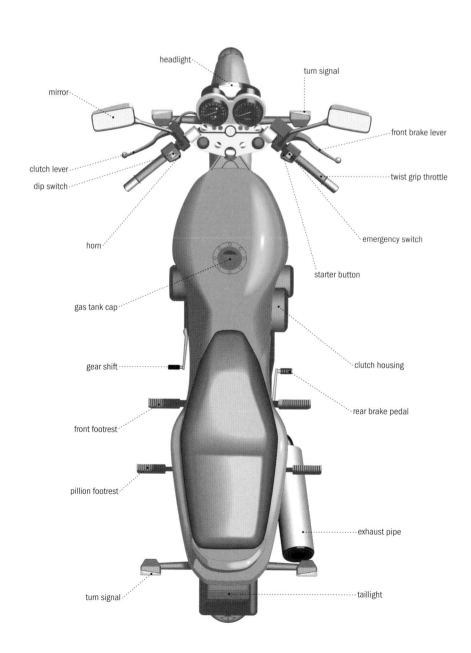

headlight

turn signal

mirror

front brake lever

clutch lever

dip switch

twist grip throttle

horn

emergency switch

starter button

gas tank cap

clutch housing

gear shift

rear brake pedal

front footrest

pillion footrest

exhaust pipe

turn signal

taillight

examples of motorcycles

motor scooter

seat

mirror

luggage rack

apron

floorboard

off-road motorcycle

seat

telescopic front fork

knobby tread tire

touring motorcycle

moped

carrier

kickstand

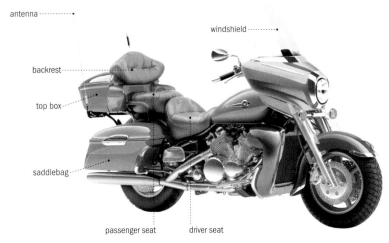

antenna

windshield

backrest

top box

saddlebag

passenger seat

driver seat

4 X 4 all-terrain vehicle

rear cargo rack

seat

gas tank

handgrip

rear fender

bumper

muffler

front shock absorber

gearshift lever

bicycle

parts of a bicycle

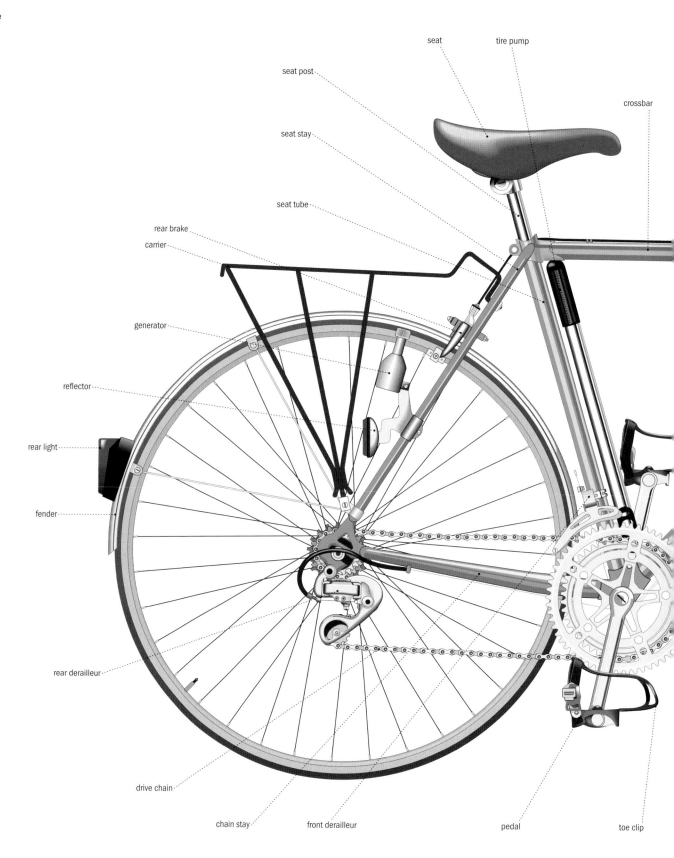

seat

tire pump

crossbar

seat post

seat stay

seat tube

rear brake

carrier

generator

reflector

rear light

fender

rear derailleur

drive chain

chain stay

front derailleur

pedal

toe clip

bicycle

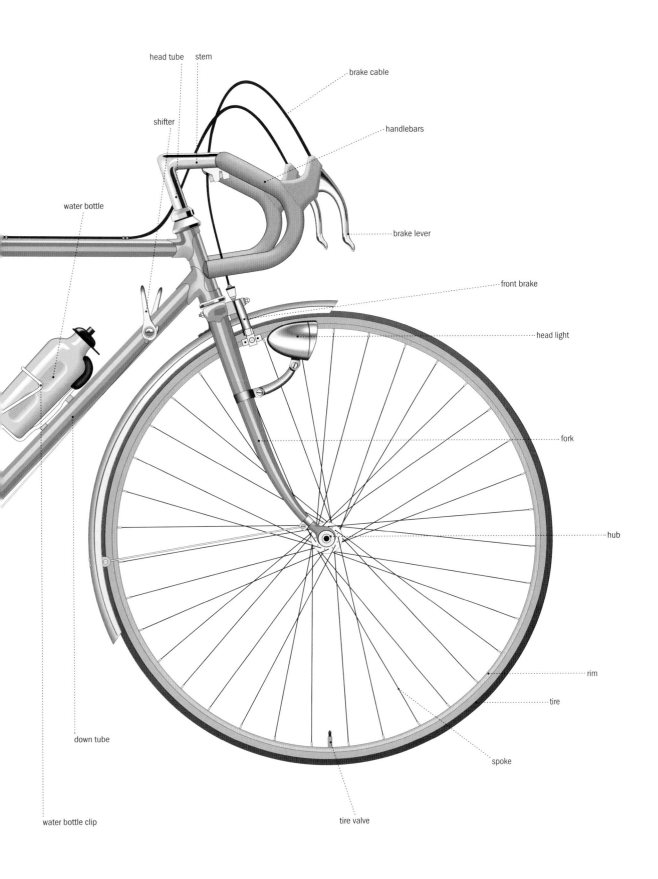

head tube   stem

brake cable

shifter

handlebars

water bottle

brake lever

front brake

head light

fork

hub

rim

tire

spoke

down tube

tire valve

water bottle clip

bicycle

power train

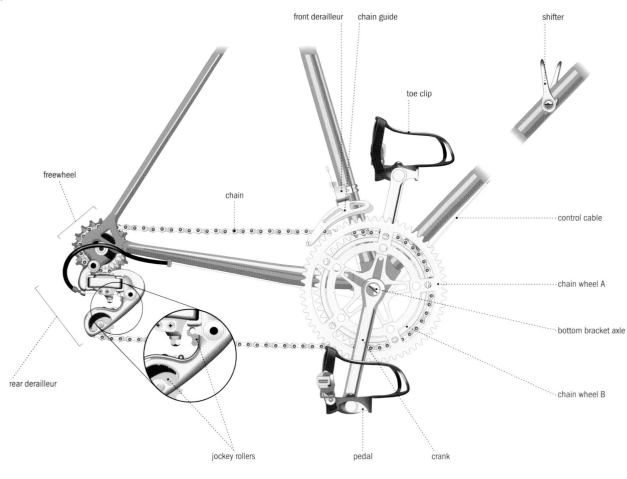

front derailleur · chain guide · shifter · toe clip · freewheel · chain · control cable · chain wheel A · bottom bracket axle · rear derailleur · chain wheel B · jockey rollers · pedal · crank

accessories

lock

protective helmet · tool kit · bicycle bag · child carrier

child's tricycle

examples of bicycles

BMX bike

Dutch bicycle

mountain bike

city bicycle

road bicycle

touring bicycle

tandem bicycle

TRANSPORT AND MACHINERY

passenger station

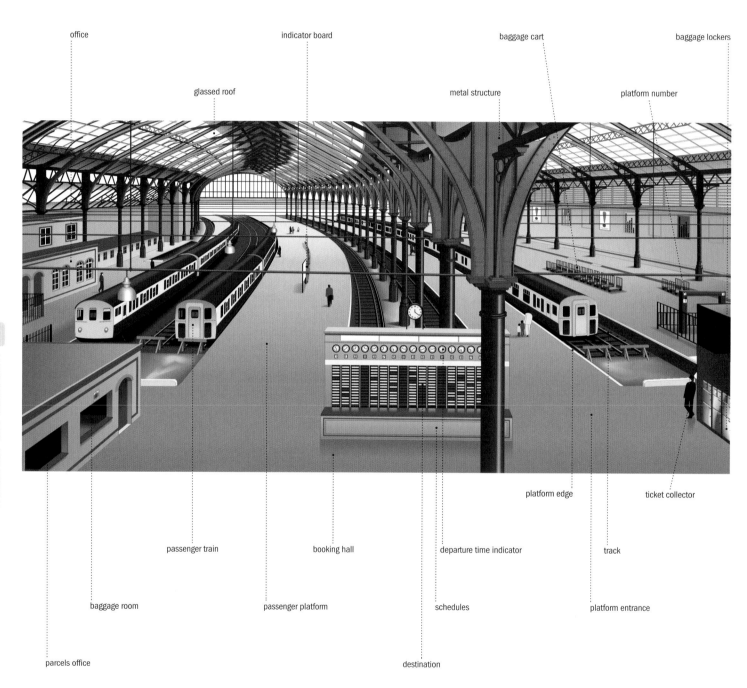

office

indicator board

baggage cart

baggage lockers

glassed roof

metal structure

platform number

platform edge

ticket collector

passenger train

booking hall

departure time indicator

track

baggage room

passenger platform

schedules

platform entrance

parcels office

destination

passenger station

station platform

commuter train

main line

suburban commuter railroad

subsidiary track

bumper

level crossing

parking

platform shelter

footbridge

semaphore

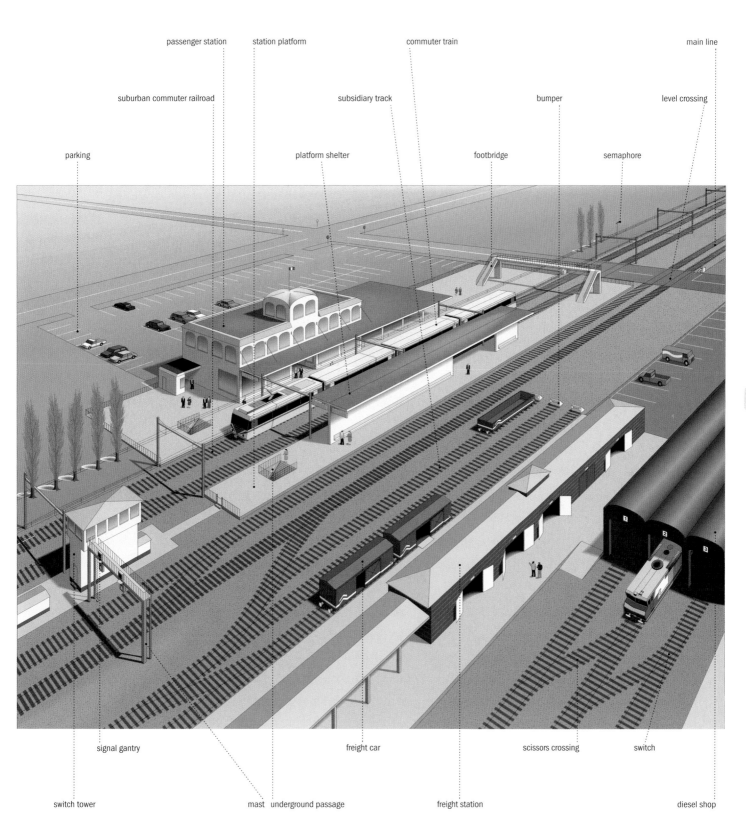

signal gantry

freight car

scissors crossing

switch

switch tower

mast underground passage

freight station

diesel shop

types of passenger cars

coach car

luggage rack   vestibule

adjustable seat   center aisle

vestibule door

sleeping car

berth   toilet

linen   sleeping compartment   wheelchair

corridor connection

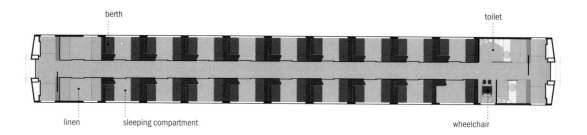

dining car

dining section   steward's desk   storage space

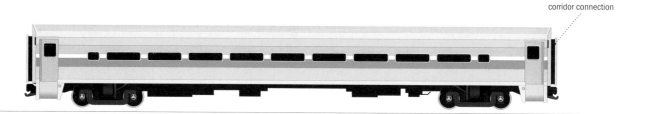

kitchen   crew's locker

panoramic window   grab handle

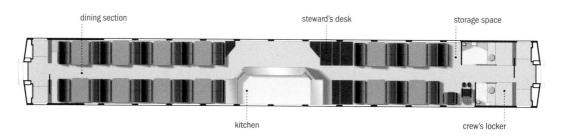

high-speed train

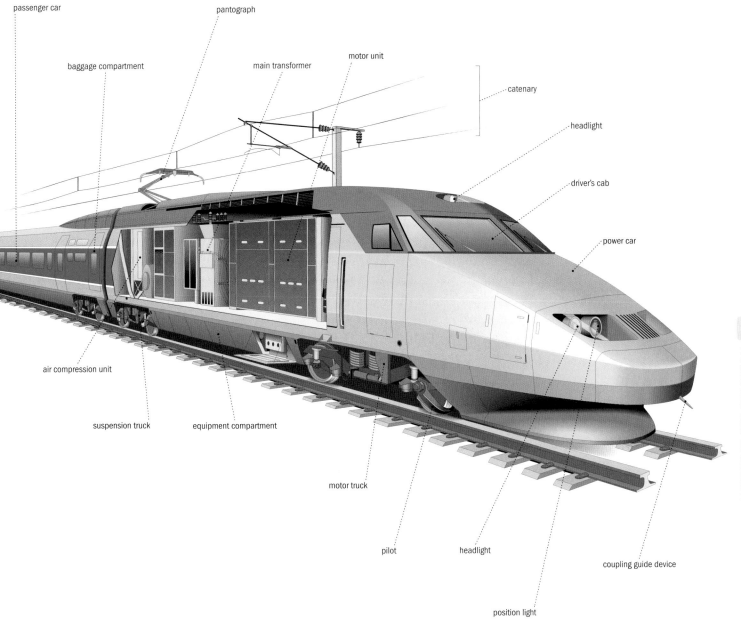

passenger car

pantograph

baggage compartment

main transformer

motor unit

catenary

headlight

driver's cab

power car

air compression unit

suspension truck

equipment compartment

motor truck

pilot

headlight

position light

coupling guide device

diesel-electric locomotive

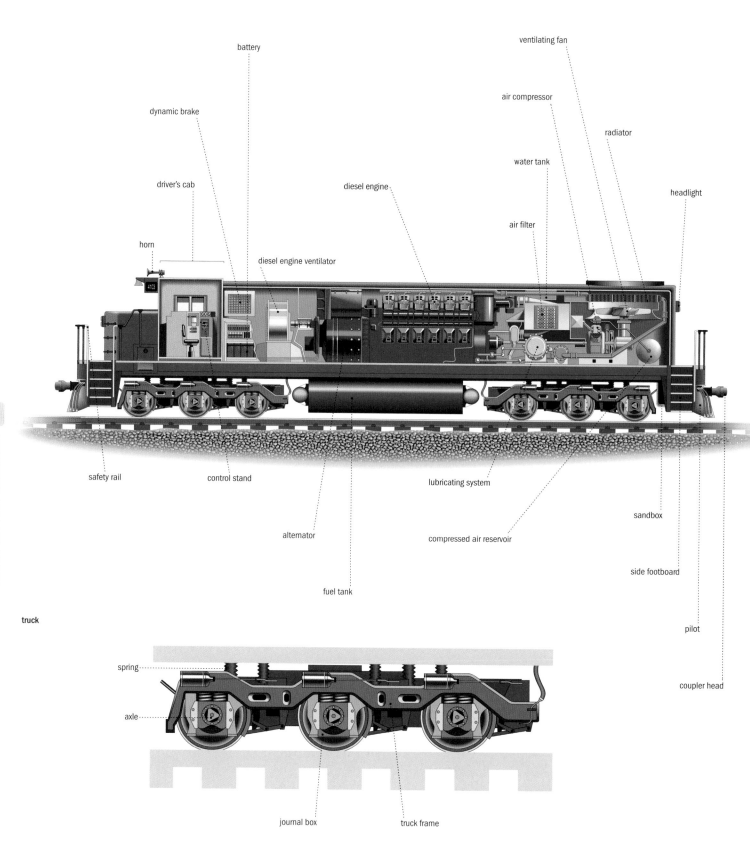

battery

ventilating fan

air compressor

radiator

dynamic brake

water tank

driver's cab

diesel engine

headlight

air filter

horn

diesel engine ventilator

safety rail

control stand

lubricating system

sandbox

alternator

compressed air reservoir

side footboard

fuel tank

pilot

truck

coupler head

spring

axle

journal box

truck frame

box car

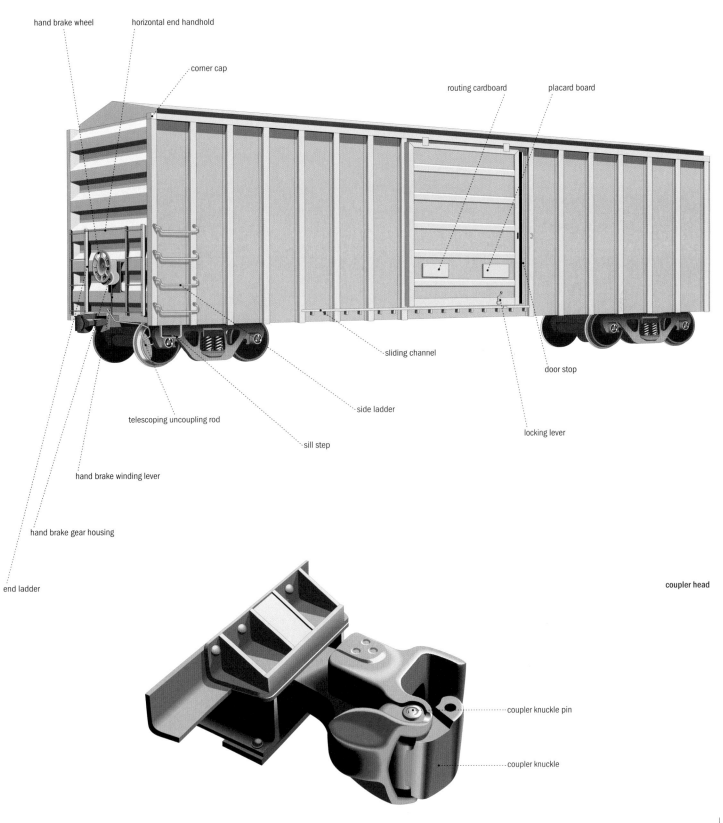

hand brake wheel

horizontal end handhold

corner cap

routing cardboard

placard board

sliding channel

door stop

side ladder

locking lever

telescoping uncoupling rod

sill step

hand brake winding lever

hand brake gear housing

end ladder

coupler head

coupler knuckle pin

coupler knuckle

TRANSPORT AND MACHINERY

car

examples of freight cars

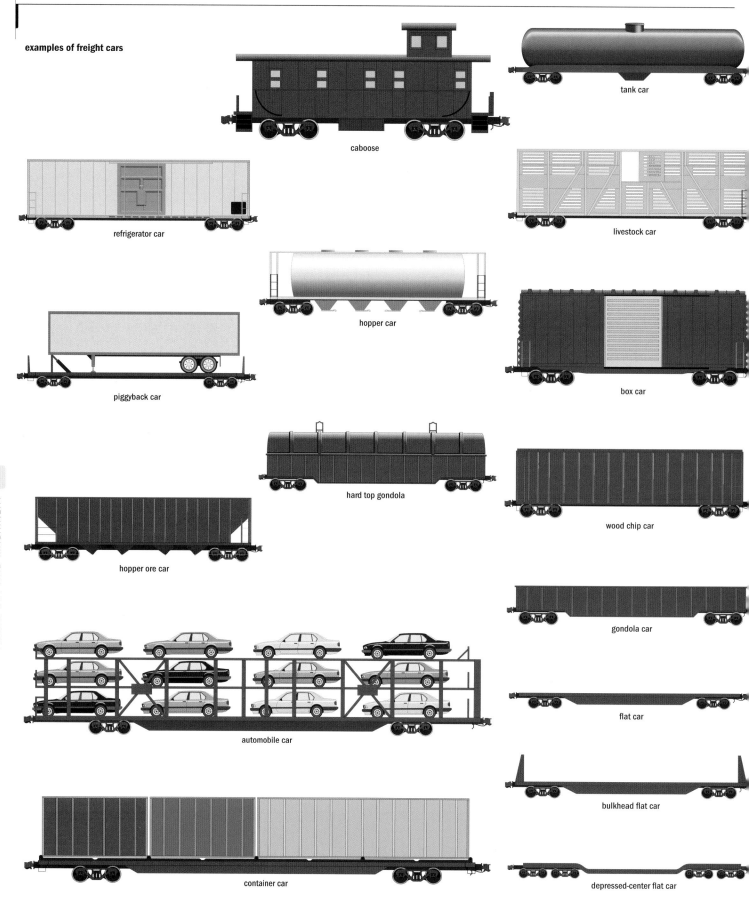

caboose

tank car

refrigerator car

livestock car

hopper car

piggyback car

box car

hard top gondola

wood chip car

hopper ore car

gondola car

automobile car

flat car

bulkhead flat car

container car

depressed-center flat car

TRANSPORT AND MACHINERY

yard

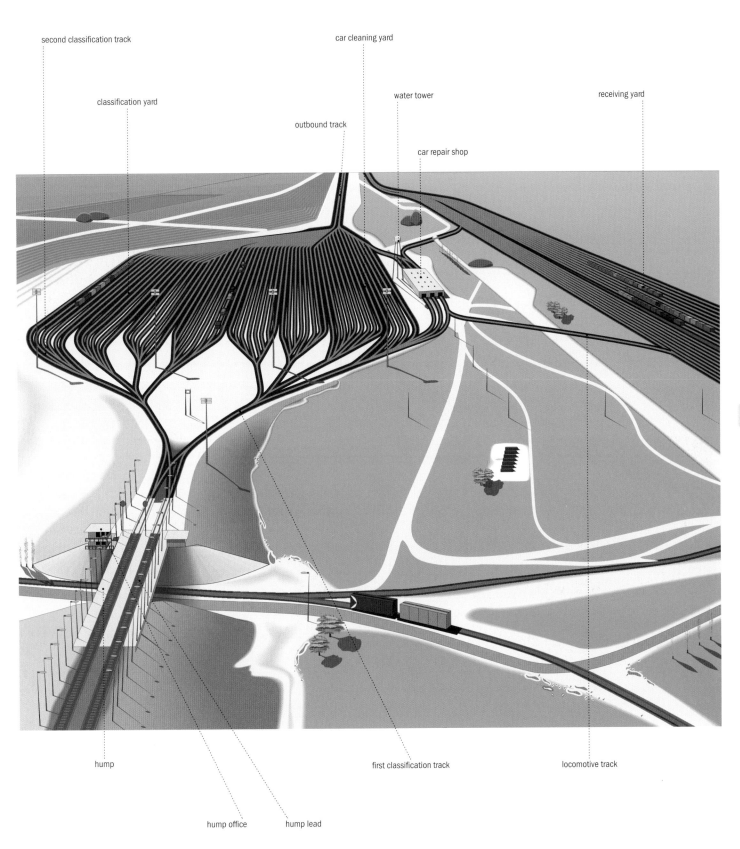

second classification track

classification yard

car cleaning yard

outbound track

water tower

car repair shop

receiving yard

hump

hump office

hump lead

first classification track

locomotive track

railroad track

rail joint

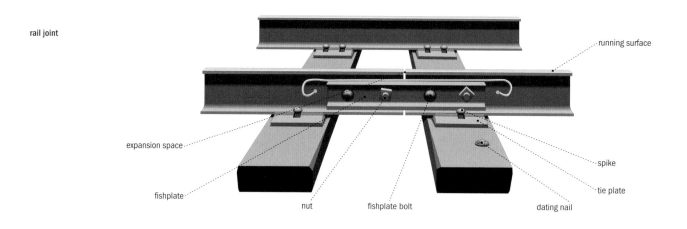

running surface

expansion space

spike

fishplate

tie plate

nut   fishplate bolt   dating nail

remote-controlled switch

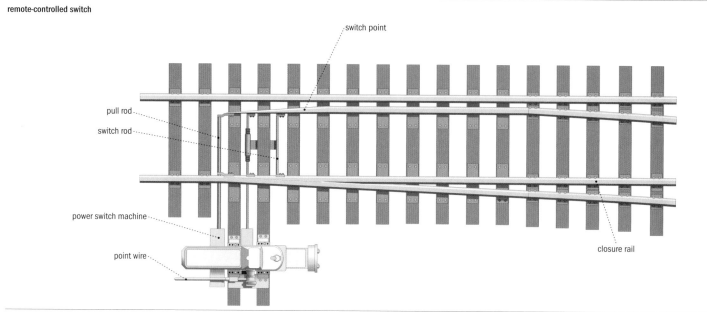

switch point

pull rod

switch rod

power switch machine

point wire

closure rail

manually-operated switch

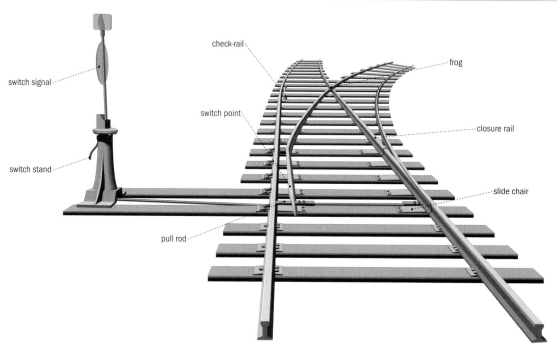

check-rail

frog

switch signal

switch point

closure rail

switch stand

slide chair

pull rod

railroad track

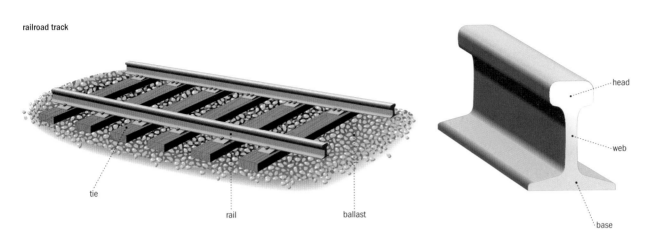

tie

rail

ballast

rail section

head

web

base

highway crossing

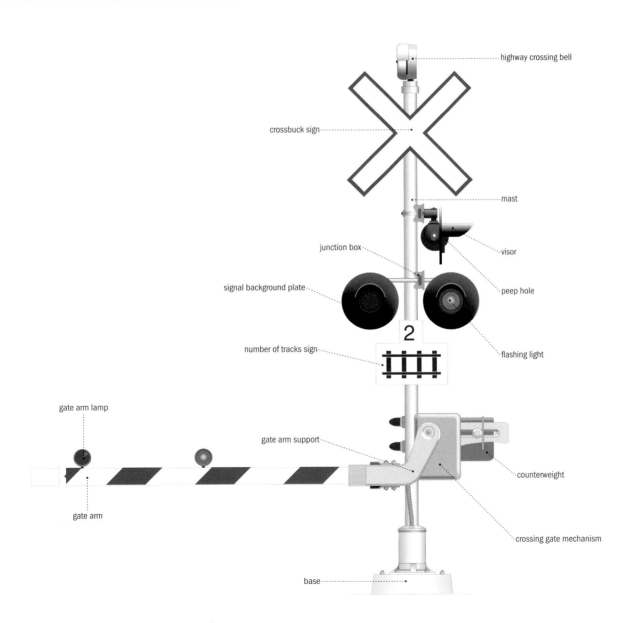

highway crossing bell

crossbuck sign

mast

junction box

visor

signal background plate

peep hole

flashing light

number of tracks sign

gate arm lamp

gate arm support

counterweight

gate arm

crossing gate mechanism

base

subway

subway station

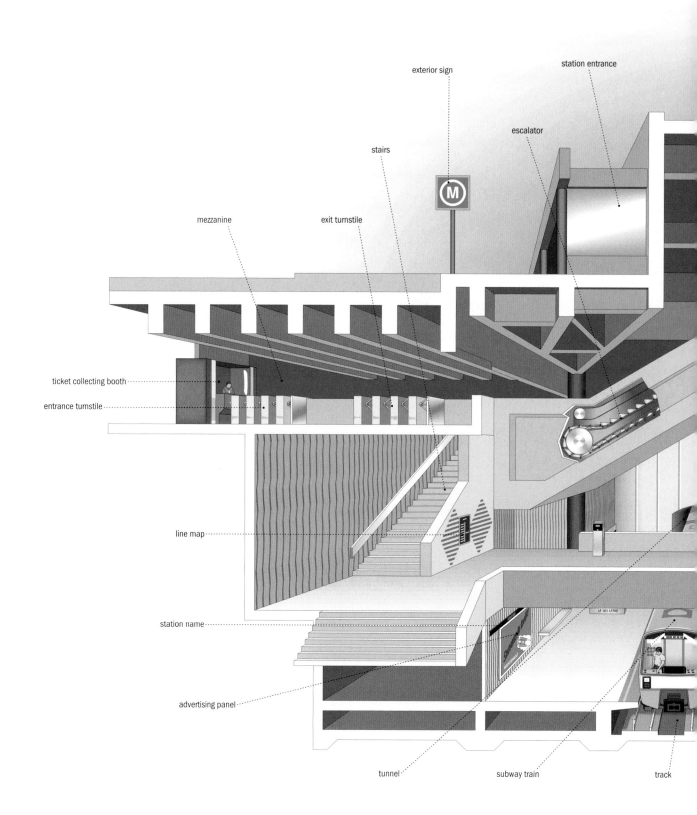

exterior sign

station entrance

escalator

stairs

mezzanine

exit turnstile

ticket collecting booth

entrance turnstile

line map

station name

advertising panel

tunnel

subway train

track

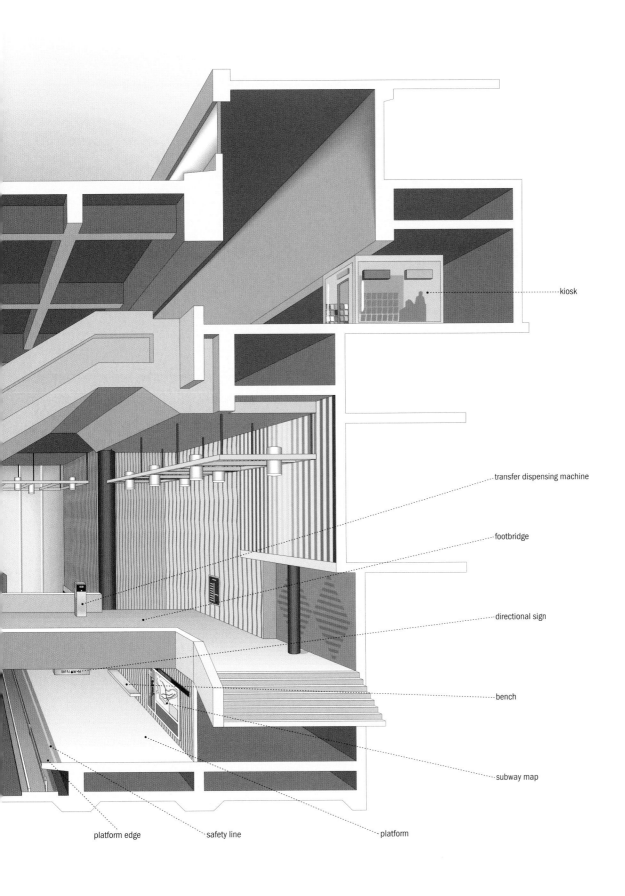

kiosk

transfer dispensing machine

footbridge

directional sign

bench

subway map

platform edge

safety line

platform

subway

TRANSPORT AND MACHINERY

passenger car

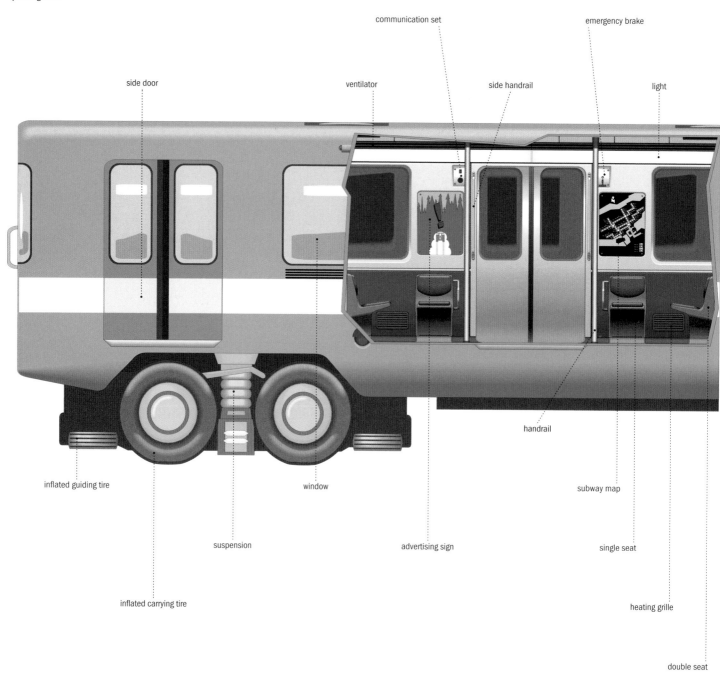

communication set

emergency brake

side door

ventilator

side handrail

light

handrail

inflated guiding tire

window

subway map

single seat

suspension

advertising sign

heating grille

inflated carrying tire

double seat

subway train

motor car

trailer car

motor car

truck and track

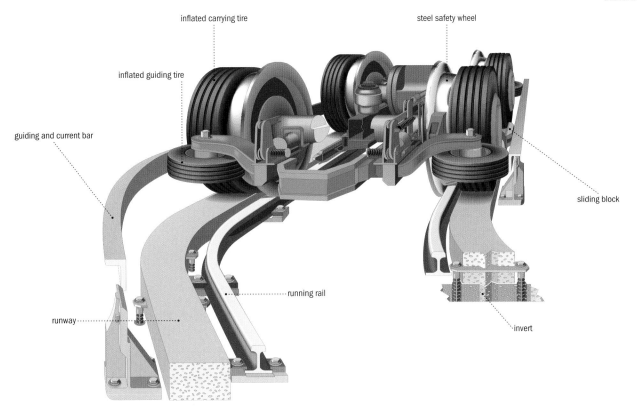

inflated carrying tire

steel safety wheel

inflated guiding tire

guiding and current bar

sliding block

running rail

runway

invert

streetcar

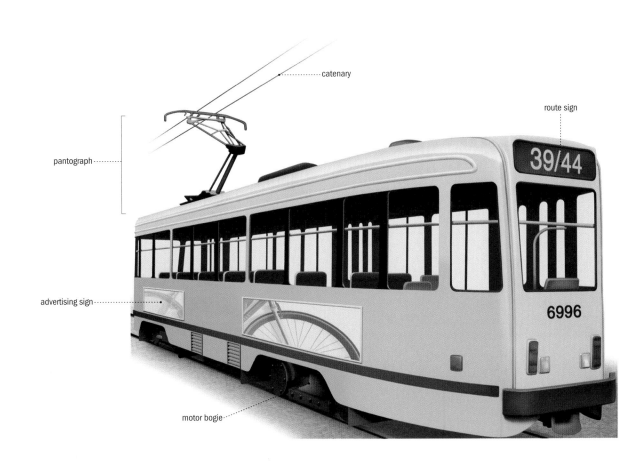

catenary

route sign

pantograph

advertising sign

motor bogie

harbor

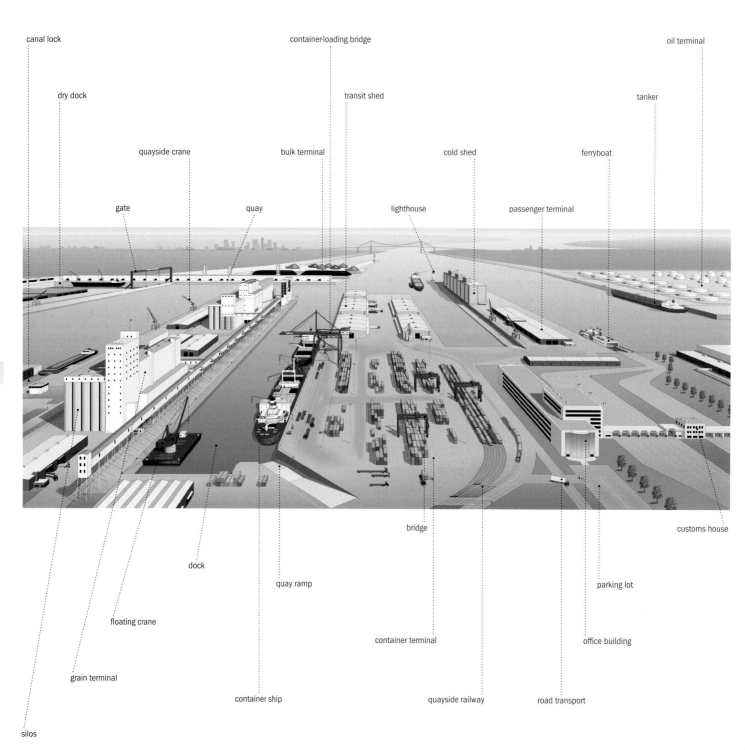

canal lock

container-loading bridge

oil terminal

dry dock

transit shed

tanker

quayside crane

bulk terminal

cold shed

ferryboat

gate

quay

lighthouse

passenger terminal

bridge

customs house

dock

quay ramp

parking lot

floating crane

container terminal

office building

grain terminal

container ship

quayside railway

road transport

silos

canal lock

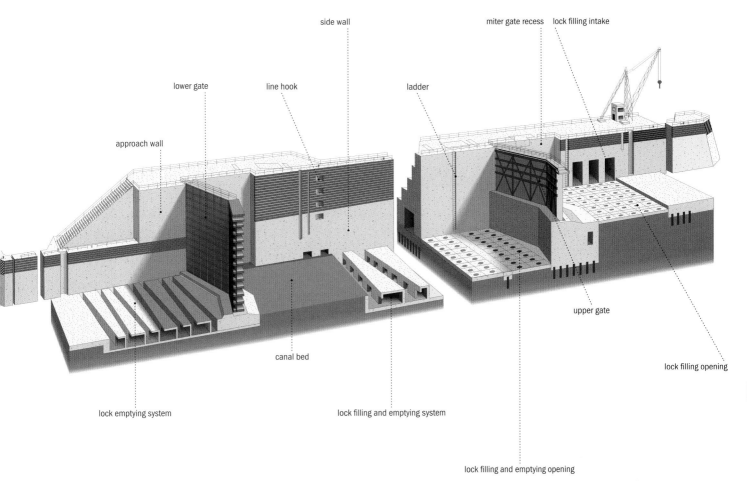

side wall

miter gate recess   lock filling intake

lower gate   line hook   ladder

approach wall

lock filling opening

canal bed

upper gate

lock emptying system   lock filling and emptying system

lock filling and emptying opening

canal lock: side view

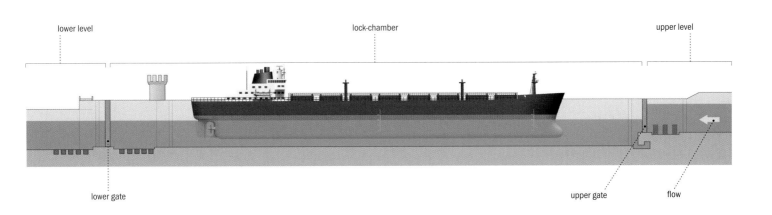

lower level   lock-chamber   upper level

lower gate   upper gate   flow

ancient ships

longship

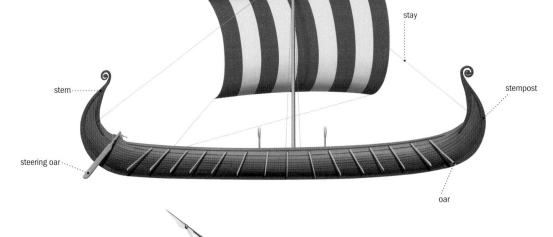

stay

stern

stempost

steering oar

oar

galley

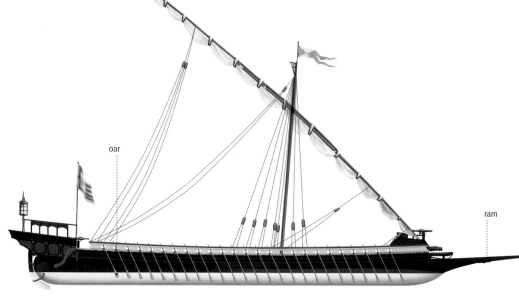

oar

ram

trireme

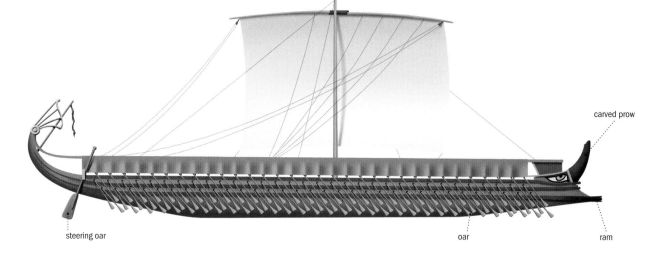

carved prow

steering oar

oar

ram

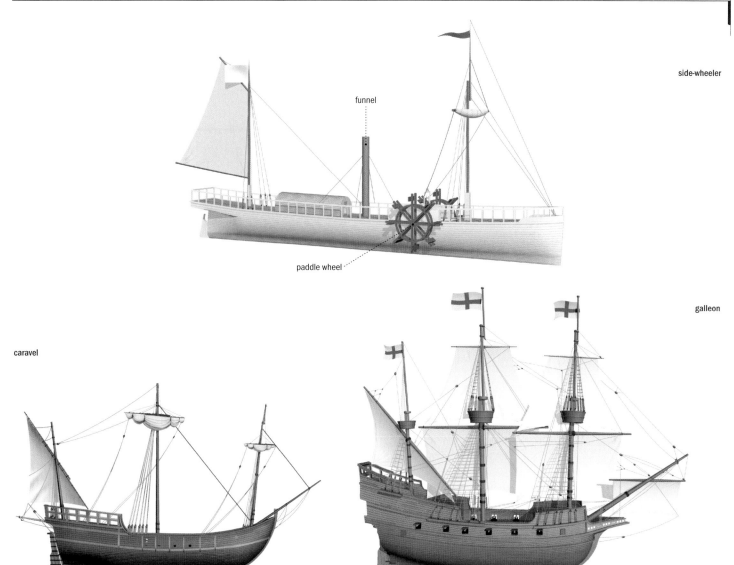

side-wheeler

funnel

paddle wheel

galleon

caravel

traditional ships

outrigger canoe

dugout canoe

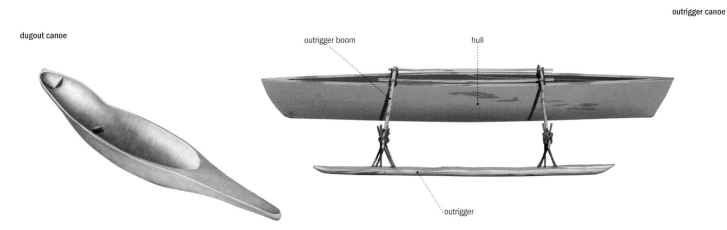

outrigger boom

hull

outrigger

traditional ships

junk

TRANSPORT AND MACHINERY

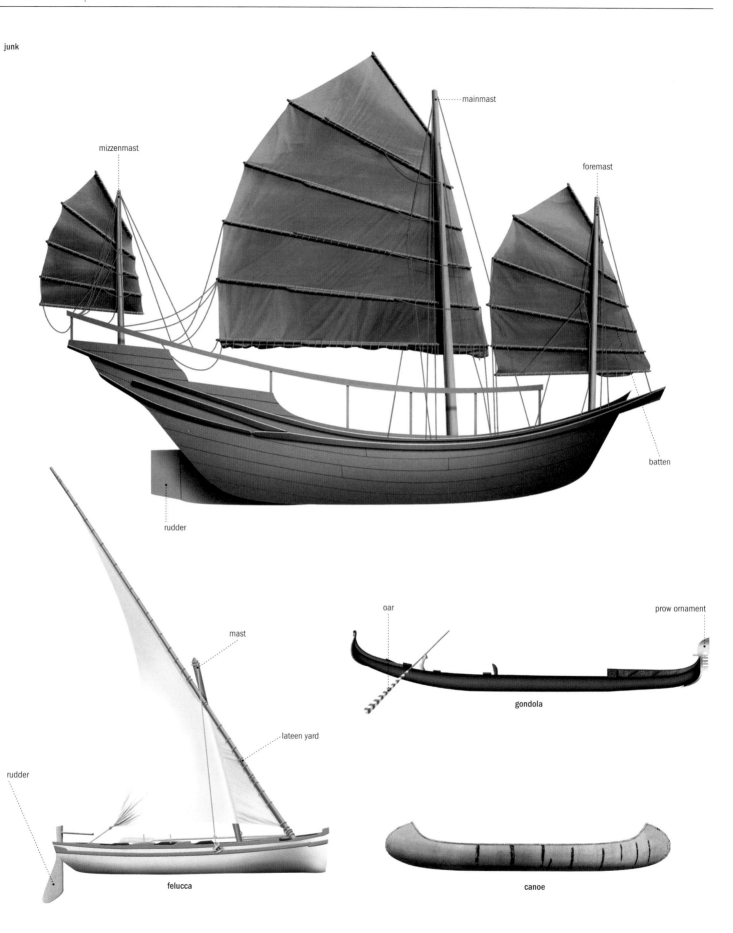

mizzenmast

mainmast

foremast

batten

rudder

oar

prow ornament

gondola

mast

lateen yard

rudder

felucca

canoe

examples of sails

gaff sail

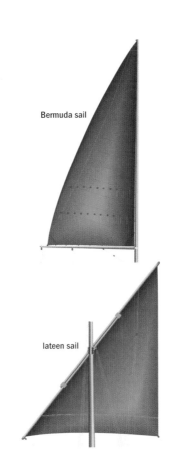

Bermuda sail

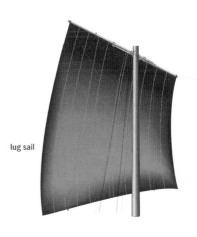

lug sail

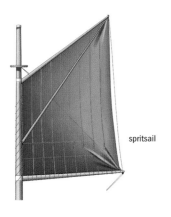

spritsail

lateen sail

square sail

examples of rigs

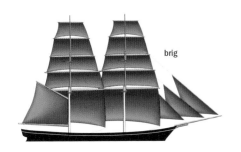

brig

ketch

brigantine

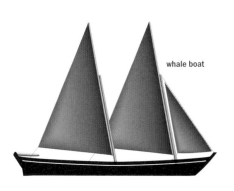

whale boat

schooner

Marconi cutter

TRANSPORT AND MACHINERY

four-masted bark

TRANSPORT AND MACHINERY

masting and rigging

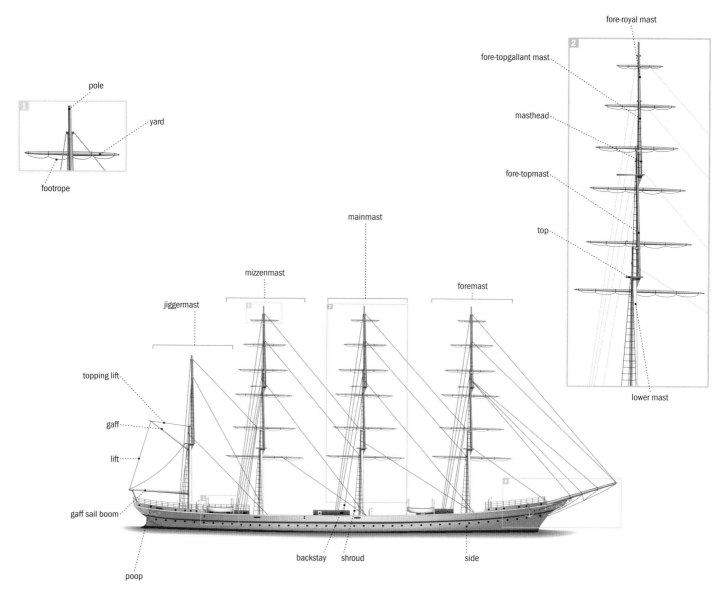

fore-royal mast

fore-topgallant mast

masthead

fore-topmast

top

lower mast

pole

yard

footrope

mainmast

mizzenmast

jiggermast

foremast

topping lift

gaff

lift

gaff sail boom

poop

backstay shroud side

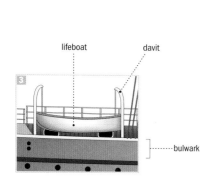

lifeboat davit

bulwark

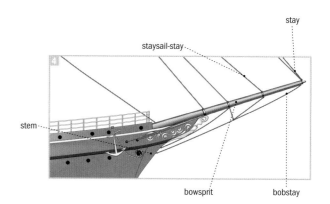

stay

staysail-stay

stem

bowsprit bobstay

sails

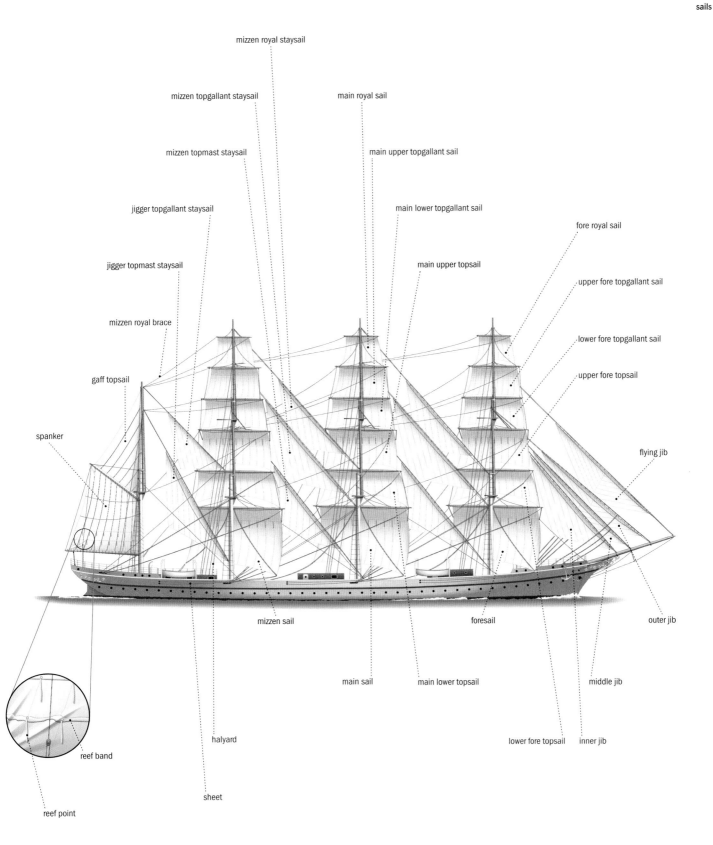

mizzen royal staysail

mizzen topgallant staysail

main royal sail

mizzen topmast staysail

main upper topgallant sail

jigger topgallant staysail

main lower topgallant sail

fore royal sail

jigger topmast staysail

main upper topsail

upper fore topgallant sail

mizzen royal brace

lower fore topgallant sail

gaff topsail

upper fore topsail

spanker

flying jib

mizzen sail

foresail

outer jib

main sail

main lower topsail

middle jib

reef band

halyard

lower fore topsail

inner jib

reef point

sheet

examples of boats and ships

drill ship

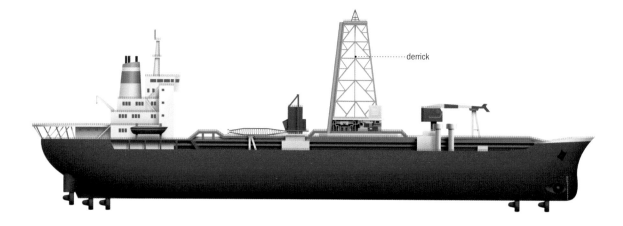

derrick

bulk carrier

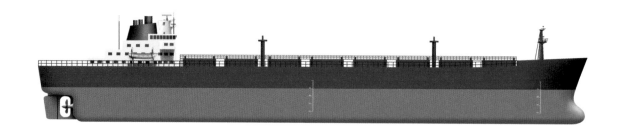

container ship

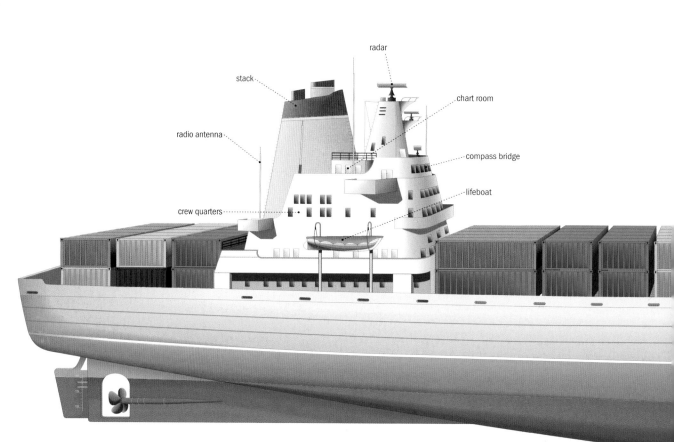

radar

stack

chart room

radio antenna

compass bridge

lifeboat

crew quarters

hovercraft

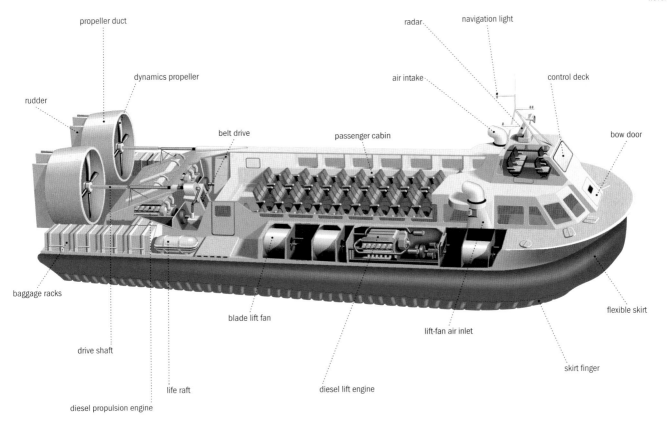

propeller duct

dynamics propeller

rudder

radar

navigation light

control deck

air intake

belt drive

passenger cabin

bow door

baggage racks

flexible skirt

blade lift fan

drive shaft

lift-fan air inlet

life raft

diesel lift engine

skirt finger

diesel propulsion engine

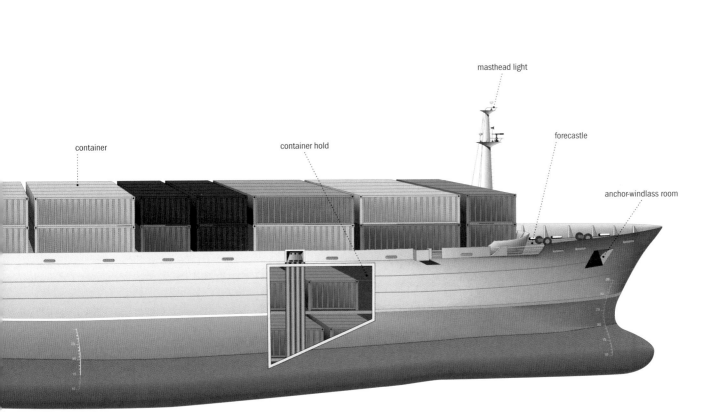

masthead light

container

container hold

forecastle

anchor-windlass room

examples of boats and ships

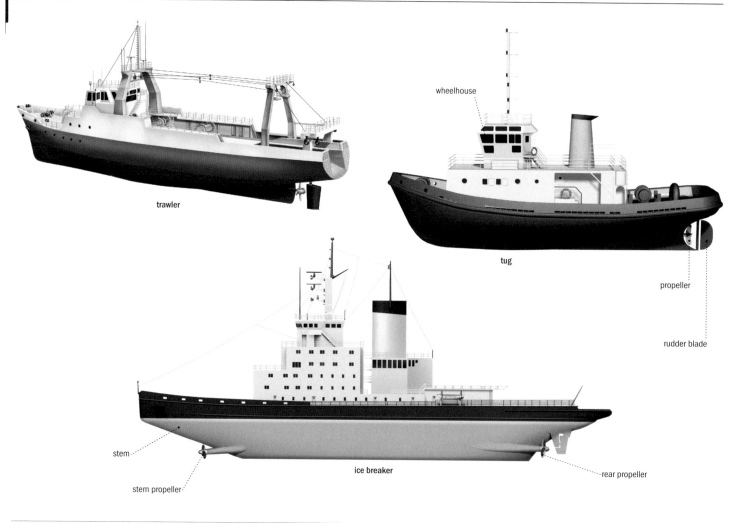

trawler

wheelhouse

tug

propeller

rudder blade

stem

stem propeller

ice breaker

rear propeller

tanker

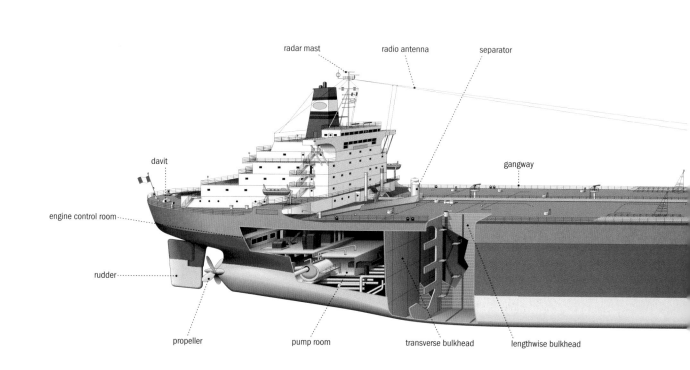

radar mast

radio antenna

separator

davit

gangway

engine control room

rudder

propeller

pump room

transverse bulkhead

lengthwise bulkhead

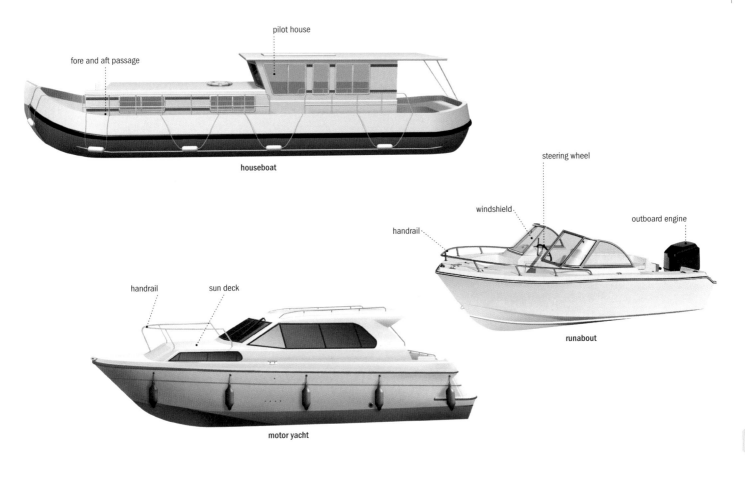

pilot house

fore and aft passage

houseboat

steering wheel

windshield

handrail

outboard engine

runabout

handrail

sun deck

motor yacht

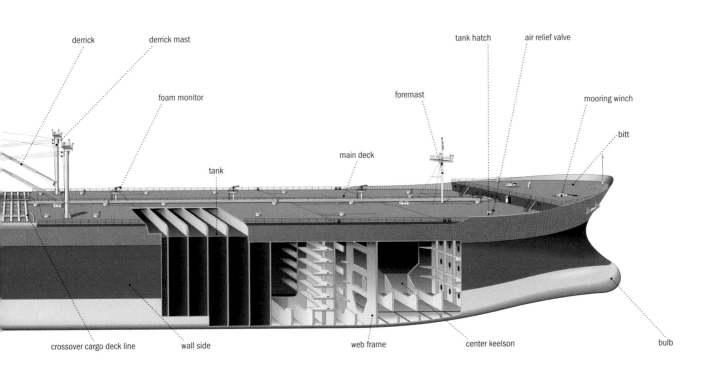

derrick

derrick mast

tank hatch

air relief valve

foam monitor

foremast

mooring winch

main deck

bitt

tank

crossover cargo deck line

wall side

web frame

center keelson

bulb

examples of boats and ships

ferry

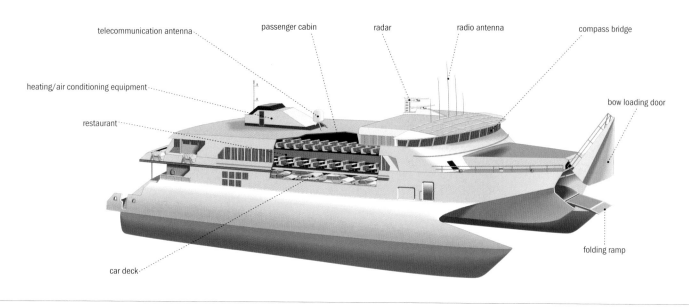

telecommunication antenna

passenger cabin

radar

radio antenna

compass bridge

heating/air conditioning equipment

bow loading door

restaurant

folding ramp

car deck

passenger liner

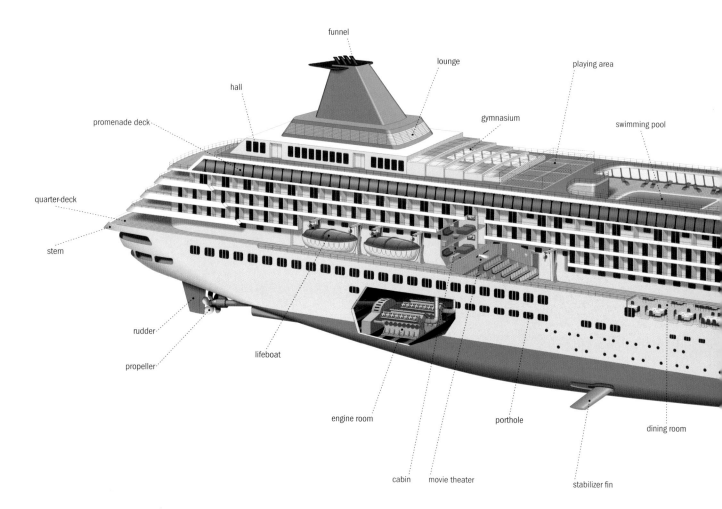

funnel

lounge

playing area

hall

gymnasium

swimming pool

promenade deck

quarter-deck

stern

rudder

propeller

lifeboat

engine room

cabin

movie theater

porthole

stabilizer fin

dining room

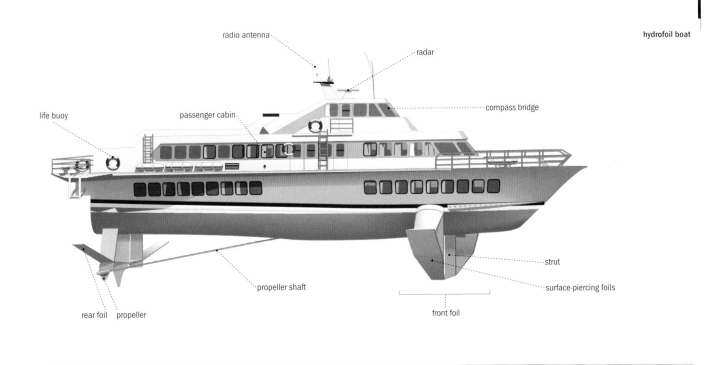

radio antenna

radar

compass bridge

life buoy

passenger cabin

strut

propeller shaft

surface-piercing foils

rear foil   propeller

front foil

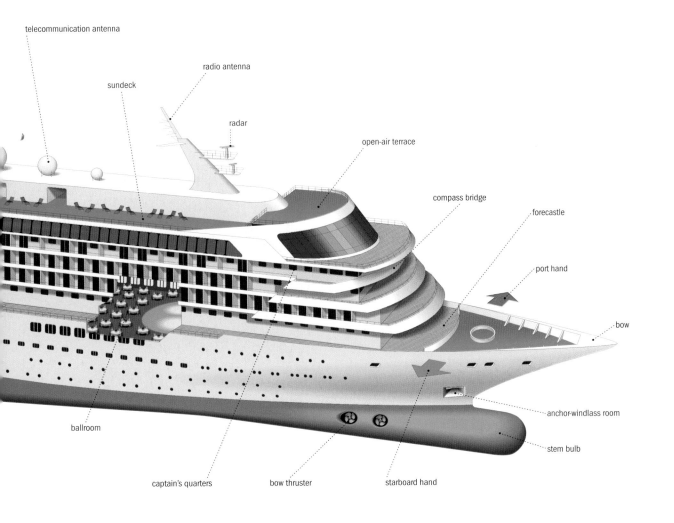

telecommunication antenna

radio antenna

sundeck

radar

open-air terrace

compass bridge

forecastle

port hand

bow

anchor-windlass room

ballroom

stem bulb

captain's quarters

bow thruster

starboard hand

anchor

ship's anchor

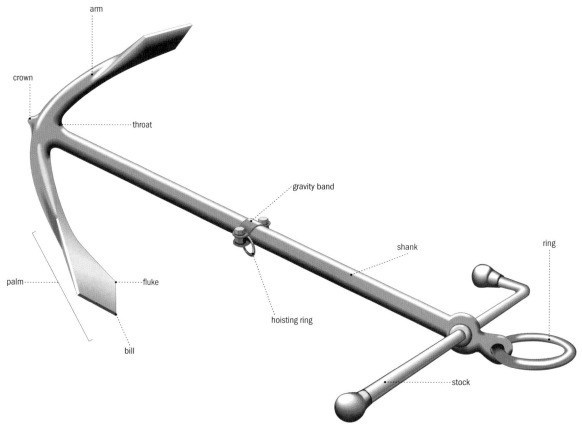

arm

crown

throat

gravity band

shank

ring

palm

fluke

hoisting ring

bill

stock

examples of anchors

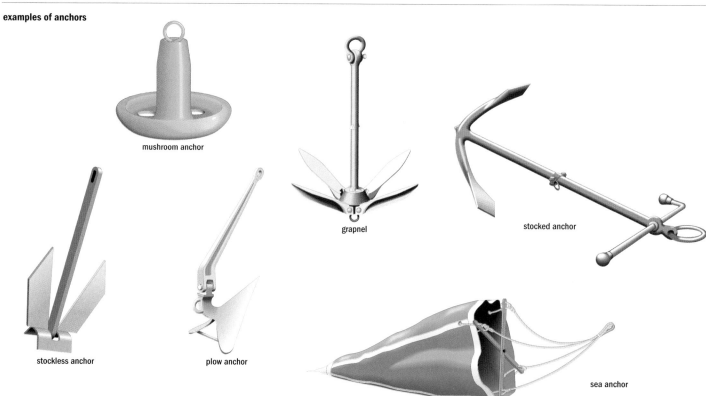

mushroom anchor

grapnel

stocked anchor

stockless anchor

plow anchor

sea anchor

life-saving equipment

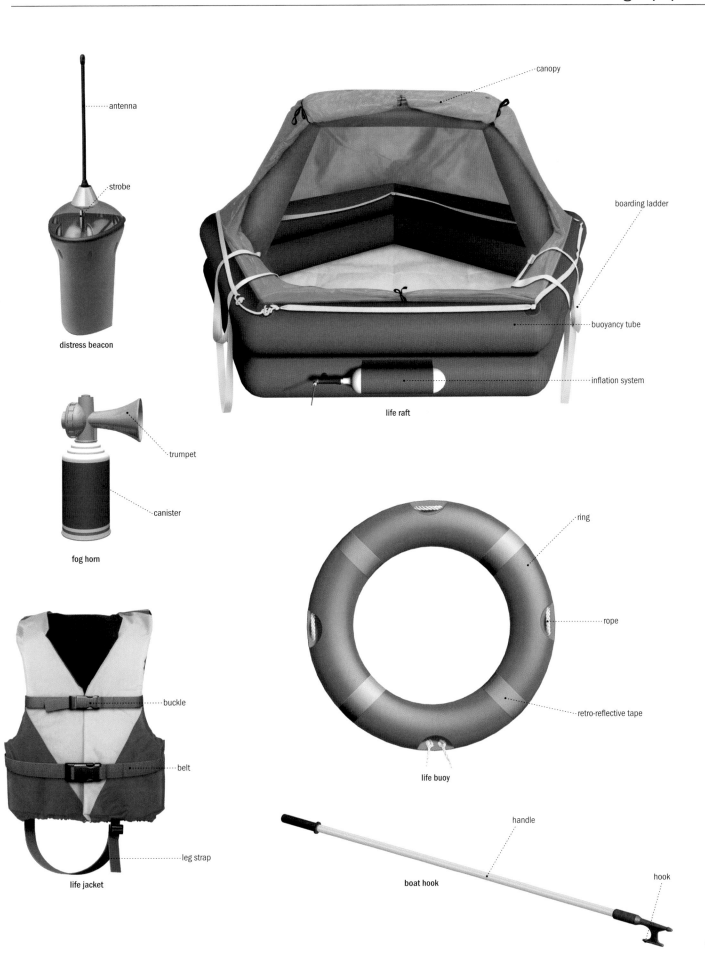

antenna

strobe

distress beacon

trumpet

canister

fog horn

buckle

belt

leg strap

life jacket

canopy

boarding ladder

buoyancy tube

inflation system

life raft

ring

rope

retro-reflective tape

life buoy

handle

hook

boat hook

navigation devices

sextant

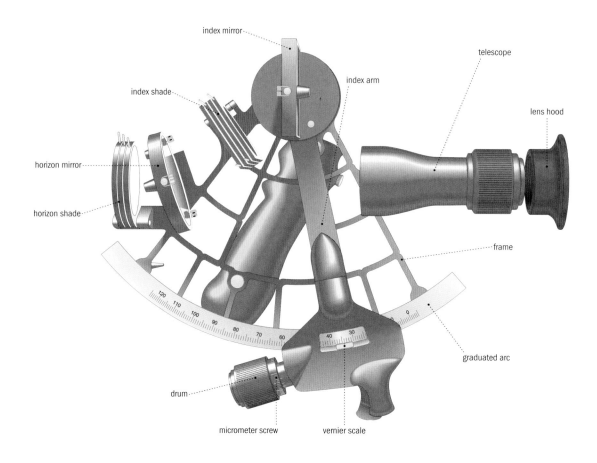

index mirror

telescope

index arm

lens hood

index shade

horizon mirror

horizon shade

frame

120 110 100 90 80 70 60

40 30

graduated arc

drum

micrometer screw

vernier scale

liquid compass

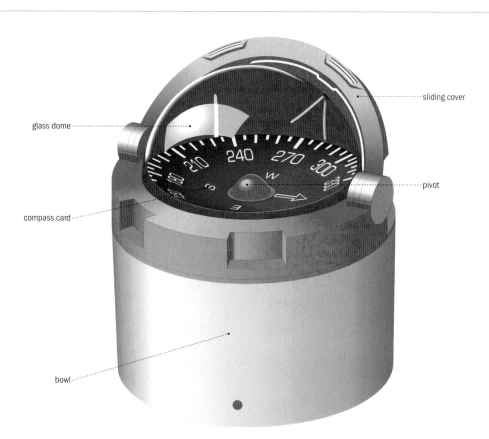

sliding cover

glass dome

210 240 270 300

W

pivot

compass card

bowl

echo sounder

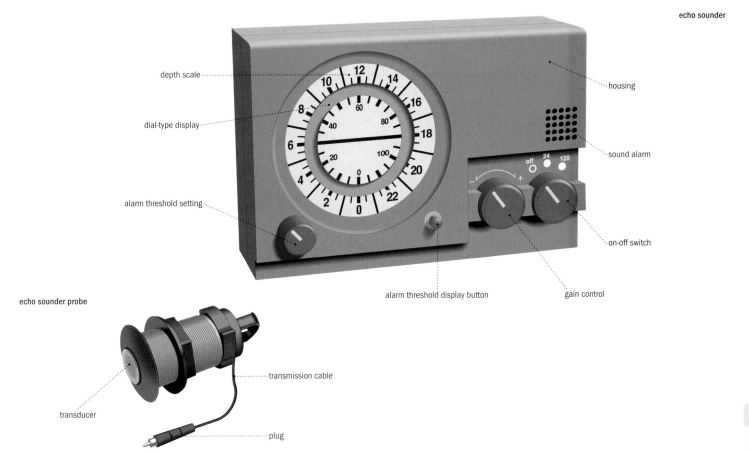

depth scale

dial-type display

alarm threshold setting

housing

sound alarm

on-off switch

alarm threshold display button

gain control

echo sounder probe

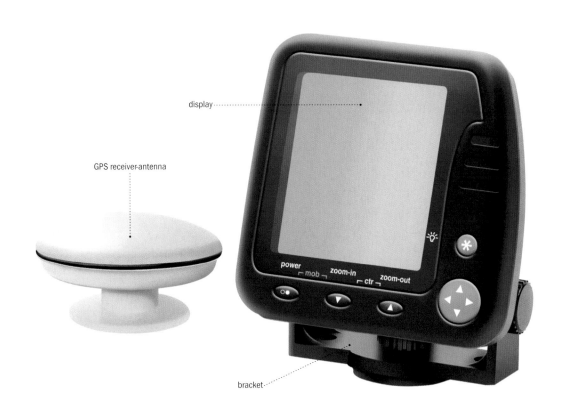

transmission cable

transducer

plug

satellite navigation system

display

GPS receiver-antenna

power

zoom-in

zoom-out

mob

ctr

bracket

maritime signals

TRANSPORT AND MACHINERY

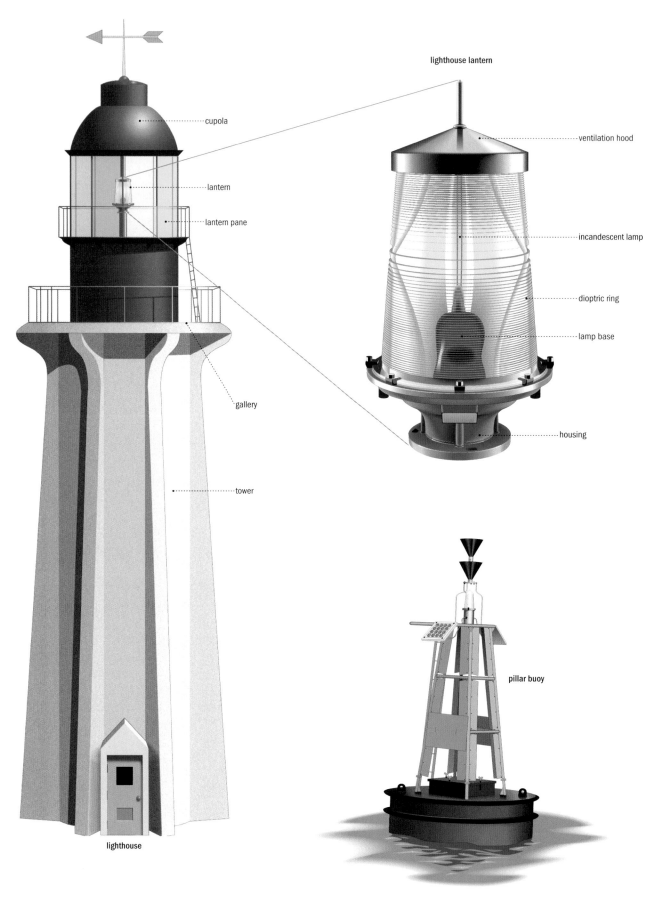

cupola

lantern

lantern pane

gallery

tower

lighthouse

lighthouse lantern

ventilation hood

incandescent lamp

dioptric ring

lamp base

housing

pillar buoy

conical buoy

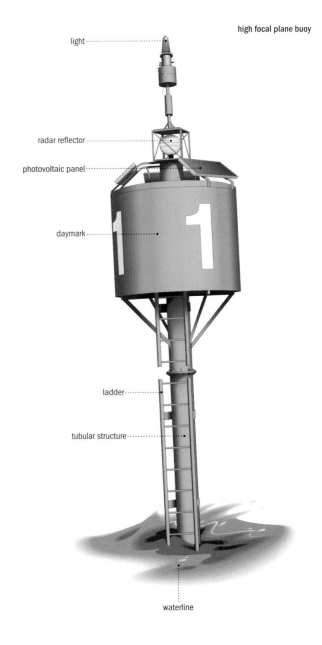

high focal plane buoy

light

radar reflector

photovoltaic panel

daymark

ladder

tubular structure

waterline

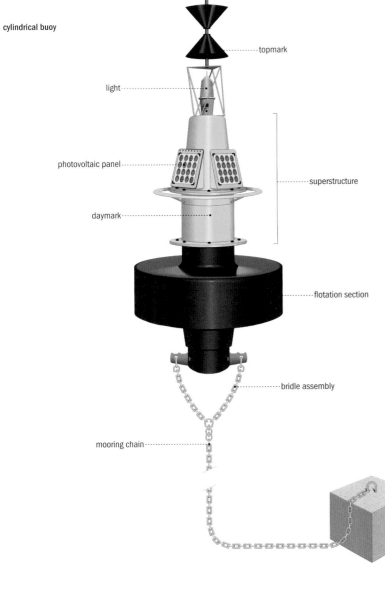

cylindrical buoy

topmark

light

photovoltaic panel

superstructure

daymark

flotation section

bridle assembly

mooring chain

sinker

maritime buoyage system

cardinal marks

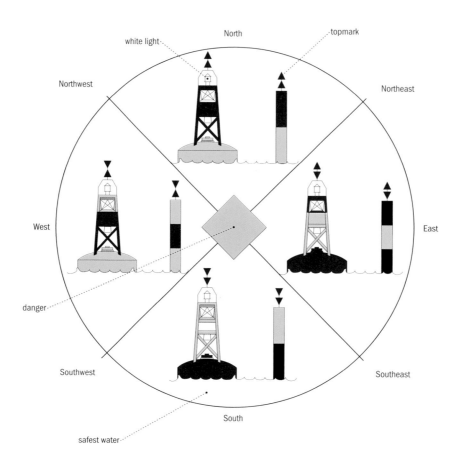

buoyage regions

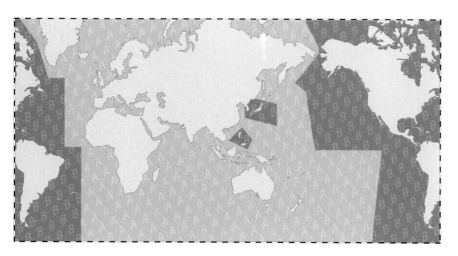

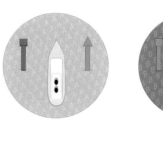

rhythm of marks by night

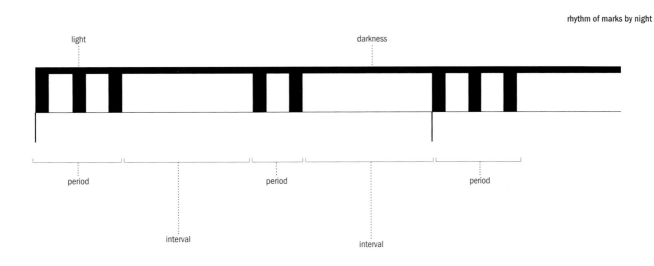

light   darkness

period   period   period

interval   interval

daymarks (region B)

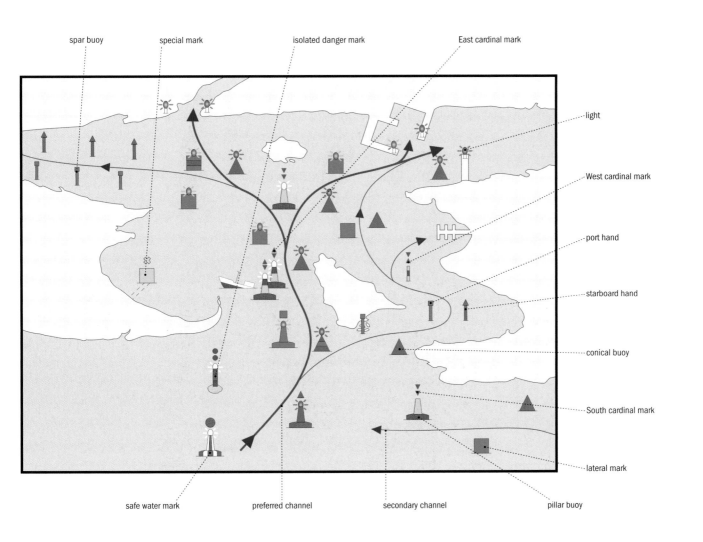

spar buoy   special mark   isolated danger mark   East cardinal mark

light

West cardinal mark

port hand

starboard hand

conical buoy

South cardinal mark

lateral mark

safe water mark   preferred channel   secondary channel   pillar buoy

TRANSPORT AND MACHINERY

airport

high-speed exit taxiway

control tower cab

control tower

access road

taxiway

by-pass taxiway

taxiway

apron

service road

apron

passenger terminal   maintenance hangar   parking area

telescopic corridor   service area   boarding walkway   taxiway line   radial passenger loading area

TRANSPORT AND MACHINERY

airport

passenger terminal

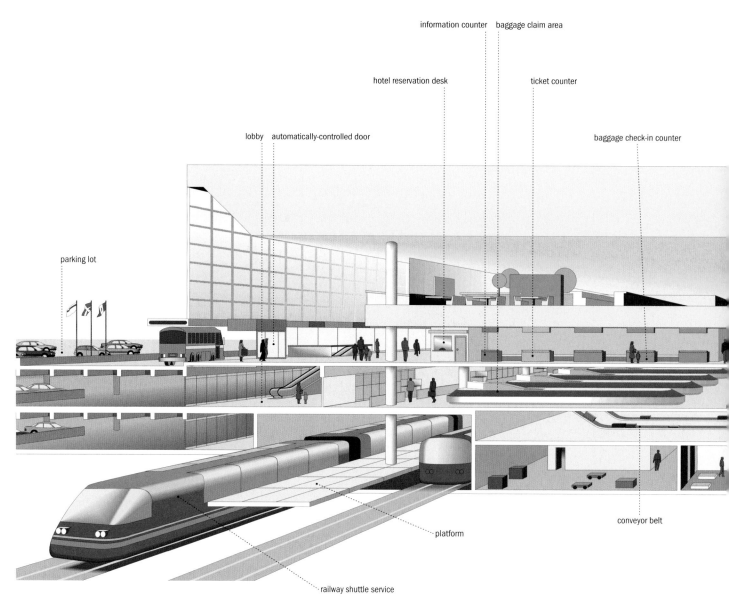

information counter   baggage claim area

hotel reservation desk   ticket counter

lobby   automatically-controlled door   baggage check-in counter

parking lot

conveyor belt

platform

railway shuttle service

TRANSPORT AND MACHINERY

runway

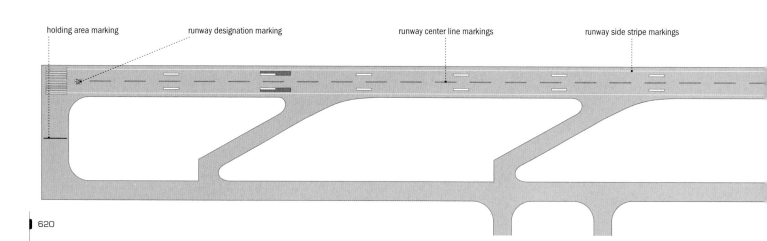

holding area marking   runway designation marking   runway center line markings   runway side stripe markings

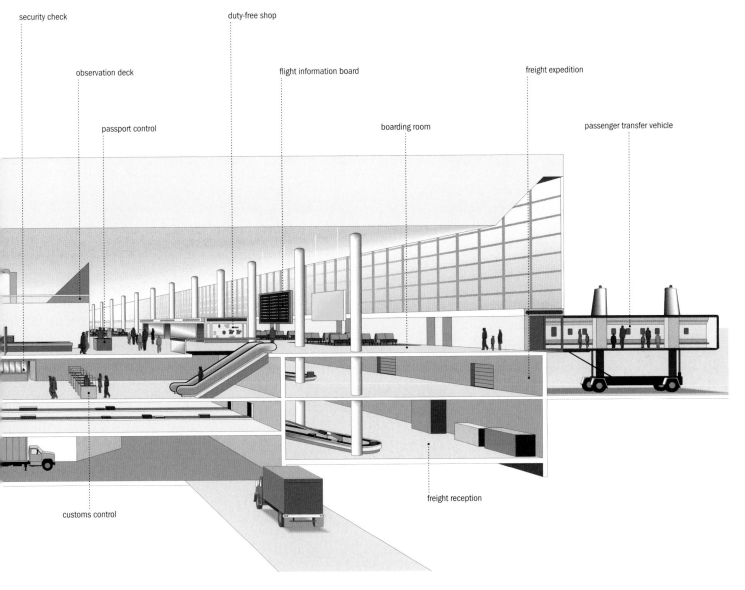

security check

observation deck

passport control

duty-free shop

flight information board

boarding room

freight expedition

passenger transfer vehicle

customs control

freight reception

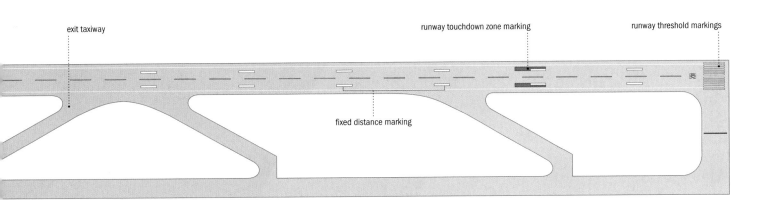

exit taxiway

runway touchdown zone marking

runway threshold markings

fixed distance marking

TRANSPORT AND MACHINERY

airport

ground airport equipment

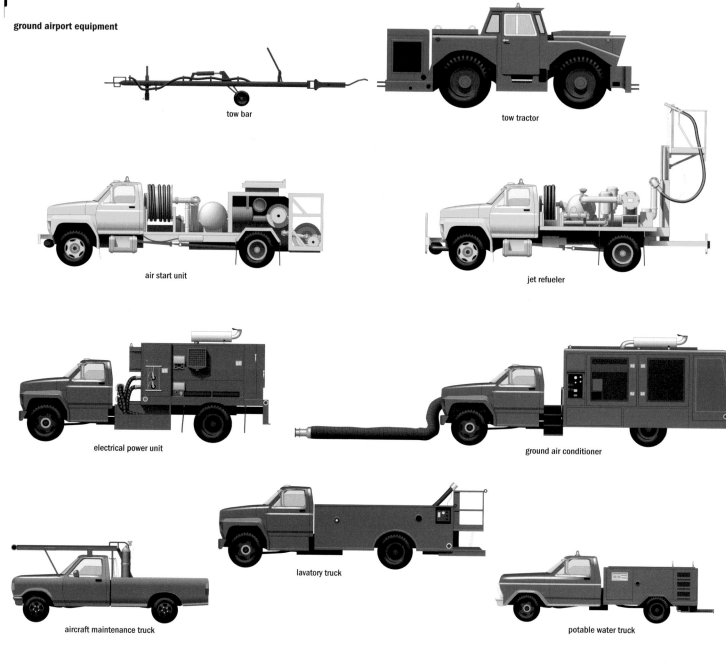

tow bar

tow tractor

air start unit

jet refueler

electrical power unit

ground air conditioner

lavatory truck

aircraft maintenance truck

potable water truck

127

wheel chock

boom truck

TRANSPORT AND MACHINERY

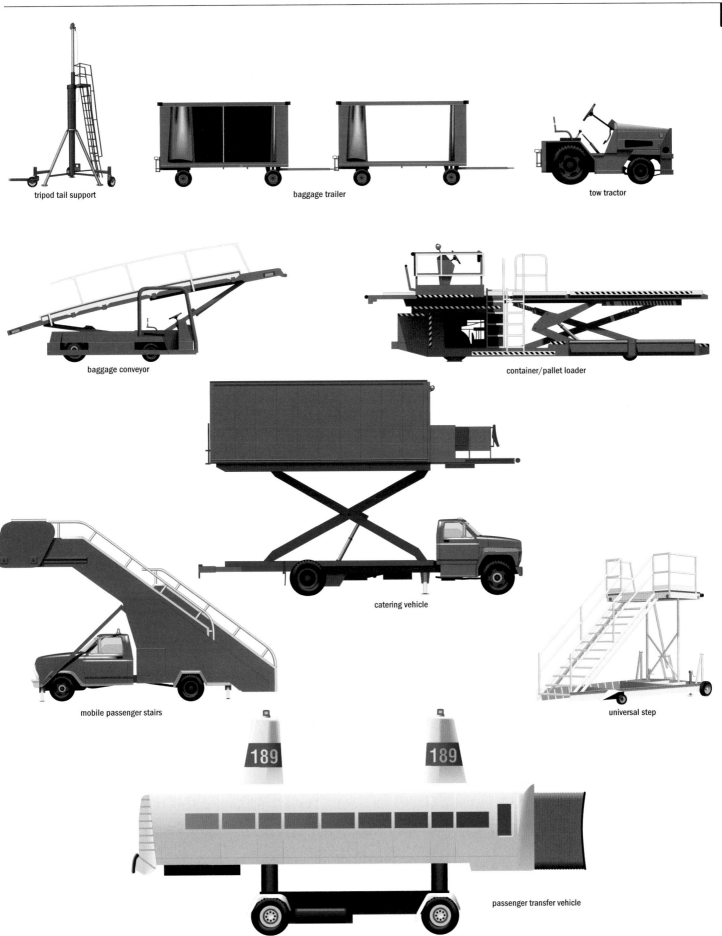

tripod tail support

baggage trailer

tow tractor

baggage conveyor

container/pallet loader

catering vehicle

mobile passenger stairs

universal step

passenger transfer vehicle

long-range jet

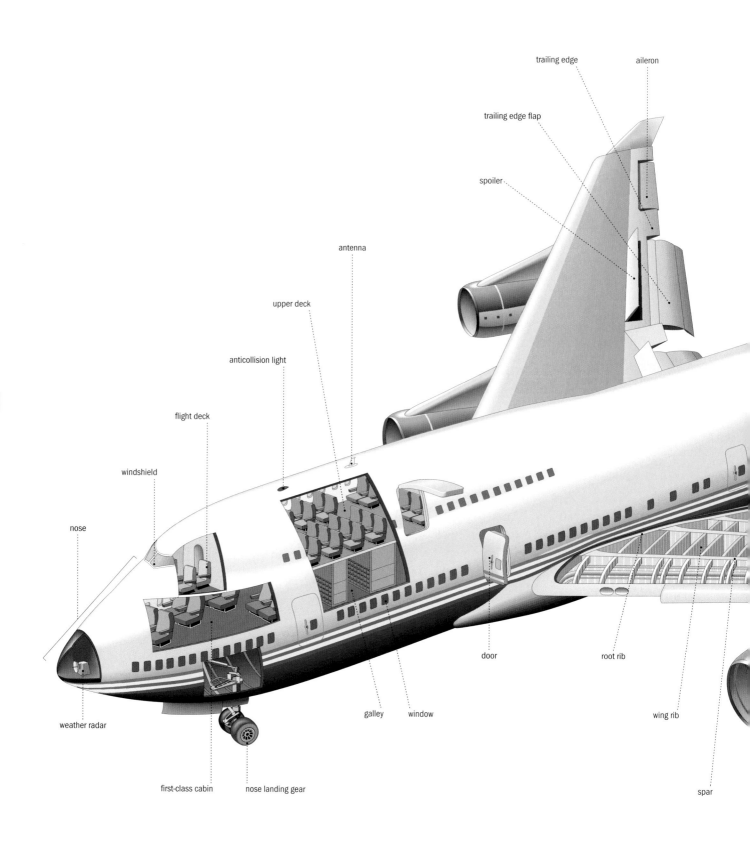

trailing edge

aileron

trailing edge flap

spoiler

antenna

upper deck

anticollision light

flight deck

windshield

nose

weather radar

first-class cabin

nose landing gear

galley

window

door

root rib

wing rib

spar

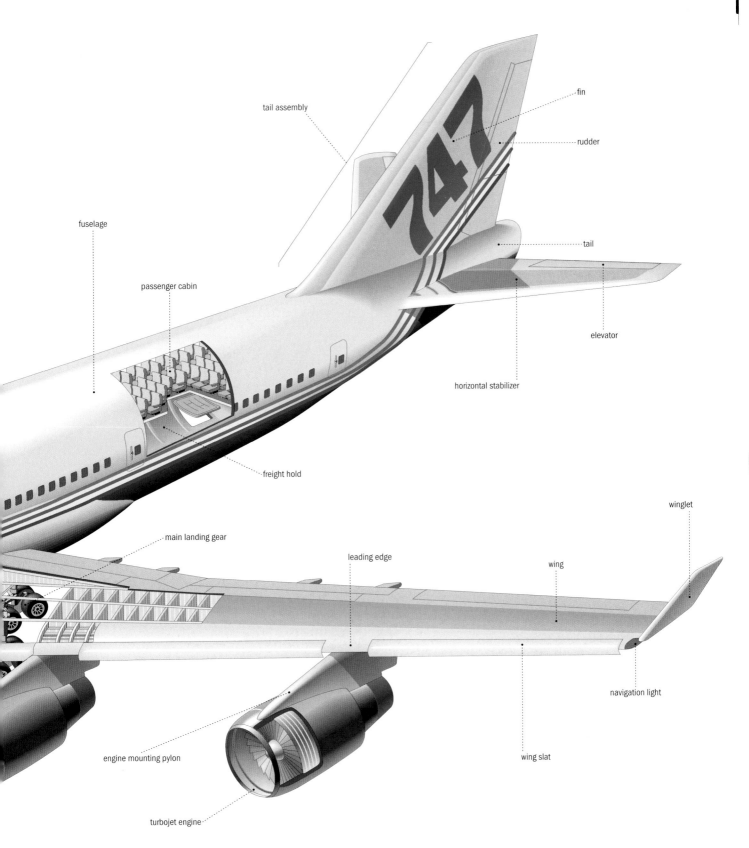

tail assembly

fin

rudder

fuselage

tail

passenger cabin

elevator

horizontal stabilizer

freight hold

winglet

main landing gear

leading edge

wing

navigation light

engine mounting pylon

wing slat

turbojet engine

flight deck

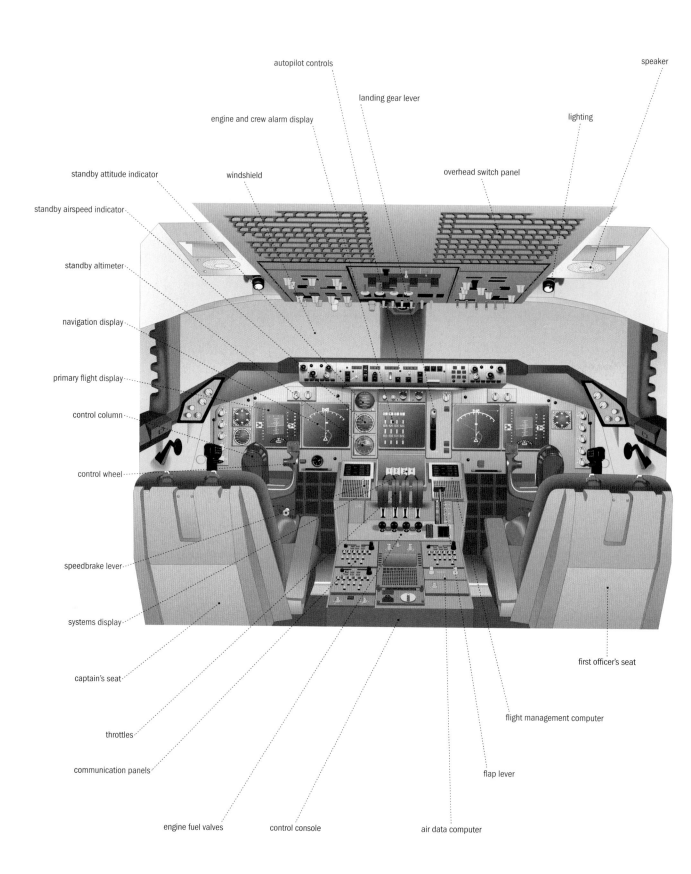

autopilot controls

speaker

landing gear lever

engine and crew alarm display

lighting

standby attitude indicator

windshield

overhead switch panel

standby airspeed indicator

standby altimeter

navigation display

primary flight display

control column

control wheel

speedbrake lever

systems display

first officer's seat

captain's seat

flight management computer

throttles

communication panels

flap lever

engine fuel valves

control console

air data computer

turbofan engine

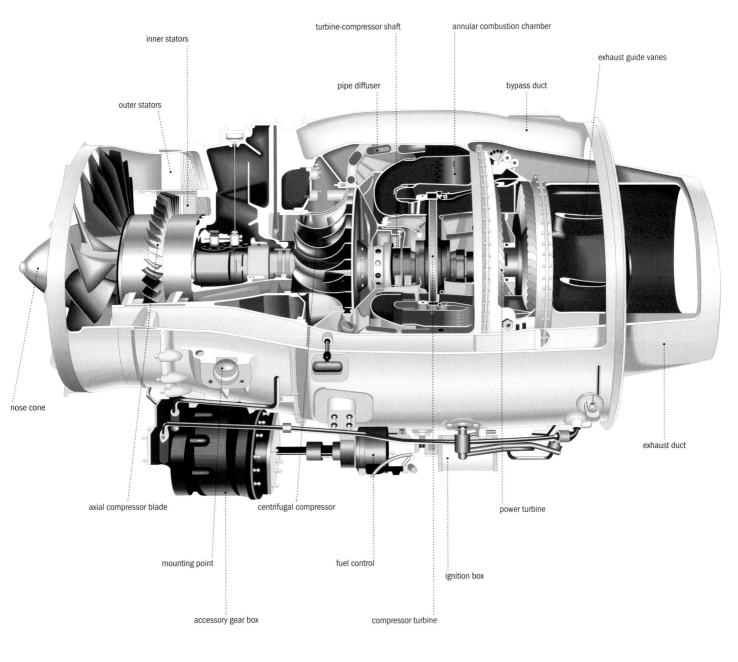

turbine-compressor shaft

annular combustion chamber

inner stators

exhaust guide vanes

pipe diffuser

bypass duct

outer stators

nose cone

axial compressor blade

centrifugal compressor

power turbine

exhaust duct

mounting point

fuel control

ignition box

accessory gear box

compressor turbine

fan

compression

combustion

exhaust

examples of airplanes

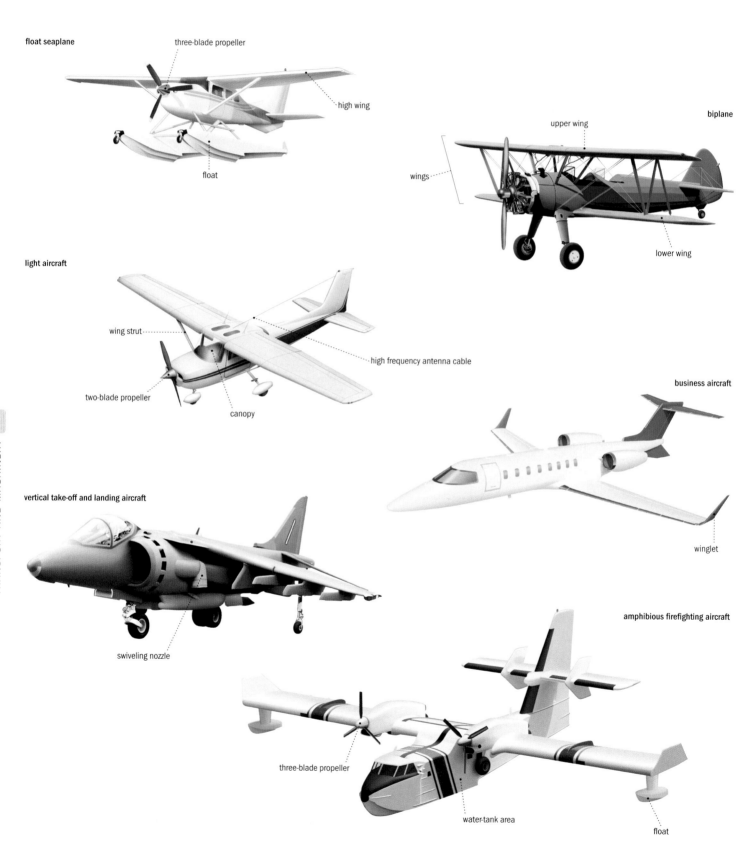

float seaplane

three-blade propeller

high wing

float

biplane

upper wing

wings

lower wing

light aircraft

wing strut

high frequency antenna cable

two-blade propeller

canopy

business aircraft

winglet

vertical take-off and landing aircraft

swiveling nozzle

amphibious firefighting aircraft

three-blade propeller

water-tank area

float

examples of airplanes

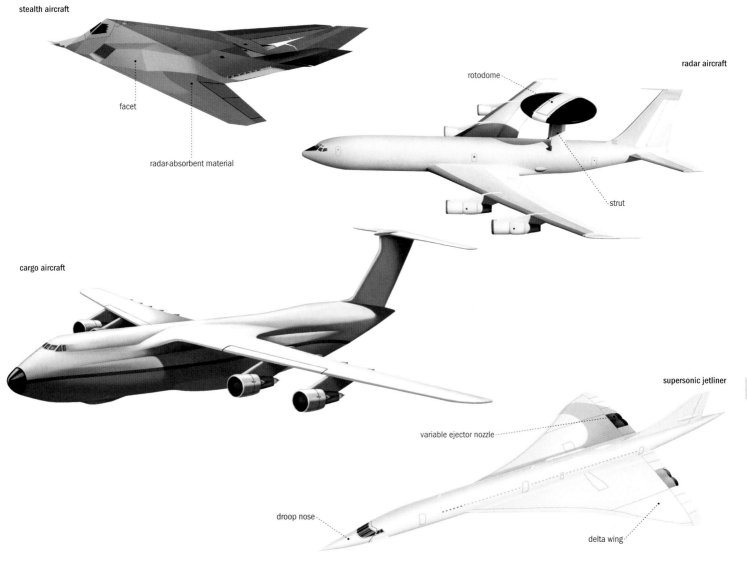

stealth aircraft

facet

radar-absorbent material

radar aircraft

rotodome

strut

cargo aircraft

supersonic jetliner

variable ejector nozzle

droop nose

delta wing

examples of tail shapes

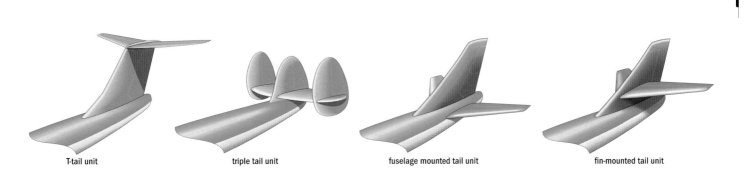

T-tail unit

triple tail unit

fuselage mounted tail unit

fin-mounted tail unit

examples of wing shapes

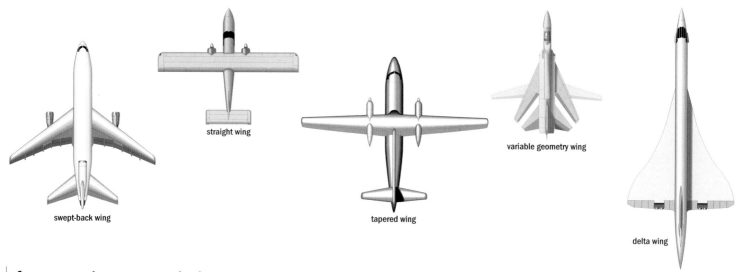

swept-back wing

straight wing

tapered wing

variable geometry wing

delta wing

forces acting on an airplane

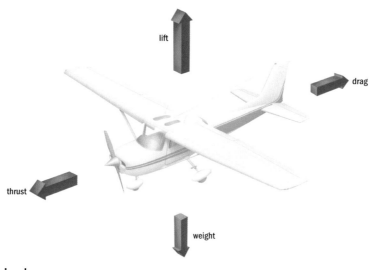

lift

drag

thrust

weight

movements of an airplane

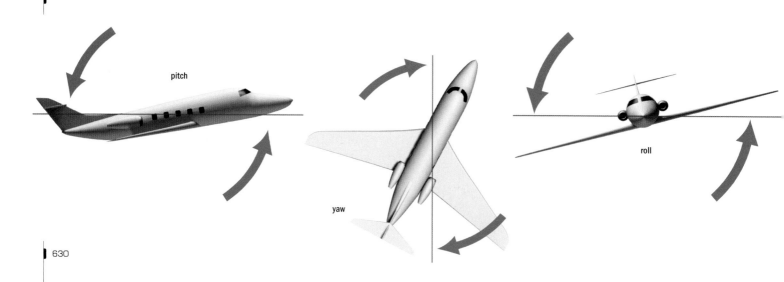

pitch

yaw

roll

TRANSPORT AND MACHINERY

helicopter

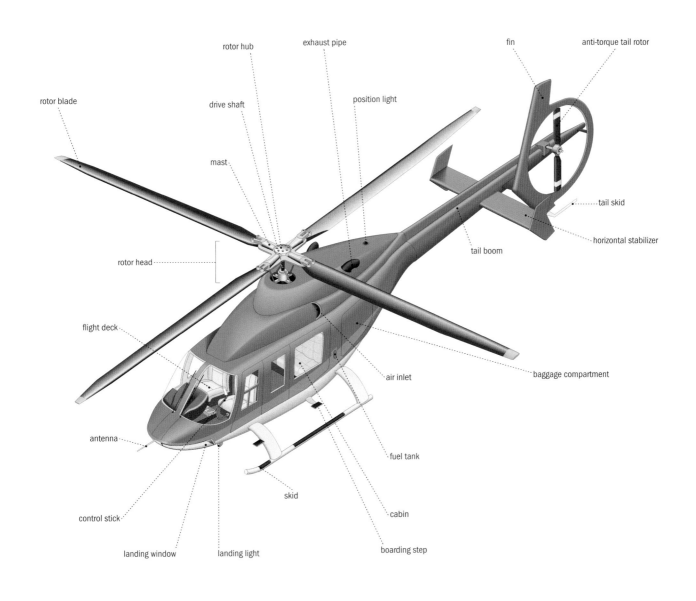

rotor hub

exhaust pipe

fin

anti-torque tail rotor

drive shaft

position light

rotor blade

mast

tail skid

horizontal stabilizer

rotor head

tail boom

flight deck

baggage compartment

air inlet

antenna

fuel tank

skid

cabin

control stick

boarding step

landing window

landing light

examples of helicopters

tactical transport helicopter

water bomber helicopter

ambulance helicopter

belly tank

material handling

forklift truck

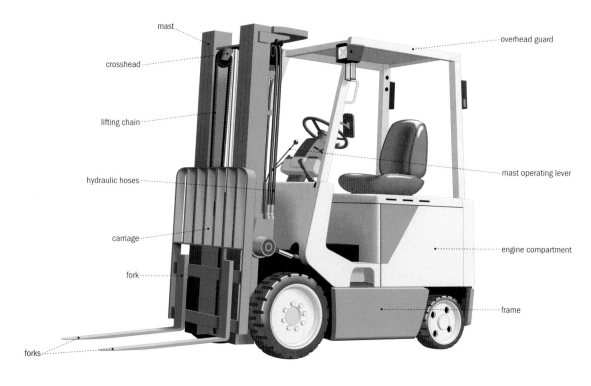

mast

crosshead

lifting chain

hydraulic hoses

carriage

fork

forks

overhead guard

mast operating lever

engine compartment

frame

pallets

wing pallet

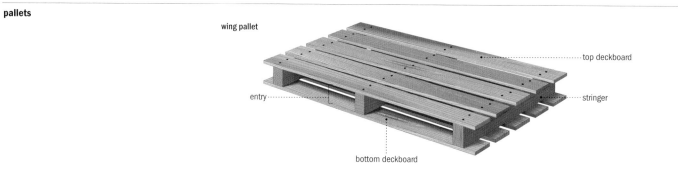

top deckboard

entry

stringer

bottom deckboard

box pallet

side

pallet

block

half-side

double-decked pallet

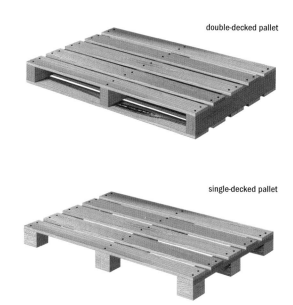

single-decked pallet

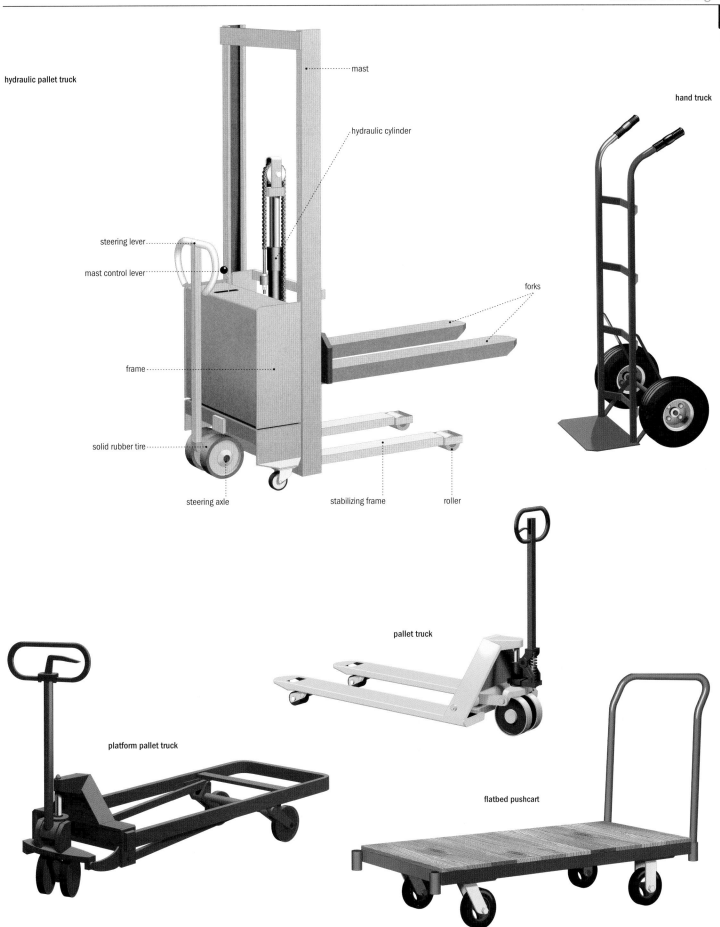

hydraulic pallet truck

mast

hydraulic cylinder

hand truck

steering lever

mast control lever

forks

frame

solid rubber tire

steering axle

stabilizing frame

roller

pallet truck

platform pallet truck

flatbed pushcart

cranes

TRANSPORT AND MACHINERY

tower crane

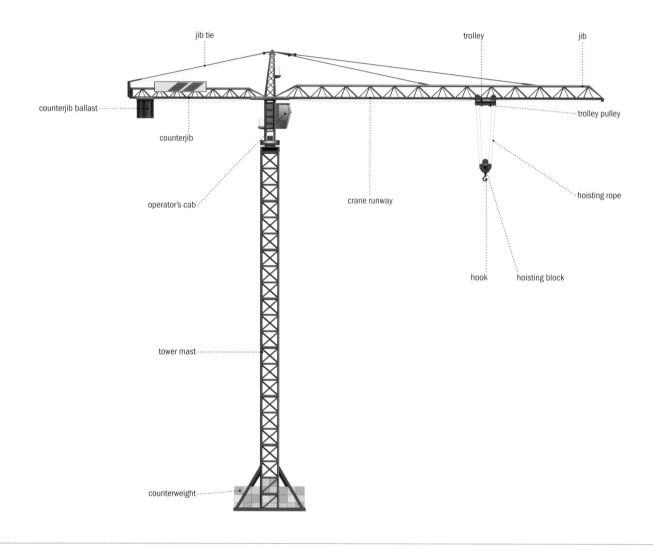

jib tie

trolley

jib

counterjib ballast

counterjib

operator's cab

trolley pulley

crane runway

hoisting rope

hook

hoisting block

tower mast

counterweight

truck crane

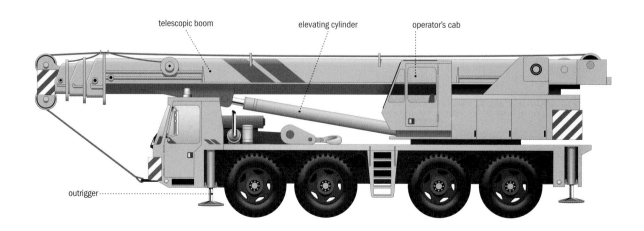

telescopic boom

elevating cylinder

operator's cab

outrigger

cranes

gantry crane

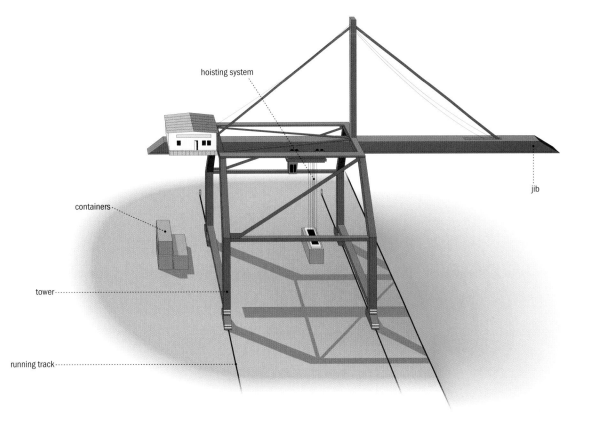

hoisting system

containers

jib

tower

running track

container

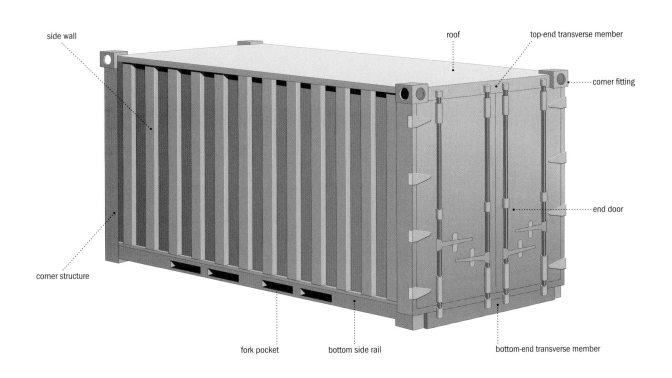

side wall

roof

top-end transverse member

corner fitting

end door

corner structure

fork pocket

bottom side rail

bottom-end transverse member

TRANSPORT AND MACHINERY

bulldozer

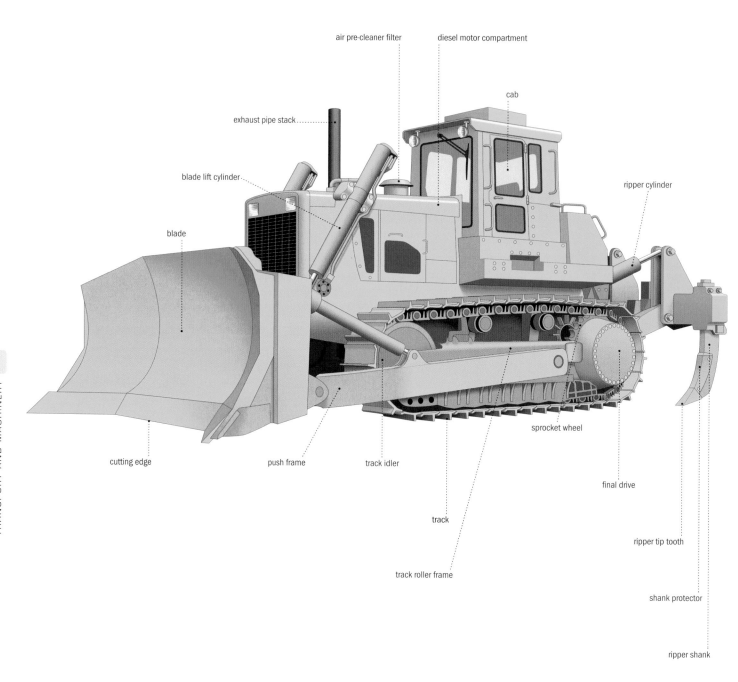

air pre-cleaner filter

diesel motor compartment

cab

exhaust pipe stack

blade lift cylinder

ripper cylinder

blade

cutting edge

push frame

track idler

sprocket wheel

final drive

track

ripper tip tooth

track roller frame

shank protector

ripper shank

crawler tractor

blade

ripper

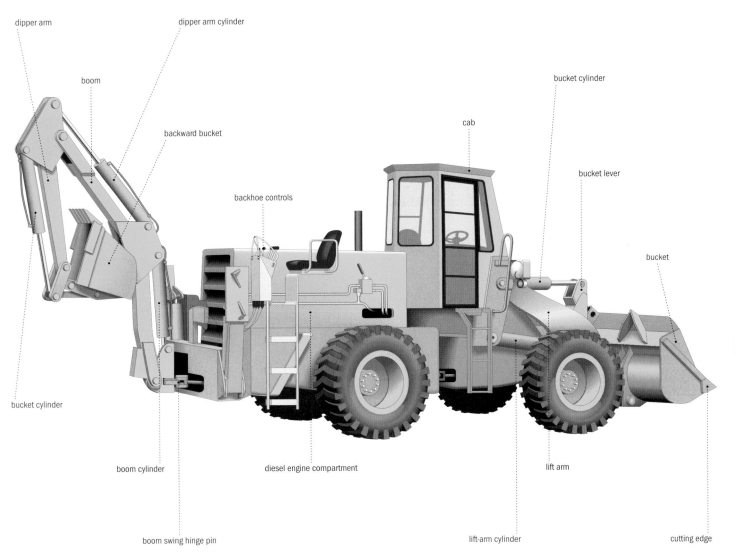

dipper arm

dipper arm cylinder

boom

bucket cylinder

cab

backward bucket

bucket lever

backhoe controls

bucket

bucket cylinder

boom cylinder

diesel engine compartment

lift arm

cutting edge

boom swing hinge pin

lift-arm cylinder

front-end loader

wheel tractor

backhoe

scraper

tractor engine compartment

gooseneck

steering cylinder

elevator

draft tube

bowl

cutting edge

draft arm

hydraulic shovel

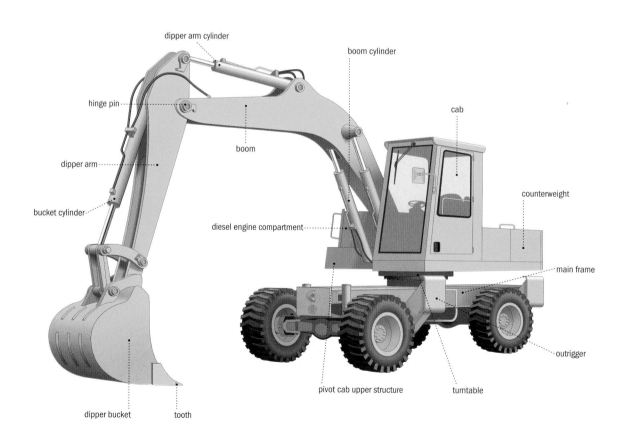

dipper arm cylinder

boom cylinder

hinge pin

cab

dipper arm

boom

bucket cylinder

counterweight

diesel engine compartment

main frame

dipper bucket

tooth

pivot cab upper structure

turntable

outrigger

grader

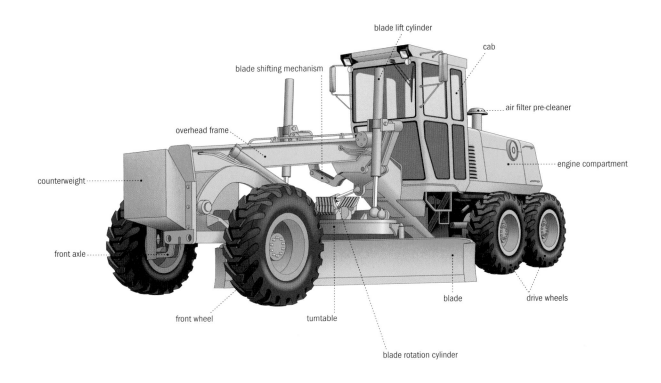

blade lift cylinder

cab

blade shifting mechanism

air filter pre-cleaner

overhead frame

engine compartment

counterweight

front axle

front wheel

turntable

blade

drive wheels

blade rotation cylinder

dump truck

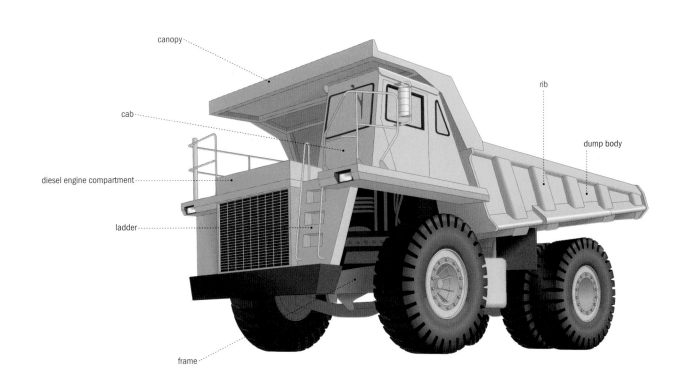

canopy

cab

rib

dump body

diesel engine compartment

ladder

frame

tractor

tractor: rear view

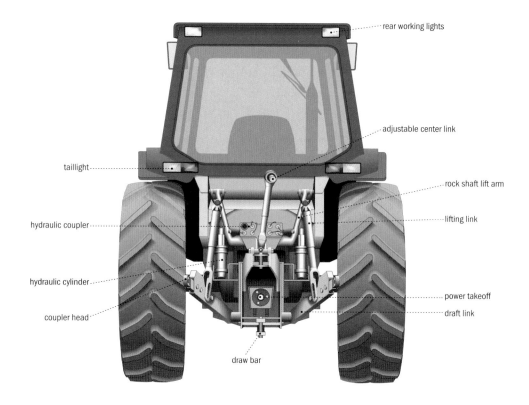

rear working lights

adjustable center link

taillight

rock shaft lift arm

lifting link

hydraulic coupler

hydraulic cylinder

power takeoff

coupler head

draft link

draw bar

tractor: front view

steering wheel

exhaust stack

fender

cab

rim

headlight

counterweight

engine compartment

front wheel

step

driving wheel

tread bar

ribbing plow

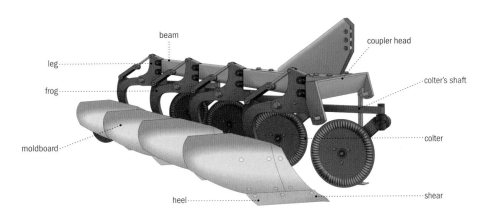

beam

coupler head

leg

colter's shaft

frog

colter

moldboard

heel

shear

tandem disc harrow

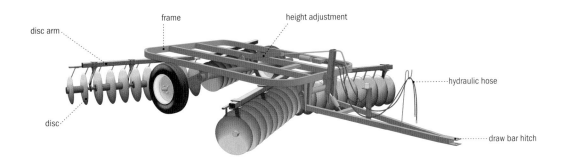

frame

height adjustment

disc arm

hydraulic hose

disc

draw bar hitch

cultivator

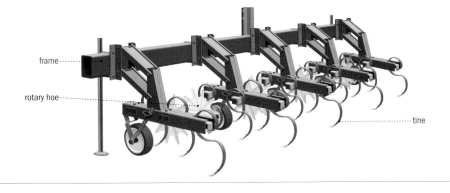

frame

rotary hoe

tine

manure spreader

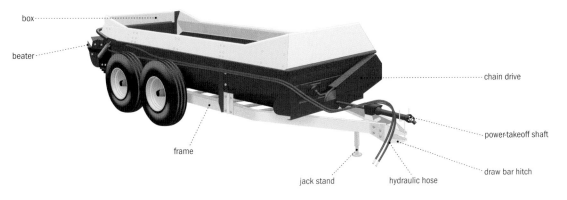

box

beater

chain drive

power-takeoff shaft

frame

draw bar hitch

jack stand

hydraulic hose

agricultural machinery

rake

height adjustment

frame

rake bar

tooth

flail mower

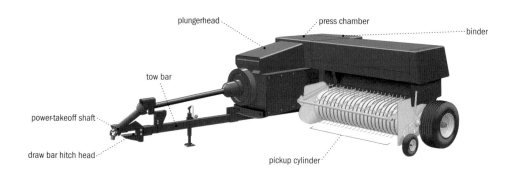

tooth

pickup reel

tow bar

hydraulic hose

crushing roll

cutter bar

draw bar hitch head

hay baler

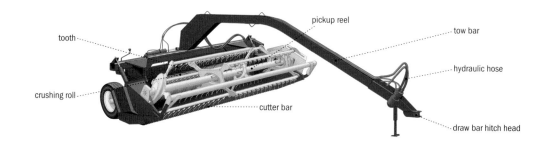

plungerhead

press chamber

binder

tow bar

power-takeoff shaft

draw bar hitch head

pickup cylinder

forage harvester

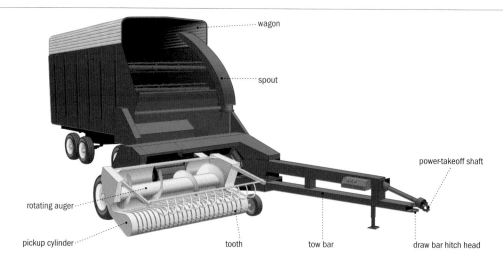

wagon

spout

power-takeoff shaft

rotating auger

pickup cylinder

tooth

tow bar

draw bar hitch head

seed drill

forage blower

grain tube

hopper

chain drive

colter

covering disk

press wheel

disk spacing lever

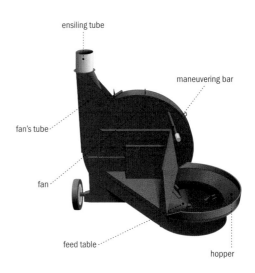

ensiling tube

maneuvering bar

fan's tube

fan

feed table

hopper

combine harvester

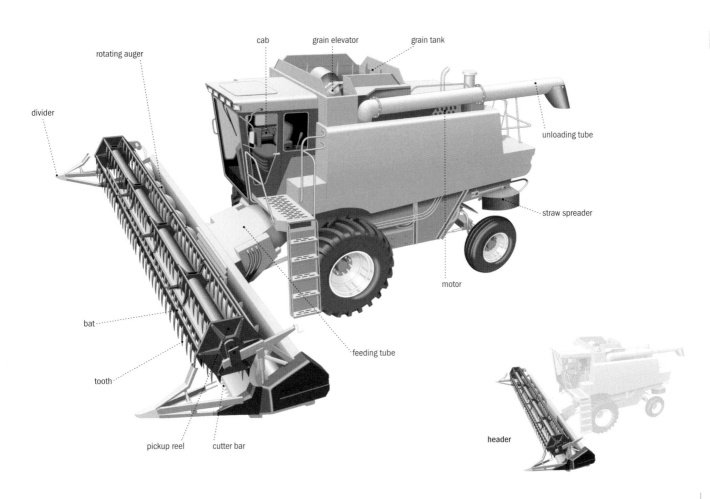

rotating auger

cab

grain elevator

grain tank

divider

unloading tube

straw spreader

bat

motor

tooth

feeding tube

pickup reel

cutter bar

header

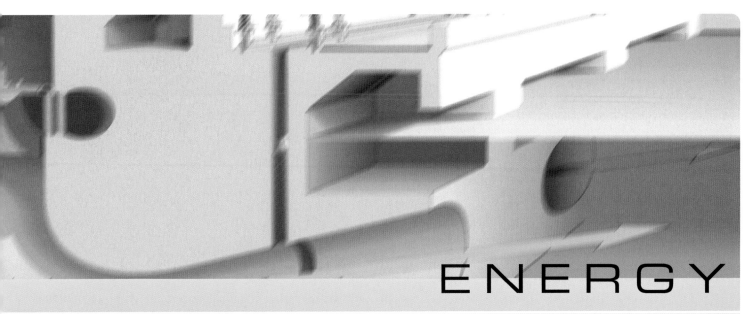

ENERGY

production of electricity from geothermal energy

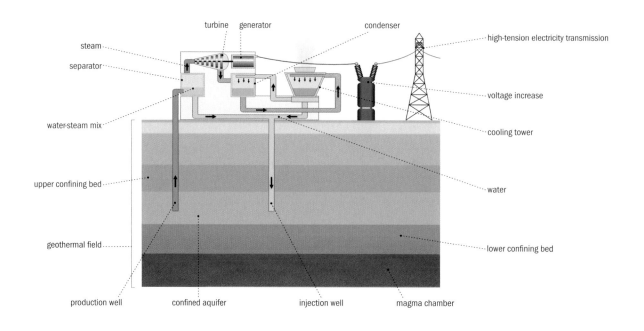

turbine generator condenser high-tension electricity transmission

steam

separator

voltage increase

cooling tower

water-steam mix

upper confining bed

water

geothermal field

lower confining bed

production well confined aquifer injection well magma chamber

thermal energy

production of electricity from thermal energy

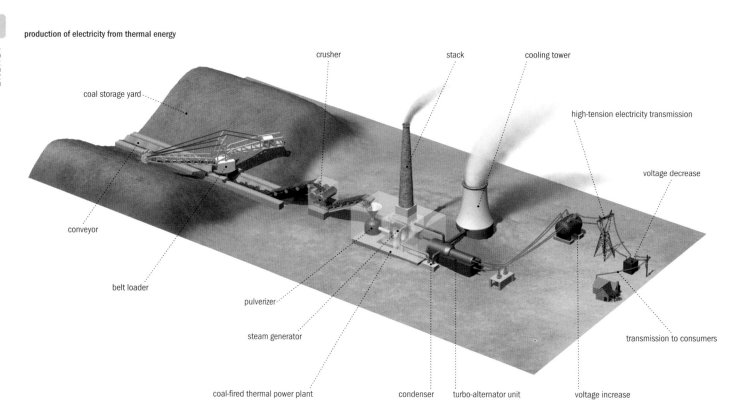

crusher stack cooling tower

coal storage yard

high-tension electricity transmission

voltage decrease

conveyor

belt loader

transmission to consumers

pulverizer

steam generator

coal-fired thermal power plant condenser turbo-alternator unit voltage increase

ENERGY

coal mine

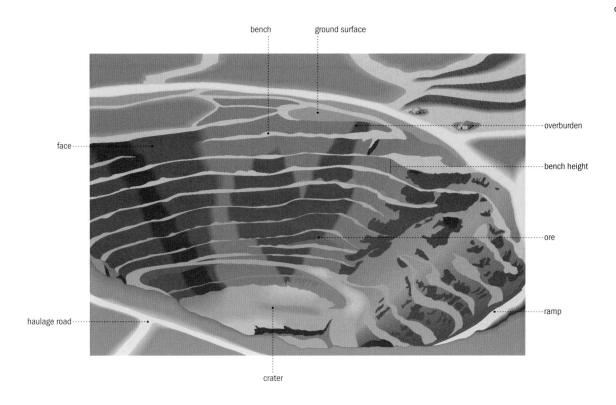

bench   ground surface

face

overburden

bench height

ore

ramp

haulage road

crater

ENERGY

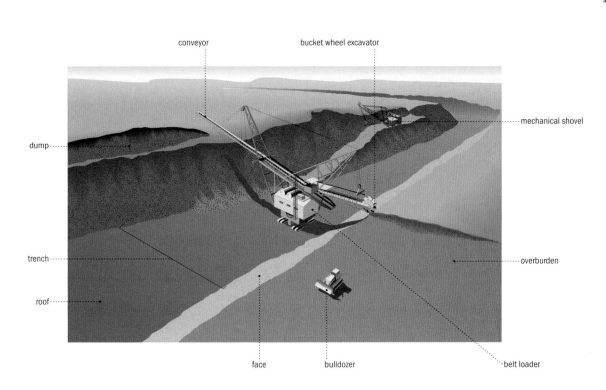

conveyor   bucket wheel excavator

mechanical shovel

dump

trench

overburden

roof

face   bulldozer

belt loader

coal mine

jackleg drill

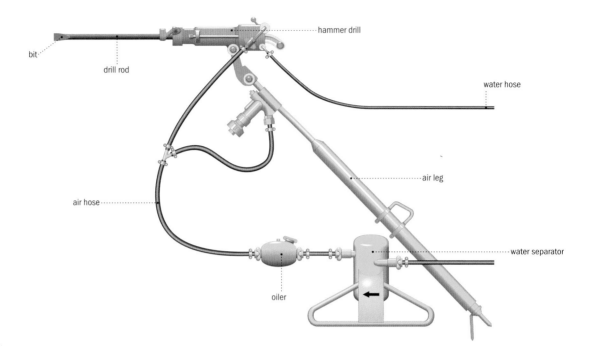

bit

drill rod

hammer drill

water hose

air leg

air hose

water separator

oiler

maintenance shop

pithead

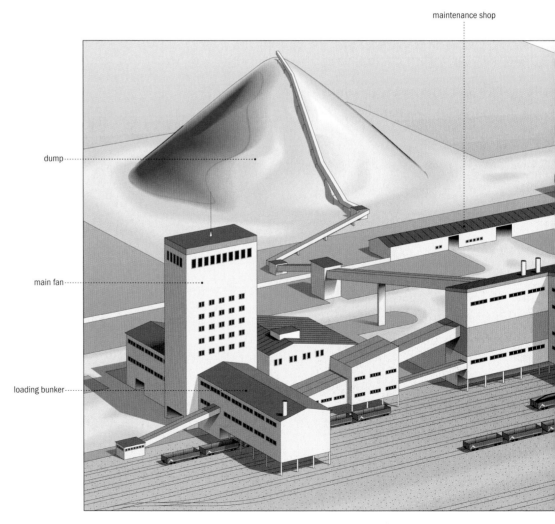

dump

main fan

loading bunker

ENERGY

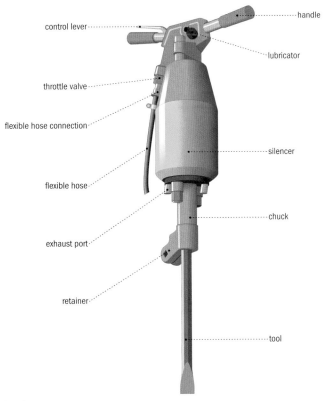

control lever

handle

lubricator

throttle valve

flexible hose connection

silencer

flexible hose

chuck

exhaust port

retainer

tool

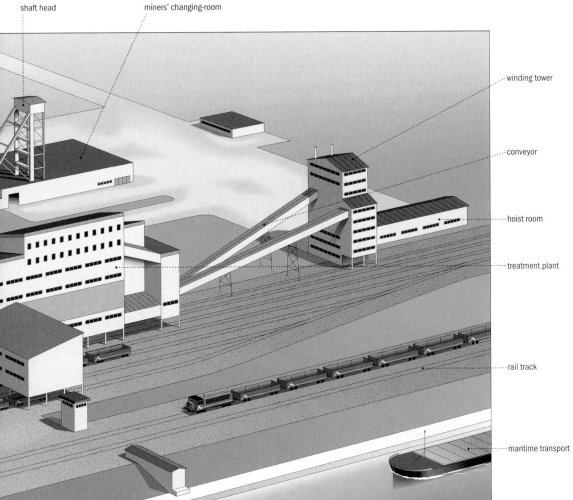

shaft head

miners' changing-room

winding tower

conveyor

hoist room

treatment plant

rail track

maritime transport

ENERGY

coal mine

underground mine

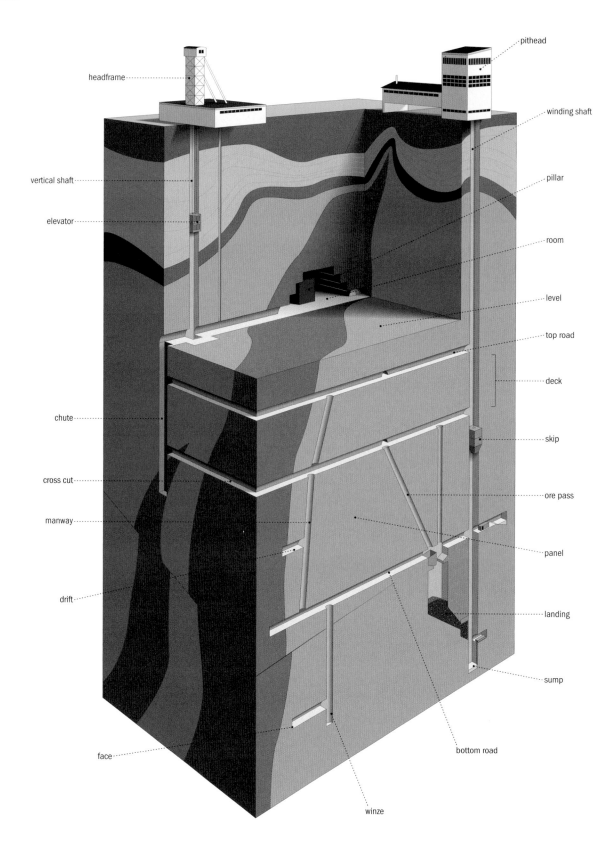

headframe

vertical shaft

elevator

chute

cross cut

manway

drift

face

winze

pithead

winding shaft

pillar

room

level

top road

deck

skip

ore pass

panel

landing

sump

bottom road

oil

surface prospecting

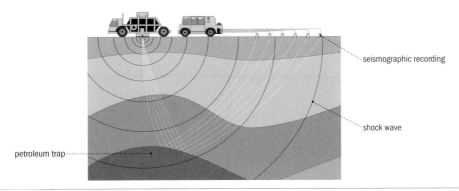

seismographic recording

shock wave

petroleum trap

drilling rig

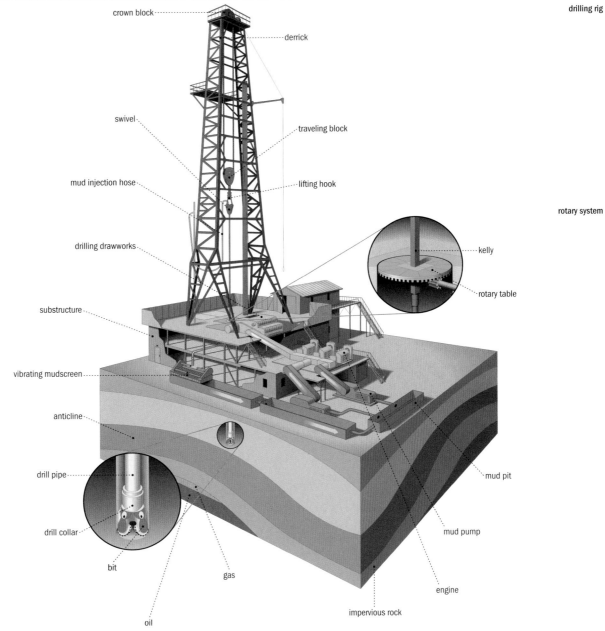

crown block

derrick

swivel

traveling block

mud injection hose

lifting hook

rotary system

drilling drawworks

kelly

rotary table

substructure

vibrating mudscreen

anticline

mud pit

drill pipe

drill collar

mud pump

bit

gas

engine

oil

impervious rock

production platform

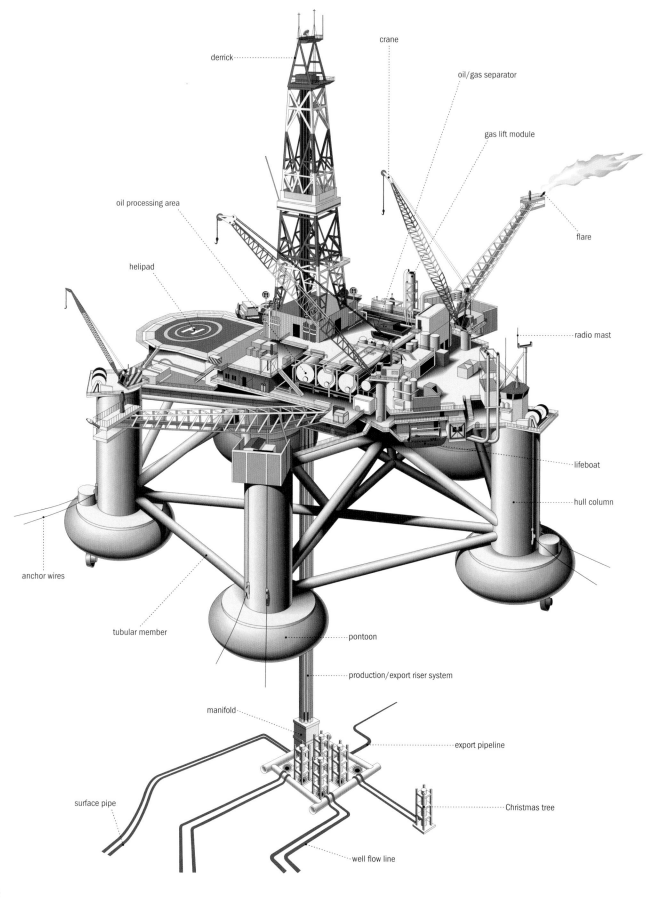

derrick

crane

oil/gas separator

gas lift module

oil processing area

flare

helipad

radio mast

lifeboat

hull column

anchor wires

tubular member

pontoon

production/export riser system

manifold

export pipeline

surface pipe

Christmas tree

well flow line

offshore prospecting

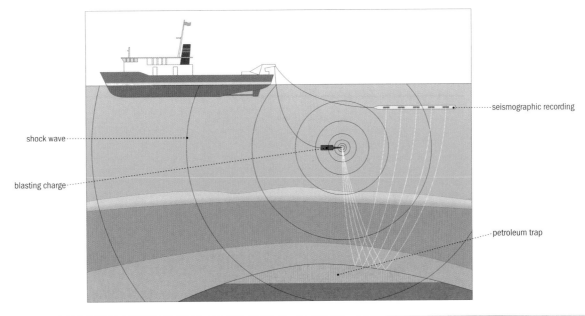

seismographic recording

shock wave

blasting charge

petroleum trap

offshore drilling

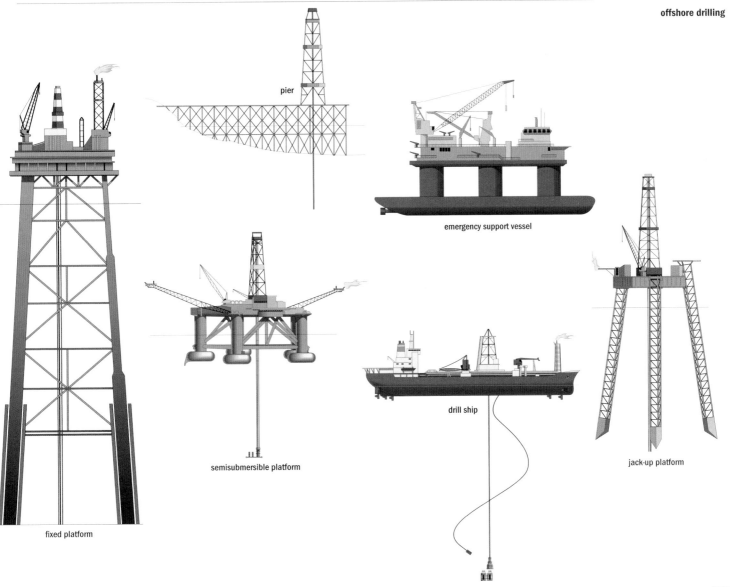

pier

emergency support vessel

semisubmersible platform

drill ship

jack-up platform

fixed platform

ENERGY

Christmas tree

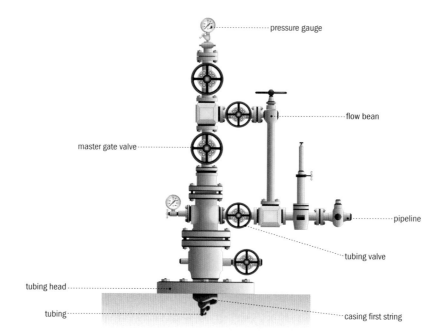

pressure gauge

flow bean

master gate valve

pipeline

tubing valve

tubing head

tubing

casing first string

crude-oil pipeline

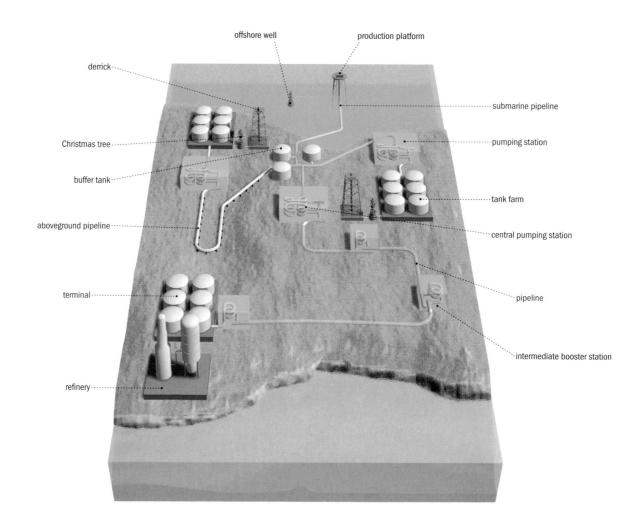

offshore well

production platform

derrick

submarine pipeline

Christmas tree

pumping station

buffer tank

tank farm

aboveground pipeline

central pumping station

terminal

pipeline

intermediate booster station

refinery

fixed-roof tank

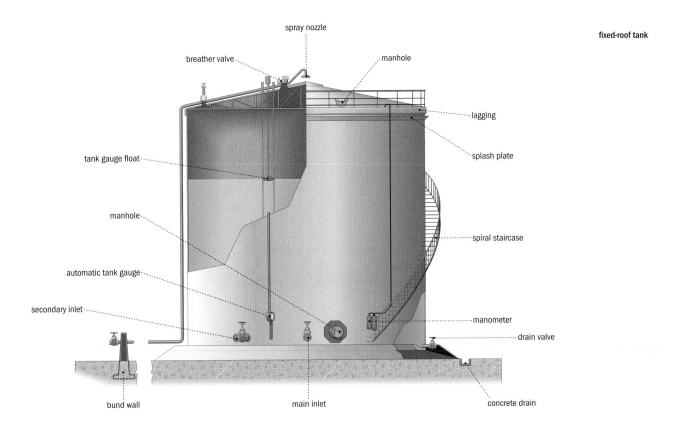

spray nozzle

breather valve

manhole

tank gauge float

manhole

automatic tank gauge

secondary inlet

lagging

splash plate

spiral staircase

manometer

drain valve

bund wall

main inlet

concrete drain

floating-roof tank

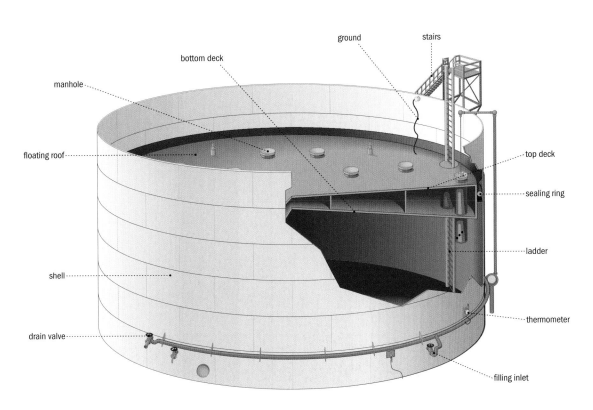

ground

stairs

bottom deck

manhole

floating roof

shell

drain valve

top deck

sealing ring

ladder

thermometer

filling inlet

refinery products

petrochemical industry

petrochemicals

propane

cooling

chemical treatment

jet fuel

catalytic reforming plant

gasoline

gasoline

kerosene

kerosene

lamp oil

fractionating tower

diesel oil

heavy gasoline

heating oil

bunker oil

fuel oil

marine diesel

fractionating tower

tubular heater

long residue

greases

solvent extraction unit

lubricating oils

lubricants plant

vacuum distillation

paraffins

storage tank

asphalt still

asphalt

crude oil

hydroelectric complex

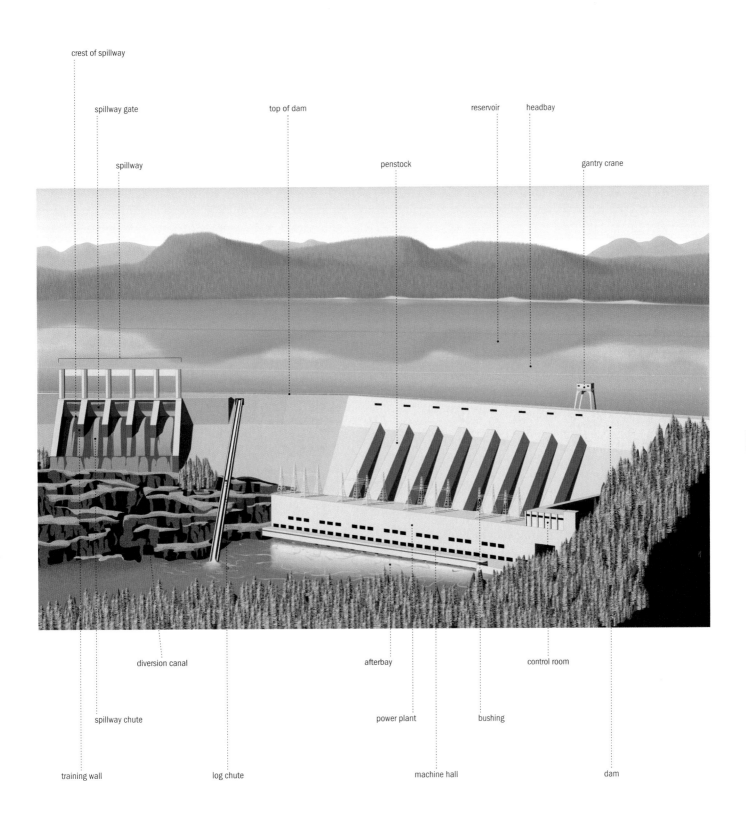

crest of spillway

spillway gate

top of dam

reservoir

headbay

spillway

penstock

gantry crane

diversion canal

afterbay

control room

spillway chute

power plant

bushing

training wall

log chute

machine hall

dam

hydroelectric complex

cross section of a hydroelectric power plant

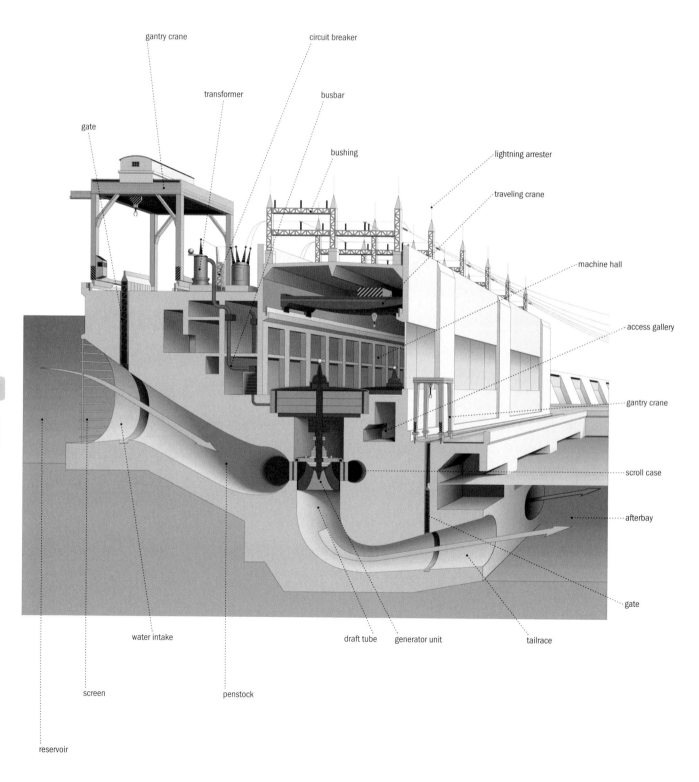

gantry crane

circuit breaker

transformer

busbar

gate

bushing

lightning arrester

traveling crane

machine hall

access gallery

gantry crane

scroll case

afterbay

gate

ENERGY

water intake

draft tube

generator unit

tailrace

screen

penstock

reservoir

generator unit

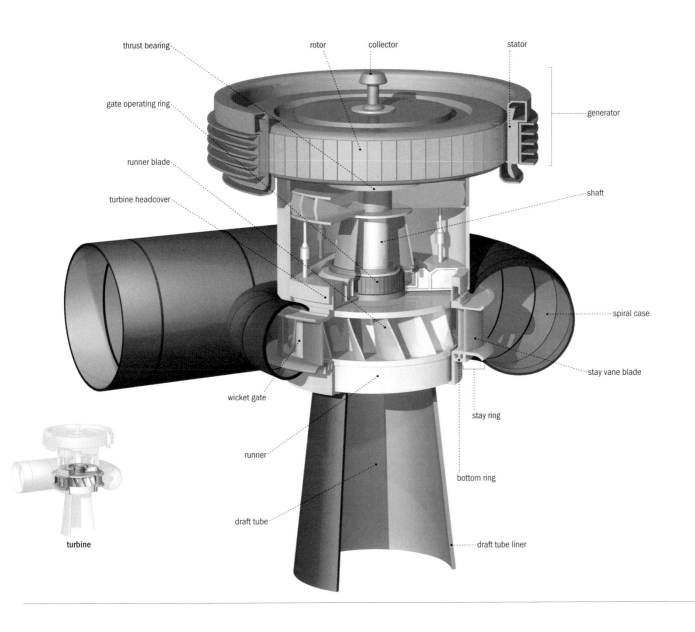

thrust bearing

rotor

collector

stator

gate operating ring

generator

runner blade

shaft

turbine headcover

spiral case

stay vane blade

wicket gate

stay ring

runner

bottom ring

draft tube

draft tube liner

turbine

runners

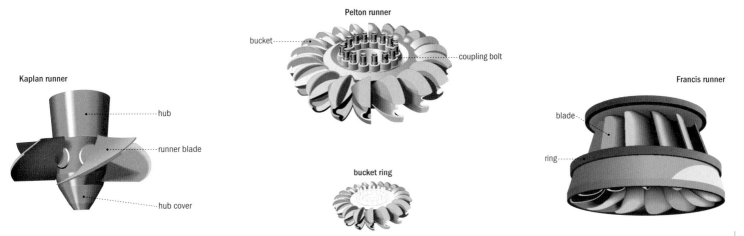

Kaplan runner

hub

runner blade

hub cover

Pelton runner

bucket

coupling bolt

bucket ring

Francis runner

blade

ring

examples of dams

buttress dam

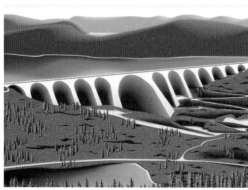

cross section of a buttress dam

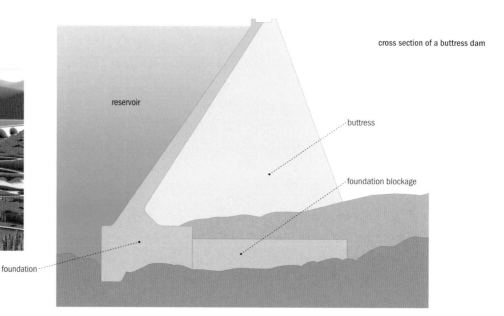

reservoir

buttress

foundation blockage

foundation

embankment dam

cross section of an embankment dam

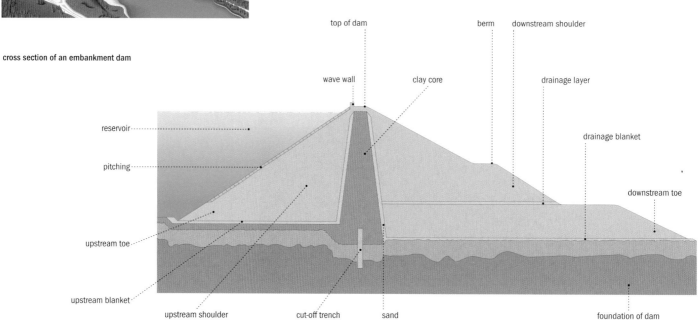

top of dam

berm   downstream shoulder

wave wall   clay core

drainage layer

drainage blanket

reservoir

pitching

downstream toe

upstream toe

upstream blanket

upstream shoulder   cut-off trench   sand   foundation of dam

cross section of an arch dam

arch dam

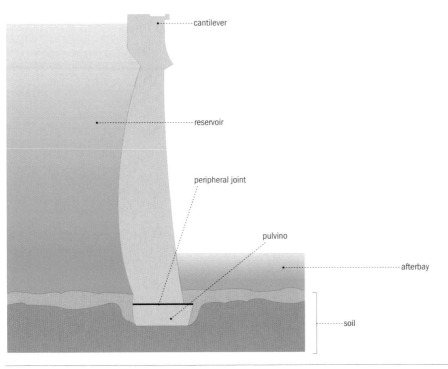

- cantilever
- reservoir
- peripheral joint
- pulvino
- afterbay
- soil

cross section of a gravity dam

gravity dam

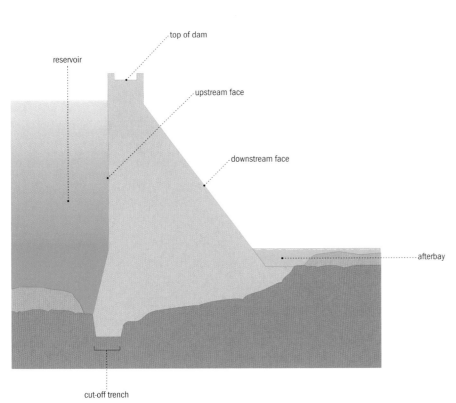

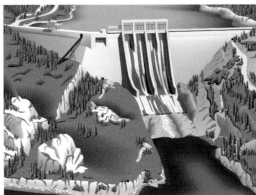

- reservoir
- top of dam
- upstream face
- downstream face
- afterbay
- cut-off trench

ENERGY

steps in production of electricity

ENERGY

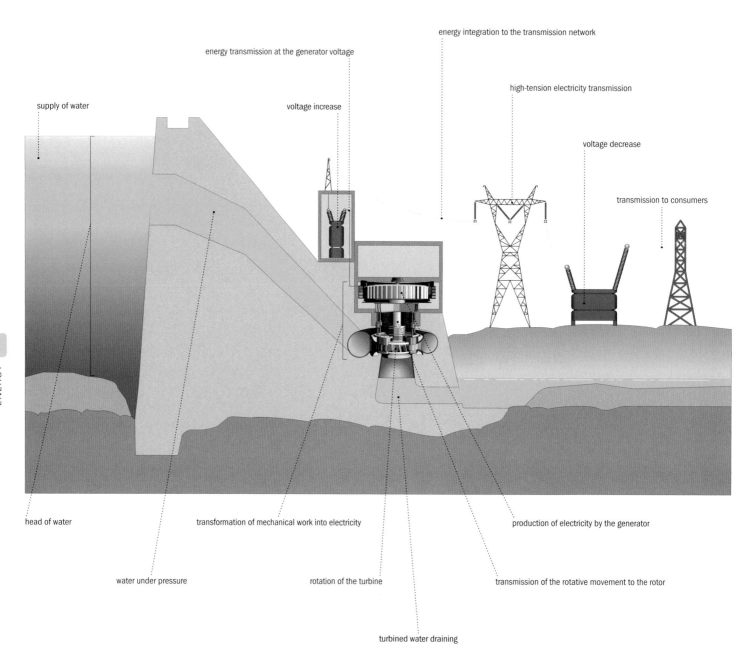

energy integration to the transmission network

energy transmission at the generator voltage

high-tension electricity transmission

supply of water

voltage increase

voltage decrease

transmission to consumers

head of water

transformation of mechanical work into electricity

production of electricity by the generator

water under pressure

rotation of the turbine

transmission of the rotative movement to the rotor

turbined water draining

electricity transmission

overhead connection

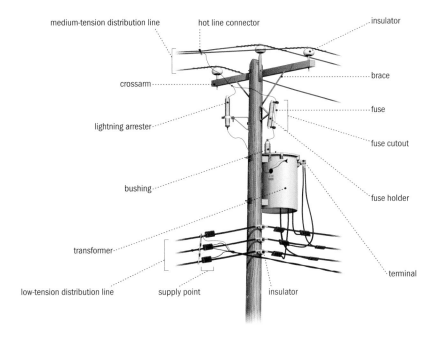

medium-tension distribution line   hot line connector   insulator

crossarm

brace

fuse

lightning arrester

fuse cutout

bushing

fuse holder

transformer

terminal

low-tension distribution line   supply point   insulator

pylon

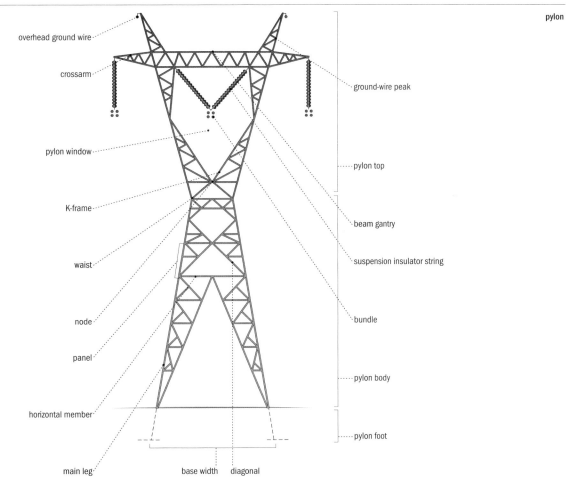

overhead ground wire

crossarm

ground-wire peak

pylon window

pylon top

K-frame

beam gantry

waist

suspension insulator string

node

bundle

panel

pylon body

horizontal member

pylon foot

main leg   base width   diagonal

ENERGY

tidal power plant

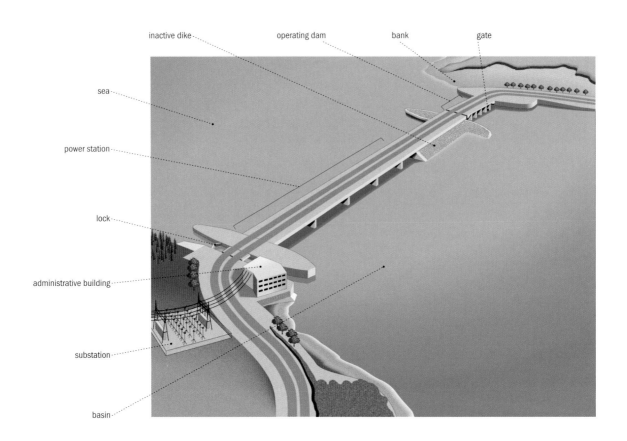

inactive dike · operating dam · bank · · · · · · · · · · · · · · · · · · gate

sea

power station

lock

administrative building

substation

basin

cross section of a power plant

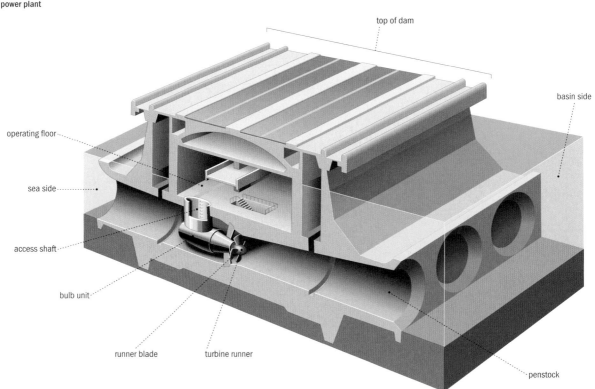

top of dam

basin side

operating floor

sea side

access shaft

bulb unit

runner blade · · · · · · · · · · turbine runner

penstock

ENERGY

production of electricity from nuclear energy

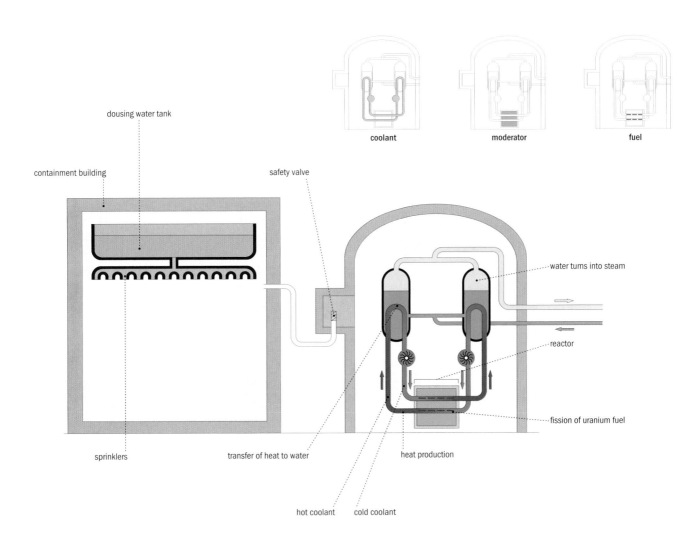

coolant

moderator

fuel

dousing water tank

containment building

safety valve

water turns into steam

reactor

fission of uranium fuel

sprinklers

transfer of heat to water

heat production

hot coolant

cold coolant

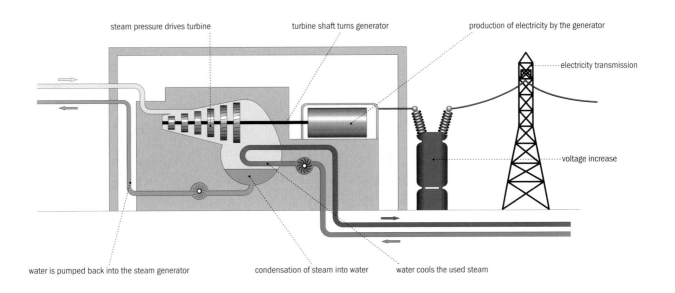

steam pressure drives turbine

turbine shaft turns generator

production of electricity by the generator

electricity transmission

voltage increase

water is pumped back into the steam generator

condensation of steam into water

water cools the used steam

fuel handling sequence

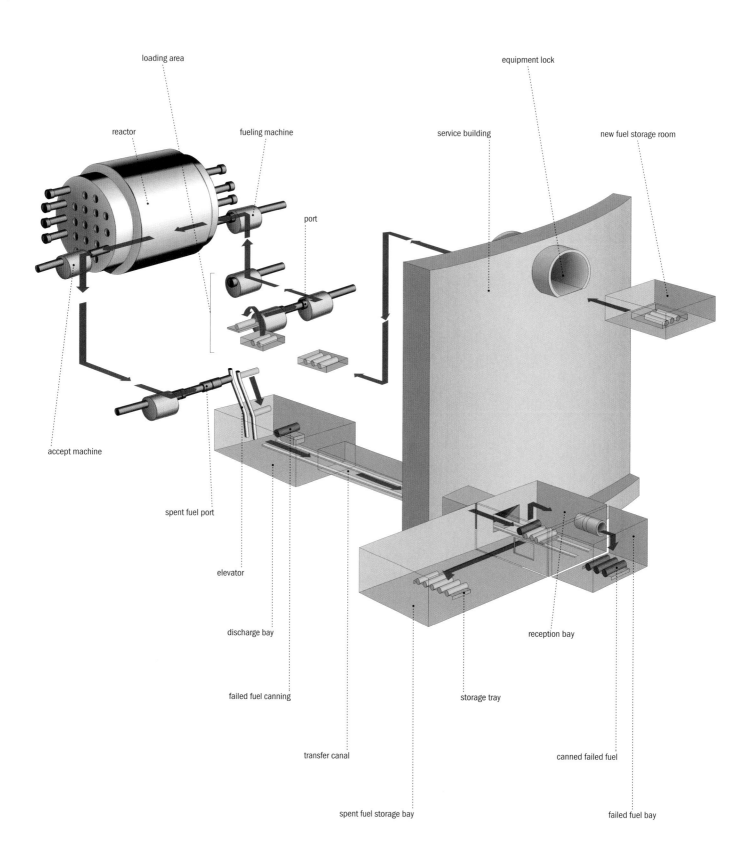

loading area

equipment lock

reactor

fueling machine

service building

new fuel storage room

port

accept machine

spent fuel port

elevator

discharge bay

reception bay

failed fuel canning

storage tray

transfer canal

canned failed fuel

spent fuel storage bay

failed fuel bay

ENERGY

fuel bundle

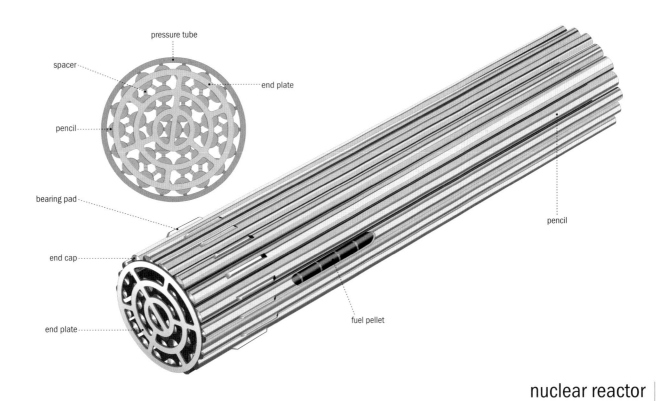

pressure tube

spacer

end plate

pencil

bearing pad

end cap

pencil

end plate

fuel pellet

nuclear reactor

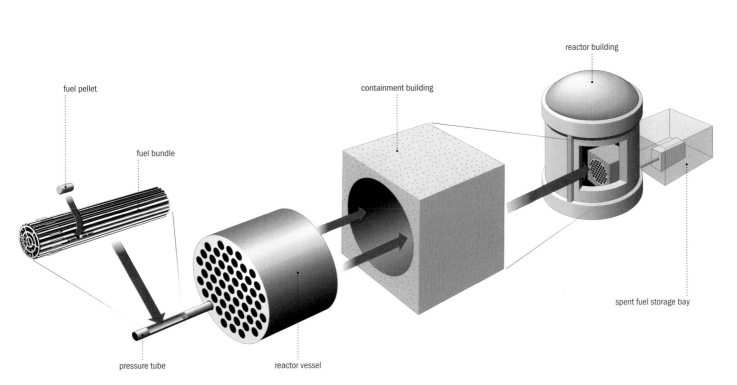

fuel pellet

fuel bundle

containment building

reactor building

spent fuel storage bay

pressure tube

reactor vessel

nuclear generating station

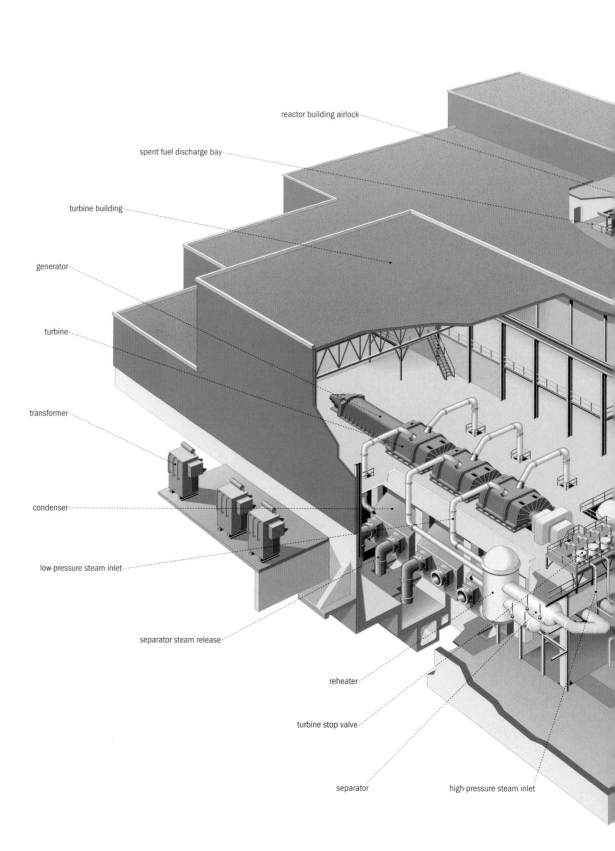

reactor building airlock

spent fuel discharge bay

turbine building

generator

turbine

transformer

condenser

low-pressure steam inlet

separator steam release

reheater

turbine stop valve

separator

high-pressure steam inlet

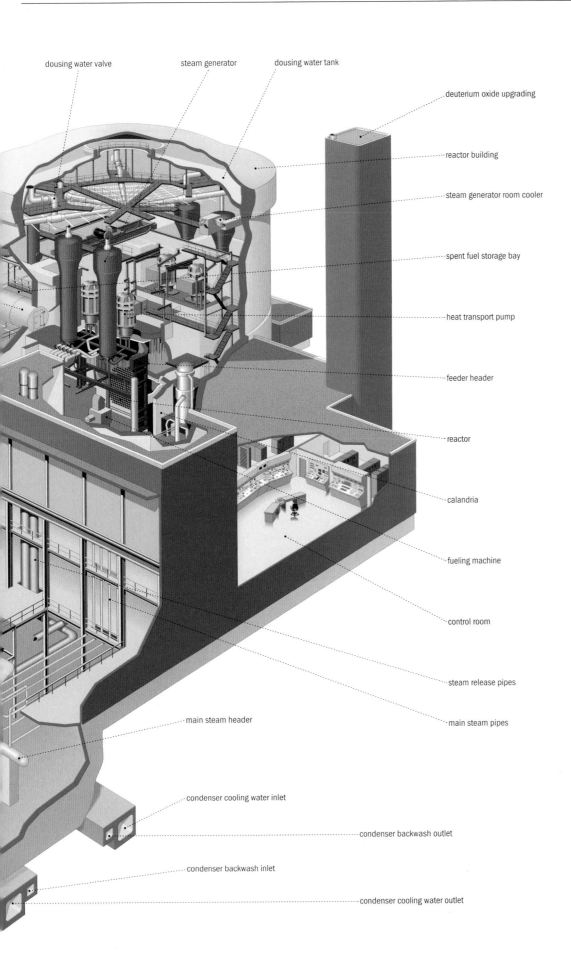

dousing water valve

steam generator

dousing water tank

deuterium oxide upgrading

reactor building

steam generator room cooler

spent fuel storage bay

heat transport pump

feeder header

reactor

calandria

fueling machine

control room

steam release pipes

main steam header

main steam pipes

condenser cooling water inlet

condenser backwash outlet

condenser backwash inlet

condenser cooling water outlet

carbon dioxide reactor

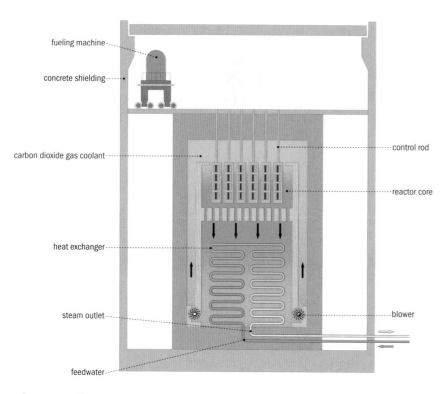

fueling machine

concrete shielding

carbon dioxide gas coolant

heat exchanger

steam outlet

feedwater

control rod

reactor core

blower

fuel: natural uranium

moderator: graphite

coolant: carbon dioxide

heavy-water reactor

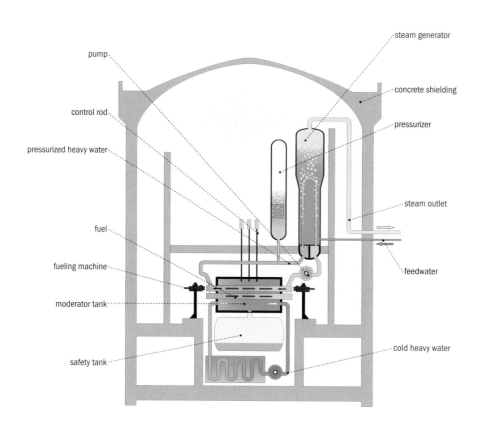

pump

control rod

pressurized heavy water

fuel

fueling machine

moderator tank

safety tank

steam generator

concrete shielding

pressurizer

steam outlet

feedwater

cold heavy water

fuel: natural uranium

moderator: heavy water

coolant: pressurized heavy water

pressurized-water reactor

fuel: enriched uranium

moderator: natural water

coolant: pressurized water

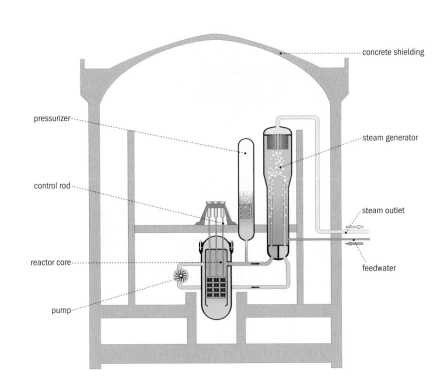

concrete shielding

pressurizer

steam generator

control rod

steam outlet

reactor core

feedwater

pump

boiling-water reactor

fuel: enriched uranium

moderator: natural water

coolant: boiling water

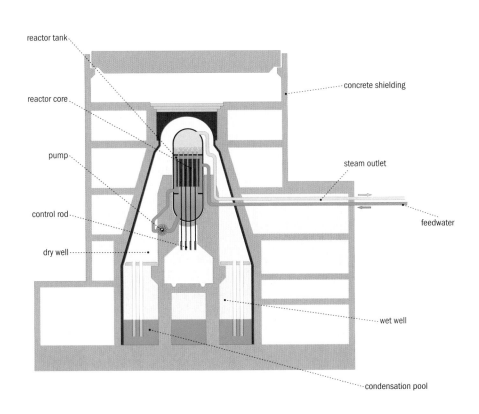

reactor tank

reactor core

concrete shielding

pump

steam outlet

control rod

feedwater

dry well

wet well

condensation pool

solar cell

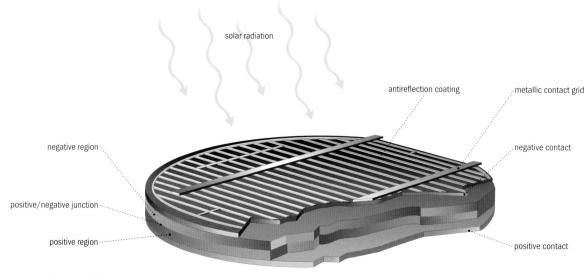

solar radiation

antireflection coating

metallic contact grid

negative region

negative contact

positive/negative junction

positive region

positive contact

flat-plate solar collector

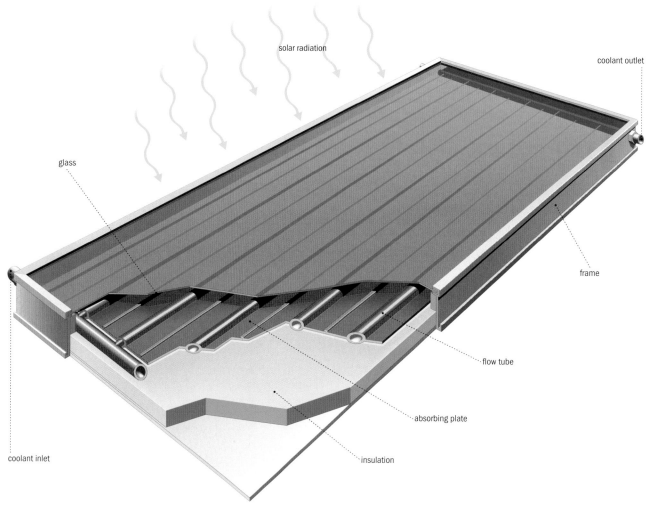

solar radiation

coolant outlet

glass

frame

flow tube

coolant inlet

absorbing plate

insulation

solar-cell system

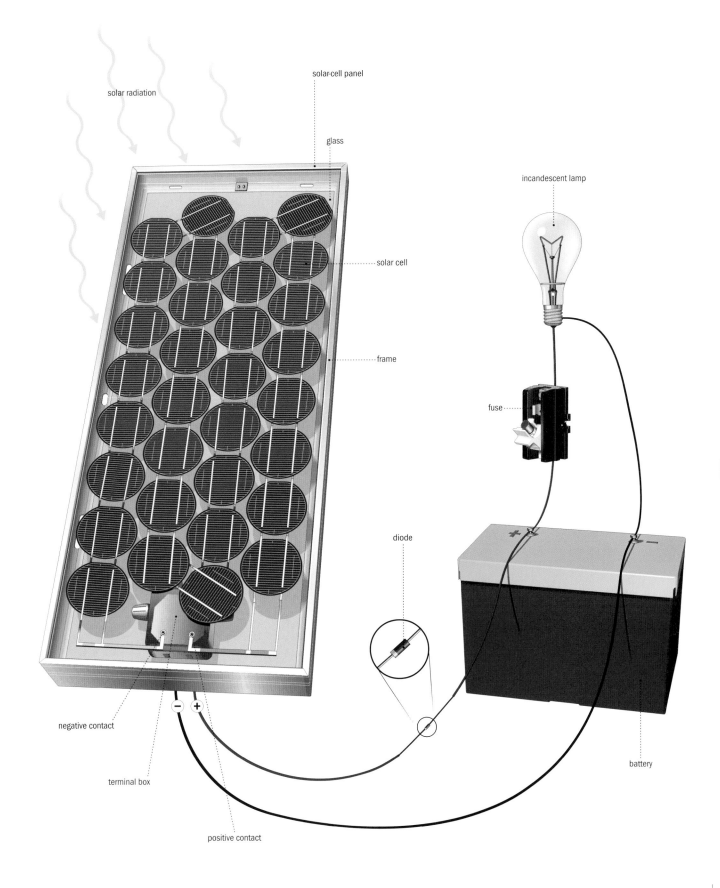

solar radiation

solar-cell panel

glass

solar cell

frame

incandescent lamp

fuse

diode

negative contact

terminal box

positive contact

+

−

battery

solar furnace

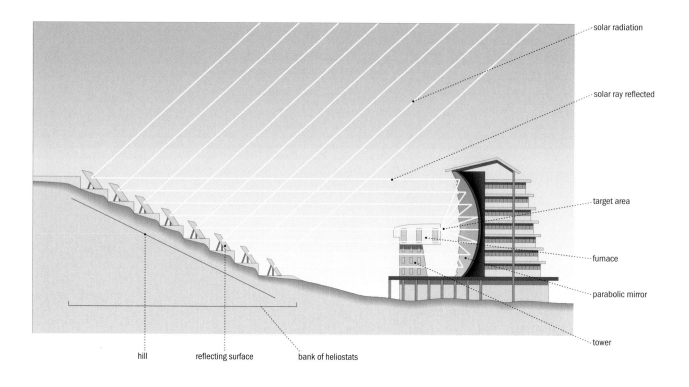

solar radiation

solar ray reflected

target area

furnace

parabolic mirror

tower

hill

reflecting surface

bank of heliostats

production of electricity from solar energy

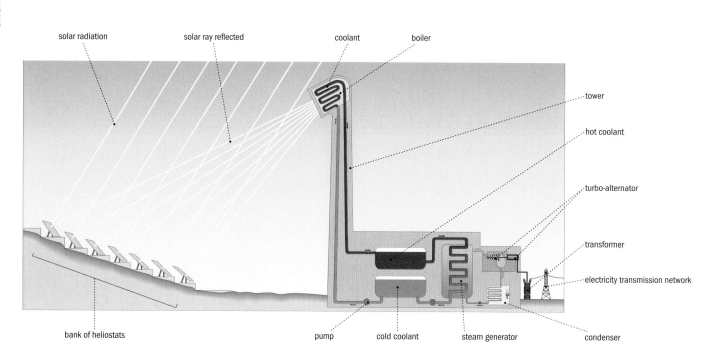

solar radiation

solar ray reflected

coolant

boiler

tower

hot coolant

turbo-alternator

transformer

electricity transmission network

bank of heliostats

pump

cold coolant

steam generator

condenser

solar house

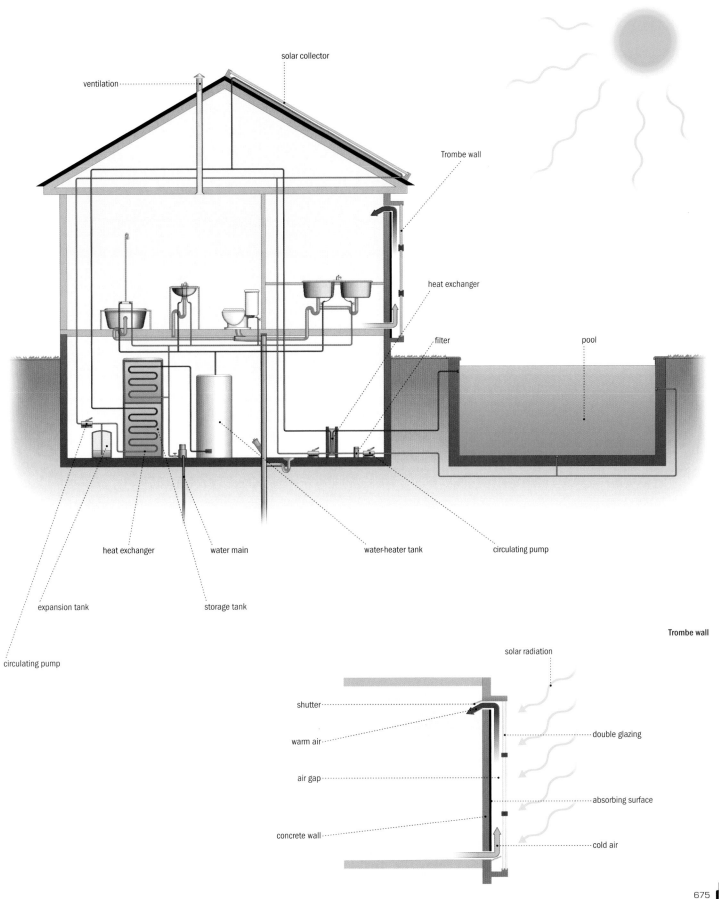

ventilation

solar collector

Trombe wall

heat exchanger

filter

pool

heat exchanger

water main

water-heater tank

circulating pump

expansion tank

storage tank

circulating pump

Trombe wall

solar radiation

shutter

warm air

double glazing

air gap

concrete wall

absorbing surface

cold air

windmill

tower mill

post mill

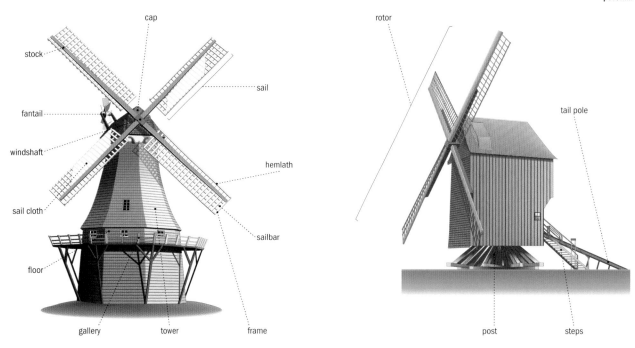

cap

stock

sail

fantail

windshaft

hemlath

sail cloth

floor

sailbar

gallery   tower   frame

rotor

tail pole

post   steps

wind turbines and electricity production

vertical-axis wind turbine

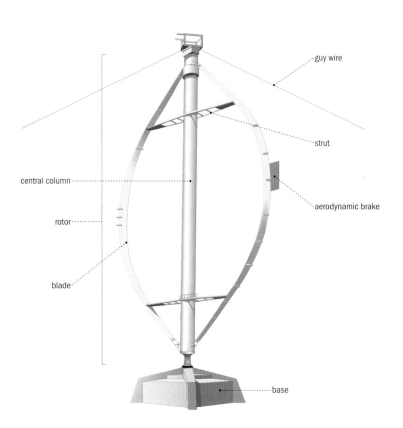

guy wire

strut

central column

aerodynamic brake

rotor

blade

base

horizontal-axis wind turbine

nacelle cross-section

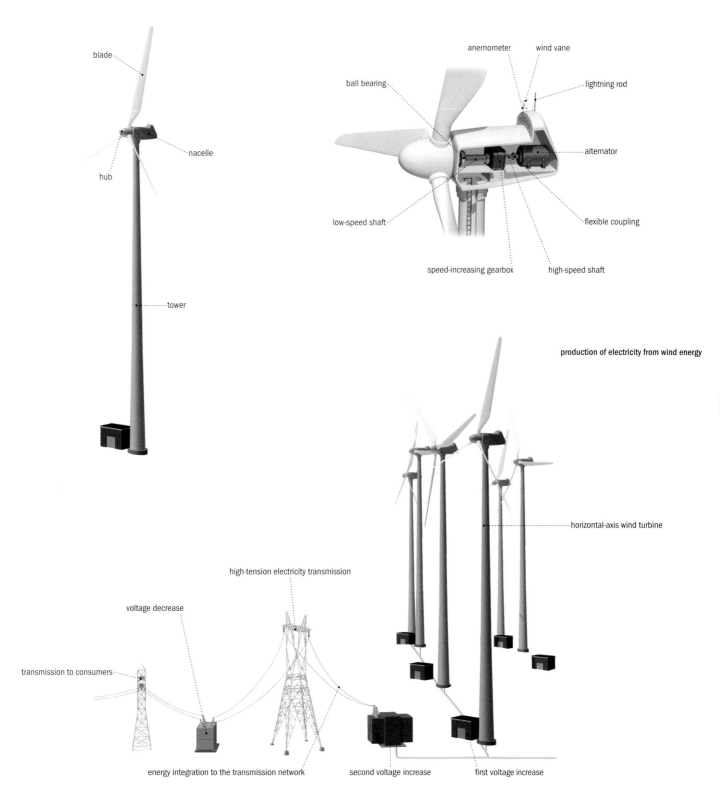

blade

nacelle

hub

tower

anemometer

wind vane

ball bearing

lightning rod

alternator

low-speed shaft

flexible coupling

speed-increasing gearbox

high-speed shaft

production of electricity from wind energy

horizontal-axis wind turbine

high-tension electricity transmission

voltage decrease

transmission to consumers

energy integration to the transmission network

second voltage increase

first voltage increase

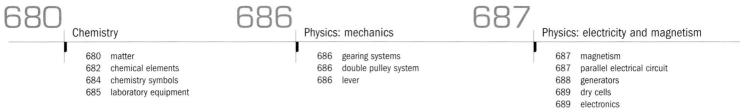

SCIENCE

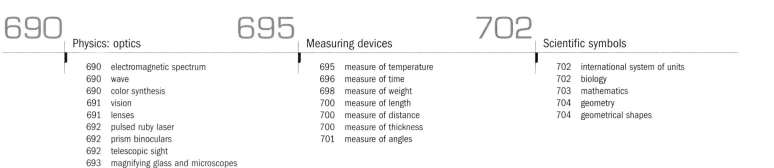

matter

atom

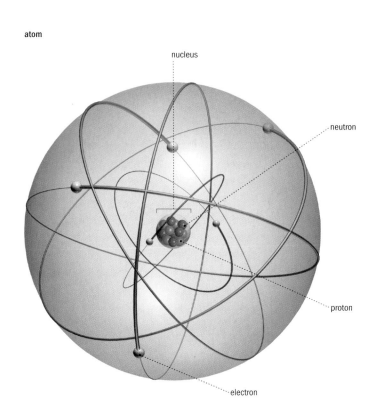

nucleus

neutron

proton

electron

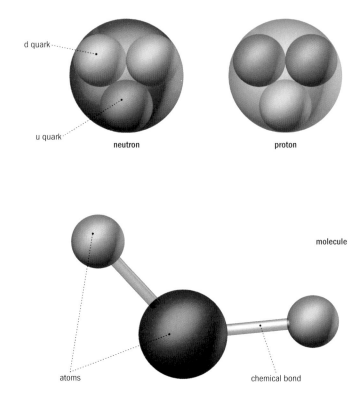

d quark

u quark

neutron

proton

molecule

atoms

chemical bond

states of matter

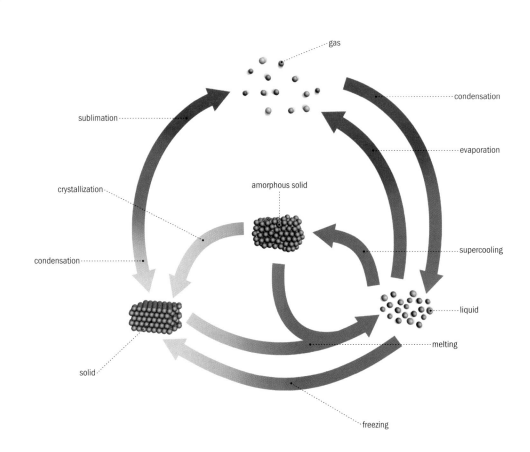

gas

condensation

evaporation

sublimation

supercooling

crystallization

amorphous solid

condensation

liquid

melting

solid

freezing

nuclear fission

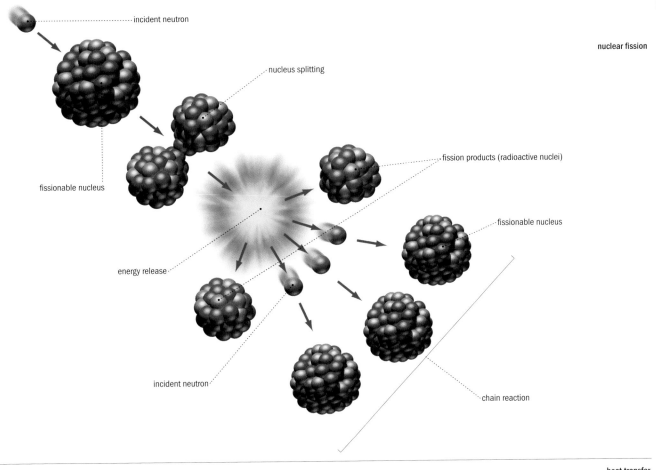

incident neutron

nucleus splitting

fissionable nucleus

fission products (radioactive nuclei)

energy release

fissionable nucleus

incident neutron

chain reaction

heat transfer

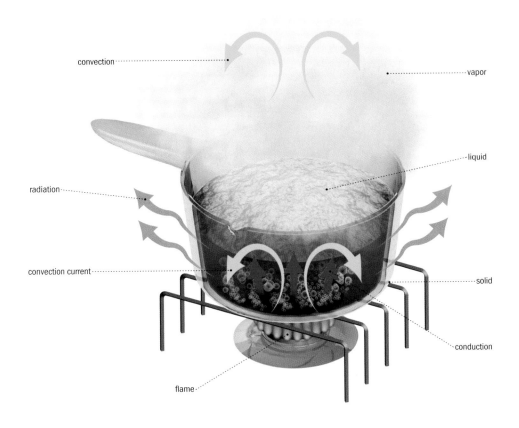

convection

vapor

radiation

liquid

convection current

solid

conduction

flame

chemical elements

table of elements

1 H																	2 He
3 Li	4 Be											5 B	6 C	7 N	8 O	9 F	10 Ne
11 Na	12 Mg											13 Al	14 Si	15 P	16 S	17 Cl	18 Ar
19 K	20 Ca	21 Sc	22 Ti	23 V	24 Cr	25 Mn	26 Fe	27 Co	28 Ni	29 Cu	30 Zn	31 Ga	32 Ge	33 As	34 Se	35 Br	36 Kr
37 Rb	38 Sr	39 Y	40 Zr	41 Nb	42 Mo	43 Tc	44 Ru	45 Rh	46 Pd	47 Ag	48 Cd	49 In	50 Sn	51 Sb	52 Te	53 I	54 Xe
55 Cs	56 Ba	57 La	72 Hf	73 Ta	74 W	75 Re	76 Os	77 Ir	78 Pt	79 Au	80 Hg	81 Tl	82 Pb	83 Bi	84 Po	85 At	86 Rn
87 Fr	88 Ra	89 Ac	104 Rf	105 Db	106 Sg	107 Bh	108 Hs	109 Mt	110 Uun	111 Uuu	112 Uub						

58 Ce	59 Pr	60 Nd	61 Pm	62 Sm	63 Eu	64 Gd	65 Tb	66 Dy	67 Ho	68 Er	69 Tm	70 Yb	71 Lu
90 Th	91 Pa	92 U	93 Np	94 Pu	95 Am	96 Cm	97 Bk	98 Cf	99 Es	100 Fm	101 Md	102 No	103 Lr

atomic number

symbol

1 H hydrogen

alkali metals

- 3 Li lithium
- 11 Na sodium
- 19 K potassium
- 37 Rb rubidium
- 55 Cs cesium
- 87 Fr francium

alkaline earth metals

- 4 Be beryllium
- 12 Mg magnesium
- 20 Ca calcium
- 38 Sr strontium
- 56 Ba barium
- 88 Ra radium

semi-metals (metalloids)

- 5 B boron
- 14 Si silicon
- 32 Ge germanium
- 33 As arsenic
- 34 Se selenium
- 51 Sb antimony
- 52 Te tellurium

other metals

- 13 Al aluminum
- 31 Ga gallium
- 49 In indium
- 50 Sn tin
- 81 Tl thallium
- 82 Pb lead
- 83 Bi bismuth
- 84 Po polonium

transition metals

21 Sc	scandium	39 Y	yttrium	72 Hf	hafnium	104 Rf	rutherfordium
22 Ti	titanium	40 Zr	zirconium	73 Ta	tantalum	105 Db	dubnium
23 V	vanadium	41 Nb	niobium	74 W	tungsten	106 Sg	seaborgium
24 Cr	chromium	42 Mo	molybdenum	75 Re	rhenium	107 Bh	bohrium
25 Mn	manganese	43 Tc	technetium	76 Os	osmium	108 Hs	hassium
26 Fe	iron	44 Ru	ruthenium	77 Ir	iridium	109 Mt	meitnerium
27 Co	cobalt	45 Rh	rhodium	78 Pt	platinum	110 Uun	ununnilium
28 Ni	nickel	46 Pd	palladium	79 Au	gold	111 Uuu	unununium
29 Cu	copper	47 Ag	silver	80 Hg	mercury	112 Uub	ununbium
30 Zn	zinc	48 Cd	cadmium				

non-metals

6 C	carbon	9 F	fluorine	17 Cl	chlorine	53 I	iodine
7 N	nitrogen	15 P	phosphorus	35 Br	bromine	85 At	astatine
8 O	oxygen	16 S	sulfur				

chemical elements

noble gases

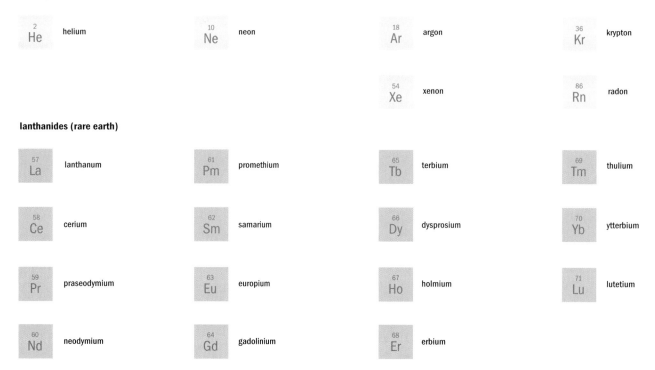

2 He helium	10 Ne neon	18 Ar argon	36 Kr krypton
		54 Xe xenon	86 Rn radon

lanthanides (rare earth)

57 La lanthanum	61 Pm promethium	65 Tb terbium	69 Tm thulium
58 Ce cerium	62 Sm samarium	66 Dy dysprosium	70 Yb ytterbium
59 Pr praseodymium	63 Eu europium	67 Ho holmium	71 Lu lutetium
60 Nd neodymium	64 Gd gadolinium	68 Er erbium	

actinides

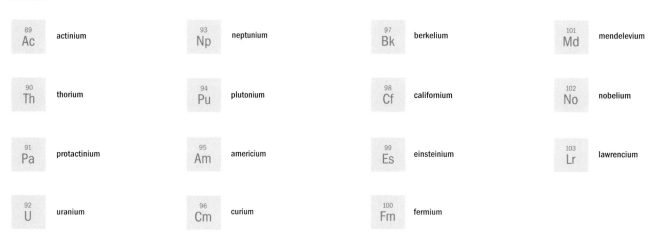

89 Ac actinium	93 Np neptunium	97 Bk berkelium	101 Md mendelevium
90 Th thorium	94 Pu plutonium	98 Cf californium	102 No nobelium
91 Pa protactinium	95 Am americium	99 Es einsteinium	103 Lr lawrencium
92 U uranium	96 Cm curium	100 Fm fermium	

chemistry symbols

negative charge   positive charge   reversible reaction   reaction direction

laboratory equipment

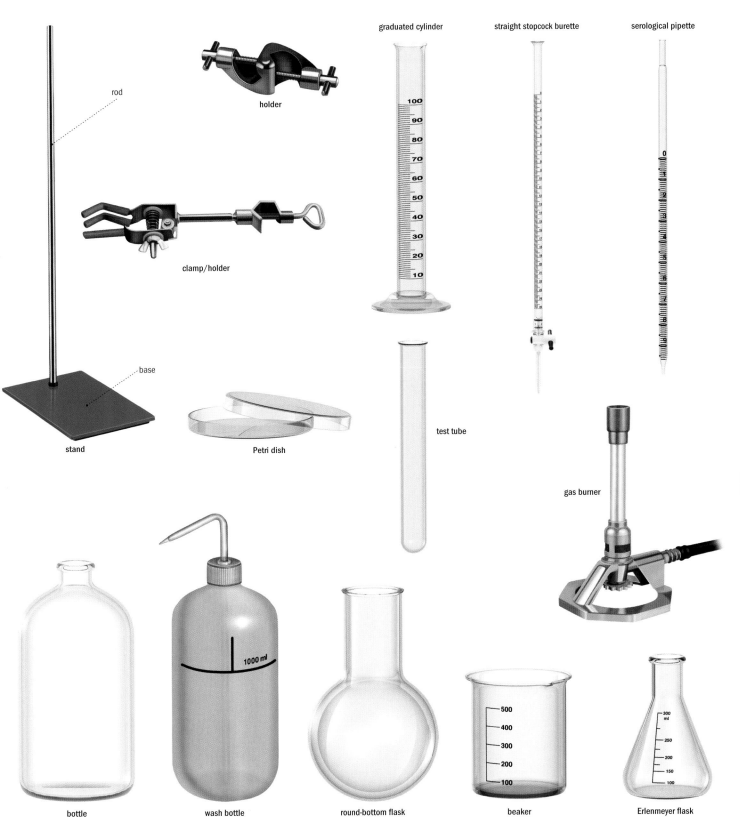

rod

holder

clamp/holder

base

stand

Petri dish

graduated cylinder

straight stopcock burette

serological pipette

test tube

gas burner

SCIENCE

1000 ml

bottle

wash bottle

round-bottom flask

beaker

Erlenmeyer flask

gearing systems

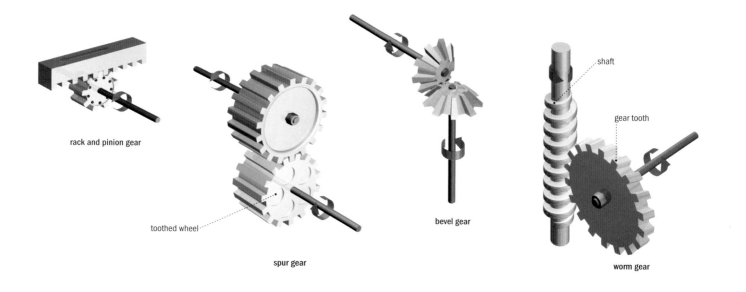

rack and pinion gear

toothed wheel

spur gear

bevel gear

shaft

gear tooth

worm gear

double pulley system

pulley

rope

effort

load

lever

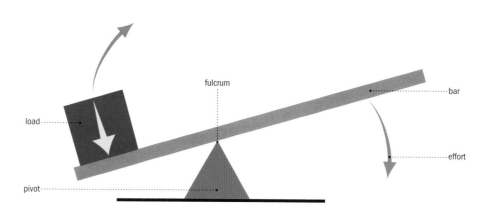

fulcrum

bar

load

effort

pivot

magnetism

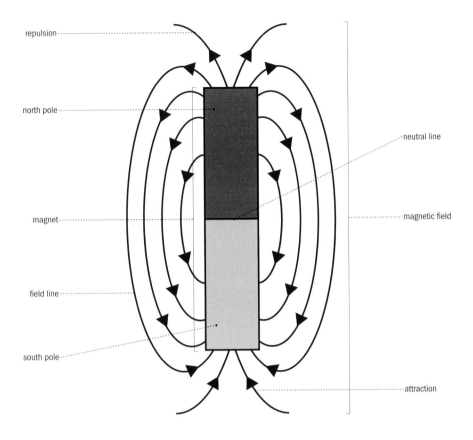

repulsion

north pole

neutral line

magnet

magnetic field

field line

south pole

attraction

parallel electrical circuit

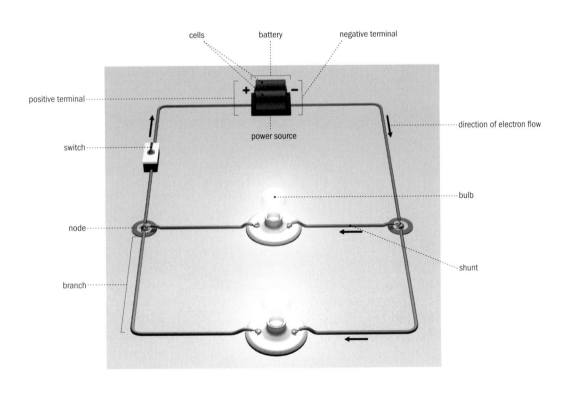

cells

battery

negative terminal

positive terminal

direction of electron flow

switch

power source

bulb

node

shunt

branch

generators

dynamo

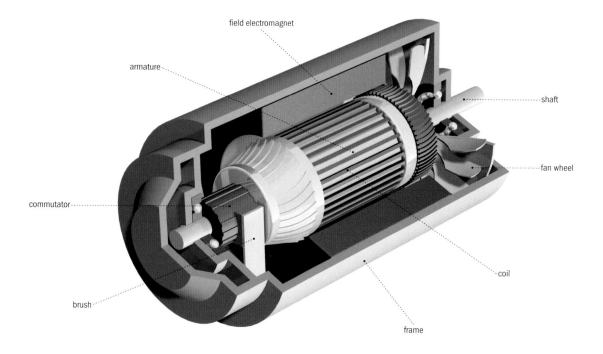

field electromagnet

armature

shaft

commutator

fan wheel

coil

brush

frame

alternator

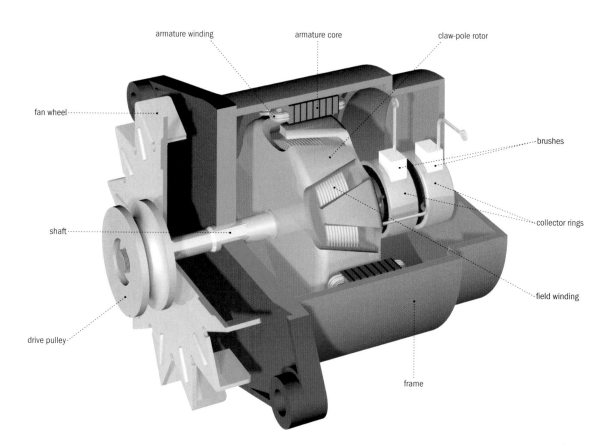

armature winding

armature core

claw-pole rotor

fan wheel

brushes

shaft

collector rings

drive pulley

field winding

frame

SCIENCE

dry cells

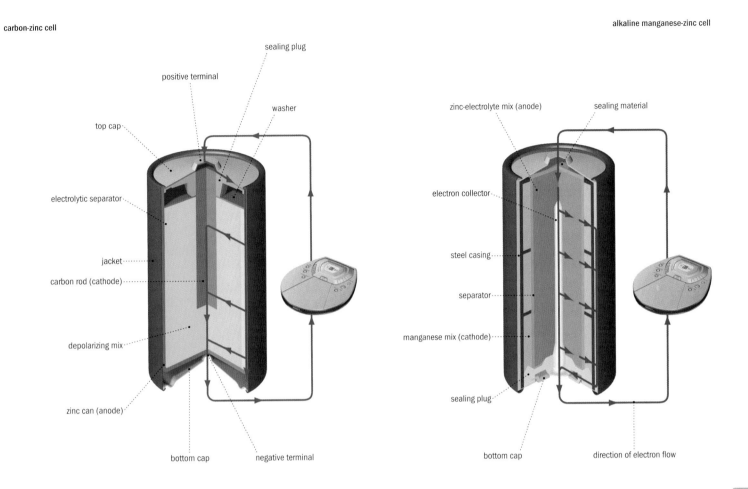

carbon-zinc cell

sealing plug

positive terminal

washer

top cap

electrolytic separator

jacket

carbon rod (cathode)

depolarizing mix

zinc can (anode)

bottom cap

negative terminal

alkaline manganese-zinc cell

zinc-electrolyte mix (anode)

sealing material

electron collector

steel casing

separator

manganese mix (cathode)

sealing plug

bottom cap

direction of electron flow

electronics

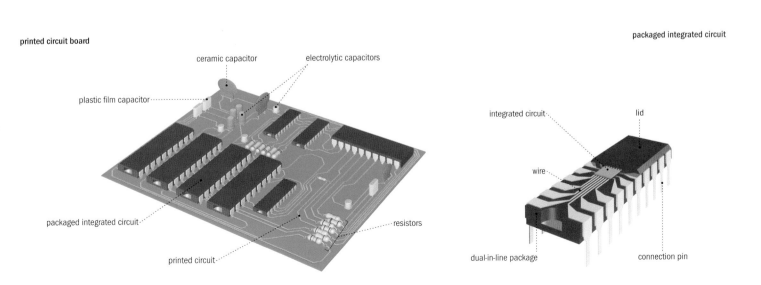

printed circuit board

ceramic capacitor

electrolytic capacitors

plastic film capacitor

packaged integrated circuit

printed circuit

resistors

packaged integrated circuit

integrated circuit

lid

wire

dual-in-line package

connection pin

electromagnetic spectrum

microwaves

ultraviolet radiation

radio waves

infrared radiation

X-rays

gamma rays

visible light

wave

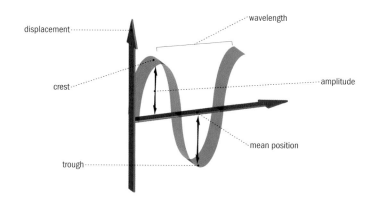

displacement

wavelength

crest

amplitude

mean position

trough

color synthesis

additive color synthesis

subtractive color synthesis

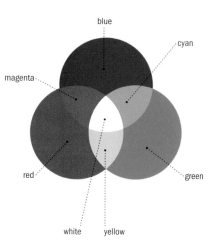

blue

cyan

magenta

red

white   yellow

green

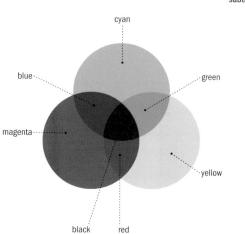

cyan

blue

green

magenta

yellow

black   red

SCIENCE

vision

normal vision

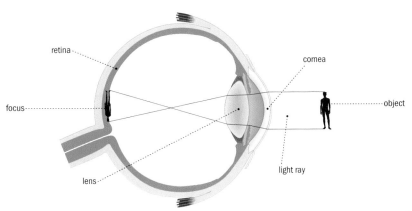

retina

cornea

focus

object

lens

light ray

vision defects and corrective lenses

myopia

hyperopia

astigmatism

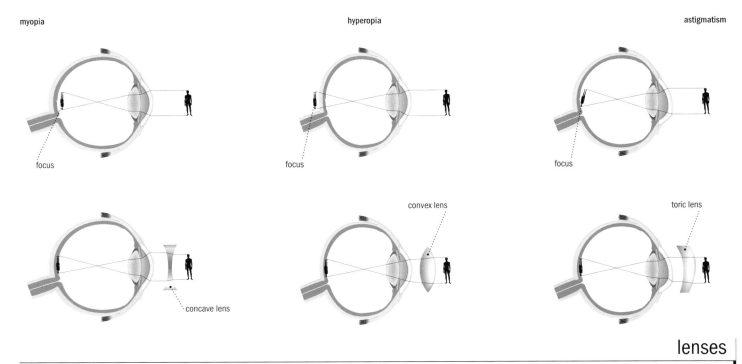

focus

focus

focus

concave lens

convex lens

toric lens

lenses

converging lenses

diverging lenses

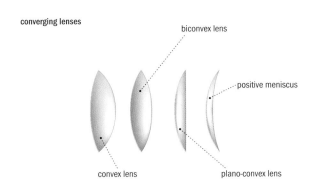

biconvex lens

positive meniscus

convex lens

plano-convex lens

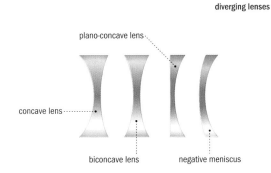

plano-concave lens

concave lens

biconcave lens

negative meniscus

pulsed ruby laser

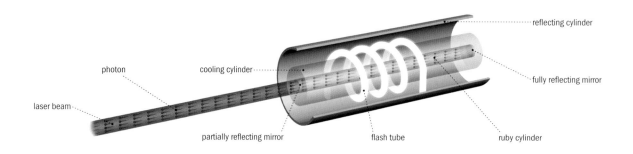

reflecting cylinder

photon

cooling cylinder

fully reflecting mirror

laser beam

partially reflecting mirror

flash tube

ruby cylinder

prism binoculars

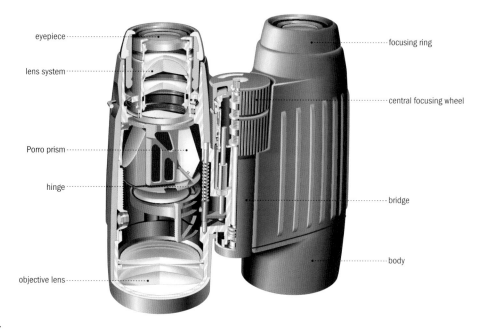

eyepiece

focusing ring

lens system

central focusing wheel

Porro prism

hinge

bridge

body

objective lens

telescopic sight

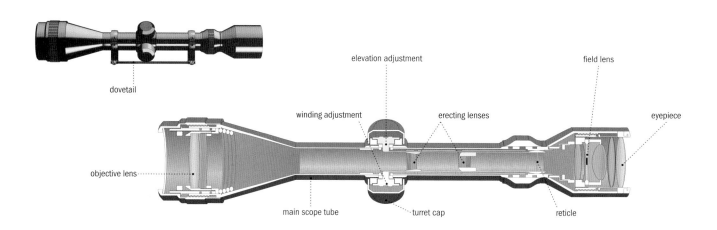

dovetail

elevation adjustment

field lens

winding adjustment

erecting lenses

eyepiece

objective lens

main scope tube

turret cap

reticle

magnifying glass and microscopes

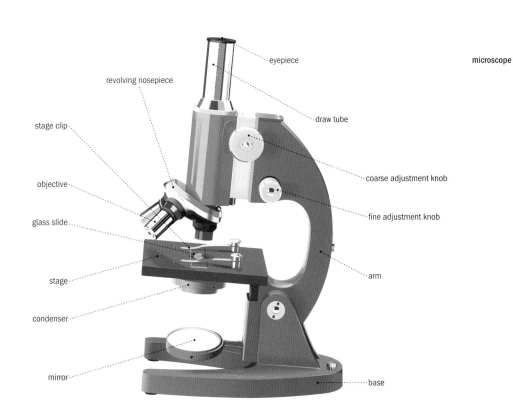

microscope

eyepiece

revolving nosepiece

draw tube

stage clip

coarse adjustment knob

objective

fine adjustment knob

glass slide

stage

arm

condenser

mirror

base

magnifying glass

binocular microscope

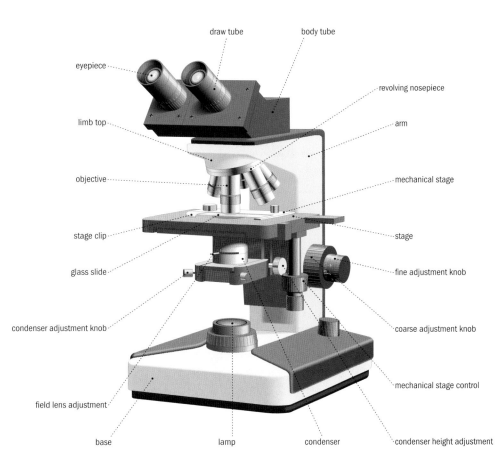

draw tube

body tube

eyepiece

revolving nosepiece

limb top

arm

objective

mechanical stage

stage clip

stage

glass slide

fine adjustment knob

condenser adjustment knob

coarse adjustment knob

mechanical stage control

field lens adjustment

base

lamp

condenser

condenser height adjustment

SCIENCE

magnifying glass and microscopes

cross section of an electron microscope

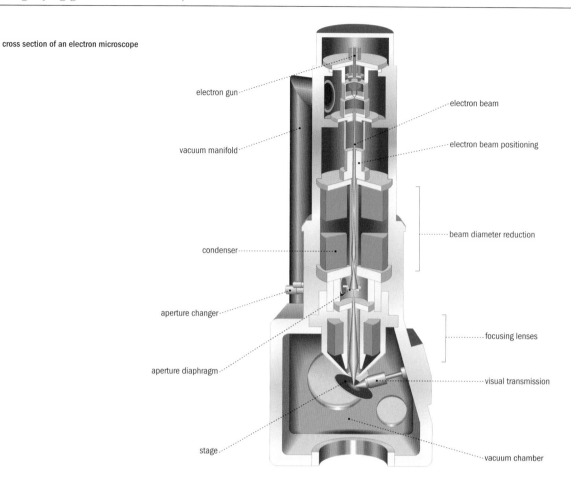

electron gun

electron beam

vacuum manifold

electron beam positioning

beam diameter reduction

condenser

aperture changer

focusing lenses

aperture diaphragm

visual transmission

stage

vacuum chamber

electron microscope elements

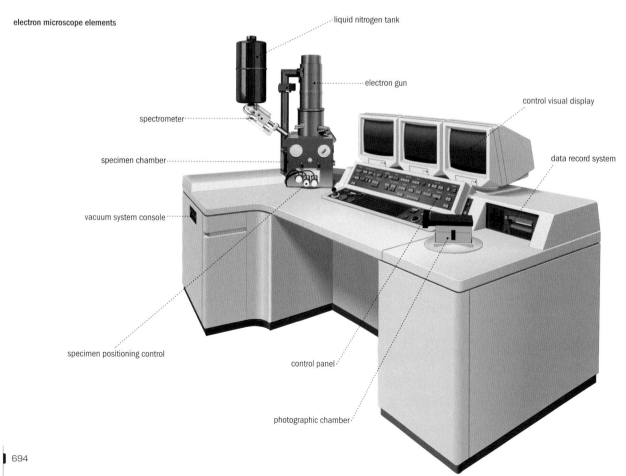

liquid nitrogen tank

electron gun

spectrometer

control visual display

specimen chamber

data record system

vacuum system console

specimen positioning control

control panel

photographic chamber

SCIENCE

thermometer

clinical thermometer

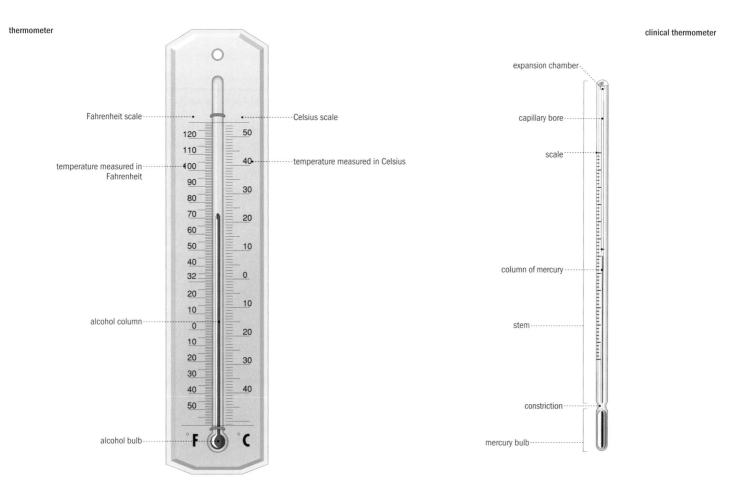

Fahrenheit scale

Celsius scale

temperature measured in Fahrenheit

temperature measured in Celsius

alcohol column

alcohol bulb

expansion chamber

capillary bore

scale

column of mercury

stem

constriction

mercury bulb

bimetallic thermometer

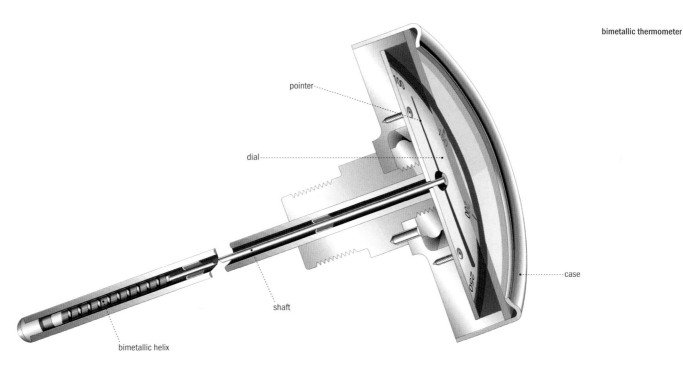

pointer

dial

case

shaft

bimetallic helix

measure of time

stopwatch

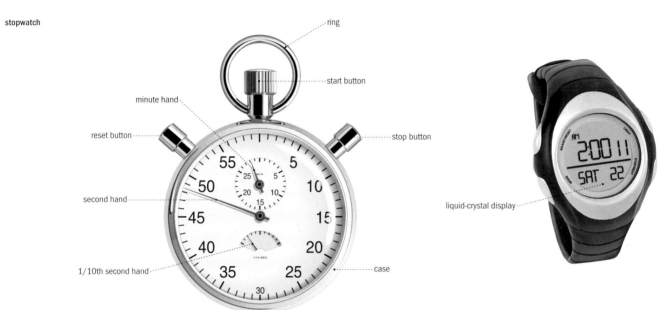

ring
start button
minute hand
reset button
stop button
second hand
55
5
50
10
45
15
40
20
1/10th second hand
35
25
30
case

25 MIN 5
20 10
15
1/10 SEC

digital watch

liquid-crystal display

2:00 11
SAT 22

mechanical watch

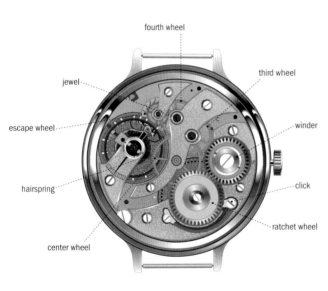

fourth wheel
third wheel
jewel
escape wheel
winder
hairspring
click
ratchet wheel
center wheel

analog watch

dial
crown
strap

11 12 1
10 2
9 3
8 4
7 6 5

sundial

gnomon
shadow
dial

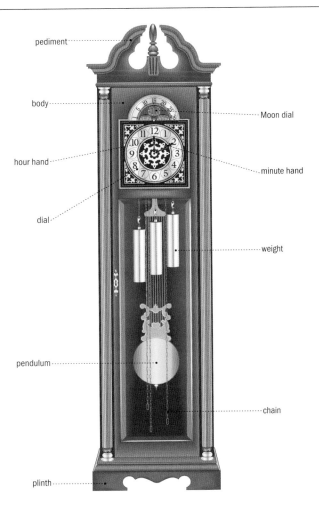

pediment

body

Moon dial

hour hand

minute hand

dial

weight

pendulum

chain

plinth

weight-driven clock mechanism

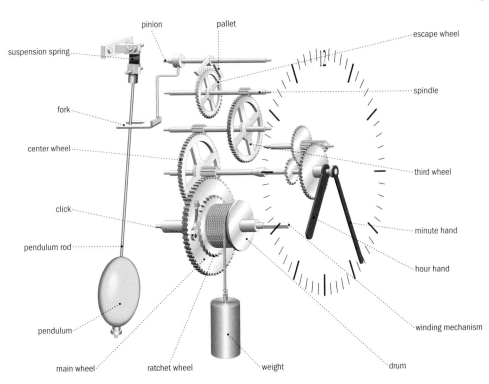

pinion

pallet

escape wheel

suspension spring

spindle

fork

center wheel

third wheel

click

minute hand

pendulum rod

hour hand

pendulum

winding mechanism

main wheel

ratchet wheel

weight

drum

measure of weight

beam balance

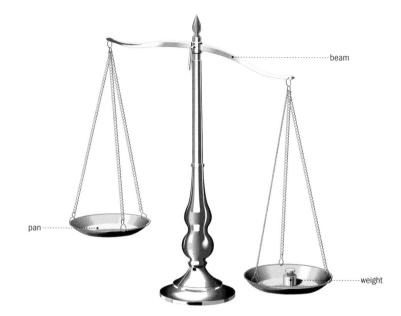

- beam
- pan
- weight

steelyard

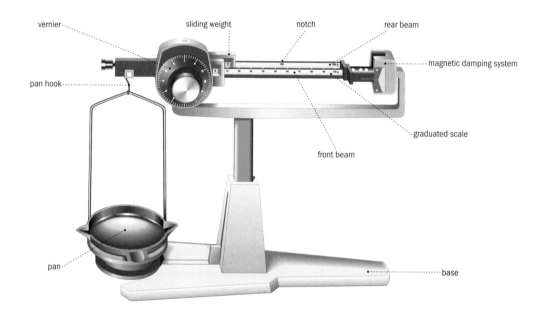

- vernier
- sliding weight
- notch
- rear beam
- pan hook
- magnetic damping system
- graduated scale
- front beam
- pan
- base

Roberval's balance

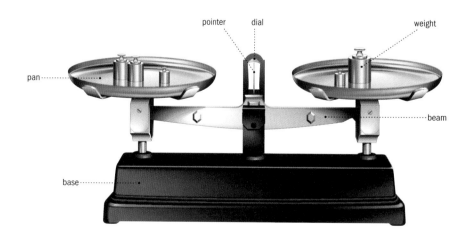

- pointer
- dial
- weight
- pan
- beam
- base

SCIENCE

spring balance

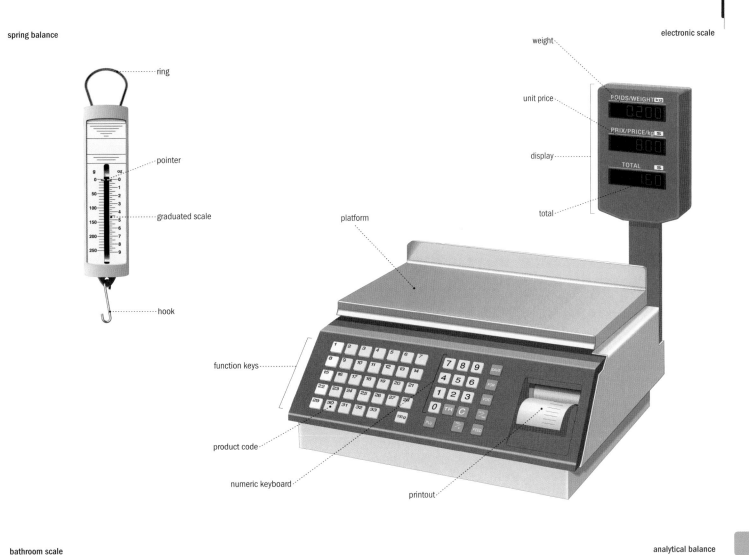

ring

pointer

graduated scale

g oz
0 — 0
50 — 1
100 — 2
— 3
150 — 4
— 5
200 — 6
— 7
250 — 8
— 9

hook

electronic scale

weight

unit price

display

total

FOIDS/WEIGHT kg

0.200

PRIX/PRICE/kg $

8.00

TOTAL $

1.60

platform

function keys

1 2 3 4 5 6 7
8 9 10 11 12 13 14
15 16 17 18 19 20 21
22 23 24 25 26 27 28
29 30 31 32 33

7 8 9
4 5 6
1 2 3
0 TR C

SAVE
FOR
VOID
FEED

100 g
PLU

product code

numeric keyboard

printout

bathroom scale

digital display

000

weighing platform

analytical balance

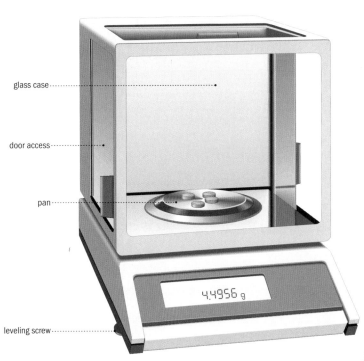

glass case

door access

pan

4.4956 g

leveling screw

measure of length

ruler

scales

measure of distance

pedometer

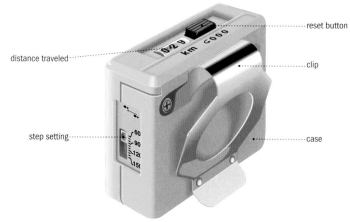

distance traveled ···········

step setting ···········

reset button

clip

case

measure of thickness

vernier caliper

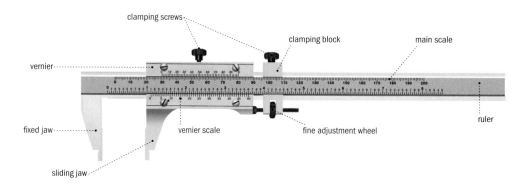

clamping screws ·

vernier ···········

fixed jaw ···········

sliding jaw ···········

clamping block

main scale

vernier scale

fine adjustment wheel

ruler

micrometer caliper

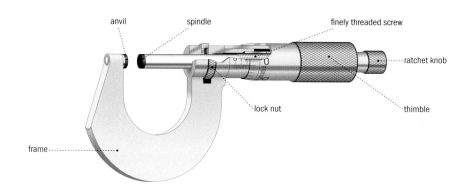

anvil

spindle

finely threaded screw

ratchet knob

lock nut

thimble

frame ···········

SCIENCE

measure of angles

theodolite

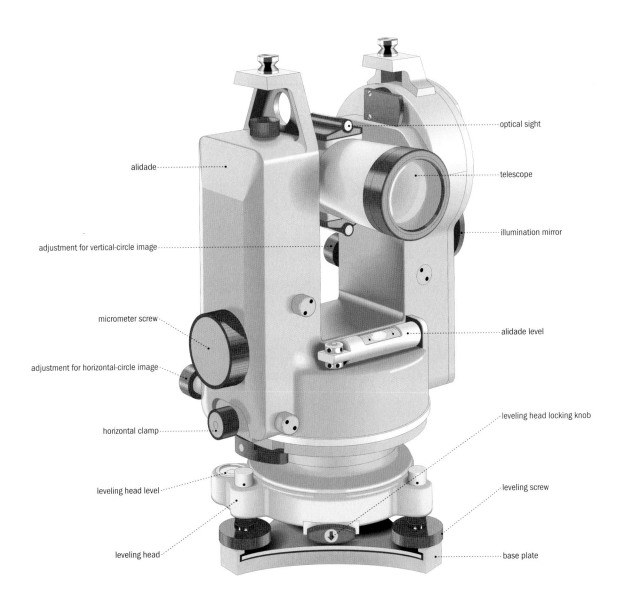

optical sight

telescope

alidade

illumination mirror

adjustment for vertical-circle image

micrometer screw

alidade level

adjustment for horizontal-circle image

horizontal clamp

leveling head locking knob

leveling head level

leveling screw

leveling head

base plate

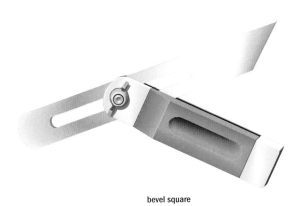

bevel square

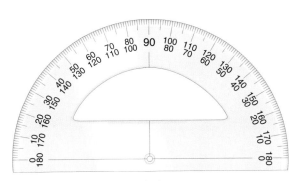

protractor

international system of units

unit of electric current

A
ampere

unit of electric potential difference

V
volt

unit of electric resistance

Ω
ohm

unit of electric charge

C
coulomb

unit of power

W
watt

unit of frequency

Hz
hertz

unit of luminous intensity

cd
candela

unit of energy

J
joule

unit of length

m
meter

unit of mass

kg
kilogram

unit of pressure

Pa
pascal

unit of force

N
newton

unit of time

s
second

unit of amount of substance

mol
mole

unit of radioactivity

Bq
becquerel

unit of Celsius temperature

°C
degree Celsius

unit of thermodynamic temperature

K
kelvin

biology

female

blood factor negative

birth

male

Rh+
blood factor positive

death

mathematics

− minus/negative	**+** plus/positive	**X** multiplied by	**÷** divided by	**=** equals
≠ is not equal to	is approximately equal to	is equivalent to	**≡** is identical with	**≢** is not identical with
± plus or minus	**≤** is less than or equal to	**>** is greater than	**≥** is greater than or equal to	**<** is less than
∅ empty set	**∪** union of two sets	**∩** intersection of two sets	**⊂** is included in/is a subset of	**%** percent
∈ is an element of	**∉** is not an element of	**∑** sum	**√** square root of	**½** fraction
	∞ infinity	**∫** integral	**!** factorial	

Roman numerals

I one	**V** five	**X** ten
L fifty	**C** one hundred	**D** five hundred

M one thousand

geometry

degree

minute

second

pi

perpendicular

is parallel to

is not parallel to

right angle

obtuse angle

acute angle

geometrical shapes

examples of angles

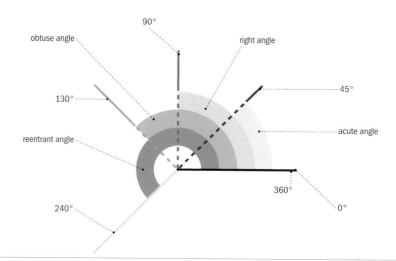

obtuse angle · 90° · right angle
130°
45°
reentrant angle · acute angle
240° · 360° · 0°

plane surfaces

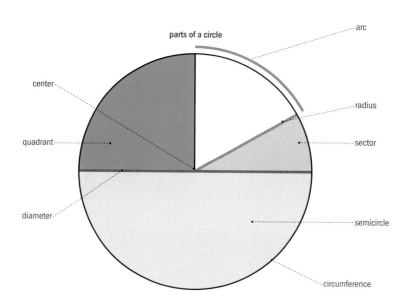

parts of a circle
arc
center
radius
quadrant
sector
diameter
semicircle
circumference

geometrical shapes

polygons

triangle

square

rectangle

rhombus

trapezoid

parallelogram

quadrilateral

regular pentagon

regular hexagon

regular heptagon

regular octagon

regular nonagon

regular decagon

regular hendecagon

regular dodecagon

solids

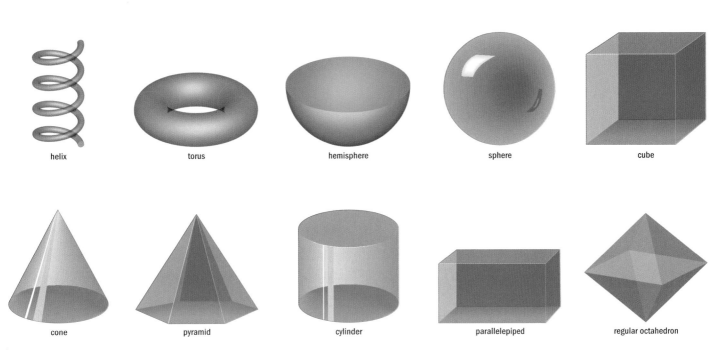

helix

torus

hemisphere

sphere

cube

cone

pyramid

cylinder

parallelepiped

regular octahedron

SCIENCE

SOCIETY

agglomeration

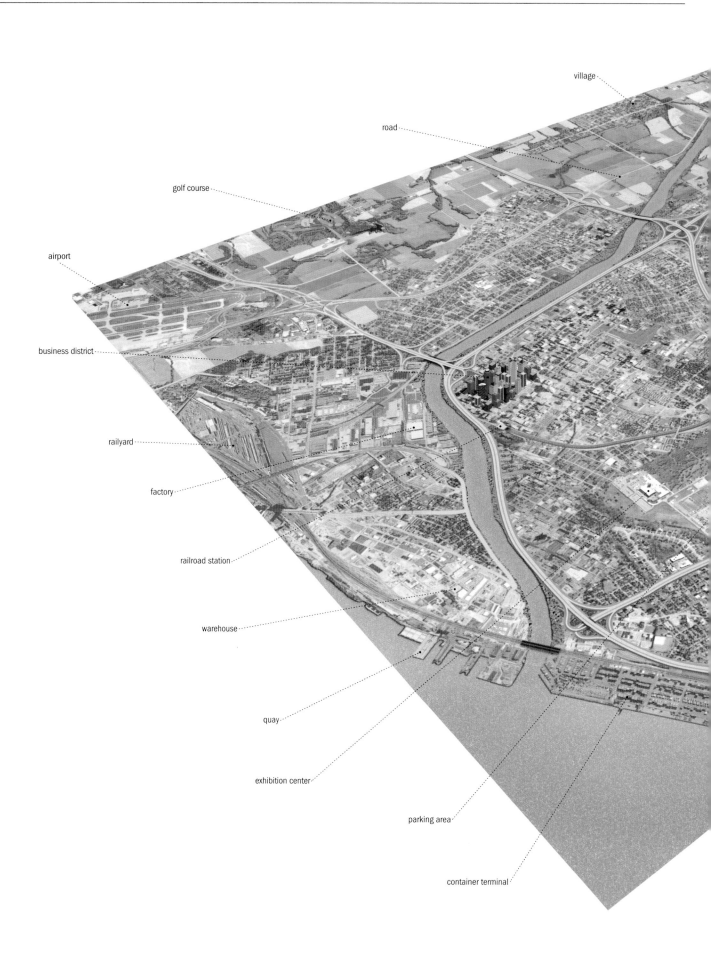

village

road

golf course

airport

business district

railyard

factory

railroad station

warehouse

quay

exhibition center

parking area

container terminal

track

peripheral freeway

freeway

landfill

interchange

shopping center

residential district

country

commercial zone

suburb

stadium

downtown

refinery

industrial area

port

sports complex

downtown

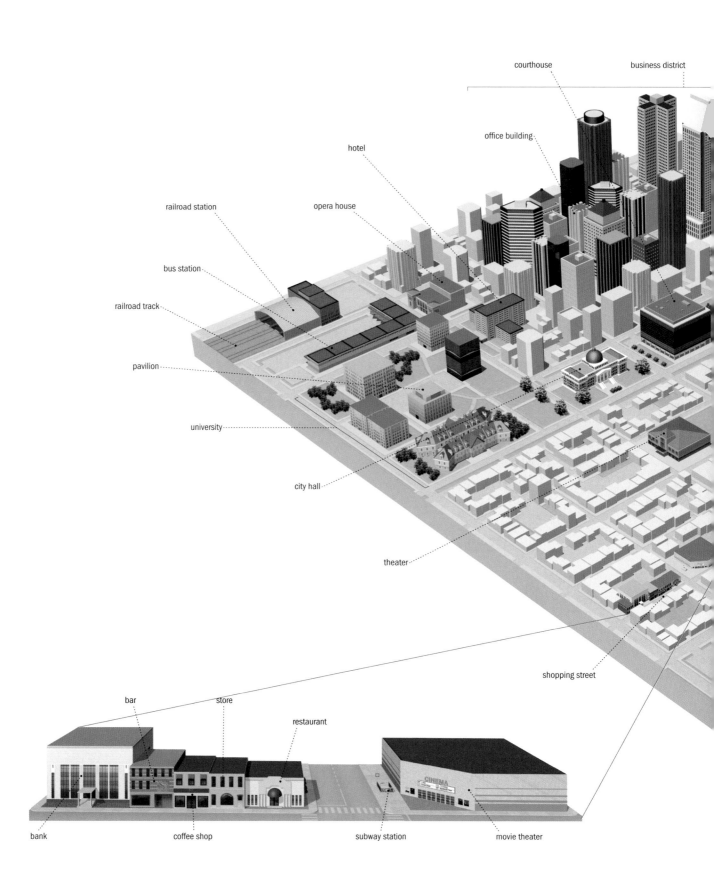

courthouse

business district

office building

hotel

opera house

railroad station

bus station

railroad track

pavilion

university

city hall

theater

shopping street

bar

store

restaurant

bank

coffee shop

subway station

movie theater

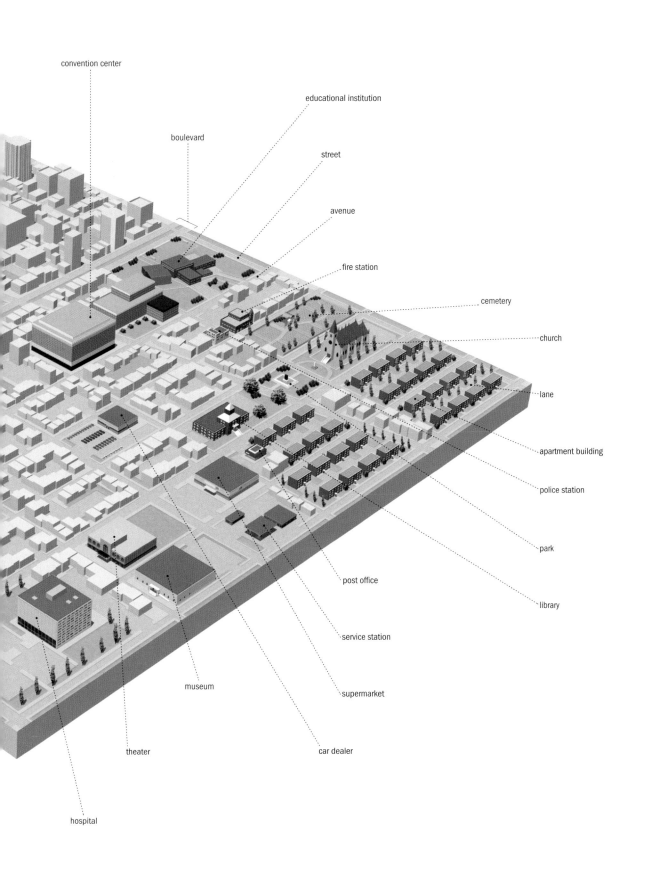

convention center

educational institution

boulevard

street

avenue

fire station

cemetery

church

lane

apartment building

police station

park

library

service station

post office

supermarket

car dealer

museum

theater

hospital

cross section of a street

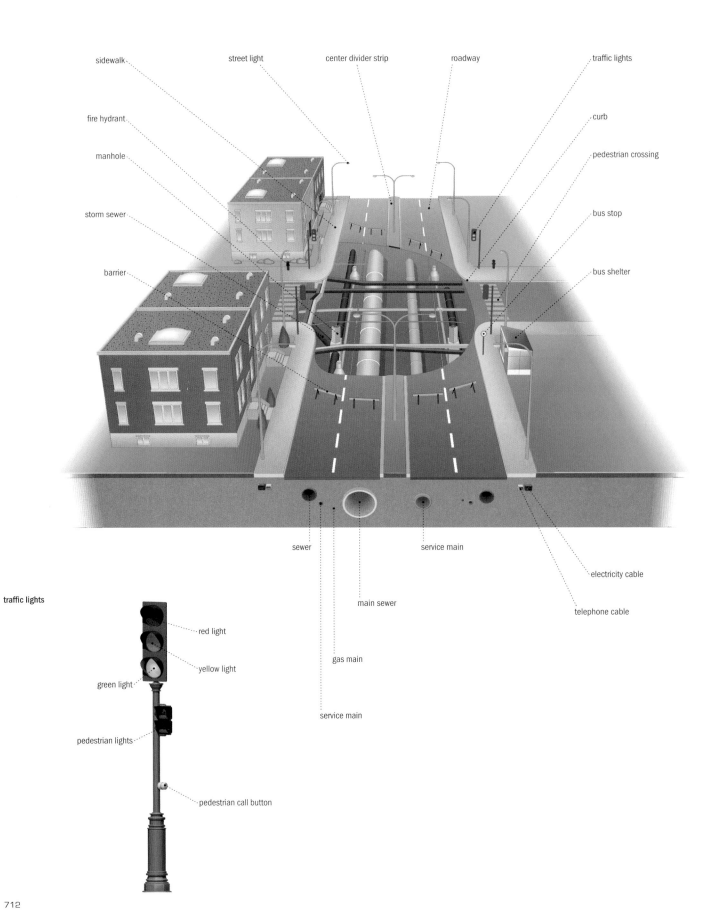

sidewalk

street light

center divider strip

roadway

traffic lights

fire hydrant

curb

manhole

pedestrian crossing

storm sewer

bus stop

barrier

bus shelter

sewer

service main

electricity cable

main sewer

telephone cable

traffic lights

red light

yellow light

green light

gas main

pedestrian lights

service main

pedestrian call button

office building

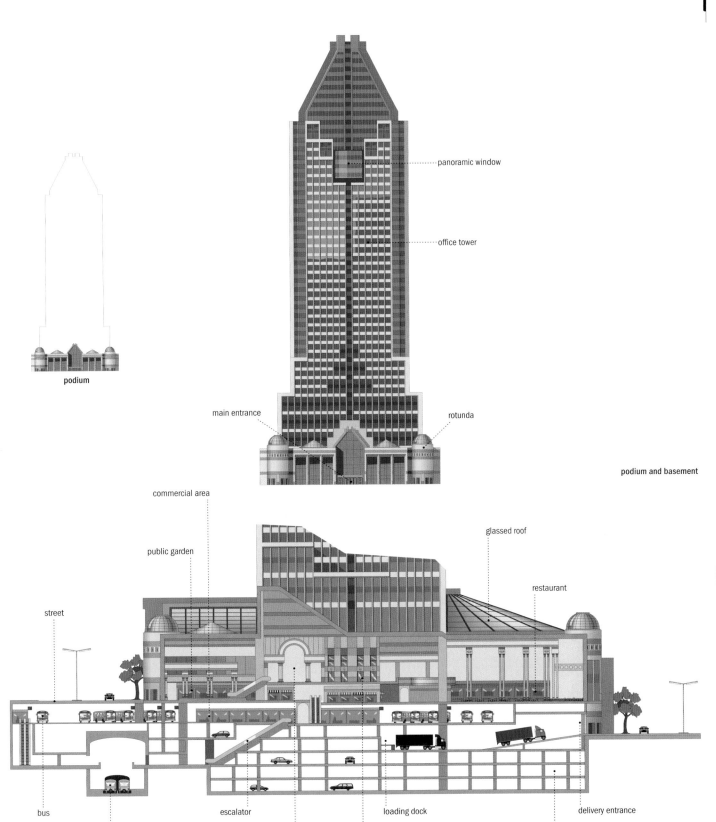

podium

panoramic window

office tower

main entrance

rotunda

podium and basement

commercial area

glassed roof

public garden

restaurant

street

bus

escalator

loading dock

delivery entrance

subway

lobby

elevator

parking

shopping center

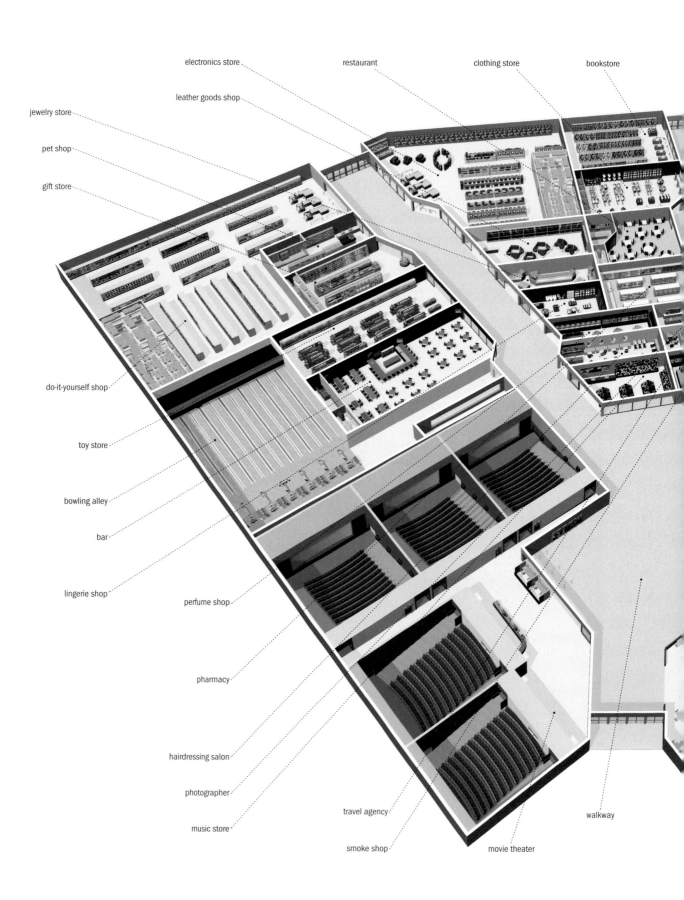

electronics store

restaurant

clothing store

bookstore

leather goods shop

jewelry store

pet shop

gift store

do-it-yourself shop

toy store

bowling alley

bar

lingerie shop

perfume shop

pharmacy

hairdressing salon

photographer

music store

travel agency

smoke shop

movie theater

walkway

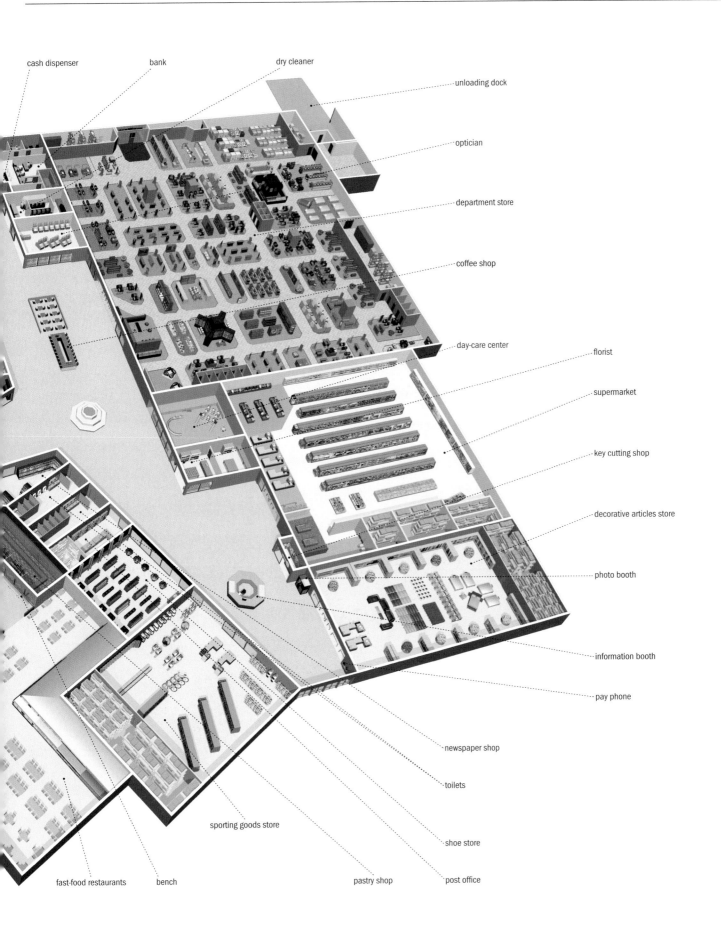

cash dispenser

bank

dry cleaner

unloading dock

optician

department store

coffee shop

day-care center

florist

supermarket

key cutting shop

decorative articles store

photo booth

information booth

pay phone

newspaper shop

toilets

sporting goods store

shoe store

fast-food restaurants

bench

pastry shop

post office

department store

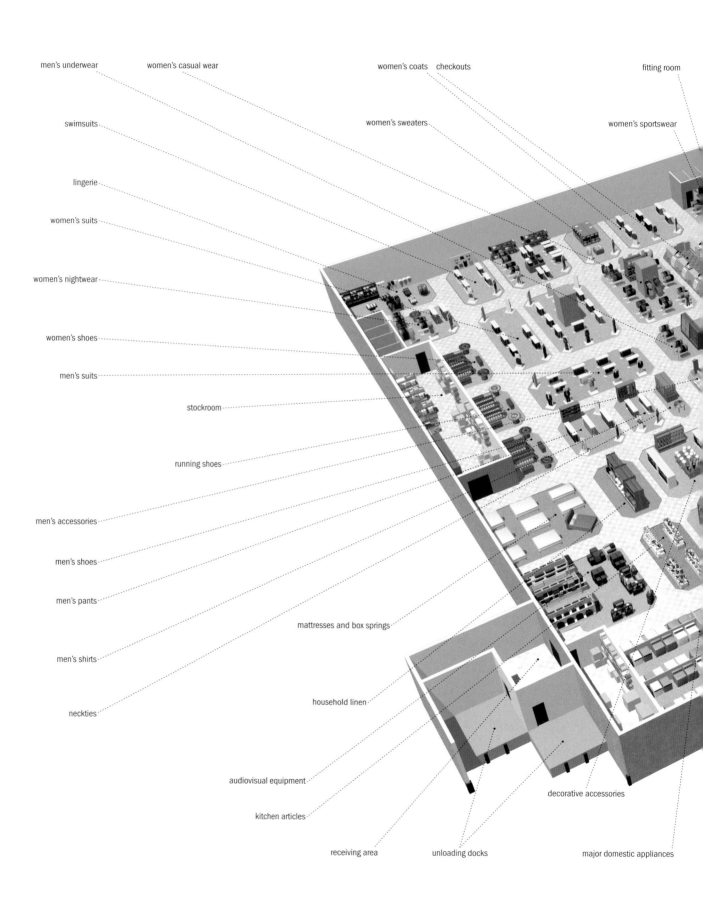

men's underwear
women's casual wear
women's coats   checkouts
fitting room

swimsuits
women's sweaters
women's sportswear

lingerie

women's suits

women's nightwear

women's shoes

men's suits

stockroom

running shoes

men's accessories

men's shoes

men's pants

mattresses and box springs

men's shirts

household linen

neckties

audiovisual equipment

decorative accessories

kitchen articles

receiving area   unloading docks   major domestic appliances

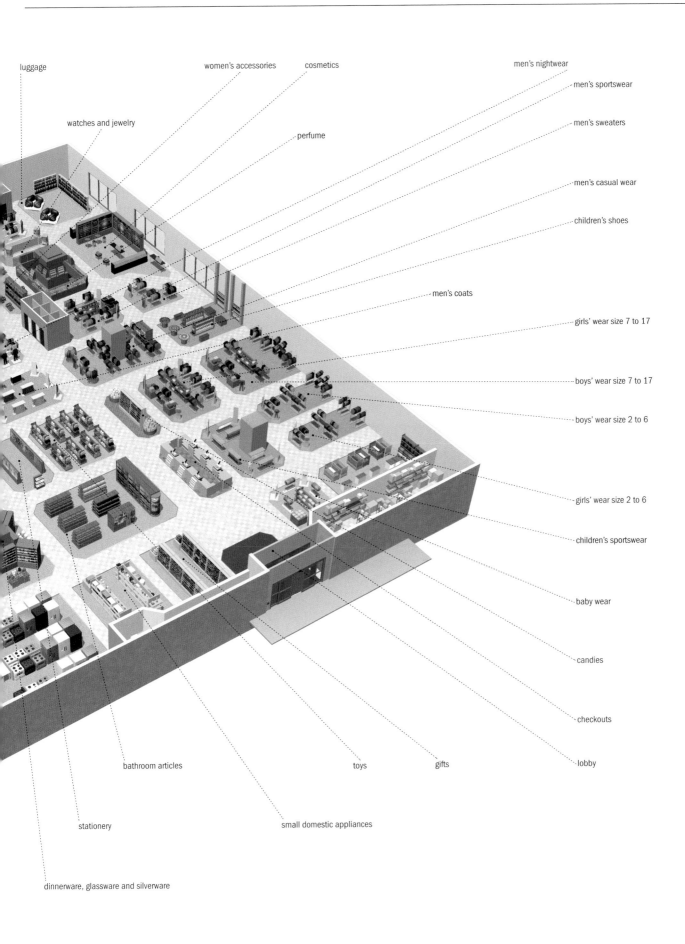

luggage

women's accessories

cosmetics

men's nightwear

watches and jewelry

perfume

men's sportswear

men's sweaters

men's casual wear

children's shoes

men's coats

girls' wear size 7 to 17

boys' wear size 7 to 17

boys' wear size 2 to 6

girls' wear size 2 to 6

children's sportswear

baby wear

candies

checkouts

lobby

bathroom articles

toys

gifts

stationery

small domestic appliances

dinnerware, glassware and silverware

convention center

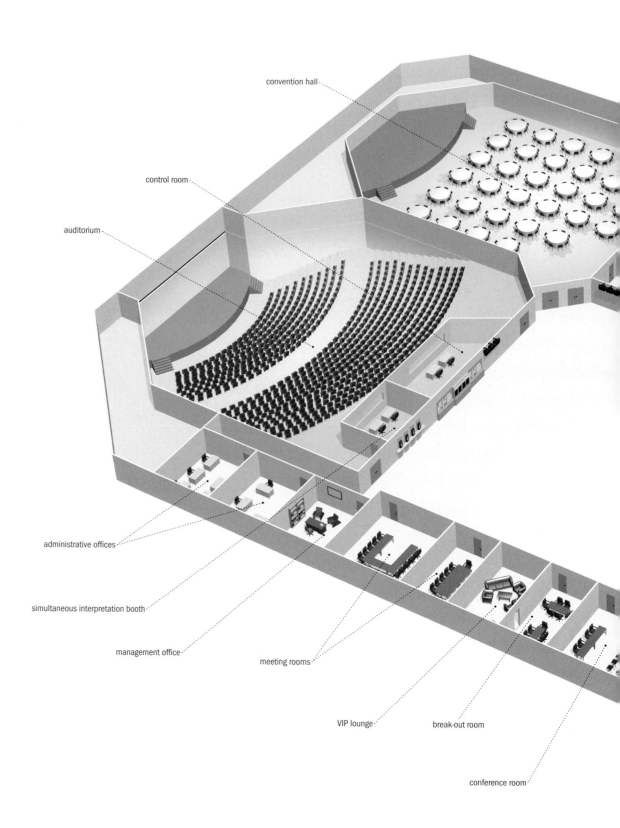

convention hall

control room

auditorium

administrative offices

simultaneous interpretation booth

management office

meeting rooms

VIP lounge

break-out room

conference room

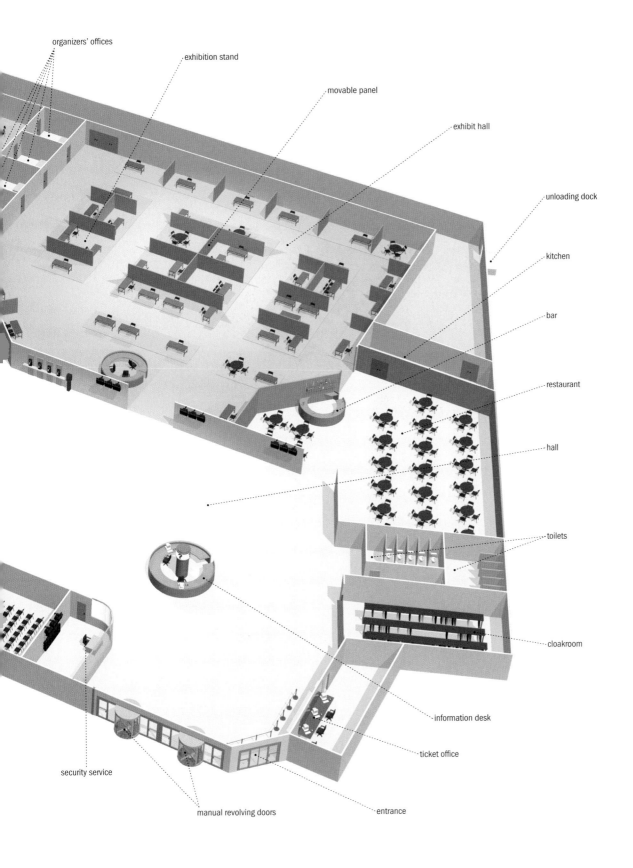

organizers' offices

exhibition stand

movable panel

exhibit hall

unloading dock

kitchen

bar

restaurant

hall

toilets

cloakroom

information desk

ticket office

security service

manual revolving doors

entrance

restaurant

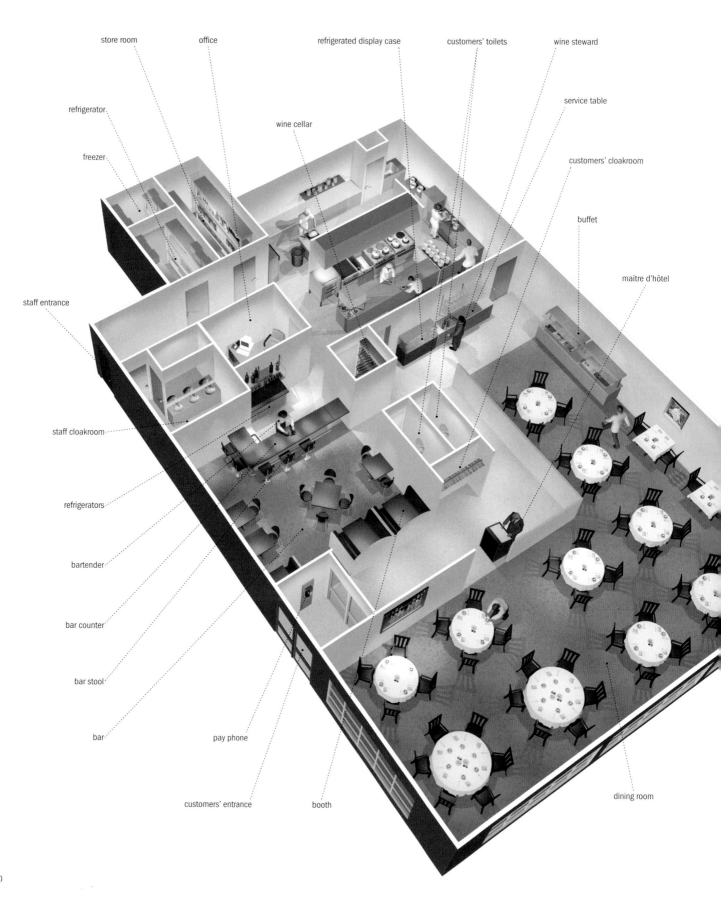

store room

office

refrigerated display case

customers' toilets

wine steward

refrigerator

wine cellar

service table

freezer

customers' cloakroom

buffet

maître d'hôtel

staff entrance

staff cloakroom

refrigerators

bartender

bar counter

bar stool

bar

pay phone

customers' entrance

booth

dining room

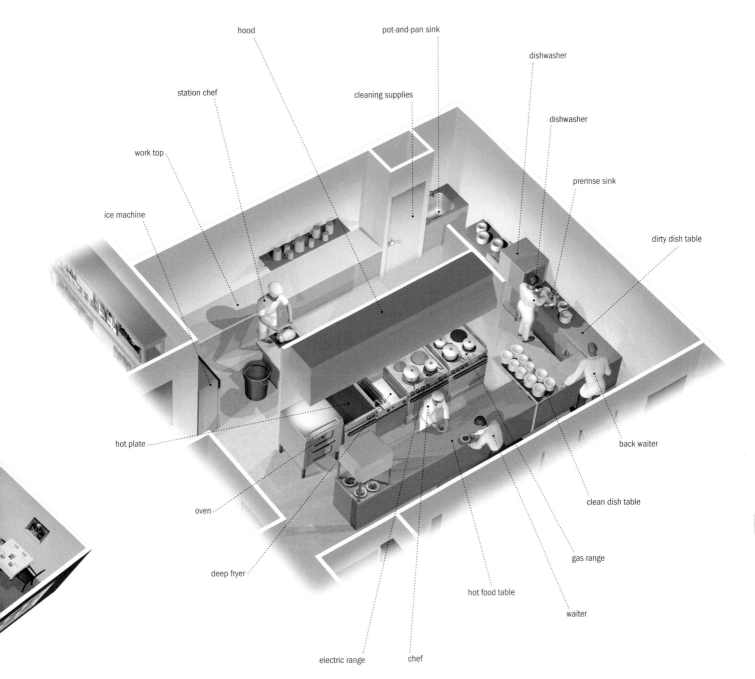

hood

pot-and-pan sink

dishwasher

station chef

cleaning supplies

dishwasher

work top

prerinse sink

ice machine

dirty dish table

hot plate

back waiter

oven

clean dish table

deep fryer

gas range

hot food table

electric range

chef

waiter

menu

wine list

check

self-service restaurant

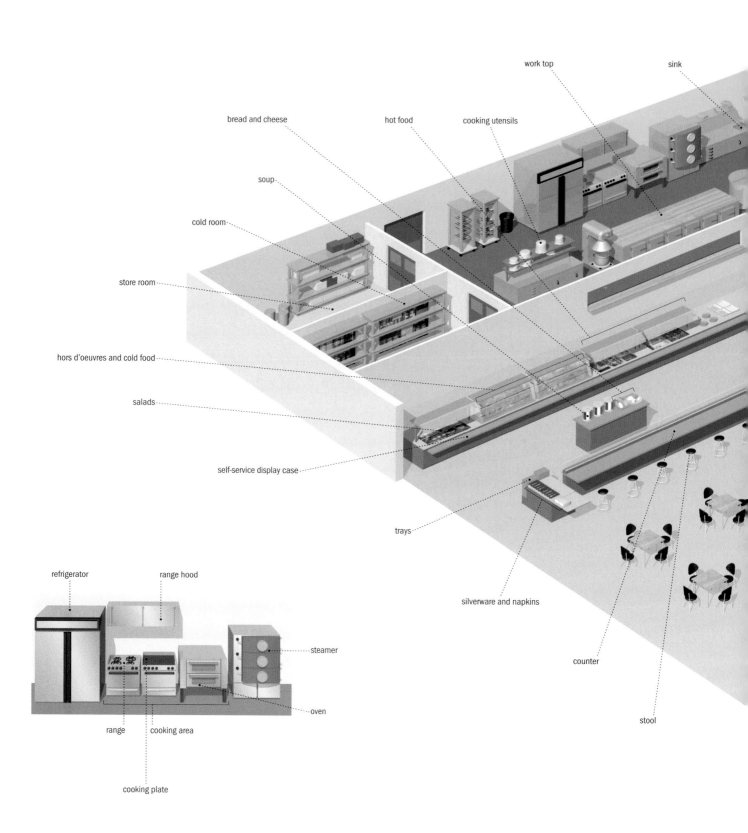

work top

sink

bread and cheese

hot food

cooking utensils

soup

cold room

store room

hors d'oeuvres and cold food

salads

self-service display case

trays

refrigerator

range hood

silverware and napkins

steamer

counter

oven

range

cooking area

stool

cooking plate

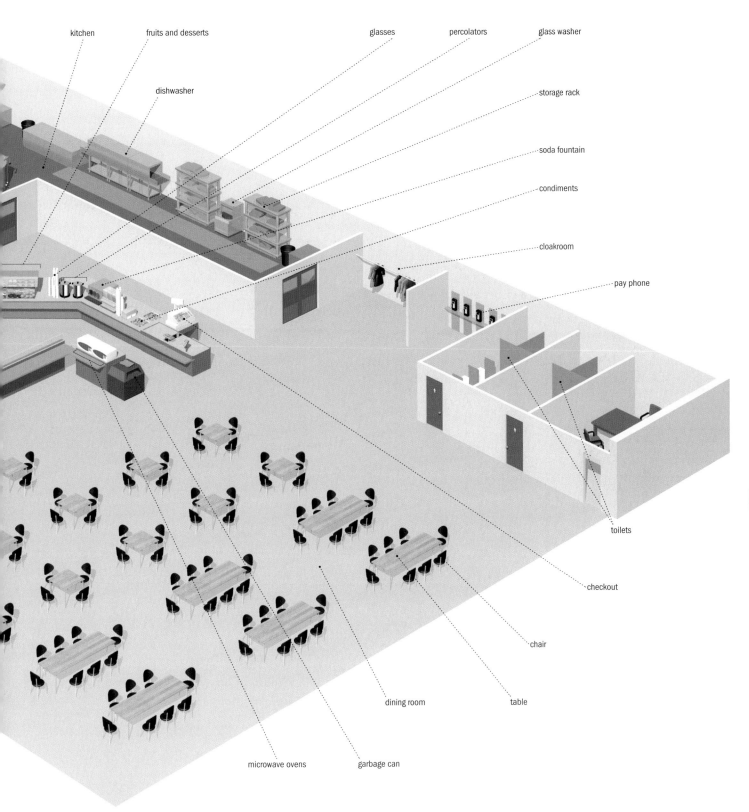

kitchen

fruits and desserts

dishwasher

glasses

percolators

glass washer

storage rack

soda fountain

condiments

cloakroom

pay phone

toilets

checkout

chair

dining room

table

microwave ovens

garbage can

hotel

reception level

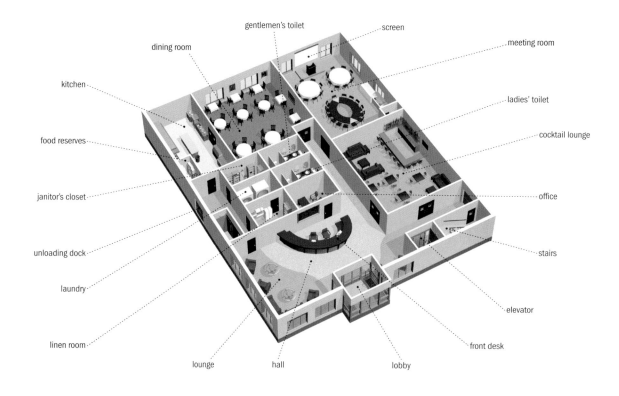

gentlemen's toilet

screen

dining room

meeting room

kitchen

ladies' toilet

food reserves

cocktail lounge

janitor's closet

office

unloading dock

stairs

laundry

elevator

linen room

front desk

lounge

hall

lobby

hotel rooms

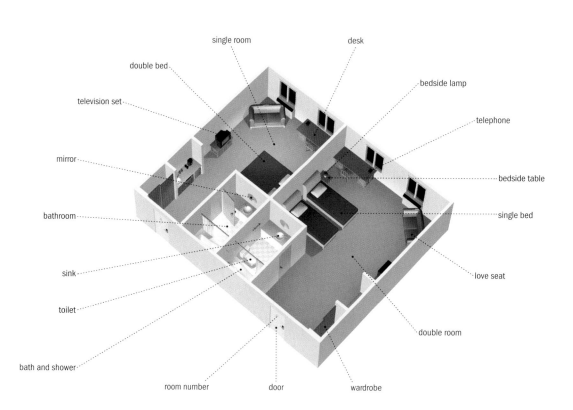

single room

desk

double bed

bedside lamp

television set

telephone

mirror

bedside table

bathroom

single bed

sink

love seat

toilet

double room

bath and shower

room number

door

wardrobe

SOCIETY

common symbols

men's rest room

women's rest room

wheelchair access

no wheelchair access

camping (trailer and tent)

picnic area

picnics prohibited

camping (tent)

camping prohibited

camping (trailer)

hospital

coffee shop

telephone

restaurant

pharmacy

police

first aid

service station

fire extinguisher

information

information

lost and found articles

currency exchange

taxi transportation

SOCIETY

prison

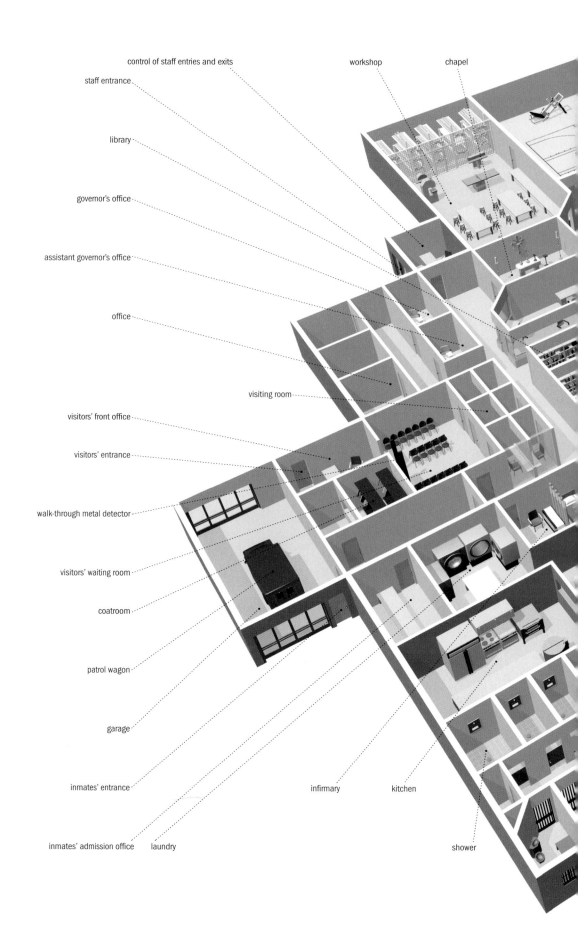

control of staff entries and exits

staff entrance

library

governor's office

assistant governor's office

office

workshop

chapel

visiting room

visitors' front office

visitors' entrance

walk-through metal detector

visitors' waiting room

coatroom

patrol wagon

garage

inmates' entrance

infirmary

kitchen

inmates' admission office   laundry

shower

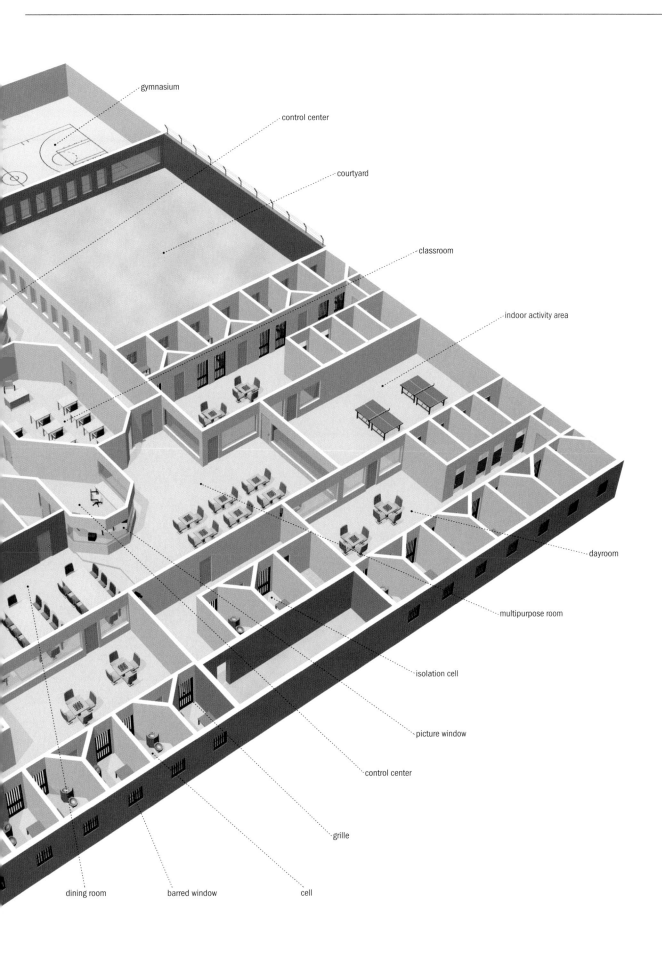

gymnasium

control center

courtyard

classroom

indoor activity area

dayroom

multipurpose room

isolation cell

picture window

control center

grille

dining room

barred window

cell

court

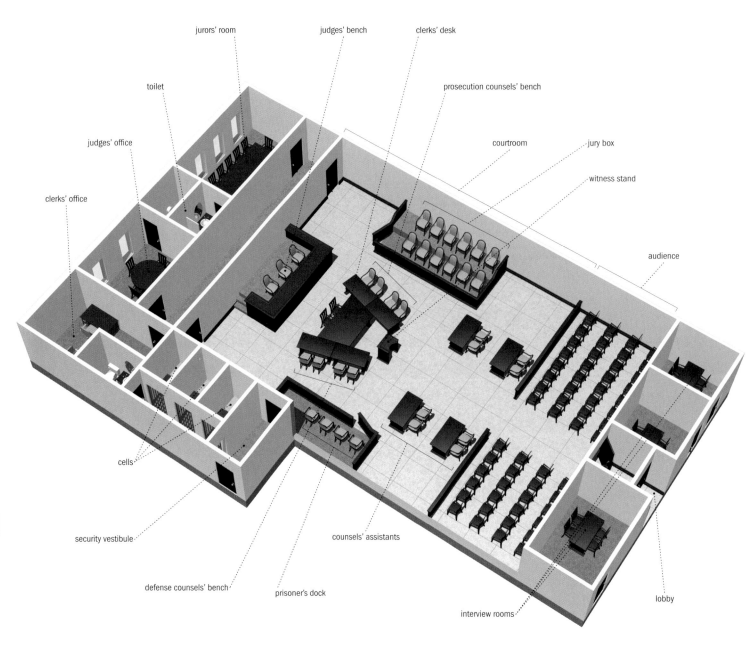

jurors' room

judges' bench

clerks' desk

prosecution counsels' bench

toilet

judges' office

courtroom

jury box

witness stand

clerks' office

audience

cells

security vestibule

counsels' assistants

defense counsels' bench

prisoner's dock

interview rooms

lobby

examples of currency abbreviations

dollar

cent

rupee

euro

new shekel

peso

yen

pound

money and modes of payment

coin: obverse

banknote: front

initials of the issuing bank

security thread

hologram foil strip

date

watermark

official signature

color shifting ink

edge

portrait

serial number

coin: reverse

banknote: back

flag of the European Union

serial number

outer ring

motto

denomination

denomination

name of the currency

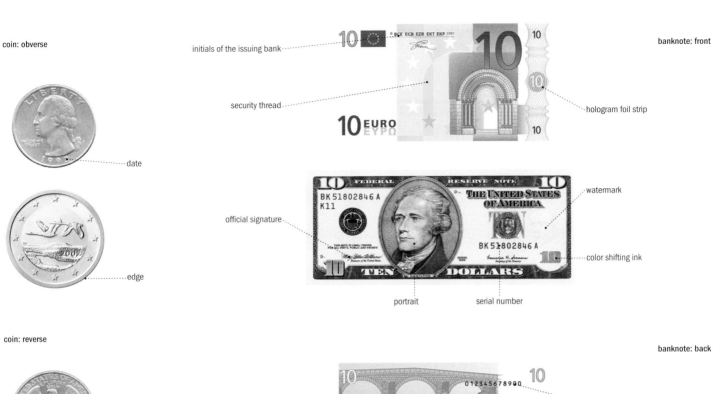

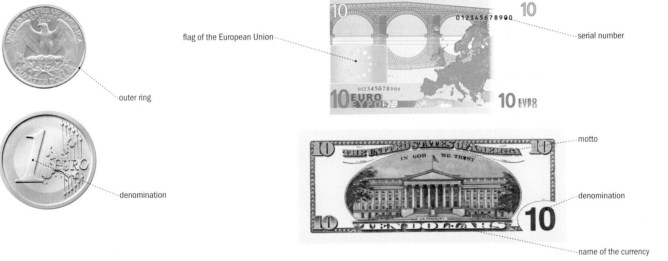

magnetic stripe

credit card

cardholder's signature

card number

checks

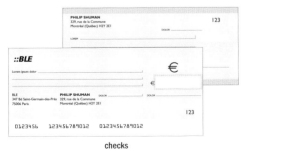

cardholder's name

expiration date

traveler's check

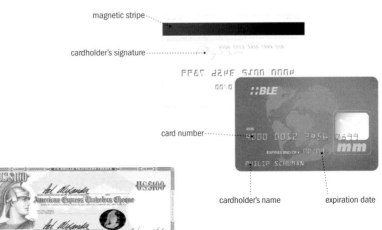

bank

cash dispenser

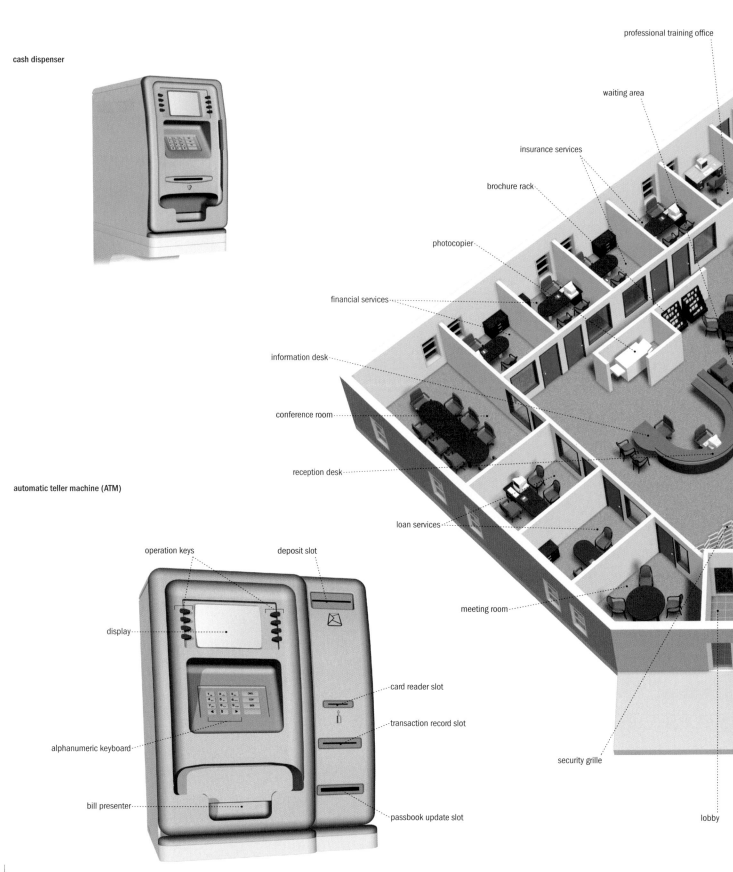

professional training office

waiting area

insurance services

brochure rack

photocopier

financial services

information desk

conference room

reception desk

loan services

meeting room

security grille

lobby

automatic teller machine (ATM)

operation keys

deposit slot

display

card reader slot

transaction record slot

alphanumeric keyboard

bill presenter

passbook update slot

SOCIETY

staff lounge

janitor's closet

cloakroom

customer service

toilet

director's office

secretary's office

safe deposit box

vault

safe

coupon booth

wicket

line

debit card

card number

4000 0012 7659 3456

business wicket

cash supply

automatic teller machine

night deposit box

personal identification number (PIN) pad

confirmation key

electronic payment terminal

power-on/paper-detect light

paper feed button

transaction receipt

display

account identification

operation keys

card reader slot

programmable function keys

alphanumeric keyboard

library

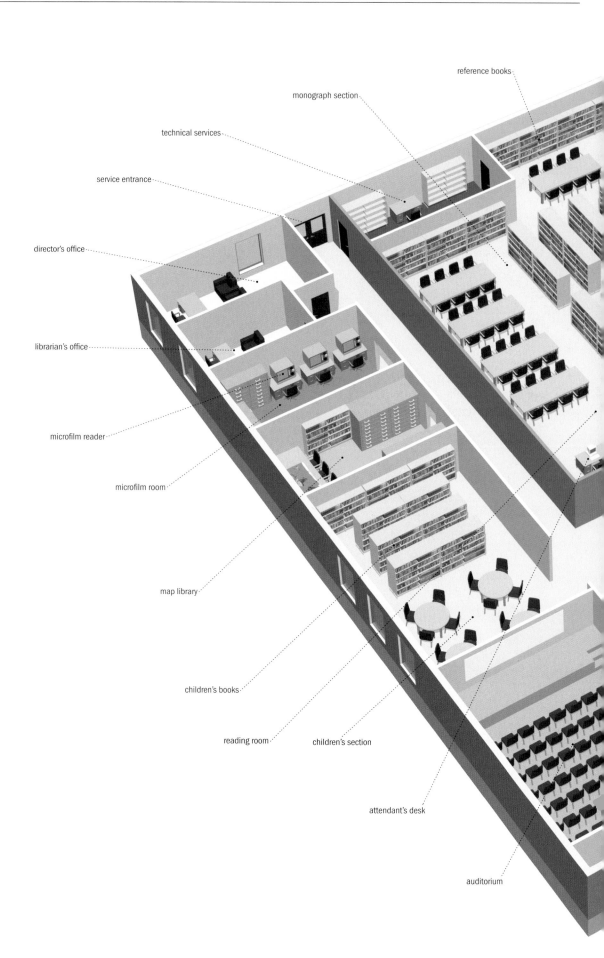

reference books

monograph section

technical services

service entrance

director's office

librarian's office

microfilm reader

microfilm room

map library

children's books

reading room

children's section

attendant's desk

auditorium

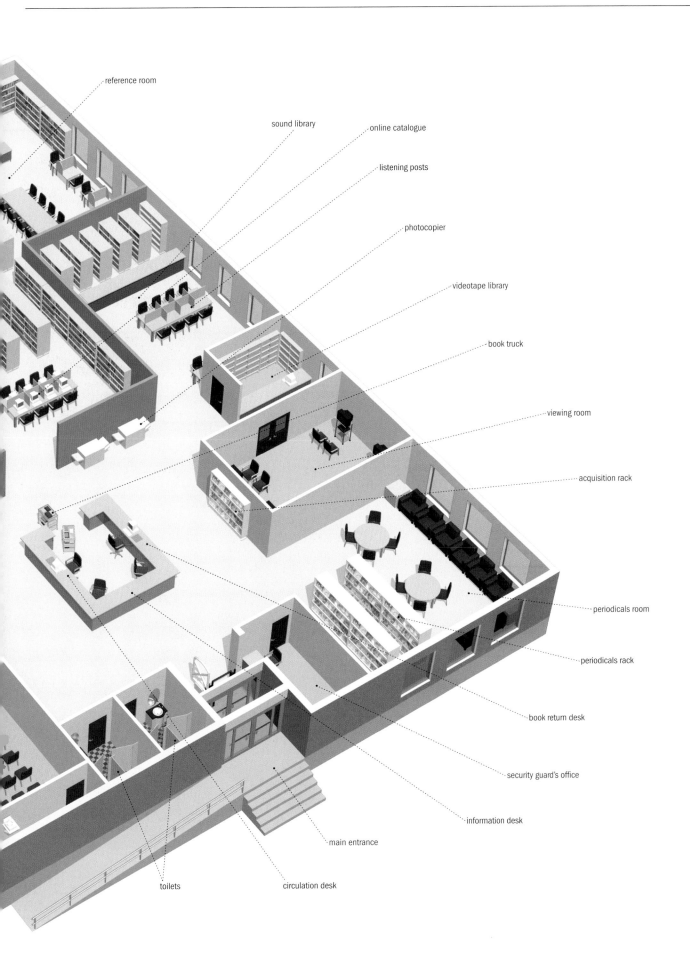

reference room

sound library

online catalogue

listening posts

photocopier

videotape library

book truck

viewing room

acquisition rack

periodicals room

periodicals rack

book return desk

security guard's office

information desk

main entrance

toilets

circulation desk

school

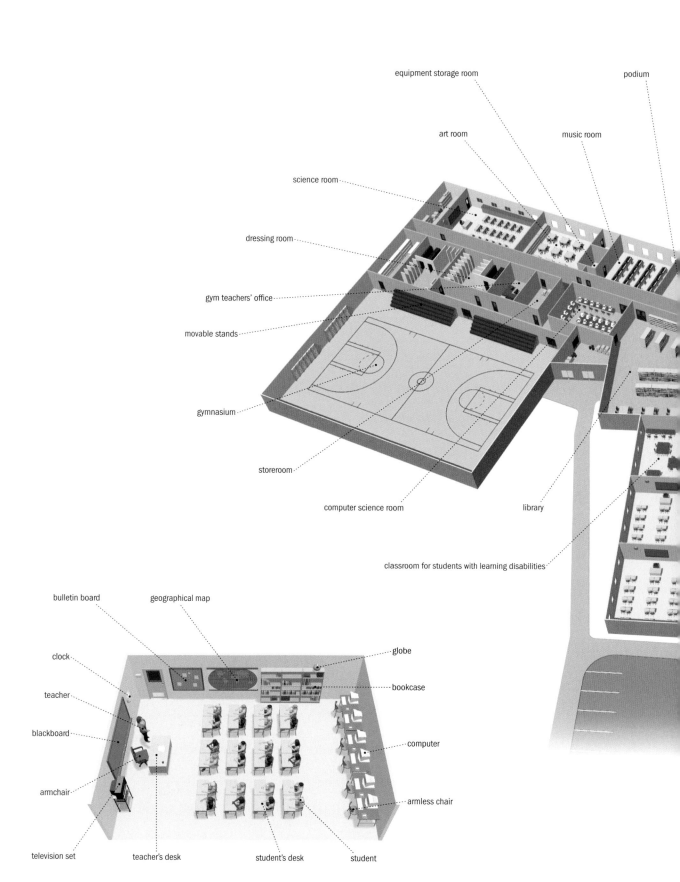

equipment storage room

podium

art room

music room

science room

dressing room

gym teachers' office

movable stands

gymnasium

storeroom

computer science room

library

classroom for students with learning disabilities

classroom

bulletin board

geographical map

clock

globe

teacher

bookcase

blackboard

computer

armchair

armless chair

television set

teacher's desk

student's desk

student

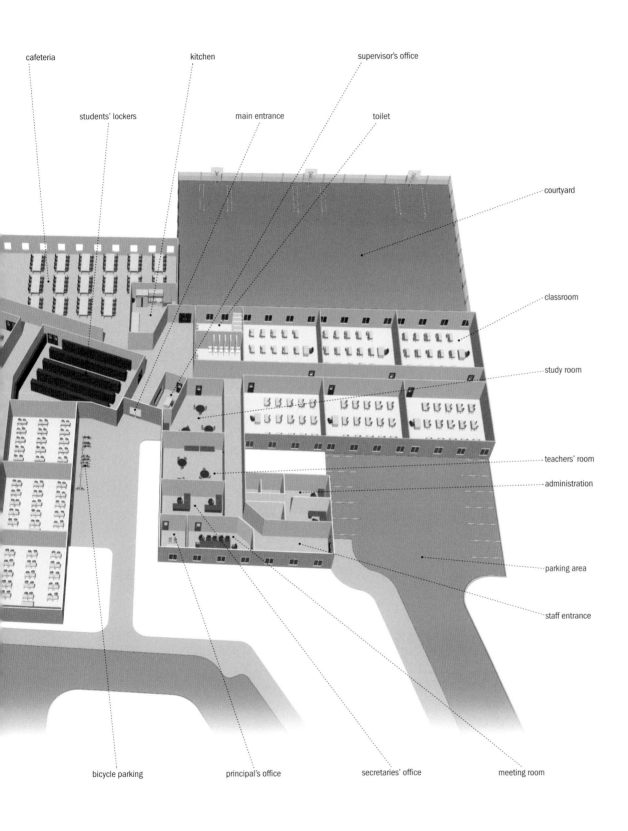

cafeteria

students' lockers

kitchen

main entrance

supervisor's office

toilet

courtyard

classroom

study room

teachers' room

administration

parking area

staff entrance

bicycle parking

principal's office

secretaries' office

meeting room

chronology of religions

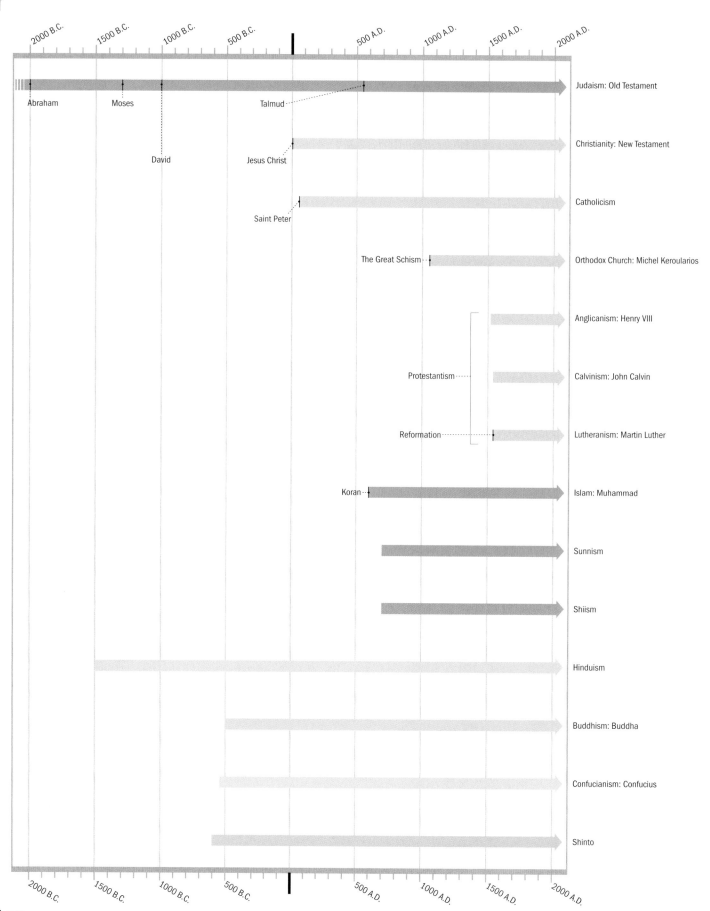

2000 B.C.	1500 B.C.	1000 B.C.	500 B.C.		500 A.D.	1000 A.D.	1500 A.D.	2000 A.D.

Judaism: Old Testament

Abraham   Moses   Talmud

David

Jesus Christ   Christianity: New Testament

Saint Peter   Catholicism

The Great Schism   Orthodox Church: Michel Keroularios

Anglicanism: Henry VIII

Protestantism   Calvinism: John Calvin

Reformation   Lutheranism: Martin Luther

Koran   Islam: Muhammad

Sunnism

Shiism

Hinduism

Buddhism: Buddha

Confucianism: Confucius

Shinto

SOCIETY

Catholic church

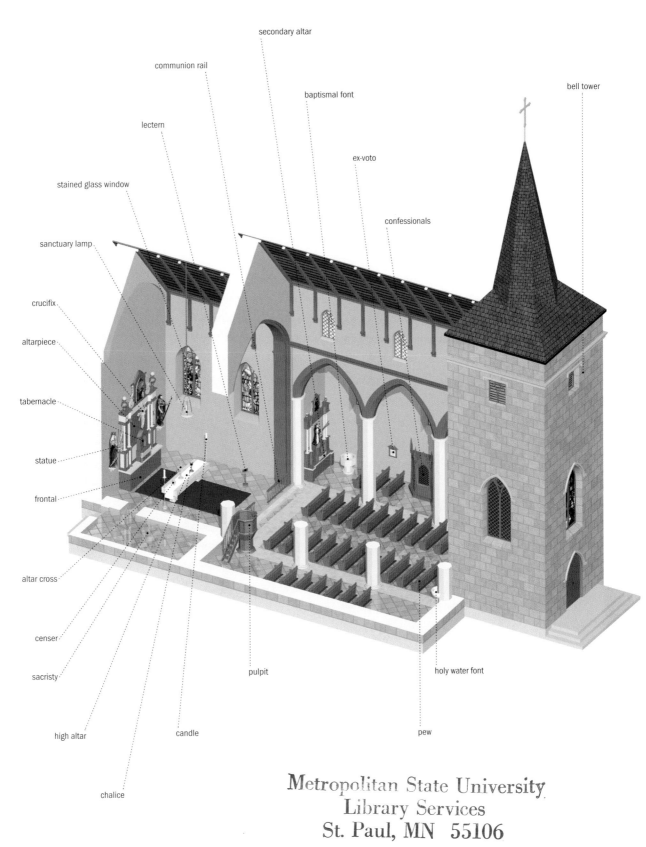

secondary altar

communion rail

baptismal font

lectern

ex-voto

stained glass window

bell tower

confessionals

sanctuary lamp

crucifix

altarpiece

tabernacle

statue

frontal

altar cross

censer

sacristy

pulpit

holy water font

high altar

candle

pew

chalice

Metropolitan State University
Library Services
St. Paul, MN 55106

synagogue

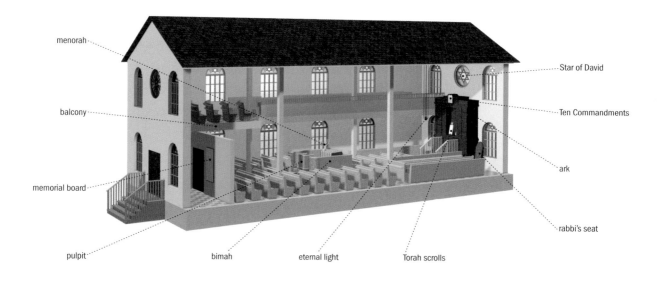

menorah

balcony

memorial board

pulpit

bimah

eternal light

Torah scrolls

Star of David

Ten Commandments

ark

rabbi's seat

mosque

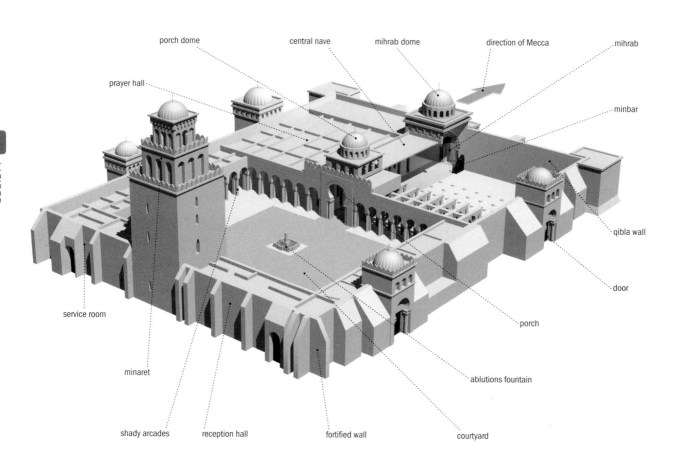

porch dome

central nave

mihrab dome

direction of Mecca

mihrab

prayer hall

minbar

qibla wall

door

service room

minaret

shady arcades

reception hall

fortified wall

courtyard

ablutions fountain

porch

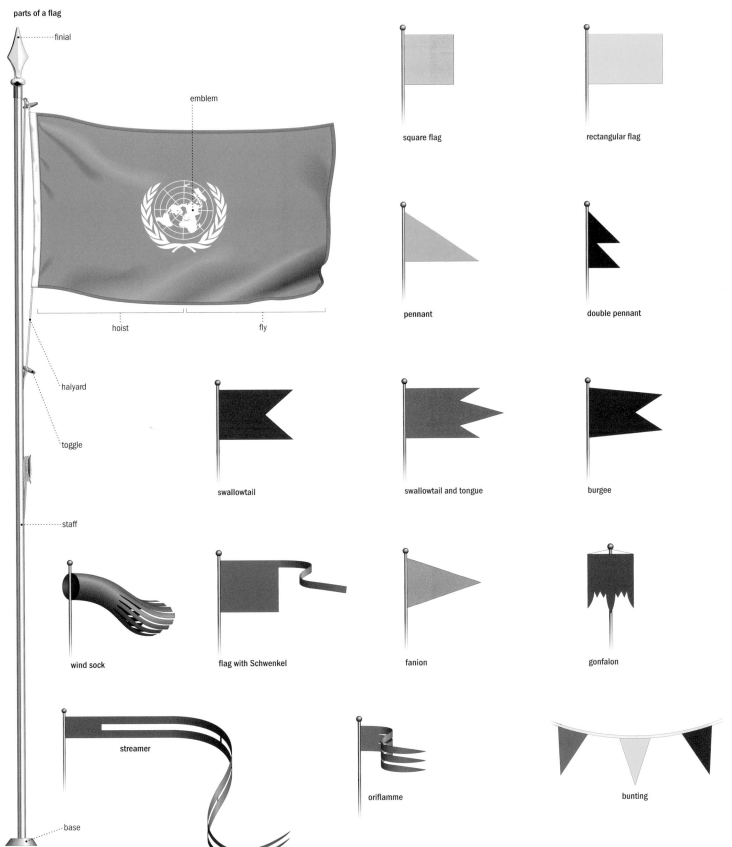

flag shapes

parts of a flag

finial

emblem

hoist

fly

halyard

toggle

staff

base

square flag

rectangular flag

pennant

double pennant

swallowtail

swallowtail and tongue

burgee

wind sock

flag with Schwenkel

fanion

gonfalon

streamer

oriflamme

bunting

heraldry

shield divisions

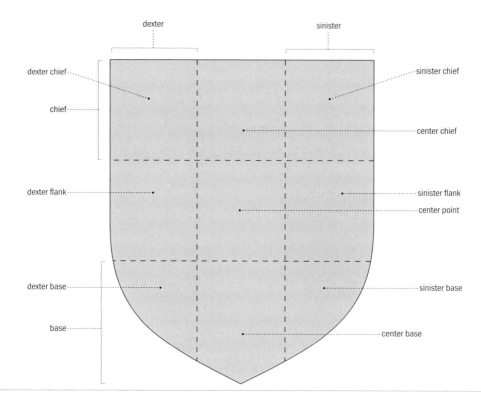

examples of partitions

per fess

party

per bend

quarterly

examples of ordinaries

chief

chevron

pale

cross

examples of metals

examples of furs

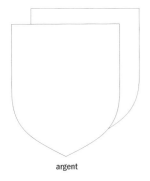

argent

or

ermine

vair

examples of charges

lion passant

fleur-de-lis

eagle

crescent

mullet

examples of colors

azure

gules

vert

purpure

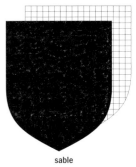

sable

SOCIETY

flags

Americas

1 Canada

2 United States of America

3 Mexico

4 Honduras

5 Guatemala

6 Belize

7 El Salvador

8 Nicaragua

9 Costa Rica

10 Panama

11 Colombia

12 Venezuela

13 Guyana

14 Suriname

15 Ecuador

16 Peru

17 Brazil

18 Bolivia

19 Paraguay

20 Chile

21 Argentina

22 Uruguay

Caribbean Islands

23 The Bahamas

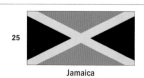

24 Cuba

25 Jamaica

26 Haiti

SOCIETY

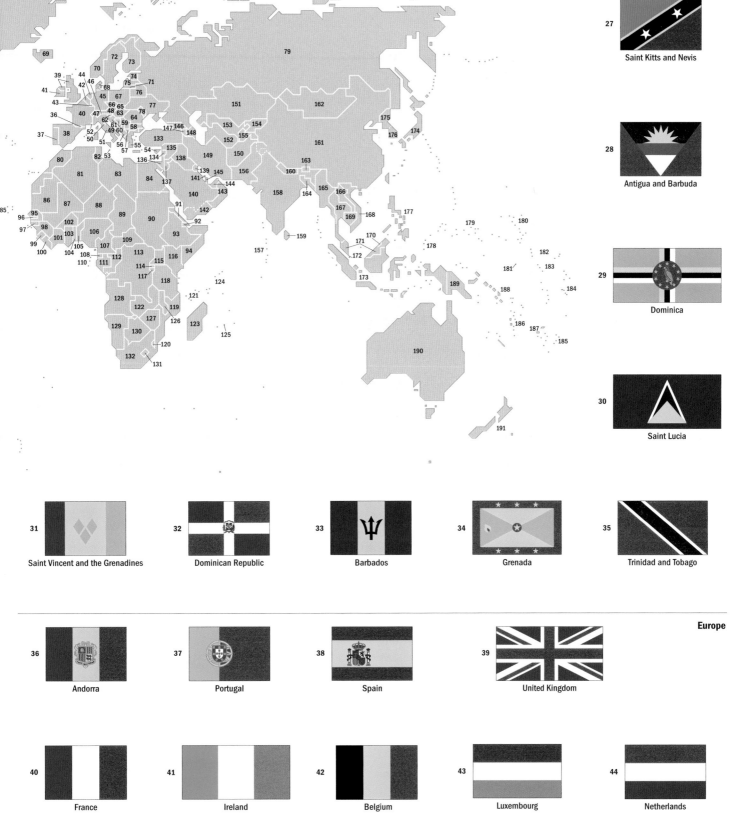

27 Saint Kitts and Nevis

28 Antigua and Barbuda

29 Dominica

30 Saint Lucia

31 Saint Vincent and the Grenadines

32 Dominican Republic

33 Barbados

34 Grenada

35 Trinidad and Tobago

Europe

36 Andorra

37 Portugal

38 Spain

39 United Kingdom

40 France

41 Ireland

42 Belgium

43 Luxembourg

44 Netherlands

flags

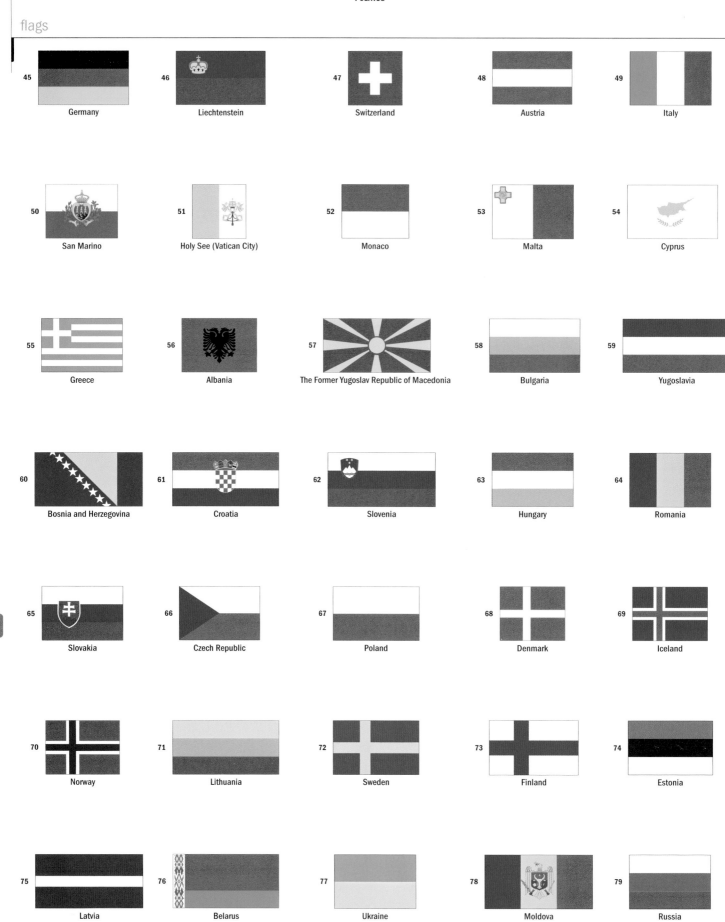

45 Germany

46 Liechtenstein

47 Switzerland

48 Austria

49 Italy

50 San Marino

51 Holy See (Vatican City)

52 Monaco

53 Malta

54 Cyprus

55 Greece

56 Albania

57 The Former Yugoslav Republic of Macedonia

58 Bulgaria

59 Yugoslavia

60 Bosnia and Herzegovina

61 Croatia

62 Slovenia

63 Hungary

64 Romania

65 Slovakia

66 Czech Republic

67 Poland

68 Denmark

69 Iceland

70 Norway

71 Lithuania

72 Sweden

73 Finland

74 Estonia

75 Latvia

76 Belarus

77 Ukraine

78 Moldova

79 Russia

SOCIETY

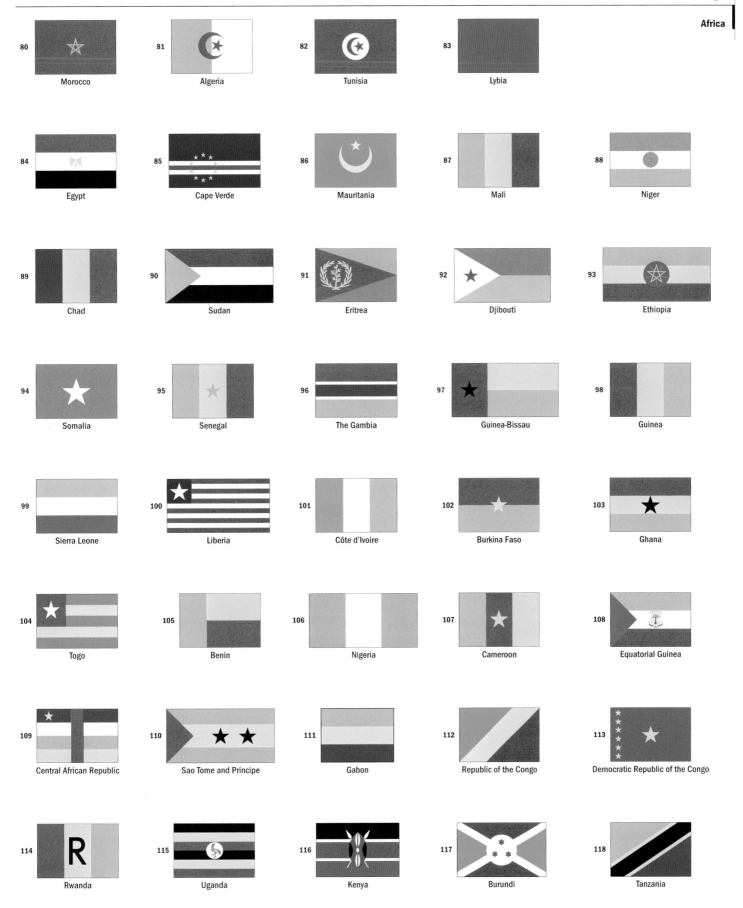

80 Morocco

81 Algeria

82 Tunisia

83 Lybia

84 Egypt

85 Cape Verde

86 Mauritania

87 Mali

88 Niger

89 Chad

90 Sudan

91 Eritrea

92 Djibouti

93 Ethiopia

94 Somalia

95 Senegal

96 The Gambia

97 Guinea-Bissau

98 Guinea

99 Sierra Leone

100 Liberia

101 Côte d'Ivoire

102 Burkina Faso

103 Ghana

104 Togo

105 Benin

106 Nigeria

107 Cameroon

108 Equatorial Guinea

109 Central African Republic

110 Sao Tome and Principe

111 Gabon

112 Republic of the Congo

113 Democratic Republic of the Congo

114 Rwanda

115 Uganda

116 Kenya

117 Burundi

118 Tanzania

SOCIETY

flags

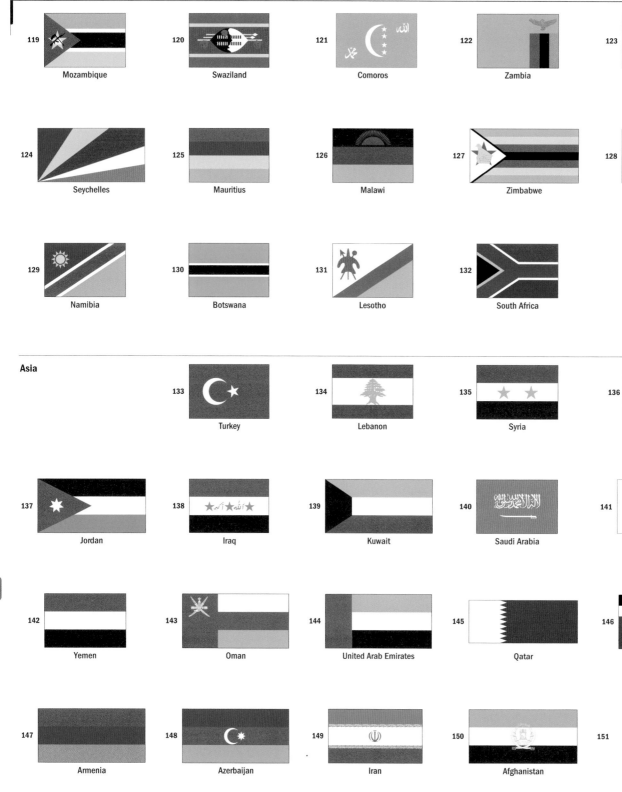

119 Mozambique	120 Swaziland
121 Comoros	122 Zambia
123 Madagascar	
124 Seychelles	125 Mauritius
126 Malawi	127 Zimbabwe
128 Angola	
129 Namibia	130 Botswana
131 Lesotho	132 South Africa

Asia

133 Turkey	134 Lebanon
135 Syria	136 Israel
137 Jordan	138 Iraq
139 Kuwait	140 Saudi Arabia
141 Bahrain	
142 Yemen	143 Oman
144 United Arab Emirates	145 Qatar
146 Georgia	
147 Armenia	148 Azerbaijan
149 Iran	150 Afghanistan
151 Kazakhstan	

Turkmenistan 152

Uzbekistan 153 Kyrgyzstan 154

Tajikistan 155

Pakistan 156

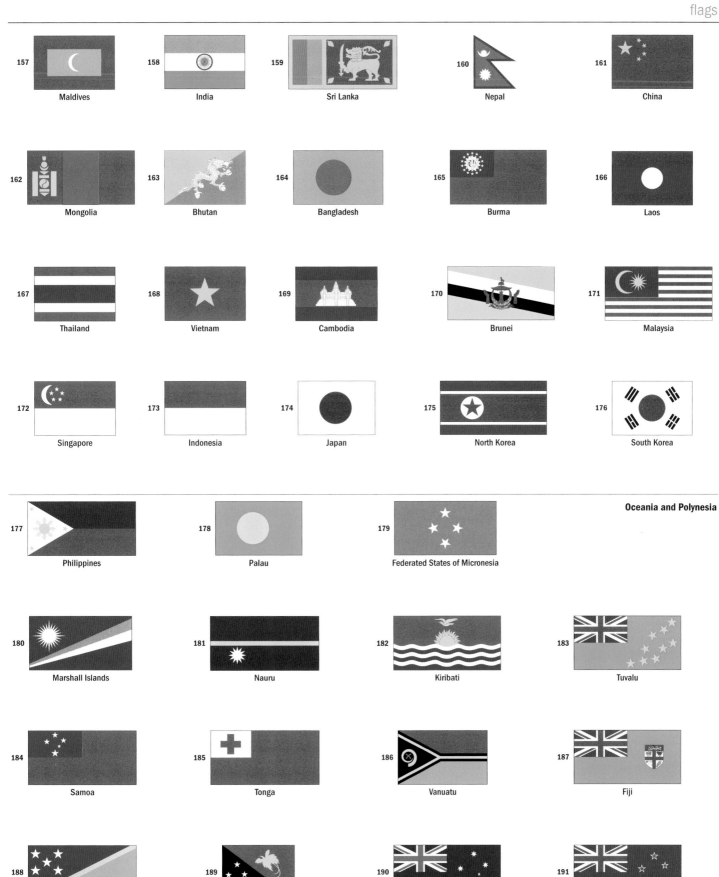

157 Maldives

158 India

159 Sri Lanka

160 Nepal

161 China

162 Mongolia

163 Bhutan

164 Bangladesh

165 Burma

166 Laos

167 Thailand

168 Vietnam

169 Cambodia

170 Brunei

171 Malaysia

172 Singapore

173 Indonesia

174 Japan

175 North Korea

176 South Korea

Oceania and Polynesia

177 Philippines

178 Palau

179 Federated States of Micronesia

180 Marshall Islands

181 Nauru

182 Kiribati

183 Tuvalu

184 Samoa

185 Tonga

186 Vanuatu

187 Fiji

188 Solomon Islands

189 Papua New Guinea

190 Australia

191 New Zealand

SOCIETY

weapons in the Stone Age

polished stone hand axe

flint arrowhead

flint knife

weapons in the age of the Romans

Roman legionary

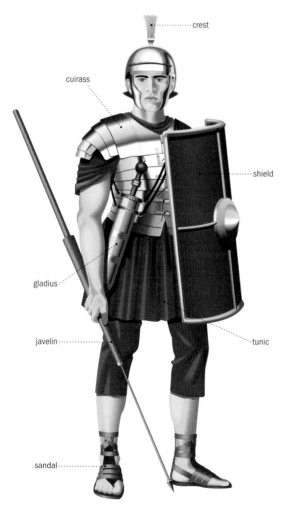

crest

cuirass

shield

gladius

javelin

tunic

sandal

Gallic warrior

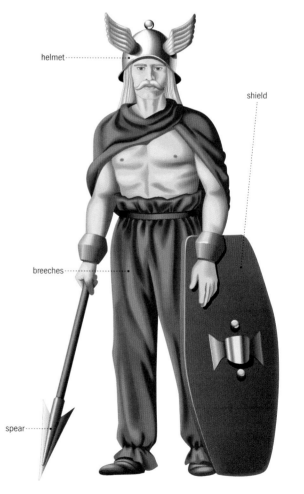

helmet

shield

breeches

spear

SOCIETY

armor

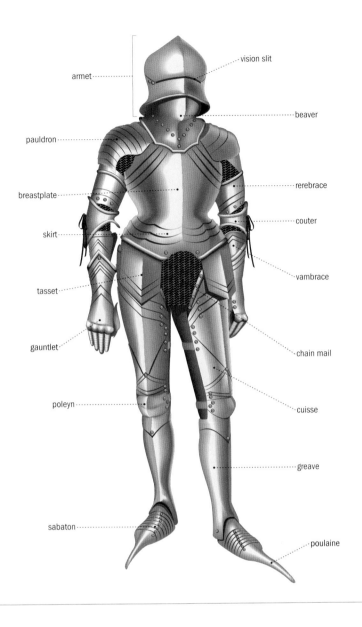

armet
- vision slit
- armet
- beaver
- pauldron
- rerebrace
- breastplate
- couter
- skirt
- vambrace
- tasset
- gauntlet
- chain mail
- poleyn
- cuisse
- greave
- sabaton
- poulaine

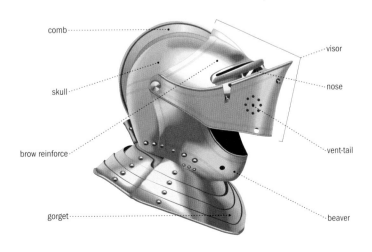

- comb
- visor
- skull
- nose
- brow reinforce
- vent-tail
- gorget
- beaver

bows and crossbow

crossbow

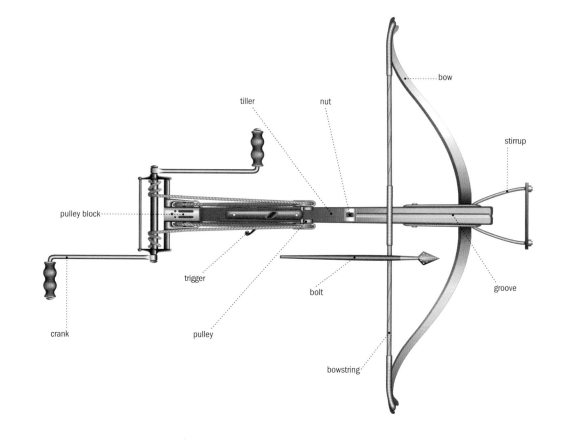

tiller

nut

bow

stirrup

pulley block

trigger

bolt

groove

crank

pulley

bowstring

bow

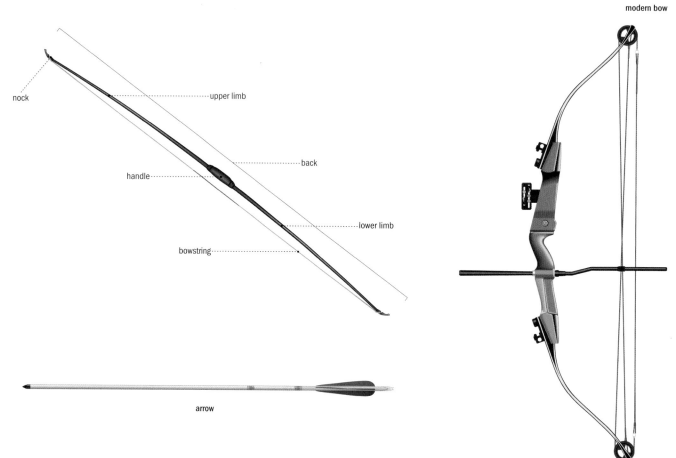

modern bow

nock

upper limb

back

handle

lower limb

bowstring

arrow

thrusting and cutting weapons

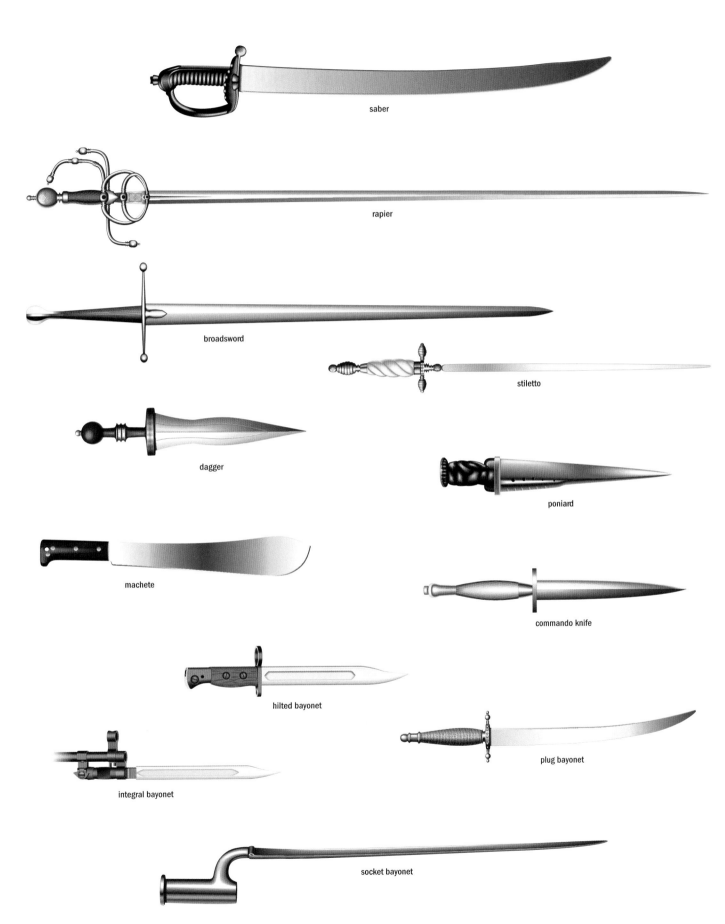

saber

rapier

broadsword

stiletto

dagger

poniard

machete

commando knife

hilted bayonet

plug bayonet

integral bayonet

socket bayonet

SOCIETY

harquebus

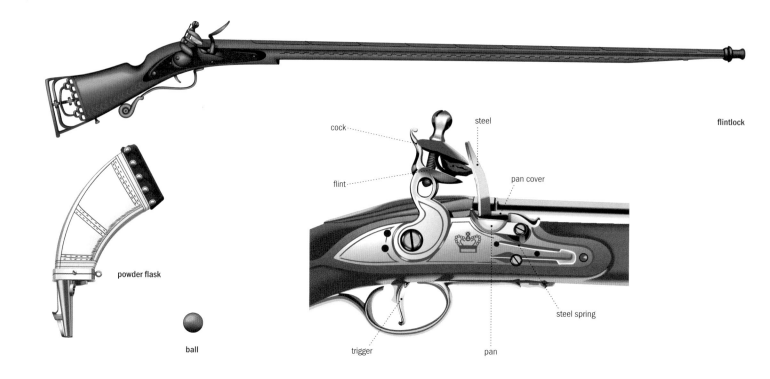

cock

steel

flint

pan cover

flintlock

powder flask

steel spring

ball

trigger

pan

seventeenth century cannon and mortar

firing accessories

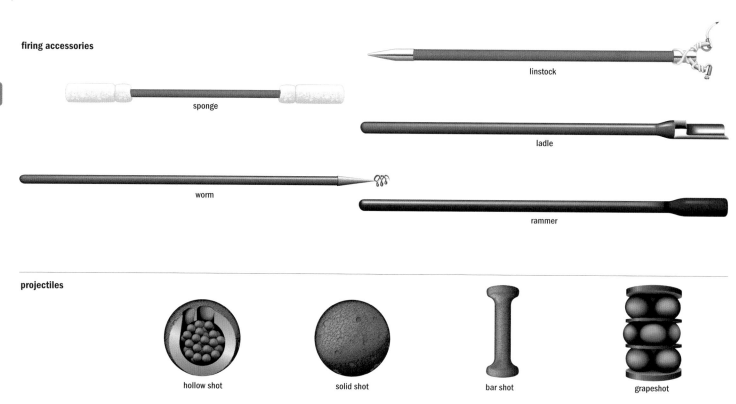

linstock

sponge

ladle

worm

rammer

projectiles

hollow shot

solid shot

bar shot

grapeshot

cross section of a muzzle loading

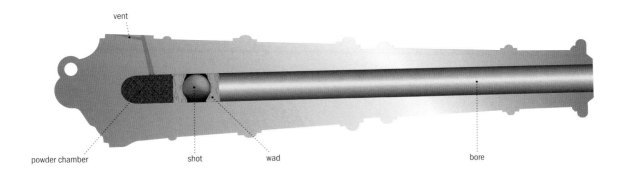

vent

powder chamber　　　　shot　　　wad　　　　　　　　　bore

muzzle loading

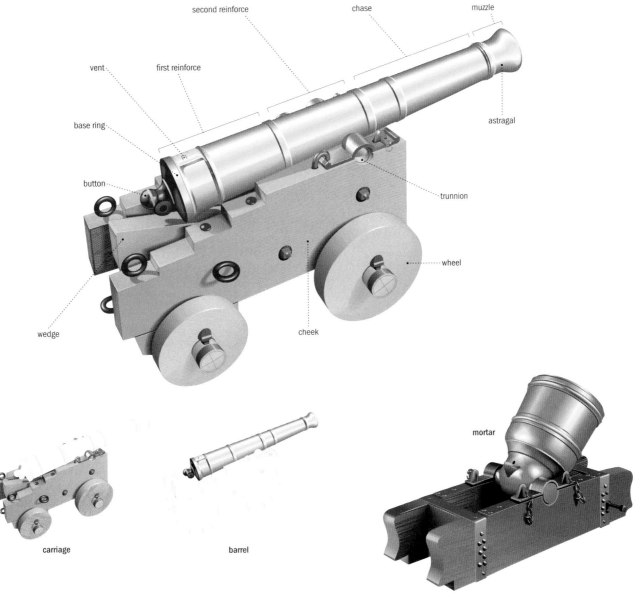

second reinforce　　　　　chase　　　　muzzle

vent　　　first reinforce

astragal

base ring

button

trunnion

wheel

wedge　　　　　　　　　　　cheek

mortar

carriage　　　　　　　barrel

submachine gun

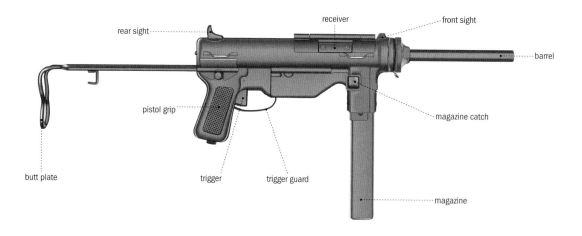

rear sight ·········

receiver

front sight ·········

barrel

pistol grip ·········

magazine catch

butt plate

trigger

trigger guard

magazine

pistol

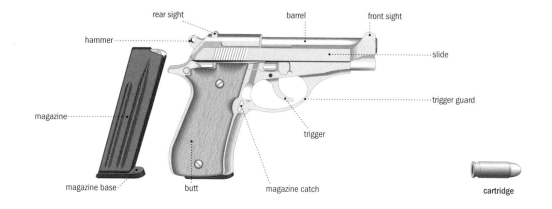

rear sight

barrel

front sight

hammer ·········

slide

magazine ·········

trigger guard

magazine base ·········

butt

magazine catch

trigger

cartridge

revolver

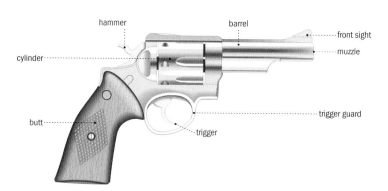

hammer

barrel

front sight

cylinder ·········

muzzle

butt ·········

trigger guard

trigger

automatic rifle

receiver rear sight barrel

bolt assist mechanism ejection port barrel jacket front sight housing

charging handle

handguard flash hider

pistol grip

magazine

butt trigger safety

light machine gun

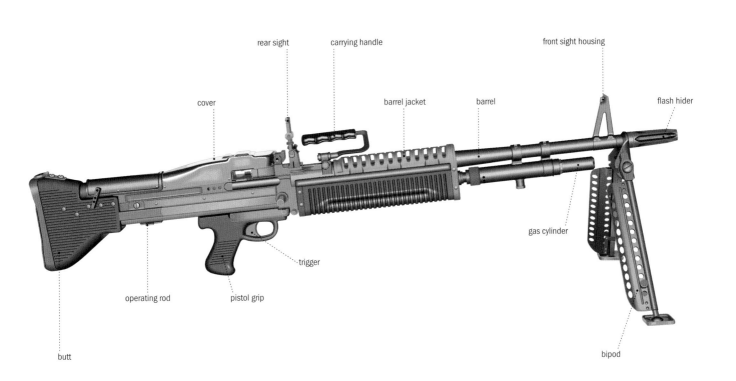

rear sight carrying handle front sight housing

cover barrel jacket barrel flash hider

gas cylinder

trigger

operating rod pistol grip

butt bipod

modern howitzer

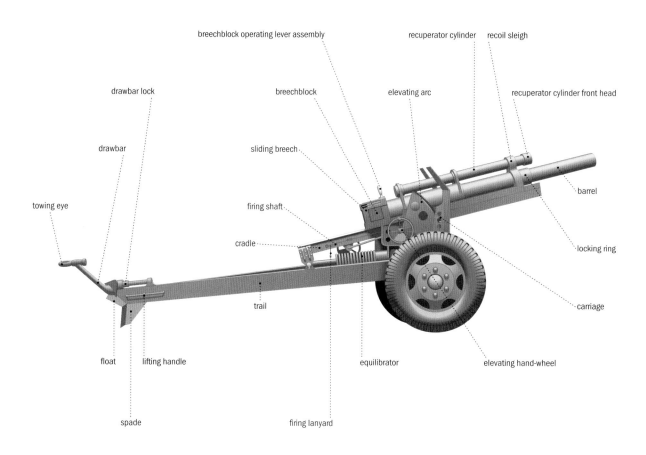

breechblock operating lever assembly

recuperator cylinder   recoil sleigh

drawbar lock

breechblock   elevating arc

recuperator cylinder front head

drawbar

sliding breech

towing eye

firing shaft

cradle

barrel

locking ring

trail

carriage

float   lifting handle

equilibrator

elevating hand-wheel

spade

firing lanyard

modern mortar

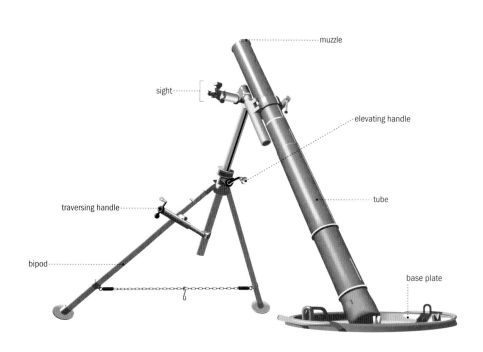

muzzle

sight

elevating handle

traversing handle

tube

bipod

base plate

hand grenade

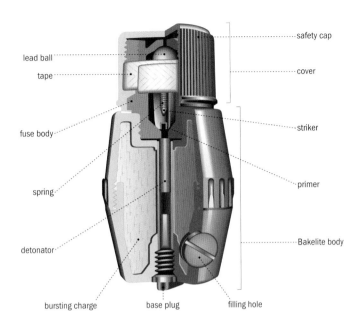

safety cap

lead ball

tape

cover

fuse body

striker

spring

primer

detonator

Bakelite body

bursting charge

base plug

filling hole

bazooka

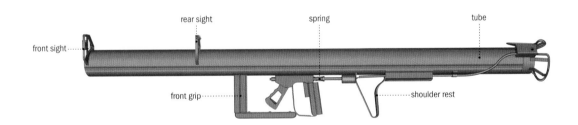

rear sight

spring

tube

front sight

front grip

shoulder rest

recoilless rifle

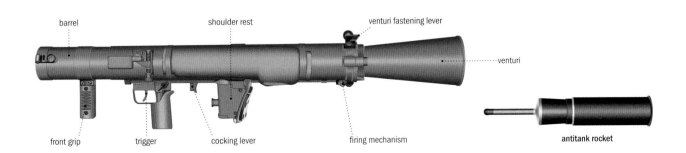

barrel

shoulder rest

venturi fastening lever

venturi

front grip

trigger

cocking lever

firing mechanism

antitank rocket

antipersonnel mine

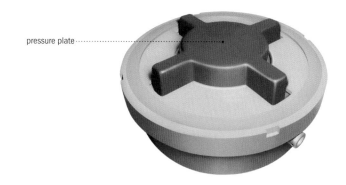

pressure plate

tank

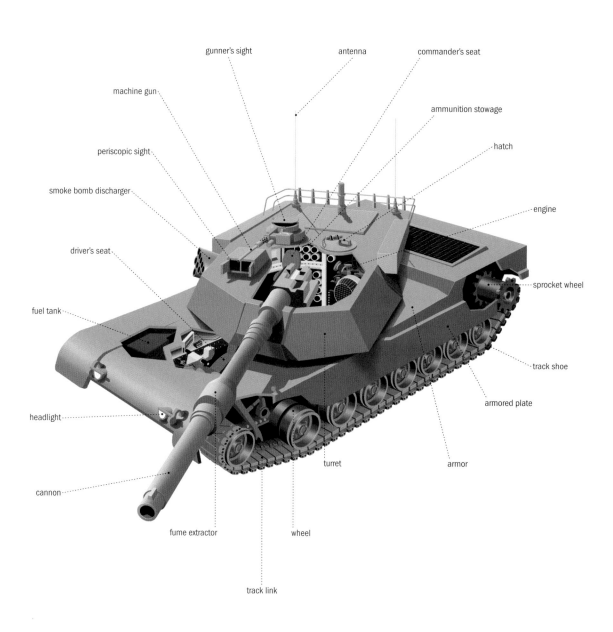

gunner's sight

antenna

commander's seat

machine gun

ammunition stowage

periscopic sight

hatch

smoke bomb discharger

engine

driver's seat

sprocket wheel

fuel tank

track shoe

armored plate

headlight

armor

cannon

turret

fume extractor

wheel

track link

missiles

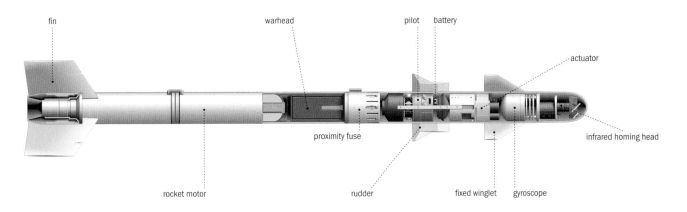

fin

warhead

pilot battery

actuator

infrared homing head

proximity fuse

rocket motor

rudder

fixed winglet gyroscope

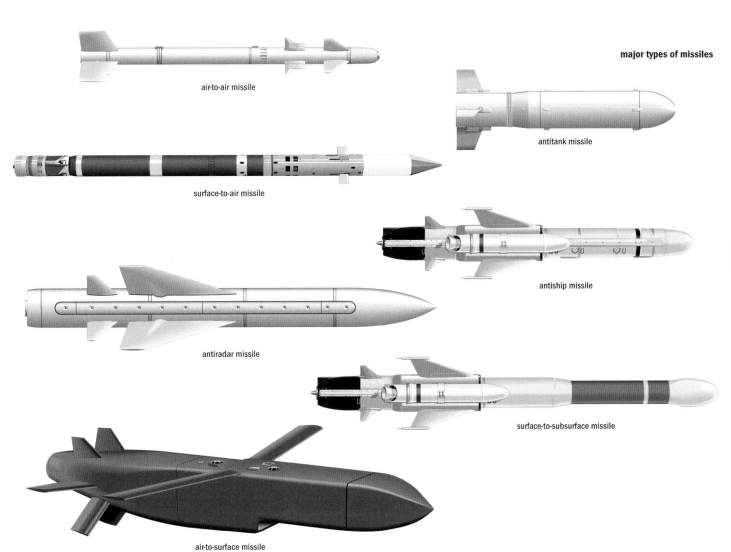

major types of missiles

air-to-air missile

antitank missile

surface-to-air missile

antiship missile

antiradar missile

surface-to-subsurface missile

air-to-surface missile

SOCIETY

combat aircraft

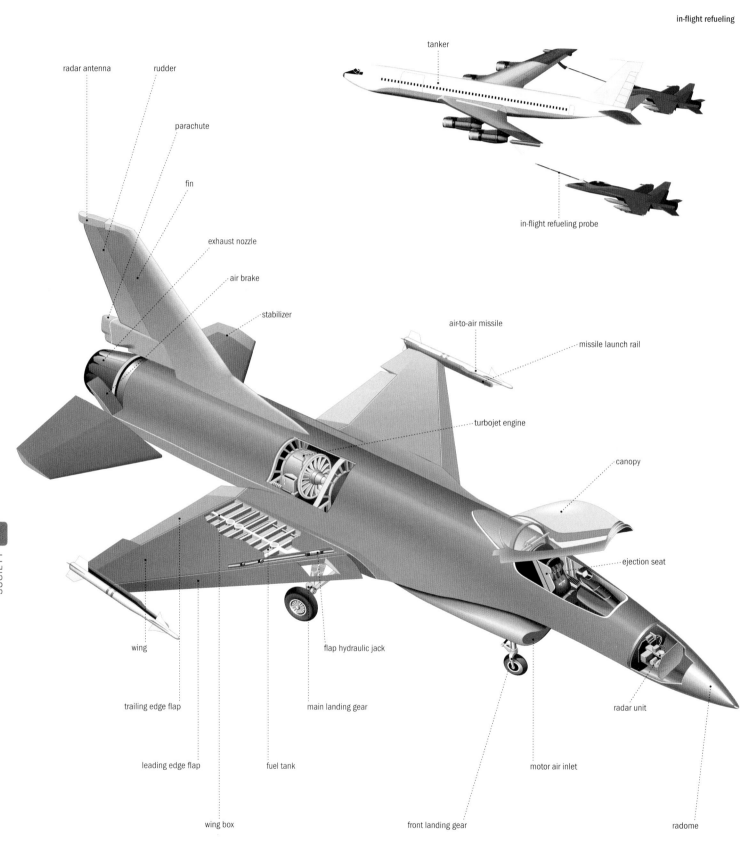

in-flight refueling

tanker

in-flight refueling probe

radar antenna

rudder

parachute

fin

exhaust nozzle

air brake

stabilizer

air-to-air missile

missile launch rail

turbojet engine

canopy

ejection seat

wing

flap hydraulic jack

radar unit

trailing edge flap

main landing gear

leading edge flap

fuel tank

motor air inlet

radome

wing box

front landing gear

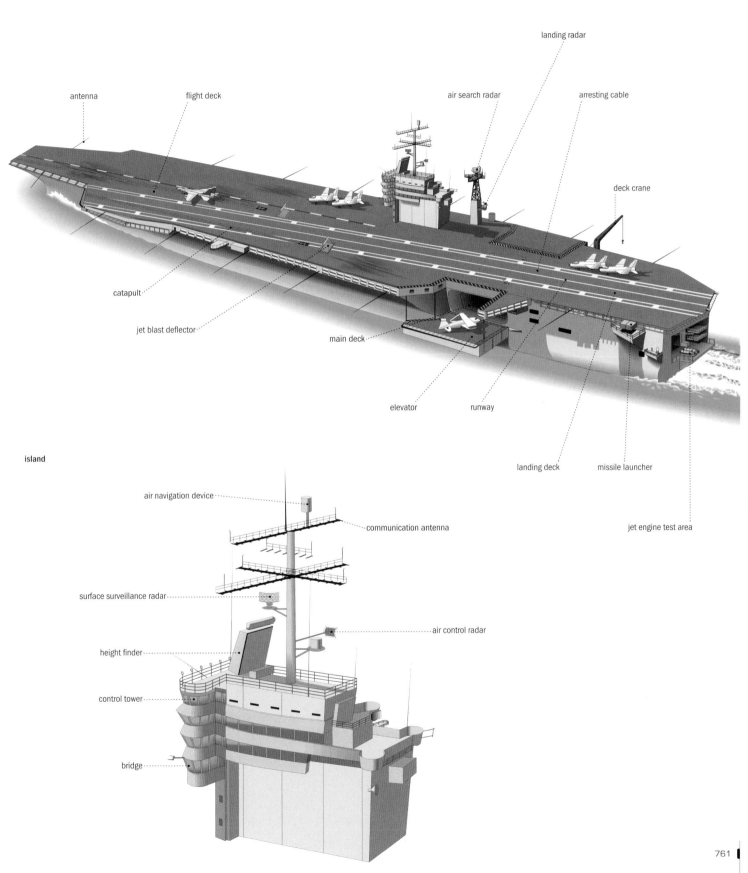

landing radar

antenna

flight deck

air search radar

arresting cable

deck crane

catapult

jet blast deflector

main deck

elevator

runway

landing deck

missile launcher

island

air navigation device

communication antenna

surface surveillance radar

air control radar

height finder

control tower

bridge

jet engine test area

frigate

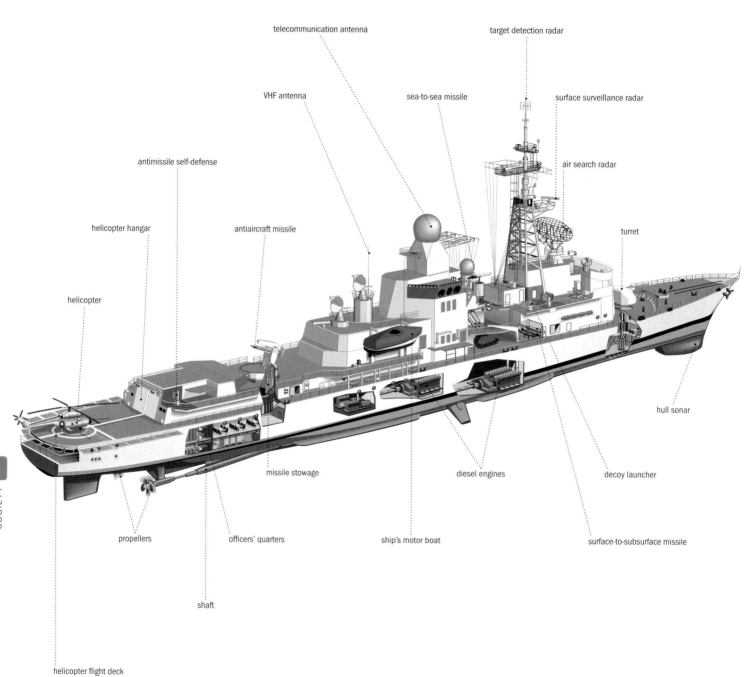

telecommunication antenna

target detection radar

VHF antenna

sea-to-sea missile

surface surveillance radar

antimissile self-defense

air search radar

helicopter hangar

antiaircraft missile

turret

helicopter

hull sonar

missile stowage

diesel engines

decoy launcher

propellers

officers' quarters

ship's motor boat

surface-to-subsurface missile

shaft

helicopter flight deck

nuclear submarine

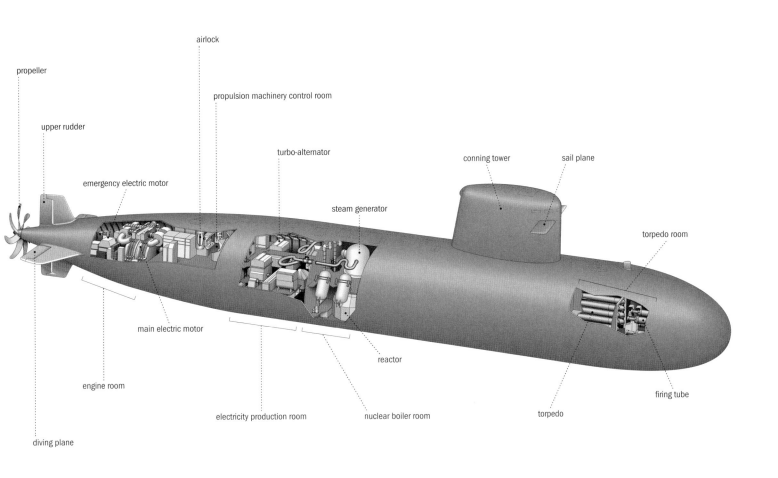

propeller

airlock

upper rudder

propulsion machinery control room

emergency electric motor

turbo-alternator

conning tower

sail plane

steam generator

torpedo room

main electric motor

reactor

firing tube

engine room

torpedo

diving plane

electricity production room

nuclear boiler room

conning tower

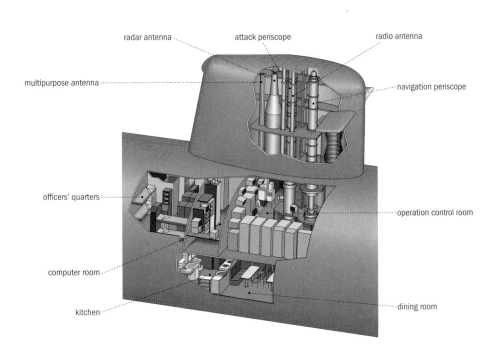

radar antenna

attack periscope

radio antenna

multipurpose antenna

navigation periscope

officers' quarters

operation control room

computer room

dining room

kitchen

fire prevention

fire station

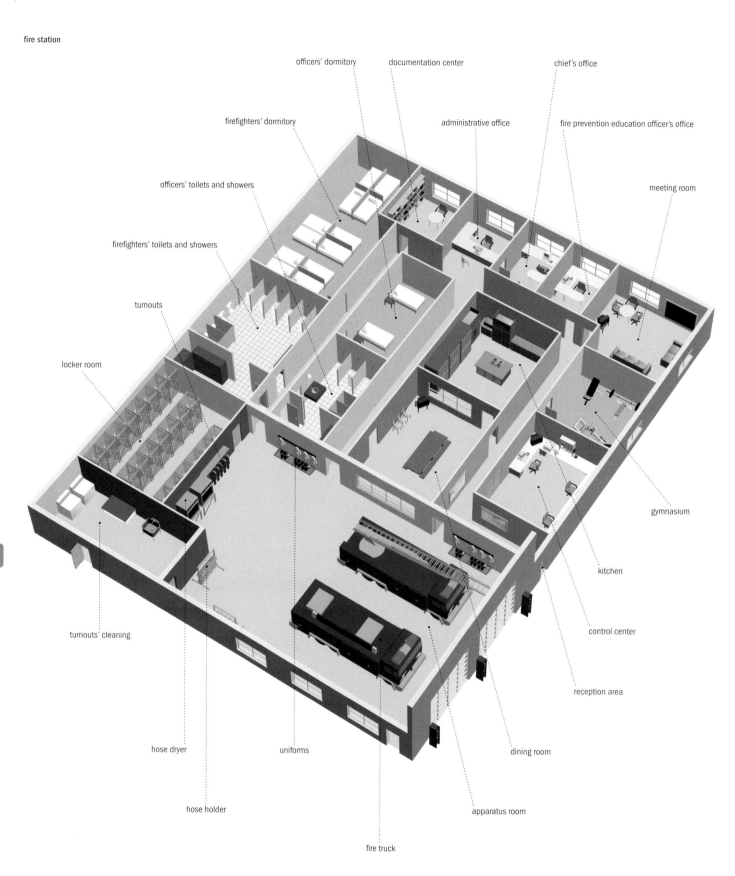

officers' dormitory

documentation center

chief's office

firefighters' dormitory

administrative office

fire prevention education officer's office

officers' toilets and showers

meeting room

firefighters' toilets and showers

turnouts

locker room

gymnasium

turnouts' cleaning

kitchen

control center

reception area

hose dryer

uniforms

dining room

hose holder

apparatus room

fire truck

hand lamp

firefighter

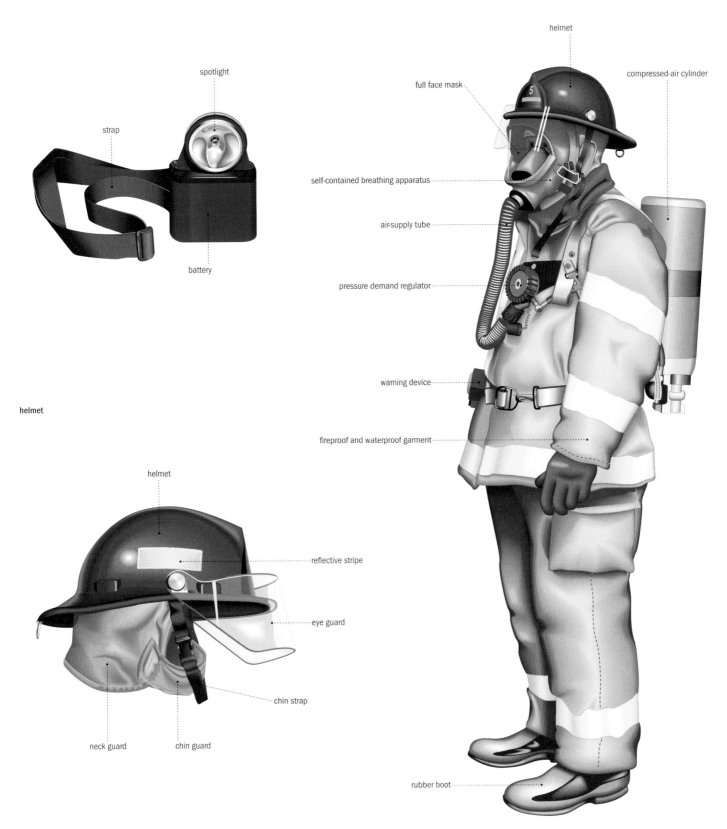

spotlight

strap

battery

helmet

full face mask

compressed-air cylinder

self-contained breathing apparatus

air-supply tube

pressure demand regulator

warning device

helmet

fireproof and waterproof garment

helmet

reflective stripe

eye guard

chin strap

neck guard

chin guard

rubber boot

fire prevention

fire engines

pumper

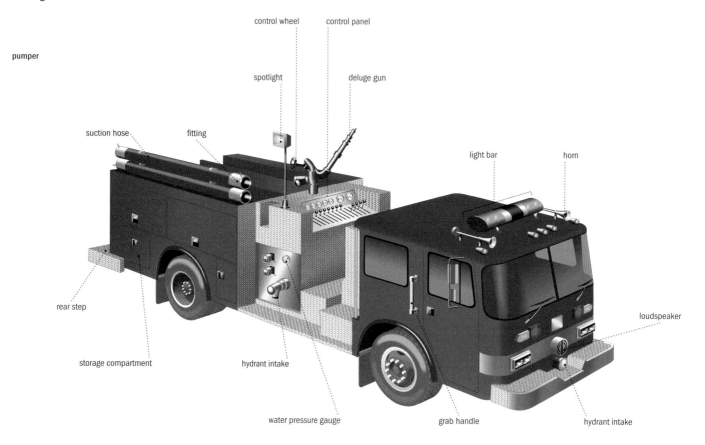

control wheel

control panel

spotlight

deluge gun

suction hose

fitting

light bar

horn

rear step

loudspeaker

storage compartment

hydrant intake

water pressure gauge

grab handle

hydrant intake

aerial ladder truck

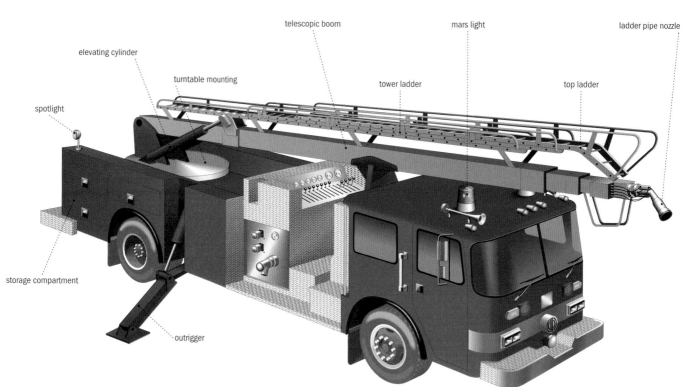

telescopic boom

mars light

ladder pipe nozzle

elevating cylinder

turntable mounting

tower ladder

top ladder

spotlight

storage compartment

outrigger

fire hydrant

cover

base

test button

indicator light

smoke detector

fire-fighting materials

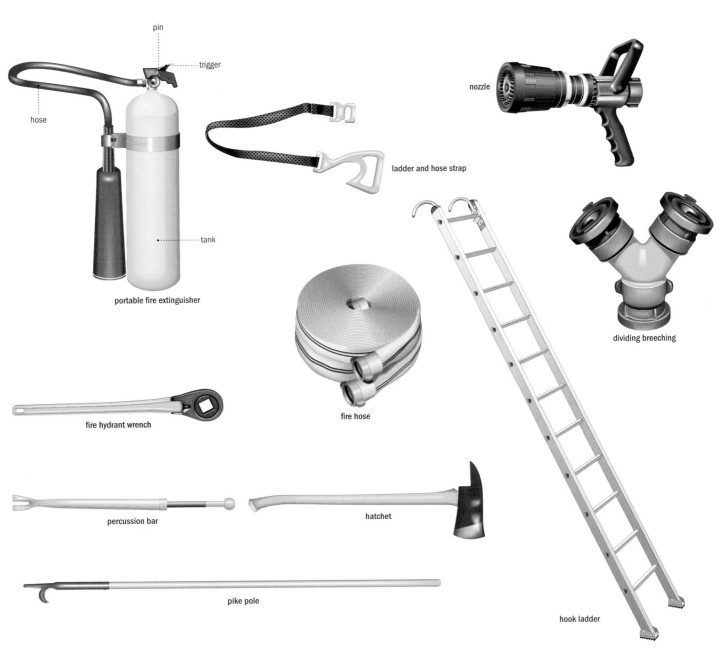

pin

trigger

hose

nozzle

ladder and hose strap

tank

portable fire extinguisher

dividing breeching

fire hose

fire hydrant wrench

percussion bar

hatchet

pike pole

hook ladder

SOCIETY

crime prevention

police station

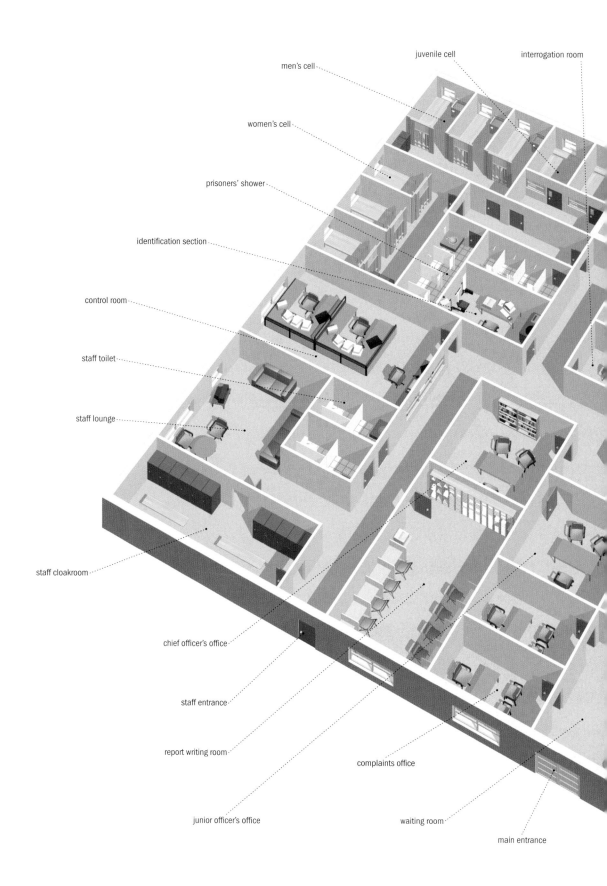

men's cell

juvenile cell

interrogation room

women's cell

prisoners' shower

identification section

control room

staff toilet

staff lounge

staff cloakroom

chief officer's office

staff entrance

report writing room

complaints office

junior officer's office

waiting room

main entrance

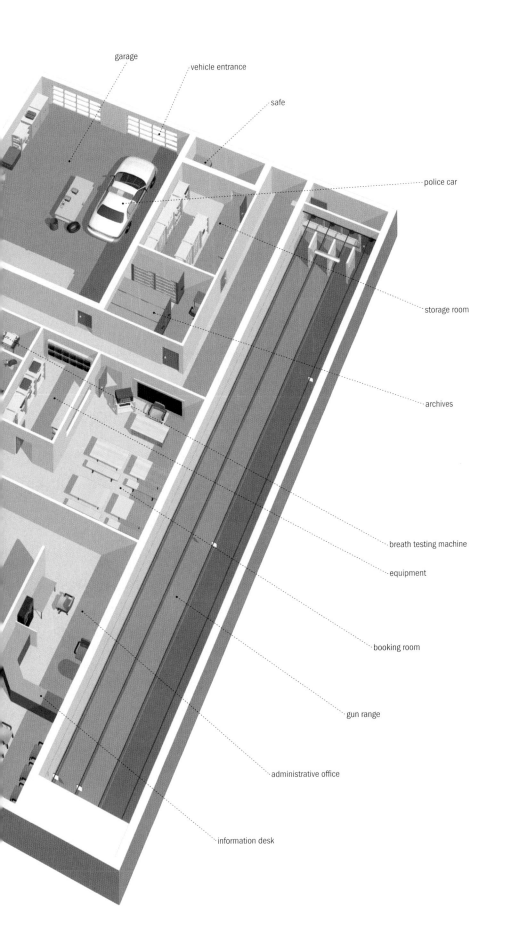

garage

vehicle entrance

safe

police car

storage room

archives

breath testing machine

equipment

booking room

gun range

administrative office

information desk

crime prevention

police officer

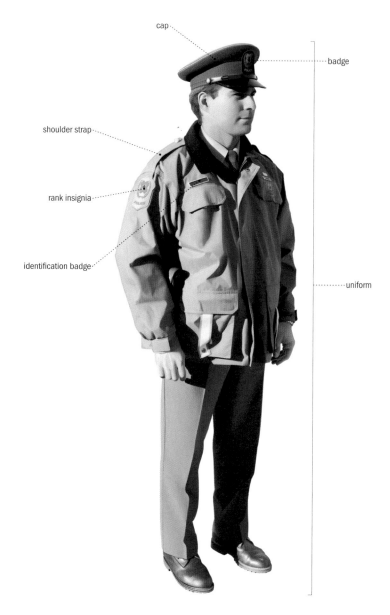

cap

badge

shoulder strap

rank insignia

identification badge

uniform

duty belt

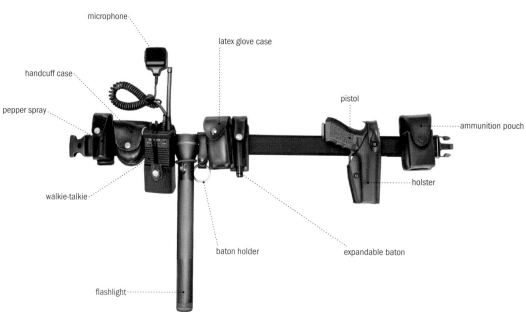

microphone

latex glove case

handcuff case

pistol

pepper spray

ammunition pouch

holster

walkie-talkie

baton holder

expandable baton

flashlight

dashboard equipment

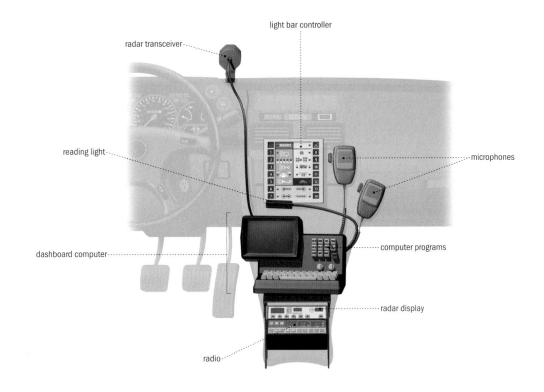

radar transceiver

light bar controller

reading light

microphones

dashboard computer

computer programs

radar display

radio

police car

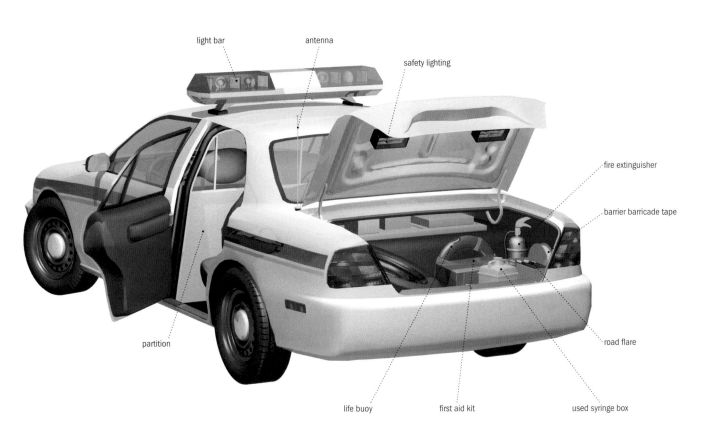

light bar

antenna

safety lighting

fire extinguisher

barrier barricade tape

partition

road flare

life buoy

first aid kit

used syringe box

ear protection

safety earmuffs

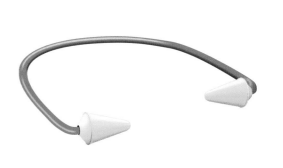

headband

foam cushion

earplugs

eye protection

safety glasses

safety goggles

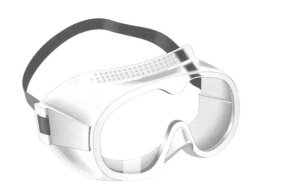

head protection

hard hat

rib

peak

suspension band   headband

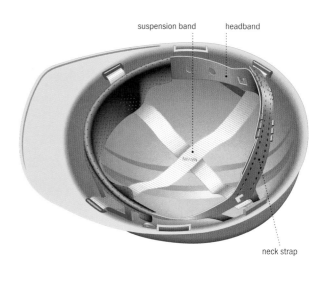

neck strap

respiratory system protection

respirator

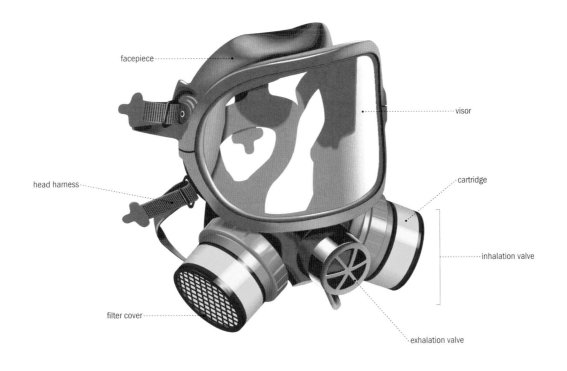

facepiece

visor

head harness

cartridge

inhalation valve

filter cover

exhalation valve

half-mask respirator

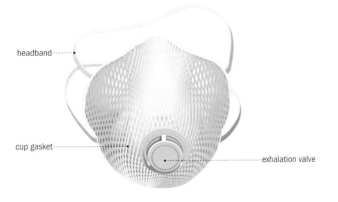

headband

cup gasket

exhalation valve

foot protection

safety boot

toe guard

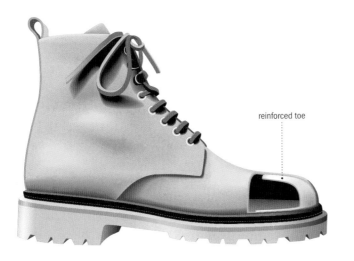

reinforced toe

safety symbols

dangerous materials

corrosive

electrical hazard

explosive

flammable

radioactive

poison

protection

eye protection

ear protection

head protection

hand protection

foot protection

respiratory system protection

ambulance

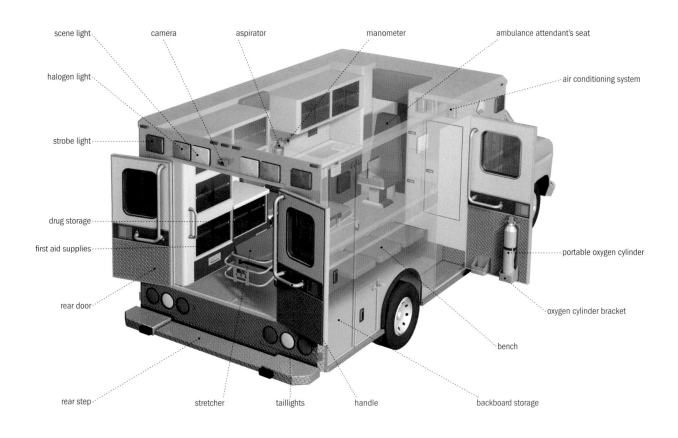

scene light
camera
aspirator
manometer
ambulance attendant's seat

halogen light
air conditioning system

strobe light

drug storage

first aid supplies

portable oxygen cylinder

rear door

oxygen cylinder bracket

bench

rear step
stretcher
taillights
handle
backboard storage

first aid equipment

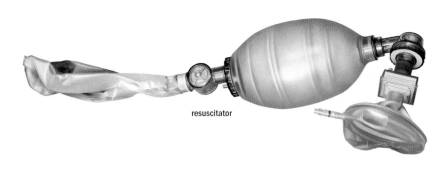

resuscitator

oxygen mask

oropharyngeal airway

cervical collar

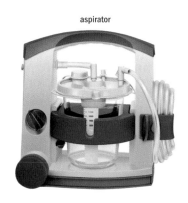

aspirator

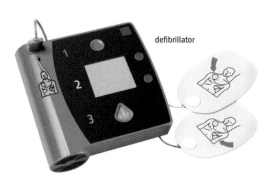

defibrillator

SOCIETY

first aid equipment

stethoscope

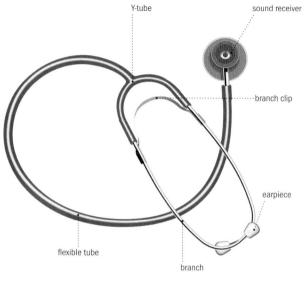

Y-tube
sound receiver
branch clip
earpiece
flexible tube
branch

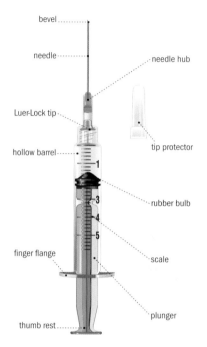

bevel
needle
needle hub
Luer-Lock tip
tip protector
hollow barrel
rubber bulb
finger flange
scale
plunger
thumb rest

latex glove

syringe for irrigation

cot

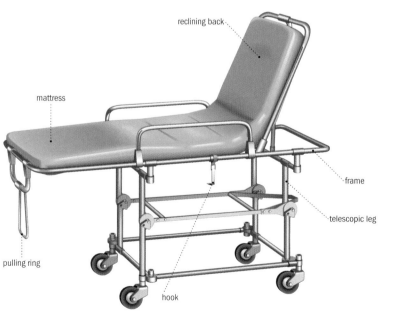

reclining back
mattress
frame
telescopic leg
pulling ring
hook

SOCIETY

stretcher

first aid kit

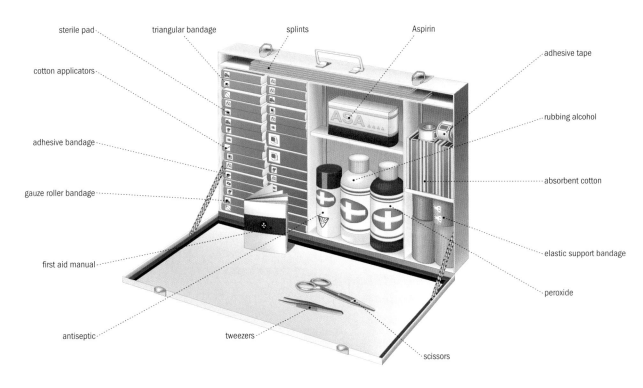

sterile pad

triangular bandage

splints

Aspirin

adhesive tape

cotton applicators

rubbing alcohol

adhesive bandage

absorbent cotton

gauze roller bandage

elastic support bandage

first aid manual

peroxide

antiseptic

tweezers

scissors

clinical thermometers

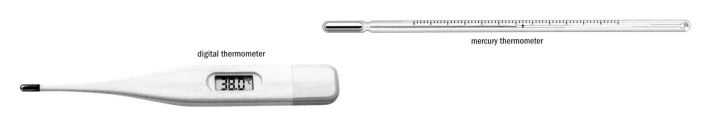

mercury thermometer

digital thermometer

blood pressure monitor

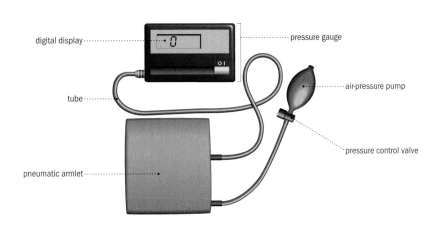

digital display

pressure gauge

air-pressure pump

tube

pressure control valve

pneumatic armlet

SOCIETY

hospital

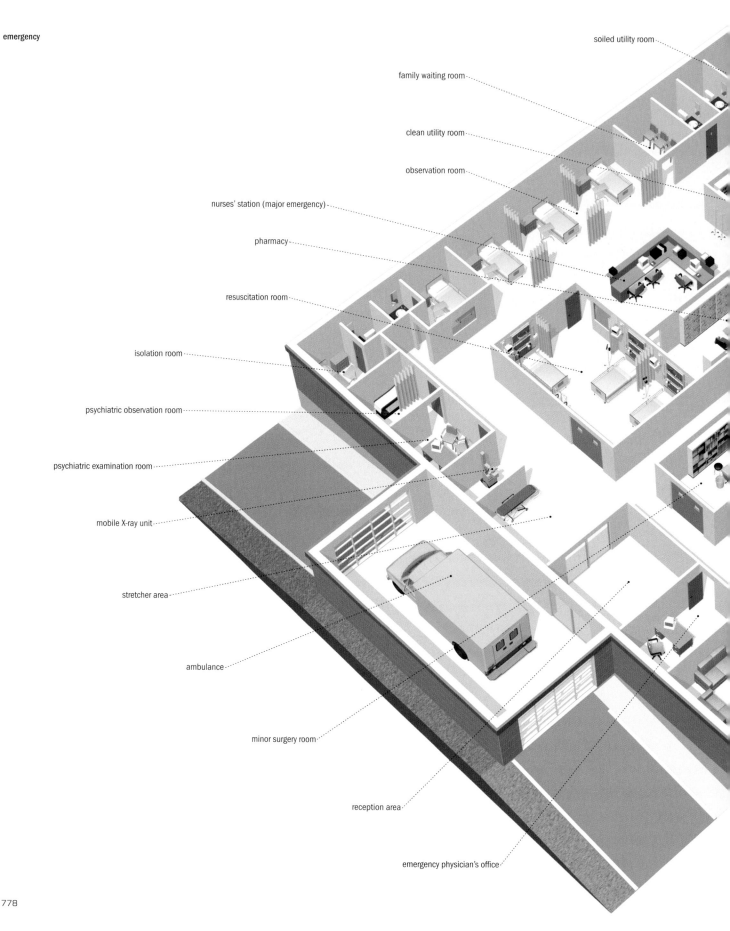

emergency

soiled utility room

family waiting room

clean utility room

observation room

nurses' station (major emergency)

pharmacy

resuscitation room

isolation room

psychiatric observation room

psychiatric examination room

mobile X-ray unit

stretcher area

ambulance

minor surgery room

reception area

emergency physician's office

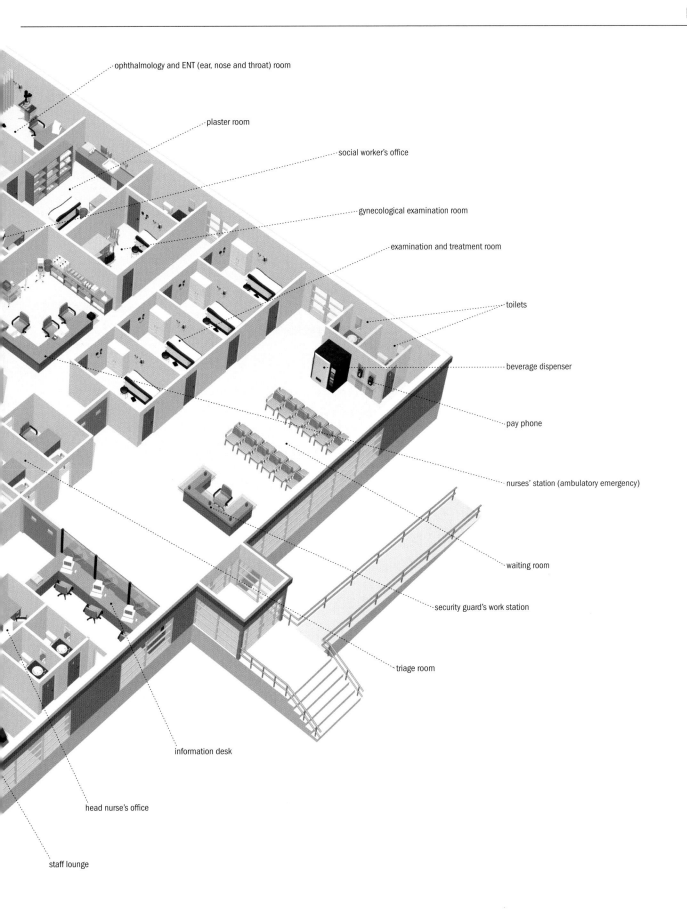

ophthalmology and ENT (ear, nose and throat) room

plaster room

social worker's office

gynecological examination room

examination and treatment room

toilets

beverage dispenser

pay phone

nurses' station (ambulatory emergency)

waiting room

security guard's work station

triage room

information desk

head nurse's office

staff lounge

hospital

patient room

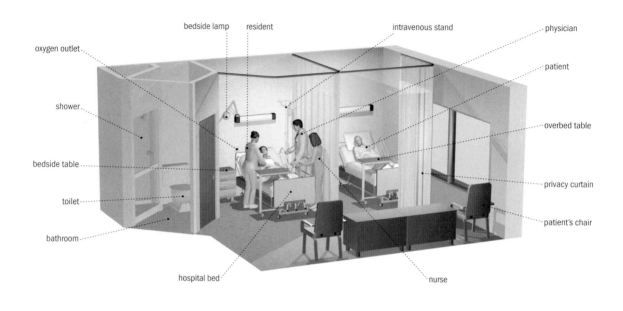

bedside lamp   resident   intravenous stand   physician

oxygen outlet

patient

shower

overbed table

bedside table

toilet

privacy curtain

bathroom

patient's chair

hospital bed

nurse

operating suite

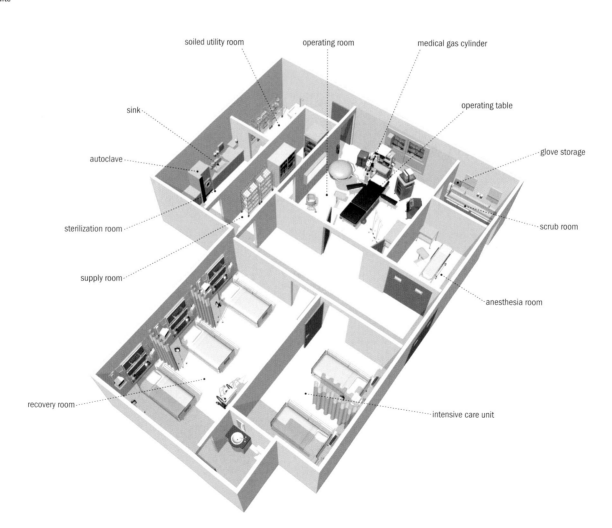

soiled utility room   operating room   medical gas cylinder

sink

operating table

autoclave

glove storage

sterilization room

scrub room

supply room

anesthesia room

recovery room

intensive care unit

ambulatory care unit

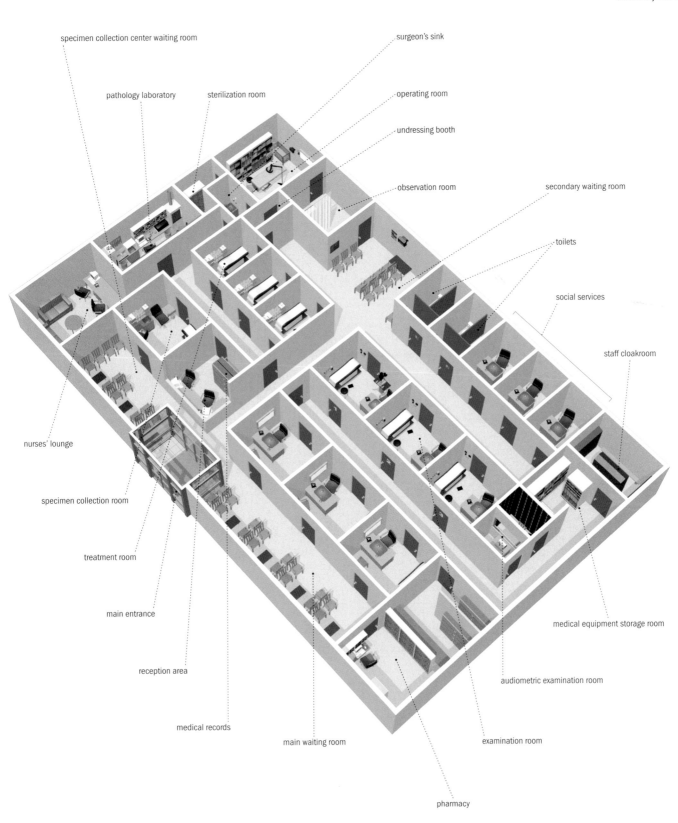

specimen collection center waiting room

pathology laboratory

sterilization room

surgeon's sink

operating room

undressing booth

observation room

secondary waiting room

toilets

social services

staff cloakroom

nurses' lounge

specimen collection room

treatment room

main entrance

reception area

medical records

main waiting room

pharmacy

examination room

audiometric examination room

medical equipment storage room

walking aids

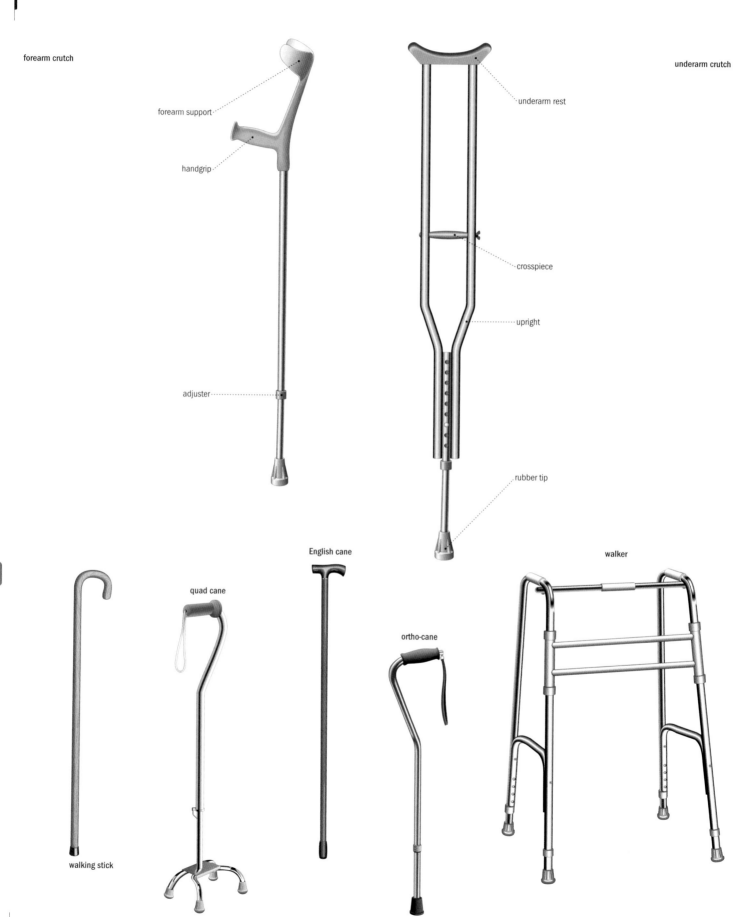

forearm crutch

forearm support

handgrip

adjuster

underarm crutch

underarm rest

crosspiece

upright

rubber tip

English cane

quad cane

ortho-cane

walker

walking stick

wheelchair

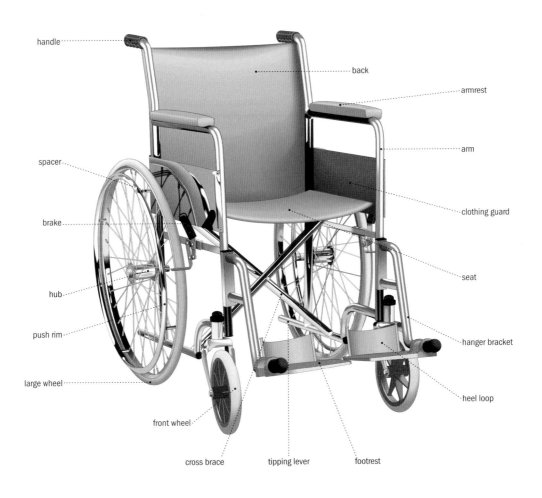

handle

back

armrest

arm

spacer

clothing guard

brake

seat

hub

push rim

hanger bracket

large wheel

heel loop

front wheel

cross brace

tipping lever

footrest

forms of medications

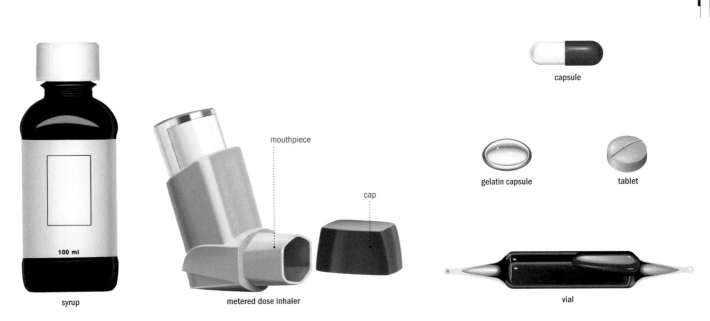

syrup

mouthpiece

cap

metered dose inhaler

capsule

gelatin capsule

tablet

100 ml

vial

family relationships

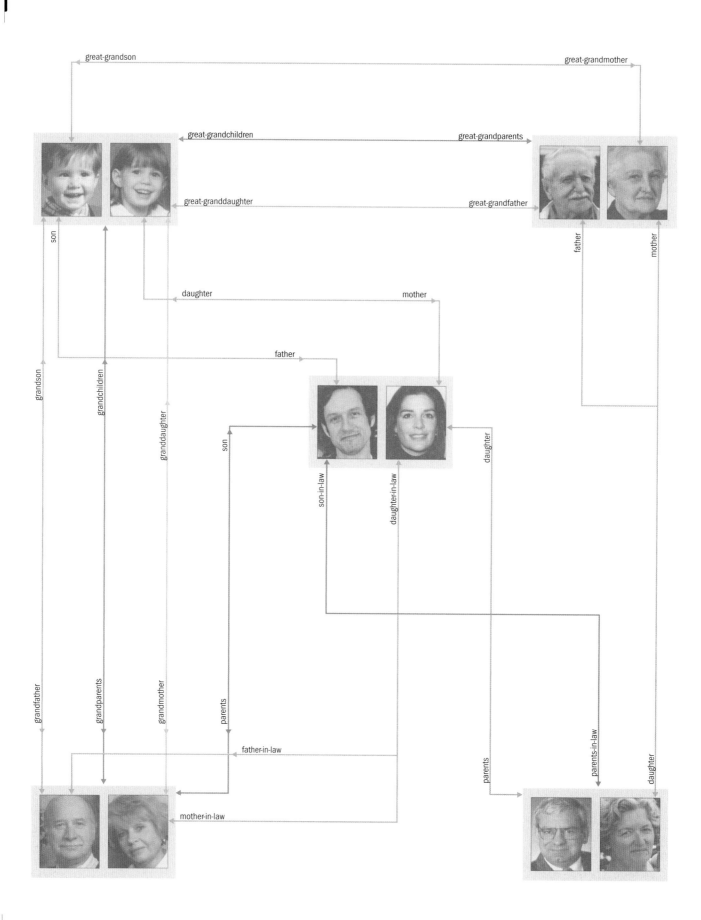

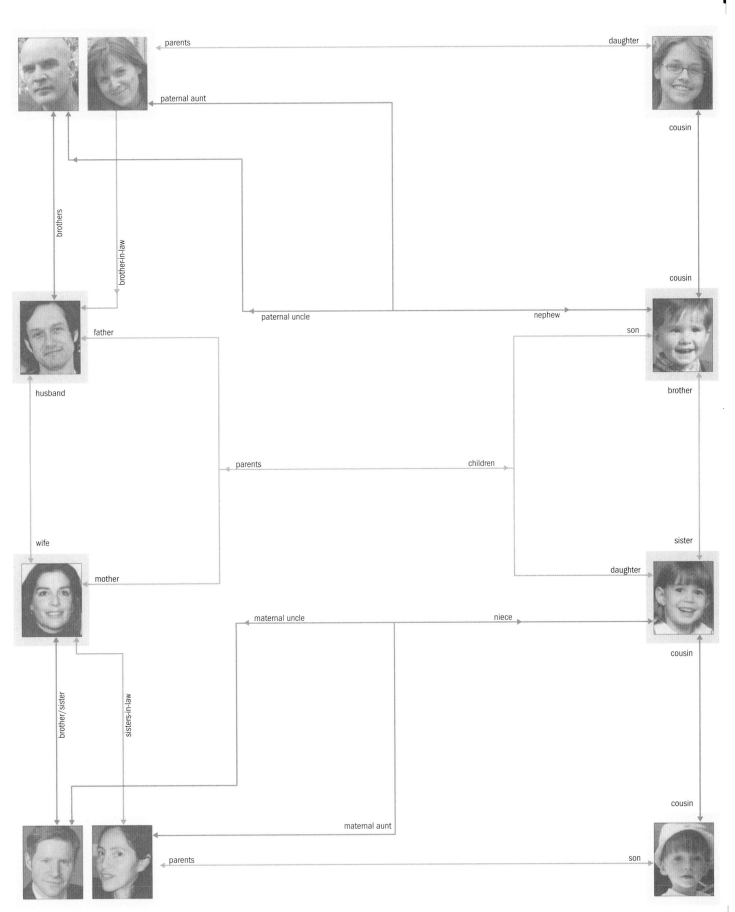

parents

daughter

cousin

paternal aunt

brothers

brother-in-law

cousin

paternal uncle

nephew

father

son

husband

brother

parents

children

wife

sister

mother

daughter

maternal uncle

niece

cousin

brother/sister

sisters-in-law

cousin

maternal aunt

parents

son

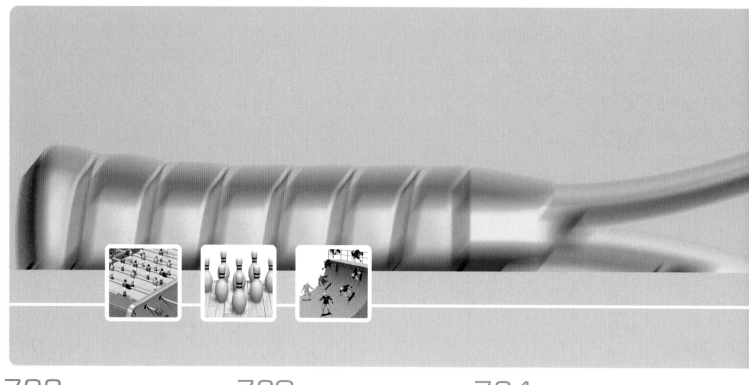

SPORTS AND GAMES

sports complex

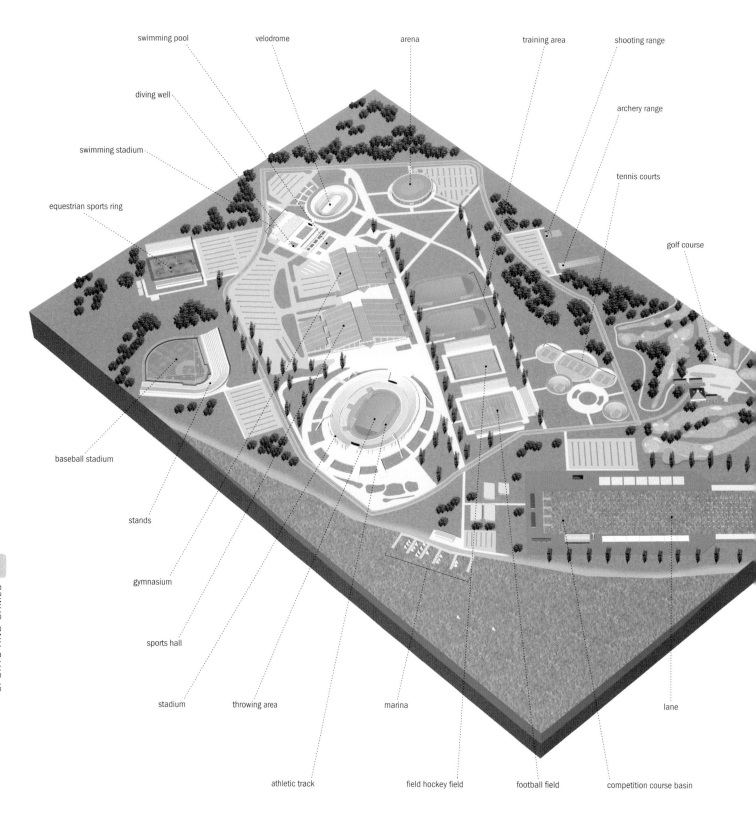

swimming pool

velodrome

arena

training area

shooting range

diving well

archery range

swimming stadium

tennis courts

equestrian sports ring

golf course

baseball stadium

stands

gymnasium

sports hall

stadium

throwing area

marina

athletic track

field hockey field

football field

lane

competition course basin

scoreboard

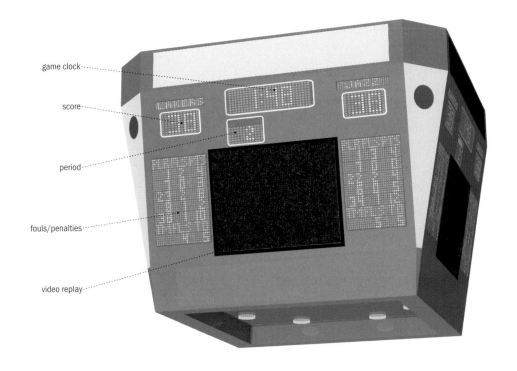

game clock

score

period

fouls/penalties

video replay

competition

draw

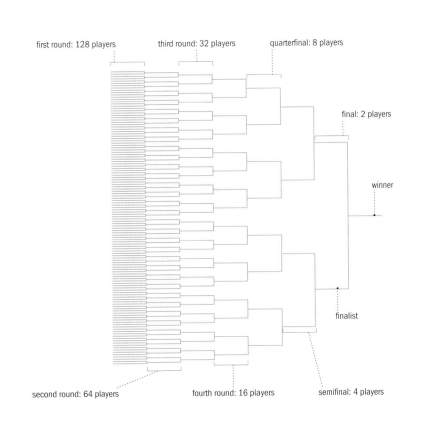

first round: 128 players

third round: 32 players

quarterfinal: 8 players

final: 2 players

winner

finalist

second round: 64 players

fourth round: 16 players

semifinal: 4 players

SPORTS AND GAMES

arena

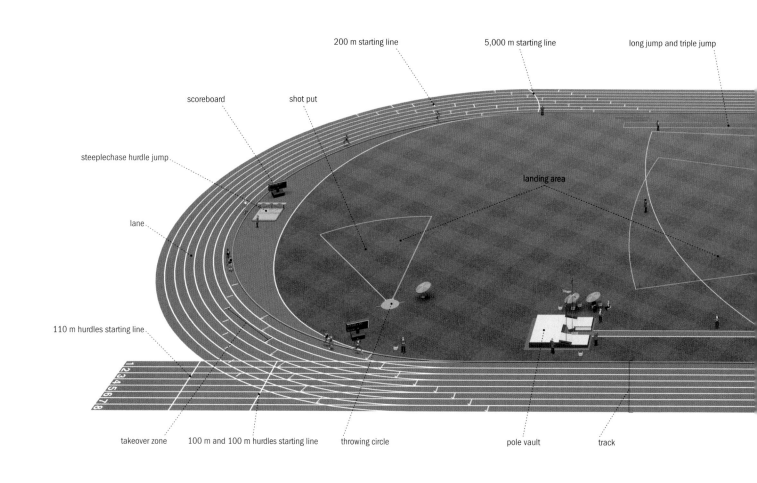

200 m starting line

5,000 m starting line

long jump and triple jump

scoreboard

shot put

steeplechase hurdle jump

landing area

lane

110 m hurdles starting line

1 2 3 4 5 6 7 8

takeover zone

100 m and 100 m hurdles starting line

throwing circle

pole vault

track

equipment

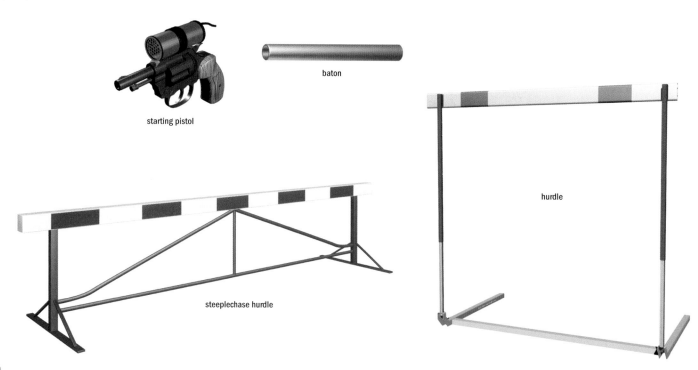

starting pistol

baton

hurdle

steeplechase hurdle

arena

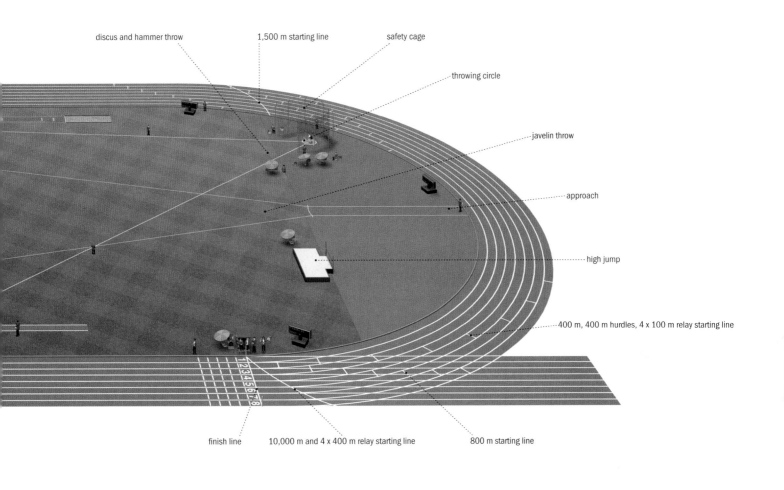

discus and hammer throw
1,500 m starting line
safety cage
throwing circle
javelin throw
approach
high jump
400 m, 400 m hurdles, 4 x 100 m relay starting line
finish line
10,000 m and 4 x 400 m relay starting line
800 m starting line

athlete: starting block

shirt
number
shorts
pedal
track shoe
notch
starting line
anchor
lane line
rack
spike
block
base

SPORTS AND GAMES

jumping

high jump

crossbar

upright

landing area

pole vault

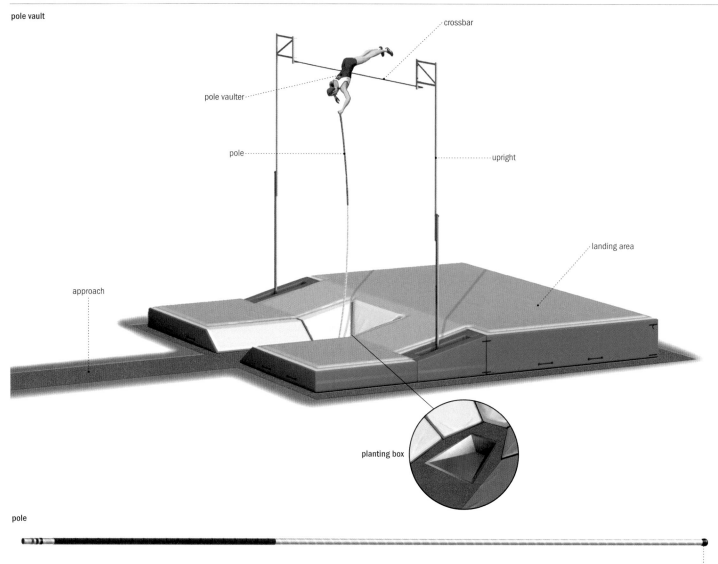

crossbar

pole vaulter

pole

upright

landing area

approach

planting box

pole

tip

long jump and triple jump

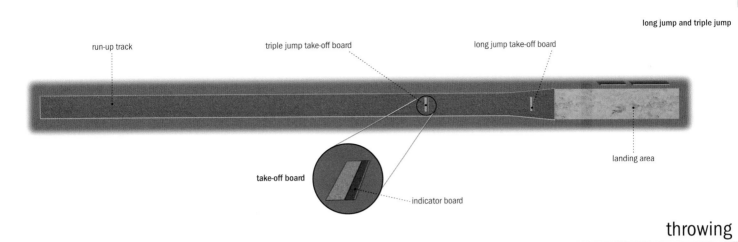

run-up track

triple jump take-off board

long jump take-off board

landing area

take-off board

indicator board

throwing

javelin

tip

shaft

grip

metal head

hammer

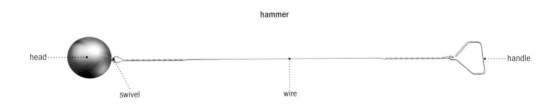

head

handle

swivel

wire

shot

discus

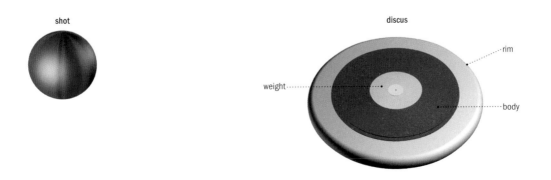

rim

weight

body

baseball

player positions

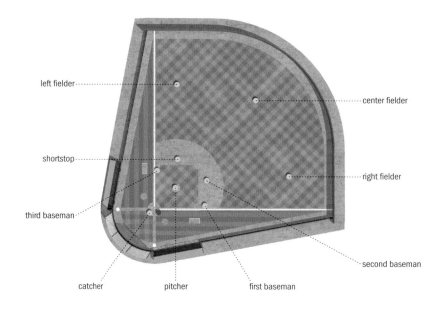

left fielder

center fielder

shortstop

right fielder

third baseman

second baseman

catcher

pitcher

first baseman

field

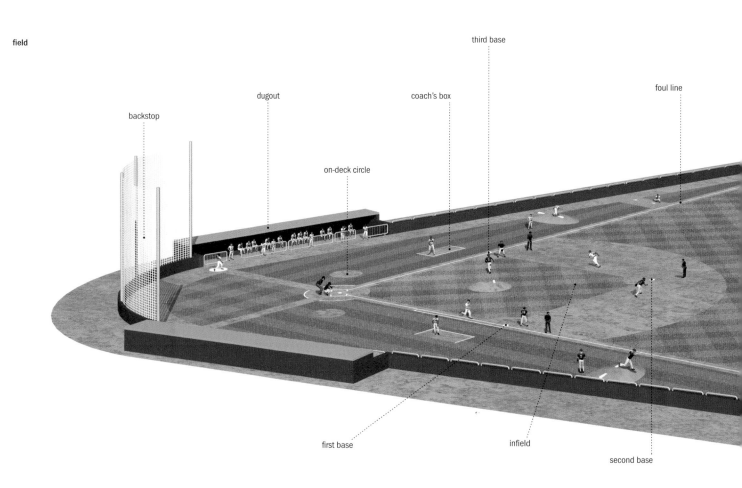

third base

dugout

coach's box

foul line

backstop

on-deck circle

first base

infield

second base

pitch

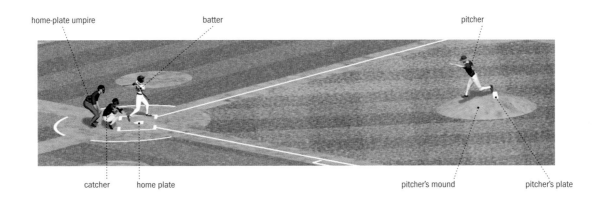

home-plate umpire   batter   pitcher

catcher   home plate   pitcher's mound   pitcher's plate

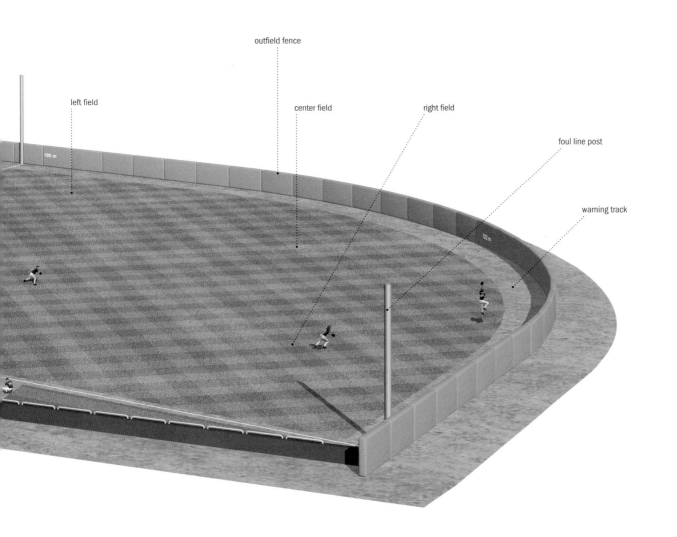

outfield fence

left field   center field   right field

foul line post

warning track

baseball

baseball

catcher

batter

bat

batter's helmet

throat protector

mask

frame

chest protector

catcher's glove

team shirt

undershirt

batting glove

pants

stirrup sock

spiked shoe

toe guard   leg guard

knee pad

ankle guard

baseball

bat

knob   handle   crest   hitting area

fielder's glove

cross section of a baseball

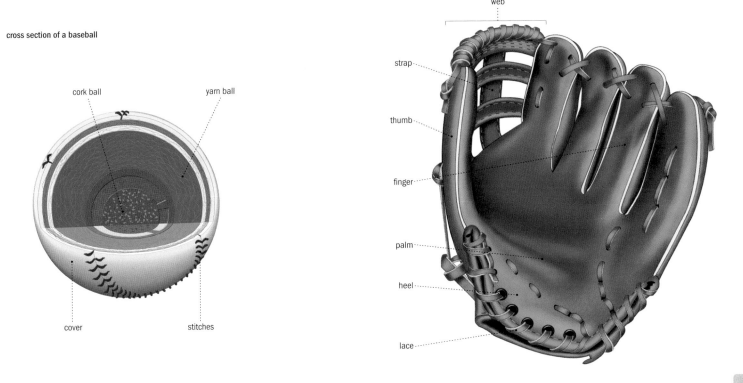

cork ball   yarn ball

web

strap

thumb

finger

palm

heel

lace

cover   stitches

softball

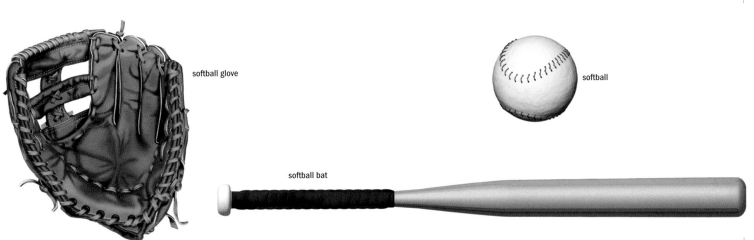

softball glove

softball

softball bat

SPORTS AND GAMES

cricket

cricket player: batsman

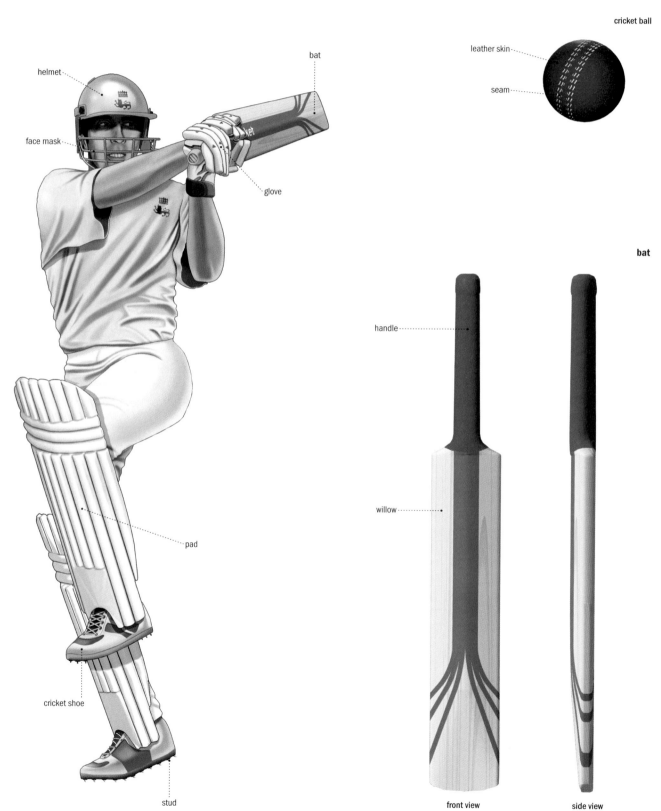

cricket ball

leather skin

seam

helmet

bat

face mask

glove

bat

handle

willow

pad

cricket shoe

front view

side view

stud

field

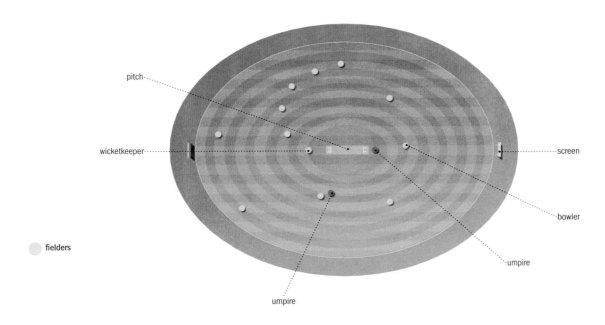

pitch

wicketkeeper

fielders

screen

bowler

umpire

umpire

wicket

bail

stump

pitch

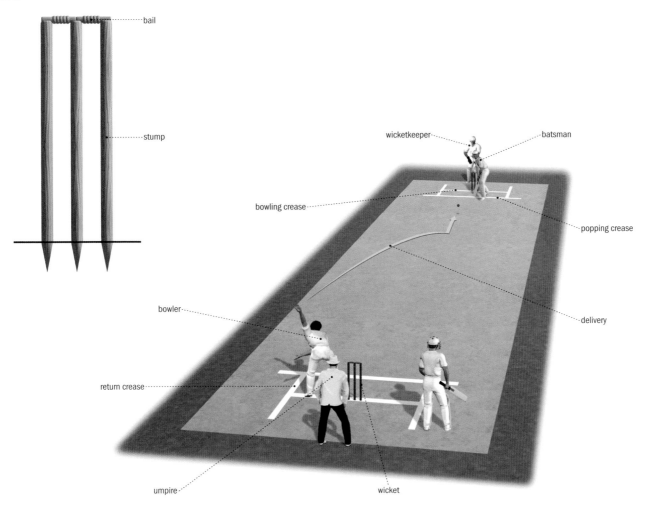

wicketkeeper

batsman

bowling crease

popping crease

bowler

delivery

return crease

umpire

wicket

field hockey

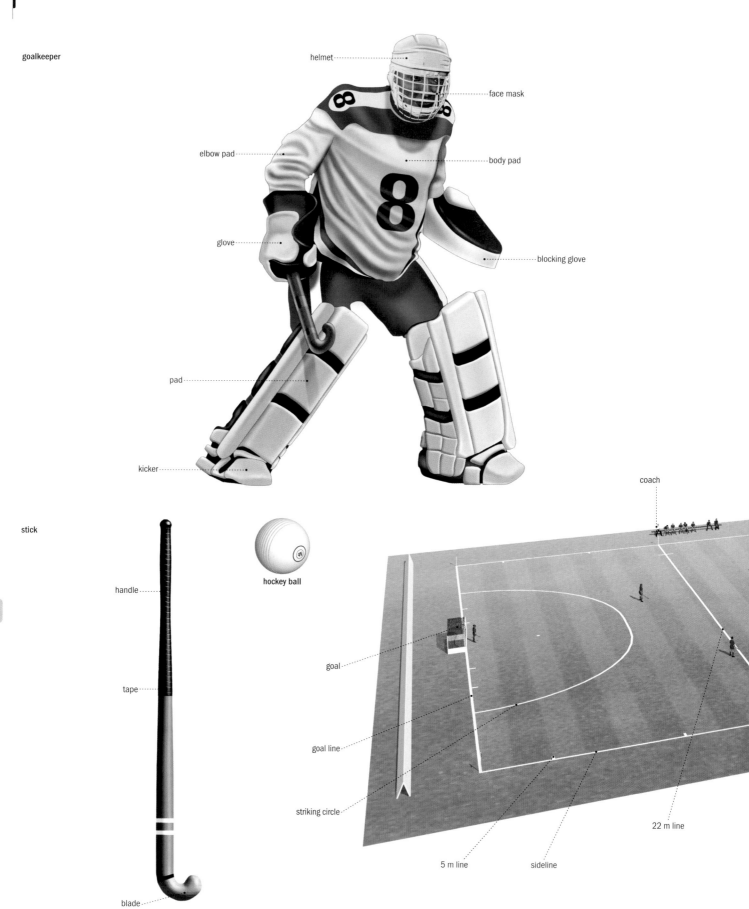

goalkeeper

helmet

face mask

elbow pad

body pad

glove

blocking glove

pad

kicker

coach

stick

handle

hockey ball

tape

goal

goal line

striking circle

22 m line

blade

5 m line

sideline

field player

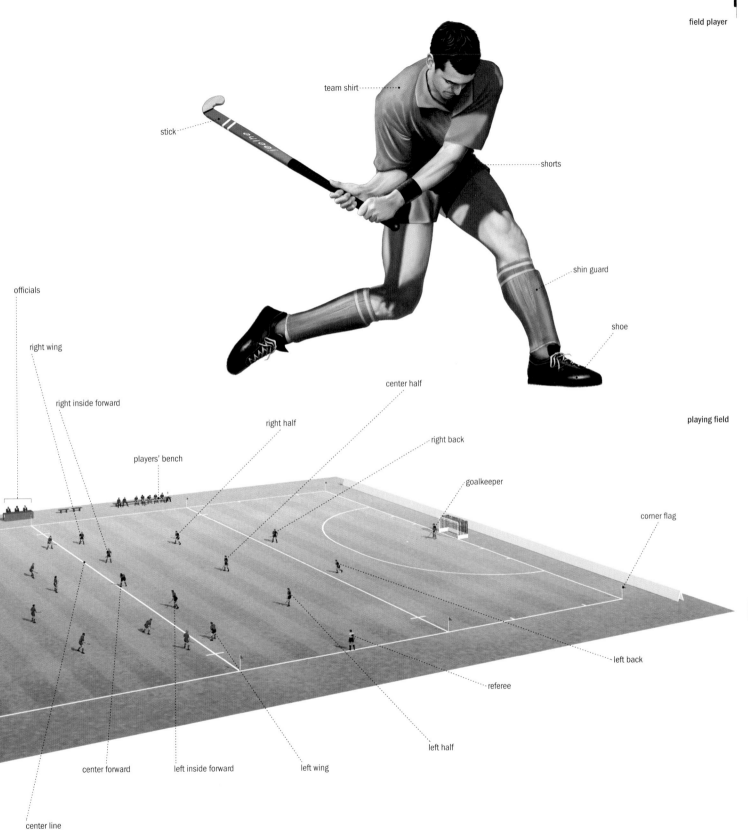

team shirt

stick

shorts

shin guard

officials

shoe

right wing

center half

right inside forward

right half

playing field

right back

players' bench

goalkeeper

corner flag

left back

referee

left half

center forward

left inside forward

left wing

center line

soccer

soccer player

team shirt

goalkeeper's gloves

shorts

interchangeable studs

soccer shoe

shin guard

sock

soccer ball

playing field

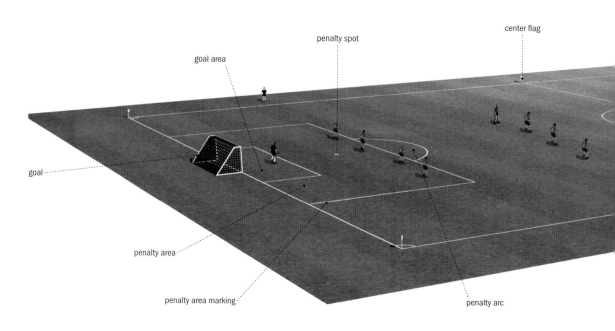

penalty spot

center flag

goal area

goal

penalty area

penalty area marking

penalty arc

player positions

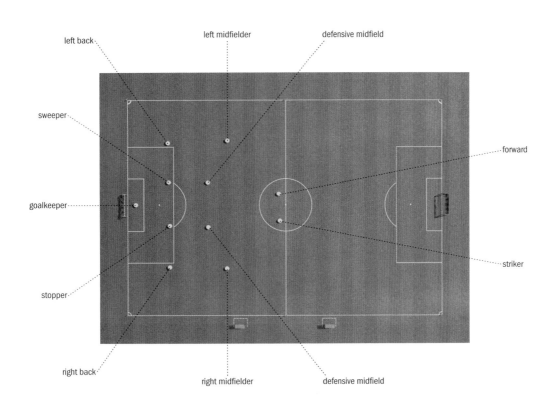

left back

left midfielder

defensive midfield

sweeper

goalkeeper

stopper

right back

right midfielder

defensive midfield

forward

striker

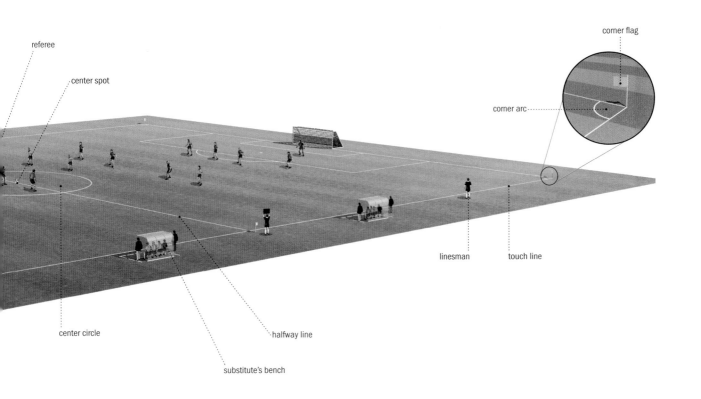

referee

center spot

corner flag

corner arc

center circle

halfway line

substitute's bench

linesman

touch line

rugby

players' positions

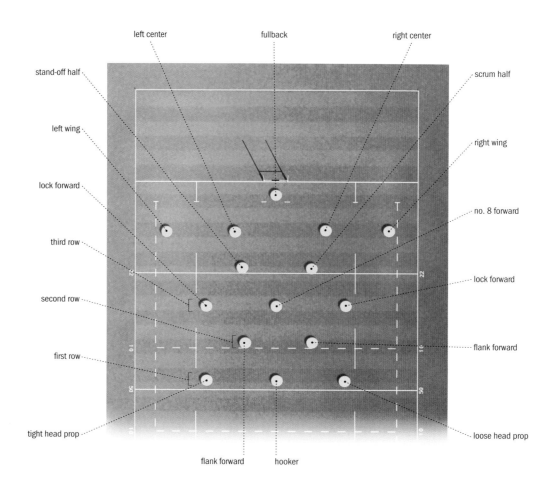

left center   fullback   right center

stand-off half

scrum half

left wing

right wing

lock forward

no. 8 forward

third row

lock forward

second row

flank forward

first row

tight head prop

loose head prop

flank forward   hooker

field

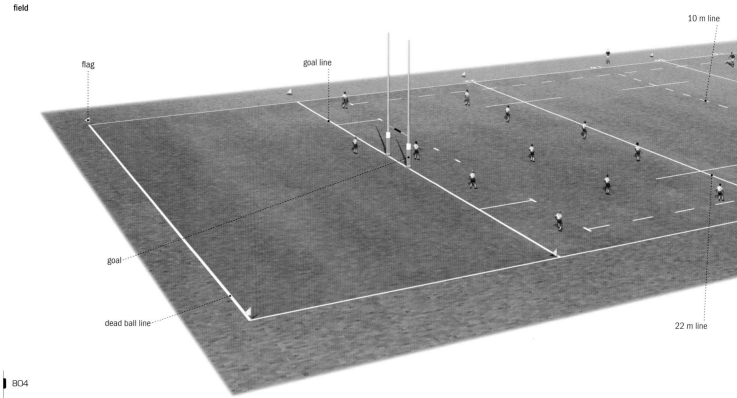

10 m line

flag   goal line

goal

dead ball line

22 m line

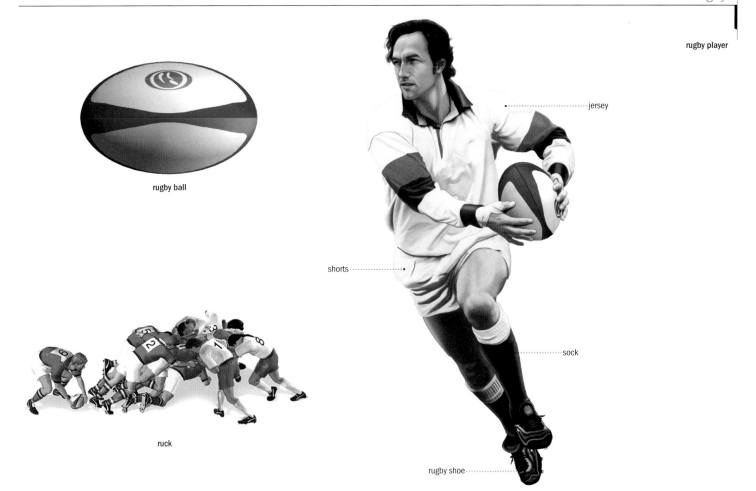

rugby ball

jersey

shorts

sock

ruck

rugby shoe

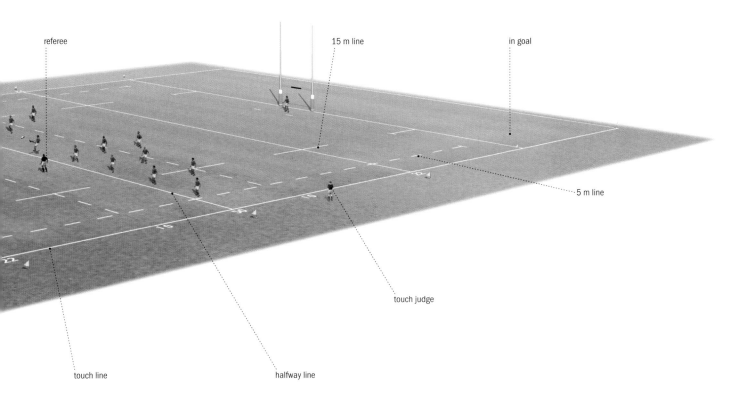

referee

15 m line

in goal

5 m line

touch judge

touch line

halfway line

American football

scrimmage: defense

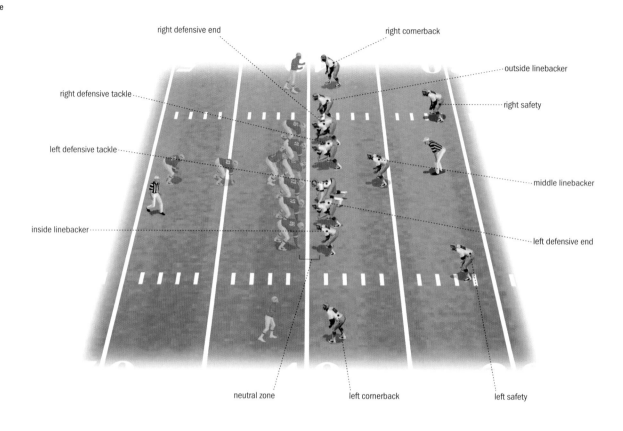

right defensive end

right cornerback

outside linebacker

right defensive tackle

right safety

left defensive tackle

middle linebacker

inside linebacker

left defensive end

neutral zone

left cornerback

left safety

playing field for American football

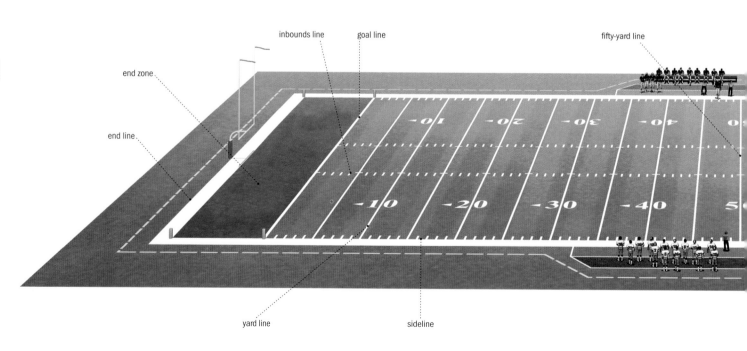

inbounds line

goal line

fifty-yard line

end zone

end line

yard line

sideline

scrimmage: offense

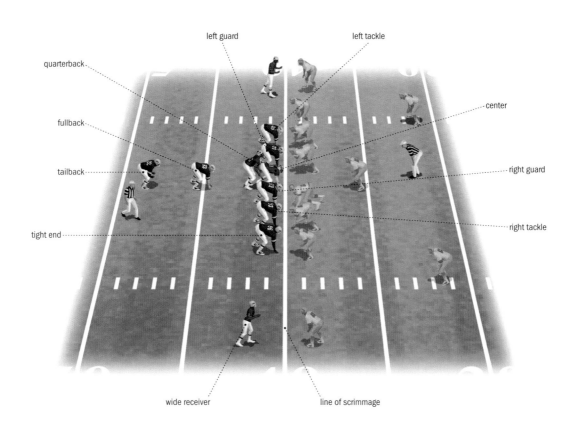

left guard

left tackle

quarterback

center

fullback

tailback

right guard

tight end

right tackle

wide receiver

line of scrimmage

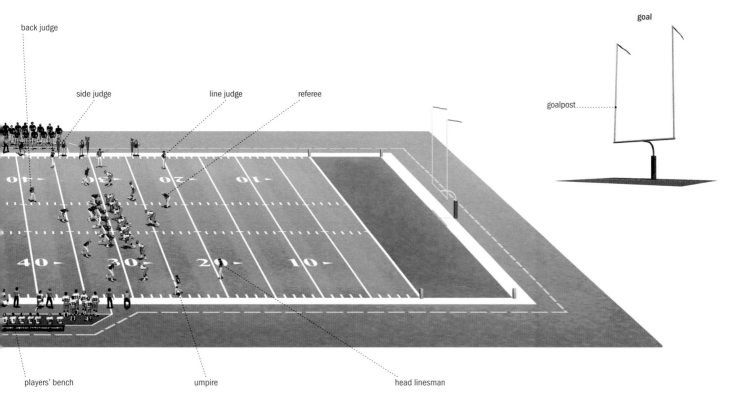

back judge

side judge

line judge

referee

goal

goalpost

players' bench

umpire

head linesman

American football

football player

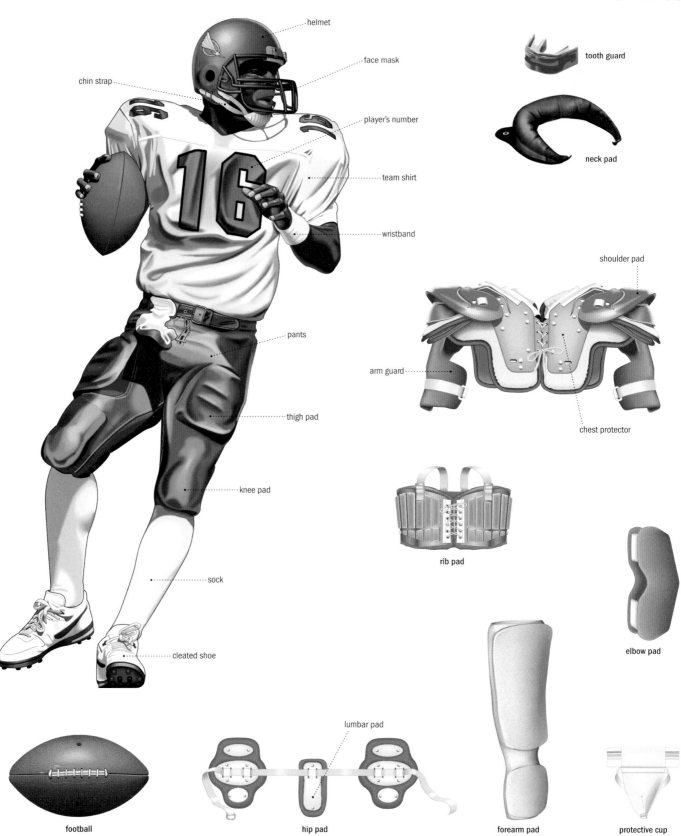

helmet

face mask

chin strap

player's number

team shirt

wristband

pants

thigh pad

knee pad

sock

cleated shoe

tooth guard

neck pad

shoulder pad

arm guard

chest protector

rib pad

elbow pad

football

lumbar pad

hip pad

forearm pad

protective cup

Canadian football

playing field for Canadian football

goal line

end zone

center line

goal

players' bench

netball

court

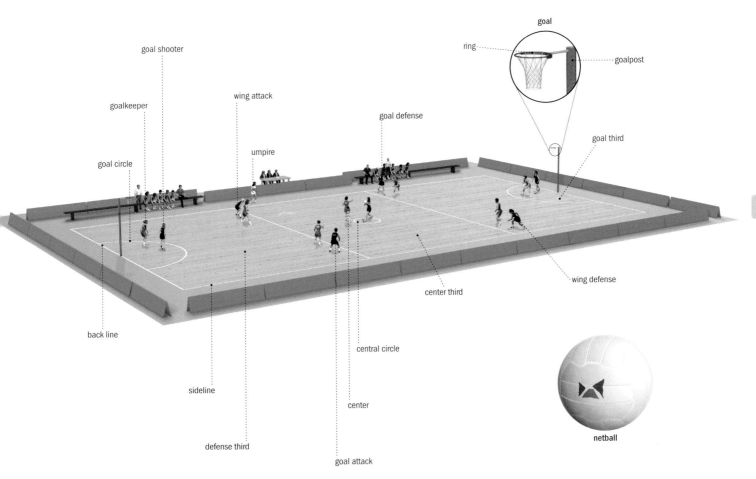

goal

ring

goalpost

goal shooter

wing attack

goalkeeper

goal defense

goal circle

umpire

goal third

wing defense

back line

center third

sideline

central circle

center

defense third

goal attack

netball

basketball

basketball player

basketball

player's number

shirt

shorts

shoe

court

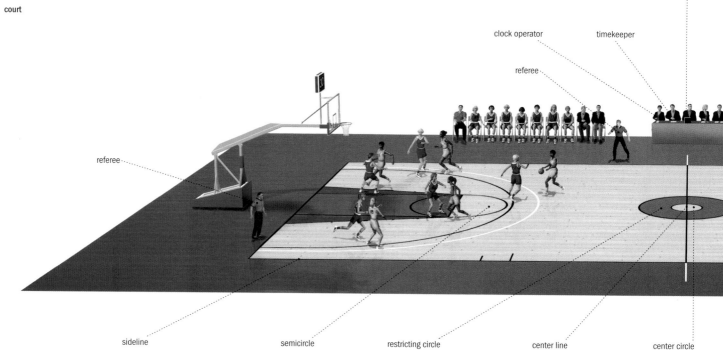

scorer

clock operator

timekeeper

referee

referee

sideline

semicircle

restricting circle

center line

center circle

player positions

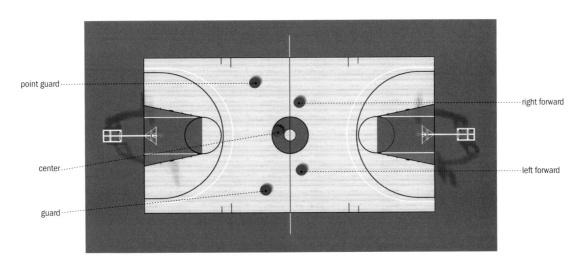

point guard

right forward

center

left forward

guard

backstop

backboard

rim

net

basket

backboard support

padded upright

padded base

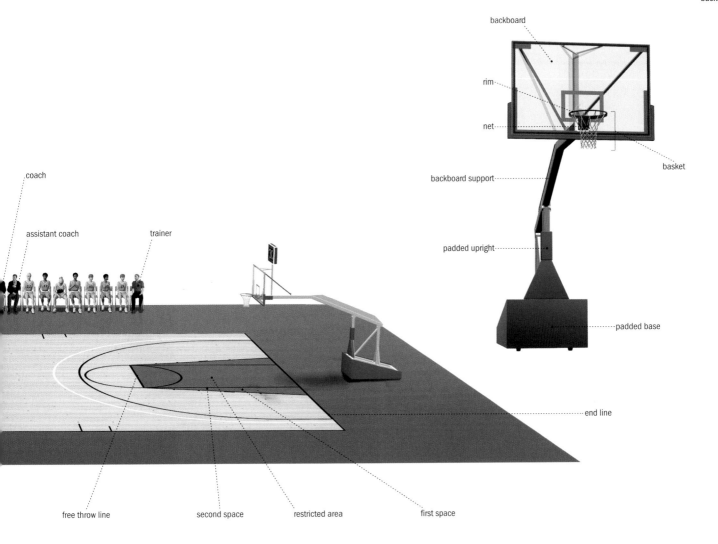

coach

assistant coach   trainer

free throw line   second space   restricted area   first space

end line

volleyball

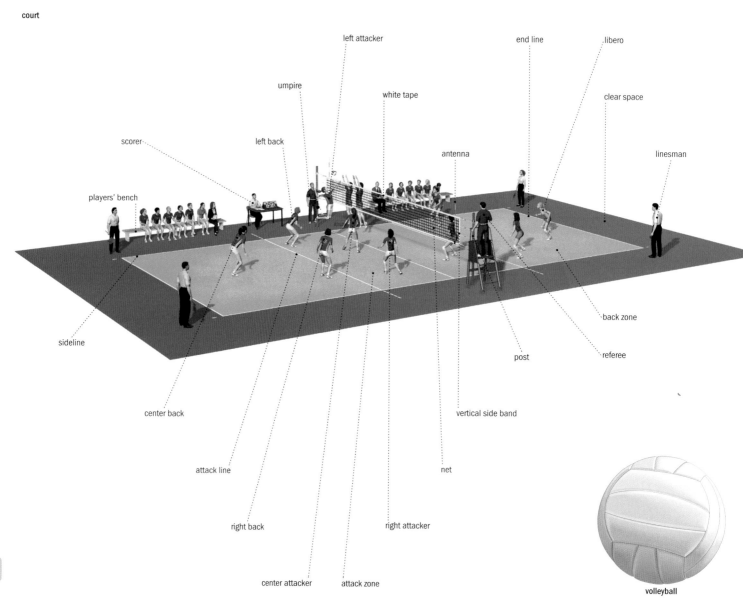

court

scorer

players' bench

sideline

center back

attack line

right back

center attacker

attack zone

left back

umpire

left attacker

white tape

antenna

net

vertical side band

right attacker

post

referee

back zone

end line

libero

clear space

linesman

volleyball

techniques

dig

bump

serve

beach volleyball

court

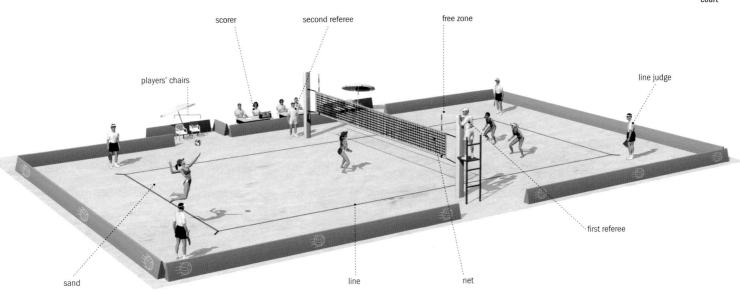

players' chairs

scorer

second referee

free zone

line judge

sand

line

net

first referee

beach volleyball

tip

spike

block

handball

player positions

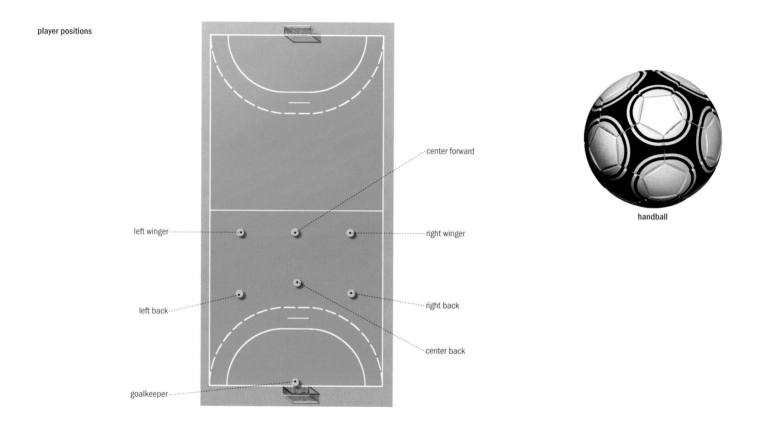

center forward

left winger

right winger

left back

right back

center back

goalkeeper

handball

court

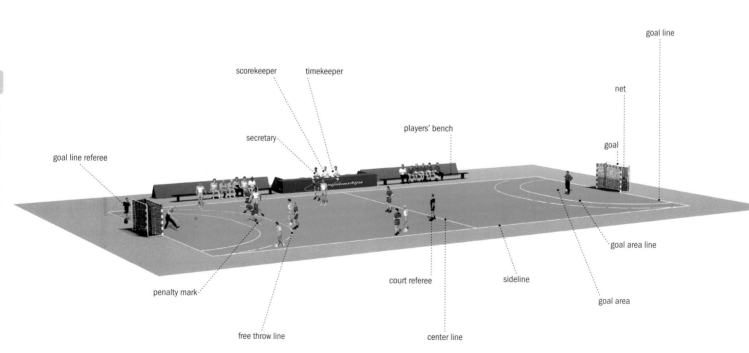

goal line

scorekeeper

timekeeper

net

players' bench

secretary

goal

goal line referee

goal area line

penalty mark

court referee

sideline

goal area

free throw line

center line

table tennis

table

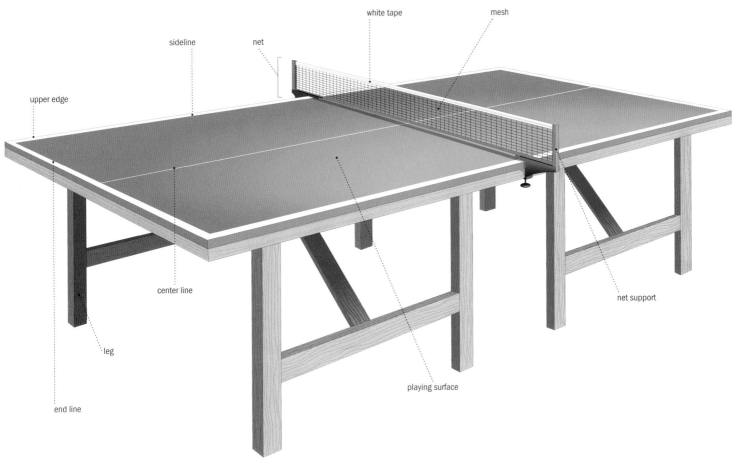

white tape

mesh

sideline

net

upper edge

net support

center line

leg

playing surface

end line

table tennis paddle

table tennis ball

types of grips

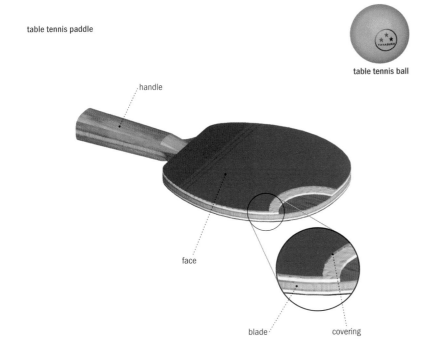

handle

face

blade

covering

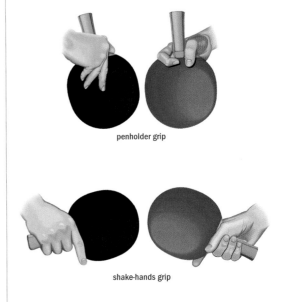

penholder grip

shake-hands grip

badminton

court

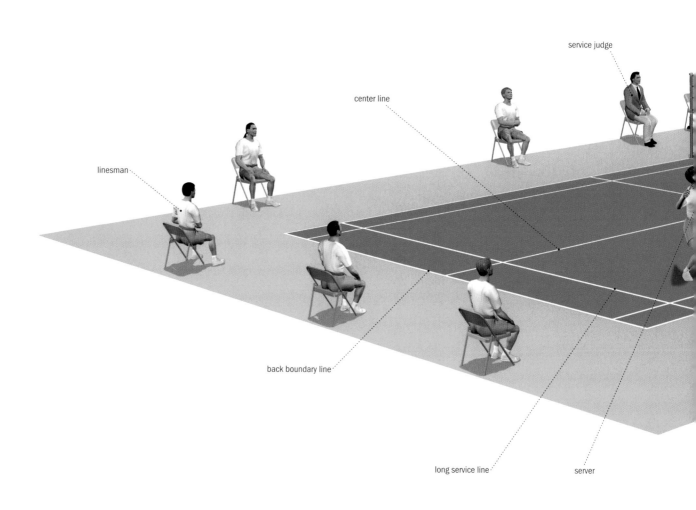

service judge

center line

linesman

back boundary line

long service line

server

badminton racket

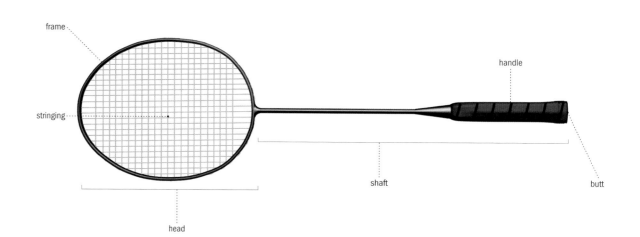

frame

handle

stringing

shaft

butt

head

SPORTS AND GAMES

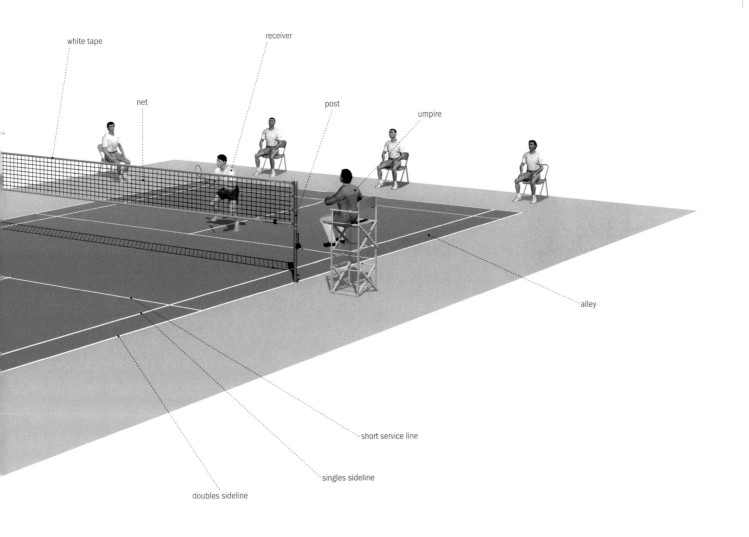

white tape

receiver

net

post

umpire

alley

short service line

singles sideline

doubles sideline

service zones

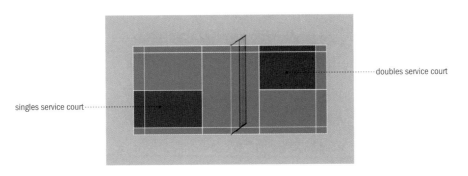

doubles service court

singles service court

synthetic shuttlecock

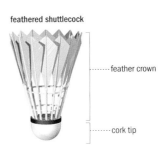

feathered shuttlecock

feather crown

cork tip

racquetball

court

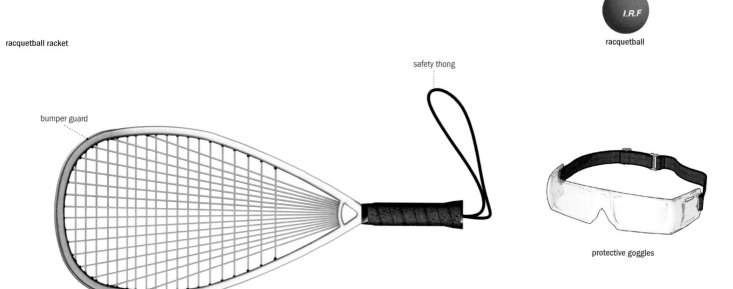

back wall

referee

center court

sidewall

ceiling

front wall

service line

service zone

frontcourt

service box line

service box

door

receiving line

line judge

short line

floor

backcourt

racquetball racket

safety thong

I.R.F

racquetball

bumper guard

protective goggles

squash

court

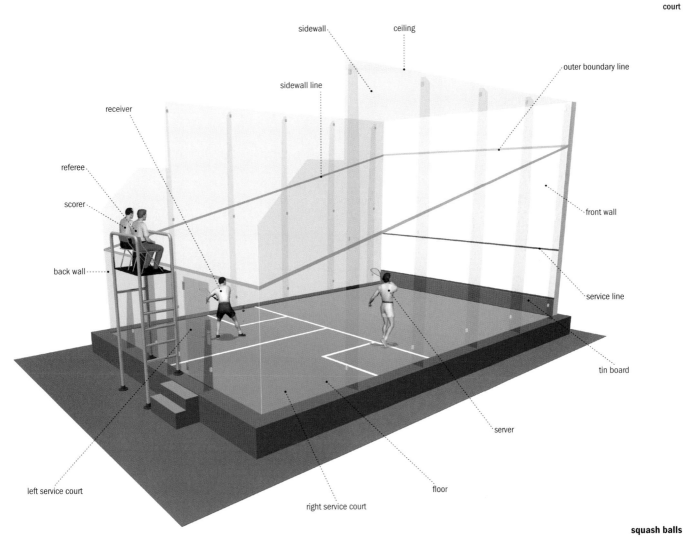

sidewall

ceiling

outer boundary line

sidewall line

receiver

front wall

referee

scorer

service line

back wall

tin board

server

left service court

floor

right service court

squash balls

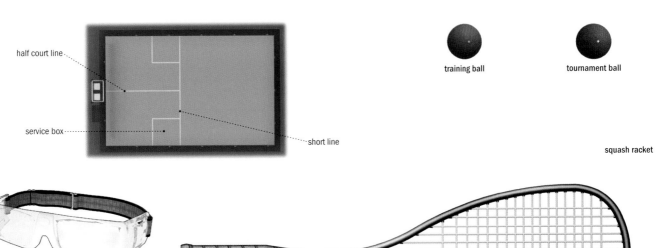

half court line

training ball

tournament ball

service box

short line

squash racket

protective goggles

SPORTS AND GAMES

tennis

court

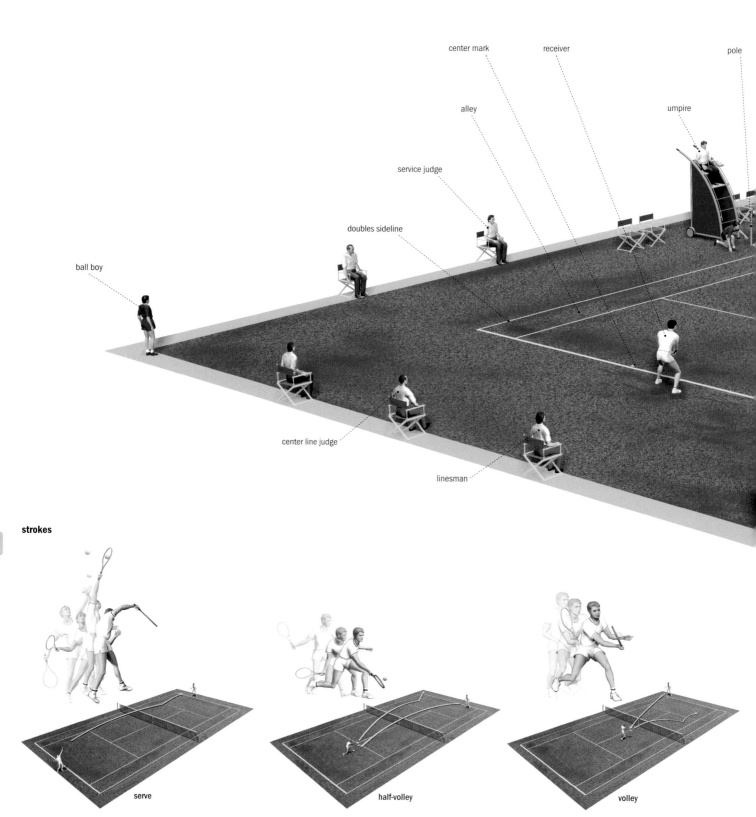

center mark

receiver

pole

alley

umpire

service judge

doubles sideline

ball boy

center line judge

linesman

strokes

serve

half-volley

volley

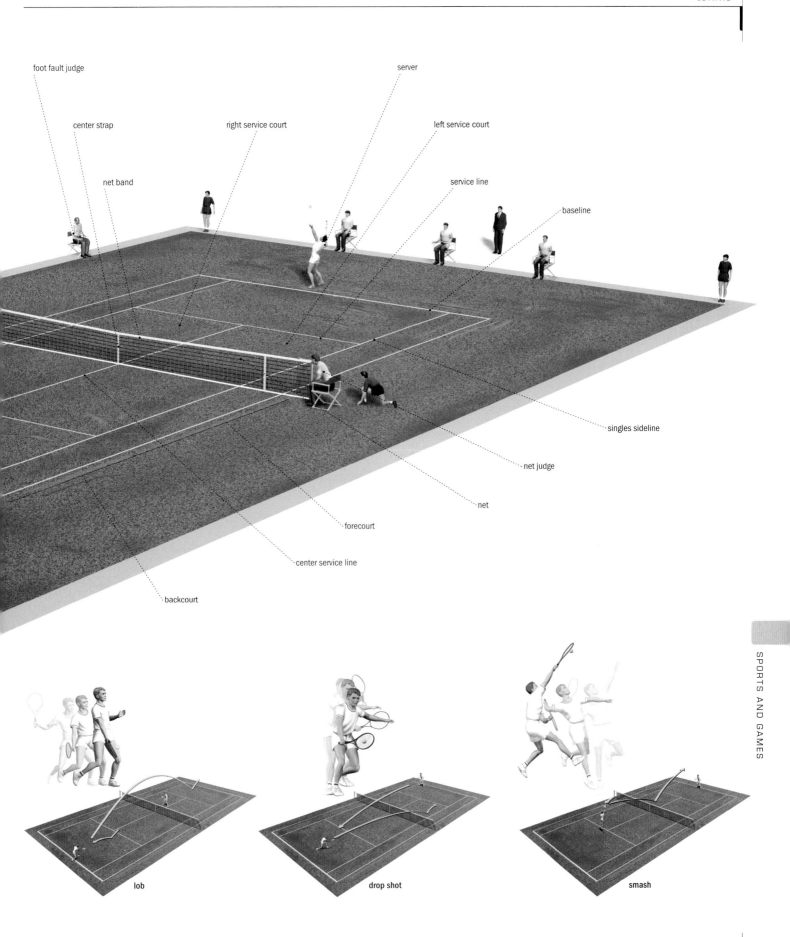

foot fault judge

server

center strap

right service court

left service court

net band

service line

baseline

singles sideline

net judge

net

forecourt

center service line

backcourt

lob

drop shot

smash

tennis

tennis racket

frame

head

stringing

shoulder

throat

shaft

handle

butt

tennis ball

tennis player

polo shirt

skirt

wristband

sock

tennis shoe

scoreboard

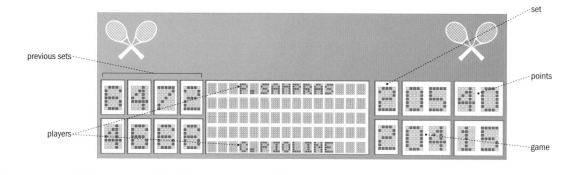

set

previous sets

points

players

game

playing surfaces

grass

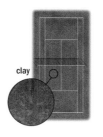

clay

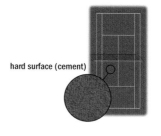

hard surface (cement)

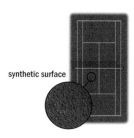

synthetic surface

rhythmic gymnastics

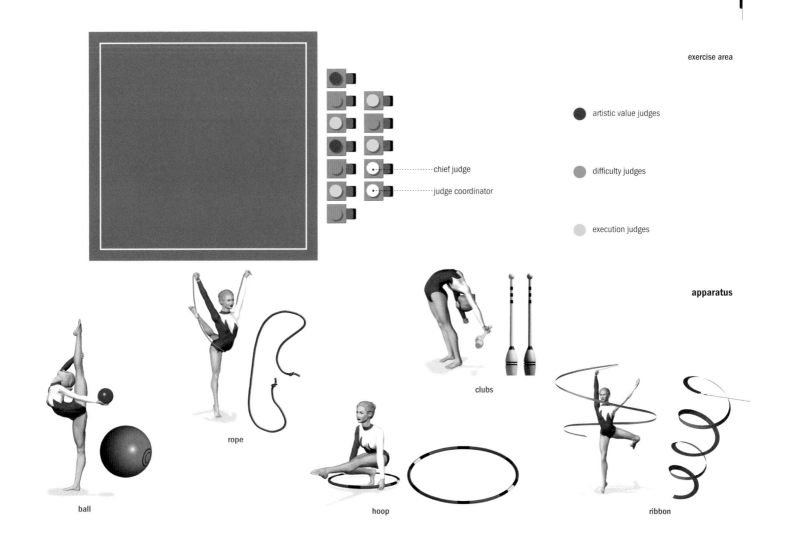

exercise area

chief judge

judge coordinator

● artistic value judges

● difficulty judges

○ execution judges

apparatus

ball

rope

hoop

clubs

ribbon

trampoline

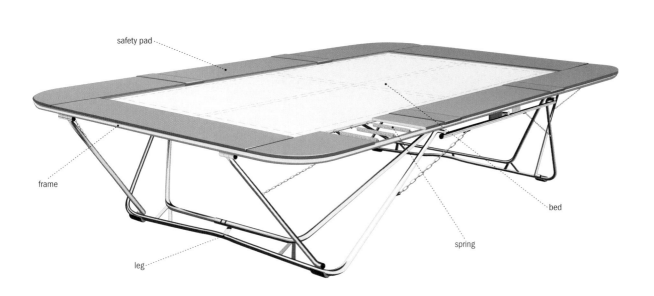

safety pad

frame

leg

spring

bed

gymnastics

event platform

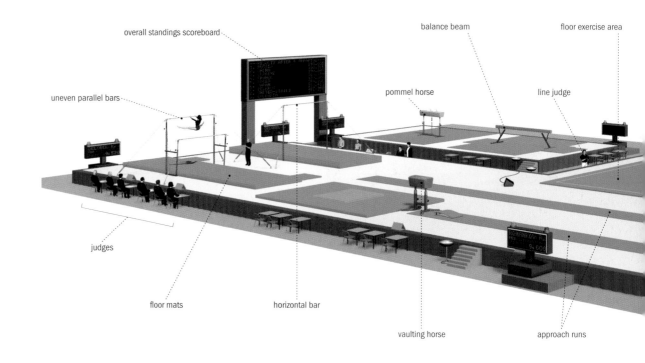

overall standings scoreboard

balance beam

floor exercise area

uneven parallel bars

pommel horse

line judge

judges

floor mats

horizontal bar

vaulting horse

approach runs

uneven parallel bars

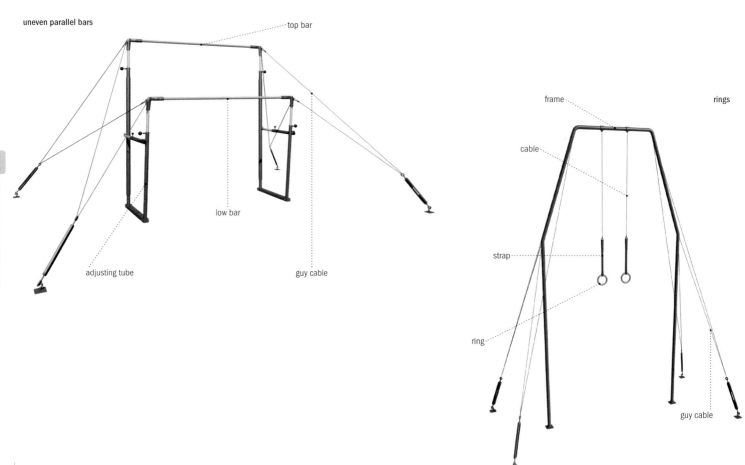

top bar

frame

rings

cable

low bar

strap

adjusting tube

guy cable

ring

guy cable

scoreboard

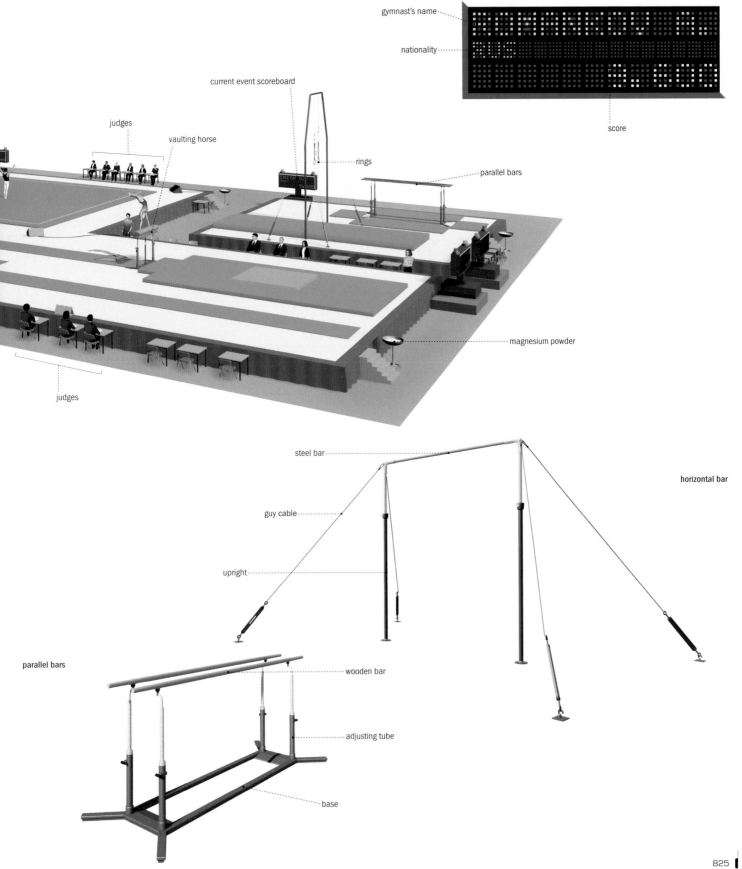

gymnast's name

nationality

score

current event scoreboard

judges

vaulting horse

rings

parallel bars

magnesium powder

judges

steel bar

horizontal bar

guy cable

upright

parallel bars

wooden bar

adjusting tube

base

gymnastics

pommel horse

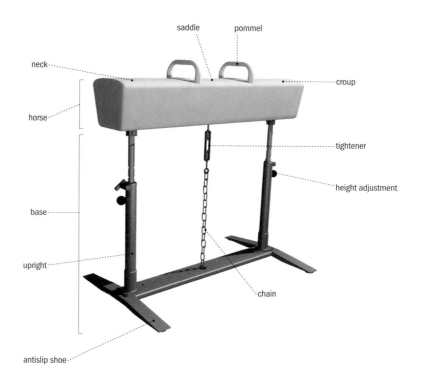

saddle

pommel

neck

croup

horse

tightener

height adjustment

base

upright

chain

antislip shoe

balance beam

upright

beam

height adjustment

vaulting horse

springboard

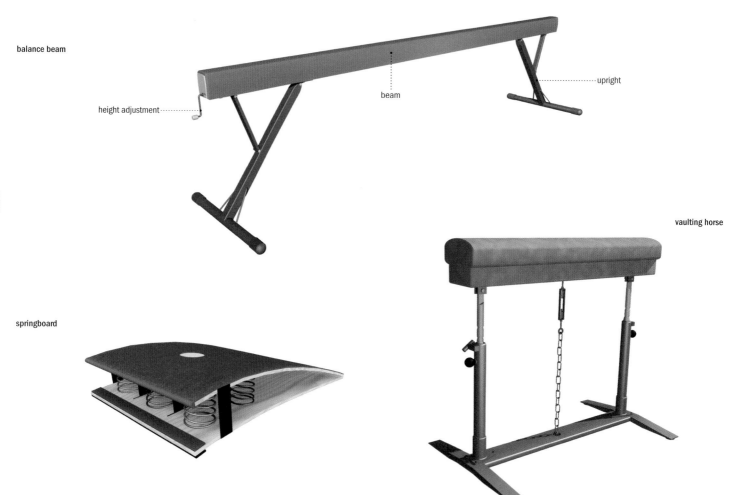

water polo

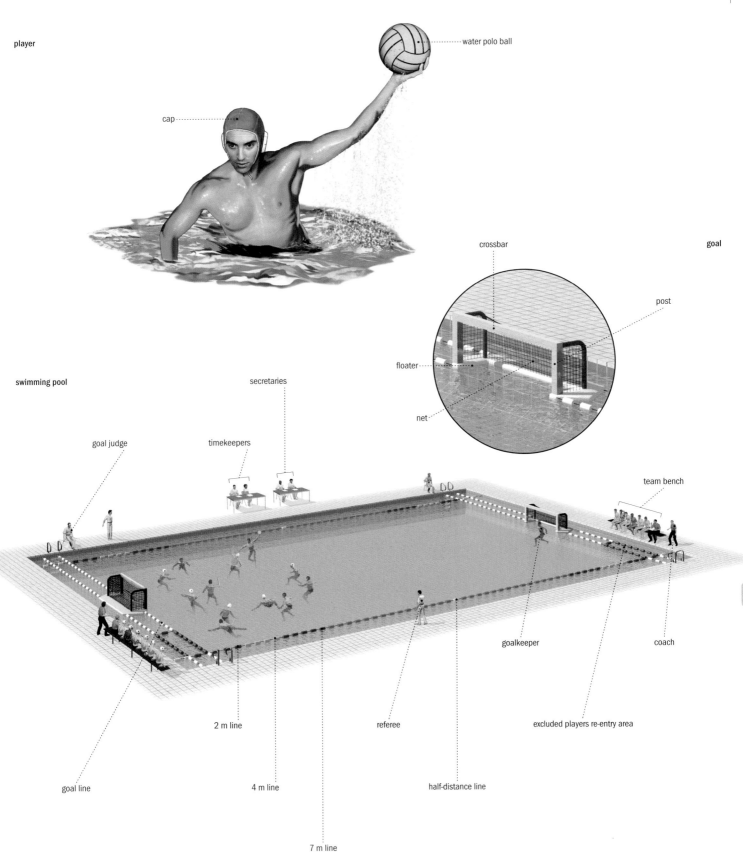

player

water polo ball

cap

crossbar

goal

post

floater

net

swimming pool

secretaries

goal judge

timekeepers

team bench

goalkeeper

coach

2 m line

referee

excluded players re-entry area

goal line

4 m line

half-distance line

7 m line

diving

starting positions

flights

reverse

inward

backward

forward

armstand

tuck position

straight position

pike position

diving installations

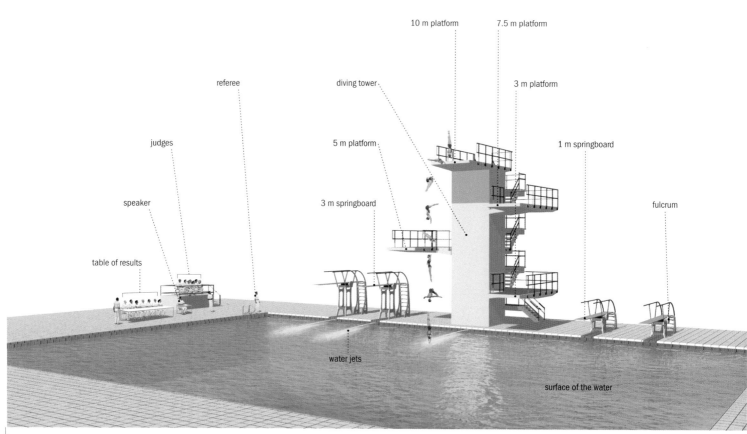

10 m platform

7.5 m platform

referee

diving tower

3 m platform

judges

5 m platform

1 m springboard

speaker

3 m springboard

fulcrum

table of results

water jets

surface of the water

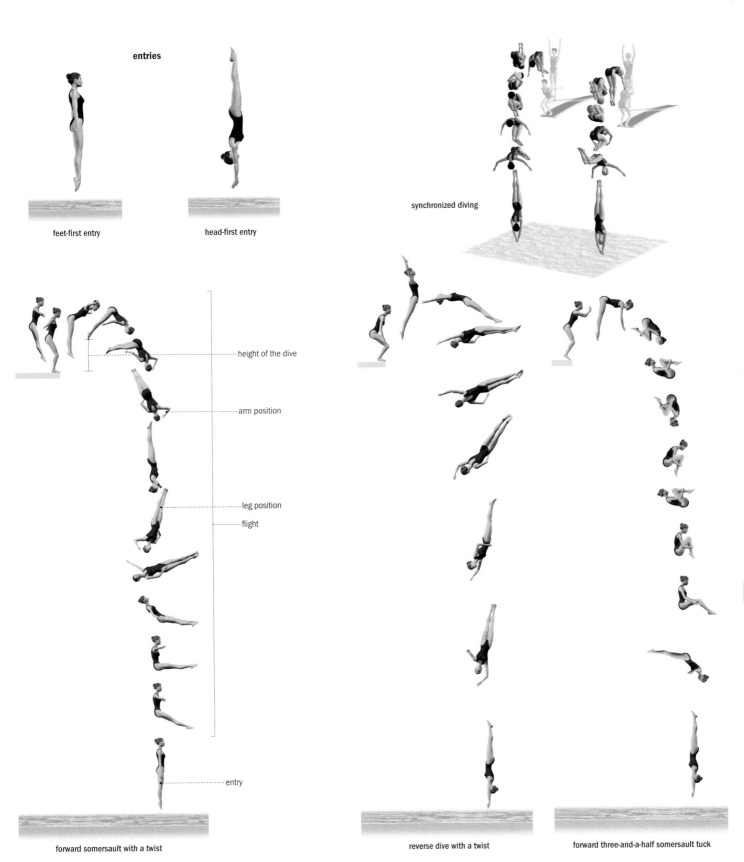

entries

feet-first entry

head-first entry

synchronized diving

height of the dive

arm position

leg position

flight

entry

forward somersault with a twist

reverse dive with a twist

forward three-and-a-half somersault tuck

swimming

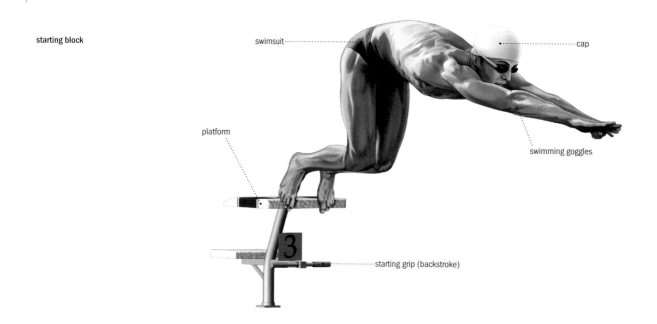

starting block

swimsuit

cap

platform

swimming goggles

starting grip (backstroke)

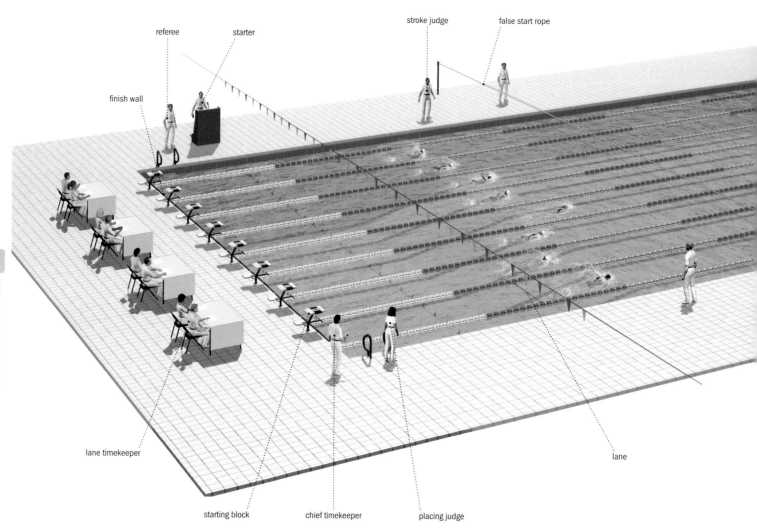

referee

starter

stroke judge

false start rope

finish wall

lane timekeeper

starting block

chief timekeeper

placing judge

lane

scoreboard

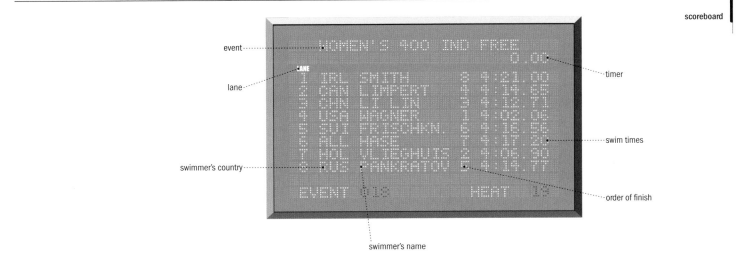

event

timer

lane

swim times

swimmer's country

order of finish

swimmer's name

competitive course

backstroke turn indicator

sidewall

turning wall

turning judges

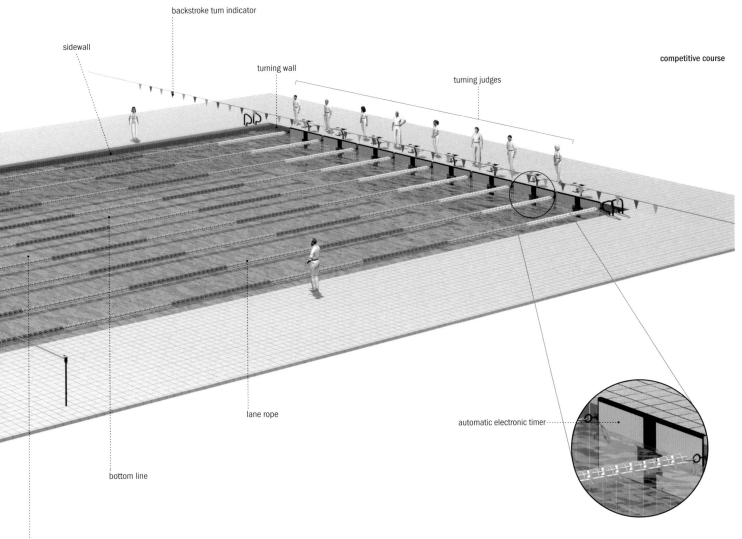

lane rope

automatic electronic timer

bottom line

swimming pool

types of strokes

front crawl stroke

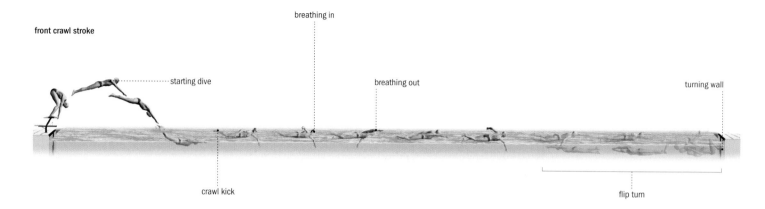

breathing in

starting dive

breathing out

turning wall

crawl kick

flip turn

breaststroke

breaststroke kick

breaststroke turn

butterfly stroke

butterfly kick

butterfly turn

backstroke

backstroke start

flip turn

sailing

points of sailing

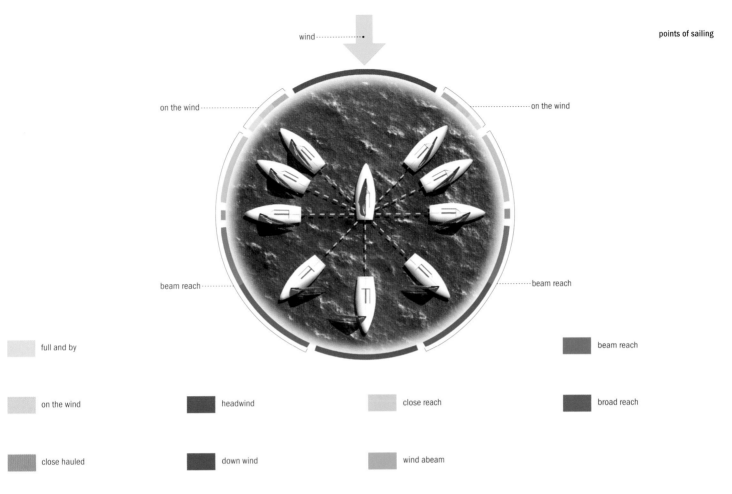

wind

on the wind

on the wind

beam reach

beam reach

full and by

beam reach

on the wind

headwind

close reach

broad reach

close hauled

down wind

wind abeam

course

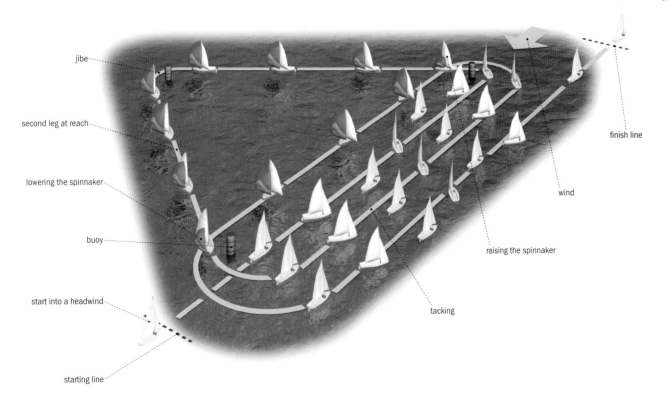

jibe

second leg at reach

lowering the spinnaker

buoy

start into a headwind

starting line

finish line

wind

raising the spinnaker

tacking

sailboat

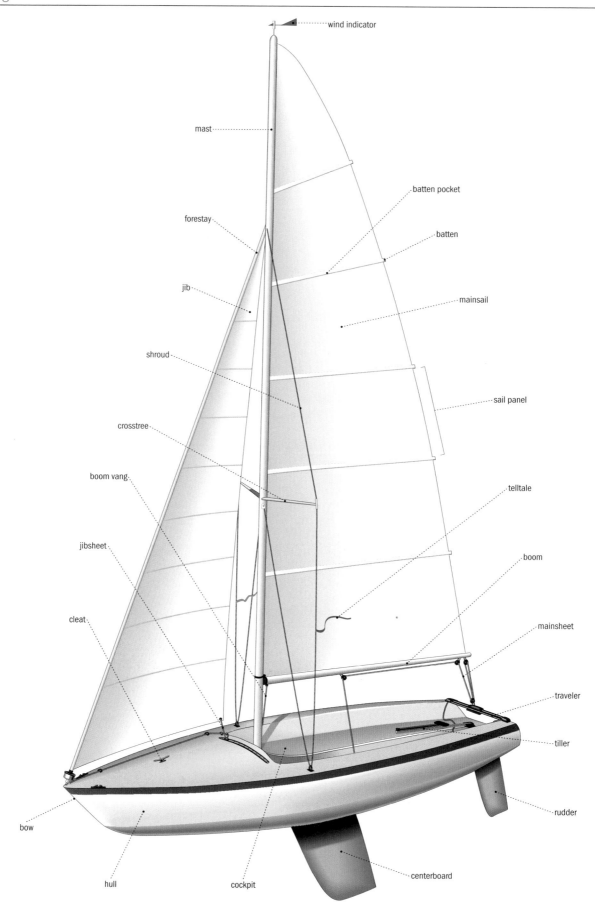

wind indicator

mast

batten pocket

forestay

batten

jib

mainsail

shroud

sail panel

crosstree

boom vang

telltale

jibsheet

boom

cleat

mainsheet

traveler

tiller

bow

rudder

hull

cockpit

centerboard

multihulls

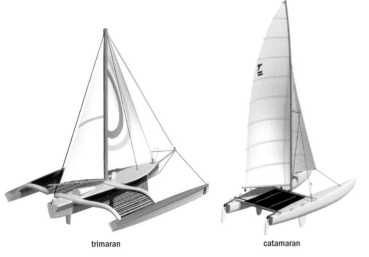

trimaran

catamaran

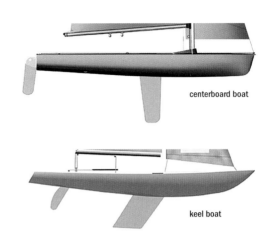

centerboard boat

keel boat

upperworks

snap shackle

hank

shackle

fairlead

cleat

winch

turnbuckle

clam cleat

sheet lead

traveler

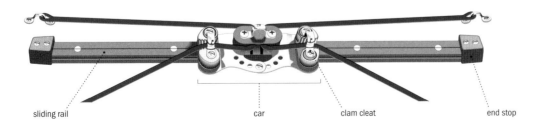

sliding rail

car

clam cleat

end stop

sailboard

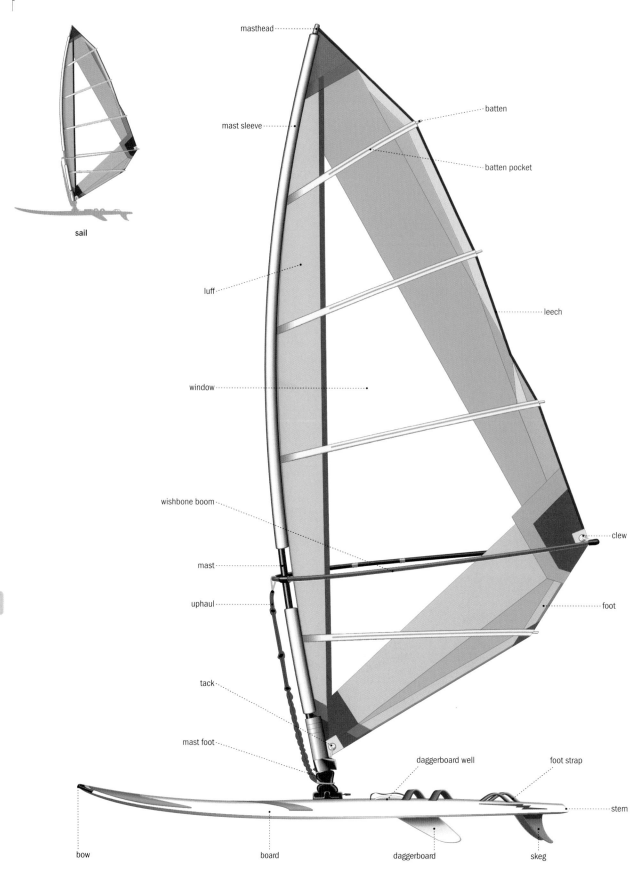

sail

masthead

batten

mast sleeve

batten pocket

luff

leech

window

wishbone boom

clew

mast

uphaul

foot

tack

mast foot

daggerboard well

foot strap

stern

bow

board

daggerboard

skeg

canoe-kayak: whitewater

canoe

single-bladed paddle

kayak

double-bladed paddle

spray skirt

whitewater

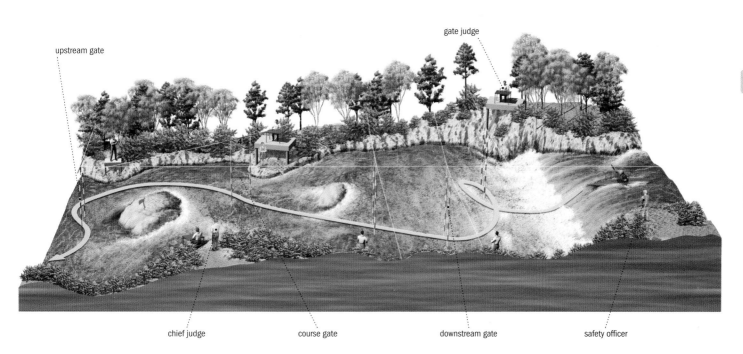

upstream gate

gate judge

chief judge   course gate   downstream gate   safety officer

SPORTS AND GAMES

rowing and sculling

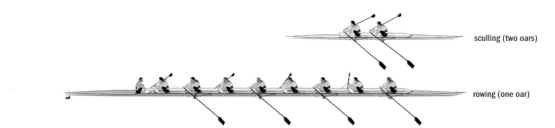

sculling (two oars)

rowing (one oar)

types of oars

sculling oar

grip · rubber sheath · blade

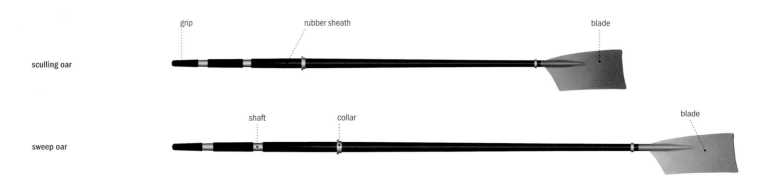

sweep oar

shaft · collar · blade

parts of a boat

rudder cable · coxswain's seat · foot stretcher · sliding seat

rudder

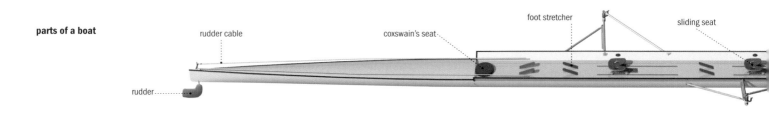

basin

starting zone · aligner · course umpire · start buoys · course buoys

starter

starting jetty

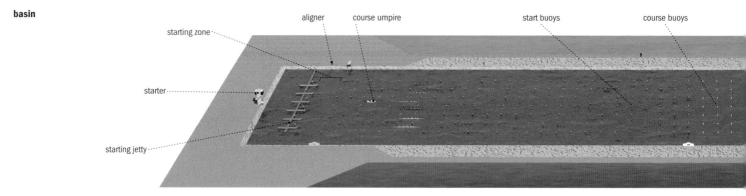

canoe-kayak: flatwater racing

C1 canoe

deck

forestem

single-bladed paddle

rowing and sculling

sculling boats

single scull

coxless double

sweep boats

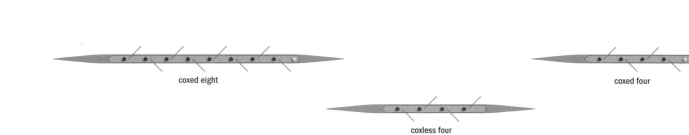

coxed pair

coxless pair

coxed eight

coxed four

coxless four

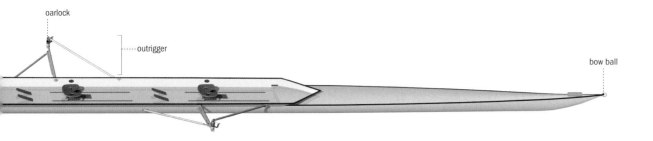

oarlock

outrigger

bow ball

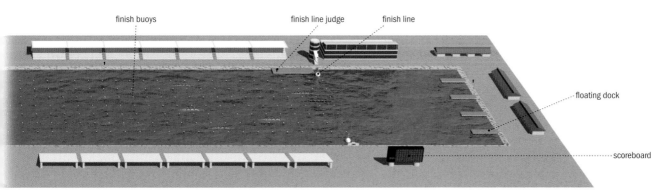

finish buoys

finish line judge

finish line

floating dock

scoreboard

canoe-kayak: flatwater racing

K1 kayak

double-bladed paddle

tapered end

seat

rudder

water skiing

examples of skis

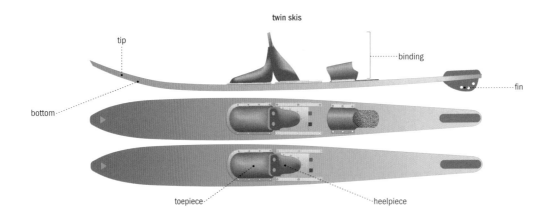

twin skis

tip

binding

fin

bottom

toepiece

heelpiece

slalom ski

back binding

front binding

jump skis

figure ski

tail

examples of handles

handle

double handle

figure skiing handle

tow line

toe strap

tow bar

surfing

surfer

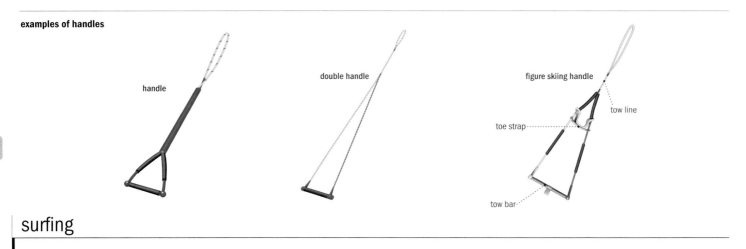

surfboard

skeg

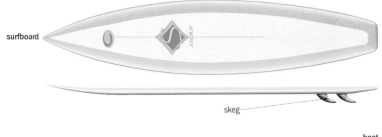

boot

SPORTS AND GAMES

scuba diving

scuba diver

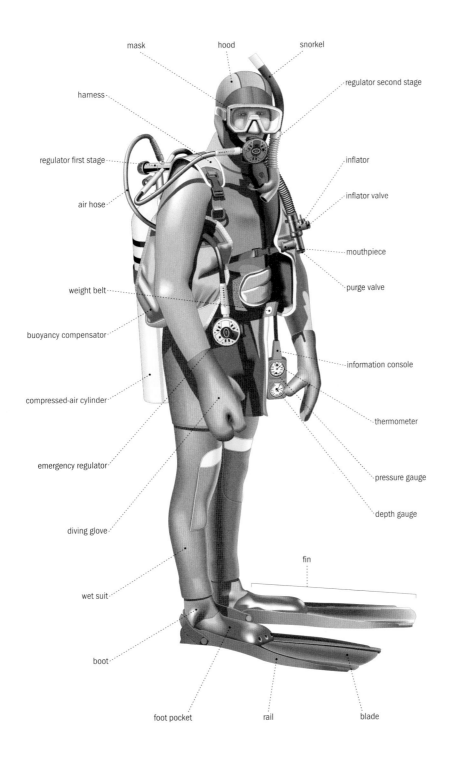

mask
hood
snorkel
regulator second stage
harness
regulator first stage
inflator
inflator valve
air hose
mouthpiece
weight belt
purge valve
buoyancy compensator
information console
compressed-air cylinder
thermometer
emergency regulator
pressure gauge
depth gauge
diving glove
fin
wet suit
boot
foot pocket
rail
blade

knife

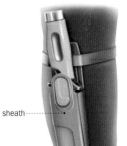

sheath

strap

speargun

boxing

boxer

headgear

glove

boxing trunks

punching ball

punching bag

ring

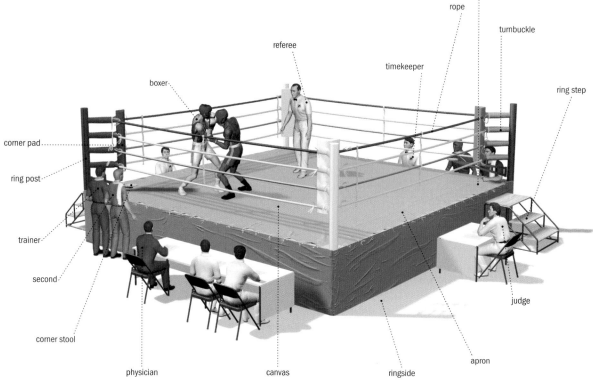

corner

rope

turnbuckle

referee

timekeeper

ring step

boxer

corner pad

ring post

trainer

second

corner stool

physician

canvas

ringside

apron

judge

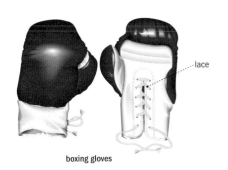

boxing gloves

lace

bandage

protective cup

mouthpiece

wrestling

wrestler

starting positions

crouching position (freestyle wrestling)   standing position (Greco-Roman wrestling)

singlet

wrestling shoe

wrestling area

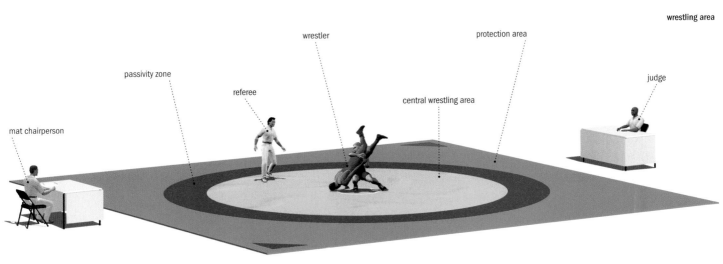

passivity zone

wrestler

protection area

referee

judge

central wrestling area

mat chairperson

judo

mat

scorers and timekeepers

scoreboard

medical team

contestant

safety area

contest area

referee

judge

danger area

examples of holds and throws

judogi

jacket

holding

stomach throw

sweeping hip throw

major outer reaping throw

major inner reaping throw

naked strangle

trousers

belt

arm lock

one-arm shoulder throw

karate

karateka

karate-gi

obi

contest area

referee's line

competitors' line

competition area

arbitration committee

corner judge

scorekeeper

timekeeper

referee

karateka

kung fu

kung fu practitioner

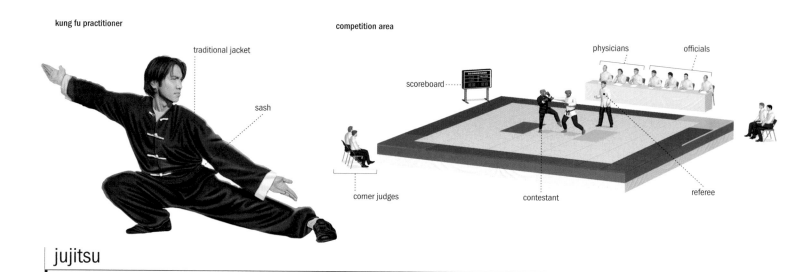

traditional jacket

sash

competition area

physicians

officials

scoreboard

corner judges

contestant

referee

jujitsu

competition area

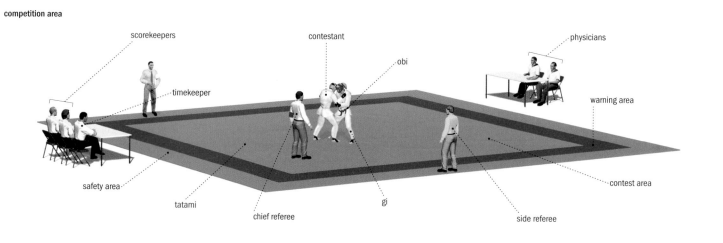

scorekeepers

contestant

obi

physicians

timekeeper

warning area

safety area

tatami

chief referee

gi

side referee

contest area

aikido

aikidoka

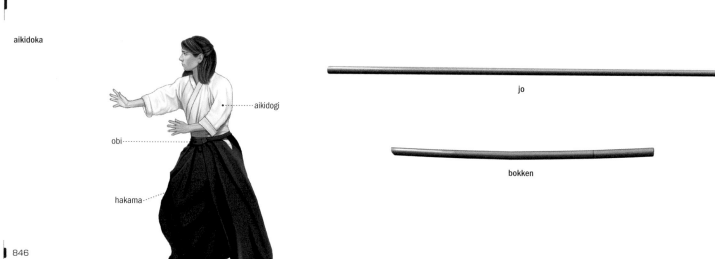

aikidogi

obi

hakama

jo

bokken

kendo

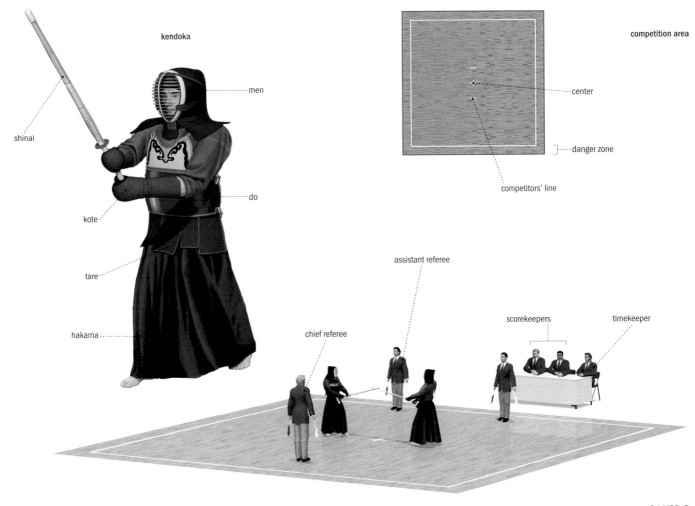

kendoka

shinai

men

do

kote

tare

hakama

competition area

center

danger zone

competitors' line

assistant referee

chief referee

scorekeepers

timekeeper

sumo

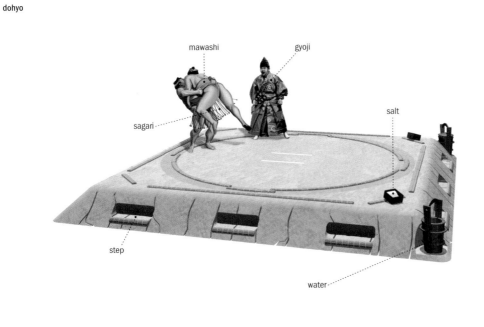

dohyo

mawashi

gyoji

sagari

salt

step

water

mage

sumotori

fencing

fencer

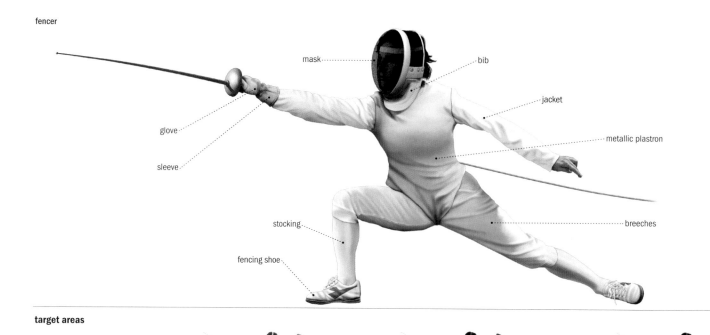

mask
bib
jacket
metallic plastron
glove
sleeve
breeches
stocking
fencing shoe

target areas

foilist

épéeist

sabreur

piste

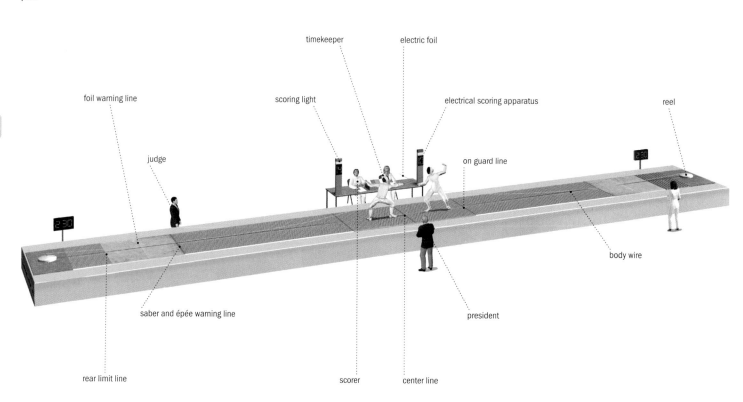

timekeeper
electric foil
foil warning line
scoring light
electrical scoring apparatus
reel
judge
on guard line
body wire
saber and épée warning line
president
rear limit line
scorer
center line

positions

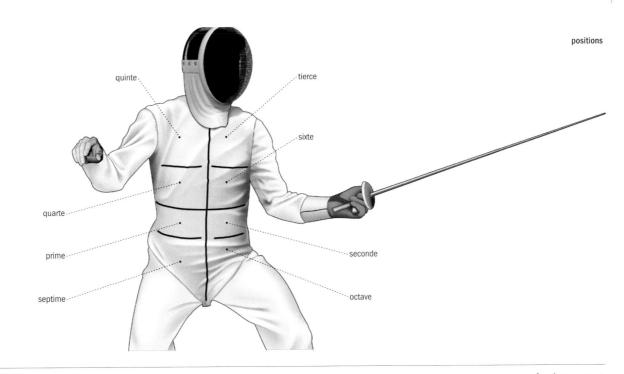

quinte

tierce

sixte

quarte

prime

seconde

septime

octave

fencing weapons

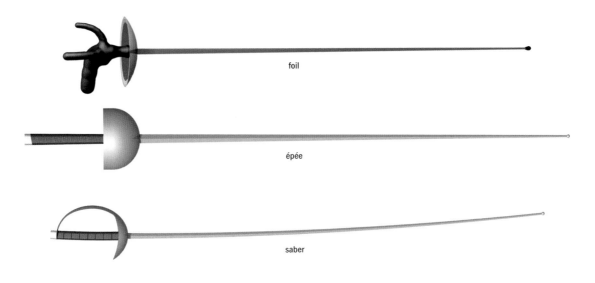

foil

épée

saber

parts of the weapon

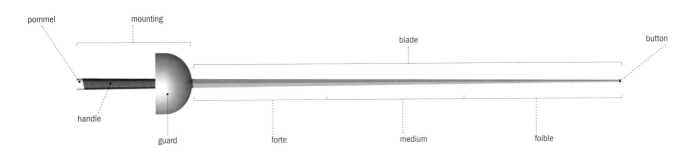

pommel

mounting

blade

button

handle

guard

forte

medium

foible

weightlifting

barbell

wristband

weightlifting belt

sleeveless jersey

trunks

knee wrap

strap

weightlifting shoe

clean and jerk

snatch

fitness equipment

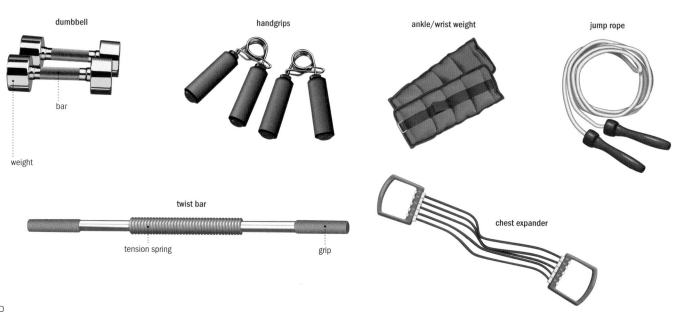

dumbbell

handgrips

ankle/wrist weight

jump rope

bar

weight

twist bar

tension spring

grip

chest expander

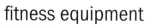

barbell

collar

disk

bar

sleeve

stationary bicycle

resistance adjustment

handlebar

seat

timer

height adjustment

speedometer

footstrap

brake

pedal

flywheel

weight machine

cable

lateral bar

pectoral deck

press bar

bench

leg curl bar

leg extension bar

triceps bar

weights

stair climber

rowing machine

oar

push-up stand

hydraulic resistance

foot support

sliding seat

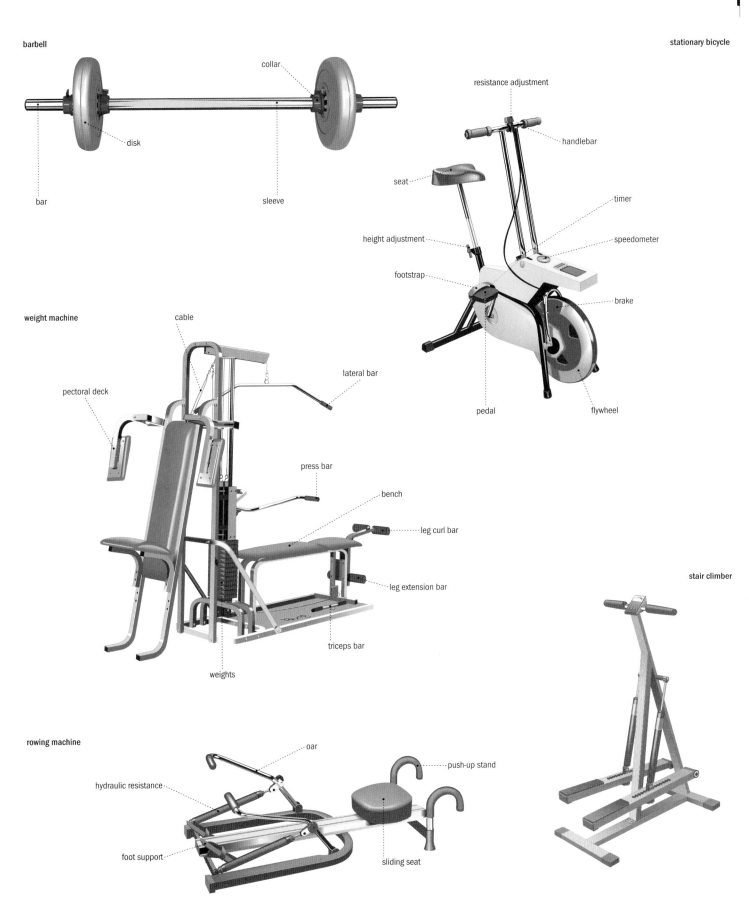

show-jumping

obstacles

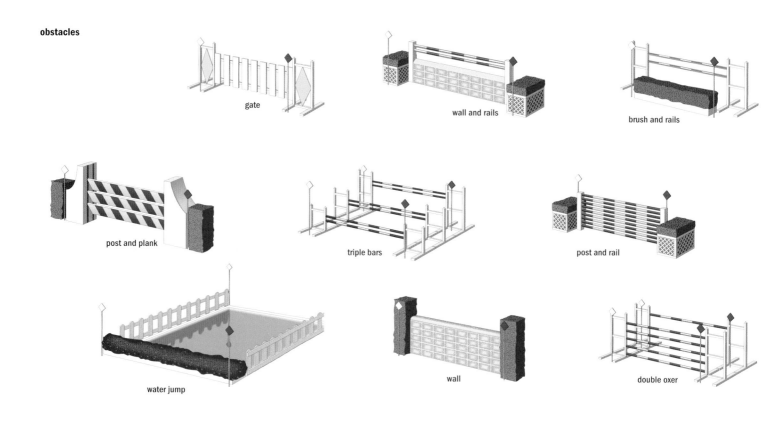

gate

wall and rails

brush and rails

post and plank

triple bars

post and rail

water jump

wall

double oxer

competition ring

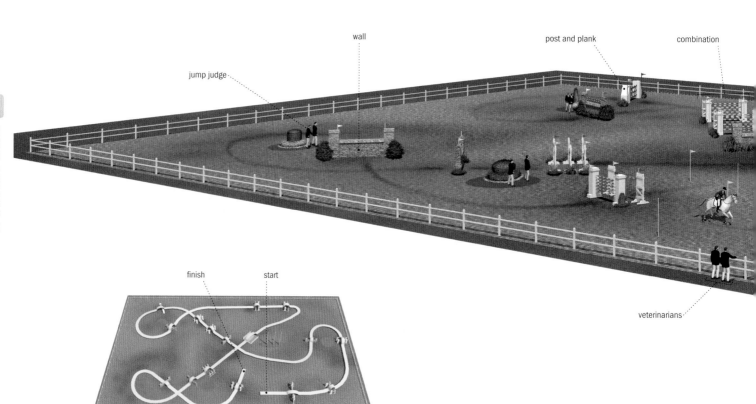

jump judge

wall

post and plank

combination

veterinarians

finish

start

rider

riding jacket

riding cap

jodhpurs

saddle

riding glove

saddlecloth

riding crop

stirrup iron

breastplate

shin boot

surcingle

coronet boot

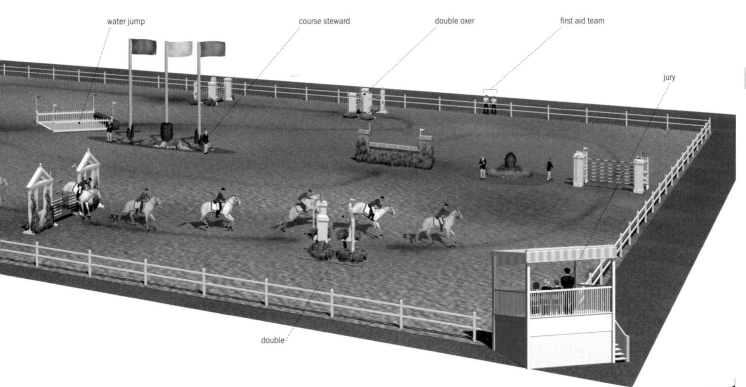

water jump

course steward

double oxer

first aid team

jury

double

riding

bridle

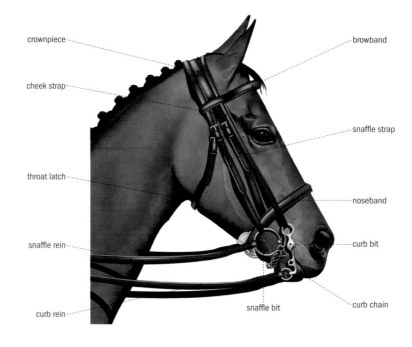

crownpiece

browband

cheek strap

snaffle strap

throat latch

noseband

snaffle rein

curb bit

curb rein

snaffle bit

curb chain

snaffle bit

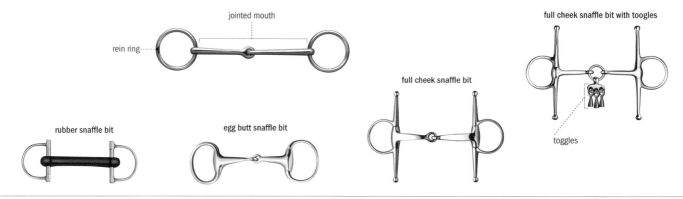

jointed mouth

rein ring

full cheek snaffle bit with toogles

full cheek snaffle bit

rubber snaffle bit

egg butt snaffle bit

toggles

curb bit

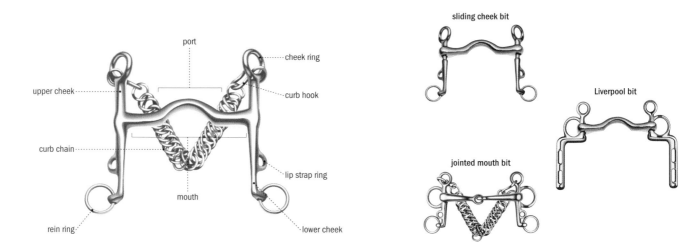

port

cheek ring

upper cheek

curb hook

curb chain

sliding cheek bit

lip strap ring

Liverpool bit

mouth

jointed mouth bit

rein ring

lower cheek

riding

saddle

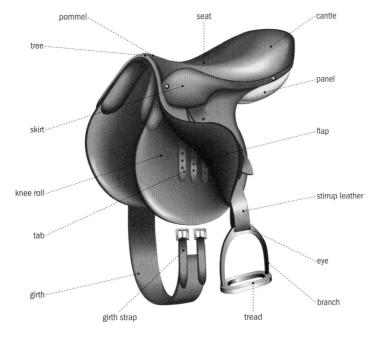

pommel · seat · cantle
tree · panel
skirt · flap
knee roll · stirrup leather
tab · eye
girth · branch
girth strap · tread

dressage

rider

jacket
glove
saddle
boot
stirrup iron
surcingle

show ring

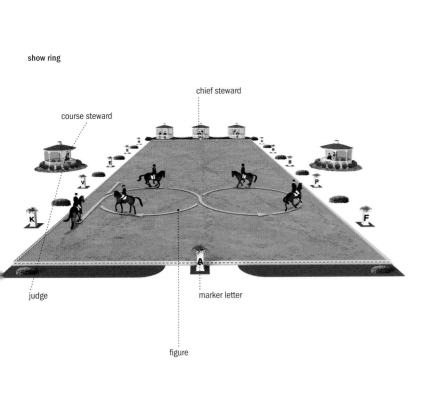

chief steward
course steward
judge · marker letter
figure

horse racing: turf

jockey and racehorse

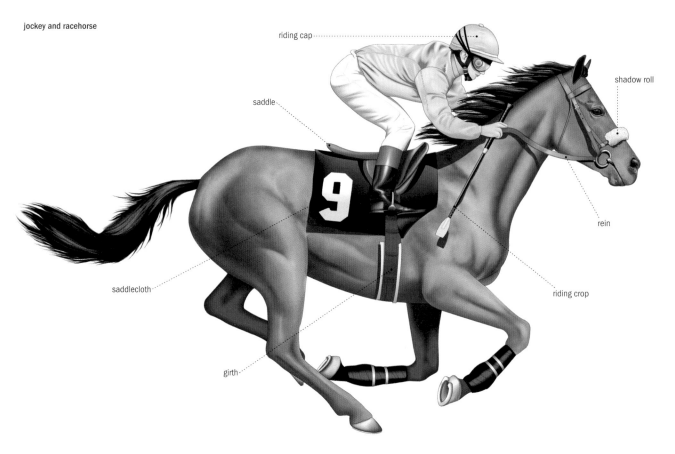

riding cap

shadow roll

saddle

rein

saddlecloth

riding crop

girth

racetrack

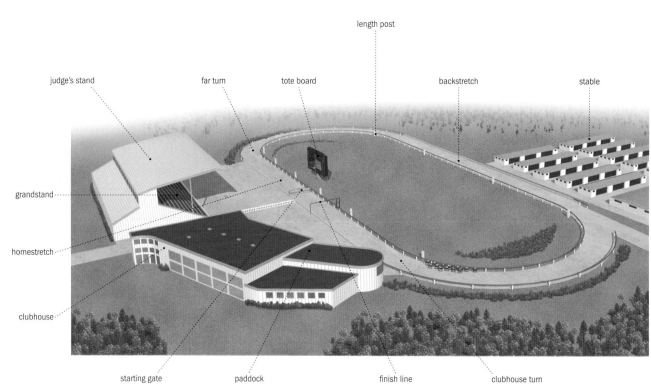

length post

judge's stand

far turn

tote board

backstretch

stable

grandstand

homestretch

clubhouse

starting gate

paddock

finish line

clubhouse turn

horse racing: harness racing

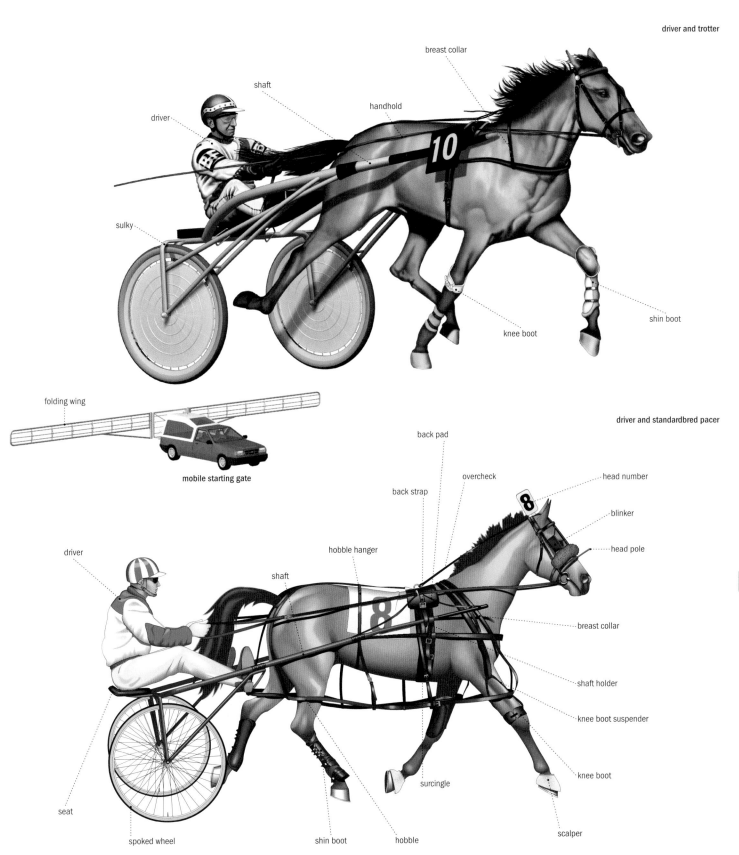

driver and trotter

breast collar

shaft

handhold

driver

sulky

folding wing

mobile starting gate

shin boot

knee boot

driver and standardbred pacer

back pad

overcheck

head number

back strap

blinker

head pole

hobble hanger

driver

shaft

breast collar

shaft holder

knee boot suspender

seat

knee boot

spoked wheel

shin boot

hobble

surcingle

scalper

SPORTS AND GAMES

polo

rider and horse

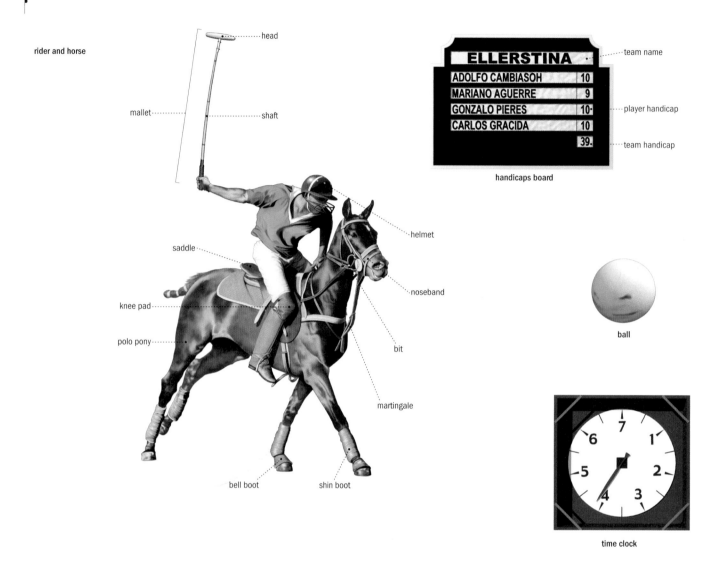

head

mallet

shaft

helmet

saddle

noseband

knee pad

polo pony

bit

martingale

bell boot

shin boot

ELLERSTINA

ELLERSTINA	
ADOLFO CAMBIASOH	10
MARIANO AGUERRE	9
GONZALO PIERES	10·
CARLOS GRACIDA	10
	39.

team name

player handicap

team handicap

handicaps board

ball

time clock

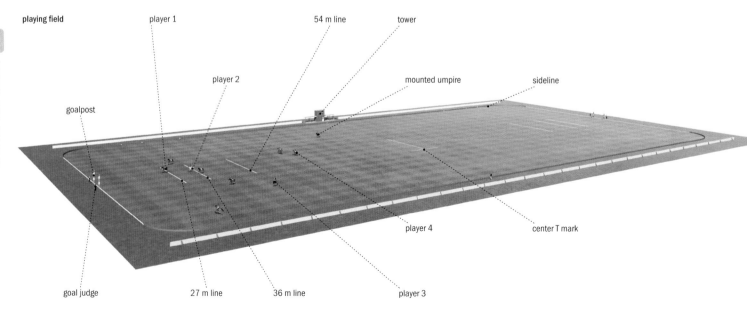

playing field

player 1

54 m line

tower

player 2

mounted umpire

sideline

goalpost

player 4

center T mark

goal judge

27 m line

36 m line

player 3

SPORTS AND GAMES

archery

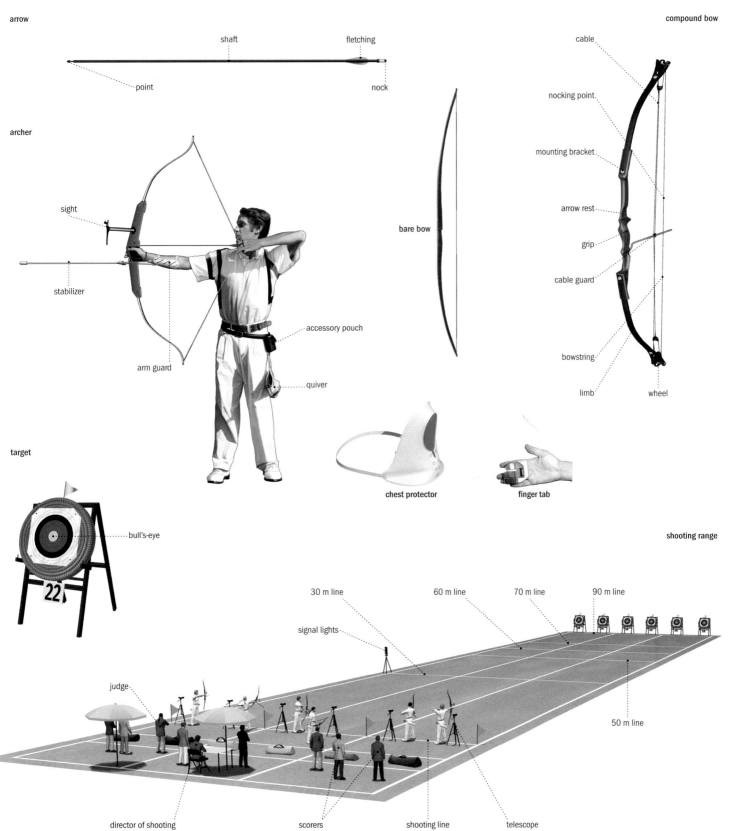

arrow

shaft

fletching

point

nock

compound bow

cable

nocking point

mounting bracket

arrow rest

grip

cable guard

bowstring

limb

wheel

archer

sight

stabilizer

arm guard

accessory pouch

quiver

bare bow

chest protector

finger tab

target

bull's-eye

22

shooting range

30 m line

signal lights

60 m line

70 m line

90 m line

judge

50 m line

director of shooting

scorers

shooting line

telescope

SPORTS AND GAMES

shotgun shooting

shotgun

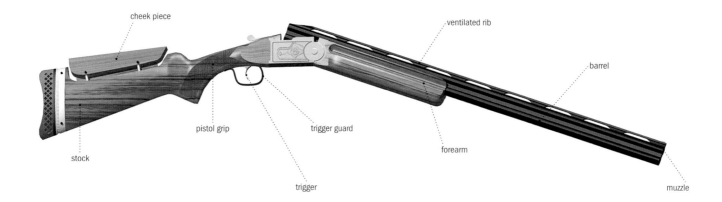

cheek piece

ventilated rib

barrel

pistol grip

trigger guard

forearm

stock

trigger

muzzle

plastic case

clay target

base

cartridges

clay target

trap machine

shooting range

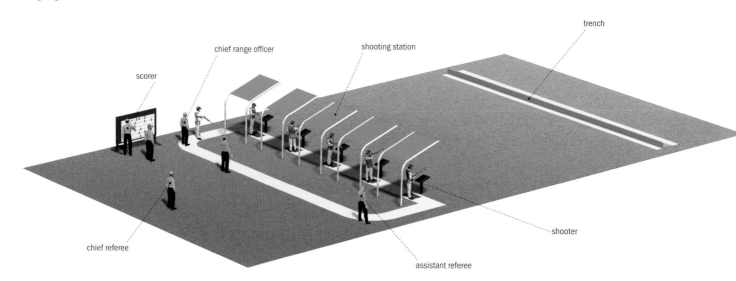

trench

chief range officer

shooting station

scorer

shooter

chief referee

assistant referee

rifle shooting

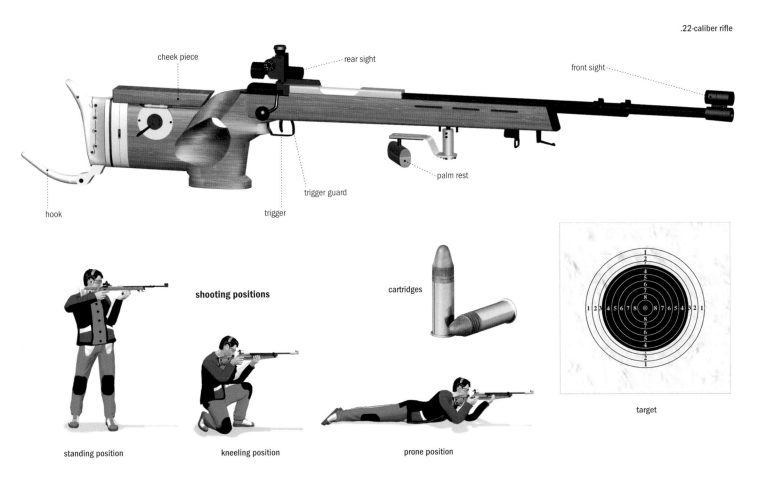

.22-caliber rifle

cheek piece

rear sight

front sight

hook

trigger

trigger guard

palm rest

shooting positions

cartridges

target

standing position

kneeling position

prone position

pistol shooting

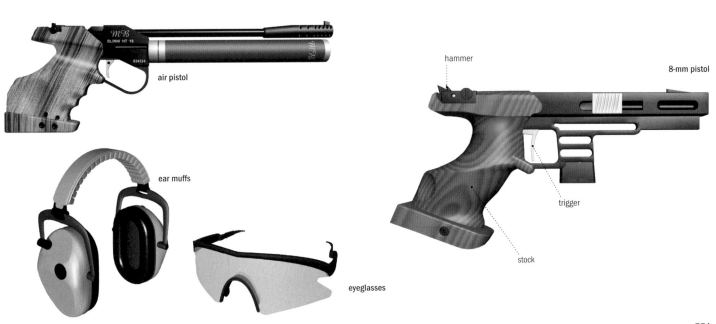

air pistol

hammer

8-mm pistol

ear muffs

trigger

eyeglasses

stock

billiards

SPORTS AND GAMES

carom billiards

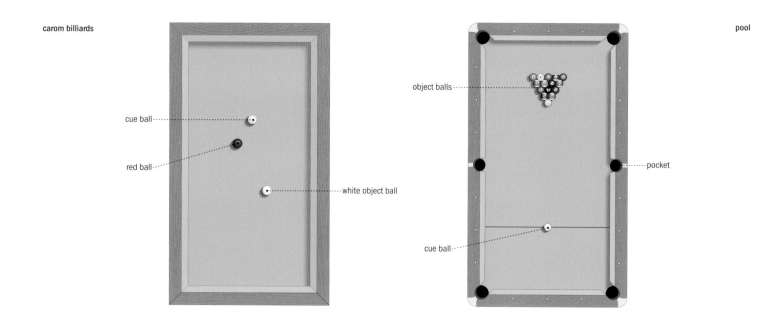

cue ball

red ball

white object ball

pool

object balls

pocket

cue ball

table

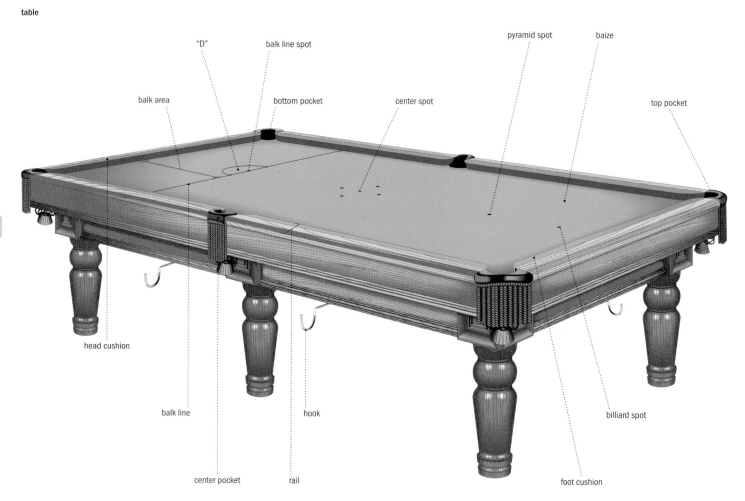

"D"

balk line spot

pyramid spot

baize

balk area

bottom pocket

center spot

top pocket

head cushion

balk line

hook

billiard spot

center pocket

rail

foot cushion

snooker

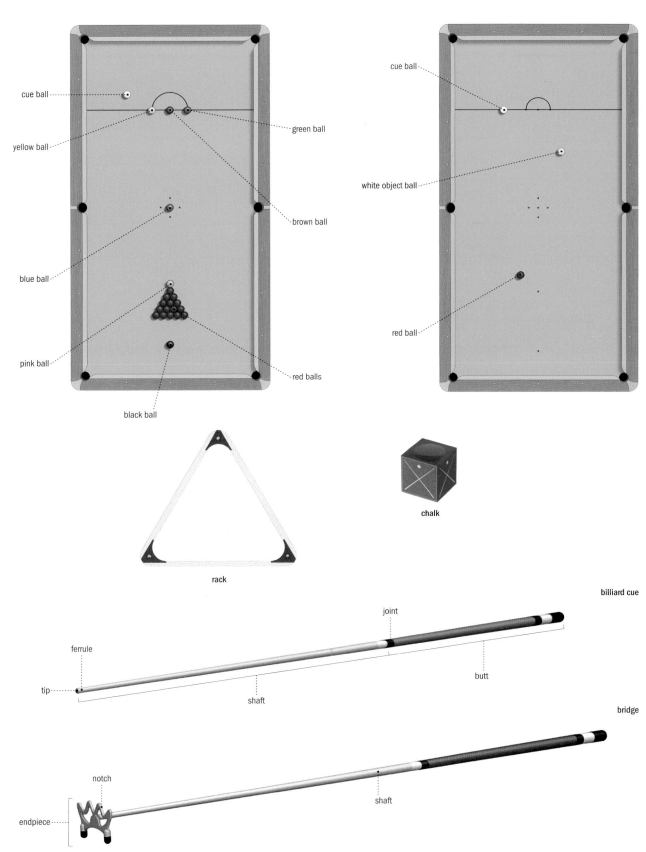

cue ball

yellow ball

green ball

brown ball

blue ball

pink ball

red balls

black ball

cue ball

white object ball

red ball

rack

chalk

billiard cue

joint

ferrule

butt

tip

shaft

bridge

notch

shaft

endpiece

lawn bowling

bowls

jack

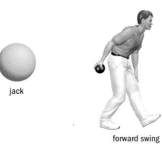

forward swing

bowling technique

follow-through

bowling technique

green

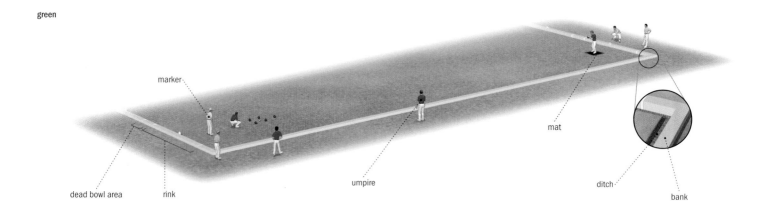

marker

mat

dead bowl area

rink

umpire

ditch

bank

petanque

playing field

referee

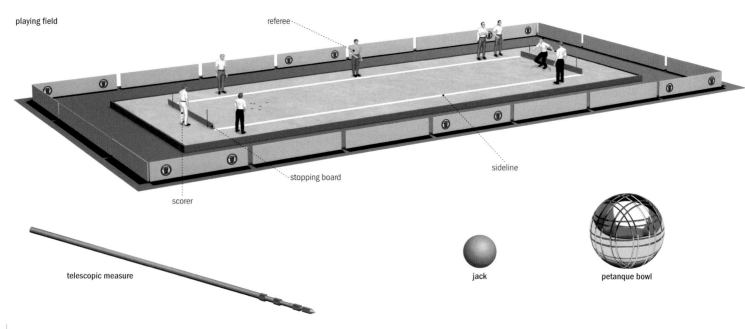

scorer

stopping board

sideline

telescopic measure

jack

petanque bowl

bowling

examples of pins

American duckpin

tenpin

candlepin

fivepin

Canadian duckpin

setup

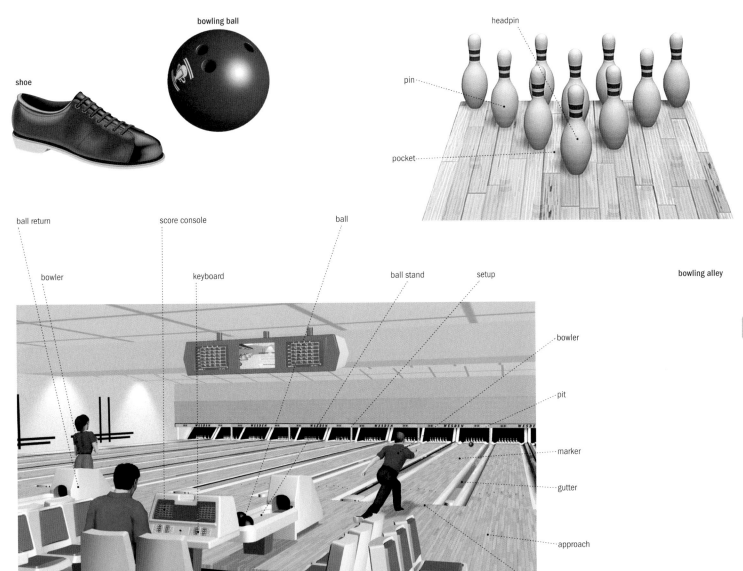

bowling ball

shoe

headpin

pin

pocket

ball return

score console

ball

bowler

keyboard

ball stand

setup

bowling alley

bowler

pit

marker

gutter

approach

foul line

golf

course

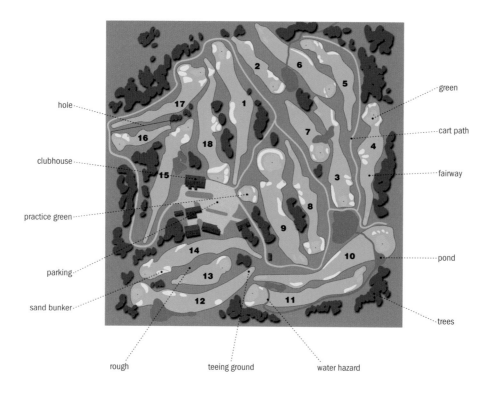

hole

green

cart path

clubhouse

fairway

practice green

parking

pond

sand bunker

trees

rough

teeing ground

water hazard

holes

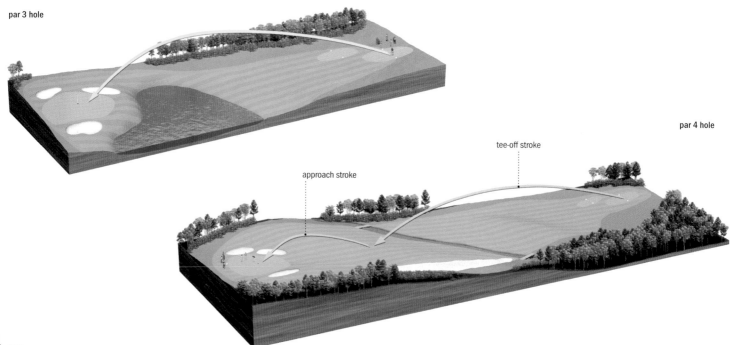

par 3 hole

par 4 hole

tee-off stroke

approach stroke

types of golf clubs

golf ball

grip

shaft

cover

dimple

tee

face

head

cross section of a golf ball

cover

rubber thread

core

putter

iron

wood

par 5 hole

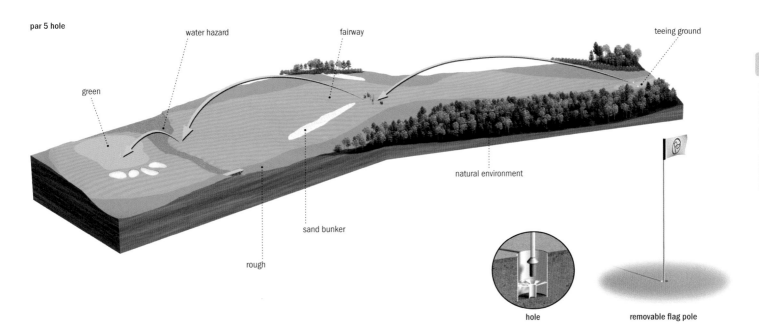

water hazard

fairway

teeing ground

green

natural environment

rough

sand bunker

hole

removable flag pole

golf

wood

iron

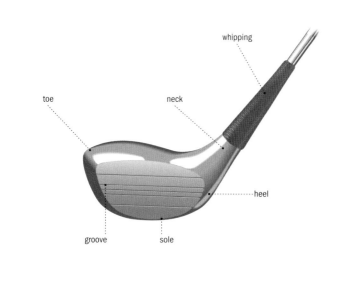

whipping

ferrule

toe

neck

neck

toe

heel

groove

sole

groove

sole

heel

driver

3-wood

5-wood

putter

3-iron

4-iron

5-iron

6-iron

7-iron

8-iron

9-iron

pitching wedge

lob wedge

sand wedge

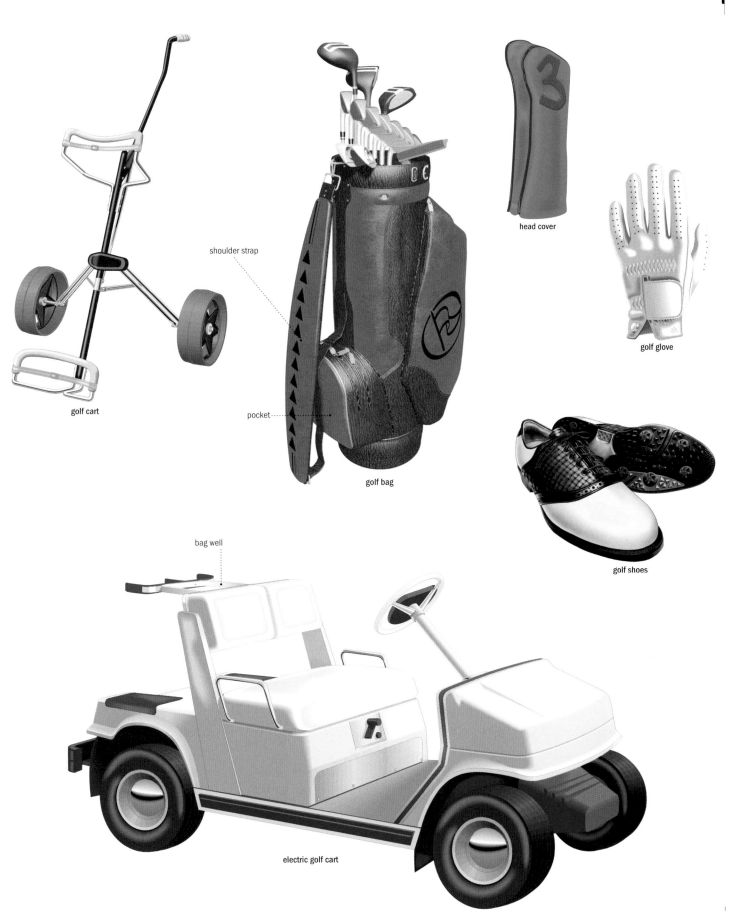

head cover

golf glove

shoulder strap

golf cart

pocket

golf bag

golf shoes

bag well

electric golf cart

road racing

road-racing bicycle and cyclist

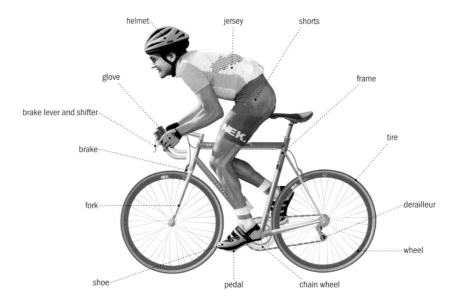

helmet   jersey   shorts

glove   frame

brake lever and shifter

brake   tire

fork   derailleur

                                wheel

shoe   pedal   chain wheel

road cycling competition

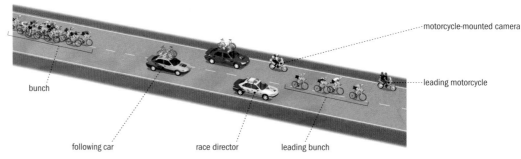

motorcycle-mounted camera

bunch   leading motorcycle

following car   race director   leading bunch

mountain biking

cross-country bicycle and cyclist   downhill bicycle and cyclist

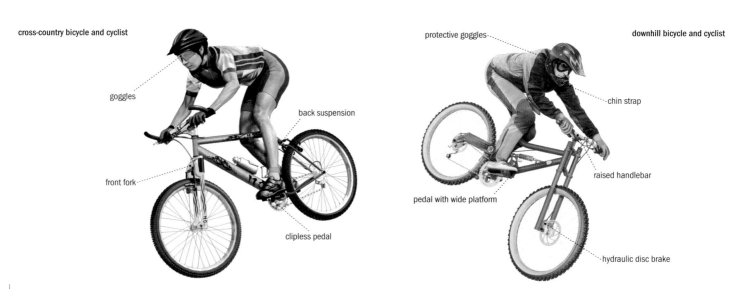

protective goggles

goggles   chin strap

                back suspension

front fork   raised handlebar

                                pedal with wide platform

                clipless pedal

                                hydraulic disc brake

track cycling

pursuit bicycle and racer

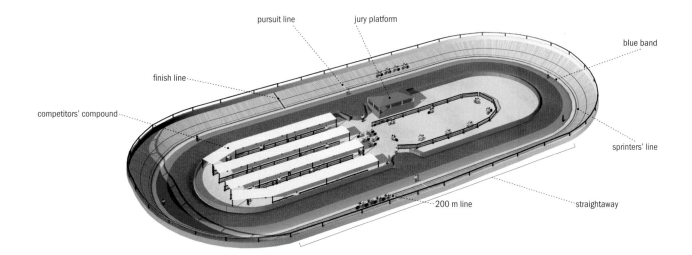

seat tube

helmet

handlebar

solid rear wheel

handlebar grip

track

pursuit line

jury platform

blue band

finish line

competitors' compound

sprinters' line

200 m line

straightaway

BMX

helmet

half-pipe

glove

handlebars

single chain wheel

foot pegs

single sprocket

car racing

driver

balaclava

undergarment

flame-resistant driving suit

crash helmet

shoe

ear plugs/earbuds

wet-weather tire

gloves

dry-weather tire

checkered flag

starting grid

pole position

track

circuit

starting line

pits

chicane

gravel bed

pit lane

curb

tire barrier

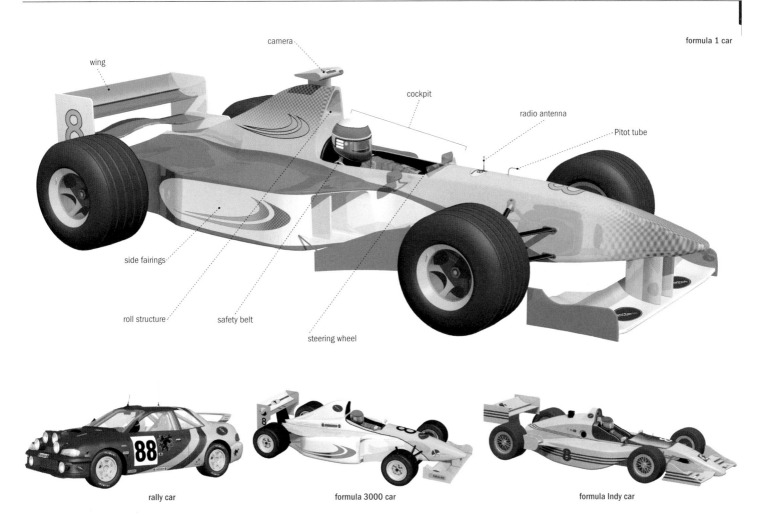

formula 1 car

camera

wing

cockpit

radio antenna

Pitot tube

side fairings

roll structure

safety belt

steering wheel

rally car

formula 3000 car

formula Indy car

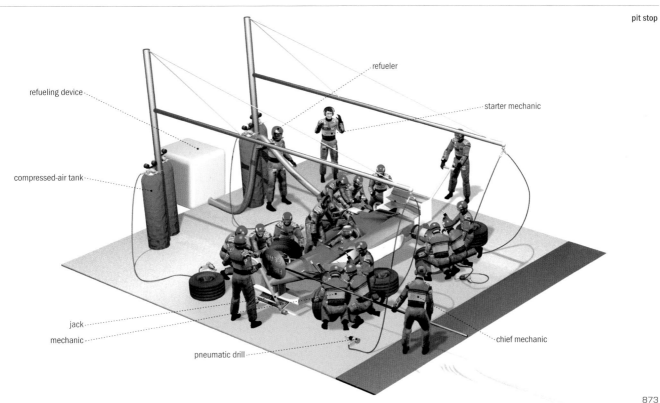

pit stop

refueler

refueling device

starter mechanic

compressed-air tank

jack

mechanic

chief mechanic

pneumatic drill

motorcycling

speed grand prix motorcycle and rider

full face helmet

visor

neck support

glove

racing suit

rub protection

boot

disk brake

wheel

air intake for engine cooling

tire

course

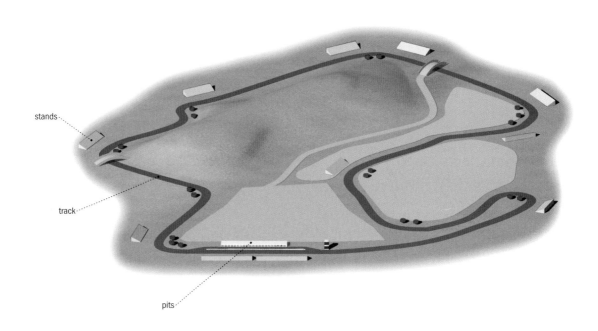

stands

track

pits

trial motorcycle

rally motorcycle

motocross and supercross motorcycle

protective suit

glove

pants

helmet

protective goggles

hand protector

number plate

fork

nubby tire

boot

protective plate

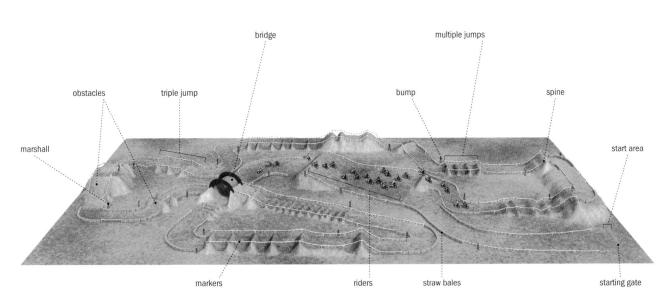

supercross circuit

bridge

multiple jumps

obstacles

triple jump

bump

spine

marshall

start area

markers

riders

straw bales

starting gate

personal watercraft

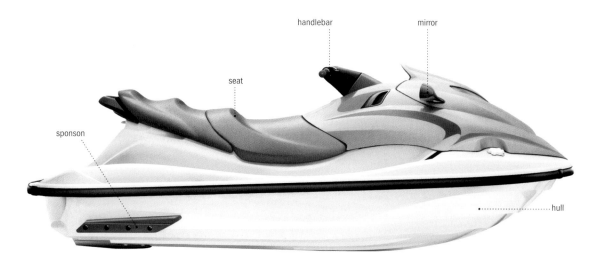

handlebar

mirror

seat

sponson

hull

snowmobile

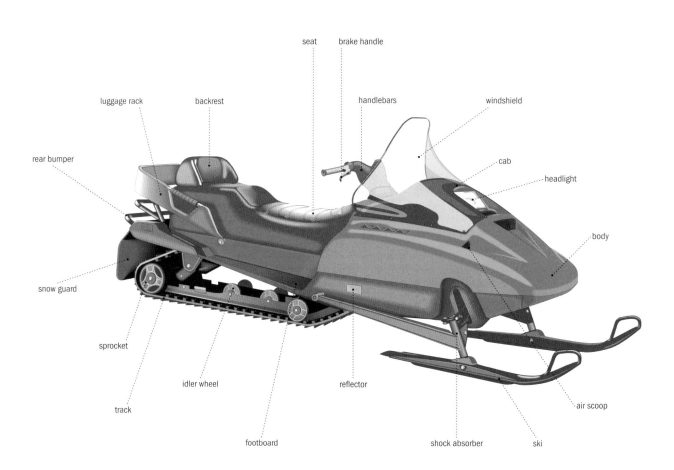

seat

brake handle

luggage rack

backrest

handlebars

windshield

rear bumper

cab

headlight

body

snow guard

sprocket

idler wheel

reflector

air scoop

track

footboard

shock absorber

ski

curling

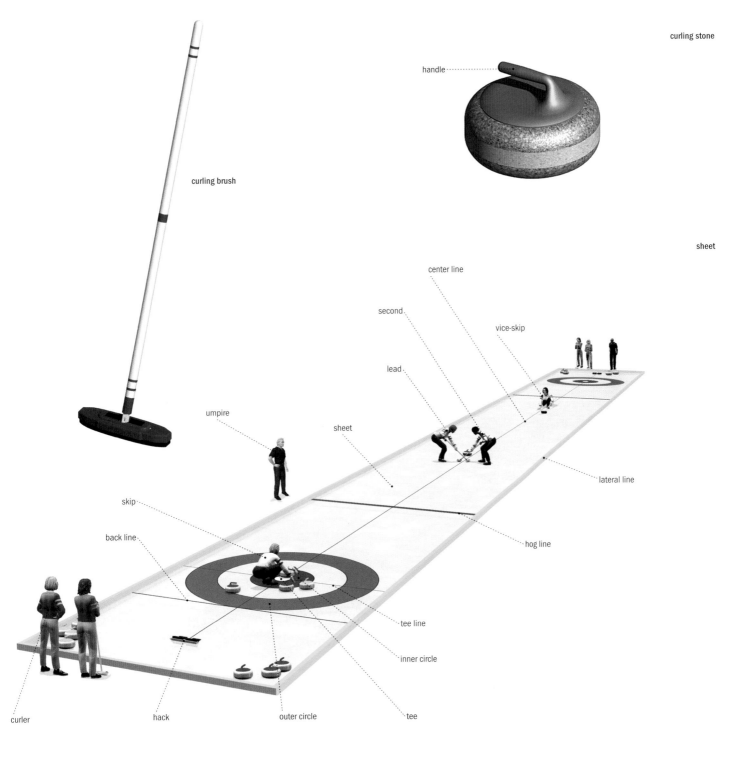

curling stone

handle

curling brush

sheet

center line

second

vice-skip

lead

umpire

sheet

lateral line

skip

back line

hog line

tee line

inner circle

curler

hack

outer circle

tee

house

free guard zone

ice hockey

ice hockey player

visor

helmet

team's emblem

player's number

glove

pants

stocking

skate

blade

rink

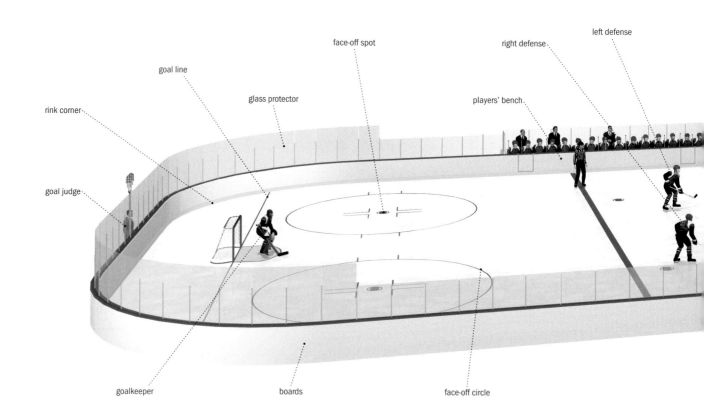

rink corner

goal line

glass protector

face-off spot

right defense

left defense

players' bench

goal judge

goalkeeper

boards

face-off circle

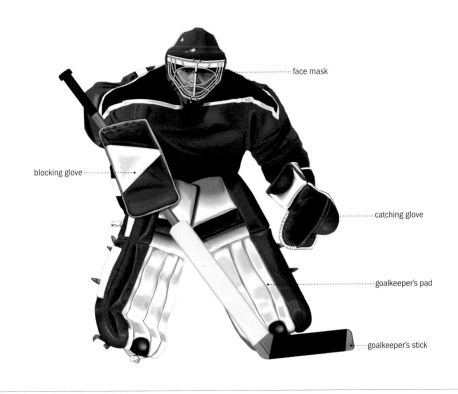

goalkeeper

face mask

blocking glove

catching glove

goalkeeper's pad

goalkeeper's stick

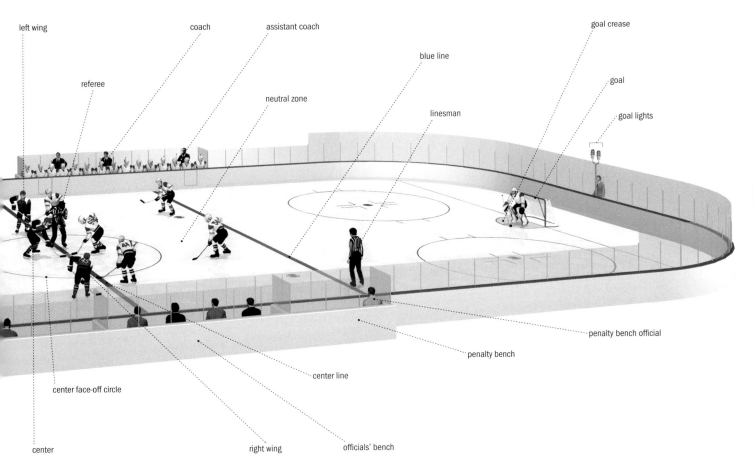

left wing

coach

assistant coach

goal crease

referee

blue line

goal

neutral zone

goal lights

linesman

center face-off circle

penalty bench official

penalty bench

center line

center

right wing

officials' bench

ice hockey

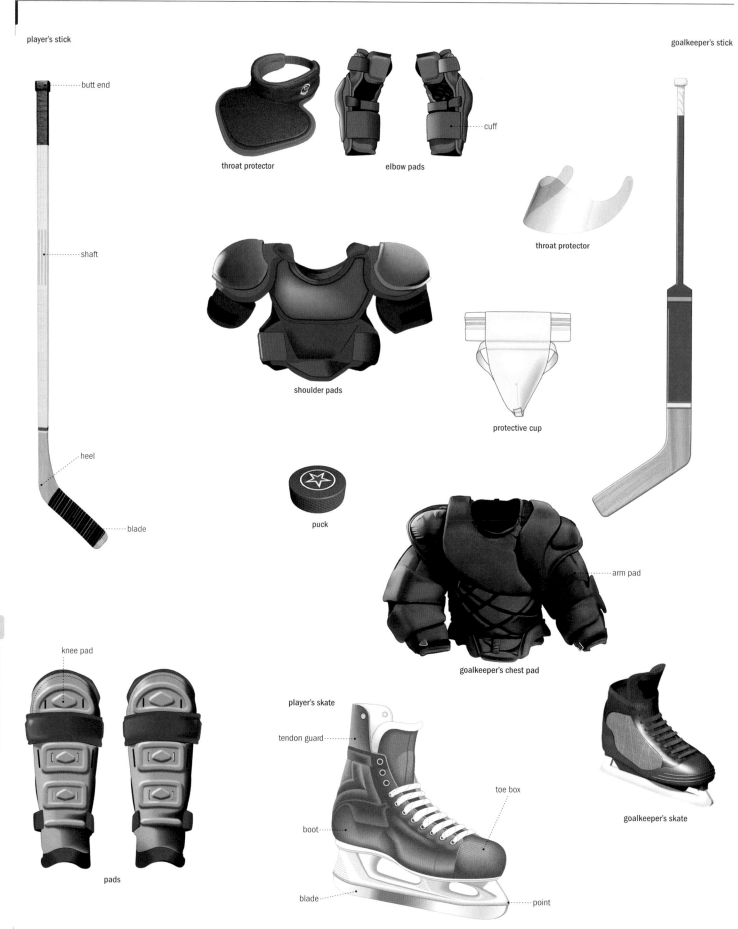

player's stick

butt end

shaft

heel

blade

throat protector

elbow pads

cuff

shoulder pads

throat protector

protective cup

puck

goalkeeper's stick

goalkeeper's chest pad

arm pad

knee pad

pads

player's skate

tendon guard

boot

toe box

blade

point

goalkeeper's skate

figure skating

figure skate

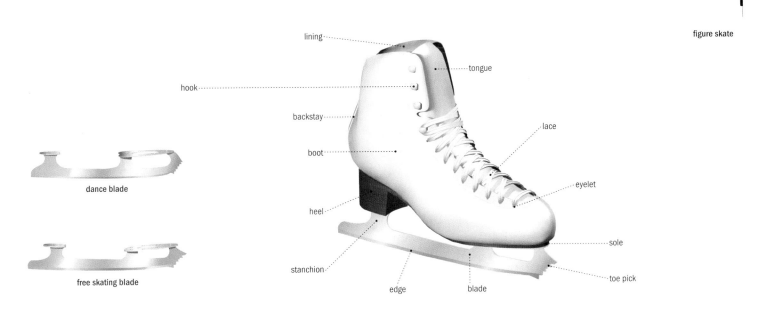

lining
tongue
hook
backstay
lace
boot
heel
eyelet
stanchion
sole
edge
blade
toe pick

dance blade

free skating blade

examples of jumps

salchow

axel

toe loop

flip

lutz

rink

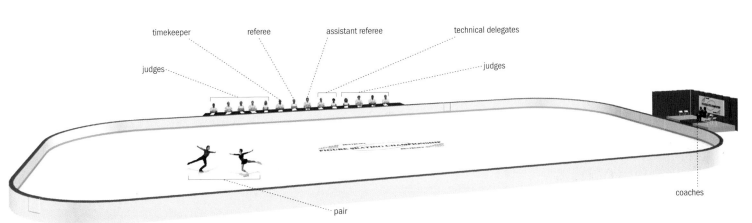

timekeeper
referee
assistant referee
technical delegates
judges
judges

coaches

pair

speed skating

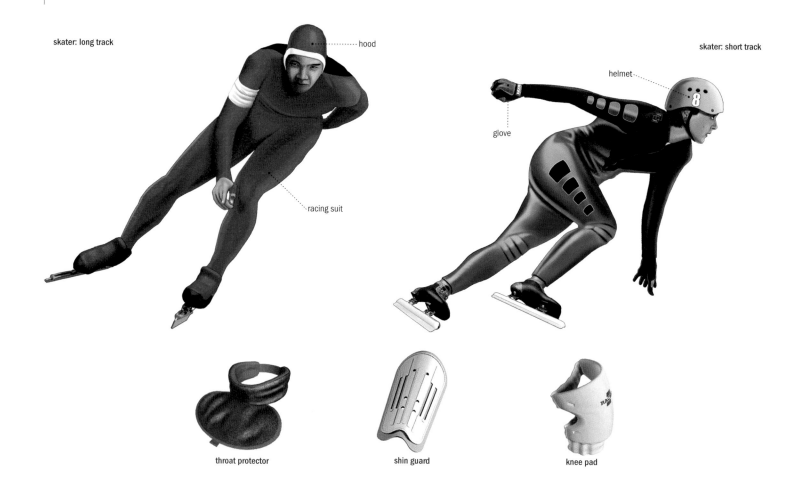

skater: long track

hood

racing suit

skater: short track

helmet

glove

throat protector

shin guard

knee pad

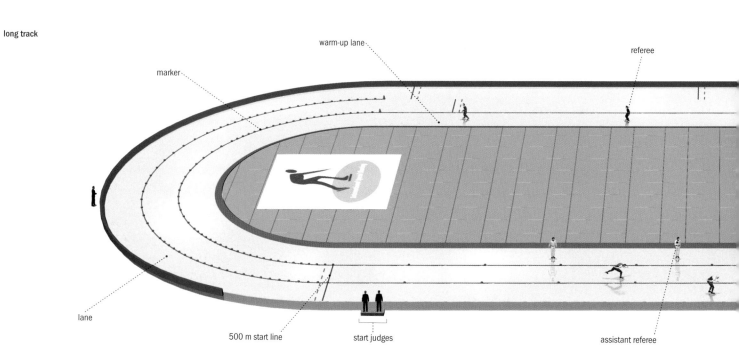

long track

warm-up lane

referee

marker

lane

500 m start line

start judges

assistant referee

speed skates

clapskate

short track skate

short track

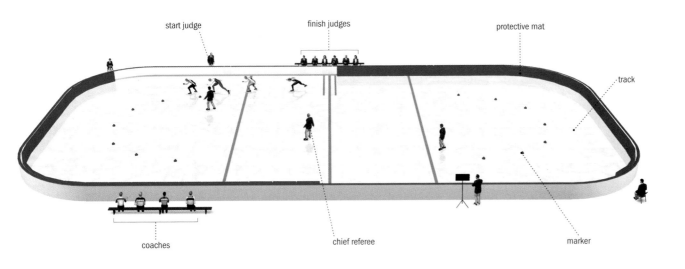

start judge

finish judges

protective mat

track

coaches

chief referee

marker

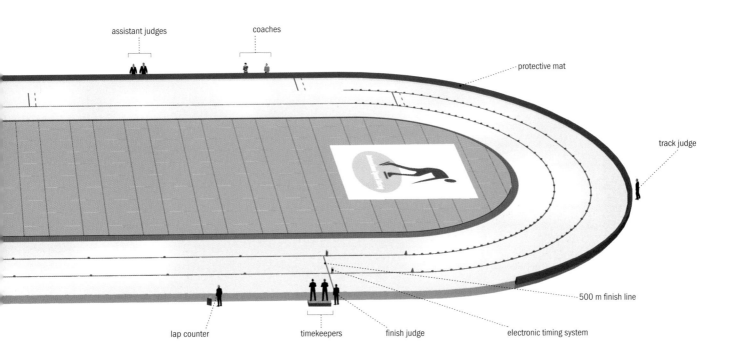

assistant judges

coaches

protective mat

track judge

500 m finish line

lap counter

timekeepers

finish judge

electronic timing system

bobsled

four-person bobsled

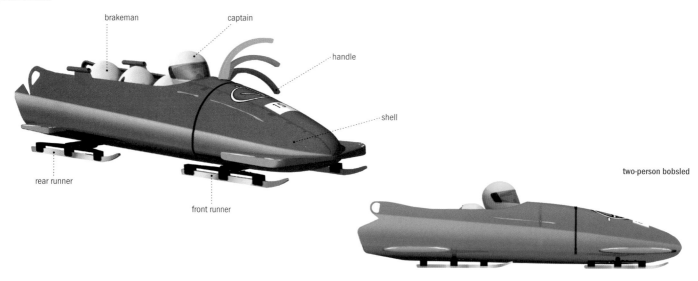

brakeman

captain

handle

shell

rear runner

front runner

two-person bobsled

luge

luge racer

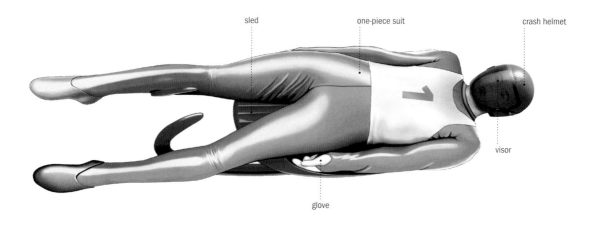

sled

one-piece suit

crash helmet

visor

glove

singles luge

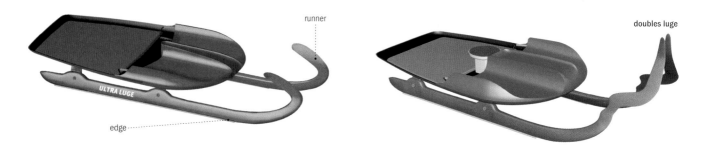

runner

doubles luge

ULTRA LUGE

edge

skeleton

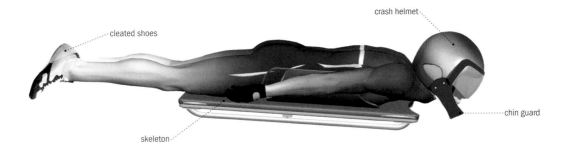

cleated shoes
crash helmet
chin guard
skeleton

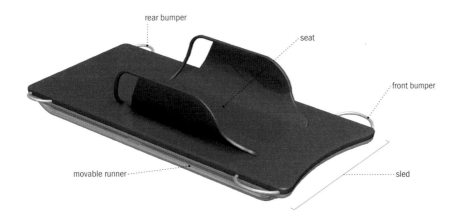

rear bumper
seat
front bumper
movable runner
sled

track

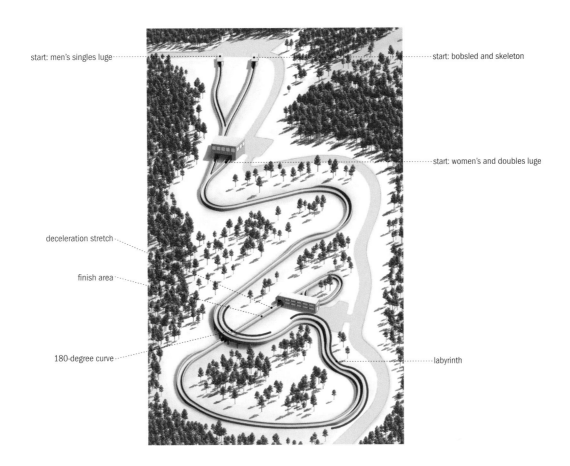

start: men's singles luge
start: bobsled and skeleton
start: women's and doubles luge
deceleration stretch
finish area
180-degree curve
labyrinth

SPORTS AND GAMES

ski resort

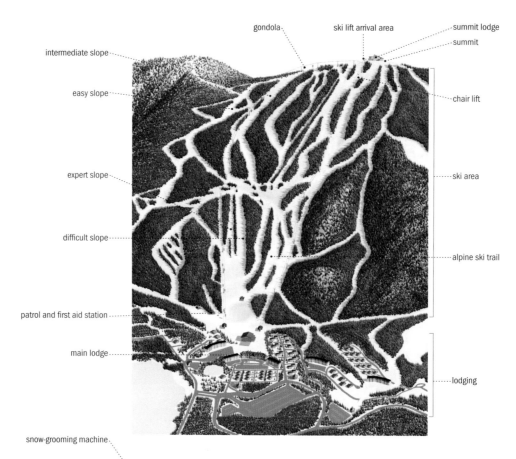

intermediate slope

gondola

ski lift arrival area

summit lodge

summit

easy slope

chair lift

expert slope

ski area

difficult slope

alpine ski trail

patrol and first aid station

main lodge

lodging

snow-grooming machine

ski school

T-bar

chair lift departure area

cross-country ski trail

skiers' lodge

gondolas departure area

ice rink

condominium

hotel

mountain lodge

information desk

village

parking

snowboarder

hard boot

helmet

goggles

coveralls

shin guard

glove

snowboard

flexible boot

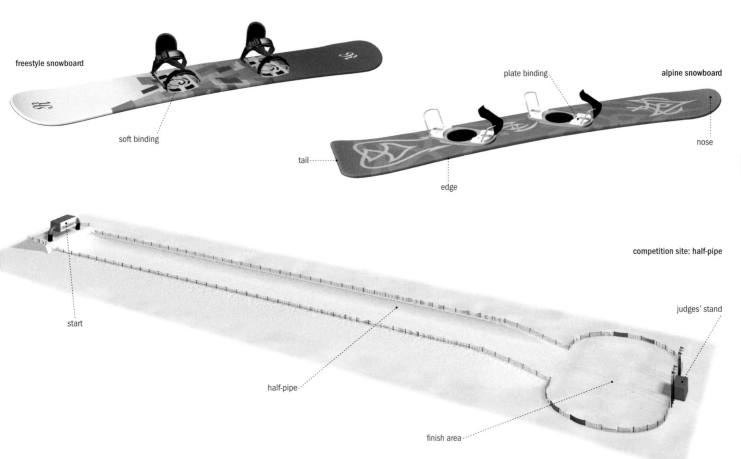

freestyle snowboard

plate binding

alpine snowboard

soft binding

nose

tail

edge

competition site: half-pipe

start

half-pipe

judges' stand

finish area

alpine skiing

alpine skier

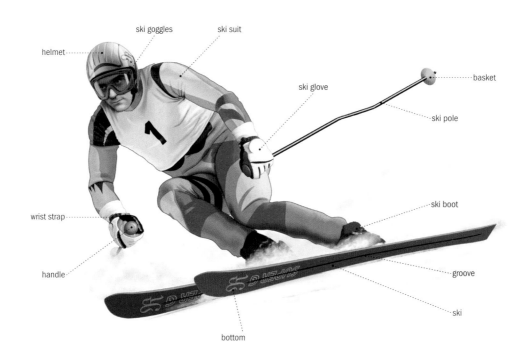

ski goggles

ski suit

helmet

ski glove

basket

ski pole

ski boot

wrist strap

groove

handle

ski

bottom

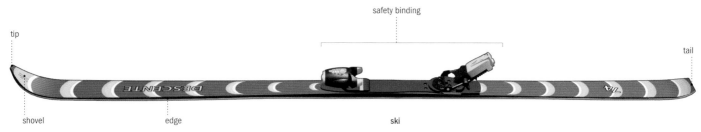

safety binding

tip

tail

shovel

edge

ski

examples of skis

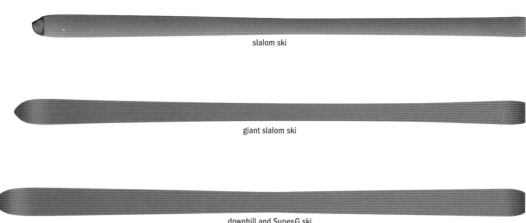

slalom ski

giant slalom ski

downhill and Super-G ski

technical events

downhill

super giant (super-G) slalom

giant slalom

special slalom

ski boot

inner boot

upper cuff

upper

tongue

upper shell

upper strap

buckle

adjusting catch

hinge

sole

lower shell

safety binding

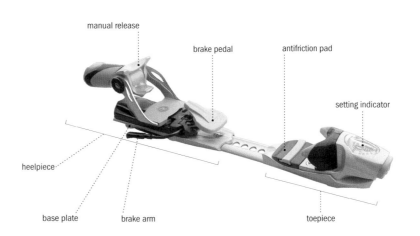

manual release

brake pedal

antifriction pad

setting indicator

heelpiece

base plate

brake arm

toepiece

freestyle skiing

course: moguls competition

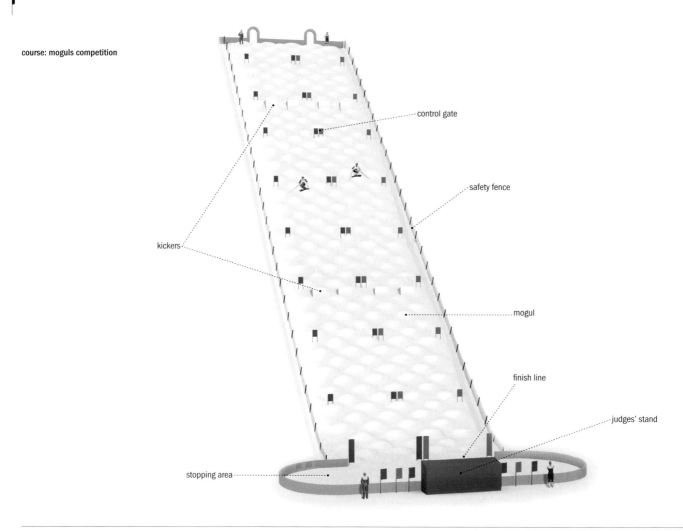

control gate

safety fence

kickers

mogul

finish line

judges' stand

stopping area

aerial site

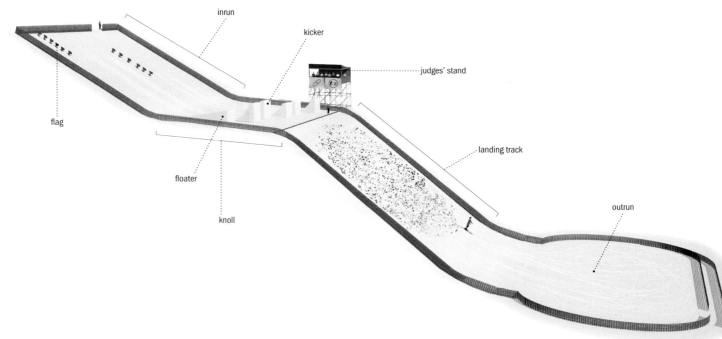

inrun

kicker

judges' stand

flag

landing track

floater

outrun

knoll

ski jumping

jumping technique

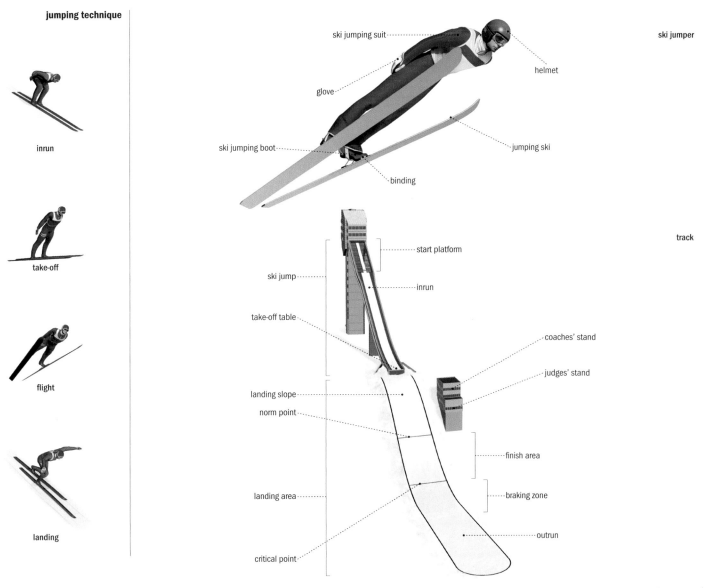

inrun

take-off

flight

landing

ski jumping suit

helmet

glove

ski jumper

ski jumping boot

jumping ski

binding

start platform

ski jump

inrun

track

take-off table

coaches' stand

judges' stand

landing slope

norm point

finish area

landing area

braking zone

critical point

outrun

speed skiing

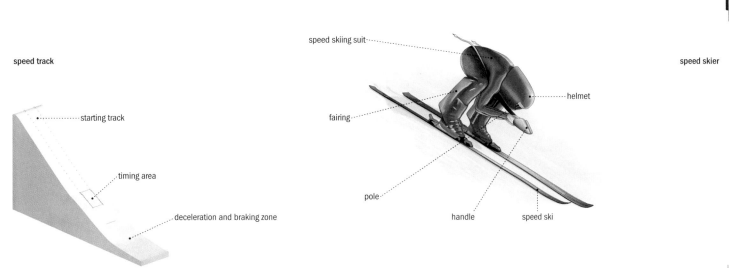

speed skiing suit

speed track

speed skier

helmet

fairing

starting track

timing area

pole

deceleration and braking zone

handle

speed ski

cross-country skiing

cross-country skier

turtleneck

ski hat

pole grip

waxing kit

cork

ski suit

pole shaft

ski pole

wrist strap

wax

scraper

cross-country ski

glove

boot

binding

shovel

cross-country ski

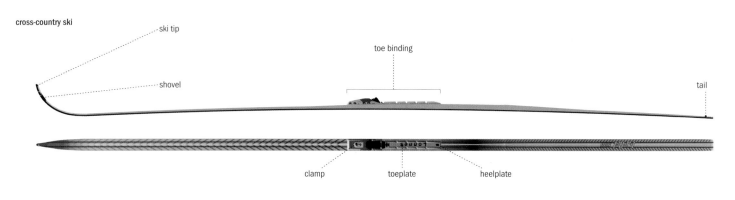

ski tip

toe binding

shovel

tail

clamp

toeplate

heelplate

skating step

diagonal step

skating kick

gliding phase

pushing phase

gliding phase

pushing phase

biathlon

shooting positions

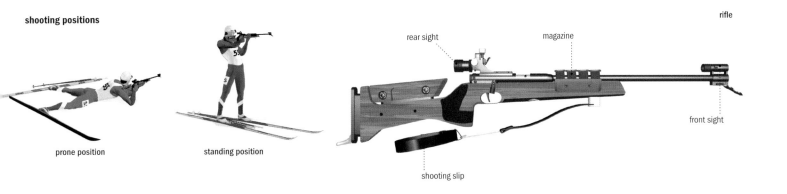

prone position

standing position

rifle

rear sight

magazine

front sight

shooting slip

shooting range

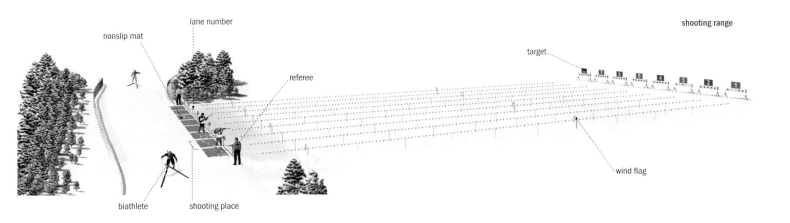

nonslip mat

lane number

referee

target

wind flag

biathlete

shooting place

snowshoes

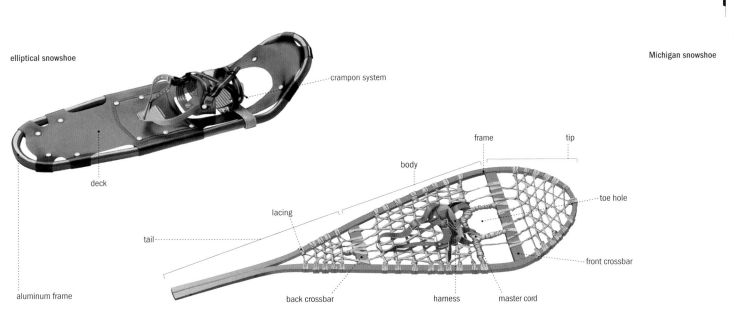

elliptical snowshoe

Michigan snowshoe

crampon system

frame

tip

body

deck

toe hole

lacing

tail

front crossbar

aluminum frame

back crossbar

harness

master cord

skateboarding

skateboard

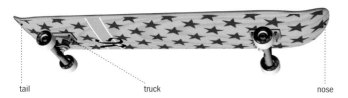

tail · truck · nose

grip tape

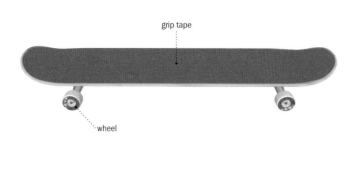

wheel

skateboarder

knee pad

elbow pad

helmet

coping

ramp

platform

coping

vertical section

flat

guard rail

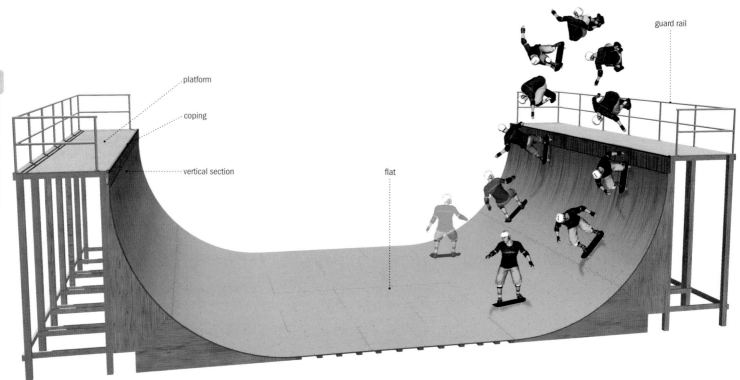

in-line skating

acrobatic skate

inner boot

upper shell

frame

wheel

skater

helmet

elbow pad

knee pad

wrist guard

in-line speed skate

in-line skate

in-line hockey skate

inner boot

upper shell

adjusting buckle

boot

axle

heel stop

wheel

truck

sky diving

sky diver

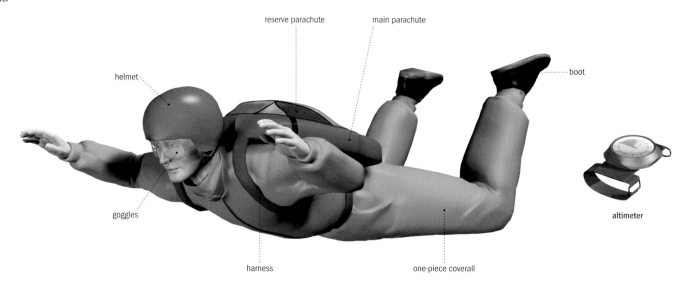

reserve parachute   main parachute

helmet

boot

goggles

altimeter

harness

one-piece coverall

canopy

parachute

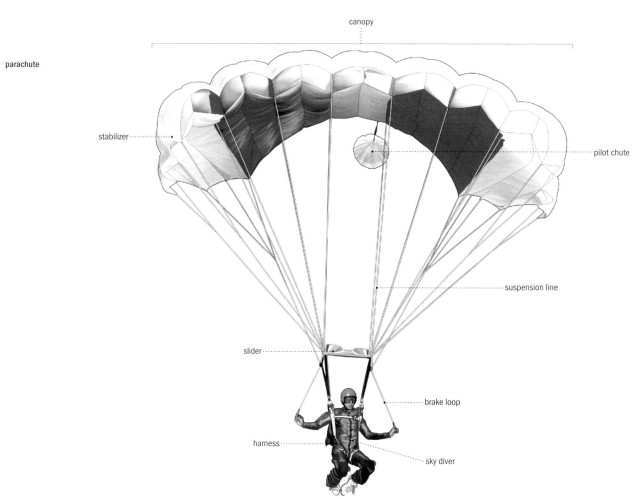

stabilizer

pilot chute

suspension line

slider

brake loop

harness

sky diver

paragliding

canopy

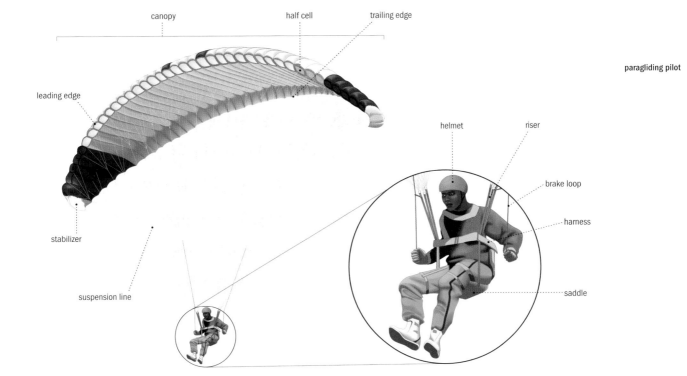

canopy   half cell   trailing edge

paragliding pilot

leading edge

helmet   riser

brake loop

harness

stabilizer

saddle

suspension line

hang gliding

hang glider

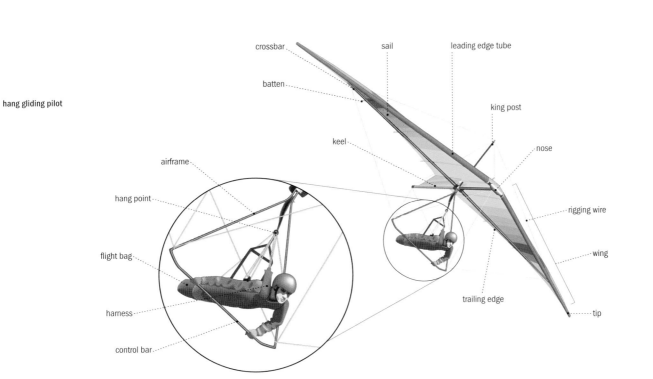

crossbar   sail   leading edge tube

batten

hang gliding pilot

king post

keel

nose

airframe

hang point

flight bag

rigging wire

harness

wing

trailing edge

control bar

tip

glider

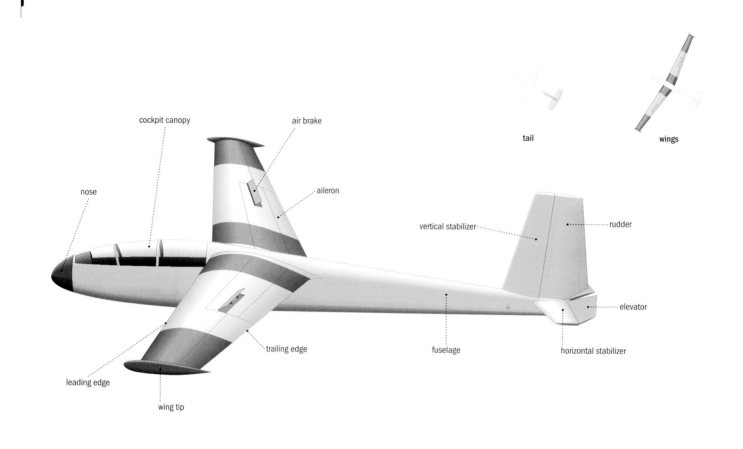

cockpit canopy

air brake

nose

aileron

tail

wings

vertical stabilizer

rudder

elevator

trailing edge

fuselage

horizontal stabilizer

leading edge

wing tip

cockpit

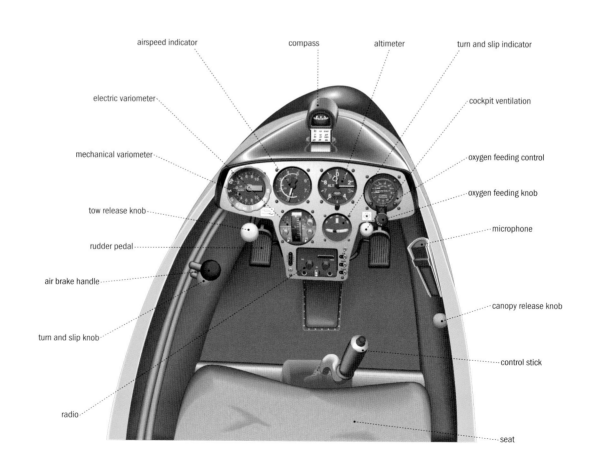

airspeed indicator

compass

altimeter

turn and slip indicator

electric variometer

cockpit ventilation

mechanical variometer

oxygen feeding control

oxygen feeding knob

tow release knob

microphone

rudder pedal

air brake handle

canopy release knob

turn and slip knob

control stick

radio

seat

ballooning

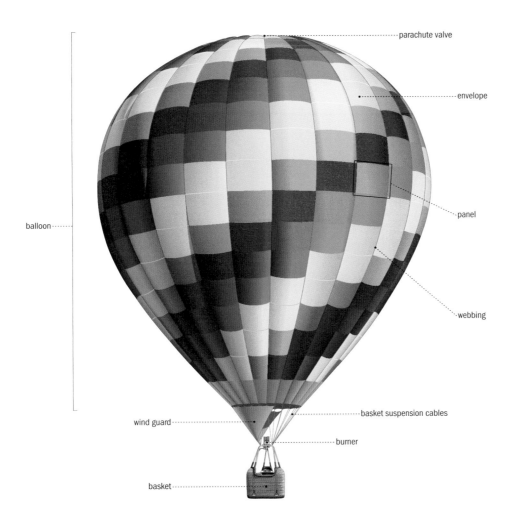

parachute valve

envelope

panel

balloon

webbing

wind guard

basket suspension cables

burner

basket

fuel lines

burner

heating coil

load support

blast valve

variometer

flight instruments

altimeter

thermometer

padding

wicker basket

basket handle

hardwood base

rock climbing

rock climber

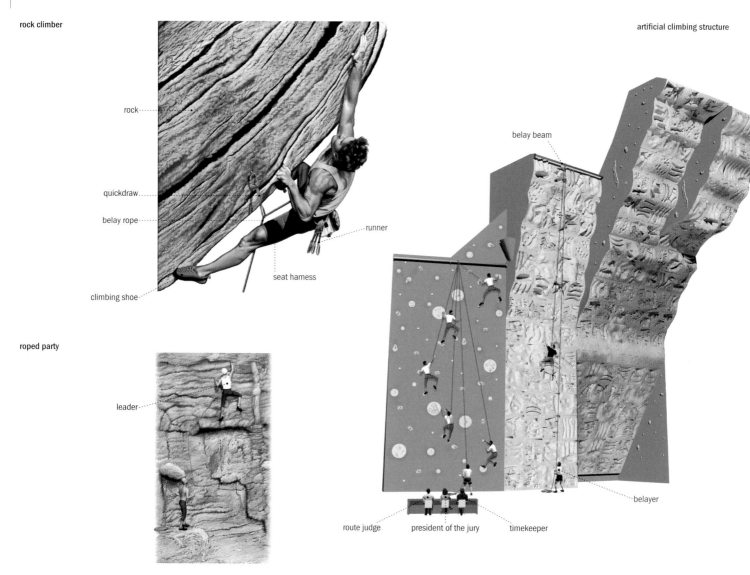

artificial climbing structure

rock

quickdraw

belay rope

climbing shoe

runner

seat harness

belay beam

roped party

leader

belayer

route judge   president of the jury   timekeeper

equipment

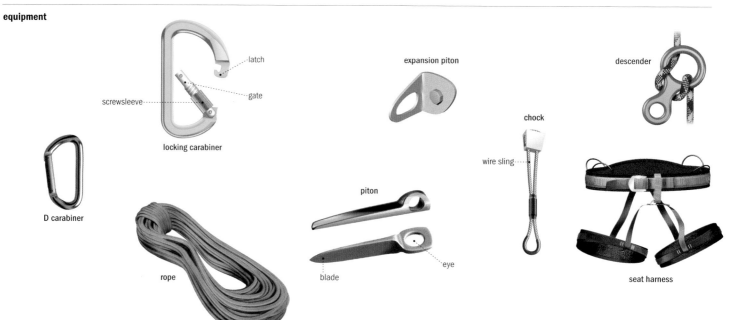

latch

screwsleeve

gate

locking carabiner

expansion piton

descender

chock

wire sling

D carabiner

piton

rope

blade

eye

seat harness

mountaineer

handholds

foothold

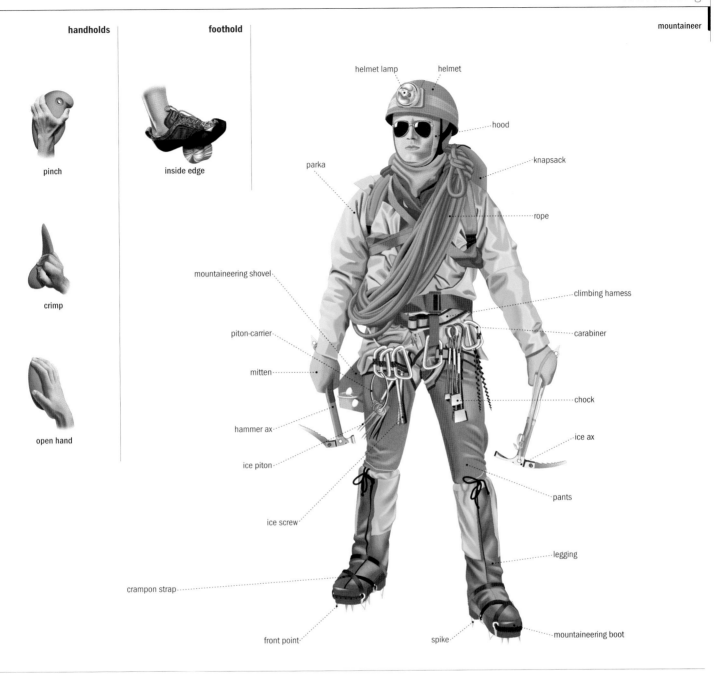

pinch

crimp

open hand

inside edge

helmet lamp

helmet

hood

parka

knapsack

rope

mountaineering shovel

climbing harness

piton-carrier

carabiner

mitten

chock

hammer ax

ice ax

ice piton

pants

ice screw

legging

crampon strap

front point

spike

mountaineering boot

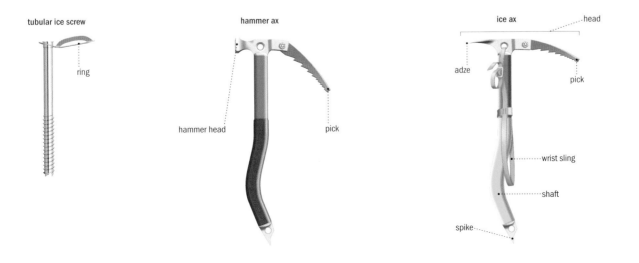

tubular ice screw

ring

hammer ax

hammer head

pick

ice ax

head

adze

pick

wrist sling

shaft

spike

camping

examples of tents

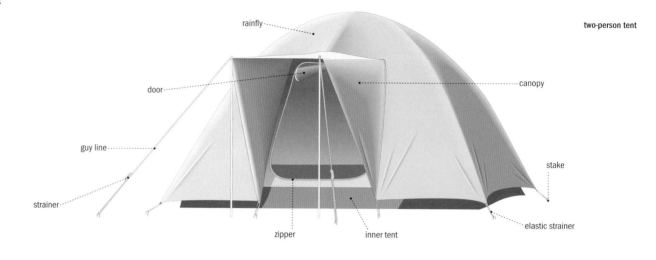

rainfly

door

guy line

strainer

zipper

inner tent

two-person tent

canopy

stake

elastic strainer

family tent

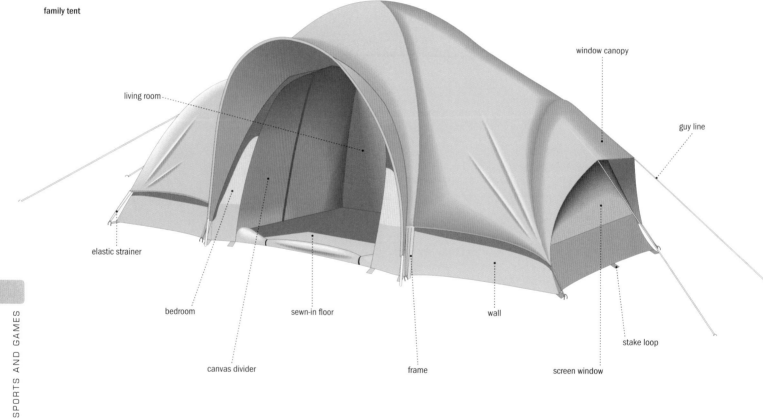

living room

window canopy

guy line

elastic strainer

bedroom

canvas divider

sewn-in floor

frame

wall

screen window

stake loop

wagon tent

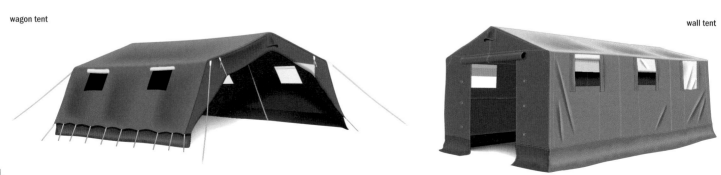

wall tent

pup tent

rainfly

roof pole

inner tent

elastic strainer

door

stake loop

sewn-in floor

stake

one-person tent

dome tent

pop-up tent

propane or butane accessories

lantern

globe

burner frame

pressure regulator

pump

leakproof cap

tank

heater

double-burner camp stove

burner

wire support

tank

single-burner camp stove

control valve

camping

examples of sleeping bags

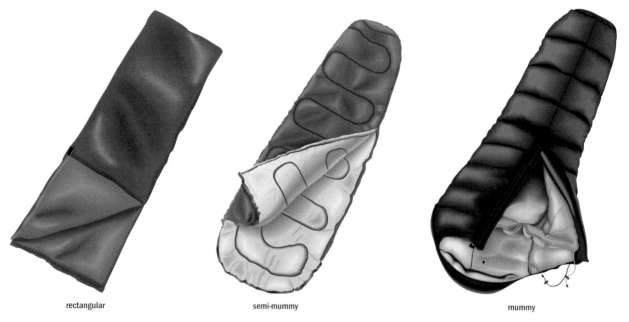

rectangular   semi-mummy   mummy

bed and mattress

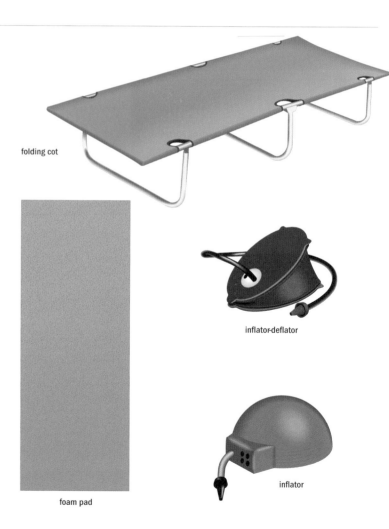

folding cot

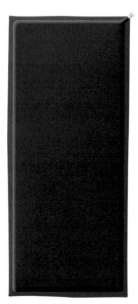

inflator-deflator

inflator

air mattress   self-inflating mattress   foam pad

cutlery set

cooking set

belt loop

spoon

sheath

fork

knife

plate

saucepan

handle

frying pan

coffee pot

cup

camping equipment

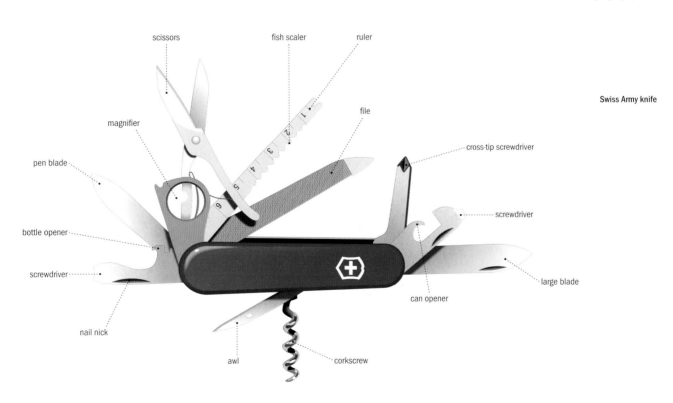

scissors

fish scaler

ruler

Swiss Army knife

magnifier

file

pen blade

cross-tip screwdriver

bottle opener

screwdriver

screwdriver

large blade

can opener

nail nick

awl

corkscrew

camping

backpack

shoulder strap

side compression strap

waist belt

top flap

tightening buckle

front compression strap

strap loop

folding shovel

vacuum bottle

bottle

stopper

cup

hurricane lamp

canteen

cooler

water carrier

bow saw

knife

leather sheath

sheath

folding grill

hatchet

magnetic compass

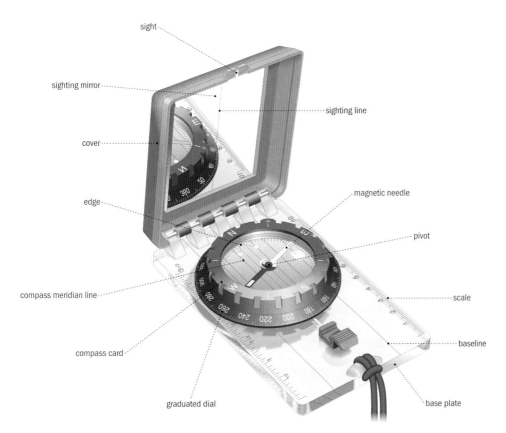

sight

sighting mirror

sighting line

cover

edge

magnetic needle

pivot

compass meridian line

scale

baseline

compass card

graduated dial

base plate

knots

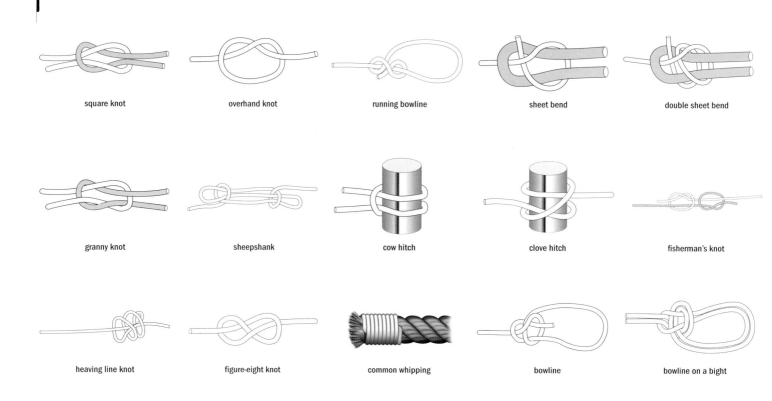

square knot

overhand knot

running bowline

sheet bend

double sheet bend

granny knot

sheepshank

cow hitch

clove hitch

fisherman's knot

heaving line knot

figure-eight knot

common whipping

bowline

bowline on a bight

short splice

forming

completion

cable

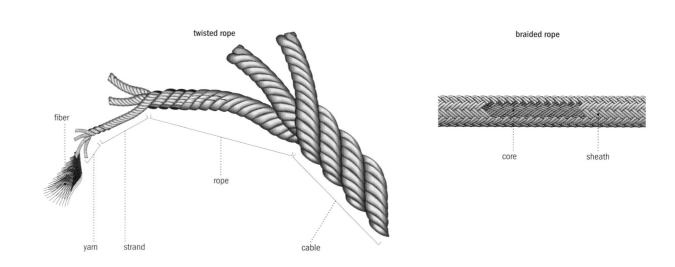

twisted rope

braided rope

fiber

rope

yarn

strand

cable

core

sheath

flyfishing

fly reel

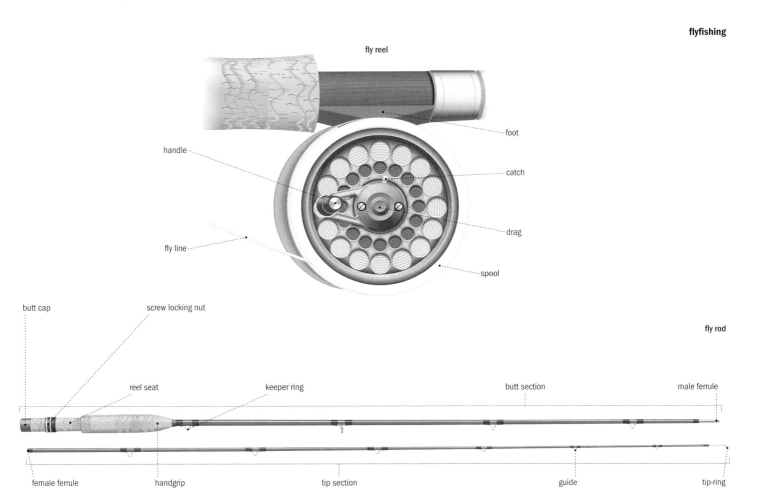

handle

foot

catch

drag

fly line

spool

butt cap

screw locking nut

fly rod

reel seat

keeper ring

butt section

male ferrule

female ferrule

handgrip

tip section

guide

tip-ring

artificial fly

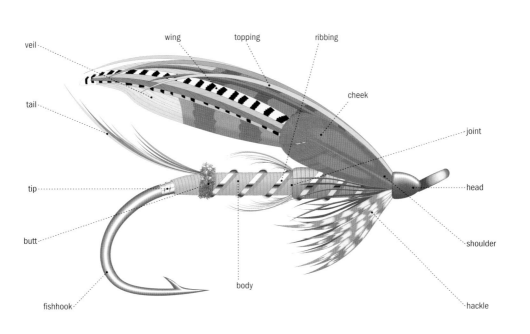

veil

wing

topping

ribbing

tail

cheek

tip

joint

butt

head

body

shoulder

fishhook

hackle

casting

spinning rod

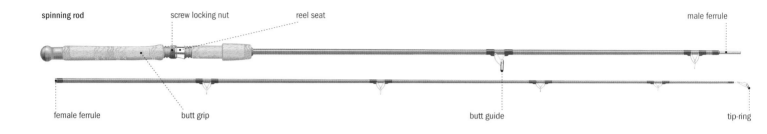

screw locking nut   reel seat   male ferrule

female ferrule   butt grip   butt guide   tip-ring

open-face spinning reel

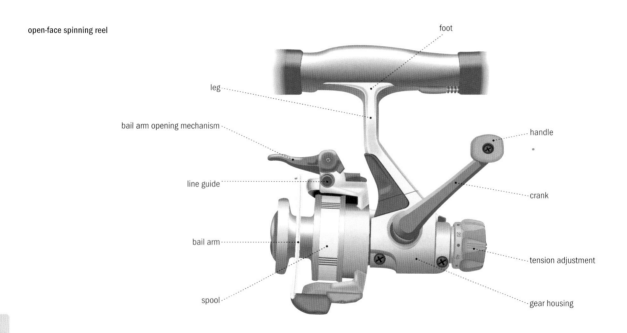

foot

leg

bail arm opening mechanism   handle

line guide   crank

bail arm   tension adjustment

spool   gear housing

baitcasting reel

spool-release mechanism

star drag wheel

spool

spool axle   crank

stand

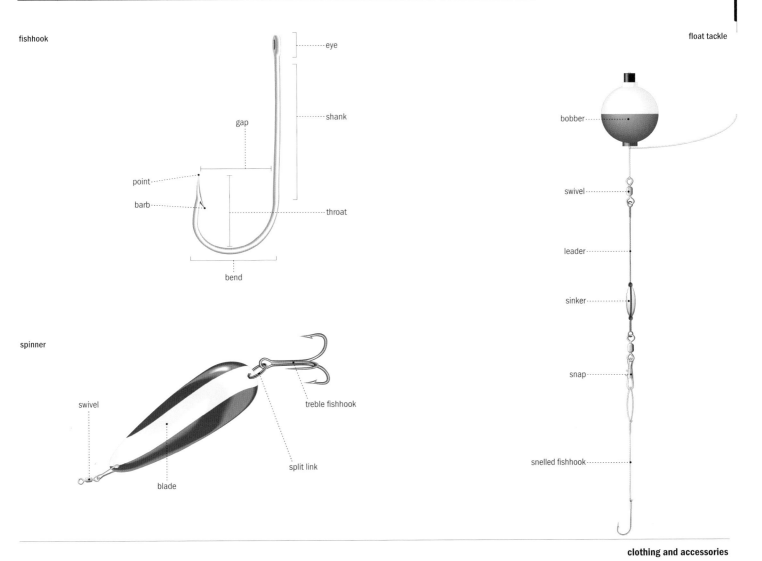

fishhook

eye

shank

gap

point

barb

throat

bend

float tackle

bobber

swivel

leader

sinker

snap

snelled fishhook

spinner

swivel

treble fishhook

split link

blade

clothing and accessories

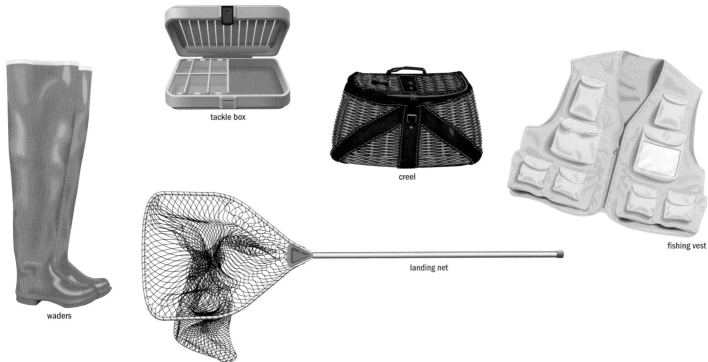

tackle box

creel

fishing vest

waders

landing net

hunting

rifle (rifled bore)

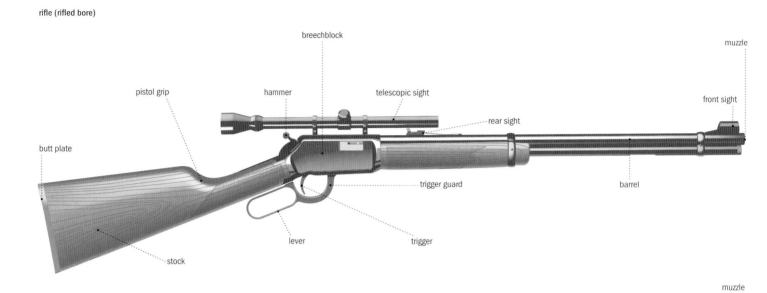

breechblock

muzzle

pistol grip

hammer

telescopic sight

front sight

rear sight

butt plate

trigger guard

barrel

lever

trigger

stock

shotgun (smooth-bore)

muzzle

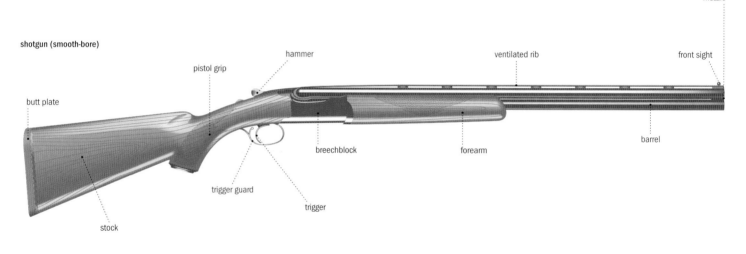

hammer

ventilated rib

front sight

pistol grip

butt plate

barrel

breechblock

forearm

trigger guard

trigger

stock

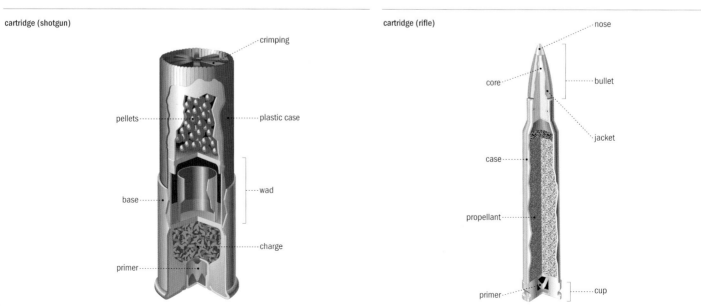

cartridge (shotgun)

crimping

pellets

plastic case

wad

base

charge

primer

cartridge (rifle)

nose

core

bullet

jacket

case

propellant

primer

cup

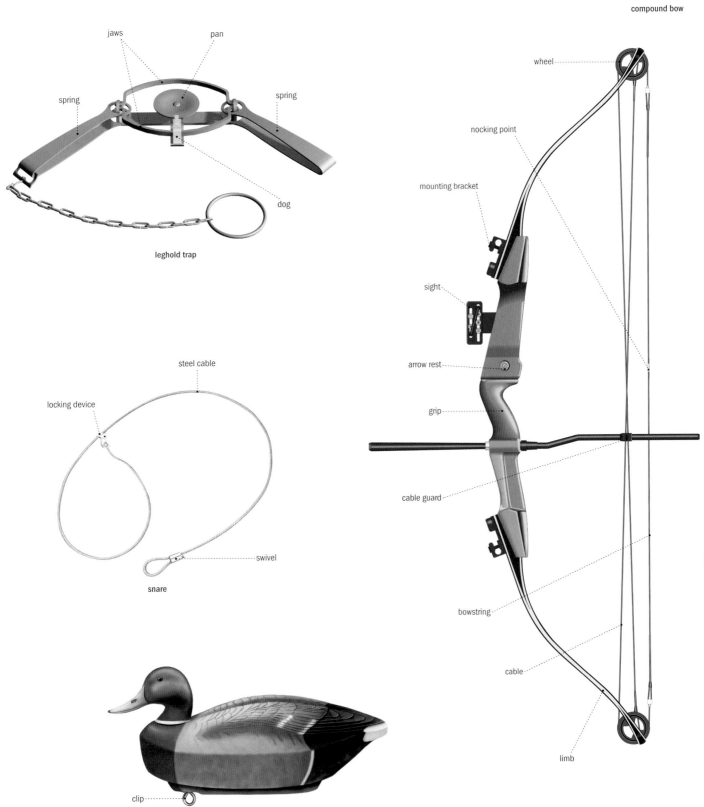

compound bow

jaws   pan

spring   spring

dog

leghold trap

wheel

nocking point

mounting bracket

sight

arrow rest

grip

cable guard

bowstring

cable

limb

steel cable

locking device

swivel

snare

clip

decoy

dice and dominoes

ordinary die

poker die

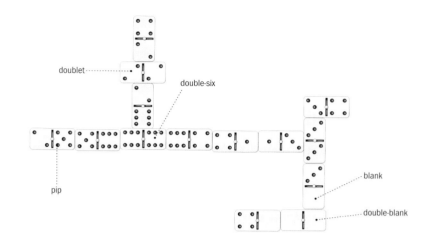

doublet

double-six

pip

blank

double-blank

cards

symbols

heart

diamond

club

spade

joker

ace

king

queen

jack

standard poker hands

high card

one pair

two pairs

three-of-a-kind

straight

flush

full house

four-of-a-kind

straight flush

royal flush

board games

backgammon

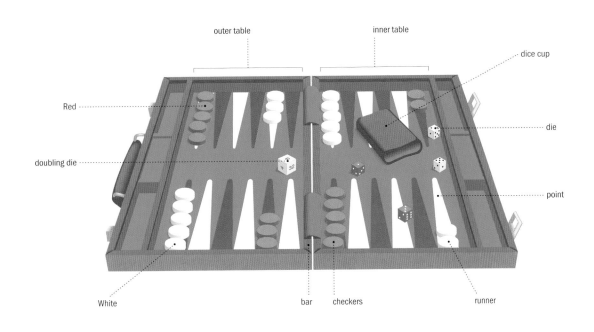

outer table
inner table
dice cup

Red
die

doubling die

point

White
bar   checkers   runner

Monopoly

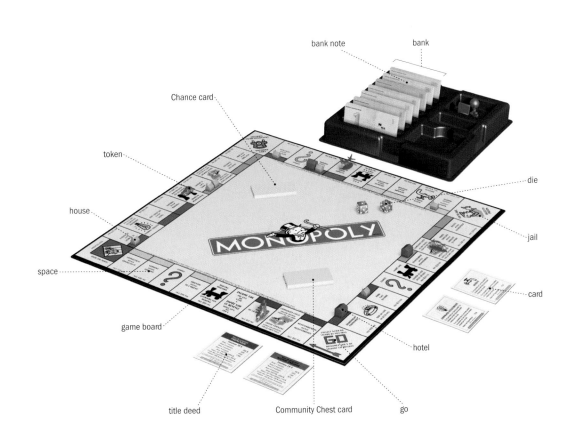

bank note   bank

Chance card

token
die

house
jail

space
card

game board
hotel

title deed   Community Chest card   go

board games

chess

chessboard

queen's side   king's side

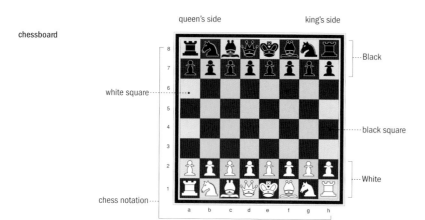

Black

white square

black square

White

chess notation

types of movements

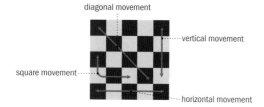

diagonal movement

vertical movement

square movement

horizontal movement

chess pieces

pawn

rook

bishop

knight

king

queen

go

board

handicap spot

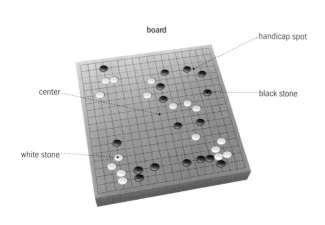

center

black stone

white stone

major motions

connection

capture

contact

checkers

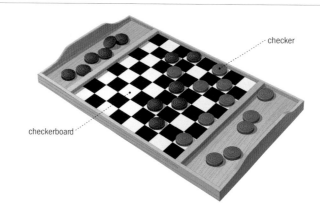

checker

checkerboard

SPORTS AND GAMES

jigsaw puzzle

piece

picture

board

mah-jongg

square

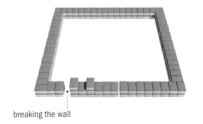

breaking the wall

East

South

North

West

wall

suit tiles

circles

characters

bamboos

honor tiles

winds

dragons

flowers

flower tiles

season tiles

video entertainment system

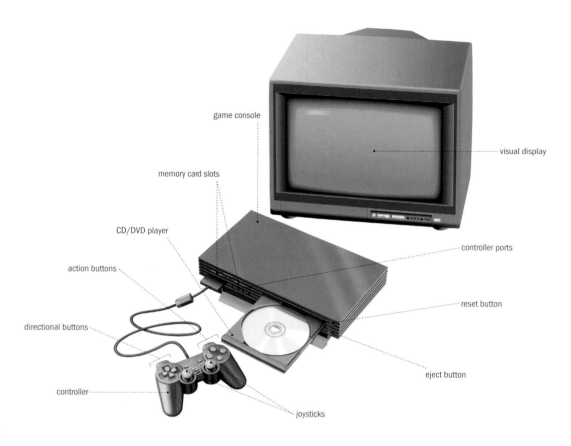

game console

visual display

memory card slots

CD/DVD player

action buttons

controller ports

reset button

directional buttons

eject button

controller

joysticks

darts

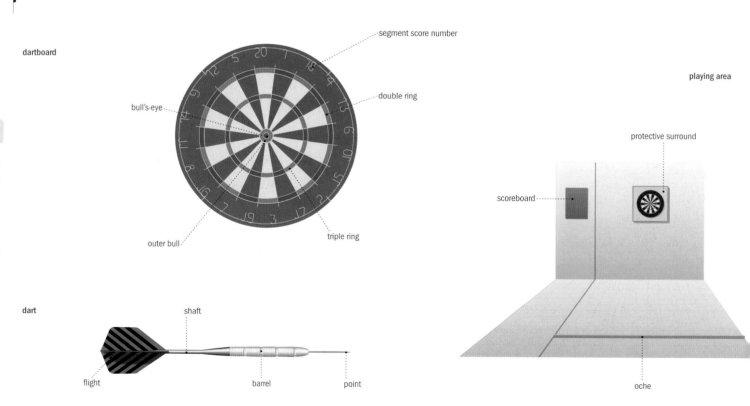

dartboard

segment score number

playing area

bull's-eye

double ring

protective surround

scoreboard

outer bull

triple ring

dart

shaft

flight

barrel

point

oche

roulette table

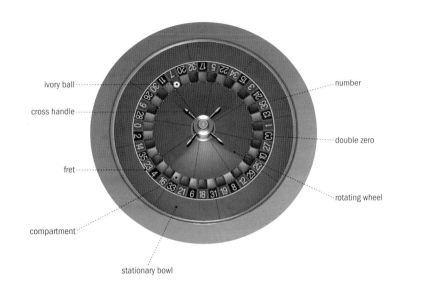

American roulette wheel

ivory ball

cross handle

fret

compartment

stationary bowl

number

double zero

rotating wheel

French roulette wheel

American betting layout

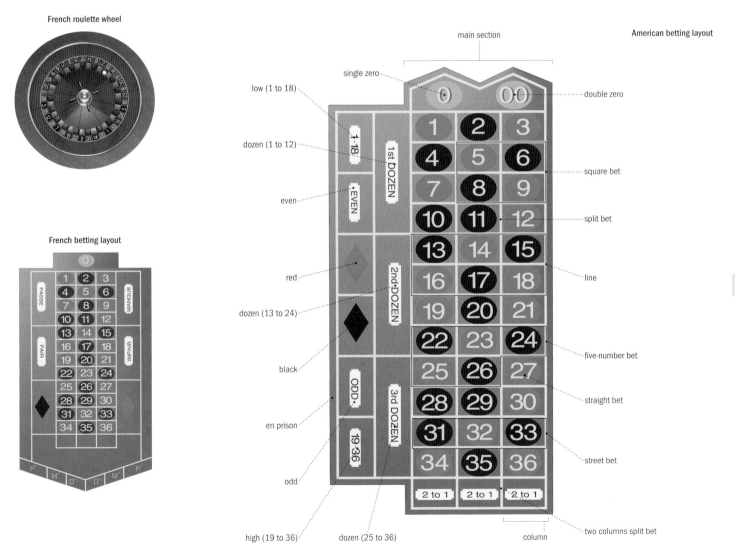

main section

single zero

low (1 to 18)

dozen (1 to 12)

even

red

dozen (13 to 24)

black

en prison

odd

high (19 to 36)

dozen (25 to 36)

double zero

square bet

split bet

line

five-number bet

straight bet

street bet

column

two columns split bet

French betting layout

slot machine

cross section

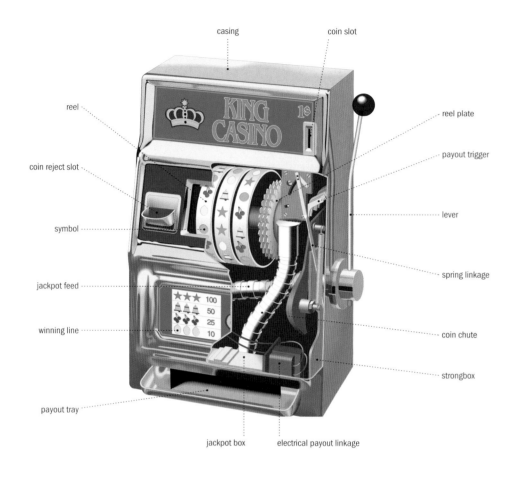

casing   coin slot

reel

coin reject slot

symbol

jackpot feed

winning line

payout tray

jackpot box   electrical payout linkage

reel plate

payout trigger

lever

spring linkage

coin chute

strongbox

KING CASINO 1$

★★★ 100
50
25
10

soccer table

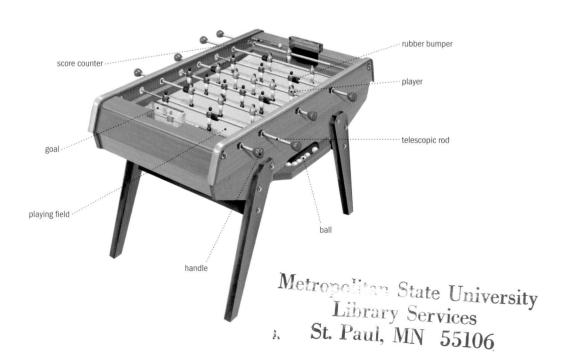

score counter

goal

playing field

handle

rubber bumper

player

telescopic rod

ball

SPORTS AND GAMES

Index

ASTRONOMY > 2-25;   EARTH > 26-71;   VEGETABLE KINGDOM >72-89;   ANIMAL KINGDOM > 90-143;   HUMAN BEING > 144-177;   FOOD AND KITCHEN > 178-241;   HOUSE > 242-295;
DO-IT-YOURSELF AND GARDENING > 296-333;   CLOTHING > 334-371;   PERSONAL ADORNMENT AND ARTICLES > 372-391;   ARTS AND ARCHITECTURE > 392-465;   COMMUNICATIONS AND
OFFICE AUTOMATION > 466-535;   TRANSPORT AND MACHINERY > 536-643;   ENERGY > 644-677;   SCIENCE > 678-705;   SOCIETY > 706-785;   SPORTS AND GAMES > 786-920

921

INDEX

ASTRONOMY > 2-25; EARTH > 26-71; VEGETABLE KINGDOM >72-89; ANIMAL KINGDOM > 90-143; HUMAN BEING > 144-177; FOOD AND KITCHEN > 178-241; HOUSE > 242-295;
DO-IT-YOURSELF AND GARDENING > 296-333; CLOTHING > 334-371; PERSONAL ADORNMENT AND ARTICLES > 372-391; ARTS AND ARCHITECTURE > 392-465; COMMUNICATIONS AND
OFFICE AUTOMATION > 466-535; TRANSPORT AND MACHINERY > 536-643; ENERGY > 644-677; SCIENCE > 678-705; SOCIETY > 706-785; SPORTS AND GAMES > 786-920

923

INDEX

924

INDEX

ASTRONOMY > 2-25; EARTH > 26-71; VEGETABLE KINGDOM >72-89; ANIMAL KINGDOM > 90-143; HUMAN BEING > 144-177; FOOD AND KITCHEN > 178-241; HOUSE > 242-295;
DO-IT-YOURSELF AND GARDENING > 296-333; CLOTHING > 334-371; PERSONAL ADORNMENT AND ARTICLES > 372-391; ARTS AND ARCHITECTURE > 392-465; COMMUNICATIONS AND
OFFICE AUTOMATION > 466-535; TRANSPORT AND MACHINERY > 536-643; ENERGY > 644-677; SCIENCE > 678-705; SOCIETY > 706-785; SPORTS AND GAMES > 786-920

925

INDEX

INDEX

gearbox 423, 552
gearing systems 686
gearshift lever 552, 556, 575, 577
gelatin capsule 783
gemstones, cuts 375
generator 563, 578, 646, 659, 668
generator unit 658, 659
generators 688
Genoa salami 216
gentlemen's toilet 427, 509, 724
geographical map 734
geography 28
geology 42
geometrical shapes 704
geometry 704
Georgia 746
geostationary orbit 60
geostationary satellite 60
geothermal and fossil energy 646
geothermal energy 646
geothermal field 646
germ 85
German 469
German mustard 200
German rye bread 205
German salami 216
German shepherd 130
Germanic languages 469
germanium 682
Germany 744
germination 77
geyser 44
Ghana 745
ghee 210
gherkin 188
gi 846
giant slalom 889
giant slalom ski 888
giant water bug 101
gibbon 139
Gibraltar, Strait 32
gift store 714
gifts 717
gill 76, 106
gill slits 108
gills 105, 109
ginger 199
ginkgo nuts 193
Giraffe 12
giraffe 129
girder 252
girdle 367, 374
girls' wear (size 2 to 6) 717
girls' wear (size 7 to 17) 717
girth 855, 856
girth strap 855
gizzard 116
glacial cirque 46
glacial lake 48
glacier 46, 48, 66
glacier tongue 46
glacis 409
gladius 748
glans penis 169
glass 672, 673
glass bottle 223
glass case 699
glass collection unit 71
glass cover 291
glass dome 612
glass lens 385
glass protector 878
glass recycling container 71
glass slide 693
glass sorting 71
glass sphere 58
glass washer 723
glass-fronted display cabinet 279
glassed roof 250, 582, 713
glasses 723
glassware 225
glider 898
gliding joint 156
gliding phase 892
global warming 68
globe 734, 903
globular cluster 9
glossae 99
glottis 112
glove 20, 798, 800, 842, 848, 855,
   870, 871, 874, 875, 878, 882, 884,
   887, 891, 892
glove compartment 556
glove finger 346
glove storage 780
glove, back 346
glove, palm 346
gloves 346, 872

glucose 78
glue 254
glue stick 534
gluteal nerve 166
gluteus maximus 151
gnocchi 206
gnomon 696
go 915, 916
goal 800, 802, 804, 807, 809, 814,
   827, 879, 920
goal area 802, 814
goal area line 814
goal attack 809
goal circle 809
goal crease 879
goal defense 809
goal judge 827, 858, 878
goal lights 879
goal line 800, 804, 806, 809, 814,
   827, 878
goal line referee 814
goal shooter 809
goal third 809
goalkeeper 800, 801, 803, 809, 814,
   827, 878, 879
goalkeeper's chest pad 880
goalkeeper's gloves 802
goalkeeper's pad 879
goalkeeper's skate 880
goalkeeper's stick 879
goalkeeper's stick 880
goalpost 807, 809, 858
goat 128
goat's milk 210
goat's-milk cheeses 210
goatfish 219
gob hat 341
Gobi Desert 33
goggles 318, 870, 887, 896
gold 683
goldfinch 118
golf 866
golf bag 869
golf ball 867
golf ball, cross section 867
golf cart 869
golf cart, electric 869
golf clubs, types 867
golf course 708, 788
golf glove 869
golf shoes 869
Golgi apparatus 74, 94
gonad 95, 105, 106
gondola 181, 600, 886
gondola car 588
gondolas departure area 886
gonfalon 739
gong 437, 449
gonopore 95, 104
goose 120, 213
goose egg 213
goose-neck 255
gooseberries 192
gooseneck 638
gored skirt 357
gorge 47, 48
gorget 749
Gorgonzola 211
gorilla 138
gorilla, morphology 139
gorilla, skeleton 138
Gothic cathedral 410
gouache 396
gouache cakes 397
gouache tube 397
gouge 401
gour 47
government organization 525
governor tension sheave 417
governor's office 726
GPS receiver-antenna 613
grab handle 567, 570, 584, 766
gracile 151
grade slope 244
grader 639
graduated arc 612
graduated cylinder 685
graduated dial 907
graduated scale 698, 699
grafting knife 330
grain 300
grain elevator 643
grain of wheat, section 85
grain tank 643
grain terminal 596
grain tube 643
Grand Canyon 30
grand gallery 402
grandchildren 784

granddaughter 784
grandfather 784
grandfather clock 697
grandmother 784
grandparents 784
grandson 784
grandstand 856
granitic layer 42
granivorous bird 117
granny knot 908
granulated sugar 209
granulation 6
grape 86
grape leaf 86
grape leaves 186
grape, section 83
grapefruit 194
grapefruit knife 229
grapes 192
grapeshot 752
graphic arts 420
graphic equalizer 498
grapnel 610
grass 822
grassbox 332
grasshopper 102
grassland 66
grate 290
grater 230
grave accent 473
gravel 253, 263
gravel bed 872
gravity band 610
gravity dam 661
gravity dam, cross section 661
gravy boat 226
gray matter 167, 168
grease well 239
greases 656
Great Australian Bight 29
Great Barrier Reef 29
Great Bear 13
Great Dane 131
Great Dividing Range 29
great green bush-cricket 101
great horned owl 119
Great Lakes 30
great organ manual 444
Great Sandy Desert 29
great saphenous vein 160
great scallop 217
Great Schism 736
Great Victoria Desert 29
great-grandchildren 784
great-granddaughter 784
great-grandfather 784
great-grandmother 784
great-grandparents 784
great-grandson 784
greater alar cartilage 175
greater covert 115
greater trochanter 153
greave 749
Greco-Roman wrestling 843
Greece 744
Greek 469
Greek bread 204
Greek temple 403
Greek temple, plan 403
Greek theater 402
green 400, 690, 864, 866, 867
green alga 75
green ball 863
green beam 494
green bean 191
green cabbage 186
green coffee beans 208
green gland 107
green light 712
green onion 184
green peas 190
green pepper 198
green russula 183
green sweet pepper 188
green tea 208
green walnut 84
greenhouse 182
greenhouse effect 68
greenhouse effect, enhanced 68
greenhouse effect, natural 68
greenhouse gas 68
greenhouse gas concentration 68
Greenland 30
Greenland Sea 28
Grenada 743
grenade 757
Grenadines 743
greyhound 131
grid 494

grid system 36
griddle 239
grille 261, 403, 432, 550, 561, 727
grinding wheel 308
grip 428, 793, 838, 850, 859, 867,
   913
grip handle 303
grip tape 894
gripping tools 310
grocery bags 181
groin 146, 148
groove 229, 424, 453, 750, 868, 888
ground 272, 655
ground air conditioner 622
ground airport equipment 622
ground beef 214
ground bond 272
ground clamp 318
ground connection 272
ground electrode 562
ground fault circuit interrupter 272
ground lamb 215
ground moraine 46
ground pepper 199
ground pork 215
ground sill 409
ground surface 647
ground terminal 497
ground veal 214
ground wire 272, 273
ground-wire peak 663
ground/neutral bus bar 272
grounded receptacle 263
groundhog 123
grounding prong 274
grow sleepers 368
growth line 104, 105
Gruyère 211
Guarani 469
guard 229, 255, 316, 811, 849
guard rail 291, 894
guardhouse 408, 409
Guatemala 742
guava 197
guide 909
guide bar 331
guide handle 308
guide roller 499
guiding and current bar 595
guiding tower 542
guillotine trimmer 484
Guinea 745
guinea fowl 120, 212
guinea pig 123
Guinea, Gulf 34
Guinea-Bissau 745
guitar 440, 441
gules 741
gulf 38
Gulf of Aden 33, 34
Gulf of Alaska 30
Gulf of Bothnia 32
Gulf of California 30
Gulf of Carpentaria 29
Gulf of Guinea 34
Gulf of Mexico 30
Gulf of Oman 33
Gulf of Panama 31
gum 159, 174
gun 315
gun body 320
gun flap 352
gun range 769
gunnard 219
gunner's sight 758
gusset 386, 388
gusset pocket 359, 360
Gutenberg discontinuity 42
gutta 404
gutter 244, 865
guy cable 824, 825
guy line 902
guy wire 676
Guyana 742
guyot 49
gym teachers' office 734
gymnasium 608, 727, 734, 764, 788
gymnast's name 825
gymnastics 823, 824
gynecological examination room 779
gyoji 847
gypsum board 299
gypsum tile 299
gyroscope 759

H

hack 877

hackle 909
hacksaw 303, 314
haddock 221
hafnium 683
hail 64
hail shower 57
hair 147, 149, 172, 439
hair bulb 172
hair clip 380
hair conditioner 379
hair dryer 382
hair follicle 172
hair roller 380
hair roller pin 380
hair shaft 172
hair stylist 428
hairbrushes 380
haircolor 379
haircutting scissors 382
hairdressing 380
hairdressing salon 714
hairpin 380
hairspring 696
Haiti 742
hakama 846, 847
half barb 56
half cell 897
half court line 819
half handle 229
half indexing 528
half note 435
half rest 435
half-distance line 827
half-glasses 385
half-mask respirator 773
half-pipe 871, 887
half-pipe, competition site 887
half-side 632
half-slip 366
half-through arch bridge 541
half-volley 820
halfway line 803, 805
halibut 221
hall 250, 608, 719, 724
hallah 205
halo 9
halogen desk lamp 286
halogen light 775
halyard 603, 739
ham knife 229
hamate 154
hammer 317, 442, 443, 754, 793,
   861, 912
hammer ax 901
hammer butt 443
hammer drill 648
hammer felt 443
hammer head 901
hammer loop 313
hammer rail 442, 443
hammer shank 443
hammer throw 791
hamster 123
hand 139, 147, 149, 154, 173
hand blender 236
hand brake 552
hand brake gear housing 587
hand brake wheel 587
hand brake winding lever 587
hand cultivator 325
hand drill 307
hand fork 325
hand grenade 757
hand hole 535
hand lamp 765
hand miter saw 303
hand mixer 236
hand mower 332
hand post 433
hand protection 774
hand protector 331, 875
hand rest 516
hand shield 318
hand tools 325
hand truck 633
hand vacuum cleaner 288
hand vice 422
hand wash in lukewarm water 347
hand wheel 452
hand-warmer pocket 353, 355
hand-warmer pouch 360
hand-wheel 425
handbags 387
handball 814
handcuff case 770
handgrip 574, 577, 782, 909
handgrips 850
handguard 755
handheld computer 527

ASTRONOMY > 2-25;   EARTH > 26-71;   VEGETABLE KINGDOM >72-89;   ANIMAL KINGDOM > 90-143;   HUMAN BEING > 144-177;   FOOD AND KITCHEN > 178-241;   HOUSE > 242-295;
DO-IT-YOURSELF AND GARDENING > 296-333;   CLOTHING > 334-371;   PERSONAL ADORNMENT AND ARTICLES > 372-391;   ARTS AND ARCHITECTURE > 392-465;   COMMUNICATIONS AND
OFFICE AUTOMATION > 466-535;   TRANSPORT AND MACHINERY > 536-643;   ENERGY > 644-677;   SCIENCE > 678-705;   SOCIETY > 706-785;   SPORTS AND GAMES > 786-920

933

ASTRONOMY > 2-25;   EARTH > 26-71;   VEGETABLE KINGDOM >72-89;   ANIMAL KINGDOM > 90-143;   HUMAN BEING > 144-177;   FOOD AND KITCHEN > 178-241;   HOUSE > 242-295;
DO-IT-YOURSELF AND GARDENING > 296-333;   CLOTHING > 334-371;   PERSONAL ADORNMENT AND ARTICLES > 372-391;   ARTS AND ARCHITECTURE > 392-465;   COMMUNICATIONS AND
OFFICE AUTOMATION > 466-535;   TRANSPORT AND MACHINERY > 536-643;   ENERGY > 644-677;   SCIENCE > 678-705;   SOCIETY > 706-785;   SPORTS AND GAMES > 786-920

935

ASTRONOMY > 2-25;   EARTH > 26-71;   VEGETABLE KINGDOM >72-89;   ANIMAL KINGDOM > 90-143;   HUMAN BEING > 144-177;   FOOD AND KITCHEN > 178-241;   HOUSE > 242-295;
DO-IT-YOURSELF AND GARDENING > 296-333;   CLOTHING > 334-371;   PERSONAL ADORNMENT AND ARTICLES > 372-391;   ARTS AND ARCHITECTURE > 392-465;   COMMUNICATIONS AND
OFFICE AUTOMATION > 466-535;   TRANSPORT AND MACHINERY > 536-643;   ENERGY > 644-677;   SCIENCE > 678-705;   SOCIETY > 706-785;   SPORTS AND GAMES > 786-920

937

INDEX

ASTRONOMY > 2-25; EARTH > 26-71; VEGETABLE KINGDOM >72-89; ANIMAL KINGDOM > 90-143; HUMAN BEING > 144-177; FOOD AND KITCHEN > 178-241; HOUSE > 242-295;
DO-IT-YOURSELF AND GARDENING > 296-333; CLOTHING > 334-371; PERSONAL ADORNMENT AND ARTICLES > 372-391; ARTS AND ARCHITECTURE > 392-465; COMMUNICATIONS AND
OFFICE AUTOMATION > 466-535; TRANSPORT AND MACHINERY > 536-643; ENERGY > 644-677; SCIENCE > 678-705; SOCIETY > 706-785; SPORTS AND GAMES > 786-920

939

INDEX

ASTRONOMY > 2-25; EARTH > 26-71; VEGETABLE KINGDOM >72-89; ANIMAL KINGDOM > 90-143; HUMAN BEING > 144-177; FOOD AND KITCHEN > 178-241; HOUSE > 242-295; DO-IT-YOURSELF AND GARDENING > 296-333; CLOTHING > 334-371; PERSONAL ADORNMENT AND ARTICLES > 372-391; ARTS AND ARCHITECTURE > 392-465; COMMUNICATIONS AND OFFICE AUTOMATION > 466-535; TRANSPORT AND MACHINERY > 536-643; ENERGY > 644-677; SCIENCE > 678-705; SOCIETY > 706-785; SPORTS AND GAMES > 786-920

941

INDEX

ASTRONOMY > 2-25;   EARTH > 26-71;   VEGETABLE KINGDOM >72-89;   ANIMAL KINGDOM > 90-143;   HUMAN BEING > 144-177;   FOOD AND KITCHEN > 178-241;   HOUSE > 242-295;
DO-IT-YOURSELF AND GARDENING > 296-333;   CLOTHING > 334-371;   PERSONAL ADORNMENT AND ARTICLES > 372-391;   ARTS AND ARCHITECTURE > 392-465;   COMMUNICATIONS AND
OFFICE AUTOMATION > 466-535;   TRANSPORT AND MACHINERY > 536-643;   ENERGY > 644-677;   SCIENCE > 678-705;   SOCIETY > 706-785;   SPORTS AND GAMES > 786-920

943

INDEX

ASTRONOMY > 2-25;   EARTH > 26-71;   VEGETABLE KINGDOM >72-89;   ANIMAL KINGDOM > 90-143;   HUMAN BEING > 144-177;   FOOD AND KITCHEN > 178-241;   HOUSE > 242-295;
DO-IT-YOURSELF AND GARDENING > 296-333;   CLOTHING > 334-371;   PERSONAL ADORNMENT AND ARTICLES > 372-391;   ARTS AND ARCHITECTURE > 392-465;   COMMUNICATIONS AND
OFFICE AUTOMATION > 466-535;   TRANSPORT AND MACHINERY > 536-643;   ENERGY > 644-677;   SCIENCE > 678-705;   SOCIETY > 706-785;   SPORTS AND GAMES > 786-920

951

INDEX

water pressure gauge 766
water separator 648
water service pipe 262
water skiing 840
water spider 102
water strider 102
water table 47, 70
water tank 241, 261, 384, 586
water tower 589
water turns into steam 665
water under pressure 662
water-heater tank 266, 675
water-heater tank, electric 266
water-level selector 292
water-level tube 288
water-steam mix 646
water-tank area 628
watercolor 396
watercolor cakes 397
watercolor tube 397
watercourse 48, 70
watercress 187
waterfall 47, 48
watering can 328
watering tools 328
watering tube 573
waterline 615
watermark 729
watermelon 195
waterproof pants 368
waterspout 63
watt 702
wave 49, 690
wave base 49
wave clip 380
wave guide 489
wave height 49
wave length 49
wave wall 660
wavelength 690
wax 892
wax bean 191
wax crayon drawing 396
wax crayons 396
wax gourd 188
wax seal 265
waxed paper 222
waxing gibbous 7
waxing kit 892
weapon, parts 849
weapons 748
weapons in the age of the Romans 748
weapons in the Stone Age 748
weasel 134
weather map 54, 55
weather radar 54, 624
weather satellite 54
weather satellites 60
weather symbols, international 56
weatherboard 247, 249
weaving 460
weaving pattern brush 456
weaving pattern lever 456
weaving principle, diagram 463
weaving, accessories 462
web 110, 117, 591, 797
web frame 607
webbed foot 110
webbed toe 117
webbing 459, 555, 899
Webcam 517
Weddell Sea 29
wedding ring 376
wedge 444, 753
wedge lever 309
weeder 325
weeding hoe 326
weekender 389
weeping willow 88
weft 460, 461
weft thread 463
weighing platform 699
weight 472, 630, 697, 698, 699, 793, 850
weight belt 841

weight machine 851
weight, measure 698
weight-driven clock mechanism 697
weightlifting 850
weightlifting belt 850
weightlifting shoe 850
weights 851
welding curtain 318
welding tools 318
welding torch 319
well flow line 652
Welsh 469
welt 342, 348
welt pocket 348, 354, 360
West 37, 616, 917
West cardinal mark 617
West Coast mirror 569, 570
West Indies 30
West-Northwest 37
West-Southwest 37
Western hemisphere 35
Western meridian 36
wet suit 841
wet well 671
wet-weather tire 872
Whale 10, 12
whale 137
whale boat 601
wheat 85, 203
wheat, grain 85
wheat: spike 85
wheel 320, 323, 389, 423, 454, 560, 570, 753, 758, 859, 870, 874, 894, 895, 913
wheel chock 622
wheel cover 551
wheel cylinder 559
wheel guard 308
wheel head 464
wheel loader 637
wheel mouse 516
wheel speed sensor 559
wheel stud 559
wheel tractor 637
wheelbarrow 323
wheelchair 584, 783
wheelchair access 725
wheelchair lift 569
wheelchair ramp 394
wheelhouse 606
whelk 217
whipping 868
whipping cream 210
whisk 232
whisker 122, 132
whistle 240
white 690
White 915, 916
white blood cell 162
white bread 205
white cabbage 186
white chocolate 208
white dwarf 8
white light 616
white line 127
white matter 167, 168
white mustard 198
white object ball 862, 863
white onion 184
white pepper 198
white rice 207
white square 916
white stone 916
white tape 812, 815, 817
white wine glass 225
white-tailed deer 128
whitewater 837
whitewater, canoe-kayak 837
whiting 221
whole note 435
whole rest 435
whole-wheat flour 204
wholegrain mustard 200
wholemeal bread 205
whorl 104, 105

wicker basket 899
wicket 731, 799
wicket gate 659
wicketkeeper 799
wide 472
wide area network 523
wide receiver 807
wide-angle lens 478
wife 785
wigwam 418
wild boar 128
wild rice 203
Wilkes Land 29
willow 798
winch 417, 573, 835
winch controls 573
wind 56, 69, 70, 833
wind abeam 833
wind arrow 56
wind chest 445
wind chest table 445
wind deflector 570
wind direction 55
wind direction, measure 59
wind duct 445
wind energy 676
wind flag 893
wind guard 899
wind indicator 834
wind instruments 446
wind sock 739
wind speed 55
wind strength, measure 59
wind supply 445
wind synthesizer controller 451
wind trunk 445
wind turbine, horizontal-axis 677
wind turbines 676
wind vane 58, 59, 677
windbag 432
windbreaker 353
winder 696
winding adjustment 692
winding mechanism 285, 697
winding shaft 650
winding tower 649
windmill 676
window 238, 239, 249, 251, 290, 386, 485, 551, 554, 567, 594, 624, 836
window accessories 282
window canopy 902
window curtain 282
window regulator handle 554
window sill 252
window tab 532
windows 386
windows, examples 415
winds 917
windscreen 488
windshaft 676
windshield 550, 570, 574, 577, 607, 624, 626, 876
windshield wiper 550, 557
windshield wiper blade 557
wine 180
wine cellar 720
wine list 721
wine steward 720
wine vinegar 201
wing 23, 97, 98, 115, 338, 416, 625, 760, 873, 897, 909
wing attack 809
wing box 760
wing covert 115
wing defense 809
wing membrane 140
wing nut 311
wing pallet 632
wing rib 624
wing shapes, examples 630
wing slat 625
wing strut 628
wing tip 898
wing vein 96
wing, bird 115

winglet 625, 628
wings 140, 430, 628, 898
wings, bat 140
winner 789
winning line 920
winter 54
winter precipitations 64
winter solstice 54
winter sports 877
winter tire 560
winze 650
wiper 557
wiper arm 557
wiper switch 556
wire 689, 793
wire beater 236
wire brush 449
wire cutter 317
wire nut 317
wire sling 900
wire stripper 317
wire support 903
wireless communication 505
wireless network interface card 522
wishbone boom 836
withers 124, 130
witness stand 728
wok 234
wok set 234
Wolf 11
wolf 134
Wolof 468
woman 148
women's accessories 717
women's casual wear 716
women's cell 768
women's clothing 355
women's coats 716
women's gloves 346
women's headgear 341
women's nightwear 716
women's rest room 725
women's shoes 343, 716
women's sportswear 716
women's suits 716
women's sweaters 716
won ton skins 207
wood 300, 867, 868
wood carving 401
wood chip car 588
wood chisel 309
wood ear 183
wood engraving 421
wood firing 256
wood flooring 253, 254
wood flooring arrangements 254
wood flooring on cement screed 254
wood flooring on wooden structure 254
wood frog 111
wood ray 87
wood-based materials 300
woodbox 256
woodcut 421
wooden bar 825
wooden modeling tools 464
woodpecker 118
woods 39
woodwind family 437
woofer 10, 502
Worcestershire sauce 200
word correction 528
work bench and vise 312
work furniture 511
work lead 318
work sheet 395
work top 721, 722
worker 99
working area 10
working pressure gauge 319
working surface 312
workshop 726
workstation 509
worm 462, 573, 752
worm gear 686
wraparound dress 356

wraparound skirt 357
wrapover top 359
wrapper 390
wrenches 311, 315
wrestler 843
wrestling 843
wrestling area 843
wrestling shoe 843
wrist 130, 140, 147, 149, 156, 173
wrist guard 895
wrist sling 901
wrist strap 888, 892
wrist-length glove 346
wristband 808, 822, 850
writing brush 470
writing case 387
writing instruments 470

X

X-band antenna 40
X-ray unit, mobile 778
X-rays 690
xenon 684
xylophone 437, 449

Y

Y-branch 269
Y-tube 776
yak 129
yard 589, 602
yard line 806
yard-long beans 190
yarn 908
yarn ball 797
yarn clip 457
yarn feeder 456
yarn rod 457
yarn tension unit 457
yaw 630
yellow 400, 690
yellow ball 863
yellow light 712
yellow onion 184
yellow sweet pepper 188
yellow-green 400
yellowjacket 101
Yemen 746
yen 728
Yiddish 469
yield 544, 546
yogurt 210
yoke 284, 349, 353, 359
yoke skirt 357
yolk 117
Yoruba 468
ytterbium 684
yttrium 683
Yucatan Peninsula 30
Yugoslavia 744
yurt 418

Z

Zambia 746
zebra 128
zenith 10
zest 82
zester 229
Zimbabwe 746
zinc 683
zinc can 689
zinc-electrolyte mix 689
zipper 353, 369, 377, 389, 453, 902
zipper line 455
zirconium 683
zither 432
zona pellucida 170
zoom lens 478, 492, 496
zucchini 188
Zulu 468
zygomatic bone 152, 158